A Manual of Style for Contract Drafting

FOURTH EDITION

Kenneth A. Adams

AMERICAN BAR ASSOCIATION
Business Law Section

Printed in the United States of America.

21 20 19 18 17   5 4 3 2 1

ISBN: 978-1-63425-964-4

Discounts are available for books ordered in bulk. Special consideration is given to state bars, CLE programs, and other bar-related organizations. Inquire at Book Publishing, ABA Publishing, American Bar Association, 321 N. Clark Street, Chicago, Illinois 60654-7598.

www.ShopABA.org

To Joanne K. Adams

CONTENTS

CHAPTER 6   Defined Terms 167

CHAPTER 7   Sources of Uncertain Meaning in Contract Language 185

CHAPTER 8   *Reasonable Efforts* and Its Variants 193

LIST OF TABLES

LIST OF FIGURES

FOREWORD

Vice Chancellor J. Travis Laster
Court of Chancery of the State of Delaware

To Fellow Students of the Contractual Arts:

A Manual of Style for Contract Drafting is an essential resource for anyone who works with contracts. Its author, Ken Adams, has produced an impressively innovative, intelligent, and thorough work.

As a judge, I regularly confront transactions where something has gone wrong. Often, it's because the governing agreement wasn't as clear as it could have been. Better contract drafting would lead to fewer disputes. Fewer disputes should mean happier clients.

As practiced in most organizations, contract drafting remains an unscientific activity, conducted mostly by consulting and largely duplicating earlier precedents of questionable quality and relevance. I know that firsthand. While practicing law before joining the Delaware Court of Chancery, a meaningful part of my time was spent commenting on merger agreements and other contracts that carried a high risk of litigation. By bluntly characterizing the current state of the art, I am not suggesting that contract drafters do not take their jobs seriously, nor implying that they do not give extensive thought to the provisions they draft. They do. But all too often, a question is answered or a debate resolved by sticking with language that seems to have worked in the past, trusting that it will work again.

Putting such a precedent-driven activity on a more rational footing is not an easy task. The first step is to establish a comprehensive set of guidelines for the building blocks of contract prose. That's what the *Manual* offers.

I have been a fan of the *Manual* since Ken began his campaign to modernize the preparation of agreements. I've found it compelling enough to cite in one of my opinions. See *Airborne Health, Inc. v. Squid Soap, LP*, 984 A.2d 126, 140 (Del. Ch. 2009). Now in its fourth edition, the *Manual* has reached a level of maturity in its scope and approach.

Ken takes a firm stand on how best to express many fundamental contract concepts. At the same time, he does not always insist on a particular outcome. The best reference works offer enough explication to allow the reader to appreciate the guidance yet opt for a different destination. The *Manual* achieves that balance. You don't have to buy into every position it takes to benefit from consulting it.

Ken hasn't been mindlessly dogmatic either. He constantly probes his work for weaknesses, and he encourages others to do so too. Commendably, he has adjusted his views when the weight of evidence warrants, as you can tell by comparing the different editions of the *Manual*.

Contract drafters undoubtedly will benefit from adopting Ken's recommendations. Judges and litigators will benefit from reading it too. Much of the text consists of detailed discussion, on a level unmatched in my experience, about what makes traditional contract language confusing. Ken offers grammatical and historical insights, and he provides helpful explanations about how familiar phrases were originally supposed to work. He frequently illustrates his analyses with examples of judicial decisions that likely surprised the original drafters, because the judges seem to have ascribed dispositive meaning to technical contract language using little more than their own wits and a copy of Strunk and White. (Doubtless I have been guilty of that failing at times.) My judicial colleagues would do well to become passingly familiar with the *Manual*, which offers interpretive guidance free of the biased perspective that necessarily permeates an advocate's brief. And litigators could improve their arguments by applying Ken's interpretive recommendations.

This is not to say that if you cite the *Manual* to me or to an another judge, your client will win. In some cases, the *Manual* recommends departing from existing practice and adopting a different approach. There, Ken's analysis offers less guidance for existing agreements that hew to older approaches. But even then, the *Manual* provides insight by illustrating an alternative means of addressing a topic.

I hope you find this book useful, as I have, and consult it often. If you do, I suspect you will be less likely to appear in my court (or any other). And if a dispute nevertheless arises, you will be more likely to occupy the linguistic high ground.

Happy drafting!

WHAT HAS CHANGED

Welcome to the fourth edition of *A Manual of Style for Contract Drafting*.

As with the second and third editions, this edition represents a substantial upgrade. But you won't find changes to the design, or extensive surgery to what came before.

I've expanded my treatment of a few topics; I've moved some sections from one chapter to another; and I've done some tweaking throughout. Otherwise, the third edition has held up well.

Instead, the biggest change is that I've added discussion of many new topics, the result of a further four years of work on the words and phrases used to construct contract provisions. That includes consulting for a broad range of clients, more than a thousand blog posts, around 20 articles, dozens of public and in-house "Drafting Clearer Contracts" seminars around the world, and three semesters of teaching at law school.

Here's an overview of the changes:

- *Introduction*. Revised and expanded. This is where you will now find discussion of the notion of "tested" contract language, which was previously in chapter 1.

- *Chapter 1 (The Characteristics of Optimal Contract Language)*. Slightly revised.

- *Chapter 2 (The Front of the Contract)*. Contains expanded discussion of the traditional recital of consideration and addresses several new topics.

- *Chapter 3 (Categories of Contract Language)*. Revised to include many new topics, including "throat-clearing" (3.25–.28) and consolidating deal points (3.29). It also contains many new examples of dysfunctional verb structures. The discussion of *represents and warrants* has been expanded. And just as Pluto is no longer a planet, language of belief is no longer a category of contract language; instead, chapter 13 now contains a section on belief.

- *Chapter 4 (Layout)*. Now includes a second *MSCD* enumeration scheme, the hanging-indent scheme.

- *Chapter 5 (The Back of the Contract)*. Largely unchanged.

- *Chapter 6 (Defined Terms)*. Revised to include several new topics, including abbreviations as defined terms (6.9–.12) and circular definitions (6.17–.23).

- *Chapter 7 (Sources of Uncertainty in Contract Language)*. Significantly revised, rearranged, and expanded.

- *Chapter 8 (Reasonable Efforts and Its Variants)*. The part dealing with the function of *efforts* standards, variants of *efforts* standards, and what *efforts* standards mean has been entirely rewritten.

- *Chapter 9* (Material *and* Material Adverse Change). Revised to propose use of *nontrivial* to avoid ambiguity in use of *material* (9.21–.23). Added a discussion of which noun *material* should modify (9.38–.39). And in this chapter and elsewhere, all instances of *representation* have been changed to *statement of fact*, consistent with the recommendations in chapter 3. Otherwise, largely unchanged.

- *Chapter 10 (References to Time).* Covers several new topics.

- *Chapter 11 (Ambiguity of the Part Versus the Whole).* Includes a new section on whether singular means plural (11.3–.14) and a new section on using *and* instead of *or*, and vice versa (11.97–.100). Also discusses recent caselaw on use of *all* (11.105–.111). Otherwise largely unchanged.

- *Chapter 12 (Syntactic Ambiguity).* Includes an expanded discussion of the serial comma (12.57–.76) and how to avoid syntactic ambiguity by restructuring (12.77–.81). Otherwise largely unchanged.

- *Chapter 13 (Selected Usages).* Covers many new topics.

- *Chapter 14 (Numbers and Formulas).* Expanded discussion of using words or digits to express numbers. Otherwise largely unchanged.

- *Chapter 15 (Internal Rules of Interpretation).* Renamed and rearranged; otherwise largely unchanged.

- *Chapter 16 (Typography).* Largely unchanged.

- *Chapter 17 (Drafting as Writing).* Largely unchanged.

- *Chapter 18 (Amendments).* Largely unchanged.

- *Chapter 19 (Letter Agreements).* Slightly revised.

The third edition contained a chapter 20 (Drafting Corporate Resolutions). It has been deleted: with the new materials added to this edition, it became more obvious that that topic was out of place in this manual.

The third edition also contained an appendix 2 (Statement of Style for Contract Drafting). It too has been deleted; its place will be taken by a new, shorter style guide (see p. xli). What was appendix 1 in the third edition is now the sole appendix to this edition, except that instead of containing three versions, as in the third edition, it now consists of two versions, the annotated "before" version and the redrafted "after" version. Because I thought few readers would find it useful, I omitted the unannotated "before" version.

For a more detailed list of changes, go to http://www.adamsdrafting.com/writing/mscd/mscd4changes.

I've changed only two recommendations made in previous editions. The first is that previous editions of this manual recommended using *significant* and *material* as defined terms. This manual now recommends that instead of *significant* you use the word *nontrivial*, without defining it (see 9.21), and defining *material* is treated as optional (see 9.30).

The second is that this manual now recommends not indenting the first line of unenumerated text (see 16.55).

Given the scope and ambition of this manual, those changes are modest.

ACKNOWLEDGMENTS

I remain in the debt of those I acknowledged in previous editions. Furthermore, just as friends, clients, seminar participants, and readers helped me with previous editions, many have helped with this edition. Some did so indirectly over the years, by telling me about interesting developments, asking thoughtful questions, and pointing out my mistakes. Others did so directly, by volunteering to read the manuscript. I thank them all, but I can't resist singling out a stalwart few: Mark Anderson, Michael Fleming, Gregory M. Harris, Vance R. Koven, Chris Lemens, and Steven H. Sholk.

I continue to be fortunate that Rodney Huddleston, coauthor of *The Cambridge Grammar of the English Language*, was willing to devote time to saving me from embarrassing myself.

And I thank my family for good-naturedly supporting me in my quixotic bid to build a reputation, and a livelihood, on how to write contracts clearly.

In particular, I thank my father-in-law Stephen Kourepinos, who died last year. He was an ebullient man, and a workhorse. He was also thoughtful and generous, although he would deny it if accused.

After living in Switzerland for three years, in 1998 my wife Joanne and I returned to the United States with our infant daughter, Sydney. We needed time to figure out what would come next, so we moved in with Steve and Toni—his wife and Joanne's mother. It was a situation no one thought ideal.

Early in our time with Steve and Toni, I parked myself at their dining room table and announced that I was writing a book about contract drafting. (It turned into my first book, a precursor to this manual.) They would have been entitled to think I was fooling myself. More to the point, we didn't have a home, and I had yet to find a new job. I will forever be grateful to Steve for not informing me, in the salty manner of a Boston-raised son of Greek immigrants, that he expected me to provide for my family before indulging in fantasies.

Instead, he and Toni cheerfully supported me in my first step in what has been a 20-year adventure. I'm glad Steve saw my efforts bear fruit.

ABOUT THIS MANUAL

The Purpose of This Manual

This manual offers guidelines for clear and concise contract language. If you're making decisions regarding contract language without consulting it, it's overwhelmingly likely that you're copy-and-pasting, relying on flimsy conventional wisdom, or improvising.

If you draft contracts and follow the recommendations in this manual, your contracts will be clearer and shorter and will express the transaction more accurately. That will allow you and your organization to save time and money, reduce risk, and compete more effectively. If you review or negotiate contracts, this manual will help you determine whether deal points are articulated sensibly and will help you spot and address potential sources of uncertain meaning. If you interpret contracts—for example, if you're involved in dispute resolution—this manual will help you ascertain meaning and determine what's causing any confusion.

This manual should be useful for readers in every contract ecosystem—a solo or small-firm general practitioner handling a broad range of contracts, from leases to separation agreements; a contract manager responsible for negotiating contracts with customers; a "BigLaw" associate preparing mergers-and-acquisitions contracts; an in-house lawyer overhauling their company's template sales contracts; a paralegal reviewing confidentiality agreements their company is being asked to sign; a judge considering how to interpret a contested contract provision.

No other work addresses in comparable detail the words and phrases that make up contract provisions. And other works—including some by prominent commentators—offer analysis that too often doesn't withstand scrutiny. This manual isn't squeamish about citing examples: the marketplace of ideas requires that you not only develop your own ideas but also challenge those offered by others.

Why a Manual of Style?

A manual of style can be used as a resource by any person or organization seeking to write more clearly and consistently. For three reasons, a manual of style would be especially useful to those who draft, review, negotiate, or interpret contracts.

First, compared to other kinds of writing (expository, narrative, and persuasive), contract prose is limited and stylized—except for recitals (see 2.129), it only regulates conduct, states facts, and allocates risk. That's why this manual can attempt to be comprehensive in scope.

Second, it's best to be precise in contracts—the stakes are often high enough to justify disputes over nuances (see 1.33). Using this manual would help you be precise.

And third, contracts benefit from consistency of usages, because differences in wording can unexpectedly affect meaning (see 1.63). Using this manual would help you be consistent.

What This Manual Covers

One way to think of this manual is that it doesn't cover what you say in a contract, it covers how to say it. But that's an oversimplification, because meaning doesn't arise in a vacuum, independent of usages. Instead, how you say something can affect meaning in unexpected ways. So this manual inevitably includes plenty of the what-to-say with the how-to-say-it.

Like any book about how to write clearly, this manual covers a broad range of topics. But it doesn't cover all of them exhaustively. For example, it can offer only some examples of redundancy (see 1.37)—it's not a legal dictionary. It also doesn't discuss entire provisions, although it does consider terminology used in, for example, indemnification provisions.

This manual doesn't deal with consumer contracts—contracts between businesses and individual consumers—although much of what it says could be applied to such contracts. Instead, it's intended for those who draft, review, negotiate, or interpret business contracts—contracts between businesses that either are experienced in handling transactions or are represented by legal counsel.

This manual doesn't limit itself to standard contract usages. Instead, it recommends the clearest and most concise usages over those with nothing but tradition going for them. If a recommendation departs markedly from what is traditional, that's noted.

To keep this manual practical, it dispenses with footnotes, it cites authorities sparingly, and it limits some explication. It does without a bibliography, because it attempts to offer the most authoritative treatment, from the perspective of the contract drafter, of the topics it covers.

The appendix contains two versions of a contract: the "Before" version, annotated with footnotes to explain its drafting shortcomings; and the "After" version, redrafted to comply with the recommendations in this manual. The difference between the "Before" version and the "After" version shows the cumulative effect of a rigorous approach to drafting usages, big and small. Readers might find that the footnotes in the annotated "Before" version allow them to locate quickly those parts of this manual that discuss a given topic.

To illustrate the analysis, this manual contains many examples of contract language. Except as indicated, they're not presented as models. Indented examples of contract language are in a sans serif typeface; indented quotations from caselaw or commentary use the same typeface as the rest of the text.

Using this Manual Internationally

English is used in contracts around the world, not just contracts between companies from English-speaking countries. English has become the lingua franca of international business. A Swedish company and a Japanese company might opt to have contracts between them be in English, rather than Swedish or Japanese. And a German company in an international group might require that its contracts with other German companies be in English.

But for anyone working with English-language contracts who isn't a native English speaker, there's no such thing as a beginner's level in English-language contracting. A contract must address what's required for the transaction; no one would accept as a valid excuse that the English of a drafter, reviewer, or negotiator was limited. And the stakes are high.

On the other hand, because contracts prose is limited and stylized, it's likely to be less encumbered with peculiarities of English than are other kinds of writing. Those who aren't native English speakers should find it easier to gain command of contracts prose. This manual will help.

Anyone drafting contracts in English can safely use this manual. In the prose used, contracts drafted in the United States, the United Kingdom, Australia, and Canada share the same features. Differences in terminology exist, but are trivial. For example, whereas Commonwealth drafters use *completion*, U.S. drafters prefer *closing*. This manual recommends eliminating some of those differences in terminology by dispensing with the Commonwealth usages *amongst* and *whilst* (see 13.23), *clause* (see 4.9), *endeavours* (see 8.91), *forthwith* (see 10.126), and *procure* (see 3.145).

Differences in spelling are likewise trivial. For example, in American English, *license* is both a noun and a verb, whereas in other varieties of English, *licence* is the noun and *license* is the verb.

The Significance of Caselaw

This manual cites caselaw as part of its analysis of different usages—mostly opinions by federal and state courts in the United States, but also opinions by English, Canadian, and Australian courts, along with, it so happens, one opinion from each of Ireland, Singapore, and South Africa.

Court opinions tell us which usages risk causing disputes and how judges misinterpret contract language. Because the prose of English-language contracts is so similar the world over, the lessons from caselaw are universal. An Illinois case involving syntactic ambiguity is as relevant to drafters in Australia as it is to those in the United States.

This manual doesn't cite caselaw to support attributing a specific meaning to a particular usage. For one thing, courts tend to be overly confident of their understanding of how English works. But more to the point, a contract should speak directly to the reader, in standard English (see 1.28), without relying on caselaw to breathe meaning into it. (See p. xxxvii regarding the notion of "tested" contract language.)

Readers have asked how the recommendations in this manual have fared in the courts. That's like assessing how law-abiding someone is by how often juries acquit them. Contracts drafted consistent with this manual shouldn't end up in court because of a fight over confusing contract language.

But sometimes contract parties pick fights for no good reason. And sometimes judges make bad decisions to achieve a desired outcome, or they make mistakes. A court might give a usage a meaning different from what this manual says you can expect, or it might attribute significance to a usage this manual says is pointless. For example, see 3.73 (regarding caselaw holding that *shall* can mean *should*) and 2.176–.178 (regarding caselaw attributing significance to a backstop recital of consideration).

Both the law and the English language are intricate, sprawling things, so you can expect this sort of caselaw glitch occasionally. An errant court opinion is no reason for this manual to retreat from any of its recommendations.

TRADITIONAL CONTRACT LANGUAGE IS DYSFUNCTIONAL

The Scale of the Dysfunction

The notion that the prose of contracts can and should be clear and modern is catching on. One sign is that this manual is now in its fourth edition. And people evidently do consult this manual. A modest example: ten years ago the concluding clause this manual recommends (see 5.4) started appearing in contracts filed on the U.S. Securities and Exchange Commission's EDGAR system, where public companies file their "material" contracts.

But have no illusions. Contracts drafted without the benefit of rigorous guidelines—most contracts—remain awash in dysfunction. The details differ, but the effect is consistent: readers must wade through a slurry of archaisms, redundancy, chaotic verb structures, overlong sentences, and confusing terminology. In short, traditional contract language.

It's not as if the dysfunction of traditional contract language is a problem for only nonlawyers. Everyone is in the same fog, although some are in denial.

It doesn't matter how exalted the law firm, company, or trade group—they mostly churn out dysfunction. The poor quality of their contracts is at odds with the aura of proficiency and dependability that such organizations seek to foster.

The Primary Cause of Dysfunction

A defining characteristic of contract drafting is that each new transaction inevitably resembles previous transactions. It makes sense to copy contracts used in those other transactions, adjusting them as needed to reflect the new transaction.

That should be a source of efficiency, but if you're using word processing, the result is a pathology this manual calls "passive drafting":

- You don't have the time or perhaps the expertise to reassess precedent contracts and templates, so you copy them, on faith, assuming that they worked before and so will work again.
- Because you're copying, you don't need guidelines.
- Because you're copying, no one needs to be trained.

The alternative to passive drafting is "active drafting":

- You follow a comprehensive set of guidelines for modern contract language.
- You're trained in how to draft and review contracts consistent with those guidelines.
- You copy from only templates and precedent contracts that comply with those guidelines.

RESISTANCE TO CHANGING TRADITIONAL LANGUAGE

Claiming That Traditional Language "Works"

Those who want to improve contract language face obstacles. For one thing, you encounter the claim that traditional contract language "works." See, e.g., Kenneth A. Adams, *Where Are the Data Showing that Traditional Contract Language Is Dysfunctional?*, Adams on Contract Drafting (20 Feb. 2017), http://www.adamsdrafting.com/where-are-the-data/. That notion assumes a binary world in which contracts work or don't work. In fact, contracts are clear or less clear, working with them is less time-consuming or more time-consuming, and they present less risk of dispute over confusing prose or more risk. And caselaw is full of instances of confusing traditional usages causing a dispute.

Claiming That Traditional Language Has Been "Tested"

A more nuanced argument against changing traditional contract language is that doing so would be risky—traditional contract language has been litigated, or "tested," so it has an established, or "settled," meaning.

Here's how one commentator expressed it: "[C]areful writing can even be counterproductive if the result is to re-draft language that has been previously interpreted by a court as having a particular meaning. Ironically, in such a case, changing the words—even for the better—can only increase uncertainty." Robert C. Illig, *A Business Lawyer's Bibliography: Books Every Dealmaker Should Read*, Journal of Legal Education 585, 625 (May 2012).

This argument suffers from three weaknesses, each fatal. First, because courts have scrutinized some traditional contract terminology but not the full range of contract usages, the notion of "tested" contract language applies only narrowly.

Second, the notion of "tested" contract language suggests that all courts ascribe the same set meaning to individual usages. That's not so. How courts interpret usages depends on the circumstances of each case and the semantic acuity of the judge, and can vary over time and among jurisdictions.

And third, if parties to a contract had to ask a court to determine the meaning of a particular provision, that's because the contract failed to state clearly the intent of the parties. Why rely on wording that created confusion? Instead, express meaning clearly, so you needn't gamble on a court attributing the desired meaning to a contract. Courts have to clean up whatever messes they're presented with, but this manual is free to recommend ways to avoid confusion. The Delaware Chancery Court has acknowledged as much, noting "the difference between the roles served by courts and judges, on the one hand, and commentators like Adams, on the other." *GRT, Inc. v. Marathon GTF Technology, Ltd.*, No. CIV.A. 5571-CS, 2011 WL 2682898, at *14 n.79 (Del. Ch. 11 July 2011).

So although some lawyers will continue to claim that "tested" contract language is safer than expressing meaning clearly, it's a lazy platitude.

The Dead Hand of Inertia

The arguments that traditional language "works" and that it has been "tested" are advanced by those who seem disinclined to do the hard work of considering, usage by usage, what is clearest and most concise. Instead, it seems likely that what motivates these objections is a basic urge: inertia.

People are wary of creative thinking, preferring instead to tackle a task by using what they already know, even if the result is inferior. This instinct is universal: you can find examples in medicine, in sports, and in cooking. Because contract drafting is inherently precedent-driven, it's particularly prone to inertia. (For more on the role of inertia in contract drafting, see the "Inertia" category of the Adams on Contract Drafting blog, http://www.adamsdrafting.com/category/inertia/.)

Even in debate over individual usages, one can attribute to inertia the way some commentators invoke obscurantist rationalizations to explain confusing terminology.

Inertia can operate through several mechanisms. One is "learned helplessness"—if you copy-and-paste traditional contract language for long enough, you might find it difficult to accept that there's an alternative. Another is "cognitive dissonance"—if you have no alternative to copy-and-pasting, that could lead you to idealize traditional contract language. A third is peer pressure—you see the merit of a modern alternative to a traditional usage, but you're reluctant to draw attention to yourself by making the change. And a fourth could be described as the no-smoke-without-fire school of contract interpretation—the notion that if enough people who work with contracts ascribe to a particular view, that view must have merit.

Underestimating Complexity

Another factor impeding change is that many lawyers aren't equipped to assess the quality of contract drafting. The delusion that one drafts well is easy to catch and hard to shake, particularly in the absence of proper training, rigorous guidelines, and a critical readership. If more attention has been paid to litigation writing than to writing contracts clearly, it's likely because litigators write for an outside audience—judges. Unless a problem arises, a contract's only readers are likely to be the lawyers who drafted and negotiated it and, to a greater or lesser extent, their clients. Usually that's not a critical readership.

Even those inclined to improve contracts underestimate what's involved. For example, law firms often assign the task of preparing templates to those who are perhaps least qualified for the task—junior lawyers with time on their hands. And some company lawyers newly converted to the cause of "plain English" contracts assume that all that's required is common sense and a copy of *Plain English for Lawyers* from law school.

Lawyers are also prone to assuming that they can figure out the implications of individual usages based on their own understanding—usually limited—of English and what sounds right. But in contracts, where the stakes are often high and prose can be subjected to extraordinary scrutiny, things are not always as they seem. To get a sense of that, you only have to skim chapter 11 (Ambiguity of the Part Versus the Whole).

Judges share this overconfidence: you will find in this manual many examples of judges considering the implications of a contract usage and reaching a conclusion that make no sense. Although courts mostly don't accept expert testimony on ambiguity, except as to technical terms, courts would benefit from admitting testimony of experts in contract language.

Legalistic Hairsplitting

And it doesn't help to bring to contract drafting and interpretation a hairsplitting legalistic mindset. If you read into contract usages a meaning that isn't established or that's at odds with how the English language works, you confuse matters and risk straying into nonsense. Three prime examples of that are legalistic interpretations of *represents and warrants* (see 3.374), *efforts* standards (see 8.15), and *indemnify and hold harmless* (see 13.419).

CHANGE AT THE LEVEL OF THE INDIVIDUAL

The Other Side's Draft

Using a manual of style when considering a draft contract involves selling change. What that requires depends on which side prepared the draft.

If you're reviewing the other side's draft, a certain etiquette applies. Your task isn't to turn their draft into a thing of beauty. You look only for whatever doesn't reflect the deal as you understand it and whatever could create confusion. You give a pass to those features of traditional contract language that don't make sense but aren't confusing. Examples include use of a traditional recital of consideration (see 2.166), benign overuse of *shall* (see 3.85), and archaisms in the front and back of the contract. Asking the other side to change such things risks needlessly antagonizing them.

Features that are worth flagging include anything that should be a condition that's instead expressed as an obligation (see 3.359), inherently confusing usages (for example, *indemnify and hold harmless*; see 13.419), and instances of ambiguity. If they've caused disputes, it's worth flagging even seemingly minor glitches, for example throat-clearing verb structures (see 3.25) and use of *may* in restrictive relative clauses (see 3.459).

If whoever prepared the other side's draft is a traditionalist, you might have to explain to them what prompted you to request a change. Citing this manual might facilitate that discussion by demonstrating that your proposed change is based on an internationally recognized set of guidelines.

Your Draft

If you're drafting, the first bit of selling you might have to do is to someone senior to you at your organization. Assess their expectations. Are they a traditionalist? If so, are they open-minded? You might mention this manual to them and see whether that starts a conversation. If they're not receptive to modern drafting, then give them what they expect, making strategic concessions on usages that don't affect meaning but being gently persistent if something matters.

Then there's the task of selling a clear and modern draft to those on the other side of the transaction. It shouldn't be an ordeal. With only a few exceptions, contract language that complies with the recommendations in this manual doesn't draw attention to itself. It simply eliminates the stumbling blocks, the repetition, the redundancy, the obscure legalisms, the archaisms, and the inconsistencies. What's left is the deal, which is what readers will focus on. That means you might not get a pat on the back for your drafting prowess, but readers will get to the substance with less delay and confusion, so your job will be easier. That should be sufficient reward.

But contract drafting is a precedent-driven part of a notoriously conservative profession, so you shouldn't be surprised if you encounter resistance. People are prone to attacking what they don't understand, so to limit pushback consider explaining to the other side in advance what's behind the usages in your draft. That could be accomplished by this email cover note:

> The language used in the attached draft complies with the recommendations in Kenneth A. Adams, *A Manual of Style for Contract Drafting* (ABA 4th ed. 2017).

That book recommends replacing many traditional drafting usages with clearer alternatives, so some usages you see routinely might be absent from this draft. Please don't ask that traditional usages be added to this draft unless that would make the contract clearer or would better reflect what the parties have agreed on.

And please check what *A Manual of Style for Contract Drafting* has to say about any usage you're inclined to add to this draft. It might be problematic in ways you hadn't considered.

It's in the interests of both sides not to spend time making, or even discussing, changes that are unrelated to the deal and changes that risk creating confusion or making the contract harder to read.

Any pushback is likely to be in proportion to the bargaining leverage the other side feels it has. Your resistance to the pushback would presumably depend on the circumstances. If it's a one-off deal, you might be willing to indulge the other side by making changes that pointlessly add traditional usages.

You might react differently if the draft is one of your core commercial templates, as the whole point of templates is to limit the changes you make from deal to deal. Consider taking a firm stance even when it comes to, say, your use of a lowercase *a* in *this agreement* (see 2.125). Although it's a usage that has no deal significance and tends to befuddle traditionalists, little is gained by throwing it to the wolves. Anyone who is so dogmatic as to get worked up about *this agreement* is likely to have a problem with other modern usages, so you're likely to find yourself discussing those usages too.

Using *this agreement* could actually work to your advantage, as it offers a convenient way to set ground rules for negotiations over contract wording. It appears early in the contract, and the explanation for it is simple. Getting the other side to accept *this agreement* might well pave the way for their accepting other novel usages. If someone nevertheless insists on your using a capital *A*, you'll know that you're dealing with a reactionary who is willing to ignore the convention that you don't meddle with the other side's draft without good reason. It's best to know that early on, so you can adjust.

More generally, be realistic about the extent to which you as an individual can follow the recommendations in this manual. If you're working with an organization's traditional templates or standard industry contracts, you might have little opportunity. Even if you have control over your drafting, retooling traditional contract language takes time. It might be best to take an incremental approach, starting first with those provisions you get the most use out of, so you get a quicker return on the time invested.

CHANGE AT THE LEVEL OF THE ORGANIZATION

A Style Guide as Foundation

If you want your organization's contracts to be clear and consistent, your first step should be to adopt a style guide.

Even if all contracts personnel at an organization are informed consumers of modern contract language, that doesn't make for an efficient contract process, as too much would be at the whim of individuals with different experience, aptitudes, and training. What's needed is centralized initiatives.

The foundation for an efficient contract process is a style guide for contract usages. It's unlikely that the drafters in an organization would independently choose the same usages, so the only way to achieve consistency would be to impose consistency through a style guide. The idea of using a style guide is catching on. A good example is how in 2015, Adobe Systems Incorporated disseminated publicly the 30-page *Adobe Legal Department Style Guide*.

For an organization to prepare a suitably comprehensive style guide from scratch would be challenging, considering the expertise and time required. Even 30 pages wouldn't cover the territory adequately.

This manual might seem like a style guide, but it's too lengthy and too detailed to be used by all contracts personnel in your organization. Instead, this manual would likely be appropriate for those who work extensively with contract language.

But it's suitable as a foundation for a style guide. That's why the author of this manual expects to publish with the American Bar Association a shorter work entitled *Drafting Clearer Contracts: A Concise Style Guide for Organizations*. It makes sense for one style guide to become the accepted standard, in the manner of *The Chicago Manual of Style*, which is widely used in the United States for general publishing. Time will tell if *Drafting Clearer Contracts* serves that function for contract drafting.

Training and Templates

Once you have a style guide, the next step is to train your contracts personnel to draft and review contracts consistent with the style guide. But that isn't enough. People draft contracts by copying, so if you want clear and modern contracts, you need clear and modern templates.

That sounds like a lot of work, but it isn't if you go about it sensibly. Enlist suitable contract-language expertise and, if required, subject-matter expertise. And don't indulge in "drafting by committee," with those involved angling to include in templates their pet contract usages, usually based on whatever conventional wisdom they've picked up.

Surrendering Autonomy

Besides inertia, an obstacle to acceptance of this manual or use of a style guide within an organization is that lawyers generally resist efforts to standardize their work. Individual autonomy has long been an integral part of being a lawyer.

In particular, it's commonplace to hear lawyers refer to their own or someone else's drafting "style." The implication is that each drafter draws on a palette of alternative yet equally valid usages.

But that's inconsistent with what's required for optimal contract language. (The word "style" in the title of this manual isn't an endorsement of the notion of drafting styles. Instead, the title was loosely intended to invoke the ambition of *The Chicago Manual of Style*.) The only criterion for judging contract prose is how clear it is. When a drafter has several alternative usages available to accomplish a drafting goal, one will generally be clearer than the others. It would make sense for all drafters to employ only the clearest usages.

Even if those alternative usages are equally clear, having all the members of an organization employ the same usage would eliminate confusion and make it easier to move blocks of text from one contract to another.

Lawyers should be willing to surrender autonomy over the building blocks of contract language. The freedom to recycle a grab-bag of usages based on some combination of limited research, uncertain conventional wisdom, and expediency isn't freedom worth preserving. Just as use of standardized, high-quality brick, stone, and steel doesn't prevent architects and builders from being creative, use of standardized contract usages doesn't stifle creativity in articulating a transaction. Instead, it enhances creativity, because it leaves you more time to focus on substance and makes you more confident that you're being clear and concise.

Specialization

But an efficient contract process can involve more than individual lawyers surrendering autonomy. As the heft of this manual suggests, acquiring a command of the full range of issues lurking in contract language takes time. That investment pays off, but perhaps not for everyone. In larger organizations, greater complexity generally leads to greater specialization—it doesn't make economic sense for everyone in the organization to be a specialist, and not everyone will have the aptitude.

The realities of the contract-drafting process suggest that for a substantial organization to achieve high quality and maximum efficiency, what's required is not only standardization but also specialization. For an organization with a sufficient volume of contracts requiring customization, specialization can readily be achieved through automated contract drafting. Information technology allows you to create contracts not by copy-and-pasting from precedent contracts but by completing an annotated online questionnaire and selecting from among the options offered. A few specialists prepare the text used in an automated system.

Aside from whether an organization can achieve economies of scale to justify implementing an automated system for creating contracts, the obstacles to specialization are cultural. They're the same as those that impede standardization, except that specialization involves not just surrendering autonomy but also, for some, relinquishing any role in contract drafting. For those organizations that can overcome those obstacles, the potential rewards are clear.

CHANGE AT THE LEVEL OF THE INDUSTRY

Just as within an organization it doesn't make sense to leave individuals to draft contracts entirely as they see fit, it also doesn't make sense to have each company create its own templates for standard commercial contracts. Information technology now offers alternative ways to compile contract language, but each has shortcomings.

Utopians see potential in crowdsourcing, with individuals collaborating to create contracts that reflect collective wisdom. But nothing useful has been created using that approach. Given how complicated contracts are, and given what's at stake, you need strong editorial control, but that's antithetical to the notion of crowdsourcing. And it's hard to imagine someone with appropriate expertise volunteering to spearhead a crowdsourcing initiative without being paid.

Free online repositories of contracts have come and gone, offering little or no quality control, consistency, customization, guidance, or credibility. And there's always the U.S. Securities and Exchange Commission's EDGAR system. It's free, and you get what you pay for.

Some services use information technology to parse EDGAR and other repositories of contracts, displaying the different ways that contracts address particular issues.

You get to see exactly what's in the contracts, but that's unrelated to whether a provision is drafted clearly, accurately reflects the deal or the law, or is even relevant to the user's needs.

Some vendors offer curated templates. At the bottom end of the market, they offer rubbish for free or for a nominal amount. The top end of the market offers you traditional BigLaw drafting, with all its shortcomings.

Real progress would require automated templates that comply with a style guide and are created with strong editorial control and suitable subject-matter expertise. An example of what that might look like is a highly customized confidentiality-agreement template created by the author of this manual, using the software Contract Express. (For more information, go to http://www.adamscontracts.com/nda.)

THE CHARACTERISTICS OF OPTIMAL CONTRACT LANGUAGE

1.1   Form follows function. The limited function of contracts—regulating conduct, stating facts, and allocating risk—has implications for the nature of contract language. Treating contracts as just another form of legal writing can lead you astray.

1.2   This chapter considers the general characteristics of clear and concise contract language. It identifies principles this manual invokes in analyzing individual usages. You might find it worthwhile to revisit this chapter occasionally, just to remind yourself of the underlying principles. You can apply these principles when considering usages not examined in this manual.

CONTRACT LANGUAGE SHOULD BE CLEAR

1.3   Obviously, contracts should be clear, but traditional contract language is unclear in different ways.

Omit Archaisms

1.4   Traditional contract drafting is full of archaic usages. This manual considers many—for example, use of *whereas* in recitals (see 2.143).

1.5   Inertia might explain how archaisms survive, but it's also likely that many drafters think, at least subconsciously, that archaisms add gravitas, making it more likely that clients and others will take contracts seriously. (Occasionally some are bold enough to say so publicly.) It's preposterous to think that despite the time and cost involved in entering into a transaction, and despite the importance to the parties of whatever goals they seek to accomplish, parties need contract archaisms to put them in an appropriate frame of mind.

1.6   Instead, archaisms create distance between the text and the reader—they tell the reader that they're entering into an occult, counterintuitive world. If readers expect archaisms, it's only because they're unaware that there's an alternative. It's hard to imagine that once presented with a contract free of archaisms, any rational reader would miss them.

Omit Problematic Terms of Art

1.7   Contract language includes legal terms of art—words and phrases that have a specialized doctrinal meaning. They serve as shorthand for legal concepts, allowing those concepts to be articulated with a minimum of fuss.

1.8   Legal terms of art add complexity, but that can be difficult to avoid. Contracts are as complex as the transactions they embody, and many transactions are highly technical. Expressing that complexity usually requires specialized terminology. Purging contracts of all that terminology can result in contracts that fail to articulate the intended meaning clearly and efficiently.

1.9   For example, it would be awkward not to use the term of art *security interest* in drafting a contract in which a party grants a security interest. Similarly, it likely would be awkward to draft a security agreement without using the noun *perfection* or the verb *perfect*, both of which are terms of art relating to security interests.

1.10   But a feature of traditional contract drafting is reliance on three kinds of flawed legal terms of art, namely those that are unnecessary, those that are improvised, and those that are unduly complex. (More generally, this manual uses the word *jargon* as shorthand for unhelpful terms of art.)

UNNECESSARY TERMS OF ART

1.11   Lawyers are prone to using doctrinal terms of art in contracts even though simpler terminology is available, rendering those terms of art unnecessary.

1.12   For example, in a security agreement, why use *hypothecate* regarding a security interest? Why not simply use *grant*? *Hypothecate* means to pledge without delivery of title and possession. That meaning goes beyond the function required of the verb in language granting a security interest. And that meaning isn't otherwise necessary, as the security agreement itself will specify what the terms of the security interest are. *Hypothecate* might have value as shorthand for court opinions or scholarly texts, but that's very different from what's required for a contract. Using *grant* in granting language in a security agreement wouldn't prevent that grant from being a hypothecation, if the remainder of the granting language is consistent with that meaning. If it isn't, using *hypothecate* instead wouldn't fix that.

1.13   What characterizes an unnecessary term of art is a discrepancy between the meaning conveyed by the term of art and the semantic function required of it in a contract—an unnecessary term of art is a dollar word or phrase doing a nickel's worth of work. That might lead some to assume that no other terminology could convey the same meaning. And some might assume that use of the term is by itself sufficient to ensure that the underlying concept applies to the provision in question, regardless of what the provision otherwise says.

1.14   An example of the second problem is how some contend that a statement of fact can't support an action for misrepresentation unless it's introduced by the word *represents*. And that a statement of fact that uses the word *represents* can't support an action for breach of warranty. (See 3.380–.397.)

1.15   Other examples of unnecessary terms of art are *allonge* (see 13.14), *attorn* (see 13.93), *novation* (see 13.615), and *subrogation* (see 13.752).

IMPROVISED TERMS OF ART

1.16   Unnecessary terms of art arise when doctrinal terminology is shoehorned into contracts. By contrast, improvised terms of art arise when lawyers and judges seek to graft doctrinal implications onto terminology otherwise free of them.

1.17   Drafters have long added the phrase *hold harmless* after *indemnify*, presumably for the rhetorical flourish it offers. But many lawyers and some judges haven't been able to resist the urge to claim that *hold harmless* conveys a distinct meaning (see 13.420). Similarly, in everyday English the phrase *best efforts* serves a specific rhetorical function, but many lawyers and some judges ignore that and instead invent baseless distinctions in the various flavors of *efforts* standards (see chapter 8).

1.18   The urge to improvise terms of art arises from the rule of interpretation that every word in a provision should be given effect. Applied zealously, that rule requires attributing significance to every stray word or phrase in a contract and to every variation in terminology, even if they can be explained as a rhetorical device.

UNDULY COMPLEX TERMS OF ART

1.19   A third category of problematic terms of art consists of those with a meaning that's fairly well established but that's also sufficiently complex that drafters are quick to use them without fully appreciating the implications. Three examples are *consequential damages* (see 13.161), *coupled with an interest* (see 13.199), and *time is of the essence* (see 13.829). The result of using an unduly complex term of art might be that the provision in question is held unenforceable or has unanticipated consequences.

REPLACING TERMS OF ART

1.20   Contracts would be clearer if instead of using terms of art that fall into the three categories described above, drafters were to use straightforward alternatives.

1.21   But replacing a particular term of art might not be feasible—doing so might prompt too much fruitless debate. The notion of replacing a term of art can seem shockingly novel—for example, using *states* instead of *represents and warrants* (see 3.416). You must weigh the risks of confusion against the transaction costs of change.

1.22   One way to facilitate change would be to not only use the term of art but also explain what it means. For examples of such explanations, see 13.208–.209 regarding the phrase *coupled with an interest* and 13.616 regarding the term *novation*.

1.23   Another way to facilitate change would be to use the term of art in a section heading and use the clearer alternative in the section text. For examples, see 13.95, 13.890. That approach could conceivably violate an internal rule of interpretation stating that headings are for convenience only, but that rule of interpretation is of little use (see 15.17).

1.24   But replacing some terms of art would likely pass unnoticed. See, for example, 13.887–.888 regarding an alternative to the verb *warrant*.

1.25   Replacing terms of art not only makes life easier for the reader, it can also help the drafter realize that although terms of art might suggest professionalism, problematic terms of art distract from articulating the deal effectively.

1.26   If you're contemplating replacing a term of art, first check whether courts attribute significance to use of that term in a contract, as opposed to alternative ways of expressing the same meaning. Sensibly, U.S. courts tend not to insist on specific wording.

TERMS OF ART IN LANGUAGES OTHER THAN ENGLISH

1.27   If an English-language contract is governed by the law of a jurisdiction where court proceedings are conducted in a language other than English, and if that contract contains terms of art, translating those terms of art can have unpredictable consequences. If someone translates, say, a Dutch term of art into English when drafting the contract, what might happen during dispute-resolution proceedings is that the court translates the English version back into something other than the original Dutch term of art. To avoid that sort of mishap, it would be prudent to include the non-English original after the English translation, in italics and in parentheses. An example: "This agreement constitutes an assignment agreement (*overeenkomst van opdracht*) under the Dutch Civil Code."

Use Standard English

1.28   Eliminating archaisms and terms of art goes a long way toward turning traditional contract prose into a specialized version of standard English— the English used by educated native English speakers. That's what you should aim for.

1.29   This manual doesn't use the terms *plain English* or *plain language*. Because those terms first came to public attention in connection with simplifying consumer documents, they can be understood, or misunderstood, as applying only to the simplified language required of consumer contracts. Here's an example of that from Charles M. Fox, *Working with Contracts: What Law School Doesn't Teach You* 73 (2d ed. 2008):

> The audience for commercial contracts is sophisticated business people and their lawyers. The notion that complex commercial contracts should be written in plain English, so as to be understood by people who would never be expected to read them is an unreasonable extension of the plain English movement.

1.30   That misses the point. No commentator favors "dumbing down" business contracts to make them as accessible as documents intended to be read by consumers—a misconceived notion, because a contract is necessarily as complex as the transaction it embodies. Instead, the idea is that by using standard English, a drafter can articulate a transaction without recourse to usages that interfere gratuitously with the ability of the reader to understand the contract. Whether they're aware of it or not, lawyers, clients, and anyone else who must read a business contract would benefit if it were written in standard English.

1.31   And you can dismiss the notion that you must stick with traditional contract language because it "works" or has been "tested." See p. xxxvii

1.32   Furthermore, don't assume that the meaning given a word or phrase for logic rules will apply to contracts. Instead, you can expect the standard English interpretation to prevail. Two examples are *or* (see 11.56) and *if and only if* (see 1.59).

CONTRACT LANGUAGE SHOULD BE PRECISE

1.33   Traditionalists maintain that traditional contract legalese is precise. It isn't, as this manual amply demonstrates.

1.34   Real precision makes it harder for a disgruntled contract party to claim, or for a judge to find, a meaning that the drafter hadn't intended. For example, real precision allows drafters to distinguish between conditions and obligations (see 3.356–.362) and to eliminate potentially mischievous alternative meanings associated with *and* and *or* (see 11.21–.85). The enemy of precision is uncertain meaning. Chapter 7 discusses the sources of uncertain meaning.

1.35   It's easy to denigrate precision. "Wordsmithing" is a term that's popular among red-meat-eating deal makers. It refers to minions figuring out, away from negotiations, how to express a deal point. It's also used dismissively of someone whose supposed pedanticism is hindering the deal. Either way, the term "wordsmithing" suggests that once parties agree on a deal point, expressing it is a formality.

1.36   Instead, it's routine for nuances in wording to cause disputes. That's because the deal is what the contract says it is, not some abstraction—how the drafter articulates a deal provision determines its meaning. Precise contract language should be a priority, not an afterthought.

CONTRACT LANGUAGE SHOULD OMIT REDUNDANCY

1.37   Redundancy is a hallmark of traditional contract legalese, but it's pernicious—it adds unnecessary words and can create confusion. It comes in different forms.

Limit the Use of Strings

1.38   Lawyers have long strung together words, and rare is the contract that doesn't include strings of two, three, or more synonyms or near-synonyms. (Pairs of words are "couplets" and groups of three are "triplets.")

1.39   Some strings, for example *goods and chattels,* presumably reflect that in medieval England the primary language of legal expression gradually shifted from Latin to French to English. Rather than rely on just one language to express a concept, scribes were in the habit of using words from two or three languages.

1.40   But because of its rhythmical appeal, lexical doubling has been with us since the dawn of English. And it has been too long entrenched in legal language to be explained by a narrow historical circumstance. Contract drafters continually improvise new strings, such as the requirement in a share purchase agreement that Smith *sell, convey, assign, transfer, and deliver* the shares to Jones.

1.41   Presumably one attraction of strings is that they add pomp to contract prose. Strings also appeal to risk-averse lawyers, allowing them to finesse the often-tricky task of selecting the best word.

1.42   But strings are problematic in three respects. First, if one of the words expresses the intended meaning, the others are extraneous—at best, they simply clog up the works.

1.43   Second, courts routinely invoke the principle that in interpreting legal documents, every word should be given meaning and nothing should be treated as superfluous. That explains litigation over the meaning of, for example, the phrase *indemnify and hold harmless* (see 13.422–.425). Don't be surprised if a court attributes unanticipated meaning to an element in a string.

1.44   And third, a drafter might use a string more than once in a contract, with minor but potentially mischievous variants. For example, if one provision refers to *losses, liabilities, damages, and claims* and another to *losses, liabilities, and damages,* a party to a dispute might try to convince a court that omission of *claims* from the second string is significant.

1.45   You can safely prune many traditional synonym strings, as the extra words are surplusage. This manual considers several such strings, including *books and records* (see 13.119) and *costs and expenses* (see 13.196).

1.46   Don't rely on strings incorporating overly subtle distinctions if you can express the intended meaning more clearly using a different approach. For example, see 13.37 regarding devising clearer alternatives to *arising out of or relating to.*

1.47   As for improvised strings, consider the example mentioned in 1.40—a requirement in a share purchase agreement that Smith *sell, convey, assign, transfer, and deliver* the shares to Jones. Just as *purchase* would be adequate to reflect the transaction from the perspective of Jones, Smith can simply sell the shares. *Convey, assign,* and *transfer* reflect concepts implicit in a sale. Address in a section on closing procedures whatever *deliver* covers.

1.48   Similarly, instead of saying that Acme *grants, assigns, conveys, mortgages, pledges, hypothecates, and transfers* a security interest, saying just *grants* should be sufficient. But instead of picking one word in a string, consider whether an alternative approach would allow you to convey the intended meaning more clearly. Compare the string in italics in the first example below with the language in italics in the second example. The intended scope of the first might be broader than that expressed in the second, but it would be clearer to express any broader meaning by referring explicitly in the second to any relevant contexts instead of stringing together legal functions.

> … except that the Employee may transfer the Employee's rights under this agreement to the Employee's *personal or legal representatives, executors, administrators, heirs, distributees, devisees, and legatees.*

> … except that the Employee's rights under this agreement may be transferred *by will or intestate succession.*

1.49   Strings can arise in autonomous definitions, as risk-averse drafters are prone to adding every conceivable example of the thing being defined:

> "**Permit**" means any consent, authorization, registration, filing, lodgment, permit, franchise, agreement, notarization, certificate, permission, license, approval, direction, declaration, authority, or exemption … .

1.50   In such contexts, consider using instead the phrase *however referred to*, to make it clear that the definition refers to a concept—in this case, anything that could be described as a permit, regardless of the word used to describe it:

> "**Permit**" means a permit, however referred to, … .

1.51   But strings are sometimes necessary to ensure that a provision covers the universe of possibilities. For example, a seller might state in a share purchase agreement that the shares are free of any *lien, community property interest, equitable interest, option, pledge, security interest, or right of first refusal.* This string might include redundancy, but don't eliminate every element except, say, *lien* unless you're confident that *lien* covers the other terms.

1.52   So consider every component of a synonym string to determine whether it conveys a meaning that is distinct, and helpfully so, from the meaning of each other component. If you use a string more than once, use identical wording each time or replace it with a defined term (see 6.2).

Reject Needless Elaboration

1.53   Contract provisions often refer not only to a general term but also to its constituent components, even though the scope of the general term is clear. This manual uses the phrase *needless elaboration* to describe this phenomenon. It's equivalent to saying, "I don't eat fish, whether freshwater or saltwater," instead of just saying, "I don't eat fish," which conveys the same meaning.

1.54   A contract example of needless elaboration is stating that a party is releasing *all claims whether at law or in equity.* Saying instead *all claims* would be just as comprehensive and would use fewer words. (Besides, for U.S. contracts, such references have a musty air to them, as most states have abolished the distinction between actions at law and suits in equity.)

1.55 Needless elaboration sometimes occurs when a provision lists elements of the general term before the general term, as in *all taxes imposed by any federal, state, or local governmental body*. Referring simply to any *governmental body* would be not only more concise but also more comprehensive, in that a jurisdiction might have a level of government better described by a term other than *federal, state,* or *local*.

1.56 Needless elaboration also occurs when drafters use a general term and list examples of items that obviously fall within that general term, with the list either coming after the general term (and usually introduced by *including*) or coming before the general term. For a discussion of the confusion that can cause, see 13.354–.386.

CONTRACT LANGUAGE SHOULDN'T SEEK TO EXPLAIN, TELL A STORY, OR PERSUADE

1.57 Because contracts serve only to regulate conduct, state facts, and allocate risk, drafters should be cautious about using words associated primarily with expository, narrative, or persuasive prose—words such as *therefore, because* (see 13.110), and *furthermore*.

1.58 Don't add rhetorical emphasis to provisions that already express the desired meaning. Rhetorical emphasis consists of words and phrases that serve only to say, "and we really mean it!" It adds unnecessary words, doesn't affect meaning, and quickly becomes grating.

1.59 The fix for rhetorical emphasis is deleting it or replacing it with something else. Below is a list of words and phrases used for rhetorical emphasis, and after each is an example using that word or phrase. In three examples (*at no time, if and only if,* and *under no circumstances*) a suggested replacement is noted in brackets; in the other examples, you would simply delete the rhetorical emphasis.

> **absolutely**: The Lessee must *absolutely* refrain from performing actions involving cooking and/or frying in the Leased Property … .
>
> **at no time**: The Escrow Agent shall *at no time* [read not] acquire any ownership interest in the Offering Proceeds.
>
> **completely**: … the Executive shall keep the terms of this agreement *completely* confidential … .
>
> **fully**: The Consultant is wholly and *fully* responsible for any taxes owed to any governmental authority … .
>
> **if and only if**: This agreement will become effective *if and only if* [read *only if*] Acme issues the Shares before the Termination Date.
>
> **in all respects**: This agreement is *in all respects* governed by Minnesota law.

in any manner: No benefit payable under the Plan is subject *in any manner* whatsoever to alienation, sale, transfer, assignment, pledge, attachment, or encumbrance of any kind.

in any way: … none of the Buyer Indemnitees will be liable *in any way* for any injury, loss, or damage arising out of any such entry that occurs to Seller or any of Seller's representatives under this agreement.

it is emphasized that: *It is emphasized that* the designer of the unit is not entitled to design or change anything outside the bounds of the unit.

of any kind: No benefit payable under the Plan is subject in any manner whatsoever to alienation, sale, transfer, assignment, pledge, attachment, or encumbrance *of any kind*.

strictly: The Company guarantees payment of the Guaranteed Obligations *strictly* in accordance with the terms of this agreement and the Notes.

under no circumstances: The Depositary will *under no circumstances* [read *not*] be liable for any incidental, indirect, special, consequential, or punitive damages.

whatsoever: No Lender has any right of action *whatsoever* against the Administrative Agent.

wholly: The Consultant is *wholly* and fully responsible for any taxes owed to any governmental authority … .

1.60   Some of these words and phrases can be combined, as in *wholly and fully* and *in any manner whatsoever*. A word or phrase can constitute rhetorical emphasis in one context and serve a different function—legitimate or not so legitimate—in a different context.

1.61   Don't use typography for rhetorical emphasis (see 16.36).

CONTRACT LANGUAGE SHOULD OMIT REPETITION

1.62   A drafter should never say the same thing twice in a contract, whether it's a party's address (see 2.72), a number (see 14.1–.19) or anything else. Repetition not only adds unnecessary words, it also invites dispute. Redundancy (see 1.37) differs from repetition, in that redundancy involves surplusage in saying something as opposed to saying something twice.

CONTRACT LANGUAGE SHOULD EMPLOY USAGES CONSISTENTLY

1.63   Usages should be consistent, to avoid having unintended meaning attributed to inconsistent usages.

1.64   Within a contract, don't use the same word or phrase to convey different meanings—that might create confusion about which meaning you intend in any one context. In traditional drafting, the word most abused in that regard is *shall* (see 3.80). And don't use two or more different words or phrases to convey the same meaning: readers (and judges) might assume that differences in wording are intended to convey differences in meaning.

1.65   Any organization would benefit if all its contracts were to draw from the same set of usages—ideally, the consistency in language and layout of a company's or a law firm's contracts would make it impossible to determine which individual had drafted what.

1.66   See the introduction for advice on how to overcome obstacles to consistency and how to use this manual (or a style guide based on it) to achieve consistency.

2

THE FRONT OF THE CONTRACT

2.1   It's standard for a contract to consist of the front of the contract, the body of the contract—what the parties are agreeing to—and the back of the contract. The front consists of the title, the introductory clause, any recitals, and the lead-in. In longer contracts, it might include one or more of a cover sheet, a table of contents, and an index of definitions. (Regarding "frontloading"—the practice of pulling selected provisions out of the body of a commercial contract and placing them at the top of the contract—see 4.91.)

THE TITLE

2.2   The title of a contract is generally placed at the top center of the first page, in all capital letters (see sample 1). (If design considerations are important, you could use instead, or in addition, another form of emphasis or a different typeface or point size; see 16.55.) The title should simply state, without a definite or indefinite article, the kind of agreement involved, as in *EMPLOYMENT AGREEMENT* and *OPTION AGREEMENT*.

SAMPLE 1 ▪ TITLE AND INTRODUCTORY CLAUSE

ASSET PURCHASE AGREEMENT

This asset purchase agreement is dated 25 September 2017 and is between HASTINGS WASTE MANAGEMENT, INC., a Delaware corporation ("**Hastings**"), JORVIK RECYCLING SYSTEMS, LTD., a New York corporation ("**Hastings Sub 1**"; together with Hastings, the "**Hastings Parties**"), and JARROW HOLDINGS LLC, a Delaware limited liability company ("**Jarrow**").

2.3   Be concise. Don't use a title that looks at a transaction from different perspectives. For example, don't use as a title *AGREEMENT OF PURCHASE AND SALE*—every purchase entails a sale, so say either *PURCHASE AGREEMENT* or *SALE AGREEMENT* (omitting the unnecessary *of* in the process). Which you choose would presumably be a function of which side you represent.

2.4   And resist the urge to cram several elements of a transaction into the title: *LICENSE, SUPPLY, MARKETING, AND DISTRIBUTION AGREEMENT*. Consider using instead a broader, conceptual title, perhaps one that reflects the business goal.

2.5   Don't be too concise. Giving a contract the title *PURCHASE AGREEMENT* leaves the reader wondering what's being sold. Consider using a more informative title, such as *ASSET PURCHASE AGREEMENT* or *SECURITIES PURCHASE AGREEMENT*. Don't use just *AGREEMENT* unless you really can't come up with a more informative title, perhaps because the contract is unusual or because the deal consists of a grab bag of different elements.

2.6   Don't include party names in the title. The reader will figure out quickly enough that Acme is a party without your calling the contract *ACME SOFTWARE LICENSE AGREEMENT*.

2.7   Don't use jargon in the title. As the title for an agreement between shareholders, *BUY-SELL AGREEMENT* is not only repetitive in the manner described in 2.3 but also uninformative. Use instead *SHAREHOLDERS AGREEMENT* or some variant. (Regarding the title to use for an agreement between shareholders, see 13.726.)

2.8   If you can give a contract a standard title, do so—contract drafting doesn't prize variety for its own sake.

2.9   Don't feel you must track the terminology of state statutes. For example, statutes in Delaware, Nevada, New York, and some other states use the term *plan of merger*, meaning essentially a document that states the terms of a merger. So it's commonplace for drafters to give merger agreements a title that includes the phrase *plan of merger*. But if you were to file in Delaware a certificate of merger that is accompanied by, or refers to, a merger agreement bearing the title *MERGER AGREEMENT* rather than the more cumbersome *AGREEMENT AND PLAN OF MERGER,* the office of the Delaware secretary of state wouldn't reject the certificate of merger for using improper terminology—they're sensibly of the view that if a merger agreement contains the information that the statute requires of a plan of merger, the title is irrelevant. The same applies to articles of merger filed in Nevada and a certificate of merger filed in New York, and it's likely that other states are equally sensible.

2.10 Similarly, don't let use of the term "plan of exchange" in state statutes governing share exchanges dissuade you from using the title *SHARE EXCHANGE AGREEMENT* rather than *SHARE EXCHANGE AGREEMENT AND PLAN OF EXCHANGE* or a variant.

2.11 Most contracts use the word *agreement* in the title rather than *contract*, perhaps because *agreement* sounds more genteel than *contract*, with its two /k/ sounds. But *contract* is unobjectionable. The word *agreement* has a broader meaning than does the word *contract*, in that *agreement* can refer to an informal arrangement, but it's clear that's not the intended meaning when *agreement* is used in the title of a contract.

2.12 Some contracts use something other than *agreement* or *contract* in the title. A lease is a contract. So is an insurance policy. And by tradition, contracts stating the terms of bonds, debentures, or trusts often use the term *indenture* (see 13.442).

2.13   If a company routinely enters into a kind of contract, it might want to supplement the title, for example by adding additional information in parentheses immediately below the title. For example, it might be helpful to specify beneath the title *TRADEMARK LICENSE AGREEMENT* which mark is being licensed, and in which territory. (Alternatively, such information could be frontloaded; see 4.91.)

2.14   Regarding the title to give amendments or amended and restated contracts, see 18.5.

THE INTRODUCTORY CLAUSE

2.15   After the title comes the introductory clause, which states the type of agreement involved, perhaps the date of the agreement (depending on the circumstances), and the parties to the agreement (see sample 1).

Know All Men by These Presents

2.16   Occasionally the introductory clause is itself introduced by the egregiously archaic *know all men by these presents*, usually in all capitals. It's a stodgy translation of the Latinism *noverint universi*, meaning "know all persons." It means, in effect, "take notice," and as such it serves no purpose other than to mark the drafter as someone in thrall to the archaic.

Format

2.17   The introductory clause in sample 1 is formatted as a single paragraph; that's the general practice in the United States.

2.18   The elements of the introductory clause could instead be broken up, or "tabulated," so that each stands by itself. (Regarding tabulation of enumerated clauses, see 4.41.) In England and other Commonwealth nations, the preference is for tabulating the introductory clause, with some drafters also giving headings, such as *DATE* and *PARTIES*, to the different components. (That's consistent with the approach to document design for contracts in those countries; see 4.73.) This manual doesn't recommend tabulating the introductory clause, as doing so results in the introductory clause taking up more space without making it appreciably easier to read. But it can make sense to tabulate if the number of parties and the information to be included would otherwise make the introductory clause bulky.

Reference to the Type of Agreement

2.19   Begin the introductory clause with *This*, then repeat the type of agreement stated in the title. Thereafter, use just *this agreement* (see 2.124). Using instead just *agreement* in the introductory clause would be unobjectionable, but this manual recommends using the full reference, so it appears once in the text of the contract. And beginning the introductory clause with *This* helps make it a complete sentence, so it's easier to read than would otherwise be the case.

2.20   Use all lowercase letters for the introductory clause's reference to the type of agreement. It would be distracting to emphasize it with all capital letters, as the title is in all capital letters (see 2.2). Don't use initial capitals in this reference or any other reference to a particular contract: a reference to a contract shouldn't be treated like the title of a book or movie. The words *merger agreement* in a reference to *the merger agreement dated 22 October 2016 between Acme and Dynaco* are no more deserving of initial capitals than is the word *book* in *Here's the book Aunt Mildred gave me.*

2.21   Using initial capitals in a reference to an agreement would be appropriate if it were a defined term—if, for example, *the merger agreement dated 22 October 2016 between Acme and Dynaco* were given the defined term *the Merger Agreement.* But the introductory-clause reference to the type of agreement involved isn't a defined term. And it shouldn't be the definition of a defined term either (see 2.124).

What Verb to Use

2.22   To be a sentence, the introductory clause needs a verb. Use *is dated,* because it's simpler and clearer than *is made* and *is entered into* and the couplet *is made and entered into.* (Regarding couplets, see 1.38.)

Date

WHETHER TO INCLUDE

2.23   Date a contract by stating the date in the introductory clause or by providing for those signing the contract to date their signatures. If signatures are to be dated, have the contract state that it will be effective when the last party signs (see 5.5–.7).

2.24   Stating the date in the introductory clause is the more usual way of dating a contract, but dating the signatures makes sense in three contexts.

2.25   First, although it's commonplace for one or more parties to sign a contract on a date other than the date stated in the introductory clause (see 2.33), that could be confusing if the discrepancy were more than a few days (see 2.36).

2.26   Second, for compliance purposes a company might use dated signatures in some or all of its contracts to preclude use of an introductory-clause date that is other than the date the last party signed. For example, a company or its outside auditors might require that all the company's sales contracts include dated signatures, the aim being to ensure that revenue is recognized in the appropriate quarter. Someone signing a contract could intentionally use an incorrect date when stating the date of their signature, but that would likely be riskier than disingenuously relying on a misleading date in the introductory clause.

2.27   And third, if your contracts are signed electronically (see 5.68), each signature would automatically be dated.

2.28   Don't include a date in the introductory clause *and* date the signatures: using two ways to date a contract would be confusing. If you date the signatures but appreciate the ease of having a date to refer to on the first page of the contract, consider stamping at the top of the contract the date of the agreement. An alternative would be to place the signature blocks on the first page (see 4.96).

2.29   If you provide for dated signatures, you could conceivably allude to that in the introductory clause. But doing so in a way that articulates clearly the significance of signature dates would clog up the introductory clause. Instead, address in the boilerplate the implications of signature dates (see 5.6).

FUNCTION

2.30   The date stated in the introductory clause is presumed to be the date that the parties signed it, and by extension it's the date that the contract is effective, unless evidence ultimately indicates otherwise. Nothing is gained by defining the date in the introductory clause as *the Effective Date*—it's simpler to refer throughout the contract to *the date of this agreement*. (See also 2.41.)

FORMAT

2.31   To state dates, this manual uses the format *1 January 2018*. Consider using that format yourself (see 10.8–.11).

2.32   Don't use the format *this 24th day of October, 2017,* which is archaic and long-winded. Don't use two digits to state the day component of a date, as in *01 November 2017*. And don't use purely numerical dates, as in *10/9/17*, because they're not appropriate in formal writing and can cause confusion, given the different international conventions for expressing dates numerically.

DIFFERENT FROM DATE OF SIGNING DUE TO SIGNING LOGISTICS

2.33   The introductory-clause date is notionally the date that the contract was signed by the parties, but often one or more parties sign the contract before or after that date.

2.34   This timing discrepancy is often due to logistics. For example, if the closing date for a transaction slips by a day or two from the scheduled date, the parties might agree that it's not worth changing the date in each of the deal documents, or that it wouldn't be feasible to do so. And a party to a contract might not get around to signing it until a day or two after the date in the introductory clause, or might find it more convenient to sign it a day or two before the date in the introductory clause.

2.35   A conventional way of reflecting that one or more parties signed a contract on a date other than the date stated in the introductory clause is to make the introductory-clause date an *as of* date. But this manual doesn't recommend that practice, because it's simply a loose professional courtesy. Drafters observe it haphazardly, in that some always use *as of* dates, regardless of when the contract is being signed, and others never use them. If the date a contract was actually signed were to become an issue, it's unlikely that using or failing to use an *as of* date would be dispositive. Because using *as of* serves no useful purpose, omitting it would remove unnecessary words and a potential source of confusion.

2.36   If it might take more than a few days for all the parties to sign a contract, don't include a date in the introductory clause. Instead, have the parties date their signatures (see 5.5–.7). Using as the date in the introductory clause the date the contract was distributed or the date the first party signed it would be misleading, because a contract isn't effective until all parties have signed it. You could conceivably use a blank date in the introductory clause, intending to add a date once all the parties had signed, but that would invite confusion.

DIFFERENT FROM DATE OF SIGNING DUE TO TIMING OF PERFORMANCE

2.37   The traditional conventions for addressing a discrepancy between the date of signing and the timing of performance are problematic.

2.38   Drafters sometimes use in the introductory clause a date other than the date of signing if the contract provides for an arrangement that won't come into effect until after the date of signing. For example, Acme and Jones might sign Jones's employment agreement on 1 March even though Jones won't start working for Acme until two months later, on 1 May. A drafter might address this by using Jones's start date as the date in the introductory clause, in addition to or instead of the date of signing. To signal that it's not the date of signing, a drafter might describe that date as an *as of* date (see 2.35) or as *the effective date* (see 2.30) or might use the phrase *dated for reference* or *dated for reference purposes only* (primarily Canadian usages).

2.39   To capture past performance, drafters sometimes use in the introductory clause a date earlier than the date of signing, in addition to or instead of the date of signing. For example, in commercial contexts it's commonplace for the parties to reach an informal oral or written understanding on the terms, then start the process of reflecting those terms in a contract. Due to deal complexity or need for approvals, that process can be protracted, leading the parties to agree that one or both sides will start performing before the contract has been signed. Once it has been signed, the parties might use in the introductory clause the date performance started or some earlier date, to tidy up history. To indicate that the date used in the introductory clause isn't the date of signing, a drafter might use one of the signals noted in 2.38.

2.40   But it would be misleading to use in the introductory clause a date in the future to reflect delayed performance (see 2.38) or a date in the past to encompass precontract performance (see 2.39) or other circumstances, because the contract would come into existence once the parties had signed it (see 2.30). Such dating also obscures the actual time frame of the transaction.

2.41   In such situations, it would be clearer to use instead in the introductory clause the date of signing and to address other timing considerations wherever makes most sense.

2.42   For example, on 15 February Acme and Widgetco propose entering into a contract that provides for Acme to pay royalties to Widgetco based on annual sales, and the arrangement is that Acme will pay royalties for that year based on sales for the entire year, not just from 15 February. The drafter might be tempted to use 1 January of that year as the date in the introductory clause, using the signals described in 2.38 to convey that it's not the date of signing. It would be clearer instead to use in the introductory clause the date of signing and state in the provisions governing royalties that the first year's royalties are based on sales for the entire year.

2.43   Regarding precontract performance, note it in the recitals, address in the payment provisions any payment required for precontract performance, and state somewhere in the body of the contract that precontract performance is governed by the contract. The date the parties reached an informal understanding on the terms might be important, but that's different from the date the parties entered into a contract. If stating clearly what actually happened presents a problem, something is amiss.

2.44   It's clearer not to use the term *effective date* for the start date of performance, because a contract is effective when it has been signed by all the parties. Consider using instead a term such as *start date*.

2.45   Administrative convenience isn't sufficient reason to impose a phony timeline on a contract. If for recordkeeping purposes the date a contract was entered into is less significant than some other date, you could make that other date more conspicuous by stamping it at the top of the signed contract.

BROADER IMPLICATIONS

2.46   The date given a contract can have legal implications beyond performance under that contract. For example, it can affect a company's tax exposure or someone's rights under another contract. Playing games with the date of a contract—including by means of the date you use in the introductory clause—can give rise to civil or criminal liability.

2.47   Furthermore, attempting to give retroactive effect to a contract, including by using in the introductory clause a date earlier than the date of signing, can create problems if the contract is part of a series of transactions. Consider these circumstances: Bank makes a loan to Acme, then Bank transfers the loan to Investor A. Three months later, Bank transfers the same loan to Investor B. Six months after that, Investor A transfers the loan back to Bank, effective retroactively to a date before Bank's transfer to Investor B. If Investor B sues Acme for payment of the loan, Acme might argue that Investor B never acquired an interest in the loan, and the court might accept that argument. See *FH Partners, LLC v. Complete Home Concepts, Inc.*, No. WD 74653, 2012 WL 4074530 (Mo. Ct. App. Sept. 18, 2012).

Between Versus *Among*

2.48 In all cases, use *between* as the preposition in the introductory clause rather than *among* or a silly couplet (see 1.38) such as *by and between*.

2.49 It's commonly held that whereas one speaks of a contract *between* two parties, the correct preposition to use with a contract involving more than two parties is *among*. But according to *The Oxford English Dictionary,* it's not only permissible but preferable to use *between* rather than *among* with more than two parties. That the pointless distinction between *between* and *among* is generally accepted is a good indication of the state of traditional contract language.

2.50 But whether you use *between* or *among* does not affect meaning or readability, so it would be unhelpful to make an issue of it. Use *between* in your drafts. If a traditionalist insists on *among* because there are more than two parties, agreeing to make that change would be a painless concession. If the other side presents you with a draft that uses *among*, asking that it be changed to *between* might well antagonize them.

Identifying the Parties

2.51 In the introductory clause, identify each individual who is a party by their full name, and identify each legal-entity party by the full name under which it was registered in its jurisdiction of organization. Include the designation of the form of entity (*Inc., LLC, B.V., GmbH,* or other). If it would help to avoid confusion, refer also to any other name by which a party is known or was previously known.

2.52 Stating party names in all capitals helps them stand out. All capitals are harder to read (see 16.19), but that's not an issue when it's used for only a few words. Using all capitals would mask use of medial capitals—that is, use of one or more inner capital letters not preceded by a space, with the first letter either a capital (as in *HarperCollins*) or lowercase (as in *iPod*). Branding is low on the list of functions served by a contract, but if showing medial capitals in the introductory clause is important to you or a client, don't use all capitals for party names in the introductory clause.

2.53 Don't enumerate the parties—it serves no purpose.

2.54 When describing a party in the introductory clause, don't tack on *including its affiliates and direct and indirect subsidiaries* or comparable language. Because affiliates and subsidiaries aren't party to the contract and so wouldn't be bound by any of its provisions, including them in the introductory clause would create confusion. (See 2.57 regarding having a parent company enter into a contract on behalf of an affiliate.)

2.55 For a template contract that's used repeatedly with little or no customization, you could replace one or more party names by referring in the introductory clause to *the other party* [or *the parties*] *named in* *the signature blocks below*. But such economy comes at the expense of readability.

The Order of the Parties

2.56   In at least some kinds of contracts in which the parties play traditional, clearly defined roles, one can identify loose conventions for the order in which you place the parties in the introductory clause. For example, in most one-way confidentiality agreements the disclosing party comes before the recipient; in credit agreements, the debtor almost always comes before the one or more lenders; and in mergers-and-acquisitions contracts, the seller usually comes before the buyer. Because such conventions give rise to reader expectations, it's best to abide by them.

Having a Parent Company Enter into a Contract on Behalf of an Affiliate

2.57   It's commonplace that a member of a group of affiliated business organizations wants to contract with a supplier or licensor on behalf of itself and other members of the corporate group. Such an arrangement would facilitate standardization throughout the group and enhance the group's buying power while limiting transaction costs.

2.58   But such an arrangement might create problems, in that the other members of the corporate group might be third-party beneficiaries but would have no obligations under the contract, because they wouldn't be party to it.

2.59   Under Delaware law, if a contract is signed by the parent of a corporate group and is explicitly for the benefit of members of that corporate group, that might be enough for members of that corporate group to be liable under the contract, even though they're not party to the contract. See *Medicalgorithmics S.A. v. AMI Monitoring, Inc.*, C.A. No. 10948-CB (Del. Ch. 18 Aug. 2016).

2.60   But that's not necessarily the case in other jurisdictions. So it would be preferable to structure a transaction so the members of a corporate group have the benefit of a contract and the supplier or licensor are explicitly protected. Which arrangement would work best would depend on the context. Various alternatives present themselves:

- The supplier or licensor could enter into a contract with each member of the corporate group.

- The member of the corporate group could act as guarantor of the other members.

- The member of the corporate group could act as agent for the other members.

- The member of the corporate group could act as sublicensor to the other members.

- The member of the corporate group and the supplier or licensor could enter into a master agreement, with other members submitting individual statements of work under the master agreement (see 4.98).

- The supplier or licensor could permit the member of the corporate group to extend the benefit of its contract with the supplier or licensor to another member if the supplier or licensor receives a written undertaking from the other member that names the supplier or licensor as a third-party beneficiary and states that the other member will comply with the contract with the supplier or licensor as if it were party to it.

Parties with a Limited Role

2.61   One can be party to a contract with respect to only certain provisions. For example, in an acquisition, the buyer's parent might be party to the acquisition agreement solely to guarantee the buyer's obligations or solely to undertake to pay a termination fee. It's helpful to reflect a party's limited role by stating in the introductory clause before the party's name, between offsetting commas, *with respect to only* [*specified provisions*]. It makes sense to put a party with a limited role last in the introductory clause.

2.62   Neglecting to highlight that a party has a limited role might have no repercussions, because that party's role will be whatever the contract says it is. But doing so makes the arrangement clear to the parties without their having to read the entire contract. Furthermore, a party with a limited role might unexpectedly become ensnared in a provision that wasn't intended to apply to that party but arguably does anyway, because it refers generically to *a party* or *the parties*. Flagging a party's limited role could help avoid such confusion.

2.63   A party with a limited role would likely also be subject to one or more boilerplate provisions addressing governing law, notices, and related matters, whether or not they're included in the provisions specified as constituting that party's limited role.

2.64   If you highlight in the introductory clause a party's limited role, do so as well in that party's signature block (see 5.47).

Referring to Lists of Parties

2.65   The parties to a contract might be sufficiently numerous that it would be impractical to list them in the introductory clause. That's often the case with loan agreements and securities purchase agreements.

2.66   In a loan agreement, one alternative would be to refer to the lenders as follows in the introductory clause: *the financial institutions listed as Lenders on the signature pages of this agreement*. That would distinguish the lenders from the other parties whose names appear on the signature pages.

2.67   Another alternative would be to refer to the lenders as *the financial institutions listed in schedule A*. That would be preferable if in addition to identifying the lenders you want to provide information about the lenders that would be out of place on the signature pages, such as addresses and other contact information. Because the list in question would be on a schedule, you wouldn't need to refer to the parties in question as being *listed as Lenders*.

Describing the Parties

CORE INFORMATION

2.68 In the introductory clause, after the name of each legal-entity party, state its jurisdiction of organization and what kind of entity it is. Be concise: use, for example, *a Delaware corporation* rather than *a corporation organized and existing under the laws of the state of Delaware*.

2.69 Distinguish a U.S. legal-entity party from any other entity bearing the same name by including its jurisdiction of organization in the introductory clause. Stating its address too would serve only to clutter up the introductory clause. If the parties must know each other's addresses for sending notices, the notices provision would be the place to state them.

2.70 In many jurisdictions outside the United States, a legal entity is given a registration number at formation. If having that number would make it easier to determine the history and status of an entity, include the number in the introductory clause. By contrast, the address of a party's registered office would, like any other entity address, be superfluous in the introductory clause.

2.71 After the name of each party that's an individual, state that he or she is an individual—*John Doe, an individual*. (The term of art *natural person* is too quaintly legalistic to be a plausible alternative.) Even without that notation, readers would likely figure out that the party is an individual, but it's simpler not to require them to make that deduction for themselves. It's also simpler to be consistent by stating after each party name in the introductory clause what kind of legal person they are.

2.72 In contrast to legal-entity parties, in many jurisdictions the simplest way to distinguish a party that's an individual from any other individual bearing the same name would be to state that party's address in the introductory clause. (In doing so, write out in full the name of any U.S. state rather than using a U.S. Postal Service abbreviation, but include the ZIP code.) But if the contract contains a notices provision, omit that party's address from the introductory clause and instead state it in the notices provision, with the other party addresses. It's convenient to put all the addresses in one place, and stating a party's address twice in a contract adds unnecessary words and invites inconsistency (see 1.62).

2.73 In some jurisdictions information other than addresses is used to distinguish individuals—for example, an individual's passport number or national identification number.

2.74 In some jurisdictions outside the United States it might be mandatory to include additional information. For example, under the Czech Civil Code registered companies must include the following information in contracts governed by Czech law: company name, registered office, company ID number, and registration in the Commercial Register.

2.75   If a party is serving an administrative function or is otherwise acting on behalf of one or more individuals or entities, indicate that in the introductory clause:

> ACME BANK, N.A., as collateral agent for the Secured Parties (in that capacity, the "**Collateral Agent**")

> JOHN DOE, as Shareholders' Representative

2.76   Any party that's wearing two hats in a transaction should be mentioned twice in the introductory clause, once in each capacity:

> ACME CAPITAL CORPORATION (in its individual capacity and not as Administrative Agent, "**Acme Capital**")

> ACME CAPITAL CORPORATION, as administrative agent for the Lenders (in that capacity, the "**Administrative Agent**")

2.77   It's redundant to use the word *solely* to emphasize that a party is acting only in a specified capacity.

A TRUST AS A PARTY TO A CONTRACT

2.78   Generally, a trust is not a legal person, so a trust cannot be party to a contract or sign a contract. The trustee is the proper signer. A trustee should sign in their fiduciary capacity, not as an individual. You accomplish that by saying in the introductory clause and in the trustee's signature block (see 5.33) that that's what they're doing: *not in her individual capacity but as trustee.* A trustee is not personally liable on a contract made in a fiduciary capacity unless the trustee exceeds their authority.

2.79   But naming a trust as a party to a contract even though it isn't a legal person doesn't necessarily render the contract invalid. See, e.g., the South African case *Standard Bank v. Swanepoel NO* (20062/2014) [2015] ZASCA 71 (22 May 2015).

2.80   Some trusts—notably Delaware statutory trusts—are by law recognized as separate legal entities and so can enter into contracts.

PERFORMANCE BY A DIVISION

2.81   If a company's performance under a contract will be handled by a division of that company, make that clear. You could do so in the recitals, or you could do so in the introductory clause by supplementing the core information for that party: *ACME CORPORATION, a Delaware corporation acting through its Widgets division ("Acme").* Because the defined-term parenthetical comes just after the reference to the division, a reader might assume that the defined term relates only to the division, not the company. But that would be an unlikely reading in this context. Using the name of the company, not the division, in the signature block for that party would eliminate any possibility of confusion (see 5.29).

2.82   Don't make the division itself party to the contract—a division lacks the capacity to enter into a legally enforceable contract, so the company might claim that the contract isn't enforceable. And don't say that the company *is represented by* the division, because that phrase is generally used to refer to an individual or entity acting on someone's behalf.

INCIDENTAL INFORMATION

2.83   Consider this introductory clause:

> This merger agreement is dated 18 January 2017 and is between DARIUS TECHNOLOGIES, INC., a California corporation ("**Parent**"), SWORDFISH ACQUISITION, INC., a California corporation ~~and a wholly owned subsidiary of parent~~ ("**Sub**"), TROMBONE SOFTWARE, INC., a Delaware corporation ("**Target**"), ~~and the stockholders of Target, namely~~ ALAN ALPHA, an individual ("**Alpha**"), BRUCE BRAVO, an individual ("**Bravo**"), and CLARENCE CHARLIE, an individual ("**Charlie**"; together with Alpha and Bravo, the "**Stockholders**").

2.84   The strikethrough text constitutes incidental information. Don't include in the introductory clause incidental information, such as information regarding relationships among the parties and what role a party has in the transaction, because doing so clutters up the introductory clause. All such information belongs in the recitals, where it would be more accessible to the reader.

2.85   As in the example in 2.83, using common nouns as defined terms for party names (see 2.104) and using defined terms to refer to parties collectively (see 2.110) can convey the essence of what otherwise might have been included in the introductory clause as incidental information.

EXTRANEOUS INFORMATION

2.86   Each of the following assertions is extraneous and shouldn't be included in the introductory clause:

• that a party is represented by a duly authorized representative	address this instead in a statement of fact (but see 5.34)
• that a party is duly organized and validly existing	address this instead in a statement of fact
• that the agreement states the binding agreement of the parties	omit—the lead-in states that the parties are agreeing to what's in the contract (see 2.160)

2.87   Generally, no purpose is served by stating, in the introductory clause or elsewhere, that the parties intend to be legally bound. The approach under U.S. law is summarized by section 21 of the *Restatement (Second) of Contracts*, which says, "Neither real nor apparent intention that a promise be legally binding is essential to the formation of a contract." Instead, formation of a contract requires an intentional act manifesting assent. But see 2.186 regarding the function under Pennsylvania law of a statement of intent to be legally bound.

2.88   By contrast, in England and in most civil-law countries, the existence of a contract depends, at least in theory, on the parties' intent to be bound. But under English law, a presumption applies that if a commercial agreement satisfies the other elements of a contract, the parties intended to be legally bound. See, e.g., *Edwards v. Skyways* [1964] 1 All ER 494.

2.89 As a practical matter, disputes regarding whether a party intended to be legally bound are comparable to disputes regarding whether under U.S. law the parties had actually entered into a contract. In both kinds of dispute, informal communications feature prominently. It would be ludicrous to argue that someone who entered into a contract articulating the complete terms of a commercial relationship might not have known that the contract was legally binding. So unless a quirk of governing law makes it necessary or advantageous to do so, don't include in a contract a statement that the parties intend to be legally bound by the contract.

Defined Terms for Party Names

2.90 Defined terms are discussed in chapter 6, but guidelines regarding their use in the introductory clause are discussed in 2.91–.123.

CREATING AND USING A DEFINED TERM FOR A PARTY NAME

2.91 Use throughout a contract a short name for each party instead of repeating its full name. Make that short name a defined term and define it in the introductory clause, even if not defining it would present no risk of confusion.

2.92 In rare instances, the short name is defined elsewhere in the contract. For example, in contracts that have as a party someone acting as a shareholders' representative, some drafters use the defined term *Shareholders' Representative* in the introductory clause (see the second example in 2.75) and define it elsewhere. That's not particularly problematic, but it can be avoided.

2.93 To create a defined term for a party name, use an integrated definition, with the defined term stated in parentheses after the party name (see 6.61). The defined term, excluding *the,* if it's used (see 2.106), should be in quotation marks and in bold for emphasis; don't bold the quotation marks. (This manual follows that convention in the samples and the indented examples of contract text, but in examples incorporated in regular paragraphs any terms being defined aren't stated in bold, to avoid distracting the reader.) Don't include introductory text in the parentheses, such as *hereinafter referred to as*—it's unnecessary. (Regarding conventions for defining terms, see chapter 6.)

2.94 When creating a defined term for the name of an entity, place the defined-term parentheses after the jurisdiction reference (see 2.68): *Excelsior Corporation, a Delaware corporation ("Excelsior")*. In an integrated definition, the term being defined should follow the definition (see 6.62). That suggests that the parenthetical should come after *Excelsior Corporation,* but it seems appropriate to place the defined-term parenthetical after *a Delaware corporation*. That's because *Excelsior Corporation* and *a Delaware corporation* are both noun phrases referring to the same thing. And placing it there presents an advantage: if when creating the defined term for a party name you take the opportunity to create additional defined terms within the same set of parentheses (if, in other words, you "stack" two or more definitions; see 6.81), placing the parentheses after the party name would make the jurisdiction reference seem like an awkward afterthought (see sample 1).

2.95   Just as it would be a mistake to tack on *including its affiliates and direct and indirect subsidiaries* or similar language when describing a party, because the affiliates and subsidiaries aren't party to the contract (see 2.54), it would be a mistake to add such language to the defined-term parenthetical— *(including its affiliates and subsidiaries, "Acme")*.

2.96   Don't state in a defined-term parenthetical that the defined term includes that party's successors. (One often sees this with parties acting on someone's behalf; see 2.75.) The contract provisions governing succession should make it clear that any successor would step into the shoes of the predecessor.

2.97   Don't use all capitals or some other form of emphasis for party-name defined terms throughout a contract—it's pointless and distracting.

THE TWO KINDS OF DEFINED TERM FOR A PARTY NAME

2.98   When selecting the defined term for a party name, you have a choice between basing it on the party's name (see 2.100–.103) or using a common noun such as *the Company* or *the Shareholder* (see 2.104–.109). Generally, defined terms based on party names make a contract slightly more accessible to the reader. But common nouns work well in the following situations: *- mistakes re title*

- if the parties play traditional, clearly defined roles, such as lender and borrower, or landlord and tenant

- if the contract focuses on a single entity, as is the case with a limited-liability-company operating agreement or a shareholders agreement

- if the identity of the signers is not yet known

2.99   Sometimes it makes sense to use a mix of the two approaches. For example, if a company uses a template software license agreement repeatedly, it would make sense, in terms of readability and corporate identity, to use in the template as the defined term for the company a defined term based on the company's name. But the party on the other side of the transaction would change with each transaction, so it would be efficient to use as the defined term for the other party a common noun such as *the Licensee*.

USING DEFINED TERMS BASED ON PARTY NAMES

2.100   If a party is an individual, you could use a defined term based on that individual's last name or, if the contract refers to two or more individuals with the same last name, that individual's first name. Add an appropriate honorific (*Mr., Ms., Dr.*) if the last name on its own is too stark, or as a sign of respect. Also, an honorific might help the reader distinguish legal-entity parties from parties who are individuals.

2.101 For companies, select a word or two from the name or use an initialism. Sargasso Realty Holdings, Inc. could be referred to as *Sargasso Realty* or simply *Sargasso,* or you could use the initialism *SRH.*

2.102 In the interest of readability, use whenever possible a defined term consisting of one or more words from an entity's name rather than an initialism. But using an initialism for a party name might nevertheless be the best option in the following situations:

- if other parties to the contract include affiliates with similar names

- if the party's name includes that initialism

- if the party is commonly known by that initialism

- if the nature of the party's name precludes something more imaginative—it would, for example, be challenging to find a noninitialism alternative to *BNJ* as a name-based defined term for Bank of New Jersey

2.103 Be careful about using as the defined term for a party name an initialism with a meaning or connotations unrelated to that party. One can imagine a contract party not being thrilled at being lumbered with the initialism *DOG* or *SAD.*

USING A COMMON NOUN AS THE DEFINED TERM FOR A PARTY NAME

2.104 If you wish to use a common noun as the defined term for a party name, you have a choice between a noun that refers to its status as a legal entity (*Company*) and one that indicates the role that the party plays in the transaction (*Seller, Employer, Lender*).

2.105 To avoid confusion, don't use paired defined terms that differ only in their final syllable, including these:

Acquiror–Acquiree

Appellant–Appellee

Assignor–Assignee

Bailor–Bailee

Covenantor–Covenantee

Donor–Donee

Employer–Employee

Endorser–Endorsee

Farmor–Farmee

Grantor–Grantee

Guarantor–Guarantee

Indemnitor–Indemnitee

Lessor–Lessee

Licensor–Licensee

Mortgagor–Mortgagee

Obligor–Obligee

Offeror–Offeree

Optionor–Optionee

Payor–Payee

Transferor–Transferee

Vendor–Vendee

Warrantor–Warrantee

2.106   If the defined term for a party name consists of a common noun, using the definite article—*the Purchaser* rather than *Purchaser*—results in prose that's less stilted, and that's worth more than the marginal economy afforded by eliminating every instance of *the* from the defined term. Some drafters prefer to omit the definite article to avoid problems with careless search-and-replace (with *the Buyer* becoming *the Acme*) if someone replaces the common-noun defined term with a name-based defined term. But paying some attention is all that's required to avoid that problem. In any event, be consistent throughout a contract in using or not using the definite article with a particular defined term—failure to do so suggests carelessness.

2.107   Don't offer alternative defined terms for a party, as in *"Widgetco" or the "Company"* or as in *"Widgetco," sometimes referred to herein as the "Company"*. Doing so serves no purpose and makes the reader responsible for remembering that *Widgetco* and *the Company* are the same.

2.108   Regarding the defined terms *Vendor*, *Seller*, and *Supplier*, it would be appropriate to use *Vendor* for a party that's in the business of selling whatever is being sold; to use *Seller* for a party that isn't; and to use *Supplier* for a party that not only is in the business of selling whatever is being sold but also is contracting to supply it over time. These distinctions are consistent with everyday usage in business, although everyday usage isn't entirely consistent. For example, in Commonwealth countries it's standard to use *vendor* for someone selling their house. *Vendor* is perhaps slightly old-fashioned, but it's informative and widely used.

2.109   Consider using *the Employee* as the default defined term for an employee in a contract with the employer. For more senior employees, the defined term *the Executive* is often used instead, but it seems unnecessary and perhaps old-fashioned to trumpet the employee's status with a defined term—it will be clear enough from the terms of the contract. An alternative would be to use the employee's last name with an honorific (see 2.100). In the United States, *executive employee* is a term with legal implications, in that the Fair Labor Standards Act provides an exemption from both minimum wage and overtime pay for employees employed as bona fide executive, administrative, professional, and outside sales employees. But what defined term you use for an employee won't affect whether that employee qualifies as an executive employee under the statute.

DEFINED TERMS USED TO REFER TO PARTIES COLLECTIVELY

2.110 Often it's helpful to use a collective defined term such as *the Shareholders*; sample 1 contains the collective defined term *the Hastings Parties*. Define such collective defined terms either in the singular or the plural, but not both (see 6.4).

2.111 But don't use *the Parties* as a collective defined term for the parties to a contract. It ostensibly spares the drafter from having to refer throughout a contract to *the parties to this agreement* (or *the parties hereto*), but one can simply refer to *the parties,* because no reasonable reader could understand such a reference to mean anything other than the parties to that contract.

2.112 A more nuanced argument for using the defined term *the Parties* relates to contract provisions stating that only the parties may enforce the contract. To preclude nonparties from enforcing a contract—something that would be an issue only if the contract contemplates intended third-party beneficiaries—make it clear in such provisions that they apply only to the named parties to the contract. If you refer simply to *the parties,* a court might hold that it includes persons other than the named parties, in particular intended third-party beneficiaries.

2.113 You could address this issue by creating the defined term *the Parties* and defining it to mean only the named parties. But a better solution would be to give the name of each party in the provision that states that only the parties may enforce the contract. Another would be to refer in that provision to *the signatories*—that would be more concise than listing all the parties, especially if there are more than two. The word *signatory* is ambiguous (see 13.731), but in this context that ambiguity wouldn't create a problem.

2.114 Creating the defined term *the Parties* instead would accomplish the same goal as naming the parties or referring to *the signatories,* but in the process would force the drafter to use throughout the contract the defined term *the Parties,* even though outside that one context the defined term would serve no purpose. Given the toll that defined terms take on readability (see 6.115), in this case the cost of using the defined term *the Parties* outweighs the limited benefit, particularly given the alternatives that are available.

PARTY OF THE FIRST PART AND *PARTY OF THE SECOND PART*

2.115 Parties to a contract were once divided into classes, or "parts," with one party identified in the introductory clause as *party of the first part* and the other as *party of the second part.* (Anyone other than a party to the contract was a *third party;* see 13.820.) The parties were referred to by those labels throught the contract. This practice had nothing to recommend it—not only was it cumbersome, it also invited confusion and litigation, given how easy it was to inadvertently transpose the labels.

2.116 In the United States this usage survives, but barely—you see it mostly in the occasional real-estate contract. Somewhat more common is use of *party of the first part* and *party of the second part* in the introductory clause but nowhere else—the parties are also given conventional defined terms in the introductory clause, and those defined terms are used throughout the contract. This usage seems particularly pointless, but it lives on; it appears to be slightly more prevalent in Commonwealth countries than in the United States.

2.117   If one or both sides to a transaction consist of more than one party, using *party of the first part* and *party of the second part* in the introductory clause would arguably be an efficient way to group the parties according to which side of the transaction they're on. But information regarding party relationships is best placed in the recitals (see 2.84). Furthermore, using common nouns as defined terms for party names and using defined terms to refer to parties collectively can efficiently convey the essence of party relationships (see 2.85).

WHEN EITHER PARTY MIGHT PLAY A GIVEN ROLE

2.118   A contract might provide for a mechanism in which either party plays a given role, with the other party playing another role. For example, either of two shareholders might have an option to buy the other out. In referring to each party when describing that mechanism, you must use a generic label instead of a party-name defined term.

2.119   The simplest way to do that would be to use *that party* and *the other party*. But that works for only the most basic provisions: if you use *that party* again after having used *the other party*, the reader might think that the second *that party* refers to *the other party*.

2.120   The 2002 International Swaps and Derivatives Association (ISDA) master agreement gets around that problem by creating the defined terms X and Y for *that party* and *the other party*, respectively:

> If a party is so required to deduct or withhold, then that party ("X") will:—
>
> (1) promptly notify the other party ("Y") of such requirement;

2.121   But X and Y are devoid of context, so the reader must remember what roles X and Y play. The same applies to using instead, say, *Party A* and *Party B*.

2.122   Less susceptible to confusion are labels that refer to the role being played. For example, *the withdrawing member* and *the remaining member*. If such labels are used often enough, it makes sense to use them as defined terms, hence *the Indemnifying Party* and *the Indemnified Party*.

2.123   Your choice of labels could have unanticipated consequences. In *Powertech Technology, Inc. v. Tessera, Inc.*, No. C 11-6121 CW, 2014 WL 171830, at *5 (N.D. Cal. 15 Jan. 2014), the court held that because a termination provision used the label "non-breaching party," a party seeking to terminate for the other party's purported breach had to substantially comply with its own obligations first. One suspects that was not what the drafter had intended. Using instead *the party claiming breach* as a label would presumably have prevented the court from so holding.

The Defined Term *This Agreement*

2.124   It's common practice to create in the introductory clause the defined term *this Agreement*. (Analogous defined terms include *this Amendment*— see 18.6—and *this Assignment*.) But this defined term is unnecessary: the definite article *this* in *this agreement* makes it clear which agreement is being referred to. The title (see 2.2) and introductory clause (see 2.15) of a contract might describe that contract as a particular kind of agreement, such as an agency agreement or a franchise agreement, but that wouldn't be an impediment to referring thereafter to *this agreement* without having made it a defined term.

2.125   And because it's best to use lowercase letters in any reference to an agreement (see 2.20), it's preferable not to use a capital *A* in *this agreement*.

2.126   Used in a provision, the term *this agreement* could in theory be interpreted as referring to some part of a contract—a section, a subsection, a sentence, an enumerated clause—rather than the entire contract. But as a practical matter, that doesn't happen. The likelihood of a party arguing that *this agreement* refers to a part of the whole, and the likelihood of a court accepting this argument, is remote.

2.127   Sometimes the defined term *this Agreement* is defined to include the attachments to the contract. That doesn't render the defined term any more useful—if a contract provision mentions an attachment, that brings the attachment within the scope of the contract, without the need to say so explicitly. (For a more general discussion of this issue, see 5.106–.109.)

2.128   Some drafters use for a contract's references to itself an initialism created from the title—for example *this CRADA* (standing for *cooperative research and development agreement*) and *this NDA* (standing for *nondisclosure agreement*). But readers don't need to be reminded at every turn what kind of contract they're reading. And although an initialism might be shorter than *agreement*, that economy is more than offset by the alphabet-soup quality of initialisms, not to mention all the capital letters, which in quantity become distracting.

RECITALS

2.129   Most contracts of any length or complexity contain, after the title and before the lead-in, one or more paragraphs referred to collectively as "recitals." The recitals in sample 2, which accompany the introductory clause in sample 1, use the format this manual recommends for recitals.

Function

2.130   The recitals to a contract state any background information that the parties regard as relevant. One can distinguish three kinds of recitals:

2.131   *Context recitals.* These describe the circumstances leading up to the parties' entering into the contract. Typical context recitals include recitals describing any relationships between the parties (see the first recital in sample 2), businesses operated by one or more parties (see the first recital in sample 2), and transactions entered into previously by one or more parties (see the second, fourth, and fifth recitals in sample 2).

SAMPLE 2   ▪   RECITALS

Hastings Sub 1 is a wholly owned subsidiary of Hastings. Hastings Sub 1 owns and operates collection and hauling operations, transfer stations, landfills, and recycling facilities in the State of New York (that business, the "**Business**"). Roger Hastings is chief executive officer of Hastings and Hastings Sub 1.

Jarrow, the Hastings Parties, Hastings Newton, Inc., a New York corporation and a wholly owned subsidiary of Hastings ("**Hastings Sub 2**"), and Raven Fund Ltd., a Bahamas corporation ("**Raven**"), are party to a letter of intent dated 12 June 2017 concerning sale to Jarrow of assets of Hastings Sub 1 and Hastings Sub 2 (the "**Letter of Intent**").

Hastings Sub 1 wants to sell to one or more persons designated by Jarrow, and Jarrow wishes to cause those persons to purchase from Hastings Sub 1, certain assets of Hastings Sub 1.

Raven asserts a security interest in all assets owned by Hastings Sub 1, and under the restructuring agreement dated 13 February 2017 between Raven, Hastings, and certain Affiliates of Hastings, Hastings Sub 1 may not sell any of its assets to Jarrow without Raven's prior written approval.

Jarrow, the Hastings Parties, Raven, and Bratton Friedman LLP, as escrow agent, are party to a deposit agreement dated 20 July 2016 (the "**Deposit Escrow Agreement**"), in accordance with which Jarrow paid to the escrow agent on 27 February 2017 a good-faith deposit of $500,000 toward the purchase price of the assets.

Concurrently with its entry into this agreement, Hastings, Hastings Sub 2, and Jarrow are entering into an asset purchase agreement providing for purchase by Jarrow of certain assets of Hastings Sub 2.

The parties therefore agree as follows:

2.132   *Purpose recitals.* These indicate succinctly and in broad terms what the parties wish to accomplish (see the third recital in sample 2). They shouldn't be used to shoehorn deal terms into the recitals.

2.133   *Simultaneous-transaction recitals.* If a contract is part of a broader transaction, these describe the other components of the transaction taking place concurrently with signing the contract (see the sixth recital in sample 2).

2.134   A complex agreement might have a dozen or more recitals. If a transaction is straightforward and lacks any back story, dispense with recitals. It's unnecessary to provide recitals that simply state, for example, that Doe wants to sell something to Holdings and that Holdings wants to purchase it from Doe, as readers could get that information from the contract title and the initial provisions of the body of the contract.

2.135   Because courts typically look to recitals just for indications of the intent of the parties on entering into the transaction, don't address in the recitals in any detail deal terms or facts. It's routine for mergers-and-acquisitions contracts to cram into the recitals information that's better placed in the body of the contract.

Giving the Recitals a Heading

2.136   Many drafters give recitals a heading, but that's unnecessary.

2.137   A traditional choice of heading is *WITNESSETH*. It's ludicrously archaic and is premised on the mistaken assumption that the word is a command in the imperative mood meaning roughly, one assumes, "Now hear this!" Instead, it's the remnant of *This agreement witnesseth that …* , with *witnesseth* presumably meaning "is evidence."

2.138   Use of an emphasized *witnesseth* in English contracts goes back to at least the early 16th century. The other standard all-capitals archaisms that clutter the front and back of the contract (see 2.143, 2.167, 5.26) have similar roots. Presumably it was thought that in documents consisting of unbroken lines of handwritten text, the reader would appreciate a graphic signal indicating a shift in topic. But what made sense hundreds of years ago makes no sense now. That the all-capitals archaisms persist is a function of the dead hand of passive drafting (see p. xxxvi).

2.139   Other possible headings for recitals are *RECITALS* or *BACKGROUND*. These represent an improvement over *WITNESSETH,* but recitals don't need a heading. Recitals can readily be identified based on their content and their position—after the introductory clause and before the lead-in. Also, the legal effect of recitals depends on their content rather than on how they are introduced. (For an anomalous Australian exception, see 5.59.) And if one is giving the recitals a heading, consistency would require giving a heading to the body of the contract (a problematic notion; see 2.213), the introductory clause, and the concluding clause. For these reasons, the recitals in sample 2 don't have a heading.

2.140   But if it would make those using a contract feel more comfortable, give the recitals an appropriate heading.

Enumeration

2.141   There's no need to number or letter each recital. Doing so would serve a purpose only if elsewhere in the contract you wish to cross-refer to a particular recital, and that shouldn't be necessary. (See 6.103–.114 regarding cross referencing to definitions of defined terms.)

Use Simple Narrative Prose

2.142   The recitals serve a storytelling function. They're the one part of a contract that calls for simple narrative prose.

2.143   So don't begin recitals with *WHEREAS,* as this meaning of *whereas*—"in view of the fact that; seeing that"—is archaic (see 2.138).

2.144   Use a conventional paragraph structure for recitals, with complete sentences rather than clauses ending in semicolons. Don't feel you have to limit yourself to the traditional one sentence per recital.

What Verb to Use in Purpose Recitals

2.145 Different verbs can be used to state in a purpose recital what the parties intend to accomplish.

2.146 If what follows the verb is another verb, here are your choices, of varying suitability (with *transfer* playing the role of the second verb):

- *wants to* [*transfer*] (not a standard option, but the most straightforward)
- *desires to* [*transfer*] (a standard option, but oddly steamy)
- *wishes to* [*transfer*] (a standard option, but a little genteel)
- *intends to* [*transfer*] (inappropriate, as it suggests a plan outside of the contract)
- *seeks to* [*transfer*] (in standard English, *seek to* plus infinitive means to try; that's not the meaning intended here)
- *would like to* [*transfer*] (too genteel)
- *is desirous of* [*transferring*] (archaic)
- *is agreeable to* [*transferring*] (awkward)

2.147 Because *wants to* is consistent with everyday English, this manual recommends *wants to*. (See the third recital in sample 2.) It would likely strike many drafters as being too blunt, but anyone offended by *wants to* is perhaps bringing to contract language a sensibility that's overly delicate.

2.148 Here are the alternatives if what follows the verb is noun-plus-verb:

- The Company *wants* the Executive to serve the Company as its chief executive officer.
- The Company *desires* that the Executive serve the Company as its chief executive officer.
- The Company *wishes* for the Executive to serve the Company as its chief executive officer.
- The Company *intends* that the Executive serve the Company as its chief executive officer.
- It is the *desire* of the Company that the Executive serve the Company as its chief executive officer.
- It is the *wish* of the Company that the Executive serve the Company as its chief executive officer.

2.149 Again, *wants* is the simplest choice.

Premature Recital References to the Agreement

2.150 A purpose recital might state that the parties propose to engage in certain activities *in accordance with this agreement* or *subject to the terms of this agreement*. But if you make a purpose recital subject to the terms of the agreement, it's no longer a general statement of intent. In effect, you're simply saying in the recital, redundantly, that the parties want to do what the contract provides. For the same reason, don't say in the recitals *this agreement contemplates*.

2.151 And a context recital might say that a party *has agreed* to do something or other *subject to the terms of this agreement*. That suggests, incongruously, two stages of agreement—first, agreement to enter into the contract, followed by entry into the contract.

2.152 It makes more sense to express in a purpose recital a general intent that isn't tied to the terms of the contract. Doing so poses no risk, as no rational court could say that a general expression of intent takes priority over the specific terms that it introduces. But obviously, a purpose recital shouldn't state a purpose that's broader than what the contract seeks to accomplish (not counting any conditions, termination provisions, and other restrictions).

2.153 So don't use in a purpose recital *in accordance with this agreement* or anything comparable, such as *upon the terms and subject to the conditions set forth in this agreement*.

Incorporation by Reference

2.154 Contracts sometimes state, either in the lead-in (as part of a traditional recital of consideration; see 2.166) or in a separate section in the body of the contract, that the recitals are *incorporated by reference* into the contract. Such statements are in response to caselaw holding that recitals aren't part of the contract, or rather don't form part of the substantive provisions. See, e.g., *Jones Apparel Group, Inc. v. Polo Ralph Lauren Corp.*, 791 N.Y.S.2d 409, 410 (App. Div. 2005).

2.155 The notion of incorporating recitals by reference is presumably intended to bring within the scope of the body of the contract any substantive provisions in the recitals. But recitals shouldn't contain substantive provisions. If a set of recitals contains substantive provisions, it would be rash to rely on incorporation by reference to clear up any resulting uncertainties. A much better fix would be to remove the substantive provisions from the recitals and place them in the body of the contract. (Regarding incorporation by reference generally, see 13.388.)

True and Correct

2.156 Provisions that seek to incorporate recitals by reference (see 2.154) routinely include a statement that the recitals are *true and correct*. Drafters who use this archaic couplet presumably seek to make actionable any facts stated in the recitals, so a party might have a remedy if any of those facts turn out to have been inaccurate.

2.157 But generally, recitals are used to convey background information that shouldn't be at issue. If a party is uncertain whether facts stated in the recitals are accurate, it would do well to include in the body of the contract, as well as or instead of in the recitals, statements of fact as to those matters by the appropriate party. That would provide a clearer foundation for a claim than would a statement that the recitals are *true and correct*.

Defined Terms in the Recitals

2.158   Defining terms in the recitals is unobjectionable, but don't clutter with definitions what should be a succinct introduction to the contract.

2.159   And don't use in the recitals defined terms that aren't defined until later in the contract, because that's inconsistent with using the recitals to introduce the reader to the transaction. If you use in the recitals a defined term that doesn't have an obvious meaning—such as *the Business, the Merger, or the Services*—and don't define it until later in the contract, you make the recitals harder to read by forcing the reader to search for and read the definition of that defined term.

THE LEAD-IN

Wording

2.160   The lead-in comes immediately after the recitals and before the body of the contract and introduces the body of the contract. If a contract doesn't contain recitals, the lead-in should say *The parties agree as follows.* If the contract does contain recitals, the lead-in should say *The parties therefore agree as follows* (see sample 2). (One could conceivably say instead *So the parties agree as follows*, but that sounds too casual.)

2.161   Don't clutter up the lead-in with extraneous verbs, as in *covenant and agree*.

2.162   Don't use *hereby* in the lead-in. *Hereby* is a feature of language of performance (see 3.35); the lead-in is language of agreement (see 3.30), not language of performance.

2.163   Don't say instead *The parties hereby enter into this agreement*. In language of performance, *hereby* means, in effect, *by means of this agreement*, so *hereby enter into this agreement* means *enter into this agreement by means of this agreement*, which doesn't make sense.

2.164   Don't refer to the parties by name in the lead-in, as doing so would serve no purpose and would just make the lead-in longer, particularly in a contract with more than two parties. (Regarding this issue in the context of the concluding clause, see 5.4.)

2.165   Sometimes when the body of the contract would otherwise consist of a single one-sentence provision, that provision is wrapped into the lead-in, with the concluding clause following. Straightforward amendments can be handled in this manner (see 18.7).

Consideration

2.166   In the United States, a standard feature of business contracts is a recital of consideration placed immediately before the body of the contract. Here's an example:

> NOW, THEREFORE, in consideration of the premises and the mutual covenants set forth herein and for other good and valuable consideration, the receipt and sufficiency of which are hereby acknowledged, the parties hereto covenant and agree as follows:

2.167   Just as you should dispense with *WITNESSETH* (see 2.137) and *WHEREAS* (see 2.143), you should also not begin a lead-in with the archaic *NOW, THEREFORE*. (You sometimes see *NOW, WHEREFORE*, with *wherefore* meaning *as a result of which*. If anything, it seems even more archaic.) And *in consideration of the premises* is an obscure way of saying "therefore."

2.168   But a bigger issue is that drafters generally shouldn't use this or any other kind of recital of consideration—they're unnecessary. To understand why, start by considering the ostensible function of recitals of consideration.

2.169   The phrase *in consideration of* can be used as a way to express, from the perspective of one side to a transaction, the exchange taking place. (The phrase *as consideration* can serve this function too. See 13.61.) Here's an example:

> In consideration of $1,000, Alpha hereby sells the Equipment to Bravo.

2.170   Such a recital of consideration might seek to express what the parties have actually bargained for. If instead what is being offered wasn't bargained for as part of an exchange, it's a pretense. In that case, the recital is said to provide for "nominal" consideration, usually a small amount of money. And if the parties never intended for the amount stated—whether bargained for or not—to be paid, that too involves pretense, and the recital is said to provide for "sham" consideration.

BACKSTOP RECITALS

2.171   That's the taxonomy of consideration you find in caselaw and commentary, but it's not complete. It doesn't explain the kind of recital of consideration routinely placed just before the body of the contract, like the one in 2.166.

2.172   Such recitals of consideration don't specify consideration but merely assert that it exists. (Deal specifics might sometimes be excluded from recitals of consideration to keep that information private, but that doesn't apply to this kind of recital of consideration.) In contracts in which such recitals occur, an exchange constituting the actual consideration is usually specified explicitly elsewhere in the contract, albeit without labeling it as consideration.

2.173   The only possible function of such recitals of consideration would be to establish that the contract is supported by consideration even if the contract otherwise doesn't state consideration or states something that isn't valid consideration. That's why this manual calls them "backstop" recitals of consideration. (A backstop is a person or thing placed at the rear of or behind something as a barrier, support, or reinforcement.) Like nominal and sham consideration, backstop recitals of consideration are a form of pretense.

2.174   But no one pays attention to backstop recitals of consideration. They're simply a standard feature of copy-and-paste drafting and as such are blithely recycled.

PRETENSE CONSIDERATION

2.175   But could a backstop recital of consideration alone be enough to establish that a contract is supported by consideration? According to commentary, the answer is no: because both nominal and sham consideration are a pretense, they don't generally constitute consideration. See 2-5 *Corbin on Contracts* § 5.17. By extension, that applies to backstop consideration too. (Option contracts and guarantees are discussed in 2.191–.201.) Instead, courts generally give a recital of consideration some weight but permit contrary evidence to be introduced. See 3 *Williston on Contracts* § 7:23; 17A *Am. Jur. 2d* Contracts § 110 (2017). That makes sense—if a backstop recital of consideration were all that it takes to establish consideration, that would nullify the requirement of consideration. Every contract would include a backstop recital of consideration and the requirement of consideration would be illusory.

2.176   But in recent years, some courts have indicated that a backstop recital of consideration supports a contract. For example, in *Network Protection Sciences, LLC v. Fortinet, Inc.*, No. C 12-01106 WHA, 2013 WL 4479336, at *6 (N.D. Cal. 20 Aug. 2013), the U.S. District Court for the Northern District of California, applying Texas law, held that a recital stating that the patents at issue were assigned "[f]or good and valuable consideration, the receipt of which is hereby acknowledged," was "conclusive" on the issue of consideration.

2.177   And in *Urban Sites of Chicago, LLC v. Crown Castle USA*, 979 N.E.2d 480, 493 (Ill. App. Ct. 2012), the contract at issue stated that the parties had entered into it "[f]or good and valuable consideration, the receipt and sufficiency of which are hereby acknowledged." The Appellate Court of Illinois pointed to that in stating, in dictum, that "the evidence contained in the record establishes that there was adequate consideration as a matter of law."

2.178   One could argue that based on these cases, it would be prudent always to include a backstop recital of consideration in a contract in case a dispute comes before a court that is misinformed regarding the law of consideration or is willing to rely on pretense consideration to achieve a given outcome. But that's too depressingly speculative a prospect to justify cluttering every contract with a backstop recital of consideration.

REBUTTABLE PRESUMPTION

2.179 There's caselaw to the effect that a recital of consideration establishes a rebuttable presumption that consideration exists. See 3 *Williston on Contracts* § 7:22. That has led one commentator to recommend including a backstop recital of consideration in contracts governed by the law of a state that recognizes the rebuttable presumption. See Tina L. Stark, *Drafting Contracts: How and Why Lawyers Do What They Do* 86 (2d ed. 2014).

2.180 But that accomplishes little. In the case of sham consideration or a backstop recital of consideration, rebutting that presumption would simply require showing lack of any payment or other exchange that could constitute consideration. Moreover, the rebuttable presumption doesn't make sense when applied to backstop recitals of consideration: they state no specific consideration, so anyone looking to rebut the presumption would have nothing specific to rebut.

2.181 More fundamentally, if you're invoking the rebuttable presumption, you're already in a fight. A characteristic of passive drafting (see p. xxxvi) is a focus on prevailing in disputes. It makes more sense to engage in active drafting, with the aim of avoiding disputes by stating the deal clearly. Those who draft or review contracts (as opposed to those who litigate contract disputes) have simple and effective alternatives to invoking in a dispute a recital of consideration that's a pretense—whether it's nominal or sham consideration or a backstop recital of consideration.

STRUCTURING CONSIDERATION

2.182 First, state any actual consideration clearly. (But don't state it as a recital of consideration; see 2.202–.206.)

2.183 Second, if a transaction lacks consideration, fix that. For example, if a party to an existing contract wants the other party to agree to a disadvantageous change in the terms, that change might be enforceable only if the party agreeing to the change has received consideration for doing so. If that consideration is lacking, then arrange for it—what constitutes consideration might depend on the jurisdiction—and state it clearly in the contract.

2.184 Third, the performing party could waive consideration and acknowledge that the other party will be relying on that waiver. Most U.S. courts would probably view reliance as an independent basis for enforcing a promise, so reliance might make a promise enforceable even in the absence of consideration. See 3 *Williston on Contracts* § 7:2. Before choosing that approach, research how this issue is handled under the governing law of the contract.

2.185 And fourth, you can take advantage of formalities offered by law as a way to establish consideration, although they're annoyingly legalistic. If the governing law requires no consideration for contracts under seal, you could make the contract one under seal (see 5.48–.59).

2.186   Under the Uniform Written Obligations Act, enacted only in Pennsylvania, a written release or promise will not be unenforceable for lack of consideration if the signer states they intend to be legally bound. Unless you're dealing with a contract governed by Pennsylvania law that might not be supported by consideration, so stating in a contract would serve no purpose (see 2.87). And in Pennsylvania, courts have limited the effect of such a statement. See *Socko v. Mid-Atlantic Systems of CPA, Inc.*, 126 A.3d 1266 (Pa. 2015) (holding that an employment agreement containing a noncompetition provision may be challenged for a lack of consideration even though the agreement states that the parties "intend to be legally bound").

2.187   Eliminating any function for pretense consideration would allow you to eliminate recitals of consideration, including backstop recitals of consideration, and all associated clutter.

2.188   One item of clutter is the phrase *good and valuable consideration*. The distinction between good consideration and valuable consideration is evidently still relevant for some real-estate deeds, because it's enshrined in, for example, Georgia statutes (Ga. Code Ann. § 13-3-41). But it's irrelevant for regular contracts. And more to the point, what matters is whether consideration exists, not what doctrinal label you can attach to it.

2.189   As regards *receipt and sufficiency*, acknowledging receipt accomplishes nothing if there was no consideration. And consideration either exists or it does not exist—it makes no sense to say that it's insufficient or sufficient. See 1-3 *Murray On Contracts* § 60[A].

2.190   Dispense with any remaining archaisms and you're left with a simple lead-in to the body of the contract (see 2.160).

OPTION CONTRACTS

2.191   Option contracts and guarantees must be considered separately.

2.192   Section 87(1) of the *Restatement (Second) of Contracts* suggests that in option contracts, a recital of nominal consideration supports a promise. Under the *Restatement*'s approach, it would be irrelevant whether the nominal consideration is paid.

2.193   Some courts have endorsed the *Restatement*'s approach—for one, the Supreme Court of Texas. See *1464-Eight v. Joppich*, 154 S.W.3d 101, 110 (Tex. 2004). So one might conclude that although in most contexts nominal or sham consideration or a backstop recital of consideration wouldn't establish consideration where none exists, it would be prudent to retain such recitals in option contracts.

2.194   But the *Restatement*'s approach remains the minority position. In jurisdictions that haven't adopted the *Restatement*'s approach, the prudent thing to do would be to set a plausible option price, recite it in the contract, and make sure it's paid.

2.195 Consider doing that even in jurisdictions that have adopted the *Restatement*'s approach. It would allow you to avoid relying on something that doesn't make sense—a sham endorsed by law.

2.196 If you wish to rely on the *Restatement*'s approach, consider using nominal consideration instead of a backstop recital of consideration—even if a court might otherwise be inclined to accept pretense consideration, it's not clear how courts would react to backstop recitals of consideration. That's because the caselaw on option contracts mostly involves a recital of a consideration for a stated amount of money, as opposed to a statement that unspecified consideration exists, and the illustrations in the *Restatement* involve purported consideration in the form of stated amounts of money.

2.197 Thankfully, you can safely dispense with consideration for option contracts governed by the law of a state that has by statute specified that option contracts need not be supported by consideration. New York is one such state (see section 5 of the New York General Obligations Law). And section 2-205 of the Uniform Commercial Code says that a firm offer to buy or sell goods is not revocable for lack of consideration.

GUARANTEES

2.198 In terms of what constitutes consideration, guarantees are analogous to option contracts.

2.199 If Alpha guarantees Bravo's debt to Charlie when Bravo incurs that debt, Charlie's willingness to lend money to Bravo is valid consideration for Alpha's promise to pay Bravo's debt. Generally, that's not the case if Alpha guarantees Bravo's debt after Bravo incurs it.

2.200 But section 88 of the *Restatement (Second) of Contracts* and section 9 of the *Restatement (Third) of Suretyship* suggest that for guarantees, a false recital of consideration would support a promise. The caselaw endorsing that approach is negligible, so it would be rash to assume that a court would endorse it for a given contract. Alpha must have a reason for guaranteeing Bravo's existing debt. Because that reason constitutes Alpha's consideration, Charlie the creditor would be better protected by having that reason stated in Alpha's guarantee instead of relying on pretense consideration.

2.201 As with option contracts, even in jurisdictions that accept a false recital of consideration for guarantees, consider stating actual consideration instead of relying on a sham. And again, as with option contracts, if you wish to rely on the *Restatements*' approach, consider using nominal consideration instead of a backstop recital of consideration.

ELIMINATING OTHER REFERENCES

2.202 As noted in 2.169, the phrases *in consideration of* and *as consideration* can be used to express part of the actual exchange taking place in a transaction, as contrasted with use of either phrase in a recital of sham or nominal consideration or in a backstop recital of consideration.

2.203   But those phrases can fail to make it clear what is happening. Consider again the example offered in 2.169:

> In consideration of $10,000, Able hereby sells the Equipment to Baker.

2.204   In this example, is the $10,000 being paid at signing? In that case, it would be clearer to say the following:

> Able hereby purchases the Equipment from Baker for $10,000, which Baker acknowledges having received from Able concurrently with the parties' signing this agreement.

2.205   Or is the $10,000 being paid later? In that case, it would be better to express payment by Able as an obligation:

> Able hereby purchases the Equipment from Baker for $10,000, which Able shall pay Baker no later than 30 days after the date of this agreement.

2.206   So besides dispensing with backstop recitals of consideration (along with nominal and sham consideration), you should be able to dispense entirely with the word *consideration* to express any part of a bargained-for exchange. Have no qualms about that—referring to consideration does not affect whether a transaction is supported by consideration. See 17A *Am. Jur. 2d* Contracts § 109 (2017).

OTHER JURISDICTIONS

2.207   It's standard to find U.S.-style backstop recitals of consideration in the lead-in of Canadian contracts. They also appear in international contracts that have some connection with the United States. Whatever the context, the analysis offered in this manual applies.

2.208   In contracts drafted in England and Australia, it's rare to encounter U.S.-style backstop recitals of consideration in the lead-in. But that shouldn't be cause for complacency, because one can find English and Australian contracts that include elsewhere in the contract provisions that reflect the same misconceptions. For example, *The parties acknowledge the receipt and sufficiency of the consideration to this agreement.*

2.209   Unlike the law in U.S. jurisdictions (with the limited exception discussed in 2.192), under English law nominal consideration is enough to support a contract. English courts give legal effect to what is a pretense.

2.210   The doctrine of consideration isn't recognized under civil law, but don't be surprised if due to copy-and-paste cross-contamination from Anglo-American contracts you see a recital of consideration in a contract governed by the law of a civil-law jurisdiction. If that happens, delete the recital of consideration.

Giving a Heading to the Body of the Contract

2.211   Some drafters insert after the lead-in and before the body of the contract a heading that introduces the body of the contract. Such headings are favored by drafters from Commonwealth countries, who are partial to naming the parts of a contract (see 2.18).

2.212 One option is *AGREEMENT*, but it's misleading, because the word *agreement* is best understood as referring to the entire contract (see 2.126). A less problematic alternative would be, for example, *OPERATIVE PROVISIONS*. Simpler still would be *THE BODY OF THE CONTRACT*.

2.213 But it serves no purpose to introduce the body of the contract twice, with the lead-in *and* a heading. Don't use such a heading.

COVER SHEET, TABLE OF CONTENTS, AND INDEX OF DEFINED TERMS

2.214 If a contract is more than 20 pages long, consider providing from the first draft onwards a table of contents that lists page numbers for articles and sections and lists all attachments. Word-processing software makes it easy to create a table of contents and keep it up to date.

2.215 Place a table of contents before the contract proper, and use a cover sheet so the first page of the table of contents isn't the first thing the reader sees. The cover sheet generally contains an edited-down and spread-out version of the introductory clause, but you could include other information, notably the name, logo, and contact information of the law firm primarily responsible for drafting the contract and the name and contact information of the lawyer handling the transaction. (Regarding the implications of including a logo, see 4.123.)

2.216 One also sees cover sheets that include a warning about confidentiality, a warning about trading in shares with knowledge of the document, or a statement that preliminary drafts of the document are not binding. The more clutter you add to a cover sheet, the less value it has as a place to put important ancillary information.

2.217 If the contract contains an index of definitions (see 6.105), place it immediately after the table of contents.

CATEGORIES OF CONTRACT LANGUAGE

3.1   Between the recitals (see 2.129) and the concluding clause (see 5.2) is the body of the contract, which contains the provisions that the parties are agreeing to—the "deal."

3.2   A clause or sentence in the body of the contract can serve one of several functions. Each function requires its own category of language, each with its own issues of usage. The categories are language of agreement, performance, obligation, discretion, prohibition, policy, declaration, intention, and recommendation. This chapter considers these categories of language, as well as how to express conditions by means of certain of these categories.

3.3   One category of contract language isn't somehow stronger or weaker than another. The phrases *mere condition* and *mere covenant* (and the latter phrase's more modern equivalent, *mere obligation*) occur in court opinions, as well as in the literature on contract law. Using the word *mere* (or *merely*) in such comparisons unhelpfully suggests that one category trumps another. Instead they serve different functions: Failure of a contract party to satisfy a condition will preclude whatever result depends on satisfaction of that condition. Failure of a contract party to comply with an obligation will entitle the other party to claim damages, and it might relieve the other party of obligations of its own. Because conditions and obligations serve different functions, it doesn't make sense to describe one category as prevailing over the other.

3.4   It makes life easier for the reader if to the extent possible you use a different verb structure for each category of contract language, consistent with the principle that you shouldn't use a word or phrase to convey more than one meaning and shouldn't use two or more words or phrases to convey the same meaning (see 1.64). This approach also helps the drafter figure out how to frame each provision (see 3.104). But the recommendations in this chapter don't invoke notional "rules" of grammar. Instead, they reflect standard English, with such adjustments as are justified to ensure clarity and reduce the risk of dispute.

3.5   This chapter begins with figure 1, a "quick reference" chart showing each category of contract language and the recommended verb structures, to make this topic more accessible.

FIGURE 1 ▪ **QUICK REFERENCE FOR THE CATEGORIES OF CONTRACT LANGUAGE**

Category of Contract Language	*Verb Structure*	*Context*	*Example*	*Ref.*
Agreement	*agree*	Used only in the lead-in	*The parties therefore agree as follows:*	3.30
Performance	*hereby +* simple present	Expresses actions performed by signing the contract	*Acme hereby purchases the Assets from Doe*	3.33–.35
ALTERNATIVE	Negative form of the present continuous	Language of policy expressing that the party isn't taking the specified action on signing the contract	*In this agreement the Buyer is not assuming any Excluded Liabilities.*	3.47
Obligation (Imposed on the Subject of the Sentence)	*shall +* infinitive	Imposes a duty on the subject of the sentence (if a party)	*Acme shall purchase the Shares from Doe.*	3.72–.74
Obligation (Imposed on Someone Other Than the Subject of the Sentence)	*must +* infinitive	The subject isn't a legal person and so cannot assume a duty	*The Closing must take place at Acme's offices.*	3.133
	must + infinitive	The subject, although a legal person, isn't a party and so cannot assume a duty	*The arbitrator must issue the award no later than 20 days after the last day of the hearing.*	3.134
ALTERNATIVE	*shall cause*	Language of obligation imposed on the subject of the sentence—used if the subject is one or more parties and the object isn't a person	*Parent shall cause the Closing to take place at Acme's offices.*	3.143–.144
	shall cause	Language of obligation imposed on the subject of the sentence—used if the subject is one or more parties and the object is an instrumentality of the subject	*Parent shall cause Sub to sell the Widget Assets.*	3.143–.144

Category of Contract Language	Verb Structure	Context	Example	Ref.
Discretion	*may +* infinitive	If the subject has the discretion to take a specified action	*The Indemnified Party may at its expense retain separate co-counsel.*	3.188
	is not required to + infinitive	Expresses absence of obligation	*Acme is not required to replace the Widget Equipment.*	3.268
	is not prohibited from + gerund	Expresses absence of prohibition	*Acme is not prohibited from removing the Widget Equipment.*	3.277
Prohibition	*shall not +* infinitive	Imposes a prohibition on the subject of the sentence	*The Customer shall not modify the Equipment without Acme's prior written consent.*	3.278
Policy	Simple present	Policies that apply on effectiveness of the contract	*New York law governs this agreement.*	3.307
	Simple present	Policies that state a time of effectiveness or lapsing of effectiveness	*This agreement terminates on 31 December 2019.*	3.307
	will + infinitive	Policies that relate to future events that might not take place or the timing of which is uncertain	*This agreement will terminate upon the closing of a Qualified IPO.*	3.307
	will + linking verb	Policies that relate to future events that might not take place or the timing of which is uncertain	*Any attempted transfer of Shares in violation of this agreement will be void.*	3.307
Condition (Generally)		A condition is a future and uncertain event or circumstance on which the existence of a legal relation depends		3.313

Category of Contract Language	Verb Structure	Context	Example	Ref.
Condition (Using a Conditional Clause)	Simple present	Used in the conditional clause	*If Jones ceases to be employed by the Company, ...* [continued in next row]	3.321
	will + infinitive	Used in the matrix clause, if the verb in a matrix clause would, absent the conditional clause, be in the present tense (*shall, may,* and *must* are unaffected by presence of a conditional clause)	[continued from previous row] *... the Option will terminate.*	3.324
Condition (Using Language of Policy)	Simple present	Introduced with a *that*-clause, whether a single condition or part of a list	*The Buyer's obligations under this agreement are subject to satisfaction of the following conditions: ... that Acme's statements of fact are accurate ... .*	3.354
	Present perfect	Introduced with a *that*-clause, whether a single condition or part of a list	*The Buyer's obligations under this agreement are subject to satisfaction of the following conditions: ... that the Buyer has received an opinion of Acme's counsel ... .*	3.354
Condition (Using Language of Obligation)	*must*	Introduced with a *to* infinitive clause or a clause beginning with *for*	*To be reimbursed, Acme must submit to Widgetco*	3.356, 3.361
Declaration	*states*	Asserts as accurate a fact the declaring party has knowledge of	*Acme states that the Equipment is listed on schedule A.*	3.416
	acknowledges	Accepts as accurate a fact the other party has knowledge of	*Acme acknowledges that the Consultant is in the business of providing services to others.*	3.436

Category of Contract Language	Verb Structure	Context	Example	Ref.
Intention	*intends that + will*	Used instead of language of policy if a given status depends on circumstances after the contract is signed	*The parties intend that the Consultant will be an independent contractor.*	3.442
Recommendation	*recommends, advises,* or *encourages + that*	Allows a party with greater bargaining power to avoid dispute by pointing out something the other party might otherwise miss	*The Company recommends that the Participant consult a legal adviser if ...*	3.452

3.6   This chapter includes tables containing one or more examples of a category of language, with each example being followed by variations on that example. Each initial example is identified by two numbers in a set of brackets, the first designating the number of the table and the second designating the number of the example within that table. For example, [3-3] denotes the third example in table 3. Each variation is given the same designation as the related initial example but is distinguished by adding a lowercase letter. For example, [3-3b] denotes the second variation on [3-3].

3.7   In addition, each example and each of its variations is annotated with the following symbols to indicate how acceptable it is:

✓✓   means this usage is recommended

✓   means that this usage, although acceptable, can be improved; that you should use it with caution; or that how acceptable it is depends on the context in which it is used

✗   means this usage isn't recommended

✗✗   means avoid this usage

GENERAL CONSIDERATIONS

Use the Third Person

3.8   In business contracts use the third person, as in *Acme shall purchase the Shares from Doe.* That's standard practice.

3.9   Some contracts are in the first and second person, using *we, us,* and *our* for one party and *you* and *your* for the other. Using both the first and second person in a contract raises the issue of how one refers to both parties collectively if *we*, *us*, and *our* are being used for one of the parties; your only recourse would be the rather awkward and potentially confusing *both of us*. Also, it's easy to imagine a reader losing track of who *we* and *you* are.

3.10   One could get around both those problems by dropping first-person pronouns in favor of a party name, but the bigger issue is whether the first and second person are suited to business contracts. The first and second person are primarily used in consumer contracts, such as insurance policies. It's safe to assume that sophisticated business people and their attorneys can do without the intimacy that use of the first and second person seeks to foster—it quickly palls, and it has a whiff of condescension about it. Furthermore, it wouldn't work in a contract with more than two parties.

Use the Active Voice Unless the Passive Voice Is Appropriate

3.11   For general writing, it's standard advice that you should be wary of using the passive voice. That applies equally to contracts.

3.12   In a sentence in the active voice, the subject of the sentence performs the action—*Marie ate the peach*. When you use a verb in the passive voice, the subject is acted on—*The peach was eaten by Marie*—and what in the active voice would have been the subject is instead the passive agent. (This manual uses the term *by*-agent to refer to the passive agent—in the example in the previous sentence, *Marie*.) When using the passive voice, you can intentionally or inadvertently omit the *by*-agent—*The peach was eaten*.

3.13   There are three drawbacks to using the passive voice. First, using the passive voice and including a *by*-agent adds unnecessary words. Second, the passive voice disrupts the normal subject–verb–object order of a sentence. And third, using the passive voice and omitting the *by*-agent obscures who the actor is. Those drawbacks apply to any form of writing, but in contract prose, the stakes are high—the consequences of obscuring the actor's identity can be drastic. So in contract prose, use the active voice unless it's clear that there's a benefit to using the passive voice. In particular, use the active voice to express action by a party.

AN EXAMPLE

3.14   For an example of what can happen if you use the passive voice and drop the *by*-agent, see *East Texas Copy Systems, Inc. v. Player*, No. 06-16-00035-CV, 2016 WL 6638865, at *1 (Tex. App. 10 Nov. 2016).

3.15   One Jason Player sold his business to East Texas Copy Systems, Inc. As part of the sale, Player was hired by Copy Systems, starting 1 July 2013. Effective 30 June 2015, Player resigned his position with Copy Systems and immediately started competing with them.

3.16   The asset purchase agreement prohibited Player from competing for two years. A separate noncompetition agreement prohibited him from competing for two years or one year after termination of his employment. The noncompetition agreement also contained the following provision:

> If Jason Player's employment with Buyer is terminated prior to two years from the date of this Agreement for any reason other than a for cause termination, this Non-Compete Agreement will no longer be binding.

3.17   The asset purchase agreement said the same thing.

3.18   After Player quit, Copy Systems demanded that he comply with the one-year restriction. Litigation followed. The trial court granted Player's motion for summary judgment and awarded his attorney fees and court costs.

3.19   On appeal, Copy Systems argued that the quoted language should be interpreted to only be effective if Copy Systems terminated Player's employment. The court disagreed, holding as follows:

> [T]he emphasis of the Disputed Clause is on the termination of Player's employment, not which party initiates the termination. Under the parties' agreement, either party could terminate the employment relationship. Therefore, we presume that the parties, by not limiting which party initiates the termination, intended that either party could initiate the termination.

3.20   The culprit in this story is use of the passive voice. In both contracts, the language at issue begins with "If Jason Player's employment with Buyer is terminated." It uses the passive voice, with no *by*-agent, so strictly speaking, these provisions would be triggered if either party were to terminate Player's employment. That can't be what Copy Systems intended, because it rendered the noncompetition provisions toothless.

3.21   From the perspective of the drafter, whether the appeals court was right in interpreting the contracts strictly is irrelevant. Instead, what matters is that this case demonstrates that if you use the passive voice, you can inadvertently drop the *by*-agent and find that you don't have the deal you expected. If you use the active voice, you're forced to include the actor, which forces you to figure out what you want to have happen.

APPROPRIATE USE OF THE PASSIVE VOICE

3.22   In general writing, sometimes you're justified in using the passive voice—among other considerations, the actor might be unimportant or unknown, or you might want to focus on the thing being acted on. That's the case with contract prose too.

3.23   Consider this example of use of the passive voice: *if a Necessary Project Approval is revoked*. One could use the active voice instead—*if a Person revokes a Necessary Project Approval*—but that would add nothing. What matters is whether an approval has been revoked, and it would be beside the point to shift the focus to who's doing the revoking, whether it be a government agency, a company, or an individual.

3.24   Here's another example: *No party will be bound by this amendment until the Parent, the Borrowers, and the Required Lenders have signed a counterpart.* It would serve no purpose to use instead the active voice, thereby shifting the focus from the parties to the amendment—*This amendment will bind no party ... .*

Throat-Clearing

3.25   A distinctive feature of traditional contract language is extraneous verb structures tacked on to the front of what would otherwise be separate sentences. This manual refers to this practice as "throat-clearing." Here's a sample of such verb structures:

    1.   Acme agrees that [Acme shall ...] .

    2.   It is agreed that ... .

    3.   Acme covenants that ... .

    4.   Acme represents that ... .

    5.   Acme represents, warrants, covenants, and agrees that ... .

    6.   Acme acknowledges that ... .

    7.   Acme warrants that ... .

    8.   Acme warrants and agrees that ... .

    9.   Acme guarantees that ... .

    10.   Acme promises that ... .

    11.   Acme intends that ... .

3.26   The first of the above examples is followed by language of obligation (see 3.70), but throat-clearing can precede any category of contract language.

3.27   A throat-clearing verb structure can be mistaken for the principal verb structure of a sentence. Of the above examples, example 1 and 2 look like language of agreement (see 3.30), example 3 looks like old-fashioned language of obligation (see 3.113), examples 4 and 6 appear to be language of declaration (see 3.371), and example 7 appears to express a warranty (see 13.884). (Examples 5 and 8 use multiple verb structures.) But throat-clearing verb structures are neutralized by the verb structure that follows, so all that throat-clearing accomplishes is to suggest a general assent to the rest of the sentence. That assent is redundant, because the essence of a contract is that the parties assent to everything in the body of the contract. That's the function of the lead-in (see 2.160).

3.28   Throat-clearing adds useless clutter to a contract, so drafters should be alert to it. So too should anyone who reviews contracts. If making a contract shorter and clearer isn't enough to justify asking the other side to remove throat-clearing from their draft, you could also point out that it can create confusion. In *UBS Securities LLC v. Highland Capital Management, L.P.*, 906 N.Y.S.2d 784 (Sup. Ct. 2009), *rev'd*, 893 N.Y.S.2d 869 (App. Div. 2010), the court attributed substantive significance to "UBS Securities and [Highland Capital] agree that … ." It was in fact meaningless throat-clearing.

Consolidating Deal Points

3.29   Drafters are prone to addressing each deal point in a separate sentence. Consolidating deal points by using one verb structure for multiple deal points allows you to address those deal points more clearly and concisely than you would otherwise. Here are two examples.

Separate	*Consolidated*
The Licensee shall make all regulatory filings. The Licensee shall decide in which countries to file for regulatory approval.	The Licensee shall make all regulatory filings in those countries in which it decides to seek Regulatory Approval for a Product.
Acme shall pay each invoice no later than 30 days after it receives that invoice. For Acme's payment of an invoice to be valid, Acme must pay that invoice by bank transfer.	Acme shall pay each invoice by bank transfer no later than 30 days after it receives that invoice.

LANGUAGE OF AGREEMENT

3.30   In "language of agreement," one or more parties state that they agree with specified contract language. Language of agreement should appear only once in a contract—in the lead-in, which states that the parties *agree as follows* (see 2.160).

3.31   Language of agreement is distinct from language of performance (see 3.33) and language of declaration (see 3.371) because it expresses a state of mind rather than a party taking an action or stating a fact. That's why it wouldn't make sense to use *hereby* in language of agreement—it's a feature of language of performance.

3.32   For an example of throat-clearing masquerading as language of agreement, see 3.25–.27.

LANGUAGE OF PERFORMANCE

3.33   In standard English, one can accomplish with a speech act, such as *I quit!*, an action involving a change in status. Speech acts also occur in contracts. One example is *Acme hereby grants the License to Smith*; for another example, see [1-1]. This manual calls such speech acts "language of performance." They use the present tense, and they express actions accomplished by signing the contract.

3.34 The term "language of performance" is unrelated to the concept of performance under a contract. Instead, it echoes the linguistics term for such a speech act—a *performative*.

TABLE 1 ■ LANGUAGE OF PERFORMANCE

[1-1]	✓✓	Acme hereby purchases the Assets from Doe.
[1-1a]	✓	Acme purchases the Assets from Doe.
[1-1b]	✗✗	The Assets are hereby purchased from Doe.
[1-1c]	✗✗	Acme is hereby purchasing the Assets from Doe.
[1-1d]	✗✗	Acme does hereby purchase the Assets from Doe.
[1-1e]	✗✗	Acme agrees to purchase the Assets from Doe.
[1-1f]	✗✗	Acme agrees to and does hereby purchase the Assets from Doe.
[1-1g]	✗✗	Acme shall purchase the Assets from Doe as of the date of this agreement.
[1-1h]	✗✗	Acme is pleased to purchase the Assets from Doe.
[1-1i]	✗✗	Acme hereby irrevocably purchases the Assets from Doe.
[1-2]	✗✗	The Buyer does not hereby assume the Excluded Liabilities.
[1-2a]	✗✗	The Buyer hereby does not assume the Excluded Liabilities.
[1-2b]	✗✗	In this agreement the Buyer is not assuming any Excluded Liabilities.
[1-3]	✗	When the Company issues a Purchase Order, it will thereby hire the Contractor to perform the services stated in that Purchase Order.
[1-3a]	✓✓	When the Company issues a Purchase Order, it will be deemed to have hired the Contractor to perform the services stated in that Purchase Order.
[1-4]	✓✓	Acme hereby grants Widgetco a license to use the Marks in … .
[1-4a]	✓	Acme hereby grants Widgetco the right to use the Marks in … .
[1-4b]	✗✗	Widgetco may use the Marks in … .
[1-4c]	✗	Acme hereby licenses to Widgetco the right to use the Marks in … .
[1-4d]	✗	Acme hereby grants to Widgetco a license to use the Marks in … .

Use of *Hereby* in Language of Performance

3.35 One helpful element of language of performance is *hereby,* which signals that the act described is being accomplished by the speech act itself. You could omit *hereby,* as in [1-1a], but this use of *hereby* is consistent with standard English. If you omit *hereby* from *Doe hereby purchases the Shares,* it would be clear from the context that the intended meaning isn't that

Doe is in the habit of purchasing certain shares. But in purely grammatical terms, one couldn't exclude that meaning without using *hereby*. *The Cambridge Grammar of the English Language*, at 860 n.3, confirms as much:

> Clauses like *I promise to return the key* and *I order you to leave* are ambiguous, having also less salient interpretations in which they are statements about my habitual behaviour ("I habitually promise to return the key / order you to leave"): in this interpretation they are not performatives since they do not themselves constitute a promise or order.

3.36   This alternative meaning is unlikely to create confusion, but it could distract readers. Eliminate the alternative meaning by using *hereby*.

3.37   In language of performance, don't replace *hereby* with *by this agreement*: the *here-* in *hereby* is best considered as relating to that language of performance rather than the agreement as a whole. It would be appropriate to replace *hereby* when it's used other than in language of performance (see 13.350).

Problematic Usages

3.38   To make it clear who the actor is (see 3.11), always use the active voice in language of performance instead of using the passive voice (as in [1-1b]).

3.39   Don't use the present continuous in language of performance, as in [1-1c]. The present continuous is used to express an event that's unfolding—that's not appropriate for language of performance. Instead, the action occurs instantaneously.

3.40   Don't use *do* as an auxiliary in language of performance, as in [1-1d]; it's an archaism. And don't use *agrees to*, as in [1-1e], because that could lead to a fight over whether it's language of performance or language of obligation (see 3.109). Combining both usages, as in [1-1f], adds to the confusion.

3.41   Don't attempt to turn language of obligation (see 3.70), such as *Acme shall grant the License to Smith*, into language of performance by adding *on the date of this agreement*, as in [1-1g]. Doing so would impose on Acme the obligation to grant the license sometime on the date of the agreement, but that would be a confusing alternative to having the grant take place simultaneously with signing the agreement.

3.42   Don't use *is pleased to* to express language of performance, as in [1-1h]. Here's an example of that usage: *The Bank is pleased to provide its commitment for the entire amount of the Facility.* Here's another: *Acme Trust is pleased to retain Doe Compliance Consulting, LLC.* The deferential tone that *is pleased to* affords might seem appropriate in a particular context, but *is pleased to* doesn't make it clear that the action in question is being accomplished by that speech act.

3.43   Be careful about using *irrevocably* (meaning "unalterably") in language of performance, as in [1-1i]. Usually *irrevocably* is redundant—when a contract party takes an action, it's implicit that absent anything in the contract to the contrary, the action can't be undone. Thus, in *irrevocably purchases*, *irrevocably waives*, *irrevocably releases*, and *irrevocably consents*, the word *irrevocably* is redundant. See, e.g., *Reyes v. Lincoln Automotive Financial Services*, No. 16-2104-CV, 2017 WL 2675363 (2d Cir. 22 June 2017) (under common law, a consent granted in a contract is irrevocable). For the same reason, don't use words like *unconditionally*, *absolutely*, and *forever* in language of performance.

3.44   But it's appropriate to use *irrevocably* with *appoint*. That's because the power to appoint a person to a position might also include the power to remove that person. If you don't want that to be the case, say so; *irrevocably* accomplishes that.

3.45   Similarly, if a party consents to ongoing conduct by another party, as opposed to a one-time action, it would be prudent to use *irrevocably*, to avoid any suggestion that the consenting party would at some point be permitted to change its mind.

Actions That Don't Work in Language of Performance

3.46   If an action relates to something other than a change of status of a person or thing, don't use language of performance. For example, it doesn't make sense to say *The Buyer hereby pays the Seller*: you can't pay someone just by saying so.

Indicating Absence of Performance

3.47   It's occasionally helpful to state that one or more parties are not taking a specified action on signing the contract. But in doing so, don't use language of performance retooled to express the negative, as in [1-2] and [1-2a]—language of performance accomplishes actions, and what you're seeking to express is the absence of action. Instead, use language of policy (see 3.305), as in [1-2b].

Future Performance

3.48   If you're looking to state the consequences of entry into a contract or issuance of a document in the future, you could conceivably use language of performance, but with *will* instead of the present tense and *thereby* instead of *hereby*, as in [1-3]. But that's not how language of performance works in standard English—it's not for accomplishing actions in the future with a speech act now. Use instead *will be deemed*, as in [1-3a]. (Regarding *deem*, see 13.216.)

In Buying and Selling

3.49   For a transaction that occurs when the contract is signed, *Acme hereby purchases the Assets from Doe* and *Doe hereby sells the Assets to Acme* are equivalent. Each verb refers not to a unilateral action but instead to transfer of whatever is being sold—if Acme is purchasing assets from Doe, it follows that Doe is selling them, and vice versa. The verb you choose simply determines which party's perspective you adopt—perhaps that of your client. It has no substantive significance.

3.50   So it's unnecessary to use both *purchase* and *sell*, as in *Acme hereby purchases the Assets from Doe and Doe hereby sells the Assets to Acme*. But in the United States, that formulation is perhaps the one used most often. That might be due to the influence of language of obligation, where reciprocity makes sense: if you omit one of *Acme shall purchase the Assets from Doe* and *Doe shall sell the Assets to Acme*, one party wouldn't be committed to the transaction.

3.51   Furthermore, drafters might feel more comfortable having the language explicitly reflect the reciprocal nature of the transaction, even at the cost of redundancy. So if you use either *purchase* or *sell*, be prepared to have someone ask you to use both. (Regarding use of *purchase* instead of *buy*, see 13.124.)

For Performance of Services

3.52   Language of obligation (see 3.70) is the default category of contract language for expressing performance of services. But if the services to be performed are such that they are used to define the parties performing them, using labels such as *agent*, *employee*, and *attorney-in-fact*, it can sound more natural to use language of performance with the verbs *appoints*, *employs*, and *retains*. The more prevalent the label, the more likely it is that language of performance is the better choice.

3.53   Here's an example expressed first using language of performance, then language of obligation:

> The Fund hereby appoints the Agent as its "Investor Servicing Agent" in accordance with this agreement.

> The Agent shall act as the Fund's "Investor Servicing Agent" in accordance with this agreement.

3.54   In that example, language of performance is the more natural choice, but it seems unnecessary in the following example, because the services in question aren't susceptible to applying a label to those who perform them:

> Acme hereby appoints ABC to perform in accordance with this agreement the administrative, bookkeeping, and pricing services stated in appendix A.

> ABC shall perform for Acme in accordance with this agreement the administrative, bookkeeping, and pricing services stated in appendix A.

Advantages of Granting Language

3.55   Language of performance using the verb *grants*, as in *Acme hereby grants Smith the License*, offers advantages over alternative ways of conveying the same meaning.

INSTEAD OF LANGUAGE OF DISCRETION

3.56   Granting language is analogous to language of discretion. Consider [1-4], [1-4a], and [1-4b]. They all convey the same meaning, but granting language using the noun *license*, as in [1-4], offers two advantages.

3.57   First, license-granting language makes it clear that discretion is being accorded regarding something that the licensor controls.

3.58   And second, using the concept of a license allows you also to use, as necessary, the concept of a sublicense. Articulating the notion of *A to B to C* using language of discretion would be trickier and wordier.

3.59   So it makes sense to use granting language in contexts where the advantages over language of discretion are relevant. It also makes sense to use granting language in the kinds of transactions where use of granting language is entrenched. In both cases, that means contracts dealing with rights to software and intellectual property.

3.60   Resist the urge to use granting language more generally. Below is an example using language of performance; below it is a version using language of discretion. The version using language of discretion is shorter and clearer.

> The Customer hereby grants Acme a perpetual, nonexclusive, and irrevocable license to use data on performance and output of the Covered Equipment … .

> During the term of this agreement and thereafter, Acme may use data on performance and output of the Covered Equipment … .

INSTEAD OF THE VERB *LICENSE*

3.61   Instead of the granting language in [1-4] you could use the verb *license*, as in [1-4c], to grant discretion. But using granting language plus the noun *license* allows the drafter to add adjectives as necessary: *nonexclusive*, *irrevocable*, *perpetual*, and so on. That's simpler than using adverbs to modify the verb *license*.

3.62   Another drawback to the verb *license* is that *Acme hereby licenses* on its own could mean that Acme is the licensee or that it's the licensor.

3.63   Use of the verb *lease* in language of performance raises the same issues, but evidently drafters have decided that the advantages of using the noun *license* don't apply to use of the verb *lease*—it would be unorthodox to say *Jones hereby grants Smith a lease* instead of *Jones hereby leases to Smith*.

USE *GRANT* INSTEAD OF *GRANT TO*

3.64   The only difference between [1-4] and [1-4d] is that in [1-4d], *hereby grants* is followed by *to*. You see both usages in contracts, but the better choice is to omit the *to*. Consider the following sentences:

> I gave John a book.

> I gave a book to John.

> *I gave to John a book.

3.65   The first sentence matches the structure of [1-4]. It's a ditransitive clause, with a direct and indirect object. The second sentence is a monotransitive clause—it has just one object—plus a prepositional phrase using *to*. See *The Cambridge Grammar of the English Language*, at 248.

3.66   When you use a monotransitive structure, the prepositional phrase conventionally comes at the end. If you have a simple direct object, it sounds odd to put the prepositional phrase before the direct object, as in the third sentence. (That's why the third sentence is marked with an asterisk.)

3.67   But if the direct object is lengthy, that can preclude putting the prepositional phrase after the direct object. That would be the case with a direct object beginning *a license to* … . Your only choice would be to put the prepositional phrase before the direct object, as in [1-4d]. But not only is the *to* oddly positioned, it's also superfluous, because without it you would have a conventional ditransitive structure, as in [1-4]. That's why the ditransitive structure is your best alternative.

3.68   Little is riding on this distinction, but it's best to have a reasoned basis for selecting among alternative usages.

3.69   This distinction applies to other verbs, including *pay*, and applies to other categories of contract language in addition to language of performance.

LANGUAGE OF OBLIGATION

3.70   "Language of obligation" is used to state any duty that a contract imposes on one or more parties. In terms of structure, language of obligation falls into two categories, depending on whether the obligation is imposed on the subject of the sentence (see 3.72) or on someone other than the subject (see 3.131).

3.71   Language of obligation also serves as one way to express contract conditions (see 3.356).

Language of Obligation Imposed on the Subject of a Sentence

USING *SHALL* TO MEAN ONLY *HAS A DUTY TO*

3.72   In the example in table 2, Acme is the subject of the sentence. To state that Acme has a duty to purchase the Shares from Doe, use *shall*, as in [2-1]. This manual recommends not using *shall* in contract drafting to express any other meaning.

TABLE 2 ▪ LANGUAGE OF OBLIGATION IMPOSED ON SUBJECT OF SENTENCE

[2-1]	✓✓	Acme shall purchase the Shares from Doe.
[2-1a]	✗	Acme must purchase … .
[2-1b]	✗	Acme will purchase … .
[2-1c]	✗✗	Acme agrees to purchase … .
[2-1d]	✗✗	Acme promises to purchase … .
[2-1e]	✗✗	Acme undertakes to purchase … .
[2-1f]	✗✗	Acme is bound to purchase … .
[2-1g]	✗✗	Acme covenants to purchase … .
[2-1h]	✗✗	Acme commits to purchasing … .
[2-1i]	✗✗	Acme has a duty to purchase … .
[2-1j]	✗✗	Acme shall be obligated to purchase … .
[2-1k]	✗	Acme is obligated to purchase … .
[2-1l]	✗✗	Acme is responsible for purchasing … .
[2-1m]	✗✗	Acme will be expected to purchase … .

3.73 Courts have long recognized use of *shall* to express obligations. For business contracts, as opposed to statutes, it's unlikely that anyone could successfully argue that instead of expressing an obligation, a particular *shall* is "discretionary" and means *may* or *should*. In *PacifiCorp v. Sempra Energy Trading Corp.*, No. CIV-04-0701 (E.D. Cal. 2 July 2004), the court held in a contract dispute that *shall* can mean *should*. But the one case it cites involved statutory interpretation, and otherwise it cites only the second edition of *Garner's Dictionary of Legal Usage* (see 3.83, 3.86). It's an outlier.

3.74 As an initial diagnostic test for use of *shall* in a provision, check whether the provision would still make sense if you were to replace *shall* with *has* [or *have*] *a duty to*. (This manual refers to this test as the *"has a duty test,"* using the word *duty* in this context simply because it's less of a mouthful than *obligation*; see 3.171.) But just because a *shall* passes the *has a duty* test doesn't mean that the provision makes sense as an obligation. It might be better phrased as a condition (see 3.356–.362).

3.75 Use of *shall* in contracts is a contentious subject, so the basis for the use of *shall* recommended in 3.72 is explained in 3.76–.108.

THE MEANING OF *SHALL* AND *WILL*

3.76 *Shall* is a modal auxiliary verb. Unlike the other auxiliaries (*be, do, have*), the modal auxiliaries (*shall, will, must, can, may, should, would, could, might*) supply information about the mood of the main verb that follows. *Shall* was originally a full verb (like *eat, walk,* and *play*) conveying obligation or compulsion, but now it's used only as an auxiliary, as is the modal *will*, which originally carried the sense of volition.

3.77   Because obligations and intentions concern future conduct, and because there's no true future tense in English similar to the present tense (*works*) and past tense *(worked), shall* and *will* also came to be used with future time.

3.78   The result is that *shall* and *will* have each been used to express modal meanings and to mark future time. A rule arose, at least in theory, and perhaps only in England, to distinguish these two uses: to express future time, use *shall* with the first person and *will* with the second or third person, and do the reverse to convey modal meanings. This cumbersome rule developed many exceptions.

3.79   The rule and its exceptions have largely been abandoned in much of the world—in common usage, use of *shall* is now largely limited to stock phrases such as *We shall overcome* and questions in the first person that seek direction or suggest politely—*Shall we go now?* But in the stylized context of the language of business contracts, which generally use only the third person (see 3.8), *shall* continues to serve as the principal means of expressing obligations.

THE PROBLEM OF OVERUSE

3.80   Contract drafters use *shall* to do more than express obligations. They use it to express future time, even in contexts where in everyday English one would use the simple present tense instead of *will*. (See, for example, [8-2b] and [16-1a].) As a result, business contracts exhibit rampant overuse of the word, making *shall* a glaring violator of the principle that in drafting, you shouldn't use a word or phrase to convey more than one meaning (see 1.64). It's as if many drafters fear that a contract provision without a *shall* would be unenforceable.

3.81   This overuse of *shall* plays a leading role in distancing contract prose from standard English, thereby making contracts harder to read. It also helps render drafters oblivious to nuances in determining how to express in a contract who is doing what, to whom, and why. This obliviousness can result in disputes, particularly over whether a provision is a condition or an obligation (see 3.357–.361).

THE MODEST BENEFITS OF ELIMINATING *SHALL*

3.82   One way to address overuse of *shall* is to be more disciplined in how you use the word—hence the recommendation in 3.72.

3.83   But some commentators on legal writing—notably Bryan Garner—advocate doing away with *shall* because it's too prone to misuse and is inconsistent with general English usage. As noted in *Garner's Dictionary of Legal Usage,* at 953, "few lawyers have the semantic acuity to identify correct and incorrect *shall*s even after a few hours of study. That being so, there can hardly be much hope of the profession's using *shall* consistently." For the anti-*shall* view from an Australian perspective, see Michèle M. Asprey, *Plain Language for Lawyers* 205–16 (4th ed. 2010).

3.84 It might be a good idea to eliminate *shall* from court rules, statutes, and consumer contracts, but it doesn't automatically follow that the same approach should be applied to business contracts—they serve a different function and address a different audience. Instead, banning *shall* from business contracts offers only modest benefits, and they're outweighed by the drawbacks.

3.85 Eliminating *shall* would prevent drafters from using *shall* instead of *will* to express future time, as in *This agreement shall terminate when the Acme Contract terminates*. But that's unlikely to result in confusion as to meaning, even though it's not ideal (see 3.308). The same applies to use of *shall* to express future time when the simple present tense would be more appropriate (see 3.307), as in *This agreement shall be governed by New York law*. Furthermore, depriving drafters of *shall* would be unlikely to make them more restrained in electing to express future time—the most likely result would be overuse of *will*.

3.86 More generally, the risks posed by *shall* can be overstated. For example, to indicate those risks, *Garner's Dictionary of Legal Usage,* at 953, points to the "more than 120 pages" devoted to *shall* in West's multivolume *Words and Phrases*. But of the cases cited, most involve the language of statutes, not contracts. At least in part, that's due to courts having recognized the discretionary *shall* (see 3.73) for interpreting statutes but not for interpreting contracts.

3.87 The only issue relating to overuse of *shall* that routinely results in contract disputes is uncertainty regarding whether a provision using *shall* is an obligation or a condition (see 3.357–.361). Replacing *shall* with *must* or any other verb wouldn't resolve that problem. Instead, you would have to supplement the provision to make it clear that you're expressing a condition (see 3.361).

USING *MUST* INSTEAD OF *SHALL*

3.88 Anyone contemplating eliminating *shall* from contracts should consider not only the modest benefits of doing so but also the drawbacks of the alternatives available to impose an obligation on the subject of the sentence.

3.89 One alternative to using *shall* to serve this function is *must* (see [2-1a]). Asprey favors this approach.

3.90 But replacing *shall* with *must* would result in *must* being used to express any obligation, whether it's imposed on the subject of a sentence— *The Company must reimburse the Consultant for all authorized expenses* (see 3.72)—or on someone else—*The Closing must take place at Acme's offices* (see 3.133). Furthermore, *must* also features in one way to express conditions (see 3.359). So using *must* for stating an obligation imposed on the subject of a sentence would result in *must* being used to convey different meanings. Muddying the distinction between obligations and conditions by using *must* for both is particularly pernicious.

USING *WILL* INSTEAD OF *MUST*

3.91   Another obstacle to using *must* as an alternative to *shall* for imposing obligations on the subject of a sentence is that many drafters consider *must* overbearing.

3.92   Asprey dismisses that objection as being "based on taste, not logic." But it's unrealistic to expect drafters to ignore issues of tone when deciding how to express obligations.

3.93   That's why in *Garner's Dictionary of Legal Usage,* at 953–54, Garner endorses use of *will* (as in [2-1b]) instead of *must:*

> In private drafting—contracts as opposed to statutes, rules, and regulations—some drafters consider *must* inappropriately bossy. The word may strike the wrong tone particularly when both parties to a contract are known quantities, such as two well-known corporations. It seems unlikely that, for example, an American car manufacturer and a Japanese car manufacturer engaging in a joint venture would want the word *must* to set forth their various responsibilities. Indeed, it seems odd to draft one's own contractual responsibilities with *must*: a lawyer for Ford Motor Company is unlikely to write *Ford must ... Ford must ... Ford must ...* . The word *will* is probably the best solution here.

3.94   This assessment is puzzling in three respects. First, why should the word you use to express obligations depend on how well-known the parties are? Second, it suggests the possibility of varying the word used to express an obligation depending on whether the obligation is imposed on the drafter's client or another party—distinction for which there's no basis in linguistics or the law. And third, the suggestion that *will* is "probably the best solution" is oddly wishy-washy.

3.95   And Garner's assessment doesn't address the two drawbacks of using *will* to impose obligations. The first is that in standard English *will* primarily expresses future time rather than obligations. *Will* is also used to express compulsion—*You will eat your spinach!*—but that use isn't directly analogous to expressing contract obligations. The second is that if you use *will* to impose an obligation on the subject of a sentence, you would also use it to impose an obligation on someone other than the subject of the sentence, as well as to express future time. Such multiple meanings are exactly what currently afflict use of *shall*.

EVERYDAY USE OF *SHALL*

3.96   Another objection to *shall* is that it makes no sense to perpetuate it in contracts, given that use of *shall* in general usage has greatly diminished (see 3.79). But because standard English isn't suited to expressing contract obligations and because of the benefit of using different verb structures for different categories of contract language, *shall* serves a real need. It shouldn't be disconcerting to have *shall* serve a broader role in contracts than it does in everyday English, given the limited and stylized nature of contract language (see p. xxxiii).

FLIGHT FROM *SHALL*?

3.97 At any one time, individual lawyers, or groups of lawyers, or conceivably entire organizations, might decline to use *shall*. But there's no sign of headlong flight from *shall*. Bryan Garner acknowledges as much, as *Garner's Modern English Usage*, at 825, says that "*shall* seems likely to persist" in legal documents. In most jurisdictions, *shall* remains overused in contracts.

3.98 Australian drafters appear more willing than others to dispense with *shall*, but review of an unscientific sample of contracts drafted by Australian law firms suggests that even in Australia, many contracts use *shall*.

MISSING THE BIGGER PROBLEM

3.99 The focus on *shall* has drawn attention away from the bigger problem—the chaotic verb structures on display in mainstream contract drafting.

3.100 Banishing *shall* addresses the most obvious symptom of the ailment, not the ailment itself. To varying degrees, contracts that don't use *shall* invariably exhibit undisciplined use of verb structures. See, e.g., Kenneth A. Adams, *Google's Services Agreement? Lots of Room for Improvement*, Adams on Contract Drafting (4 Mar. 2014), http://www.adamsdrafting.com/googles-services-agreement-lots-of-room-for-improvement/.

3.101 Using *shall* to mean only "has a duty to" (see 3.74) is a big step toward curing the ailment. It's well suited to the task, and the *has a duty* test provides a simple way to ensure that *shall* isn't used for any other purpose.

3.102 It's too pessimistic to say disciplined use of *shall* is beyond the reach of most lawyers (see 3.83). The test for disciplined use of *shall*—use it to mean only "has a duty to"—does require a modest amount of semantic acuity on the part of drafters, but no more than what's required for competent drafting.

3.103 Besides, it's too early to write most drafters off as incapable of disciplined use of *shall*—the notion that clear drafting requires complying with objective standards is still relatively novel. The key to rigorous verb use is training and reliable reference materials. That might sound unrealistic, but it's more plausible than the notion that drafters will purge their contracts of *shall* despite the uncertain benefits of doing so and the manifest shortcomings of the alternatives.

APPLYING THE *HAS A DUTY* TEST—AN EXAMPLE

3.104 To get a sense of the value of the *has a duty* test as a diagnostic tool, consider the standard arbitration clause recommended by the American Arbitration Association.

3.105 It's a piece of traditional contract drafting, with all the shortcomings that implies. In particular, it includes the following: "Any controversy or claim … shall be settled by arbitration administered by the American Arbitration Association." That *shall* fails the *has a duty* test, and it isn't amenable to a quick fix. It uses the passive voice, with the parties as the missing *by*-agent (see 3.12).

3.106   You could instead use the active voice—"The parties shall settle"—but it doesn't make sense to impose on the parties an obligation to arbitrate all disputes. Some disputes are more serious than others, and presumably a contract party would seek arbitration for only the most serious, as opposed to seeking mediation or informal negotiations or simply shrugging off the grievance.

3.107   The best way to reflect that nuance would be to use language of discretion, to allow a party to demand arbitration, while also making it clear that arbitration is the only means of dispute resolution permitted: "As the exclusive means of initiating adversarial proceedings to resolve any dispute … a party may demand that the dispute be resolved by arbitration administered by the American Arbitration Association."

3.108   For a complete analysis of the American Arbitration Association's standard arbitration clause, see Kenneth A. Adams, *The AAA Standard Arbitration Clause: Room for Improvement,* New York Law Journal, 9 Mar. 2010.

OTHER PROBLEMATIC USAGES

3.109   Some drafters rely on other verb structures to express obligations imposed on the subject of a sentence. One is *agrees to*, as in [2-1c]. Its only advantage is that it can't be used to express future time. Most drafters who use *agrees to* use it to impose an obligation, but some might use it as language of performance (see 3.33), with the idea that *Acme agrees to assign its rights* means the same thing as *Acme hereby assigns its rights*. In one dispute, a litigant attributed that meaning to *agrees to*. See *IpVenture, Inc. v. Prostar Computer, Inc.*, 503 F.3d 1324 (Fed. Cir. 2007). And it's easy to imagine those partial to *agrees to* also using it, unhelpfully, instead of *must* to express conditions (see 3.356).

3.110   Furthermore, *agrees to* is awkward when used to express an obligation that would apply only in the future, as in *If X, then Acme agrees to Y*. That could be cured by reversing the phrases, as in *Acme agrees to X, if Y*, but that won't always be feasible. And besides, *agrees to* is too clumsy to use with any frequency.

3.111   Because of these shortcomings, don't use *agrees to* to express obligations.

3.112   *Promises to* (see [2-1d]) occurs most often in the phrase *promises to pay*, which is standard in promissory notes and other negotiable instruments. But 4 Hawkland UCC Series § 3-102:10 (2016) notes that "the word 'promise' need not appear" in negotiable instruments, although "the language used must be promissory in nature." A different deal context doesn't justify using a different verb structure to express an obligation; consistency favors saying instead *shall pay*.

3.113   *Undertakes to* (see [2-1e]), *is bound to* (see [2-1f]), and *covenants to* (see [2-1g]) also have the virtue that they can't be used to express future time, but they're too awkward to be plausible alternatives to *shall*. (Regarding the noun *covenant*, see 3.165.) Couplets such as *covenants and agrees to* merely add redundancy to the shortcomings of each component. As for *commits to* plus gerund (see [2-1h]), it's too colloquial. And *is committed to* serves to express a general position—it's appropriate for press releases, not contracts.

3.114   Drafters also use *shall be obligated to* (see [2-1j]). It's inconsistent with disciplined use of *shall*, in that applying the *has a duty* test (see 3.74) yields "has a duty to be obligated," which doesn't make sense. Using *is obligated to* (see [2-1k]) represents little improvement—it's long-winded and could be understood to mean that the obligation arises not from that language but from some other source. (Regarding the British preference for *obliged* over *obligated*, see 3.269.)

3.115   The same goes for *has a duty to* (see [2-1i]), notwithstanding the role of that phrase in helping drafters use *shall* to express only a duty imposed on the subject of a sentence (see 3.74).

3.116   And *will be expected to* (see [2-1m]) is oddly circumspect, as if it would be too vulgar simply to impose an obligation. It's not clear what the consequences would be if the expectations aren't met. This formula appears in employment agreements.

USE THE INDICATIVE MOOD

3.117   The Construction Specifications Institute's *Project Delivery Practice Guide*, a widely used resource on preparing architectural specifications, recommends that you use the imperative mood to express obligations in architectural specifications. This manual doesn't endorse that recommendation.

3.118   Architectural specifications are attached to construction contracts and define the requirements for products, materials, and workmanship and for project administration and performance. They're a specialized form of contract language. *Project Delivery Practice Guide* is the only resource that recommends using the imperative mood to express contract obligations.

3.119   English has three moods—the indicative mood, the imperative mood, and the subjunctive mood. (For our purposes, we can ignore the subjunctive.) The indicative mood is the most common and is used to express facts and opinions and to pose questions. The imperative mood is used to instruct or request that someone do or not do something: *Feed the dog. Don't eat the pizza. Stop!*

3.120   Here's what *Project Delivery Practice Guide* says about mood:

> 11.3.5.2   Sentence Structure
>
> Two basic grammatical sentence moods can be used to clearly convey specification requirements:
>
> - *Imperative Mood.* The imperative mood is the recommended method for instructions covering the installation of products and equipment. The verb that clearly defines the action becomes the first word in the sentence, such as: spread adhesive with notched trowel. The imperative sentence is concise and readily understandable.
>
> - *Indicative Mood.* The indicative mood, passive voice requires the use of shall in nearly every statement. This sentence structure can cause unnecessary wordiness and monotony, such as: adhesive shall be spread with notched trowel.

3.121   But the imperative mood isn't up to expressing the full range of obligations. A set of instructions in the imperative mood can be directed at only one person—the contractor—whereas architectural specifications can also impose obligations on the owner or on the architect. If you use the imperative mood for contractor obligations, you would have to switch to the indicative mood for owner or architect obligations. That would make for an odd mix.

3.122   Even if you assume that all obligations in a set of specifications are imposed on the contractor, you would likely need to do more than bark instructions. Specifications can also feature language of discretion (*The Contractor may ...*), language of policy (*The Architect will be responsible for ...*), and conditions (*It is a condition to acceptance of the Work that ...*), all of them using the indicative mood. Switching back and forth from the imperative mood to the indicative mood would be awkward.

3.123   And what *Project Delivery Practice Guide* has to say about use of the indicative mood doesn't put it in proper perspective. If you want to avoid "unnecessary wordiness," you shouldn't limit yourself to the passive voice—it's conducive to wordiness (see 3.13). It would be a simple matter to preface a set of contractor obligations with something like *The Contractor shall do the following*, using the active voice, and state the obligations as tabulated enumerated clauses. Each such enumerated clause would be in the indicative mood and would be identical to obligations stated in the imperative (*spread adhesive with a notched trowel*).

3.124   But there's no sign of anyone outside of construction specifications emulating this aspect of *Project Delivery Practice Guide*, so use of the imperative mood in architectural specifications isn't a matter of broader concern. (A rare instance of use of the imperative mood in contracts is the phrase *Read before signing*; see 5.42.)

DON'T USE THE SIMPLE PRESENT TENSE

3.125   A model construction contract, *The New Engineering Contract*, recommends that you use the simple present tense to express obligations. This manual doesn't endorse that recommendation.

3.126   *The New Engineering Contract*, created by the Institution of Civil Engineers, a UK organization, is a guide to drafting documents for civil-engineering and construction projects. It's used in the United Kingdom and internationally. Here are two examples of how it uses the simple present tense to express obligations (emphasis added):

> ... the Contractor *keeps* accounts of his payments of actual cost ... .

> A Partner may ask another Partner to provide information that it needs to carry out work in its own contract and the other party *provides* it.

3.127   But in standard English, expressing obligations is not one of the functions of the present tense used with the third person. It's standard to use the present tense in checklists, for example the World Health Organization's surgical safety checklist ("Nurse Verbally Confirms …). But checklists remind users how best to carry out procedures—they don't impose obligations.

IS RESPONSIBLE FOR

3.128 Don't use *is responsible for* plus present participle (see [2-1l]) to express duties owed to another party. It's long-winded. It's also potentially confusing, because it's not clear whether a provision using *is responsible for* itself creates a duty or acknowledges the existence of a duty that derives from some other source.

3.129 Using *is responsible for* would, however, allow you to convey that although a party is free to handle as it wishes a particular obligation it owes to a nonparty, that party would have to bear any resulting liabilities. For example, if a transaction between Acme and Widgetco risks creating a tax liability for Acme, Widgetco's concern, strictly speaking, shouldn't be that Acme pay the tax, but that Acme not look to Widgetco to pay the tax, that Acme pay the tax if any tax authority requires Widgetco to pay the tax, and that Acme reimburse Widgetco if Widgetco ends up paying the tax. So it would make sense for the Acme–Widgetco contract to provide that Acme *is responsible for* paying any taxes. This use of *is responsible for* is language of policy.

3.130 Although in that context *is responsible for* would make more sense semantically, imposing an obligation on Acme to pay any taxes would have the same effect, because Widgetco would have a cause of action against Acme only if Widgetco were harmed by Acme's having failed to pay any taxes.

Language of Obligation Imposed on Someone Other Than the Subject of a Sentence

3.131 When a sentence expresses an obligation, the obligation can be imposed on someone other than the subject of that sentence. There are five contexts in which this occurs.

3.132 First, it occurs when a sentence that would, in the active voice, have one or more parties to the contract as the subject is instead phrased in the passive voice (2.17), causing the active object to become the passive subject and either turning the active subject into a *by*-agent, as in [3-1], or omitting it entirely, as in [3-2]. (For more on the passive voice, see 3.11–.24.)

3.133 Second, it occurs when, as in [3-3], the subject of a sentence isn't a legal person and so cannot assume a duty.

3.134 Third, it occurs when, in a sentence in the active voice (see [3-4] and [3-6]) or passive voice (see [3-6c]), the active subject or *by*-agent (whether present or not), although an individual or entity, isn't a party and so cannot be required to assume a duty.

3.135 Fourth, it occurs when, in a sentence in the active voice in which the subject is a party, the duty is, by means of the verb *receive*, as in [3-7] (see 3.151), in effect imposed on someone other than the subject, and the subject denotes the beneficiary of performance of that duty.

3.136   And fifth, it occurs when a main clause using *is entitled to*, meaning "has a right to," is used with a noun, as in [3-8], or with a passive complement clause, as in [3-1c] and [3-2d]. In such constructions it's implicit that another must provide what the subject is entitled to (see 3.152). (When *is entitled to* is used with a complement clause in the active voice, it's language of discretion; see 3.264. An exception is when it's used with *receive*; see [3-7c].)

TABLE 3	■	LANGUAGE OF OBLIGATION IMPOSED ON SOMEONE OTHER THAN THE SUBJECT OF THE SENTENCE
[3-1]	✓	Notice of any claim must be given by the Indemnified Party to the Indemnifying Party.
[3-1a]	✗✗	Notice of any claim shall be given by the Indemnified Party to the Indemnifying Party.
[3-1b]	✗	Notice of any claim will be given by the Indemnified Party to the Indemnifying Party.
[3-1c]	✗	The Indemnifying Party is entitled to be notified by the Indemnified Party of any claim.
[3-1d]	✗✗	The Indemnifying Party shall be entitled to be notified by the Indemnified Party of any claim.
[3-1e]	✓✓	The Indemnified Party shall notify the Indemnifying Party of any claim.
[3-2]	✗	The Consultant must be reimbursed for all authorized expenses.
[3-2a]	✗✗	The Consultant shall be reimbursed for all authorized expenses.
[3-2b]	✗	The Consultant will be reimbursed for all authorized expenses.
[3-2c]	✓	The Consultant must be reimbursed by the Company for all authorized expenses
[3-2d]	✗	The Consultant is entitled to be reimbursed for all authorized expenses.
[3-2e]	✗	The Consultant shall be entitled to be reimbursed for all authorized expenses.
[3-2f]	✓✓	The Company shall reimburse the Consultant for all authorized expenses.
[3-3]	✓	The Closing must take place at Acme's offices.
[3-3a]	✗✗	The Closing shall take place at Acme's offices.
[3-3b]	✗	The Closing will take place at Acme's offices.
[3-3c]	✓	The parties shall cause the Closing to take place at Acme's offices.
[3-3d]	✓✓	The parties shall hold the Closing at Acme's offices.

[3-4]	✗	Sub must sell the Widget Assets no later than 30 days after Closing.
[3-4a]	✗✗	Sub shall sell the Widget Assets … .
[3-4b]	✗✗	Sub will sell the Widget Assets … .
[3-4c]	✓✓	Parent shall cause Sub to sell the Widget Assets … .
[3-4d]	✗	Parent shall procure Sub to sell the Widget Assets … .
[3-4e]	✗	Parent shall ensure that Sub sells the Widget Assets … .
[3-4f]	✗	Parent shall require Sub to sell the Widget Assets … .
[3-5]	✗	Each Acme employee must enter into a confidentiality agreement with Acme in the form of exhibit 2.
[3-5a]	✗✗	Each Acme employee shall enter into … .
[3-5b]	✗✗	Each Acme employee will enter into … .
[3-5c]	✗	Acme shall cause each Acme employee to enter into … .
[3-5d]	✓✓	Acme shall enter into a confidentiality agreement in the form of exhibit 2 with each of its current employees, unless any one or more current Acme employees refuses, in which case Acme shall terminate those one or more current employees. Acme shall not hire as an employee any person who does not enter a confidentiality agreement with Acme in the form of exhibit 2 as a condition to becoming an Acme employee.
[3-6]	✓	The arbitrator must issue the award no later than 20 days after the last day of the hearing.
[3-6a]	✗✗	The arbitrator shall issue the award no later than 20 days after the last day of the hearing.
[3-6b]	✗✗	The arbitrator will issue the award no later than 20 days after the last day of the hearing.
[3-6c]	✗	The award must be issued no later than 20 days after the last day of the hearing.
[3-6d]	✗✗	The award shall be issued no later than 20 days after the last day of the hearing.
[3-6e]	✗✗	The award will be issued no later than 20 days after the last day of the hearing.
[3-6f]	✗	The parties shall cause the arbitrator to issue the award no later than 20 days after the hearing.
[3-7]	✓	Jones must receive a salary of $100,000 a year.
[3-7a]	✗✗	Jones shall receive a salary of $100,000 a year.
[3-7b]	✗✗	Jones will receive a salary of $100,000 a year.
[3-7c]	✗✗	Jones is entitled to receive a salary of $100,000 a year.

[3-7d]	✓✓	Widgetco shall pay Jones a salary of $100,000 a year.
[3-8]	✗	Doe is entitled to full credit for service performed on behalf of the Company.
[3-8a]	✗✗	Doe shall be entitled to full credit for service performed on behalf of the Company.
[3-8b]	✓✓	The Purchaser shall credit Doe fully for service performed on behalf of the Company.

USING *MUST* INSTEAD OF *SHALL* OR *WILL*

3.137 The first four contexts described above (see 3.132–.135) require a modal auxiliary, whether *shall*, *must*, or *will*. The traditional choice—not recommended by this manual—would be to use *shall* in this context, in addition to using it to convey an obligation imposed on the subject of a sentence.

3.138 But using *shall* when the duty is imposed on someone other than the subject would preclude using *shall* to mean only "has a duty to." As discussed in 3.101, the *has a duty* test offers a straightforward way to ensure disciplined use of *shall* and coherent use of verbs generally to express the categories of contract language. Also, giving *shall* a broader role would increase the disconnect between contract language and standard English (see 3.79).

3.139 *Must*, meaning "is required to," is the best alternative to *shall* for imposing an obligation on someone other than the subject of a sentence. Using *must* in this context offers two advantages, and they mirror the disadvantages of using *shall*. First, this use of *must* is more in keeping with general English usage. Second, it enhances clarity by allowing *shall* to be reserved for imposing a duty on the subject of a sentence. But take care to distinguish this use of *must* from use of *must* to state a condition (see 3.356).

3.140 *Will* is an inferior alternative. In duties imposed on someone other than the subject of a sentence, the weaknesses of *will* are the same as those apparent in duties imposed on the subject of a sentence (see 3.95): in general usage, *will* expresses future time rather than obligations, and using *will* to express obligations as well as futurity would likely result in the sort of confusion that those who advocate abandoning *shall* are hoping to avoid.

AVOIDING THE NEED FOR *MUST*

3.141 Usually a better alternative to replacing *shall* with *must* would be not to impose a duty on someone other than the subject of the sentence. That can be accomplished in two ways.

3.142 One way is to use the active voice rather than the passive voice. Not only does that result in clearer and more concise prose (see 3.13), it also reduces the need for *must*. So of [3-1] and [3-2] and their variants, the preferred approach is that shown in [3-1e] and [3-2f].

3.143 A second way is to make explicit, in any sentence in which the active subject or *by*-agent is incapable of assuming a duty, exactly who does owe the duty. One does this by stating that the party owing the duty *shall cause* something to happen or someone else to take a specified action.

3.144 Depending on the context, this approach can be applied to a sentence with a subject that isn't a legal person; compare [3-3] to [3-3c]. But if the subject is a legal person that isn't a party, this approach is appropriate only if the subject is an instrumentality of one or more parties. For example, it makes sense to restructure [3-4] as [3-4c]—because Sub is a wholly owned subsidiary of Parent, Parent controls Sub.

3.145 Some drafters use unhelpful variants of *shall cause*. One is *shall procure* (see [3-4d]), which is used in Commonwealth countries; it's too legalistic. Another is *shall ensure* (see [3-4e]); it's overly genteel. And a third, *shall require* (see [3-4f]), could be understood as meaning that the party in question has a duty to impose a duty on the nonparty.

3.146 It's best not to use *shall cause* if the subject of the original sentence is a nonparty that isn't an instrumentality of a party. A party can't be said to control individuals (for example, an employee or an arbitrator), because individuals might do as they see fit. That's the problem with [3-5c] and [3-6f]. And a party can't be said to control unaffiliated entities, for example contractors.

3.147 At least one court has held that a contract party breached a *shall cause* obligation by failing to control an individual. See *World of Boxing LLC v. King*, 56 F. Supp. 3d 507, 513 (S.D.N.Y. 2014). But that isn't an argument for using *shall cause* with nonparty individuals and other nonparties that a party doesn't control. Whenever you impose an obligation on someone to control something they can't really control, you're spoiling for a fight, and winning a fight is a distant second-best to avoiding the fight.

3.148 Depending on the context, you might be able to restructure a provision that has as the subject a nonparty that isn't an instrumentality of one of the parties so that instead the provision imposes an obligation on a party. Such restructuring might raise issues that had been glossed over; see for example [3-5d]. Alternatively, or in addition, state explicitly who bears the risk for conduct by a nonparty that isn't an instrumentality of a party. In particular, if the issue is conduct by a nonparty that a party doesn't control, consider imposing an obligation that reflects the limited control and incorporating a risk-allocation mechanism that addresses what happens if an outcome that the provision seeks to avoid nevertheless happens.

3.149 If such restructuring isn't possible, *must* would be your best bet (see [3-6]). It might be best to specify the implications if the nonparty fails to act as anticipated—because the provision doesn't apply to a party, it might not be evident what the remedies would be.

3.150 By selecting your verbs judiciously, you might avoid altogether any need for *shall cause* (see [3-3d]).

3.151 It's unhelpful to use *receive* to impose a duty on someone other than the subject of the sentence, as in [3-7]. The drawbacks are the same as those relating to use of the passive voice (see 3.13). In particular, note that [3-7] doesn't specify who is to pay Jones's annual salary. Instead, use *shall* to impose the duty directly on the relevant actor, as in [3-7d].

3.152 Use of *is entitled to* with a noun or a passive complement clause is analogous to provisions in the passive voice. The *by*-agent is often unexpressed, as in [3-2d] ([3-8] cannot accommodate a *by*-agent), and even when the *by*-agent is stated, as in [3-1c], the result is wordy. Furthermore, focusing on the entitled party could create problems for the entitled party: in response to a claim for breach brought by the entitled party, the party owing the obligation could claim it didn't have to perform until the entitled party had notified it that the entitled party sought performance. So don't use *is entitled to* in language of obligation and instead focus on the party owing the duty, as in [3-1e], [3-2f], and [3-8b].

3.153 A secondary issue is that *is entitled to* used with a noun or a passive complement clause doesn't require a modal auxiliary. More often than not, though, drafters provide, as in [3-1d], [3-2e], and [3-8a], that a party *shall be entitled to* rather than *is entitled to*. This use of *shall* is inconsistent with the limited use recommended in this manual (see 3.72). It also occurs in language of policy (see 3.308).

3.154 Regarding use of *is entitled to* in language of discretion, see 3.264.

Imposing Impossible Obligations

3.155 Before considering how to express a particular obligation, determine whether it makes sense to address the issue with an obligation.

3.156 What if the party that would be responsible for complying with the obligation doesn't have sufficient control to ensure compliance? What if compliance isn't feasible? Imposing the obligation regardless wouldn't make sense, could confuse readers, and could cause a court to hold that the obligation is unenforceable.

3.157 For example, if Acme wants Widgetco to obtain a landlord consent that's required for closing, it could impose on Widgetco an obligation to obtain that consent. But under its contract with Widgetco, the landlord may withhold its consent. It would make more sense for Acme to (1) impose on Widgetco an obligation to use reasonable efforts to obtain the consent (see 8.3), (2) make it a condition to closing that the landlord has provided the consent, and (3) consider imposing on Widgetco an obligation to pay Acme a termination fee, or indemnify Acme (see 13.404), if lack of the landlord's consent results in the deal not closing.

3.158　A similar approach might be a sensible alternative to imposing on a party receiving confidential information an obligation to destroy all electronic versions of that information, regardless of whether that's possible to do.

Imposing Obligations to Stop Something from Happening

3.159　To address in a contract something undesirable that might happen and that isn't completely in the control of the performing party, imposing an obligation wouldn't be enough.

3.160　A contract between Acme and Widgetco says *Acme shall not permit employees to remove Equipment from the Premises.* Acme doesn't adopt a policy regarding removing equipment from the premises, so it hasn't given employees permission to remove equipment. An employee takes equipment home, and it gets stolen. Because *permit* can also mean allowing something to happen, one can imagine a dispute over whether under the contract Acme was required to take steps to prevent employees from taking equipment home. The same applies to use of *shall not allow.*

3.161　Imagine instead that the contract says *Acme shall prohibit employees from removing Equipment from the Premises.* Acme puts up a sign to that effect but doesn't otherwise do anything. Was Acme required to do more under the contract? It's not clear.

3.162　And if the contract says *shall prevent*, does that make Acme liable if an employee takes equipment home, whatever the measures Acme took to prevent that?

3.163　The problem with these formulations is that all such scenarios raise two separate issues, so addressing them comprehensively requires two separate provisions. In the case of Acme and Widgetco, first, it would make sense for Widgetco to require that Acme take appropriate steps to prevent employees from taking equipment home; the best way to accomplish that would be with a *reasonable efforts* obligation (see 8.3). And second, Widgetco should include in the contract a risk-allocation provision making Acme liable for any Widgetco losses that result if an employee nevertheless takes equipment home.

Obligations—Some Related Terminology

3.164　Contracts use a range of terms relating to obligations, some more helpful than others.

USE *OBLIGATION*, NOT *COVENANT*

3.165　Why not use *covenant* instead of *obligation*? *Black's Law Dictionary* defines *obligation* as "A formal, binding agreement or acknowledgment of a liability to pay a certain amount or to do a certain thing for a particular person or set of persons; esp., a duty arising by contract." And it defines *covenant* as "A formal agreement or promise, usu. in a contract or deed, to do or not do a particular act; a compact or stipulation."

3.166   As such, *covenant* is a synonym of *obligation*, and many drafters use the two words interchangeably. But *covenant* has a quaint Old Testament (or *Raiders of the Lost Ark*) quality to it. (David Mellinkoff, *Mellinkoff's Dictionary of American Legal Usage* 135 (1992), says that *covenant* is "An old synonym for contract and agreement.") When given a choice between the archaic and the more modern, choose the more modern.

3.167   Don't revert to *covenant* when referring to grouped obligations that address how a party is to conduct itself between the signing and closing of a transaction, while a debt remains outstanding, or in some other context. If you switch from one word to the other depending on where you find yourself in a contract or depending on the kind of obligation involved, you're using two words to convey the same meaning (see 1.64). It would be clearer to stick with *obligation* throughout.

3.168   *Covenant* occurs in the term of art *covenant not to compete. Noncompetition provision* would be less fusty.

3.169   Don't use the phrases *affirmative covenant* and *negative covenant*, meaning an obligation to do something and an obligation not to do something. Aside from the archaic quality that *covenant* adds to those phrases, generally when referring in a contract to obligations imposed by that or any other contract, no purpose is served by distinguishing between an obligation to do something and an obligation not to do something. See also 3.170.

OBLIGATION AND *PROHIBITION*

3.170   Given that a category of contract language is language of prohibition (see 3.278), one could conceivably refer to *obligations* and *prohibitions* in contracts. But that's unnecessary, and would in fact be confusing, because it's standard to use *obligation* with respect to both doing something and not doing something. See also 3.169.

OBLIGATION VERSUS *DUTY*

3.171   The *Black's Law Dictionary* definition of *obligation* (see 3.165) suggests that it means the same thing as *duty*. And the *Restatement (Second) of Contracts* uses *duty* and *obligation* interchangeably—it uses *duty* in section 1 and uses *obligation* in section 1, comments a and b, and in section 2, comment b. But *Garner's Dictionary of Legal Usage*, at 624, distinguishes between *obligation* and *duty*:

> **obligation; duty.** Broadly speaking, the words are synonymous in referring to what a person is required to do or refrain from doing— or for the performance or nonperformance of which the person is responsible. But there are connotative nuances. An *obligation* is normally an immediate requirement with a specific reference <his child-support obligations> <Burundi's obligations under the treaty>… .
>
> A *duty* may involve legal compulsion and immediacy, but the word carries an overlay of a moral or ethical imperative <parental

duties> <fiduciary duties>. More specifically, *duty* = (1) that which one is required to do or refrain from doing, esp. as occupant of some position, role, or office; or (2) any one of a complex of rights and standards of care imposed by a legal relationship. Sense 2 appears primarily in tort law, in which writers use *duty* only to mean that there could be liability.

3.172   This manual concurs, which is why it refers to contract obligations yet refers to the implied duty of good faith (see 3.225). But whether you use *obligation* or *duty* in a contract to refer to what a party is required to do under that contract would have no implications for that transaction. Just be consistent in the terminology you use.

USING ADJECTIVES WITH *OBLIGATION*

3.173   In contracts, obligations are sometimes modified by *irrevocable, absolute,* or *unconditional*. It doesn't make sense to refer to an obligation as being *irrevocable*—you revoke something that benefits the other party, not something imposed on you. And it's not clear what *absolute* and *unconditional* are intended to accomplish in this context.

USE *COMPLY WITH*, NOT *PERFORM*

3.174   It's standard to say that one *performs* an obligation and to refer to *performance* of an obligation. But an obligation could consist of a duty not to do something (see 3.170), in which case *perform* would have to encompass sitting on your hands. That seems counterintuitive. Possible alternatives such as *discharge* and *fulfill* are no improvement.

3.175   So use instead *comply with* and the noun form *compliance with*—they would cover both action and inaction.

USING *BREACH* AS A COUNT NOUN OR A MASS NOUN

3.176   The word *breach* is used both as a noun and as a verb. It's more sober than *violation* (and *violate*) and more direct than *nonperformance* and *noncompliance* (and *fail to perform* and *fail to comply with*).

3.177   But *breach* involves subtleties. Let's consider first its use as a noun:

> Any such disclosure will constitute [*a breach*] [*breach*] of the Recipient's obligations under this section 5.2.

3.178   Both of the bracketed alternatives reflect accepted usage. The first alternative features *breach* used as a count noun, in that it can be quantified by a number. Just as one can say *Joe ate five cookies,* you can say *Acme committed multiple breaches of its obligations under the Widgetco contract.*

3.179   By contrast, in the second alternative, *breach* is used to express an abstract idea. It's used as a mass noun, like *destruction*. This kind of mass noun cannot be used in the plural and doesn't take an indefinite article—you don't say *five destructions* or *a destruction*. That's why *breach* also works without the indefinite article *a*. Because doing without the indefinite article is slightly more economical, use *breach* as a mass noun, not a count noun.

USING *BREACH* AS A COUNT NOUN OR A VERB

3.180   Consider this example:

> … its entry into this agreement and its performance of its obligations under this agreement do not … conflict with, [*result in a breach of*] [*breach*], or constitute a default under … .

3.181   The first alternative uses *breach* as a count noun; the second uses it as a verb. Using the verb is more concise.

USING *BREACH* AS A MASS NOUN OR A VERB

3.182   Let's now compare using *breach* as a mass noun and using it as a verb:

> *Mass Noun*
>
> Any such disclosure will constitute breach of the Recipient's obligations under this section 5.2.
>
> *Verb*
>
> Any such disclosure will breach the Recipient's obligations under this section 5.2.

3.183   Here too the verb is the more economical option.

3.184   And consider this example:

> Any purported assignment or delegation [*in breach of*] [*that breaches*] this section 20.4 will be void.

3.185   The first alternative consists of the mass noun *breach* used in the phrase *in breach of*; the second alternative uses the verb *breach*. Here, too, the verb is the simpler alternative.

3.186   Furthermore, using *breach* as a mass noun can result in the actor being dropped (see 17.8). Using the verb prevents that:

> *Mass Noun*
>
> In the event of breach of this section 6.7 … .
>
> *Verb*
>
> If Acme breaches this section 6.7 … .

LANGUAGE OF DISCRETION

3.187   "Language of discretion" is language stating that a party has the discretion to take or not take a specified action.

Using *May* to Convey Discretion

3.188   Discretion is primarily conveyed by means of *may*, which expresses permission or sanction. When used in an active construction, as in [4-1], *may* means "has discretion to," "is permitted to," or "is authorized to." (It would be unnecessarily wordy to use these formulations instead of *may*, as in [4-1a].) *May* can also be used in a passive construction, in which case the one or more parties that have permission are represented by a *by*-agent, as in [4-2], or are absent, as in [4-2a]. For the reasons stated in 3.13, don't use the passive; [4-2b] represents an improvement over [4-2]. (*May* can also express the possibility of something occurring; see 3.206.)

TABLE 4 ■ **LANGUAGE OF DISCRETION: *MAY***

[4-1]	✓✓	Acme may appoint one or more subcontractors.
[4-1a]	✗	Acme is authorized to … .
[4-1b]	✗	Acme is entitled to … .
[4-1c]	✗✗	Acme shall have the right to … .
[4-1d]	✗✗	Acme reserves the right to … .
[4-1e]	✗✗	Acme is permitted to … .
[4-1f]	✗✗	Acme is allowed to … .
[4-1g]	✗✗	Acme is free to … .
[4-1h]	✗✗	Acme is hereby empowered by the Customer to … .
[4-1i]	✗✗	Acme may but is not required to … .
[4-1j]	✗✗	Acme may freely … .
[4-1k]	✗✗	Acme can … .
[4-1l]	✗✗	Acme may at its sole discretion … .
[4-1m]	✗✗	The Customer hereby grants Acme the right to … .
[4-2]	✓	The Option may be exercised by Smith any time before 1 January 2018.
[4-2a]	✓	The Option may be exercised any time before 1 January 2018.
[4-2b]	✓✓	Smith may exercise the Option any time before 1 January 2018.

3.189   As with language of obligation, there are other, more long-winded alternatives to *may*. See, for example, [4-1c] through [4-1h]. In [4-1i], *but is not required to* is redundant, given that *may* expresses discretion. Similarly, in [4-1j], *freely* is redundant. And in [4-1k], *can* is inappropriate, as it expresses physical or mental ability, not discretion.

Be Explicit as to Whether Discretion Is Limited

3.190   A grant of discretion to do one thing doesn't necessarily equal a prohibition against doing other things. If a mother tells her son he may play video games, it wouldn't necessarily follow that she's forbidding him from engaging in any alternative activity.

3.191   But the presumption that a grant of discretion doesn't also entail prohibition comes up against what this manual calls "the expectation of relevance." (Relevance is a principle of linguistics. According to *The Cambridge Grammar of the English Language*, at 38, "A central principle in pragmatics … is that the addressee of an utterance will expect it to be relevant, and will normally interpret it on that basis.") The more specific a grant of discretion is, the more likely it is that the reader would conclude that the discretion is limited—otherwise there would be no point in being so specific. And the more likely a court would be to invoke the arbitrary rule of interpretation *expressio unius est exclusio alterius*—the expression of one thing implies the exclusion of others.

3.192   Consider the sentence *Acme may sell the Shares to Doe*. Maybe the parties had in mind that Acme could sell the shares to anyone—they addressed sale to Doe explicitly simply because otherwise it would have been uncertain whether Acme could sell the shares to Doe. But the expectation of relevance suggests that if the parties mentioned only Doe when authorizing Acme to sell the shares, it's because Acme was precluded from selling the shares to anyone else.

3.193   To avoid any uncertainty regarding the expectation of relevance, be explicit as to whether discretion is limited. If Acme has unlimited discretion to sell the shares, it would be preferable to say *Acme may sell the Shares to any Person*. If its discretion is limited, it would be preferable to say *The only Person to whom Acme may sell the Shares is Doe*. Or you could use language of prohibition—*Acme shall not sell the Shares to anyone other than Doe*.

3.194   See 3.201–.205 for a source of ambiguity in expressing limited discretion.

A CASE STUDY

3.195   Uncertainty over whether discretion is limited can cause disputes that lead to litigation. For example, at issue in *Arkel International, L.L.C. v. Parsons Global Services*, No. 07-474-FJP-DLD, 2008 U.S. Dist. LEXIS 1624 (M.D. La. 8 Jan. 2008), was the following forum-selection clause: "[E]ither party may institute suit in the Superior Court of the State of California for the County of Los Angeles, or, if mutually agreed to by the parties, the dispute shall be settled by arbitration in Pasadena, California."

3.196   The parties disagreed over whether the forum-selection clause provided for mandatory or permissive jurisdiction—in other words, whether a party could sue only in the specified court. The court considering this dispute held that the forum-selection clause provided for permissive jurisdiction.

3.197   If the forum-selection clause had simply stated that either party may sue in the specified California court, it would have been reasonable to conclude that it was permissive—the countervailing expectation of relevance would have been weak. But instead, the provision said that either party may sue in California or the parties may agree to arbitrate. The second alternative—arbitration—provides greater specificity and so gives greater force to the expectation of relevance—the contrast between the two alternatives specified would lose significance if unlimited other options were also available.

3.198   Imagine that you say to Frank, "You may go to the movies." That could mean "You may engage in any number of activities, one of which is going to the movies." It could also mean "The only activity that you're permitted to engage in is going to the movies." But if you say to Frank, "You may go to the movies or you may go to the library," it's more likely that you're telling Frank those are his only two choices.

3.199   Whoever drafted the forum-selection clause likely had mandatory jurisdiction in mind but didn't feel the need to make it explicit, perhaps because they were swayed by the increased expectation of relevance afforded by the reference to arbitration. Whatever they intended, they would have done better to make it explicit.

3.200   An English case involving language of discretion and the expectation of relevance is *Ener-G Holdings plc v. Hormell* [2012] EWCA Civ. 1059 (31 July 2012). The question was whether the two means of serving notice specified in the provision at issue were the only two means authorized under the contract, or whether that provision simply specified two means of service from among those permitted.

The Ambiguity Inherent in *May … Only*

3.201   Drafters often use *may … only* to convey limited discretion. The result is alternative meanings that can give rise to ambiguity. Consider the following sentence:

> Acme may close one or more Contract Stores for any reason, and in doing so it may consider only its own interests.

3.202   This sentence is ambiguous. The drafter presumably intended it to mean that Acme may consider only its own interests but would be free to consider the interests of others. But it could also mean that the only interests Acme may consider are its own. The latter meaning seems unlikely.

3.203   Now consider this sentence:

> Widgetco may sell only the 1965 Ford Mustang.

3.204   It could convey a meaning analogous to the first possible meaning of the previous example—in other words, that Widgetco may elect to sell only that car but would also be free to sell other cars instead of or in addition to the Ford Mustang, or not sell any cars. But it could also mean that the only vehicle that Widgetco may sell is the vehicle specified. In this case, the latter meaning seems the more likely.

3.205   The ambiguity engendered by *may … only* can't be avoided by repositioning *only* (see 13.617). Instead, you must come up with alternative language to express the intended meaning. Here's how one could reword the two above examples to express the intended meaning:

> Acme may close one or more Contract Stores for any reason, and in doing so it may elect to consider only its own interests.

> Widgetco shall sell no vehicle other than the 1965 Ford Mustang.

Using *May* to Convey Possibility

3.206   Besides conveying discretion, *may* can also be used to express the possibility of something occurring. The result is ambiguity, but this manual doesn't consider that sufficient reason to stop using *may*.

3.207   Consider this sentence: *The Investigator may provide the Sponsor with confidential information.* It could mean that the Investigator is authorized to provide the Sponsor with confidential information, but it could also mean that it's possible that the Investigator will do so.

3.208   Although one can usually discern from the context which meaning is intended, it would nevertheless be best to avoid this sort of confusion. If the intention were to convey possibility, you could restructure the provision in question to omit *may*. For example, the above example could be rephrased as *If the Investigator provides the sponsor with confidential information, then … .*

3.209   Alternatively, to convey the possibility of something occurring you could instead of *may* use either *might* (if it's uncertain whether the event will come to pass) or *expects to* (if it's likely that the event will come to pass and a party is the subject).

3.210   *The Cambridge Grammar of the English Language*, at 200, says that *might* "suggests a slightly lower degree of possibility" than *may*, but that's no obstacle to use of *might*—the parties to a contract would be less interested in parsing the likelihood of an event happening than in specifying the consequences if it does happen. Furthermore, the distinction is a relative one, so there's no way to assign an absolute degree of possibility to a given instance of *may* or *might*. The best you can say is that it's possible that whatever it is will come to pass.

3.211   But even if you use something other than *may* to express the possibility of something occurring, some readers might wonder whether a given *may* in fact means *might*. Online discussion suggests that some drafters are sufficiently concerned about that possibility that they've dropped *may* from their drafting in favor of *is permitted to* (see [4-1d]) or some other alternative.

3.212   But before jettisoning a word because it conveys alternative meanings, it's appropriate to examine the risks posed by the alternative meanings and the burden that change would impose.

3.213   The possibility of *may* being understood as meaning *might* doesn't create meaningful risk. Consider again the sample sentence used in 3.206: *The Investigator may provide the Sponsor with confidential information.* Party A claims that in that sentence, *may* expresses discretion; Party B claims it means *might*. It's hard to see what benefit Party B could derive from so claiming—if you accept that the Investigator might provide confidential information, it's hard to see how you could use that to argue that the Investigator isn't allowed to provide confidential information.

3.214 As regards the burden that change would impose, asking those who work with contracts to drop *may*—a basic verb structure in everyday English— in favor of a more cumbersome structure that offers no, or negligible, benefits seems counterproductive. So *may* remains the best means of expressing discretion.

May Require

3.215 The phrase *may require* is often used to frame as Party X's discretion what is best thought of as Party Y's obligation. Instead, use language of obligation:

> The Company may require a Participant to retain [read *At the Company's written request, a Participant shall retain*] the shares purchased on that Participant's behalf in the Participant's ESPP Broker Account until sale of those shares.

> The Bank may require each Borrower to establish [read *At the Bank's written request, each Borrower shall establish*] a lockbox under the control of the Bank to which all applicable Account Debtors shall forward payments on the Accounts.

3.216 Sometimes *may require* is used to indicate possibility rather than discretion:

> The issuer of these securities *may require* an opinion of counsel satisfactory to the issuer to the effect that any proposed transfer or resale is in compliance with the Act and any applicable state securities laws.

3.217 In such cases, use *might* rather than *may* (see 3.208).

3.218 The phrase *may require* is also used to convey possibility in a restrictive relative clause modifying a noun phrase. In that context *may* is superfluous; use the simple present tense instead (see 3.456):

> The Borrowers shall complete and sign such applications and supplemental agreements and provide such other documentation as the Bank *may require* [read *requires*] regarding issuance and administration of the Letters of Credit.

May Request

3.219 Related to *may require* is the phrase *may request*.

3.220 When *may request* is the main verb, its function might simply be to express that a party may ask for something—for example, assistance. But *may request* might result in an obligation being imposed on another party:

> Pending the preparation of Definitive Notes, the Issuer *may request* and the Trustee, upon receiving an Issuer Order, shall authenticate and deliver temporary Notes of that Series.

3.221   In this context, *may request* expresses an instruction, not a request. It would be simpler to omit *X may request* and instead say *at the request of X, Y shall*. In the example above, if an Issuer Order reflects the Issuer's request, that's already provided for—you could just omit *the Issuer may request and.*

3.222   But in some contracts, the follow-on obligation is omitted. Here's an example:

> ... the Trustee *may request* that the Company deliver an officers' certificate stating the names or titles of officers then authorized to take specified actions under this indenture ... .

3.223   Presumably in the above example, the Trustee's request isn't a casual one that the Company could blithely ignore. It would be best to make that clear by revising this example to incorporate the structure *at the request of X, Y shall.*

Don't Use *At Its Sole Discretion* with *May*

3.224   It's commonplace for drafters to use *at its* [or *his, her,* or *their*] *sole discretion* in language of discretion, as in *Acme may at its sole discretion terminate this agreement*, and as in [4-1l]. As explained in this section, if *at its discretion* is rhetorical emphasis, delete it. If it attempts to address a real issue, consider addressing that issue directly.

IMPLIED DUTY OF GOOD FAITH

3.225   Use of *at its sole discretion* in language of discretion suggests (1) that the language of discretion in question doesn't grant complete discretion and (2) that tacking on *at its sole discretion* remedies that. The first element of this proposition is correct—the discretion granted under a contract is limited, in that generally any party to a contract would be under a duty to exercise that discretion in good faith, at least in those jurisdictions that recognize the implied duty of good faith. That includes the United States (it has been adopted by most states and the Uniform Commercial Code) and many other countries, but excludes England.

3.226   Section 205 of the *Restatement (Second) of Contracts* states that "Every contract imposes upon each party a duty of good faith and fair dealing in its performance and its enforcement." And section 1-304 of the Uniform Commercial Code (UCC) provides that "Every contract or duty within [the UCC] imposes an obligation of good faith in its performance and enforcement." Cases invoking the duty of good faith "are legion." *Murray on Contracts* § 90[A].

3.227   Regarding language of discretion specifically, "where a party has contractual discretion to promote its own interest, the good faith requirement precludes action that would contravene the reasonable expectations of the other party." 1-5 *Murray on Contracts* § 91[A]; see also 23 *Williston on Contracts* § 63:22 (stating that "even where a defendant is given absolute discretion, it must exercise that discretion in good faith"). For a case that stands for this proposition, see *Gilson v. Rainin Instrument, LLC,*

No. 04-C-852-S, 2005 WL 1899471 (W.D. Wis. 9 Aug. 2005) (stating that the implied covenant of good faith requires each party to an agreement "to exercise any discretion afforded it by the agreement in a manner consistent with the reasonable expectations of the other party").

WORDING

3.228 *Acme may at its sole discretion* incorporates redundancy—in effect it means *Acme has the discretion, at its sole discretion, to … .* And it's not necessarily clear that *sole* adds anything—a grant of discretion to a party is necessarily to that party only.

3.229 Some drafters use *absolute* instead of, or in addition to, *sole*, but that wouldn't seem to offer any advantage over using *sole* on its own. Neither would using *uncontrolled*.

3.230 It wouldn't make sense to refer to *good-faith discretion*—if you're willing to have your discretion be subject to the duty of good faith, it would be unnecessary to modify language of discretion to say so.

3.231 As for *reasonable discretion*, that might *curtail* a party's discretion—a reasonableness standard could be interpreted as being more stringent than a good-faith standard (see 13.681).

3.232 And just *at its discretion* simply echoes the language of discretion—*Acme may at its discretion* means *Acme has the discretion, at its discretion, to … .*

ATTEMPTING TO CIRCUMVENT THE DUTY OF GOOD FAITH

3.233 It might not be clear what prompted use of an instance of *at its sole discretion.* Perhaps it simply reflects the redundancy inherent in traditional contract language, in which case it should be deleted. On the other hand, adding *at its sole discretion* to language of discretion might represent an attempt to nullify the duty to exercise discretion in good faith. The intent would be that *at its sole discretion* allows a party to exercise discretion without having its reasonableness challenged.

3.234 Some drafters use an internal rule of interpretation (see 15.2) to make it explicit that they intend to circumvent the duty of good faith. Here's an example:

> The terms "sole discretion" and "absolute discretion" regarding any determination to be made a party under this agreement mean the sole and absolute discretion of that party, without regard to any standard of reasonableness or other standard by which the determination of that party might be challenged.

3.235 Drafters also attempt to circumvent the duty of good faith by using *for any reason or no reason.* Regarding that phrase generally, see 13.293.

CASELAW

3.236 Some courts have held enforceable provisions that in effect state that a party may act unreasonably.

3.237   For example, in *Cussler v. Crusader Entertainment, LLC*, No. B208738, 2010 WL 718007 (Cal. Ct. App. 3 Mar. 2010), the California Court of Appeal rejected Crusader's argument that in failing to approve Crusader's many proposed screenplays for the film *Sahara*, the author Clive Cussler had breached the implied duty of good faith that under California law is read into every contract. The contract provided that Crusader would "not ... change the Approved Screenplay ... without Cussler's written approval exercisable in his sole and absolute discretion." (For more on this opinion and the problematic reasoning underlying it, see Kenneth A. Adams, *Whittling Away at Duty of Good Faith*, Recorder, 28 June 2011.)

3.238   And in *Automatic Sprinkler Corp. of America v. Anderson*, 257 S.E.2d 283 (Ga. 1979), the court considered "whether good faith is a prerequisite in the exercise of an absolute discretion to withhold incentive compensation." The contract at issue stated that whether to pay a terminated employee incentive compensation "will rest completely in the absolute and final discretion of the Compensation Committee of the Board of Directors." The court held that the presence or absence of good faith was irrelevant.

3.239   But cases in other jurisdictions hold otherwise. For example, in *A.W. Fiur Co. v. Ataka & Co.*, 422 N.Y.S.2d 419, 422 (App. Div. 1979), the court said, "Although the contract conferred upon [a wholly owned subsidiary of the defendant] the 'absolute and exclusive right to reject any orders for any reason whatsoever', such a contract does not import the right arbitrarily to refuse to accept orders."

3.240   In the same vein, according to section 1-302 of the UCC, "The obligations of good faith, diligence, reasonableness, and care prescribed by [the UCC] may not be disclaimed by agreement." That's what *at its sole discretion* attempts to accomplish.

3.241   The policy arguments go both ways. Having a party waive the benefit of the implied duty for a particular provision would, in states that recognize such waivers, spare the other party the risk of having its exercise of discretion challenged as lacking good faith. But that certainty comes at a cost, in that a party could use the other party's waiver of the implied duty as license to sabotage the transaction.

AN ALTERNATIVE APPROACH

3.242   Given the mixed caselaw, drafters might be tempted to adjust, depending on the governing law of the contract, how they approach the implied duty of good faith, thinking that it would be appropriate to include *at its sole discretion*, or some variant, if the contract is governed by the law of California or another jurisdiction that recognizes waivers of the implied duty of good faith.

3.243   Or drafters might be inclined to include *at its sole discretion* in all contracts— they know that courts in a particular jurisdiction would disregard that phrase, but they decide that retaining it is harmless, and it might work to their advantage if the other side is unaware of the law on the issue.

3.244   But it would be preferable to eliminate from your contracts any language that could be construed as effecting a waiver of the implied duty of good faith, even if it favors your client—doing so would reduce the likelihood of confusion or dispute.

3.245   Even in jurisdictions that construe *at its sole discretion* as effecting an enforceable waiver of the implied duty of good faith, any benefit of such a waiver is more than offset by the potential mischief of an apparent endorsement of a party's acting in bad faith (see 3.241). And the language used to articulate a waiver of the implied duty is sufficiently unclear that it could cause a dispute. Furthermore, the confused caselaw (at least in California) might make it difficult to predict whether a court would hold that a particular waiver is enforceable.

3.246   Instead, address directly whatever concern you might have been tempted to address with a waiver of the implied duty—it's unlikely that the party in question simply wants to ensure that it's free to act in bad faith.

3.247   For example, imagine that Acme wants to purchase from Widgetco several stores that sell widgets. The parties have in mind that as part of the purchase price, Acme would pay commissions based on future net sales of the stores. But Acme wants to close stores if it sees fit. Simply saying "Acme may at any time close any one or more Contract Stores" might allow Widgetco to claim that Acme was acting in bad faith if it ultimately were to close Contract Stores. And it would be reckless to assume that adding "at its sole discretion" would preclude that possibility without risk of dispute.

3.248   You could make this language of discretion more specific by making Acme's exercise of its discretion subject to conditions—for example, it may close a store only if that store fails to meet specified targets. But if Acme would prefer to avoid any meddling in its business decisions, a more promising approach would be to add specificity by having Widgetco acknowledge that certain potential adverse consequences will be irrelevant to Acme's exercise of its discretion. That could be accomplished by the following:

> Acme may close one or more Contract Stores for any reason, and in doing so it may elect to consider only its own interests and will not be required to consider the effect of any such closure on Widgetco, including any reduction in commissions that Acme pays Widgetco under this agreement.

3.249   This approach should be palatable to the other party if circumstances suggest that the party with discretion would to some extent be constrained from acting in bad faith. In the above example, closing stores presumably involves some cost to Acme.

3.250   Furthermore, a court would be less likely to view an explicit provision of that sort as an impermissible attempt to waive the duty of good faith. For example, the above scenario is based on the facts in *VTR, Inc. v. Goodyear Tire & Rubber Co.*, 303 F. Supp. 773 (S.D.N.Y. 1969). In that case, the court held that "the parties may, by express provisions of the contract, grant the right to engage in the very acts and conduct which otherwise would have been forbidden by an implied covenant of good faith and fair dealing."

3.251   And section 1-302 of the UCC states that although the obligations of good faith, diligence, reasonableness, and care may not be disclaimed by agreement, "The parties, by agreement, may determine the standards by which the performance of those obligations is to be measured if those standards are not manifestly unreasonable."

3.252   If you're unable or unwilling to craft explicit language of this sort, you could use *at its discretion* and warn the client that *at its discretion* may be ineffective to ensure it has unfettered discretion. Or you could simply omit *at its discretion* because it would be best to omit such an unstable phrase from your contracts, even if doing so precludes the possibility, however uncertain, of unfettered discretion. The latter approach seems more prudent.

3.253   Furthermore, in some contexts the approaches described in 3.246–.251 are unlikely to work. Consider the circumstances of *Cussler*, mentioned in 3.237: Assessing a screenplay is a highly subjective task, so it's unlikely that either party would have agreed to make Cussler's approval right subject to objective conditions. And Cussler's rejection of Crusader's screenplay didn't cause him to incur any direct costs, so he had little to stop him from rejecting screenplays for any reason, however justified or unjustified.

3.254   In such contexts, the prudent course to take would be to eliminate the problematic language of discretion. Regarding *Cussler*, dispute would have been avoided had the screenplay initially approved by the parties been the final screenplay, or had one or other party been given unilateral control over revisions to the screenplay.

USE OUTSIDE OF LANGUAGE OF DISCRETION

3.255   The phrase *at its sole discretion* is not only used in language of discretion. It also occurs in conditional clauses (*If Acme at its sole discretion buys more widgets*) and in restrictive relative clauses (*at a price acceptable to Widgetco in its sole discretion*).

3.256   Use of the phrase in these contexts has nothing to do with discretion granted by the contract, but it nevertheless relates to conduct that falls within the scope of the contract. Because in these contexts nothing constrains the party's action, that action could conceivably fall under the implied duty of good faith.

3.257   It would be best to treat this use of *at its sole discretion* the same way as this manual recommends treating its use in language of discretion (see 3.224): if the phrase is used in an attempt to address a deal issue, address that issue directly. If it's used out of legalistic habit, delete it.

Hereby Grants ... the Right To

3.258   One sometimes sees the formula *Party X hereby grants Party Y the right to* [verb], as in [4-1m]. It's language of discretion disguised as language of performance. *Widgetco hereby grants Acme the right to sell the Assets* means the same thing as *Acme may sell the Assets*, but uses ten words rather than five.

3.259   So instead of the formula *Party X hereby grants Party Y the right to* [verb], you're always better off using *Party Y may* [verb], as in this example:

The Borrower hereby grants to the Holder the right to [read *The Holder may*] set off against this note upon occurrence of an Event of Default ... .

When Exercising Discretion Requires Cooperation

3.260   Consider this language of discretion: *One or more Acme representatives may inspect Widgetco's financial records during business hours at Widgetco's principal office.* It doesn't simply grant discretion—it also imposes on Widgetco an unstated obligation to cooperate with Acme's representatives. That obligation is hinted at if instead of *may* you say *will be given the opportunity to*—a structure that's sometimes used in contracts.

3.261   It's clearer to make explicit any such implicit obligations: *Widgetco shall permit one or more Acme representatives to inspect Widgetco's financial records during business hours at Widgetco's principal office.*

Using *Hereby Waives the Right To* to Express Discretion

3.262   Sometimes the phrase *hereby waives the right to* is used when what you're really saying is that the other party doesn't have to do something. So say that instead:

> *Acme hereby waives any right to* [read *Photoco is not required to permit Acme to*] inspect or approve of any finished photographs.

> *The Employee hereby waives his right to receive* [read *The Company will not be required to pay the Employee*] any severance other than under this agreement.

> *The Borrower hereby waives its right to elect to make* [read *The Lender is not required to accept*] payments under this agreement in a currency other than U.S. dollars.

3.263   Regarding use of *hereby waives the right to* as a suboptimal way to express prohibition, see 3.285.

Is Entitled To

3.264   A second vehicle of discretion is *is entitled to* used with a complement clause in the active voice (unless it's used with *receive*; see 3.136). It conveys a specific meaning, but there's a clearer alternative.

3.265   Although more often than not *is entitled to* used with a complement clause in the active voice is, as in [4-1b], a wordier and therefore inferior alternative to *may*, in this context it can be distinguished from *may*.

3.266   As discussed in 3.136 and 3.152, when *is entitled to* is used with a noun or a complement clause in the passive voice, it's implicit that another party is obligated to provide what the subject of the sentence is entitled to. Similarly, *is entitled to* with an active complement clause is best used when one party's discretion depends on performance by another party. For example, in [5-1], Jones's purchase of Shares would require that Acme do whatever is required of it as the seller, and in [5-2] Smith could serve on Investco's board only if appointed. *Is entitled to* captures this nuance;

may (as in [5-1b] and [5-2a]) does not. (The active-voice alternative, *will entitle*, is awkward; see [5-1a].)

TABLE 5	■	LANGUAGE OF DISCRETION: *IS ENTITLED TO*
[5-1]	✓	No later than five days after Jones exercises the Option, Jones will be entitled to purchase a number of Shares equal to … .
[5-1a]	✗✗	Exercise of the Option will entitle Jones to purchase within five days a number of Shares equal to … .
[5-1b]	✗	No later than five days after Jones exercises the Option, Jones may purchase a number of Shares equal to … .
[5-1c]	✓✓	No later than five days after Jones exercises the Option, Acme shall sell to Jones, at Jones's election, a number of shares equal to … .
[5-2]	✓	Smith is entitled to serve on Investco's board of directors.
[5-2a]	✗	Smith may serve on Investco's board of directors.
[5-2b]	✓✓	Investco shall at Smith's option appoint Smith a member of its board of directors.

3.267   But it would be much clearer to ignore this subtle distinction and instead focus on the other party's obligation, as in [5-1c] and [5-2b]. This approach is feasible in contract drafting because of the limited number of actors; in statutory drafting, it would likely be very awkward to express *a person is entitled to vote* as language of obligation.

Is Not Required To

3.268   Use *is not required to* plus verb to convey absence of obligation (see [6-1]). (Strictly speaking, absence of obligation doesn't equal discretion, but the two are comparable, so it makes more sense to place this discussion with language of discretion instead of language of obligation.) Don't use the wordier *in no event is Acme required to*, with its rhetorical emphasis (see 1.58), or *nothing in this agreement requires Acme to*. Except to avoid confusion, don't use the wordier *this agreement does not require Acme to* or *nothing in this agreement requires Acme to*: the implication with all verb structures used to establish the categories of contract language is that they reflect agreement of the parties, not some broader reality.

3.269   Using instead *is not obligated to* might seem an appropriate choice to express absence of obligation. By contrast, *is not required to* might seem like "elegant variation"—unnecessary use of a synonym. But British drafters prefer *is not obliged to* (see [6-1a]), which sounds too conversational to American ears. To avoid these dueling usages, use *is not required to*. *Is not bound to* (see [6-1b]) is an unnecessary variant. *May not*, meaning in this context "is authorized not to," isn't suitable, because that meaning is just one of three possible meanings conveyed by *may not* (see 3.279).

3.270   The verb following *is not required to* can be used in the active voice (see [6-1] and [6-3a]) and the passive voice (see [6-3]). Use the active voice (see 3.13).

TABLE 6 ■ **LANGUAGE OF DISCRETION:** *IS NOT REQUIRED TO*

[6-1]	✓✓	Acme is not required to replace the Widget Equipment.
[6-1a]	✓	Acme is not [obligated] [obliged] to replace the Widget Equipment.
[6-1b]	✗✗	Acme is not bound to replace the Widget Equipment.
[6-1c]	✗✗	Acme shall not be required to replace the Widget Equipment.
[6-1d]	✗	Acme will not be required to replace the Widget Equipment.
[6-1e]	✗✗	Widgetco shall replace the Widget Equipment.
[6-1f]	✓	Widgetco is not entitled to have the Widget Equipment replaced.
[6-1g]	✗✗	Acme need not replace the Widget Equipment.
[6-1h]	✗✗	Acme may refuse to replace the Widget Equipment.
[6-1i]	✗✗	Widgetco does not expect Acme to replace the Widget Equipment.
[6-2]	✓	Acme is not required to reimburse the Consultant for annual expenses in excess of $10,000.
[6-2a]	✗✗	The Consultant's annual expenses must not exceed $10,000.
[6-2b]	✓✓	Acme shall reimburse the Consultant's expenses up to $10,000 per year.
[6-3]	✗	Amounts collected from Participants are not required to be held in a segregated account.
[6-3a]	✓✓	Widgetco is not required to hold in a segregated account any amounts collected from Participants.
[6-3b]	✗✗	Amounts collected from Participants shall not be required to be held in a segregated account.

3.271 Don't use, as in [6-1c] and [6-3b], *shall not be required to,* as that use of *shall* is inconsistent with using it to mean only "has a duty to" (see 3.74). And unless you're addressing the consequences of a contingent future event (see 3.307), it's better not to use *will not be required to,* as in [6-1d]: even though the obligation will continue into the future, it applies when the agreement becomes effective, so the present tense is preferable (see 3.307).

3.272 Don't confuse not imposing an obligation on Party A with imposing that obligation on Party B (see [6-1e]). The latter doesn't necessarily follow from the former.

3.273 Similarly, it doesn't make sense to impose limits on Party A if Party B's concern is simply that it not be responsible if Party A exceeds those limits. More specifically, [6-2a] prevents the consultant from incurring more than a stated amount of expenses; that's too restrictive, since Acme simply wants to limit the consultant expenses that it's required to reimburse. The latter meaning is expressed by [6-2], but it's expressed even more clearly by an obligation with a cap (see [6-2b]). For expressing performance with limits, it's better to state what has to be done rather than what doesn't have to be done.

3.274   Example [6-1f], using *is not entitled to* and a passive complement clause, is equivalent to [6-1] viewed from the perspective of Widgetco. Provisions using *is not entitled to* and a passive complement clause are, like provisions using *is entitled to* and a passive complement clause (see 3.152), analogous to provisions in the passive voice and so exhibit the shortcomings associated with the passive voice, namely wordiness and often, as in [6-1f], an absent *by*-agent. Instead of using *is not entitled to*, focus on the party not subject to the obligation. Similarly, it's best not to use *is not entitled to* plus a noun: instead of *Acme is not entitled to advance notice*, say *Roe is not required to give Acme advance notice*.

3.275   Don't use *need not*, as in [6-1g], to convey absence of obligation. Colloquially, *need* is used to indicate not only the lack of something (*I need a haircut*) but also an obligation (*You need to come to my office immediately*). But it would be unhelpful to use *need to* in a contract to express an obligation, because that function is already served by *shall* for imposing an obligation on the subject of the sentence (see 3.72). By extension, it would be unhelpful to use *need not* to preclude an obligation. Further muddying the waters is colloquial use of *need not* to mean "should not" (*Foreigners need not apply*) and "has no reason to" (*Fred need not be afraid*). The slightly old-fashioned *need not* is simply not as clear as *is not required to*.

3.276   Don't use *may refuse to* (see [6-1h]) to convey absence of obligation; the discretion to refuse to do something differs from having no obligation to do it. And don't say that one party *does not expect* the other party to do something or other (see [6-1i]). Like *will be expected to* (see 3.114), it's oddly circumspect.

Is Not Prohibited From

3.277   Use *is not prohibited from* to express absence of prohibition. (Strictly speaking, absence of prohibition doesn't equal discretion, but the two are comparable, so it makes more sense to place this discussion with language of discretion instead of language of prohibition.) Except to avoid confusion, don't use the wordier *this agreement does not prohibit Acme from* or *nothing in this agreement prohibits Acme from* (see 3.268). You could instead use *may*, but if in the absence of a contract Acme would be able to do whatever it is, it would be to Acme's advantage to avoid suggesting that its ability to so conduct itself is a function of the contract.

LANGUAGE OF PROHIBITION

Shall Not

3.278   "Language of prohibition" specifies what a contract prohibits the parties from doing. Prohibition is principally conveyed by *shall not*, meaning "has a duty not to," or *must not*, meaning "is required not to." Use *shall not* (see [7-1]) and *must not* to convey prohibition where you would use *shall* and *must*, respectively, to convey obligation. As with language of obligation, the most direct way to express prohibition is by imposing the prohibition on the subject of the sentence, using *shall not* (see [7-1]), but as with use of *shall*, that wouldn't make sense if the subject of the sentence is a nonparty (see 3.138).

TABLE 7	■	LANGUAGE OF PROHIBITION
[7-1]	✓✓	The Customer shall not modify the Equipment without Acme's prior written consent.
[7-1a]	✗	The Customer may not modify the Equipment … .
[7-1b]	✗	The Customer is not entitled to modify the Equipment … .
[7-1c]	✗✗	The Customer shall refrain from modifying the Equipment … .
[7-1d]	✗✗	The Customer hereby waives the right to modify the Equipment … .
[7-1e]	✗✗	The Customer shall never modify the Equipment … .
[7-1f]	✗✗	The Customer shall in no way modify the Equipment … .
[7-1g]	✗✗	The Customer cannot modify the Equipment … .
[7-1h]	✗✗	The Customer agrees not to modify the Equipment … .
[7-1i]	✗✗	Nothing in this agreement gives the Customer the right to modify the Equipment … .
[7-2]	✗	Neither party shall assign any of its rights … .
[7-2a]	✓	Neither party may assign any of its rights … .
[7-2b]	✗	The parties shall not assign any of their rights … .
[7-2c]	✓	Each party shall not assign any of its rights … .

Don't Use *May Not*

3.279   *May not*, meaning "is not permitted to" (see [7-1a]), is not the best choice for language of prohibition. It seems to achieve the same effect as *shall not* and *must not*, in that depriving a party of authority to take an action would be equivalent to requiring that party not to take that action. But it suffers from ambiguity that goes beyond that afflicting *may* (see 3.206): *Acme may not transfer the Shares* can mean that Acme (1) might not transfer the Shares, (2) is authorized not to transfer the Shares, or (3) isn't authorized to transfer the Shares. Readers likely would nevertheless derive the intended meaning, but presenting them with alternative meanings gives them more work to do.

Is Not Entitled To

3.280   Just as *is entitled to* with an active complement clause is best used when action by one party depends on performance by another party (see 3.266), *is not entitled to* with an active complement clause is appropriate when prohibition is based on another party's not being subject to an obligation, as in *Smith is not entitled to serve on Widgetco's board of directors*—Smith could serve on Widgetco's board only if appointed. Similarly, *Acme is not* *entitled to convert the Shares except as provided in section 3.2* captures that nuance better than *Acme shall not convert its Shares … .* Outside of that context—see for example [7-1b]—there's no need for *is not entitled to* in language of prohibition.

3.281 Although in both examples in 3.280 you could use *has no obligation* or *has no right* instead of *is not entitled to,* this manual recommends that you not do so. Using *obligation,* an abstract noun (see 17.7), makes *has no obligation* rather ponderous. As for *has no right,* the noun *right* (one definition of which is "an interest or expectation guaranteed by law") doesn't otherwise feature in language recommended in this chapter; it would be anomalous to introduce it solely in this context.

3.282 Although this manual recommends in 3.267 that one use language of obligation rather than *is entitled to* with an active complement clause, no particular benefit would be gained from an analogous fix in language of prohibition, for example rephrasing the first example in 3.280 as *Widgetco is not required to appoint Smith to its board of directors.*

Don't Use *Shall Refrain*

3.283 When someone asks you to refrain from doing something, they're being polite. The implication is that they're relying on your self-control. It's used in social contexts—*Please refrain from picking a fight with your Uncle Roger.* The consequences of failing to refrain presumably depend on the context and might be limited to mild disappointment. You also see *refrain* used when businesses deal with the public, as when a public announcement at an airport asks that you please refrain from smoking. In such contexts it's clearer a prohibition is being expressed.

3.284 For contracts, one would likely have a hard time claiming that *refrain* expresses something less than outright prohibition. But there is no reason to risk having that discussion—*shall not* expresses the intended meaning more clearly than does *shall refrain from.* Furthermore, contracts are for articulating rules and not for persuading (1.57), so they're not the place for deference exemplified by *shall refrain from.*

Don't Use *Hereby Waives the Right To* to Express Prohibition

3.285 The phrase *hereby waives the right to* and its variants (for example, *hereby waives any right to*) constitute language of performance. There's always an alternative that shows more clearly and concisely what's actually going on.

3.286 For one thing, *Acme hereby waives the right to sell the Shares* means that Acme is prohibited from doing so. It would be simpler and more concise to say *Acme shall not sell the Shares*—it confuses matters to use different verb structures to say the same thing. (See [7-1d] for another example.)

3.287 You generally see *hereby waives the right to* used in a more limited context, namely in provisions relating to how a party conducts itself in adversarial proceedings. An example: *The Purchaser hereby waives its right to pursue any other remedy.*

3.288 But there's no reason to distinguish, say, the right to sell shares from the right to assert an argument in a legal proceeding. If in the former it makes sense to use language of prohibition to express surrender of a right, then it makes sense in the latter too.

3.289 The most common example of this use of *hereby waives the right to* is for waiving the right to trial by jury. Rule 38 of the Federal Rules of Civil Procedure provides that a party may secure a jury trial by filing a jury trial demand and completing proper service on opposing parties, so to use language of prohibition, you could say *Each party shall not demand a trial by jury*. But the waiver language is universal, so you might find it expedient to stick with it.

3.290 Regarding using language of discretion instead of *hereby waives the right to*, see 3.262.

Other Suboptimal Usages

3.291 Don't use *shall never* (see [7-1e]): the notion of perpetuity inherent in *never* is overkill in this context, because *shall not* is equally comprehensive. If you want an obligation—for example, an obligation to keep information confidential—to continue perpetually, even after termination of the agreement, say so explicitly. Don't rely on *shall never* to convey that meaning, because *never* could just as well be understood to mean only until termination of the agreement.

3.292 Using *shall in no way* (see [7-1f]) is to indulge in rhetorical emphasis, adding needless words (see 1.58). It means the same thing as *shall not*, but adds a pointless flourish.

3.293 Just as using *can* in language of discretion is inappropriate (see 3.189), so is using *cannot* in language of prohibition, as in [7-1g]. And just as using *agrees to* isn't a clear way of expressing an obligation (see 3.109), *agrees not to*, as in [7-1h], isn't a clear way of expressing prohibition.

3.294 Saying that a contract doesn't authorize a party to do something, as in [7-1i], is equivalent to prohibition; it would be simpler to express it as such. If you intend a different meaning, find a clearer way to express it.

Collective Nouns

3.295 When the subject of a sentence is a collective noun such as *party* or *shareholder*, whether singular or plural, you can convey prohibition by rendering negative either the subject or the verb.

3.296 You render the subject negative by using *neither*, if the subject consists of two parties (*Neither party* ...), or *no*, if the subject consists of more than two parties (*No Shareholder* ...). When you render the subject negative, you have the choice of using as the verb *shall* (see [7-2]) or *may* (see [7-2a]). The drawback to using a negative subject with *shall* is that if you apply the *has a duty* test (see 3.74), it would appear to express the absence of duty rather than expressing prohibition. The drawback to using *may* is that it would be inconsistent to use *may* to express prohibition in this context and *shall not* elsewhere (see 3.278). Of the two, using *may* is the better option.

3.297   The alternative would be to render the verb negative. You could do so using a plural noun, as in [7-2b]. As is the case whenever a plural noun is the subject of the sentence, the question is whether the prohibition applies to the members of the group collectively as opposed to individually (see 11.16), but it's unlikely that would cause confusion. More problematic is a plural subject accompanied by the pronoun *their*, as in [7-2b]—it could be understood to mean that the object is owned collectively. Using instead a singular noun, as in [7-2c], would allow you to avoid both issues, at the cost of an extra word.

Nor Shall

3.298   Don't use *nor shall* to express negation.

3.299   *Nor* plus verb is used to express negation that follows an express negative or an idea that is negative in sense. Usually it begins a sentence, but *nor shall*, preceded by a comma, usually continues a sentence, as in this example:

> The Receiving Party shall not use Confidential Information other than as authorized by the Disclosing Party under the SOW, *nor shall* the Receiving Party disclose any Confidential Information to nonparties without the Disclosing Party's written consent.

3.300   But it's awkward to echo prohibition expressed earlier in the sentence by using a structure that places the auxiliary (*shall*) before the subject and the main verb. Instead, use language of prohibition. That would have the added benefit of avoiding using *shall* in a way that fails the *has a duty* test (see 3.74). And *nor shall* is conducive to run-on sentences.

3.301   So here's a revised version of the above example:

> The Receiving Party shall not use Confidential Information other than as authorized by the Disclosing Party under the SOW. The Receiving Party shall not disclose any Confidential Information to nonparties without the Disclosing Party's written consent.

Prohibition by Way of an Exception to Language of Discretion or Obligation

3.302   You can express prohibition with an exception to language of discretion, but there are clear and slightly less clear ways of doing so.

3.303   Consider the following: *Widgetco may sell one or more of the Vehicles except the 1965 Ford Mustang.* As a matter of logic, it could be argued that the exception excludes that vehicle from Widgetco's discretion but does no more—in other words, the provision is otherwise silent regarding that vehicle, so Widgetco could sell it without being in breach of this provision. That's a weak argument, as the expectation of relevance (see 3.192) strongly suggests that the intention was to have the exception be equivalent to language of prohibition; had the intention been to allow

Widgetco to sell the Ford Mustang, it would have made sense to omit the exception. But to avoid any chance of a dispute over meaning, say instead *Widgetco may sell one or more of the Vehicles, except that it shall not sell the 1965 Ford Mustang.* Or more concisely, *Widgetco may sell one or more of the Vehicles but not the 1965 Ford Mustang.*

3.304 You can express prohibition with an exception to language of obligation, but you have to be more explicit than with an exception to language of discretion. If the example in 3.303 were instead to read *Widgetco shall sell all Vehicles except the 1965 Ford Mustang,* as a matter of logic it could be argued that the exception excludes that vehicle from Widgetco's obligation but does no more, so Widgetco could sell the Ford Mustang without breaching the obligation. But more to the point, in this case the expectation of relevance is unrelated to whether Widgetco may sell the Ford Mustang—it suggests only that the obligation doesn't apply to the Ford Mustang. To avoid any chance of a dispute over meaning, say instead *Widgetco shall sell one or more of the Vehicles, except that it shall not sell the 1965 Ford Mustang.* It wouldn't be enough to negate the obligation.

LANGUAGE OF POLICY

3.305 Besides stating what the parties are required to do, permitted to do, or prohibited from doing, a contract will usually contain "policies," which is the term this manual uses for rules that the parties must observe but that don't, at least expressly, require or permit action or inaction.

3.306 There are two kinds of policy. First, those that state rules governing a thing, event, or circumstance (see [8-1], [8-7], and [8-8]). And second, those that address the scope, meaning, or duration of a contract or part of a contract (see [8-2] through [8-6]).

Verbs in Language of Policy

3.307 Use the present tense for those policies that apply on effectiveness of the contract (such as [8-2], [8-3], and [8-4]), even though the policy will continue to apply in the future. Use the present tense also for those policies (such as [8-5]) that state a time of effectiveness or lapsing of effectiveness—in general usage it's standard to use the present tense in this manner for situations that are to occur at a stated time in the future. But if the policy relates to future events that might not take place, as in [8-1] and [8-6], or the timing of which is uncertain, use *will.*

TABLE 8	■	LANGUAGE OF POLICY
[8-1]	✘	Any attempted transfer of Shares in violation of this agreement is void.
[8-1a]	✔✔	Any attempted transfer of Shares in violation of this agreement will be void.
[8-1b]	✘✘	Any attempted transfer of Shares in violation of this agreement shall be void.

[8-2]	✓✓	The laws of the state of New York govern all matters arising out of this agreement.
[8-2a]	✗	The laws of the state of New York will govern … .
[8-2b]	✗✗	The laws of the state of New York shall govern … .
[8-3]	✓✓	This agreement constitutes the entire agreement of the parties regarding the subject matter of this agreement.
[8-3a]	✗✗	This agreement shall constitute … .
[8-4]	✓✓	"GAAP" means generally accepted accounting principles, consistently applied.
[8-4a]	✗✗	"GAAP" shall mean … .
[8-5]	✓✓	This agreement terminates on 31 December 2019.
[8-5a]	✗	This agreement will terminate … .
[8-5b]	✗✗	This agreement shall terminate … .
[8-6]	✓✓	This agreement will terminate upon the closing of a Qualified IPO.
[8-6a]	✗	This agreement terminates … .
[8-6b]	✗✗	This agreement shall terminate … .
[8-7]	✓	Interest is payable at a rate of 8% per year.
[8-7a]	✗✗	Interest shall be payable … .
[8-7b]	✓✓	The Borrower shall pay interest … .
[8-8]	✓	The Option is exercisable until midnight at the end of 31 December 2019.
[8-8a]	✗✗	The Option shall be exercisable … .
[8-8b]	✓✓	Smith may exercise the Option … .

3.308 Don't use *shall* in language of policy: as language of policy doesn't impose obligations.

Buried-Actor Policies

3.309 Some policies focus on what is acted on, when it would be clearer to focus on the actor. This manual calls such policies "buried-actor policies." One kind of buried-actor policy features the adjectives *exercisable*, *payable*, and *recoverable*. Such buried-actor policies have two shortcomings. First, as with passive verb phrases (see 3.12), the agent can be expressed by a *by*-agent, but in contracts the agent is often omitted (see [8-7] and [8-8]), leaving unstated the party responsible for performing the action. Second, if a contract states that *the fee is payable by 20 April 2018*, that could, depending on the context, mean that the party in question is obligated to pay the fee by that date, or has discretion to pay the fee, or that timely payment of the fee is a condition. Such buried-actor policies should be rephrased as language of obligation (see [8-7b]), as language of discretion (see [8-8b]), or as conditional clauses.

3.310 A comparable source of buried-actor policies is the phrase *is due*, as in *The First Installment is due by 1 March 2018*. It would be better expressed as language of obligation: *The Purchaser shall pay the First Installment by 1 March 2018*.

3.311 Another feature of buried-actor policies is the phrase *is subject to*, as in *The Employee's position and assignments are subject to change*. Instead of saying *is subject to* plus abstract noun, with an inanimate object as the subject, use *may* plus a verb, with a party as the subject: *The Company may change the Employee's position and assignments*. Yet another example is the phrase *is eligible for*, as in *The Employee will be eligible for a bonus if … .* It would be clearer to say instead *The Company shall pay the Employee a bonus if … .*

Use of the Passive Voice

3.312 Use of the passive voice in language of policy is unremarkable (see the example in 3.24). But in some instances in which the *by*-agent (see 3.12) is missing, the missing *by*-agent is the world at large, not one or more parties. That's the case with *the Exercise Price will be adjusted*. One way to prevent any implication that action by the parties or anyone else is involved would be to use *automatically* (see 13.102). Another way would be to switch, if possible, from the passive voice (*the Option Price will be increased*) to the active voice (*the Option Price will increase*), leaving the subject unchanged. That wouldn't make sense with, for example, *will be deemed* (see 13.217–.218)—leave it as is.

EXPRESSING CONDITIONS

3.313 This section addresses not a category of contract language but instead how to express conditions in conjunction with categories of contract language. For these purposes, "condition" means a future and uncertain event or circumstance on which the existence of some particular legal relation depends.

3.314 This manual is concerned only with how to convey meaning in a contract, so terms of art ostensibly relating to conditions and applied in resolving disputes—for example, the distinction under English law between "promissory conditions" and "contingent conditions," and the three pages devoted to *condition* and its variants in *Black's Law Dictionary*—are irrelevant for our purposes.

3.315 In a contract, use the term *condition* rather than *condition precedent*, which conveys the same meaning but adds an unnecessarily legalistic flavor. You should never need to use *condition subsequent*, meaning something that, if it occurs, would bring something else to an end—it's safe to assume that its meaning is unclear to clients and many lawyers. Without using the label *condition subsequent*, simply state that if X happens, then Y will cease.

Conditional Clauses

3.316 Conditional clauses don't fall within one of the categories of contract language. Instead, they modify language of obligation, discretion, prohibition, and policy.

STRUCTURE AND FUNCTION

3.317 A sentence containing a conditional clause consists of the conditional clause, including a subordinator, and the matrix clause. In the sentence *"If Acme has not exercised the Option by 31 December 2017*, Smith may transfer the Shares to another Person," the italicized portion is the conditional clause, with *If* as the subordinator; the remainder of the sentence is the matrix clause.

3.318 The truth of the proposition in the matrix clause is a consequence of fulfillment of the condition in the conditional clause. In general usage, the most common subordinator is *if*, with the negative subordinator *unless* the next most common. Other subordinators include *where*, *when*, *as long as*, *so long as*, and *on condition that*.

3.319 When using *if* as the subordinator, it's unnecessary to use *then* to begin a matrix clause that follows. And if the conditional clause is relatively short, adding *then* to the matrix clause just adds dead weight to the sentence. But if the conditional clause is complex and either it's not lengthy enough to justify putting it after the matrix clause or it doesn't make sense to put it there (see 3.326), beginning the matrix clause with *then* might help reduce reader miscues.

3.320 For example, in the following sentence, omitting *then* from the beginning of the matrix clause might cause the reader to think for a moment that *for as long as that compulsory license is in effect* refers to how long Acme may sell a Product under the license as opposed to how long the terms of the license apply:

> If a Government Body grants to Acme a compulsory license to sell a Product in a country on terms more favorable than those in this article 8, then for as long as that compulsory license is in effect the terms of that compulsory license will control.

VERBS IN THE CONDITIONAL CLAUSE

3.321 The present tense is acceptable in all conditional clauses; see [9-1] and [9-2]. In the interest of consistency, use only the present tense, even though the present perfect is also acceptable if, as in [9-2a], satisfying the condition is a part of the transaction as opposed to a response to a contingency.

3.322 Don't use *shall* in conditional clauses. Many drafters do; see [9-1b], [9-1c], [9-2b], [9-2c], and [9-3a]. Because in this context *shall* cannot convey obligation, drafters presumably use it to express futurity. Perhaps they think that if a conditional clause uses the present tense, then the matrix clause would operate only on conditions that are met at the moment the contract becomes effective. When a conditional clause uses a dynamic verb (as in *If Roe transfers the Shares*), this fear is unwarranted. When, as in [9-3], a conditional clause uses a stative verb (that is, a verb that expresses a continuing state, such as *is*), you can alleviate this fear by adding *at any time*, as in [9-3c]. Even better, you can often sidestep the issue by switching from a stative to a dynamic verb, as in [9-3d].

TABLE 9 ■ CONDITIONAL CLAUSES		
[9-1]	✓✓	If Investco receives a Violation Notice, it shall promptly notify Widgetco.
[9-1a]	✗	If Investco has received a Violation Notice, ...
[9-1b]	✗✗	If Investco shall receive a Violation Notice, ...
[9-1c]	✗✗	If Investco shall have received a Violation Notice, ...
[9-1d]	✗	If Investco should receive a Violation Notice, ...
[9-2]	✓✓	If Acme receives a Notice of Consent, it may transfer the Shares.
[9-2a]	✓	If Acme has received a Notice of Consent, ...
[9-2b]	✗✗	If Acme shall receive a Notice of Consent, ...
[9-2c]	✗✗	If Acme shall have received a Notice of Consent, ...
[9-3]	✓	If the Borrower is in default, the Lender may accelerate the Loan.
[9-3a]	✗✗	If the Borrower shall be in default, ...
[9-3b]	✗✗	If the Borrower be in default, ...
[9-3c]	✓	If the Borrower is at any time in default, ...
[9-3d]	✓✓	If the Borrower defaults, ...

3.323   Using *should* in conditional clauses, as in [9-1d], conveys an unhelpful tentativeness. You could place *should* at the beginning of the conditional clause (*Should Investco receive* ...), but that wouldn't represent an improvement. No purpose is served by using the subjunctive, as in [9-3b].

VERBS IN THE MATRIX CLAUSE

3.324   If the verb in a matrix clause would, absent the conditional clause, be in the present tense, use *will*, as in [10-1] and [10-2], and not the present tense, as in [10-1b] and [10-2b], and not *shall*, as in [10-1a] and [10-2a], as no duty is involved.

TABLE 10 ▪ CONDITIONAL CLAUSES: THE MATRIX CLAUSE		
[10-1]	✓✓	If Jones ceases to be employed by the Company, the Option will terminate.
[10-1a]	✗✗	If … , the Option shall terminate.
[10-1b]	✗	If … , the Option terminates.
[10-2]	✓✓	If a Stockholder transfers all its Shares to a Person that is not a Stockholder, that transfer will be valid only if the Person acquiring those Shares agrees to be bound by this agreement.
[10-2a]	✗✗	If … , that transfer shall be valid only … .
[10-2b]	✗	If … , that transfer is valid only … .

3.325   The auxiliary verbs *shall*, *may*, and *must* are unaffected by the presence of a conditional clause.

POSITION OF THE CONDITIONAL CLAUSE

3.326   The traditional place for a conditional clause is at the beginning of a sentence, but you should place it elsewhere if doing so would make the provision easier to read. The longer the conditional clause, the more likely it is that the provision would be more readable with the matrix clause rather than conditional clause at the front of the sentence. If both the conditional clause and matrix clause contain more than one element, you would likely be better off expressing them as two sentences.

CHOOSING BETWEEN POSITIVE AND NEGATIVE IN THE MATRIX CLAUSE

3.327   Consider these alternatives:

1. Acme may sell the Shares only if Widgetco consents.

2. Acme shall not sell the Shares unless Widgetco consents.

3.328   The first uses language of discretion and includes a conditional clause, with *if* as the subordinator. The second uses language of prohibition, and it too includes a conditional clause, with *unless* as the subordinator. Both appear to convey the same meaning. How does one choose which to use?

3.329   A practical approach would be to select the example that better reflects what the client expects will happen or would prefer to happen. Regarding the above examples, if the client thinks it's more likely that Acme will sell the shares, or if the client prefers that Acme do so, choose the first example. If the opposite is the case, choose the second example.

3.330   But it's also relevant to consider what happens if in each of the above examples the condition isn't satisfied. In the first example, what category of contract language would apply if Widgetco doesn't consent? The expectation of relevance (see 3.191) suggests that if Widgetco doesn't consent, discretion would be removed and Acme wouldn't be permitted to sell the shares. But it's conceivable that Acme might instead be obligated to sell the shares if Widgetco doesn't consent.

3.331 And in the second example, the expectation of relevance suggests that if Widgetco consents, the prohibition would be lifted and Acme could sell if it wishes. But it's conceivable that Acme might instead be obligated to sell the shares if Widgetco consents.

3.332 If you would prefer to be specific instead of relying on the expectation of relevance to fill in the gap in each example, you would have to say the following:

> Acme shall not sell the Shares, except that it may sell the Shares if Widgetco consents.

3.333 A comparable choice can occur in language of policy that includes a conditional clause, as in these alternatives:

1. An amendment to this agreement will be effective only if it is in writing and signed by both parties.

2. An amendment to this agreement will not be effective unless it is in writing and signed by both parties.

3. No amendment to this agreement will be effective unless it is in writing and signed by both parties.

3.334 The first is expressed in positive terms and uses *if* as the subordinator; the second and third are expressed in negative terms (with negation achieved with the verb and with the subject, respectively) and use *unless* as the subordinator. The third is one word shorter than the second and so is marginally more concise.

3.335 One encounters mixed views as to whether it's preferable to express this in positive or negative terms. But because instances of parties amending a contract effectively greatly outnumber instances of ineffective amendment, this manual suggests that it's preferable to express this provision in positive terms, using the first alternative.

3.336 To see what other categories of contract language could be used to express this meaning, see 3.467.

USING *UNLESS* WITH LANGUAGE OF OBLIGATION DENOTING ACTIVITY

3.337 The opinion of the District Court for the Northern District of California in *Total Recall Technologies v. Luckey*, No. C 15-02281 WHA, 2016 WL 199796 (N.D. Cal. 16 Jan. 2016), reveals the potential for dispute when language of obligation denoting activity (as opposed to momentary action) is coupled with a conditional clause using *unless* as the subordinator.

3.338 In that dispute, the defendant Luckey argued that he had not breached the terms of the confidentiality agreement at issue, in that the nondisclosure and exclusivity provisions had never taken effect. Here's the relevant part of the contract (emphasis added by the court):

> The Receiving party shall keep all details including drawings and part suppliers of the Head Mounted Display confidential and shall not aid any other person or entity in the design of a Head Mounted Display other than the disclosing party. *Unless within a twelve month period from 1st July 2011 the receiving party has not received a minimum payment in royalties of*

> *10,000 US dollars by the disclosing party.* The exclusivity shall remain in place for a period of 10 years providing a minimum of 10,000 US dollars is paid from the disclosing party to the receiving party per annum.

3.339 The second sentence is ungrammatical; the court assumed that should have been a conditional clause modifying the first sentence. Here's what the court said about the second sentence:

> Luckey's argument that the nondisclosure and exclusivity provisions of the agreement never took effect turns on the interpretation of the italicized sentence fragment above. Luckey contends that the ten thousand dollar payment contemplated therein was a contingent event that had to occur before the exclusivity and nondisclosure obligations could take effect. Seidl's (and Total Recall's) failure to make such a payment, Luckey argues, is fatal to Total Recall's claim that Luckey breached the contract. Total Recall responds that its payment obligation was excused by Luckey's alleged breach.

> The use of the word "unless" tends to support Luckey's construction of the agreement; however, the grammatical defect in the provision renders it ambiguous at the Rule 12 stage. One possibility is that the fragment was a condition subsequent, meaning the duty to maintain confidentiality evaporated after one year (if the payment was not made). Another is that it was a condition precedent, meaning the duty never arose in the first place (since no payment was made). And, while it seems clear that zero payment was ever made, the idea that Luckey frustrated such payment and thus excused it is plausible (if barely so) at the Rule 12 stage.

3.340 But Luckey's reading of the language at issue is unreasonable. Here's why:

3.341 Obligations are expressed using two kinds of verb—those denoting momentary action and those denoting activity. Below are two versions of an obligation using a verb denoting momentary action plus a conditional clause, one using the subordinator *if* (with a positive conditional clause) and the other the subordinator *unless* (with a negative conditional clause):

> On 1 January 2018, A shall pay B $100 if C is then living in the United States.

> On 1 January 2018, A shall pay B $100 unless C is then not living in the United States.

3.342 Both versions express the same meaning.

3.343 And here are two versions of another obligation, this one using a verb denoting activity plus a conditional clause, again with one conditional clause using *if* (with a positive conditional clause) and the other the subordinator *unless* (with a negative conditional clause):

> A shall keep the information confidential if by 1 July 2012 B has paid A $10,000.

> A shall keep the information confidential unless by 1 July 2012 B has not paid A $10,000.

3.344   The version with *if* is clear—the obligation applies only after the condition has been satisfied. The version with *unless*—it's a simplified version of the language at issue in *Total Recall Technologies*—expresses a different meaning. There's nothing to suggest that the obligation wouldn't apply on entry into the contract. *Unless* is the negative counterpart of *if*, so in the context of an obligation that uses a verb denoting activity and that applies on entry into the contract, the natural reading of a conditional clause with *unless* is that satisfaction of the condition would mean that the party under the obligation would no longer have to comply with it. But that's not the meaning sought by the defendant in *Total Recall Technologies*.

3.345   That's perhaps easier to see using simpler examples:

> I'll look after your plants if you're nice to me.

> I'll look after your plants unless you're not nice to me.

3.346   The first example is clear—it's a condition to my looking after your plants that you be nice to me. It would be semantically anomalous to derive that meaning from the second example, but that meaning is analogous to the meaning sought by the defendant in *Total Recall Technologies*. The natural meaning is that I'll look after your plants, but I'll stop doing so if you're not nice to me.

3.347   So the court was mistaken in saying that "use of the word 'unless' tends to support the defendant's construction of the agreement."

3.348   To avoid this sort of dispute, whenever an obligation that uses a verb denoting activity is coupled with a conditional clause using *unless*, replace the *unless* conditional clause with *except that* plus language of discretion (using *is not required to*) and an *if* conditional clause, as in the second version below (the first version is the simplified version of the language at issue in *Total Recall Technologies*):

> A shall keep the information confidential unless by 1 July 2012 B has not paid A $10,000.

> A shall keep the information confidential, except that if by 1 July 2012 B has not paid A $10,000, A will no longer be required to keep the information confidential.

3.349   The second version also has the advantage of not relying on the expectation of relevance (see 3.191).

3.350   The version with *unless* couldn't be said to be unclear, so why change it? Because it might be prudent not only to be clear but also to avoid possible fights. Disgruntled contract parties might follow the example of the defendant in *Total Recall Technologies* and pick a fight based on ostensible confusion resulting from a verb denoting activity coupled with a conditional clause using *unless*.

Language of Policy Used to Express Conditions

3.351   When deal lawyers refer to conditions, they usually have in mind not conditional clauses but closing conditions, namely a list of requirements introduced by a main clause such as this: *The obligations of Acme under this agreement are subject to satisfaction of the following conditions … .* Closing conditions are a specialized form of language of policy.

3.352   Traditionally, each closing condition is presented as a separate sentence using *shall* in either the modal auxiliary (*shall be*) or modal perfect (*shall have been*) form. There are two problems with this approach.

STRUCTURE

3.353   When standard closing conditions are considered apart from the main clause, it isn't evident that they're conditions. To express just one condition, rather than a list of them, the appropriate form of introduction would be *The obligations of Acme under this agreement are subject to the condition that … .* Despite this, standard closing conditions are never expressed as *that*-clauses, and as a result they could conceivably be read as statements of fact (see [11-1] and [11-2]), or even language of obligation (when used with *shall*). To make it clear that one is dealing with conditions, express each closing condition as a tabulated enumerated *that*-clause (see 4.41–.53).

TABLE 11   ▪   LANGUAGE OF POLICY USED TO EXPRESS CONDITIONS

The Buyer's obligations under this agreement are subject to satisfaction of the following conditions:

[11-1]	✗ ✗	Acme's statements of fact are accurate at the Closing as though made at the Closing; … .
[11-1a]	✗ ✗	that Acme's statements of fact shall be accurate … .
[11-1b]	✗ ✗	that Acme's statements of fact must be accurate … .
[11-1c]	✗ ✗	that Acme's statements of fact will be accurate … .
[11-1d]	✗ ✗	that Acme's statements of fact be accurate … .
[11-1e]	✓ ✓	that Acme's statements of fact are accurate … .
[11-2]	✗ ✗	the Buyer has received an opinion of Acme's counsel in the form of exhibit A … .
[11-2a]	✗ ✗	that the Buyer shall have received an opinion of Acme's counsel … .
[11-2b]	✗ ✗	that the Buyer must have received an opinion of Acme's counsel … .
[11-2c]	✗ ✗	that the Buyer will have received an opinion of Acme's counsel … .
[11-2d]	✗ ✗	that the Buyer have received an opinion of Acme's counsel … .
[11-2e]	✓ ✓	that the Buyer has received an opinion of Acme's counsel … .

3.354 Using *shall* or *shall have* in closing conditions, as in [11-1a] and [11-2a], is inappropriate, because closing conditions aren't for expressing obligations. For the same reason, using *must* or *must have*, as in [11-1b] and [11-2b], is no improvement. Using *will* or *will have*, as in [11-1c] and [11-2c], is also inappropriate. Determining whether the closing conditions have been satisfied requires that one inquire on the closing date into present, not future, circumstances. Just because the conditions are specified before the closing date doesn't mean that they must be expressed in future time. Instead, use as appropriate either the present tense, as in [11-1e], or the present perfect, as in [11-2e].

3.355 Normally it would be appropriate, even desirable, to use the subjunctive in closing-condition *that*-clauses, as in [11-1d] and [11-2d], but structuring the closing conditions as tabulated *that*-clauses makes the subjunctive seem an odd choice. Use the indicative mood, as in [11-1e] and [11-2e].

Language of Obligation Used to Express Conditions

3.356 A third way to express a condition is by imposing an obligation on the subject of a sentence, but by using *must* rather than *shall*.

3.357 [12-1b] is part of a provision governing Widgetco's reimbursement of Acme's expenses. With its use of *shall,* [12-1b] is phrased as an obligation. If a court were to treat it as an obligation, failure by Acme to timely submit invoices to Widgetco would represent breach of Acme's obligation but wouldn't preclude reimbursement unless Widgetco were able to show damages caused by Acme's having submitted the invoices late.

TABLE 12 ▪ LANGUAGE OF OBLIGATION USED TO EXPRESS CONDITIONS		
[12-1]	✓✓	To be reimbursed, Acme must submit to Widgetco no later than 90 days after Acme receives it each invoice for expenses that Acme incurs.
[12-1a]	✗✗	Acme must submit to Widgetco … .
[12-1b]	✗✗	Acme shall submit to Widgetco … .
[12-1c]	✗✗	To be reimbursed, Acme need only submit to Widgetco … .

3.358 If instead this provision were expressed as a condition, Acme wouldn't be entitled to reimbursement unless it were to timely submit the related invoices. Presumably Widgetco would prefer that arrangement as providing greater certainty.

3.359 Using *must* instead of *shall*, as in [12-1a], would suggest that Acme doesn't have a duty to timely submit invoices to Widgetco—that instead it has to timely submit invoices if it wants to be reimbursed for the related expenses. But it would be reckless to rely on *must* and nothing more, as in [12-1a], to express a condition—when faced with uncertainty over whether a provision is a condition or an obligation, a court would likely hold that it's an obligation. See 1-7 *Murray on Contracts* § 103; 13 *Williston on Contracts* § 38:13. Relying on *shall* and nothing more, as in [12-1b], would render this even more likely. See, e.g., *Mind & Motion Utah Investments, LLC v. Celtic Bank Corp.*, 367 P.3d 994, 1002 (Utah 2016) (holding that the phrase "shall record Phase 1" in a contract expresses an obligation and not a condition). Using *need only*, as in [12-1c], is too colloquial.

3.360   And consider the case of *Howard v. Federal Crop Insurance Corp.*, 540 F.2d 695 (4th Cir. 1976), which involved this contract provision: "The tobacco stalks on any acreage of tobacco of types 11a, 11b, 12, 13, or 14 with respect to which a loss is claimed *shall not be destroyed* until the Corporation makes an inspection." (Emphasis added.) The court held that absent any language plainly requiring that the provision be construed as a condition, it was to be construed as a promise, so the insureds had not automatically forfeited coverage under the policy by plowing under damaged tobacco stalks.

3.361   So if you wish to use language of obligation to express a condition, add language that makes it clear that you're dealing with a condition. The simplest way to do that would be to add a *to* infinitive clause, as in [12-1], or a clause beginning with *for*.

3.362   A possible alternative to [12-1] would be to use language of obligation that incorporates a time limit: *Widgetco shall reimburse Acme for those expenses reflected in any invoice that Acme submits to Widgetco no later than 90 days after Acme receives that invoice.* Besides being a mouthful, that alternative is less clear than [12-1], in that it's silent regarding invoices submitted after 90 days. The rule of interpretation *expressio unius est exclusio alterius*—the expression of one thing implies the exclusion of others—might suggest to a court that Widgetco wasn't under any obligation regarding any such invoices. But given that courts aren't fond of all-or-nothing arrangements unless the contract gives them no choice, making it explicit that late submission of an invoice precludes reimbursement would provide greater certainty.

A Condition Doesn't Make Sense If It Can Be Ignored

3.363   If a party can ignore a condition before taking an action that's subject to satisfaction of that condition, use an obligation instead of a condition. The following explains why.

3.364   Acme has an inventory of widgets. Acme's contract with Widgetco contains this:

> It is a condition to Acme's conducting a public sale of widgets that Acme notify Widgetco in advance of the date and location of that sale.

3.365   Compare that sentence to this one:

> It is a condition to XYZ's disputing a Dynaco invoice that XYZ submit a Dispute Notice to Dynaco no later than five business days after XYZ receives that invoice.

3.366   Both sentences use language of policy to express conditions (see 3.351). But in the first, Acme is in a position to ignore the condition and conduct the public sale of widgets whether or not the condition has been satisfied. By contrast, in the second sentence, the process of disputing a Dynaco invoice under the contract's dispute mechanism can't happen without Dynaco participating.

3.367   So it doesn't make sense to state the first sentence as a condition. Structuring something as a condition makes sense only if satisfaction of the condition depends on something that is out of the control of the party that would take the action that is subject to satisfaction of the condition. Instead, the issue should be addressed in an obligation:

> Before conducting a public sale of widgets, Acme shall notify Widgetco in advance of the date and location of that sale.

3.368   That would give Widgetco a remedy if Acme doesn't notify Widgetco. By contrast, it's not clear what the consequences are of ignoring a condition.

A Condition Might Not Be the Only Condition

3.369   When something is stated as a condition, it might not be the only condition. For example, if someone tells you, "We'll let you into the party only if you're wearing a red carnation and a top hat," it's unlikely you would be admitted to the party were you wearing *only* a red carnation and a top hat, unless it were a special sort of party.

3.370   Similarly, if a contract specifies that an invoice will be valid only if it's delivered no later than 60 days after the related services were performed, presumably that isn't the only condition—other conditions might be read into the contract. For example, an invoice wouldn't be valid if it's for triple the agreed price.

LANGUAGE OF DECLARATION

3.371   "Language of declaration" declares facts using verbs of speaking. Language of declaration allows parties not simply to assert facts but to be seen to be asserting them—without the verb, it wouldn't be clear who is making the declaration.

3.372   Contracts contain two kinds of assertions of fact: If the declaring party knows a fact and the other party wants the declaring party to assert in the contract that the fact is accurate, the declaring party *states* that fact (see 3.416). (This is not a traditional usage; see 3.374.) If the other party wants the declaring party to accept in the contract that the declaring party is unable to challenge the accuracy of a fact known to the other party, the declaring party *acknowledges* that fact (see 3.436).

TABLE 13	▪	**LANGUAGE OF DECLARATION**
[13-1]	✓✓	Acme states that the Equipment is listed in schedule A.
[13-1a]	✗	Acme hereby states … .
[13-1b]	✗	Acme represents … .
[13-1c]	✗✗	Acme represents and warrants … .
[13-2]	✓✓	The Investor acknowledges that it has received a copy of each SEC Document.
[13-2a]	✗	The Investor hereby acknowledges … .

3.373   Language of declaration is analogous to language of performance—in the former a party is making a specialized declaration by a speech act, and in the latter a party is taking an action by a speech act. But one difference is that *hereby*, which is a signal of language of performance, is less commonly used with verbs of speaking, although one does see it, as in [13-1a] and [13-2a]. This manual recommends that you not use *hereby* with language of declaration.

Statements of Fact—Using *Represents and Warrants*

3.374   In the United States, *represents* and *warrants* are used in business contracts to introduce statements of fact by parties—statements relating to matters they broadly control or that fall within the scope of their operations. Sometimes only one verb is used, as in [13-1b] (using *represents*), but usually both are joined in a doublet—*represents and warrants*, as in [13-1c], in which case the statements of fact are known as *representations and warranties*.

3.375   Sometimes one or more verbs are added to *represents* and *warrants* (whether used separately or together), as in *Acme represents and acknowledges* and *Acme represents, warrants, covenants, and agrees*. That pileup of categories of contract language makes no sense, so this manual addresses use of only one or both of *represents* and *warrants* to introduce statements of fact.

3.376   A different function is served by use of the verb *warrants* and the noun *warranty* on their own, without *represents* and *representation*, regarding goods in a contract for the sale of those goods (see 13.879).

REMEDIES FOR INACCURATE STATEMENTS OF FACT

3.377   Determining what *represents* and *warrants* each mean requires considering the remedies available under U.S. law for inaccurate statements of fact in a contract.

3.378   Due to how the common law has developed, if a party's statement of fact turns out to have been inaccurate, the counterparty might be able to bring a tort-based claim for misrepresentation, a contract-based claim for breach of warranty, or both.

3.379 In that context, the simplest meaning of *representation* is that it's a statement of fact that might support a claim for misrepresentation. And the simplest meaning of *warranty* is that it's a statement of fact that might support a claim for breach of warranty.

THE REMEDIES RATIONALE

3.380 Some U.S. commentators have attempted to attribute significance to each verb in *represents and warrants*. They fall into two camps, one offering what this manual calls the "remedies rationale," the other offering what this manual calls the "timeframe rationale."

3.381 Whether a contract party can bring a claim for misrepresentation or a claim for breach of warranty for an inaccurate statement of fact made by the other party can have significant practical implications. According to the remedies rationale, a drafter can ensure that a statement of fact is treated as a representation, as a warranty, or as both by introducing that statement of fact with *represents*, *warrants*, or both, respectively, or by identifying that statement as a representation, a warranty, or both. The most vocal advocate of the remedies rationale is Tina L. Stark, in her book *Drafting Contracts: How and Why Lawyers Do What They Do* 15, 137–38 (2d ed. 2014).

3.382 The remedies rationale comes in two flavors, which this manual calls "permissive" and "restrictive." Under both the permissive remedies rationale and the restrictive remedies rationale, explicitly describing a statement of fact as a representation, a warranty, or both, by means of an introductory verb or otherwise, is sufficient to make it so.

3.383 Where the permissive and restrictive rationales differ is how they treat a statement of fact that isn't introduced by *represents* or *warrants*, or both, or otherwise explicitly characterized as a representation, a warranty, or both. Under the permissive version, such a statement of fact could still be deemed a representation or warranty, respectively, depending on the nature of the statement itself. By contrast, the restrictive version holds that a statement of fact will support a claim for misrepresentation only if it is introduced with *represents* or is known as a representation, and a statement of fact will support a claim for breach of warranty only if it is introduced with *warrants* or is known as a warranty. So under the restrictive version, failure to use *represents*, *warrants*, or both, or to otherwise explicitly characterize a statement of fact as a representation, a warranty, or both, should prevent that statement from being deemed a representation or a warranty, or both, respectively.

3.384 Stark has stated that she doesn't suggest that using *represents* or *warrants* is the only way to make something a representation or warranty. That means she in effect endorses the permissive remedies rationale. See Tina L. Stark, Comment to Kenneth A. Adams, *The Semantics Fallacy Underlying "Represents and Warrants"*, Adams on Contract Drafting (24 Sept. 2013, 2:38 PM), http://www.adamsdrafting.com/the-semantics-fallacy-underlying-represents-and-warrants/.

3.385   By contrast, Bryan Garner in effect endorses the restrictive remedies rationale. In the entry for *representations and warranties* in *Garner's Dictionary of Legal Usage*, at 775, Garner suggests that if a statement of fact is introduced by only *warrants* and not *represents*, it wouldn't constitute a representation supporting an action for misrepresentation: the drafter would be in a position to limit what sort of claims could be brought for an inaccurate statement of fact regardless of the nature of that statement of fact.

3.386   Both flavors of the remedies rationale fall short in several respects. First, *represents and warrants* is used in every kind of contract. It's well known that the law of warranties applies to the sale of goods, but even if you also consider the role of the law of warranties in negotiable instruments, bank deposits and collections, letters of credit, documents of title, and investment securities, many contracts that use *represents and warrants* would fall outside the scope of the law of warranties as it's generally understood. So treating as a warranty any contract statement of fact introduced by *warrants* or called a warranty would require extending the law of warranties to statements of fact to which the law of warranties as it's generally understood wouldn't apply. There's no principled basis for doing so.

3.387   Second, caselaw and, regarding *warranty*, the Uniform Commercial Code specify the elements of a claim for misrepresentation and a claim for breach of warranty. Allowing drafters to designate what constitutes a representation or a warranty just by saying so would render those requirements irrelevant.

3.388   Imagine that a contract contains this sentence: *Acme represents that it shall promptly replace defective Equipment.* Even though it uses *represents*, that sentence imposes an obligation, so according to caselaw on the elements of a claim for misrepresentation, it wouldn't constitute a representation supporting a claim for misrepresentation. It would elevate form over substance to suggest that use of *represents* would be enough to make that sentence a representation. (In fact, *Acme represents that* is "throat-clearing"; see 3.25.)

3.389   It would be equally bizarre to conclude, as the restrictive remedies rationale requires, that an intended remedy isn't available because it's not introduced by the appropriate verb. For example, if a party's statements of fact are introduced by neither *represents* nor *warrants*, according to the logic of the restrictive remedies rationale the counterparty would have no remedy, regardless of the nature of those statements. It would be hard to justify that.

3.390   Third, this manual is not aware of any U.S. caselaw supporting the notion that if you use *represents* in a sentence, what follows will as a matter of law constitute a representation supporting an action for misrepresentation, regardless of what the sentence says, or that if you use *warrants* in a sentence, what follows will as a matter of law constitute a warranty supporting an action for breach of warranty, regardless of what the sentence says.

3.391   As for the restrictive version of the remedies rationale, there's no meaningful support for the notion that to constitute a representation, a statement must be introduced by *represents* or called a representation, and to constitute a warranty, a statement must be introduced by *warrants* or called a warranty.

3.392   Instead, there's caselaw to the opposite effect, in that use of *represents* or *representations* in a contract hasn't precluded courts from holding that the statement in question is actually a warranty. See, e.g., *Aspect Systems, Inc. v. Lam Research Corp.*, No. CV 06-1620-PHX-NVW, 2008 WL 2705154, at *9 (D. Ariz. 26 June 2008) (describing as a "warranty" a contract provision introduced by the verb "represents"); *Quality Wash Group V, Ltd. v. Hallak*, 58 Cal. Rptr. 2d 592, 596 (Ct. App. 1996) (describing as a "warranty" a provision introduced by "makes the following representations"). And section 2-313(2) of the Uniform Commercial Code states that "[i]t is not necessary to the creation of an express warranty that the seller use formal words such as 'warrant' or 'guarantee' or that he have a specific intention to make a warranty."

3.393   Fourth, the semantics of the remedies rationale makes no sense. To permit the verb to have remedies implications, or to require it do so, is to impose on the verb a semantic function it doesn't have in standard English. It's unreasonable to expect readers to make that connection.

3.394   And fifth, what's the simplest explanation for prevalence of the couplet *represents and warrants*, as opposed to one or other verb, for introducing statements of fact other than those relating to goods? Not that after considering potential remedies if a dispute occurs, contract parties opt to make it explicit that inaccurate statements of fact could support an action for misrepresentation or an action for breach of warranty, or both.

3.395   Instead, if contract parties are presented with three options with ostensibly meaningful implications—*represents, warrants,* or *represents and warrants*—yet overwhelmingly choose *represents and warrants* regardless of the nature of the transaction, the simplest explanation is that they don't recognize they're making a choice.

3.396   That impression is reinforced by the way mergers-and-acquisitions contracts generally provide for indemnification as the exclusive remedy yet overwhelmingly use *represents and warrants*. If use of *represents and warrants* is an empty gesture there, economy of hypothesis suggests that it's an empty gesture elsewhere. It also follows that there's no reason to attribute significance to use of either *represents* or *warrants* alone.

3.397   So it's reasonable to conclude that in the United States, the remedies rationale for use of *represents* and *warrants* is of no practical relevance.

THE TIMEFRAME RATIONALE

3.398   The clearest articulation of the timeframe rationale for using *represents, warrants,* or both is that offered by the Section of Business Law of the American Bar Association in I *Model Stock Purchase Agreement with Commentary* (2d ed. 2011), which uses the phrase *represents and warrants*. At page 77, it says, "Representations are statements of past or existing facts and warranties are promises that existing or future facts are or will be true." If you take that at face value, it follows, according to I *Business Acquisitions* 170 (John W. Herz & Charles H. Baller, 2d ed. 1981), that "[a] party can, for instance, represent and warrant that as of a prior date his net worth was $75,000; he can also warrant that as of a future date his net worth will be that amount."

3.399   If one looks hard enough, one can find modest caselaw and other commentary that endorses the timeframe rationale. See, e.g., *Krys v. Henderson*, 69 S.E.2d 635, 637 (1952) ("Generally, warranties relate to future events, and representations to past or existing facts … ."). But the timeframe rationale suffers from flaws that render it untenable as an explanation of how one should use *represents* and *warrants* in contracts.

3.400   First, as with the remedies rationale, the timeframe rationale is inconsistent with the law of warranties, because it suggests that a statement of fact can be a warranty not just in contracts for the sale of goods and other contracts to which the law of warranties has been held to apply but in any kind of contract.

3.401   Second, one requirement of an action for misrepresentation is indeed that a party have made a false representation as to fact regarding a past event or present circumstance, but not a future event—when a statement as to future circumstances is made, there is no way to determine when it's made whether it's accurate or not. But nothing in the law of warranties suggests that to be a warranty a statement of fact must pertain only to existing or future facts. Instead, the Uniform Commercial Code § 2-313 says that "[a]ny affirmation of fact or promise made by the seller to the buyer which relates to the goods and becomes part of the basis of the bargain" is sufficient to create an express warranty.

3.402   And third, even if the law of warranties were to apply to every contract, and even if warranties were to pertain only to existing or future facts, the timeframe rationale would still fail because as a matter of semantics, it doesn't make sense.

3.403   For the timeframe rationale to apply to contract language, a drafter would have to choose the verb that introduces a statement of fact based on the nature of that fact. As the ABA's *Model Stock Purchase Agreement* suggests, that would be "a drafting nuisance"—drafters would have to use *represents* or *warrants* to introduce a statement of fact, depending on whether that fact is a past or existing fact or a future or existing fact, respectively. But more to the point, that exercise would be a charade. It would be evident from a statement of fact itself whether it's a past fact, existing fact, or future fact, so taking the time to make sure that the verb used to introduce that statement of fact matches its content would add no value. And the timeframe rationale suggests the bizarre result that if a statement of past fact were introduced by *warrants* instead of *represents*, it wouldn't constitute a past fact and so couldn't be used to support an action for misrepresentation.

3.404   So as an explanation for why contracts use the phrase *represents and warrants*, the timeframe rationale is as lacking as the remedies rationale.

3.405 Whereas in the United States, courts and practitioners mostly treat both *represents* and *warrants* as meaning the same thing when used to introduce a statement of fact, in England a different view prevails. There, it has been standard practice to use only *warrants*, the concern being that a claim for misrepresentation could give rise to the remedy of rescission, with the parties being returned to the situation they were in before they entered into the contract. By using only *warrants*, the party making statements of fact hopes to avoid making representations and so avoid being subject to a claim for misrepresentation.

3.406 This view was endorsed by the English High Court in *Sycamore Bidco Ltd v. Breslin* [2012] EWHC (Ch) 3443 (Eng.). Sycamore purchased the shares of a company from Breslin and another. After the transaction was consummated, Sycamore found errors in the company's audited accounts. The sellers had made statements regarding the accounts in the share purchase agreement, so Sycamore sued for breach of warranty and misrepresentation. The relevant language was introduced using the verb *warrant*, and the statements were called warranties. Sycamore argued that "the warranties are also capable of being representations so that, if there is a contravention of their terms, there is also a misrepresentation," but Justice Mann held that "I find that they are warranties only, and not representations," primarily because "[t]he warranties in this case are clearly, and at all times, described as such, and are nowhere described as representations." This is the restrictive remedies rationale, offered without explanation.

3.407 *Sycamore Bidco* isn't an anomaly. Another case to similar effect is *MAN Nutzfahrzeuge AG v. Freightliner Ltd* [2005] EWHC 2347, 2005 WL 2893816, at *32 (QBD (Comm Ct) 2005), where the court said, "By drafting the clauses in question as both representations and warranties the parties have attached different characteristics to the statements they contain which, depending on the circumstances, may give rise to different consequences and different measures of loss." And citing *Sycamore Bidco*, the Commercial Court adopted a similar approach in *Idemitsu Kosan Co Ltd v. Sumitomo Corporation* [2016] EWHC 1909 (Comm) (27 July 2016).

3.408 In fact, the restrictive remedies rationale has a long history in England. The 1603 case *Chandelor v. Lopus* 79 Eng. Rep. 3 (Ex. Ch. 1603) involved a dispute between the buyer and the seller of a bezoar stone—a concretion found in the gut of certain animals and believed by some to have occult qualities. The seller had "affirmed" to the buyer that this item was a bezoar stone. The court held that because the seller hadn't stated that he was "warranting" that the item was a bezoar stone, the buyer couldn't bring against the seller a claim for breach of warranty.

3.409 But English law is not settled on the matter. For example, the opinion in *Sycamore Bidco* discusses the 2009 High Court opinion by Justice Arnold in *Invertec Ltd v. De Mol Holding BV* [2009] EWHC 2471 (Ch). In that case, the defendants argued that because the claims were "all framed by reference to warranties" in the underlying share purchase agreement, the claimant couldn't bring a claim for misrepresentation. But the court held that "the warranties in question also amount to representations of fact." It continued (emphasis added):

> In those circumstances I cannot see any reason in principle why [the claimant] cannot claim that it was induced to enter into the agreement by *the representations made by those warranties* so as to found a misrepresentation claim if they were false, particularly if they were fraudulently made.

3.410 In other words, by finding that something called a warranty in the contract was also a representation supporting a misrepresentation remedy, Justice Arnold in effect rejected the restrictive remedies rationale. Justice Mann's perfunctory analysis in *Sycamore Bidco* provides no reason to consign *Invertec* to oblivion. *Sycamore Bidco* was greeted with deference by English practitioners, but a 2007 analysis by the London office of the international law firm Jones Day expresses little enthusiasm for the restrictive remedies rationale:

> In reality, the simple categorization of a statement as a warranty (without any further provisions) probably has little bearing on whether the statement is susceptible to being treated as a representation for purposes of [the Misrepresentation Act of 1967].

3.411 To summarize, English courts and practitioners differ from those in the United States by giving significant but not overwhelming support to the restrictive remedies rationale. Yet for English contracts, the remedies rationale suffers from some of the same weaknesses it does for U.S. contracts: First, it applies the law of warranties where it doesn't belong. Second, allowing drafters to designate what constitutes a representation or a warranty just by saying so would make a mockery of the substantive law regarding what's required to bring a claim for misrepresentation and what's required to bring a claim for breach of warranty. And third, in terms of semantics, it doesn't make sense.

Statements of Fact—Using *States* and Addressing Remedies Directly

3.412 The main problem with the verbs *represents* and *warrants*, used together or apart, is that despite lack of any plausible basis, some think they imply particular remedies. That confusion could spread, leading to time wasted in negotiations, as well as time and money wasted in contract disputes that could have been avoided.

3.413 And by using *represents* or *warrants* or both to introduce statements of fact, one unnecessarily injects jurisprudence terms of art into contracts. That makes contracts less clear, even for those who aren't inclined to see the verbs as having remedies implications. (Regarding use of terms of art generally, see 1.7.)

3.414 For U.S. contracts, one could take the position that because a no-reliance provision would provide greater protection, there's no need to concern oneself with whether introducing statements of fact with *represents and warrants* could result in unwanted tort liability. See Glenn D. West, *Reps and Warranties Redux—A New English Case, An Old Debate Regarding* *a Distinction With or Without a Difference*, Global Private Equity Watch (2 Aug. 2016), https://privateequity.weil.com/insights/reps-warranties-redux-new-english-case-old-debate-regarding-distinction-without-difference/. That leave-well-enough-alone approach might make sense for high-value, one-time transactions, where efficiency and clarity aren't high priorities. But with lower-value, high-volume deals, simpler, clearer contracts allow you to close deals faster, less expensively, and with less risk and less lawyering. In that context, *represents and warrants* is more of a nuisance than it is in the big-deal world.

3.415   There's a simple two-part alternative to *represents and warrants*: use *states* to introduce facts and address remedies directly.

USING *STATES*

3.416   The first part of the solution aims to eliminate confusion: Don't use *represents*, *warrants*, or the phrase *represents and warrants* to introduce statements of fact. Instead, introduce statements of fact using the simplest verb available, namely *states*. Other alternatives, such as *asserts* and *confirms*, carry unnecessary rhetorical baggage. And use of *states* suggests use of the corresponding noun phrase *statement of fact* instead of *representation* and *warranty*.

3.417   When introducing a series of statements of fact, say [*Party name*] *states that the following facts are accurate*, if only to ensure that you have a full independent clause before the colon that follows (see 4.37). One wouldn't need to signal that an inaccurate statement of fact can support a remedy, just as one doesn't need to signal that failure to comply with an obligation can support a remedy.

3.418   Lawyers on one or both sides of a transaction might be concerned that *states* has unknown implications for remedies. You could allay those fears by adding this to a contract: *The verb used to introduce a statement of fact in this agreement does not affect the remedies available for inaccuracy of that statement of fact.*

3.419   A drafter stuck with using *represents* or *warrants* or both could also use that sentence. That situation might arise if using *states* would meet too much resistance or provoke too much discussion. That's more likely to be the case when you propose revising the other side's draft to use *states* as opposed to using *states* in your own draft.

ADDRESSING REMEDIES DIRECTLY

3.420   The second part of the solution to problems posed by *represents* and *warrants* aims to establish clear meaning: If remedies are an issue, address remedies explicitly. Putting one's faith instead in the smoke-and-mirrors of any combination of *represents* and *warrants* is irresponsible.

3.421   Instead of using *represents and warrants* to introduce statements of fact, a drafter who embraces the remedies rationale could achieve the same effect by stating that each party may bring a claim for misrepresentation, a claim for breach of warranty, or both if the other party makes inaccurate statements of fact. And instead of using just *warrants*, a drafter who embraces the restrictive remedies rationale could achieve the same effect by stating that each party is precluded from bringing a claim for misrepresentation if the other party makes inaccurate statements of fact. One could also make it explicit that each party may instead bring a claim for breach of warranty. (The mirror-image of that provision would express the restrictive-remedies-rationale equivalent of using just *represents*.)

3.422   Electing one remedy over the other might offer advantages. For example, a claimant might prefer bringing a misrepresentation claim over a breach-of-warranty claim if doing so offers a longer statute of limitations or seems likely to permit a claim for a greater amount damages, even if the claimant would have to meet a greater burden to prevail.

3.423   But for five reasons, the utility of such provisions is uncertain. First, the likelihood of being able to enforce such provisions is mixed. Saying that a party may bring a particular kind of claim doesn't guarantee that a court would find that a party had met the requirements for that kind of claim. But courts in the United States and England generally accept that parties may exclude remedies by contract, subject to a fairness or reasonableness standard.

3.424   Second, such provisions are limited in scope. At least in the United States, a simple statement that a party is precluded from bringing a claim for misrepresentation presumably allows a claimant seeking to impose extra-contractual liability plenty of room to make mischief. The best way to protect against that is through a no-reliance provision; see 3.414.

3.425   Third, rote limiting of remedies might not make sense for a given transaction. For example, the English aversion to rescission as a remedy, regardless of the context, has the merit of simplicity but doesn't consider that rescission might sometimes be an appropriate remedy for either party, depending on the circumstances.

3.426   Fourth, for many contract parties, considering the potential sources of dispute and the remedies implications of any dispute could be distracting, time-consuming, and ultimately speculative.

3.427   And fifth, if a party wishes to control remedies, it might well elect to do so more simply and assertively by providing for indemnification or liquidated damages or by imposing limits on liability, bearing in mind that doing so effectively poses a different set of challenges.

3.428   But those issues are beyond the scope of this manual. What's relevant is that instead of using *represents*, *warrants*, or both with the aim of including or excluding particular remedies, it would be clearer to express the intended meaning explicitly, although it's a separate question whether doing so would be worthwhile.

3.429   For a more detailed version of this analysis of *represents and warrants*, see Kenneth A. Adams, *Eliminating the Phrase* Represents and Warrants *from Contracts*, 16 Tennessee Journal of Business Law 203 (2015).

Statements of Fact—Alternatives To

3.430   Drafters routinely state as facts matters more logically handled using another category of contract language.

3.431   For example, it doesn't make sense, strictly speaking, to have a party make a statement of fact regarding something over which it has no control. You could have the seller state in an asset purchase agreement that on the closing date the market price of unobtanium will be above a stated dollar amount. And doing so would in theory give the buyer a claim for damages if on the closing date the market price were less than the stated amount. But because the seller has no control over the market price, it would be rash to assume that a court would permit such a claim rather than treating it as a condition to closing. Having a party make a statement of fact regarding something over which it has no control is in effect a form of risk allocation. It would be clearer to provide for explicit risk allocation in the form of indemnification, liquidated damages, or a breakup fee.

Statements of Fact—Some Related Terminology

3.432   One breaches an obligation, but not a statement of fact (whether you call it that or a representation). Instead, a statement of fact is accurate or inaccurate. If Abigail says that it's Monday but in fact it's Tuesday, Abigail hasn't "breached" anything. Instead, she's made an inaccurate statement.

3.433   This distinction is worth pointing out for its own sake, but it might also help drafters avoid a further problem, namely inappropriately lumping statements of fact with obligations. It's commonplace for contracts to provide for the possibility of cure of not only breached obligations but also "breached" representations. But if you make an inaccurate statement of fact, you can't subsequently make it accurate.

3.434   In the same vein, a statement of fact is either accurate or inaccurate—it cannot *become* inaccurate.

3.435   Regarding contract references to survival of statements of fact, see 13.781.

Acknowledgments

3.436   Use *acknowledge* if the declaring party is accepting as accurate a fact offered by another party:

> Acme *acknowledges* that the Consultant is in the business of providing services and consulting advice to others.

> The parties *acknowledge* that breach of any obligation stated in this section 10.2 will cause irreparable harm to the Disclosing Party and that monetary damages will not provide an adequate remedy.

> Each Shareholder *acknowledges* that the Merger Shares have not been registered under the Securities Act and are instead being issued under an exemption from registration.

3.437 Having a party acknowledge a fact would preclude it from later challenging that fact. *Understand, accept,* and *concede* are used as alternatives to *acknowledge.* In the interest of consistency (see 1.63), stick with *acknowledge.*

RELATION TO RECITALS

3.438 An alternative to having Party X acknowledge that a fact asserted by Party Y is correct would be to include that fact in the recitals. (Recitals too contain assertions of fact, but they don't need language of declaration—it's clear enough without it that the parties are making the recitals jointly.) If a fact relates to the background to the transaction, it would fit in the recitals (see 2.131). But if the fact is important, have the declaring party acknowledge that fact in the body of the contract (see 2.135).

INAPPROPRIATELY USED TO INTRODUCE OTHER LANGUAGE

3.439 Use *acknowledge* only to introduce a fact asserted by another party. Don't use it to introduce language that itself falls within a category of contract language—don't indulge in throat-clearing (see 3.25). In the following two examples, *acknowledge* is used inappropriately to introduce language of obligation and language of policy, respectively:

> Each Lender ~~acknowledges that it~~ shall conduct its own independent investigation of the financial condition and affairs of each Borrower.

> ~~The parties acknowledge that this~~ [read *This*] agreement does not supersede, modify, or otherwise affect the terms of any stock options that Acme granted the Executive before the date of this agreement.

RHETORICAL EMPHASIS

3.440 Don't indulge in rhetorical emphasis (see 1.58) by using *unconditionally acknowledge* or *expressly acknowledge.*

USED WITH OTHER VERBS

3.441 It never makes sense to use *acknowledge* with another verb. For example, rather than say *Acme acknowledges and agrees that,* use *acknowledge* on its own or omit the entire phrase, if it constitutes throat-clearing (see 3.439). (Regarding *agrees that,* see 3.32.)

LANGUAGE OF INTENTION

3.442 Some aspects of a contract relationship can't be established by the parties in a contract. Instead, it's up to the courts to make the relevant determination. But it can be helpful for the parties to address such issues in a contract, using language of intention.

3.443 For example, it's commonplace for consulting agreements to contain a provision regarding the consultant's status as an independent contractor rather than an employee. What category of contract language should you use for such provisions? If you consider the possibilities, it's clear that language of intention is the logical choice.

TABLE 14 ▪ **LANGUAGE OF INTENTION**

[14-1]	✓✓	The parties intend that the Consultant will be an independent contractor.
[14-1a]	✗✗	The Consultant shall be … .
[14-1b]	✗	The Consultant will be … .
[14-1c]	✗	The Consultant acknowledges that she will be … .
[14-1d]	✗	The Consultant believes that she will be … .
[14-1e]	✗✗	The Consultant shall be construed to be … .
[14-1f]	✗	The Consultant is to be construed to be … .

3.444 Obviously, it wouldn't make sense to use language of obligation, as in [14-1a]—whether the consultant is an independent contractor isn't something that's entirely within the control of the consultant.

3.445 You could use language of policy, as in [14-1b], but whether a consultant is an independent contractor or an employee isn't something the parties can decide among themselves. Instead, it depends on the governing law and the nature of the services performed, not on the label the parties choose to apply to the relationship.

3.446 Language of declaration, or more specifically an acknowledgment, as in [14-1c], wouldn't work either: you acknowledge facts, and whether someone is an independent contractor isn't an established fact that a consultant can acknowledge at the outset of the relationship.

3.447 A statement of fact using *believes* (see 13.113), as in [14-1d], would be inappropriate, as such a statement would express the opinion of a party regarding a legal circumstance on the date of the agreement. Whether someone is a consultant or an employee can't be determined on the date of the agreement—how the relationship develops is a factor.

3.448 In such contexts, drafters routinely use *shall be construed*, as in [14-1e], but besides failing the *has a duty* test (see 3.74), it's unrealistic, as it in effect seeks to impose a duty on a nonparty. And not just any nonparty, but one that will do what it feels appropriate, thank you very much—a court. Using instead *is to be construed*, as in [14-1f], is more discreet but attempts to achieve the same result. (Regarding using verb structures to say how a court is to conduct itself, see 3.470.)

3.449 The only remaining possibility is [14-1]—language of intention. In other words, the parties intend that the consultant will be an independent contractor, but if the nature of the relationship were ever to become an issue, it would be up to a court to decide the consultant's status, based on the law and the facts.

3.450   Although a consultant's status would depend on the totality of the circumstances rather than on what label the parties apply, addressing the consultant's status in a contract using language of intention would nevertheless be worthwhile, because a court might consider what the contract says. See 19 *Williston on Contracts* § 54:2 (including among the factors that courts consider "whether the parties believe they are creating the relation of master and servant").

3.451   Aspects of a contract relationship are subject to judicial scrutiny in another respect. For example, in the United States, a court might override the parties' choice of governing law because the state specified doesn't bear a reasonable relationship to the transaction, or because applying the law of that state would be contrary to public policy of the forum state. But this and analogous instances differ from those discussed in 3.442–.443. In the latter instances, the nature of the relationship would be entirely a question of law and fact, whereas in the former, the selection of the parties applies, unless it fails to meet minimum legal requirements. Given that distinction, it would be awkward to insist on using for the governing-law provision language of intention rather than language of policy: "The parties intend that the laws of the state of New York will govern ... ." When the choice specified by the parties in a contract applies unless a court decides that it fails to meet minimum requirements, stick with language of policy.

LANGUAGE OF RECOMMENDATION

3.452   One side to a transaction might have significantly greater bargaining power than the other side; that's usually the case in, for example, a contract between a company and one of its employees. The party with the greater bargaining power might take the opportunity to include in the contract a recommendation to the other party, as in [15-1]. Presumably, with such recommendations a party seeks to avoid dispute by pointing out something the other party might otherwise miss. The alternative—letting the other party figure out such matters for itself—might ultimately work to the disadvantage of the party with the greater bargaining power, because the disparity in bargaining power might cause a court to cut the weaker party some slack.

TABLE 15 ▪ LANGUAGE OF RECOMMENDATION		
[15-1]	✓✓	The Company recommends that the Participant consult with his or her personal legal advisor if the Participant is uncertain whether the insider rules apply.
[15-1a]	✗	The Company advises the Participant to consult with his or her personal legal advisor ... .

3.453   Because *recommends* is a verb of speaking, don't use *hereby* with *recommends* (see 3.373).

3.454 You could convey the meaning of [15-1] using *advises*, as in [15-1a], but *recommends* is preferable, because having one party give another advice suggests a relationship involving trust. Other possibilities for language of recommendation include *advises*, *encourages*, and *reminds*.

3.455 An alternative to language of recommendation is having Party A acknowledge that Party B has recommended that Party A do something or other, or having Party A release Party B from any liability arising from Party A's failure to do something or other.

SHALL AND *MAY* IN RESTRICTIVE RELATIVE CLAUSES

3.456 *Shall* and *may* are used inappropriately in a construction that's unrelated to the categories of contract language—the restrictive relative clause. This topic is nevertheless included in this chapter because inappropriate uses of *shall* and *may* detract from appropriate use and might cause confusion.

Use of *Shall*

3.457 In [16-1], the restrictive relative clause is *that Acme specifies in writing*. Drafters sometimes use *shall* in restrictive relative clauses, as in [16-1a], as an alternative to *will*, out of a misguided fear that the present tense cannot be used to refer to events that will happen.

3.458 But sometimes this use of *shall* might represent an attempt to address a legitimate issue. Because [16-2] uses a stative verb (*owns*) rather than a dynamic verb (see 3.322), it's not clear whether the transfer restrictions apply only to shares owned on the date of the agreement or whether shares acquired subsequently are also included. Referring to *Shares that it shall own* isn't, however, the way to resolve this ambiguity; instead, as in [16-2b], make it clear that after-acquired shares are included.

TABLE 16 ■ MISUSE OF *SHALL* AND *MAY* IN RESTRICTIVE RELATIVE CLAUSES

[16-1]	✓✓	Jones shall pay the Purchase Price by wire transfer to any account that Acme specifies in writing.
[16-1a]	✗✗	… to any account that Acme shall specify in writing.
[16-2]	✓	Other than under the terms of this agreement, no Stockholder may transfer any Shares it owns.
[16-2a]	✗✗	… any Shares it shall own.
[16-2b]	✓✓	… any Shares it currently owns or any additional Shares it acquires.
[16-3]	✓✓	If Acme sells Assets to one or more buyers that Roe introduces to Acme …
[16-3a]	✗✗	… one or more buyers that Roe may introduce to Acme …

Use of *May*

3.459   In [16-3], the restrictive relative clause is *that Roe introduces to Acme*. If it were to include *may*, as in [16-3a], it's likely that the intended meaning of *may* would be *might*, to acknowledge that Roe might introduce no buyers to Acme. In effect, the restrictive relative clause would express the meaning *one or more buyers, if any, that Roe introduces to Acme*. But it would be redundant to add that meaning—even without it, the conditional clause in [16-3] reflects that Roe might not introduce any buyers to Acme. (For another example of this use of *may*, see 3.218.)

3.460   But in this context, *may* not only adds clutter, it also adds potential confusion. That's because another possible meaning of the restrictive relative clause in [16-3a] is *one or more buyers that Roe might introduce to Acme, whether or not Roe actually introduces them to Acme*. In other words, to fall within the scope of the restrictive relative clause, someone would simply have to be a plausible prospective buyer.

3.461   That meaning seems unlikely, in terms of how transactions work, but at least one court interpreted that way a restrictive relative clause containing *may*. *383 Madison LLC v. Bear Stearns Companies, Inc.*, No. 601570/08 2008, WL 5380443 (N.Y. Sup. Ct. 18 Dec. 2008), involved a dispute over the scope of an exemption to a right of first offer in a ground lease. The court held that because the exemption referred to an entity "with which Tenant may be merged," the exemption applied "even to those situations where a potential merger is contemplated, and it is not contingent upon the actual occurrence of a merger." In other words, the court attributed to *may* in the restrictive relative clause at issue the significance described in 3.460.

3.462   So not only does using *may* in restrictive relative clauses create ambiguity, the alternative meanings are themselves unpromising—in one meaning *may* is redundant, and the other meaning is unlikely. Most likely omitting *may* would allow you to express the meaning you intend. If not, find some other way to say what you want to say.

NOT A CATEGORY OF CONTRACT LANGUAGE: ASSUMPTIONS

3.463   A standard feature of statements of work in commercial contracts is sets of assumptions. That poses a drafting problem, in that a statement of work forms part of the contract to which it's attached, yet assumptions don't fall within the categories of contract language proposed in this manual.

3.464   The point of entering into a contract is that it forces the parties to be explicit about their transaction—there should be no place for assumptions. A set of statement-of-work assumptions is likely to raise questions: What happens if that which is assumed doesn't happen? Is the assumption in fact a condition? Is it an obligation? Or something else?

3.465   It would make sense to recast each statement-of-work assumption using whichever category of contract language is appropriate. That would likely pose a challenge for an organization's contract process, because it's standard for statements of work and the contract proper to be handled by different groups. It's likely that revising assumptions would, at least initially, result in more work being imposed on whoever handles the contract.

SELECTING WHICH CATEGORY OF CONTRACT LANGUAGE TO USE

3.466 Once you're attuned to the categories of contract language, it becomes routine to ask yourself, when drafting a provision, what category of contract language you should use. Working through the possibilities gives you a better understanding of what's at stake, making you better equipped to address the issues raised. So it's not only the reader who benefits from adept handling of the categories of contract language but also the drafter and, by extension, the client.

Amending a Contract

3.467 Determining how to say what's required to amend a contract provides an opportunity to consider which category of contract language is appropriate. Here are the possibilities:

- *Language of discretion.* The parties may amend this agreement only by a writing signed by both parties. [Using language of limited discretion presupposes the possibility of breach (if that discretion is exceeded) and a remedy for breach. That doesn't make sense in this context.]

- *Language of prohibition.* The parties shall not amend this agreement, except by written agreement of the parties. [Using language of obligation presupposes the possibility of breach and a remedy for breach. That doesn't make sense in this context.]

- *Condition using language of obligation.* To be effective, an amendment to this agreement must be in writing and signed by both parties. [This works.]

- *Language of policy.* An amendment to this agreement will be effective only if it is in writing and signed by both parties. [This works too. To see other ways this could be phrased, see 3.333.]

Giving Notice

3.468 Consider these three alternatives:

- *Language of obligation.* Jones shall submit any Dispute Notice no later than five Business Days after the related invoice is delivered. [This suggests that if Jones submits a dispute notice after five business days, it will be in breach, giving the other party a remedy for breach. That wouldn't make sense: the only appropriate response to late submission of a dispute notice is that Jones isn't entitled to dispute the invoice.]

- *Language of policy.* If Jones submits a Dispute Notice more than five business days after the related invoice is delivered, that Dispute

Notice will be void. [This conveys the intended meaning, but it addresses only what happens if Jones is late in submitting a dispute notice, and *is void* is somewhat bureaucratic in tone.]

- *Language of obligation used to express a condition.* To dispute an invoice, Jones must submit a Dispute Notice no later than five Business Days after the related invoice is delivered. [This is the best choice, because it avoids the shortcomings of the other alternatives.]

Unreasonably Withholding Consent

3.469   How should a contract address a landlord's unreasonably withholding consent to the tenant's assigning the lease? Do you prohibit the landlord from unreasonably withholding consent, or do you allow the tenant to assign if the landlord unreasonably withholds consent? Here are your choices:

- *Language of Prohibition.* The Tenant shall not assign this lease without the Landlord's consent, which the Landlord shall not unreasonably withhold. [This gives the tenant a remedy for breach if the landlord unreasonably withholds consent. Suing the landlord might not be a realistic option for the tenant, particularly if the contract states that the only remedy for breach is that the landlord will be deemed to have given consent.]

- *Carveout from Language of Prohibition.* The Tenant shall not assign this lease without the Landlord's consent, unless the Landlord unreasonably withholds consent. [This would allow the tenant to assign if the landlord is unreasonable. The landlord would be in a position to prevent the new tenant from occupying the premises, so this version wouldn't prevent a fight, but it might give the tenant leverage in negotiations.]

- *Language of Discretion.* The Tenant shall not assign this lease without the Landlord's consent, except that the Tenant may assign this lease if the Landlord unreasonably withholds consent. [This expresses the same meaning as the previous alternative, but more clearly. (For an explanation why, see 3.327–.332.)]

Stating How a Court Is to Conduct Itself

3.470   Whether or not they realize it, one way drafters try to preempt judicial discretion is by specifying in a contract what a court may do, isn't authorized to do, or must do. One example of that, [14-1f], using *is to be construed*, is discussed at 3.448, but this urge manifests itself in different ways.

3.471   Various verb structures are used to ostensibly grant a court discretion. Here's an incomplete list, with *interpret* used as a placeholder for different verbs, *interpret* and *construe* being the most common:

- *the court may interpret*
- *the court will/shall have the right to*

- *the court will/shall be entitled to interpret*
- *the court will/shall be allowed to interpret*
- *the court will/shall have the power to interpret*

3.472 All but the first of the above examples is suboptimal, for reasons discussed in this chapter. (The same applies to most of the other examples in this section.) Here's an example that uses one of these structures:

> The courts shall be entitled to modify the duration and scope of any restriction contained herein to the extent such restriction would otherwise be unenforceable, and such restriction as modified shall be enforceable.

3.473 To show that the above list is incomplete, here's an example that uses a different verb structure to say that a court has the authority to rule on the law and facts of a lawsuit:

> Each party hereby agrees that any such court shall have in personam jurisdiction over it and consents to service of process in any manner authorized by Nevada law.

3.474 Similarly, various verb structures aim to prohibit a court from doing something:

- *the court shall/may not construe*
- *no court shall/may construe*
- *X shall/may not be construed as*
- *neither X nor Y is to be construed as*
- *X is not to be construed as*
- *nothing in this agreement is to be construed as*

3.475 And there are other ways to say that a court is prohibited from doing something. Here are two examples:

> No prior drafts of this agreement or any negotiations regarding the terms contained in those drafts shall be admissible in any court to vary or interpret the terms of this agreement.

> The principal of ejusdem generis shall not be used to limit the scope of the category of things illustrated by the items mentioned in a clause introduced by the word "including."

3.476 Various verb structures aim to say that a court must do something:

- *the court shall construe*
- *the court will be required to construe*
- *X is to be construed*
- *X shall be construed*

3.477 That list, too, is incomplete. Here's an example of a different structure used to say that a court must act a certain way:

> The Service Provider agrees that in the event of such violation, Acme will, in addition to any other rights and remedies, be entitled to equitable relief by way of temporary or permanent injunction and to such other remedy as any court of competent jurisdiction may deem just and proper.

3.478 On encountering this sort of provision, a judge is likely to think, "Says who!" Contract parties have no basis for telling a court how to act, and a court might well ignore or explicitly reject anything that suggests as much. A case before the Delaware Court of Chancery, *AM General Holdings LLC v. Renco Group, Inc.*, No. CV 7639-VCN, 2015 WL 9487922, at *3 (Del. Ch. 29 Dec. 2015), provides an example of a court doing just that. A party to a contract sought a preliminary injunction, basing its claim in part on the following provision:

> The parties hereto agree that any party by whom this Agreement is enforceable shall be entitled to specific performance in addition to any other appropriate relief or remedy. Such party may ... apply to a court of competent jurisdiction for ... injunctive or such other relief as such court may deem just and proper in order to enforce this Agreement or prevent any violation hereof and, to the extent permitted by applicable law, each party waives any objection to the imposition of such relief.

3.479 This in effect requires that a court grant specific performance. The Delaware Court of Chancery denied the motion for a preliminary injunction, offering this explanation:

> Parties, however, cannot in advance agree to assure themselves (and thereby impair the Court's exercise of its well-established discretionary role in the context of assessing the reasonableness of interim injunctive relief) the benefit of expedited judicial review through the use of a simple contractual stipulation that a breach of that contract would constitute irreparable harm.

3.480 Drafters can aim for the same result without appearing to boss the court around. For example, instead of saying in a severability provision that a court must interpret the contract in a certain way if it holds that a provision is unenforceable, you could introduce the provision as follows:

> The parties acknowledge that if a dispute between the parties arises out of this agreement or the subject matter of this agreement, they would want the court to interpret this agreement as follows:

3.481 This approach has the benefit of putting the focus on the parties, not on the court.

Arbitration Provision

3.482 For another example of the diagnostic value of the categories-of-contract-language approach, see 3.104.

CHAPTER 4

LAYOUT

4.1   How the text of the body of the contract is formatted and arranged helps determine how easy it is to read.

THE *MSCD* ENUMERATION SCHEMES

4.2   This manual recommends two enumeration schemes—the "*MSCD* first-line-indent scheme" and the "*MSCD* hanging-indent scheme." Each comes in two versions, "articles" and "sections," depending on whether the sections are grouped into articles. See sample 3 for the "articles" version of the first-line indent scheme; see sample 4 for the "articles" version of the hanging-indent scheme.

4.3   The first-line-indent scheme is a more systematic version of the scheme (with many variants) used in the bigger U.S. law firms for bigger transactions. The hanging-indent scheme is a more systematic version of the kind of scheme favored for commercial transactions and favored in particular outside the United States. The first-line-indent scheme makes more efficient use of space; the hanging-indent scheme is easier to navigate. Both are logical, so take your pick.

4.4   The rest of this chapter explains why the two *MSCD* schemes look the way they do. It first considers aspects that are common to both schemes, then it considers what distinguishes them.

THE COMPONENTS OF THE BODY OF THE CONTRACT

4.5   The body of the contract is composed of sections (which can be grouped into articles), subsections, and enumerated clauses. Subdividing contract text in this manner makes it much easier to read, permits cross-referencing, and helps readers to find their way around the document.

4.6   Don't use footnotes in contracts. Footnotes make a contract harder to read and can lead readers to think that the footnote text is of lesser significance.

Articles

4.7   Whether to group into articles all sections that share a theme is a function of how long the contract is. Consider grouping sections into articles once you have more than 25 or so sections.

SAMPLE 3 ■ *MSCD* FIRST-LINE-INDENT ENUMERATION SCHEME, ARTICLES VERSION

Article 1
SALE OF ASSETS

    1.1   **Acquired Assets.** (a) Mercury hereby sells to Stratford the following assets as they exist on the date of this agreement (the "**Acquired Assets**"):

(1)   all of Mercury's accounts, notes, and other receivables (including accounts receivable) relating to the Collectibles Business, whether or not accrued and whether or not billed, as described on schedule 1.1(a)(1) (the "**Accounts Receivable**");

(2)   all goodwill associated with the Collectibles Business and all of Mercury's claims and causes of action relating to the assets and current and former customers of the Collectibles Business;

(3)   all inventory listed on schedule 1.1(a)(3);

(4)   all of Mercury's rights under each Contract relating to the Collectibles Business, each of which is listed on schedule 1.1(a)(5); and

(5)   all Mercury lists relating to the Acquired Assets and the Collectibles Business, including the Customer List.

    (b)   The assets to be conveyed to Stratford must be adjusted to reflect, in accordance with GAAP, the principle that all income and expenses attributable to the period after the Effective Date are for the account of Stratford, subject to the Management Agreement.

    1.2   **Purchase Price.** Stratford shall transfer to Mercury the following as the aggregate purchase price for the Acquired Assets (the "**Purchase Price**"):

(1)   in accordance with the stock grant agreement dated the date of this agreement between Stratford and Mercury in the form of exhibit A (the "**Stock Grant Agreement**"), shares of capital stock of Stratford;

(2)   the warrant agreement in the form of exhibit B (the "**Warrant**"); and

(3)   a cash payment of $100,000.

    1.3   **Assumed Liabilities.** Stratford hereby assumes and shall discharge when due in accordance with their terms the debts, obligations, and liabilities of Mercury listed on schedule 1.3 (the "**Assumed Liabilities**").

4.8   Some contracts use the term *section* for a group of sections. But with that approach, a reference to *section 1*, considered in isolation, could refer to a single provision or to a group of provisions. Using instead *article* distinguishes the whole from its constituent parts.

4.9   UK drafters are partial to using *clause* instead of both *article* and *section*. But in general usage *clause* refers to a part of a sentence—in particular, this manual uses the term *enumerated clause* (see 4.32)—so also using *clause* instead of *article* and *section* would result in *clause* conveying three meanings.

4.10   Give each article a simple, all-encompassing heading, using all capitals; see sample 3. All-capitals text is harder to read (see 16.19), but that's not an issue when it's used for only a few words. Using *Miscellaneous* as an article heading is acceptable—it's generally understood that it refers to a group of "boilerplate" provisions addressing governing law, notices, and other such matters.

4.11   Use digits, not words—*article 1*, not *article one*. Use Arabic rather than Roman numerals for article numbers—they're easier to read. Don't use the multiple-numeration system—use *article 1*, not *article 1.0*.

4.12   In some contracts, the first article is enumerated *article 0* (zero). Starting sequences with zero is a feature of mathematics and programming, but there's no good reason to use it for contract enumeration schemes. Perhaps it's an inside joke.

SAMPLE 4   ■   *MSCD* HANGING-INDENT ENUMERATION SCHEME, ARTICLES VERSION

Article 1
SALE OF ASSETS

1.1   **Acquired Assets**

(a)   Mercury hereby sells to Stratford the following assets as they exist on the date of this agreement (the "**Acquired Assets**"):

(1)   all of Mercury's accounts, notes, and other receivables (including accounts receivable) relating to the Collectibles Business, whether or not accrued and whether or not billed, as described on schedule 1.1(a)(1) (the "**Accounts Receivable**");

(2)   all goodwill associated with the Collectibles Business and all of Mercury's claims and causes of action relating to the assets and current and former customers of the Collectibles Business;

(3)   all inventory listed on schedule 1.1(a)(3);

(4)   all of Mercury's rights under each Contract relating to the Collectibles Business, each of which is listed on schedule 1.1(a)(5); and

(5)   all Mercury lists relating to the Acquired Assets and the Collectibles Business, including the Customer List.

(b)   The assets to be conveyed to Stratford must be adjusted to reflect, in accordance with GAAP, the principle that all income and expenses attributable to the period after the Effective Date are for the account of Stratford, subject to the Management Agreement.

1.2   **Purchase Price**

Stratford shall transfer to Mercury the following as the aggregate purchase price for the Acquired Assets (the "**Purchase Price**"):

(1)   in accordance with the stock grant agreement dated the date of this agreement between Stratford and Mercury in the form of exhibit A (the "**Stock Grant Agreement**"), shares of capital stock of Stratford;

(2)   the warrant agreement in the form of exhibit B (the "**Warrant**"); and

(3)   a cash payment of $100,000.

1.3   **Assumed Liabilities**

Stratford hereby assumes and shall discharge when due in accordance with their terms the debts, obligations, and liabilities of Mercury listed on schedule 1.3 (the "**Assumed Liabilities**").

Sections

FUNCTION

4.13　A section contains provisions relating to a particular topic. In the United States the term *section* is standard. It's a better choice than a UK alternative, *clause* (see 4.9).

4.14　In the boilerplate at the end of a contract, provisions addressing unrelated topics are sometimes lumped together in one section. Because that practice can make it harder for readers to find a particular provision, use it only when the provisions in question are sufficiently brief that giving each provision its own section would waste space. Take care when combining disparate provisions in a single section, because the context of one provision could influence interpretation of another provision in the same section. See, e.g., *Williams v. CDP, Inc.*, No. 10-1396, 2012 WL 959343 (4th Cir. 22 Mar. 2012).

4.15　Don't use subsections in such omnibus sections—if the provisions are substantial enough for each to be given its own subsection, then they're substantial enough to be turned into sections. Don't combine more than two unrelated provisions in a single section—the added economy is more than offset by the potential for confusion. And give such sections an appropriate heading (see 4.23).

ENUMERATION

4.16　Number each section. Don't add *Section* in front of each section number—it takes up space without providing any benefit. Don't bold section numbers. If sections aren't grouped into articles, number them consecutively (*1*, *2*, *3*, not *1.0*, *2.0*, *3.0*). (Whether you put a period after the section number depends on whether you're using the first-line-indent scheme or the hanging-indent scheme; see 4.55, 4.62.) If they're grouped into articles, number them using the multiple-numeration system (the sections of article 1 being numbered *1.1*, *1.2*, *1.3*, not *1.01*, *1.02*, *1.03*, with the unnecessary extra zero, or *1.1.*, *1.2.*, *1.3.*, with the superfluous extra period); see sample 3.

4.17　For section numbers, use the automatic-numbering function in word-processing software, or use specialized paragraph-numbering software. Use it also for subsections (see 4.27) and tabulated enumerated clauses (see 4.41). Doing so would spare you having to renumber provisions whenever you add, delete, or move an enumerated block of text.

4.18　Some settlement agreements—presumably ones drafted by litigators—enumerate sections using *FIRST:*, *SECOND:*, *THIRD:*, and so on, as if the contract were an old-fashioned pleading. Don't do that.

4.19　One school of thought has it that if an article contains just one section, you shouldn't enumerate that section. This manual recommends instead that you enumerate each such section, treating each article as a repository of one or more sections. That results in consistent enumeration throughout the contract. And if you cross-reference such a section, calling it *section 5.1* would give the reader a better idea of what to expect, compared with calling it *article 5*.

HEADINGS

4.20   Give each section a heading consisting of a bolded word or short phrase. Such headings make it easier to find one's way around a document. Use headline-style capitalization (see *The Chicago Manual of Style*, at 8.159).

4.21   The alternatives to bold are unappealing: Underlining is a hangover from typewriter days (see 16.21). Using all capitals would be too strident and harder to read (see 16.19). And adding italics to bold would be an unnecessary embellishment.

4.22   Many headings recur in contract after contract. Certain headings, such as *Arbitration* or *Confidentiality*, are a straightforward reflection of a section's contents. Others, such as *Further Assurances*, are cryptic terms of art. If you create a heading, make it clear and brief. Don't use a heading that seems to promise more than the section actually delivers or is otherwise misleading. (See 13.806 regarding using *Termination for Convenience* as a section heading.) Courts have refused to enforce provisions with uninformative or misleading headings, although that would seem unlikely in the case of a contract between ostensibly sophisticated parties represented by counsel. Longer contracts often include a provision stating that headings are for convenience only and are not intended to affect meaning, but such provisions are of questionable value (see 15.17).

4.23   If a section addresses two distinct issues (see 4.14), you could give it a heading consisting of a word or short phrase for each issue, separated by a semicolon (such as *Amendment; Waiver*).

4.24   Although *MISCELLANEOUS* is acceptable as an article heading (see 4.10), don't use it as a section heading. Use instead several small sections, each with an informative heading.

4.25   Don't use *etc.* to broaden a heading, as in *Notices, etc.* If a section addresses more concepts than you can comfortably refer to in the heading, that's a sign you should divide it into two or more separate sections. More generally, don't use it anywhere in contracts (see 13.266).

4.26   Put all text in the body of the contract within a section. One exception: when Acme's statements of fact constitute an article unto themselves, place the introductory language—for example, *Acme states to Widgetco that the following facts are accurate*—after the article heading but before the sections. That allows the statements of fact to be presented as sections, complete with headings, rather than as subsections. (Regarding using *states* and *statements of fact* instead of *represents* and *representations*, see 3.412.)

Subsections

4.27   Divide a section into two or more enumerated subsections if each subsection addresses different aspects of a single topic or the section would otherwise be too long to read comfortably (see 4.70). Don't divide a section into paragraphs that aren't enumerated. For an example of the confusion that can occur when a section divided into subsections includes an unenumerated paragraph, see *Karmely v. Wertheimer*, 737 F.3d 197, 209–11 (2d Cir. 2013).

4.28 Use the *(a)* hierarchy to designate subsections. If you run out of letters you could shift to the *(aa)* hierarchy, but if a section has 10 or more subsections, consider grouping them into two or more sections.

4.29 Don't use instead the multiple-numeration system, with the subsections of section 4.3 numbered 4.3.1, 4.3.2, and so forth. It has four shortcomings: First, it takes up more space than the *(a)* hierarchy. Second, it's potentially confusing: considered in isolation, *section 1.1* could refer to the first section of article 1 or the first subsection of section 1. Third, it would look odd to use the multiple-numeration system if you put the first subsection designation after the heading, as this manual recommends. And fourth, this manual recommends against using the multiple-numeration system for tabulated enumerated clauses (see 4.47), and it would look odd to start with the multiple-numeration system and then shift to the *(1)* hierarchy for first-level tabulated enumerated clauses.

4.30 An advantage to using the multiple-numeration system is that if you find yourself on a page without section enumeration, you would know from any subsection enumeration and tabulated-enumerated-clause enumeration what section they're part of. But that advantage isn't enough to offset the disadvantages.

4.31 Don't give headings to subsections—any benefit a reader might derive from subsection headings is more than offset by the way they detract from section headings. If you keep your sections a manageable length, you won't miss subsection headings.

Enumerated Clauses

FUNCTION

4.32 "Enumerated clauses" are the parts of a sentence in a section or subsection that are preceded by introductory text and are designated by a number or letter in parentheses, with the next-to-last enumerated clause followed by *and* or *or*. Here's a sample set of enumerated clauses with introductory text:

> Schedule 3.3 lists (1) the name of each financial institution in which Acme has an account or safe-deposit box, (2) the one or more names in which each account or box is held, (3) the type of account, and (4) the name of each Person authorized to draw on or have access to each account or box.

4.33 Designating the parts of a sentence in this manner highlights and renders more readable the individual components of a list or series; use enumerated clauses whenever a list or series is anything other than a short string of very brief clauses.

4.34 Because enumerated clauses are parts of a sentence, don't begin an enumerated clause with a capital letter, unless the word otherwise requires one. For the same reason, in a set of enumerated clauses the only period marking the end of a sentence should occur at the end of the last enumerated clause.

4.35   An enumerated clause could itself contain enumerated subclauses. And those subclauses could conceivably contain enumerated sub-subclauses, but three levels of enumerated clauses is generally a sign of undue complexity.

4.36   The alternative to using enumerated clauses is to make each enumerated clause into a separate provision, repeating each time the essence of the introductory text. Depending on the context, using that approach might yield clearer prose. For example, using as introductory text *Acme shall do the following* would result in enumerated clauses that lack a subject. It might be clearer to use instead separate provisions, each using *Acme shall*.

PUNCTUATION

4.37   Use a colon to introduce any set of enumerated clauses that is more than about three lines long. A colon allows readers to catch their breath before tackling the enumerated clauses. Because readers don't expect to pause at the end of a clause fragment, structure whatever precedes a colon as a full independent clause—it should contain a subject and verb and be capable of standing alone. You can easily turn into an independent clause any introductory statement that isn't one by incorporating *the following* or *as follows*. For example, *Since 30 March 2017, the Company has not: (1) incurred any obligation* ... could be rephrased as *Since 30 March 2017, the Company has not done any of the following: (1) incurred any obligation* ... .

4.38   If *the following* or *as follows* occurs in a single independent clause or the last independent clause in a compound sentence, you don't have to place *the following* or *as follows* at the end of the introductory text preceding a colon. The independent clause can be followed by one or more subordinate clauses, as in this example:

> Acme shall transfer to Widgetco each of *the following*, with its certificate of title attached:

4.39   But *the following* or *as follows* is too remote when it's separated from the colon by one or more other independent clauses, as here:

> If any of *the following* occurs and the Licensor notifies Acme it is terminating this agreement in accordance with this section 6 and includes in that notice its reason for terminating this agreement, this agreement will terminate when Acme receives that notice:

4.40   When the enumerated clauses in a sentence are long and complex or involve internal punctuation, for clarity separate them with semicolons; otherwise, separate them using commas. If the enumerated clauses in a sentence are sufficiently complex or lengthy to justify their being preceded by a colon, then separate them using semicolons rather than commas. Use commas, not semicolons, to separate enumerated clauses not preceded by a colon.

4.41   A sentence containing enumerated clauses can constitute part of a paragraph, or a paragraph unto itself, but you can instead use "tabulation" to make each enumerated clause stand alone. Each enumerated clause so treated is a "tabulated enumerated clause," as opposed to an "integrated enumerated clause"; in sample 3 and sample 4, section 1.1(a) contains five tabulated enumerated clauses and section 1.2 contains three. The more enumerated clauses there are in a sentence, and the longer they are, the more likely it is that having them stand alone would make them easier to read. For comparison, sample 5 (using the first-line-indent scheme) shows two versions of the same section, one with integrated enumerated clauses and the other with tabulated enumerated clauses.

SAMPLE 5 ▪ **INTEGRATED AND TABULATED ENUMERATED CLAUSES (USING *MSCD* FIRST-LINE-INDENT ENUMERATION SCHEME)**

Integrated Enumerated Clauses

      1.6   **Conversion of Stock.** (a) At the Effective Time, by virtue of the Merger and without any action on the part of Holdings, Sub, or PMG, the following will occur: (1) all shares of PMG common stock outstanding immediately before the Effective Time (other than shares held by PMG as treasury stock and Dissenting Shares) will be converted into the right to receive the Merger Consideration; (2) all shares of PMG common stock held at the Effective Time by PMG as treasury stock will be canceled and no payment will be made with respect to those shares; and (3) each share of capital stock of Sub outstanding immediately before the Effective Time will be converted into one validly issued, fully paid, and nonassessable share of common stock of the Surviving Corporation.

Tabulated Enumerated Clauses

      1.6   **Conversion of Stock.** (a) At the Effective Time, by virtue of the Merger and without any action on the part of Holdings, Sub, or PMG, the following will occur:

(1)   all shares of PMG common stock outstanding immediately before the Effective Time (other than shares held by PMG as treasury stock and Dissenting Shares) will be converted into the right to receive the Merger Consideration;

(2)   all shares of PMG common stock held at the Effective Time by PMG as treasury stock will be canceled and no payment will be made with respect to those shares; and

(3)   each share of capital stock of Sub outstanding immediately before the Effective Time will be converted into one validly issued, fully paid, and nonassessable share of common stock of the Surviving Corporation.

4.42   When you tabulate a set of enumerated clauses, you have the choice of either tabulating or integrating any subclauses. But you shouldn't tabulate subclauses if the enumerated clauses are integrated. The same applies to the relationship between subclauses and sub-subclauses.

4.43   Keep integrated those enumerated clauses that are not preceded by a full independent clause and a colon and are separated by commas: such enumerated clauses should be relatively short and few in number, and it would look odd to have the introductory statement end without punctuation and the tabulated enumerated clauses end with commas.

4.44   Place tabulated enumerated clauses at the end of a sentence to avoid "dangling" text, which occurs when the first part of a sentence consists of a series of tabulated enumerated clauses and the remainder starts flush left below the last enumerated clause; see sample 6 (using the hanging-indent scheme). To eliminate dangling text, restructure the provision or integrate the enumerated clauses. Similarly, end a section or subsection after a series of tabulated enumerated clauses instead of having the remaining one or more sentences as an unenumerated block of text.

SAMPLE 6   ▪   TABULATED ENUMERATED CLAUSES FOLLOWED BY DANGLING TEXT (USING *MSCD* FIRST-LINE-INDENT ENUMERATION SCHEME)

Conversion of Stock. (a) At the Effective Time, the following will occur:

(1)   all shares of PMG common stock outstanding immediately before the Effective Time (other than shares held by PMG as treasury stock and Dissenting Shares) will be converted into the right to receive the Merger Consideration;

(2)   all shares of PMG common stock held at the Effective Time by PMG as treasury stock will be canceled and no payment will be made with respect to those shares; and

(3)   each share of capital stock of Sub outstanding immediately before the Effective Time will be converted into one validly issued, fully paid, and nonassessable share of common stock of the Surviving Corporation;

in each case by virtue of the Merger and without any action on the part of Holdings, Sub, or PMG.

DANGLING TEXT

ENUMERATION

4.45   Use as the enumeration hierarchy for enumerated clauses the *(1)* series, followed by the *(A)* series for subclauses and the *(i)* series (generally called "Romanette") for sub-subclauses. This hierarchy reserves the *(a)* series for subsections, to enhance the distinction between subsections and enumerated clauses. The *(1)* series takes precedence over the *(i)* series, because it's easier to read and takes up less space.

4.46   Don't use "commingled enumeration"—in sections that aren't divided into subsections, don't use for first-level tabulated enumerated clauses the enumeration used for subsections, namely the *(a)* hierarchy (see 4.28). Because tabulated enumerated clauses serve a different function than do sections and subsections (see 4.62), commingled enumeration send mixed signals regarding how a contract is organized. Reserving the *(a)* hierarchy for subsections and using the *(1)*, *(A)*, and *(i)* hierarchies for first-, second-, and third-level enumerated clauses has the added benefit of facilitating automated enumeration.

4.47   For four reasons, it's best not to use the multiple-numeration system to enumerate tabulated enumerated clauses. First, the multiple-numeration system is suited to conveying taxonomies and emphasizes that each component is subsumed within the next level up in the hierarchy. By contrast, the components of a set of first-level tabulated enumerated clauses are simply parts of a sentence within a section or subsection; the most important relationship is between the tabulated enumerated clauses, not between the set of tabulated enumerated clauses and the section or subsection in which it's located.

4.48   Second, the multiple-numeration system wouldn't work for integrated enumerated clauses, and it would be awkward to switch enumeration depending on whether your enumerated clauses are tabulated or integrated.

4.49   Third, to avoid commingled enumeration, you would have to use the *1.1.1* hierarchy for first-level tabulated enumerated clauses, even in sections without subsections. That would look odd.

4.50   And fourth, using the multiple-numeration system for second-level tabulated enumerated clauses (for example, *6.10.4.5.3* in a contract divided into articles with respect to a section divided into subsections) would be cumbersome and might well interfere with tab settings.

4.51   Don't use bullets to enumerate tabulated enumerated clauses. Although bullets are useful in other documents, they're too informal for contracts and aren't conducive to cross-referencing.

4.52   In a set of tabulated enumerated clauses, don't have enumeration from one hierarchy followed immediately, with no intervening text, by enumeration from the next hierarchy down. For example, don't have *(2)* followed directly by *(A)* and its related clause, with the two enumerations separated only by a tab and with the *(A)* clause followed by one or more other enumerated clauses in the same hierarchy. Such arrangements are awkward and raise the question why the enumerated clauses aren't all in the same hierarchy.

4.53   Instead of using in a section or subsection two sets of tabulated enumerated clauses, each with a different enumeration hierarchy (for example the *(a)* hierarchy, but starting with *(x)*, and the *(1)* hierarchy), limit yourself to one set, either by eliminating the enumeration from one set or by placing one set in a separate section or subsection.

HEADINGS

4.54   Like subsection headings (see 4.31), headings for tabulated enumerated clauses add more clutter than they're worth.

The *MSCD* First-Line-Indent Enumeration Scheme

4.55   For sections, the *MSCD* first-line-indent scheme indents the first line (as the name suggests), with the enumeration one tab-setting in and the section heading another tab-setting farther in.

4.56   Because each section number has text immediately below, with the section heading to the right, putting a period after the section number helps it stand out. But don't put a period after the section number in the "articles" version (see 4.16).

4.57   Because the section heading is followed on the same line by text, put a period after the heading and make the period bold, like the heading (see 4.20).

4.58   Except for the first subsection of a section, each subsection uses first-line indenting, but with the indent one tab-setting farther in than section numbers, to distinguish them (see sample 3). Because sections and subsections serve the same function—grouping entire sentences, by topic, into manageable blocks of text (see 4.27)—it makes sense to have them share basically the same format. Place the first subsection designation after the section heading and on the same line, with one space on each side: placing the *(a)* on a new line would waste the better part of two lines of space and would isolate the heading, as compared with the headings of sections without subsections.

4.59   A set of tabulated enumerated clauses and the phrase introducing that set together constitute a single sentence. So tabulated enumerated clauses serve an entirely different function from sections and subsections—it doesn't make sense to have them share the same format. Instead, tabulated enumerated clauses are analogous to bullet points. That's why the first-line indent scheme uses hanging indents, but puts on the left margin the enumeration for first-level tabulated enumerated clauses, so as not to make them subservient to sections and subsections.

4.60   For four reasons, the first-line-indent scheme doesn't use first-line indents for tabulated enumerated clauses. First, staggered first-line indents, with the first line of tabulated enumerated clauses beginning one tab-setting further in compared to the first line of a subsection, would give the reader a misleading sense of how tabulated enumerated clauses relate to sections and subsections. Second, to avoid having the format look odd, you would need to adjust the first-line indents of a set of tabulated enumerated clauses depending on whether the section it occurs in contains subsections. Third, first-line indents are used to denote paragraphs; because a tabulated enumerated clause is only part of a sentence, it isn't a paragraph. And fourth, when you indent the first line of a tabulated enumerated clause to the third or fourth tab setting and leave the rest flush left, it looks odd.

4.61   If a tabulated enumerated clause itself contains enumerated subclauses and you tabulate them, use the hanging indent format again but place each subclause one tab-setting further in from the left margin.

The *MSCD* Hanging-Indent Enumeration Scheme

4.62   For sections, the *MSCD* hanging-indent scheme indents all text, not just the first line. The text of sections and subsections is indented equally, instead of having the text of subsections indented one tab setting further in, as is usually the case with hanging-indent schemes. Indenting them differently would reflect standard taxonomy logic used in outlines, but it doesn't accurately reflect the relationship between sections and subsections.

Subsections aren't one level lower than sections in a taxonomy. Instead, subsections are simply a way of structuring sections so they're easier to read. Dividing a section into subsections is analogous to cutting a cake into slices. It's misleading to indent subsections differently from sections, and it wastes space.

4.63   Instead, subsections are distinguished from sections by indenting subsection enumeration slightly more.

4.64   Because section numbers have no text around them, no purpose would be served in putting a period after each section number.

4.65   Whereas with first-line indenting it makes sense to put text after a section heading, that would be awkward with hanging indents. And if a section heading has a line to itself, there's no point putting a period at the end.

4.66   Tabulated enumerated clauses are indented one tab setting further in than sections and subsections. Tabulated enumerated clauses are in effect bullet points, so it's appropriate to put the enumeration at the left edge of the text.

Adopting an *MSCD* Enumeration Scheme

4.67   Anyone who wishes to adopt the *MSCD* enumeration scheme could conceivably do so by setting up the appropriate Microsoft Word styles. But a simpler option is available: PayneGroup, a company that provides software, training, and project-management services to law firms, businesses, and government agencies, offers "articles" and "sections" versions of both *MSCD* enumeration schemes as preloaded options in the Numbering Assistant, its inexpensive paragraph-numbering software. The Numbering Assistant allows you to quickly add, modify, and update automatic multilevel numbering schemes in Word documents. It uses native Word functionality, so you can also easily share your numbering schemes with anyone who doesn't use the software.

4.68   More information is available at www.adamsdrafting.com/resources/numbering-assistant/. If you would like a free 30-day trial of the Numbering Assistant, send an e-mail to CustomerRelations@thepaynegroup.com with the subject line "Numbering Assistant MSCD" and specify which version of Word you use. Neither the author of this manual nor the publisher receives any proceeds from sales of the Numbering Assistant.

4.69   Alternatively, go to http://www.adamsdrafting.com/resources/layouttemplates/ for Word templates of the "articles" and "sections" versions of both *MSCD* enumeration schemes.

Don't Make Blocks of Text Too Long or Too Short

4.70   At some point, a block of text becomes sufficiently long that it's appreciably harder to read—the reader runs out of steam, and it's easier to lose your place. If a section or subsection is more than about 15 lines long, consider dividing it into two or more sections or subsections, or tabulating any enumerated clauses it contains.

FIGURE 2 ▪ EXTRACT FROM A U.S. MERGERS-AND-ACQUISITIONS CONTRACT

SECTION 5.02. No Solicitation; Company Recommendation. (a) Subject to the terms of this Section 5.02(a), during the period commencing on the date hereof, (i) the Company shall and shall cause each of its Subsidiaries to, and shall instruct each of its and their respective directors, officers, employees, financial advisors, legal counsel, auditors, accountants or other agents (each, a "Representative") to, immediately cease any solicitation, knowing encouragement, discussions or negotiations with any Persons that may be ongoing with respect to an Acquisition Proposal (as defined below) and immediately instruct any Person (and any of such Person's Representatives) in possession of confidential information about the Company that was furnished by or on behalf of the Company in connection with any actual or potential Acquisition Proposal to return or destroy all such information and (ii) the Company and its Subsidiaries shall not, nor shall they authorize or knowingly permit their respective Representatives to, directly or indirectly, (A) solicit, initiate, propose or induce the making, submission or announcement of, or knowingly encourage or assist, an Acquisition Proposal, (B) furnish to any Person (other than Parent, Merger Sub or any designees of Parent or Merger Sub) any non-public information relating to the Company or any of its Subsidiaries in connection with any Acquisition Proposal, or in response to any other proposal or inquiry for a potential transaction that on its face, if the Company entered into such transaction, would breach (in the absence of Parent's consent, unless granted) clauses (d)(i), (d)(iii) (but only with respect to Material Contracts of the type described in clauses (iv) or (v) of Section 3.16(a)) or (j), (v) or (w) of Section 5.01 (the "Specified Transactions"), or afford to any Person access to the business, properties, assets, books, records or other non-public information, or to any personnel of the Company or any of its Subsidiaries (other than Parent, Merger Sub or any designees of Parent or Merger Sub) in connection with any Acquisition Proposal, or in response to any other proposal or inquiry for a potential Specified Transaction (in the absence of Parent's consent, unless granted), (iii) enter into, participate, engage in or continue or renew discussions or negotiations with any Person with respect to any Acquisition Proposal, or (iv) enter into, or authorize the Company or any of its Subsidiaries to enter into, any letter of intent, memorandum of understanding, agreement or understanding (whether written or oral, binding or nonbinding) of any kind providing for, or deliberately intended to facilitate an Acquisition Transaction (as defined below) (other than an Acceptable Confidentiality Agreement (as defined below) entered into in accordance with Section 5.02(b)) (a "Company Acquisition Agreement"). It is understood that any violation of the restrictions set forth in this Section 5.02(a) by any director, officer or a financial advisor of the Company or any of its Subsidiaries shall be

4.71   U.S. big-deal drafting is notorious for indulging in overlong blocks of text. See figure 2 for an extract from a representative example of this kind of drafting, the 2011 merger agreement providing for Google's acquisition of Motorola Mobility. Contract text that dense is difficult to read.

4.72   At the other extreme, if text is too fragmented, it turns contract prose into something resembling a shopping list or a set of instructions for assembling a bookshelf. That can disrupt the reader's flow and concentration and make it harder to keep track of what's been covered. Consider keeping the shortest components consolidated.

4.73   The too-fragmented end of the spectrum is represented by an approach to contract layout prevalent in Commonwealth countries. Figure 3 (an extract of a lending agreement drafted by a substantial Australian law firm) exhibits the characteristics of this kind of drafting: short subsections, tabulation of even short enumerated clauses, and overuse of enumerated clauses at the expense of clarity (see 4.36). Note how in figure 3 just the word "Interest" is used to introduce the second set of tabulated enumerated clauses.

FIGURE 3 ■ EXTRACT FROM AN AUSTRALIAN LENDING AGREEMENT

---

4   Interest

  4.1   **Interest**

    (a)   Subject to clause 4.1(d), the Borrower must pay to the Lender interest on each
           Advance:

      (i)   at the rate determined under clause 4.1(b) for each Interest Period for that
               Advance; and

      (ii)   in arrears on each Interest Payment Date for that Advance.

    (b)   The rate of interest for each Interest Period in respect of an Advance is the rate of
           interest per annum determined by the Lender to be the Base Rate for that Advance
           and Interest Period.

    (c)   Interest:

      (i)   accrues on a daily basis, including the first day but excluding the last day of
               the relevant Interest Period; and

4.74 With experience, gauging whether blocks of text are too long or too short becomes a matter of assessing white space on a page. You then make any adjustments necessary to maintain an appropriate balance.

Using a Two-Column Format

4.75 A two-column format is an alternative to the standard one-column format. Both *MSCD* enumeration schemes could be used in a two-column format; see sample 7 for a two-column version of the *MSCD* hanging-indent scheme. For a Word template, go to www.adamsdrafting.com/resources/templates.

4.76 A two-column format allows you to pack more words on a page. That's why it's used most often in commercial agreements—by reputation, salespeople tend to be more concerned about page count than the number of words. A two-column format also reduces the number of characters per line (see 16.39).

4.77 But a two-column format comes at a cost—the small font size it requires, which makes text harder to read. (The two-column version of the *MSCD* hanging-indent enumeration scheme uses 9-point Calibri rather than the 11-point Calibri used in the standard version.) The small font size, together with the limited room in which to mark comments by hand, conveys to the other side, in a way that might not be appreciated, that comments are discouraged. And on-screen reading of a two-column contract requires regularly scrolling back up the page as you finish reading the left-hand column and start reading the right-hand column.

4.78 Generally, minimizing a contract's page count should be a lower priority than making sure that it's concise, easy to read, and easy to work with. A two-column format should be the exception rather than the rule.

SAMPLE 7   ▪   TWO-COLUMN FORMAT OF THE *MSCD* FIRST-LINE-INDENT ENUMERATION SCHEME, ARTICLES VERSION

1.   **Acquired Assets.** (a) Mercury hereby sells to Stratford the following assets as they exist on the date of this agreement (the "**Acquired Assets**"):

(1)   all of Mercury's accounts, notes, and other receivables (including accounts receivable) relating to the Collectibles Business, whether or not accrued and whether or not billed, as described on schedule 1.1(a)(1) (the "**Accounts Receivable**");

(2)   all goodwill associated with the Collectibles Business and all of Mercury's claims and causes of action relating to the assets and current and former customers of the Collectibles Business;

(3)   all inventory listed on schedule 1.1(a)(3);

(4)   all of Mercury's rights under each Contract relating to the Collectibles Business, each of which is listed on schedule 1.1(a)(5); and

(5)   all Mercury lists relating to the Acquired Assets and the Accounts, including the Customer List.

(b)   The assets to be conveyed to Stratford must be adjusted to reflect, in accordance with GAAP, the principle that all income and expenses attributable to the period after the Effective Date are for the account of Stratford, subject to the Management Agreement.

2.   **Purchase Price.** Stratford shall transfer to Mercury the following as the aggregate purchase price for the Acquired Assets (the "**Purchase Price**"):

(1)   in accordance with the stock grant agreement dated the date of this agreement between Stratford and Mercury in the form of exhibit A (the "**Stock Grant Agreement**"), shares of capital stock of Stratford;

(2)   the warrant agreement in the form of exhibit B (the "**Warrant**"); and

(3)   a cash payment of $100,000.

3.   **Assumed Liabilities.** Stratford hereby assumes and shall discharge when due in accordance with their terms the debts, obligations, and liabilities of Mercury listed on schedule 1.3 (the "**Assumed Liabilities**").

4.   **Acquired Assets.** (a) Mercury hereby sells to Stratford the following assets as they exist on the date of this agreement (the "**Acquired Assets**"):

(1)   all of Mercury's accounts, notes, and other receivables (including accounts receivable) relating to the Collectibles Business, whether or not accrued and whether or not billed, as described on schedule 1.1(a)(1) (the "**Accounts Receivable**");

(2)   all goodwill associated with the Collectibles Business and all of Mercury's claims and causes of action relating to the assets and current and former customers of the Collectibles Business;

(3)   all inventory listed on schedule 1.1(a)(3);

(4)   all of Mercury's rights under each Contract relating to the Collectibles Business, each of which is listed on schedule 1.1(a)(5); and

(5)   all Mercury lists relating to the Acquired Assets and the Accounts, including the Customer List.

(b)   The assets to be conveyed to Stratford must be adjusted to reflect, in accordance with GAAP, the principle that all income and expenses attributable to the period after the Effective Date are for the account of Stratford, subject to the Management Agreement.

5.   **Purchase Price.** Stratford shall transfer to Mercury the following as the aggregate purchase price for the Acquired Assets (the "**Purchase Price**"):

(1)   in accordance with the stock grant agreement dated the date of this agreement between Stratford and Mercury in the form of exhibit A (the "**Stock Grant Agreement**"), shares of capital stock of Stratford;

(2)   the warrant agreement in the form of exhibit B (the "**Warrant**"); and

(3)   a cash payment of $100,000.

6.   **Assumed Liabilities.** Stratford hereby assumes and shall discharge when due in accordance with their terms the debts, obligations, and liabilities of Mercury listed on schedule 1.3 (the "**Assumed Liabilities**").

ARRANGING PROVISIONS IN THE BODY OF THE CONTRACT

4.79   Arranging the text of the body of the contract involves three processes that a drafter would engage in concurrently:

- *division*, creating sections, subsections, and, if applicable, articles

- *classification*, determining the section into which a provision should be placed

- *sequence*, ordering the sections and, if applicable, articles

Division

4.80 Custom mostly dictates what sections are included in standard kinds of contract. In commercial contracts, it usually makes sense to have sections address different deal issues. It would be artificial to divide provisions according to the category of contract language—for example, Party A's statement of facts followed by Party B's statement of facts and Party A's obligations followed by Party B's obligations. But mergers-and-acquisitions contracts are organized that way.

4.81 Whether you should group sections into articles is a function of how long the contract is (see 4.7). Whether you should divide a section into subsections depends on how long the section is and the topics it addresses (see 4.27).

Classification

4.82 Make sure each provision is in its proper place. If a contract is organized by category of contract language (see 4.80), it would risk confusion to include language of obligation among the statements of fact.

Sequence

4.83 Two factors come into play in determining the order of articles (if any) and sections.

4.84 On the one hand, more-important provisions should come before less-important provisions, and provisions consulted more frequently should come before provisions consulted less frequently. It makes sense to give readers easy access to what they need.

4.85 On the other hand, because most contracts aren't drafted from scratch but are based on models, the sequence of articles and sections is often similar from contract to contract. In an acquisition agreement, for example, the body of the contract is generally organized in this sequence: deal terms, statements of fact (traditionally known as *representations and warranties*; see 3.374), obligations, conditions to closing, termination, indemnification, and miscellaneous provisions.

4.86 Such consistency not only saves time when drafting but also enables lawyers to navigate easily around a contract and determine whether it addresses all that it should.

4.87 In some respects the conventional order of contract provisions reverses what would seem the logical order. For example, a set of statements of fact in an acquisition agreement invariably begins with statements of fact about basic matters: that Acme has been duly organized, that its entry into the agreement has been appropriately authorized, and so on. Because such matters are rarely at issue, these statements of fact could safely be pushed farther back. But any inefficiencies caused by retaining the conventional order would be negligible—a reader could readily move past those statements of fact that aren't at issue.

4.88   So it's unrealistic to expect drafters to adjust the order of provisions from transaction to transaction based on how the deal terms have affected the relative significance of each provision. Instead, it's up to the drafter to decide what balance to strike between using a conventional sequence and reflecting the priorities of a deal.

4.89   Drafters sometimes approach sequence with the aim of "burying" a contentious provision by putting it with less significant provisions. In the case of consumer contracts, burying a provision could cause the provision to be held unenforceable. That's less likely to happen with contracts between ostensibly sophisticated parties represented by counsel, but other adverse consequences could arise. For one thing, such gamesmanship could well sour a business relationship and wouldn't reflect well on whoever does the burying. And it's unlikely to fool anyone.

4.90   Regarding where to place the definition section, see 6.95.

FRONTLOADING AND BACKENDING

4.91   An exception to the standard approach to arranging provisions in the body of the contract (see 4.79) is what this manual calls "frontloading"—pulling selected information out of the body of the contract and placing it at the top of the contract.

4.92   Frontloading is a common feature of commercial agreements. A company might enter into dozens, hundreds, or thousands of transactions using a particular template. With each transaction, only certain information changes—for example, in the case of a license agreement, the date of the contract, the customer's name, the product, the term, the fees, and any identification numbers. From the company's perspective, that's the most pertinent information, so the company might elect to place it at the top of the contract, perhaps in a table.

4.93   Frontloading offers several potential advantages:

- it could make it easier for company personnel to assess the transaction and locate key information

- it could facilitate training salespeople in how to handle the contract process

- it would likely speed negotiations by highlighting the main terms

- it allows you to signal to the other side that negotiating anything outside of the frontloaded information would be a more time-consuming process, perhaps involving the legal department

4.94   But the more information you frontload, the harder it can be to digest. And departing from conventional notions of sequence can disrupt a reader's expectations regarding where to find a particular provision (see 4.86). So take information out of its conventional context and put it on the first page only if justified by the transactional and administrative benefits. For example, if a company can readily retrieve its customers' contact information through its invoicing system, nothing would be gained by frontloading it.

4.95 Also, if when frontloading you simply repeat the information in question as opposed to moving it from the body of the contract, the result would be a contract that contains the same information in two places. That's always a bad idea (see 1.62). It wouldn't be surprising if the frontloaded information were revised without making conforming changes to the body of the contract, leading to inconsistency and confusion.

4.96 Frontloading the signature blocks would allow company personnel to determine, without having to turn a page, whether a contract has been signed. But it also might encourage customers to sign the contract without paying much attention to what follows the signature blocks. Dissuading customers from negotiating the boilerplate is one thing; dissuading them from reading it is a different and more problematic notion, one that perhaps invites customers to claim later that they hadn't known what they were getting into.

4.97 Instead of frontloading deal-specific information, you could put it in a schedule—this manual refers to that as "backending." Compared with frontloading, one disadvantage is that it puts the most important information at the back of the contract. But backending makes more sense if the deal-specific information is at all voluminous.

4.98 Analogous to backending is a "master" agreement structure, with the parties specifying in a contract the general terms of transactions between them and then stating in a separate document, commonly called a statement of work or a purchase order, additional terms relating to a specific project. But that structure is a function of the serial nature of transactions between the parties, whereas frontloading and backending are driven by repeat use of a template with different counterparties.

4.99 Analogous to both frontloading and backending is the practice of handling a purchase using a purchase order supplemented by terms printed on the back of the purchase order or stated separately. Purchase orders can also be used with a "master" agreement (see 4.98).

CROSS-REFERENCES

Function

4.100 It's routine for a contract provision to refer to an article, section, subsection, or enumerated clause in that contract (in which case the reference is called an internal cross-reference) or to a provision in another contract (in which case it's called an external cross-reference).

4.101 Cross-references can also be categorized as "pointing" cross-references and "prioritizing" cross-references. A pointing cross-reference simply points to another section. For example, a termination provision might state that failure to satisfy one or more conditions stated elsewhere in the contract is grounds for termination.

4.102   Prioritizing cross-references indicate that in some respect, one provision takes priority over another. That type of cross-reference is associated with *notwithstanding*, *subject to*, and *except as provided in*. Those phrases are discussed in 13.599–.611.

4.103   Generally, the fewer cross-references in a contract, the better. A reader should be able to understand each provision on its own, without having to turn to another part of the same contract or to another contract. Prioritizing cross-references can be particularly disruptive; in quantity, they're a sign of inefficient structure.

4.104   See 6.103–.114 regarding cross-references to definitions.

Wording

4.105   In a cross-reference, state whether a section or article is being referred to, plus its enumeration. Don't add *of this agreement* after internal cross-references, or even *hereof*. It's tiresome to encounter *hereof* at every turn, and it strains credulity to suggest that without *hereof* a contract reference to *section 4.5* could be understood as referring to a section of some other contract. This issue wouldn't even be worth addressing in an internal rule of interpretation (see 15.9). And don't add the notation *above* or *below*: such notations are more annoying for the drafter and reader than they are helpful.

4.106   A provision can refer to itself—*this section 4*. If any such reference is to a section rather than to a subsection, you could omit the section number—*this section*. But don't do so—instead of including enumeration when referring to a subsection and omitting it when referring to a section, it's simpler always to include enumeration. And when referring to two or more sections, don't repeat the word *section*—say *sections 5 and 7*, not *section 5 and section 7*.

4.107   In a cross-reference to a subsection, use the word *section*—as in *this section 4(c)*—rather than the word *subsection*. It's simpler to use the same word in both contexts, and there's no risk of confusion. In the interest of consistency and to facilitate revisions, when referring to two or more subsections of the same section, repeat the section number. For example, say *section 6(b) or 6(c)* instead of *section 6(b) or (c)*. That would also spare readers momentarily thinking that the second cross-reference is the enumeration for an enumerated clause.

4.108   In referring to an enumerated clause that isn't a sentence, it's arguably preferable to refer to *clause (2) of section 4(b)* rather than *section 4(b)(2)*, because the latter suggests that you are referring to an entire provision rather than a fragment. Since nothing significant is riding on this distinction, it's unobjectionable to use the more compact formula. A cross-reference to an enumerated clause could be to an enumerated clause in a section, as in *section 7(2)*, or a subsection, as in *7(b)(2)*. In the interest of consistency and to facilitate revisions, when referring to two or more enumerated clauses occurring in the same section and, if applicable, subsection, repeat the section number and, if applicable, the subsection.

For example, say *sections 6(b)(2) and 6(b)(3)* instead of *sections 6(b)(2) and (3)*.

4.109 In cross-references, don't use initial capitals in the words *section* and *article* (see 17.34). And don't use bold, italics, underlining, or any other form of typographic emphasis for cross-references. Doing so could conceivably come in handy if you don't use automatic cross-referencing (see 4.112) and need to check internal cross-references—emphasizing them could help ensure that you don't miss any. But using Microsoft Word's "Find and Replace" function would be a more efficient way to find cross-references. And emphasized internal cross-references are more likely to distract readers than help them.

4.110 An internal cross-reference that consists of only the enumeration of what's being referred to gives the reader no indication what's addressed in the specified provision. The alternative would be to include in each cross-reference the heading of the article or section in question, as in *article 12 (Indemnification)*, but this manual doesn't recommend that practice. It gives the reader a better idea of the significance of the cross-reference, and it makes inaccurate cross-references easier to catch. But in effect it involves referring to the same section twice and as such invites inconsistency (see 1.62).

4.111 An alternative way of making it easier for readers to figure out what's addressed in the provision being referred to would be to use the Word option that allows you to insert an automated cross-reference (see 4.112) as a hyperlink.

Updating

4.112 Adding, deleting, or rearranging blocks of text would likely render inaccurate some or all internal cross-references in a contract. You could painstakingly check them each time you prepare a new draft, but that's a nuisance. You could leave them inaccurate until just before signing, but cross-references, like the table of contents (see 2.214), are of greatest use when reviewing drafts and negotiating, less so after the contract has been signed. Using Word's automatic-cross-referencing feature is a simple way to ensure that your cross-references remain up to date—it turns cross-references into field codes that adjust automatically to changes in enumeration. But it presents two challenges of its own. First, if anyone modifying a draft contract doesn't know that the cross-references are coded, chaos can result, with some cross-references being coded, some not, and some turning into error messages. Second, some software for removing metadata—potentially sensitive information automatically embedded in computer files—treats cross-reference field codes as metadata.

4.113 To avoid such problems, use automatic cross-referencing only in the master version of a draft contract. In copies you send out for comment, change the cross-reference field codes to regular text—doing so takes only a few key strokes. When preparing the next draft, make your changes to the master version and in the process update the cross-references automatically.

4.114   If cross-references would be rendered inaccurate by deleting blocks of text, one alternative to renumbering is replacing the deleted text with the bracketed notation *Intentionally omitted* and leaving the enumeration unchanged. Even an organization that uses automatic cross-references might find this technique useful: if it handles a high volume of transactions based on a template, renumbering template sections for a particular transaction might create confusion.

HEADERS AND FOOTERS

Page Numbers

4.115   Number the pages of a contract—except for the first page, which should be unnumbered—using Arabic numerals. If a contract has a cover sheet, use lowercase Roman numerals to number each page of the associated materials (the table of contents and the index of definitions, if present).

4.116   In general, follow standard practice and place page numbers in the center of the footer. But if the footer contains additional information, you might want to put the page numbers flush right and perhaps highlight their function by adding the word *Page*.

4.117   Using the notation *Page X of Y*, or *X/Y*, tells the reader how long the document is and precludes anyone from surreptitiously adding pages at the end of the contract after it has been signed. But for the contract itself, as opposed to any attachments, those advantages aren't compelling. Flipping to the signature page just once would tell readers how long a contract is—they don't need to be constantly reminded of the number of pages. And it's unlikely that anyone would attempt, let alone pull off, that sort of fraud. So perhaps the slight clutter that this notation adds outweighs the minor benefits. (Regarding using it for attachments, see 4.119.)

4.118   If a contract has more than one attachment, you can number the pages consecutively, as if the attachments are all one document, or number them nonconsecutively, with each attachment treated as a separate document. Nonconsecutive numbering makes it easier for readers to figure out where they are in an attachment. And if attachment enumeration is added to page numbers, with *C-5* designating page five of attachment C, readers could also tell which attachment they're on. But that enhanced numbering would be awkward if attachments are enumerated using section numbers (see 5.86).

4.119   On the other hand, using consecutive numbering with the notation *Page X of Y*, or *X/Y*, would allow readers to figure out quickly whether they have a complete set of attachments. Because a set of attachments can consist of more than one document and, unlike the rest of the contract, doesn't end with a signature page, the convention *Page X of Y* is more useful for attachments than for the rest of the contract.

4.120 Because using both consecutive and nonconsecutive numbering in a single set of attachments seems excessive, it's up to the drafter to consider which system would be appropriate for the transaction at hand.

Other Information

4.121 Headers and, more usually, footers are where you find file names and draft lines.

4.122 Drafters who want working drafts kept confidential might add the notation *Confidential* to the header or footer. Adding the notation *Privileged and Confidential* to drafts exchanged with the other side wouldn't make sense, but it might be appropriate for drafts that are shared only with clients and contain explanatory notes—it might help the client invoke the attorney-client privilege to shield a draft from discovery in later litigation. But it's hard to see how another notation, *Attorney Work Product*, could serve any purpose, because the work-product doctrine applies to materials prepared in anticipation of litigation, not draft contracts.

4.123 Businesses and law firms increasingly place their logo in headers and footers and on cover sheets. There's little reason to be concerned that use of an organization's logo would suggest to a court that, for purposes of the doctrine that ambiguities are to be construed against the drafter, the organization should be considered the drafter: presumably plenty of other information is available indicating who drafted what, if it comes to that.

THE BACK OF THE CONTRACT

5.1   The body of the contract is followed by the concluding clause, the signature blocks, and any attachments. This manual refers to those components collectively as "the back of the contract."

THE CONCLUDING CLAUSE

5.2   In most contracts, the signature blocks are preceded by a sentence known as the concluding clause. You could conceivably dispense with the concluding clause, as it states the obvious, but it's best to retain it, in an appropriate form—it eases what would otherwise be an abrupt transition to the signature blocks.

The Two Kinds of Concluding Clause

5.3   You have a choice of two forms of concluding clause, one for if you state the date of the agreement in the introductory clause, the other for if you have those signing the contract date their signatures (see 2.23–.28).

5.4   If you state the date of the agreement in the introductory clause, use this concluding clause: *The parties are signing this agreement on the date stated in the introductory clause.* (See sample 8.) Don't name the parties: doing so results in a less concise concluding clause, the wordiness increasing with the number of parties. (Regarding this same issue in the context of the lead-in, see 2.164.)

5.5   If the contract anticipates that those signing will date their signatures, use this concluding clause: *Each party is signing this agreement on the date stated opposite that party's signature.* (See sample 9.)

5.6   And if you have those signing date their signatures, include this provision in the boilerplate (see sample 9):

> This agreement will become effective when all parties have signed it. The date of this agreement will be the date this agreement is signed by the last party to sign it (as indicated by the date associated with that party's signature).

5.7   The above provision makes it clear that the contract becomes effective once all the parties have signed it, and it explains what date to give the contract. As such, it simply states what the law provides, but there's value to informing the parties of that. It doesn't attempt to be comprehensive. In particular, it doesn't explain that just signing a contract doesn't accomplish anything unless the other side knows that you've signed it.

SAMPLE 8 ■ CONCLUDING CLAUSE AND SIGNATURE BLOCKS, DATE STATED IN THE INTRODUCTORY CLAUSE

The parties are signing this agreement on the date stated in the introductory clause.

HASTINGS WASTE MANAGEMENT, INC.

By: _____
      Name:
      Title:

JORVIK RECYCLING SYSTEMS, LTD.

By: _____
      Name:
      Title:

_____
ROGER HASTINGS

JARROW HOLDINGS LLC

By: Raindance Associates LLC, its manager

    By: _____
        Name:
        Title:

Use *Signing* Instead of *Executing and Delivering*

5.8 In most traditional contracts, the concluding clause refers to execution and delivery of the contract by the parties. For a general discussion of *execute and deliver*, see 13.274. For the reasons explained immediately below, this manual recommends you use *signing* instead.

EXECUTE

5.9 Determining whether one should refer to execution in the introductory clause requires first establishing what it means.

5.10 *Black's Law Dictionary* says that to execute a contract means to make a document legally valid by signing it. But signing a contract isn't by itself enough to make it legally valid. Other requirements must be satisfied— for example, the signer can't somehow be incapacitated—and you can't circumvent those requirements simply by having the party state in the concluding clause that it's executing the contract.

5.11 Alternatively, executing a contract means having it signed in the name of a party by someone with authority to act on that party's behalf. See Scott

T. FitzGibbon, Donald W. Glazer & Steven O. Weise, *Glazer and FitzGibbon on Legal Opinions* § 9.4 (3d ed. 2008 & Supp. 2012). But if you're concerned whether someone signing a contract on behalf of a party has been authorized by that party, having that individual sign under a concluding clause that refers to execution shouldn't provide any comfort. (Regarding authorization generally, see 5.20.)

5.12   *Execute* also means to perform or complete a contract or duty, making "to execute a contract" potentially confusing.

5.13   So if *execute* means something other than simply *sign*, that additional meaning is irrelevant for purposes of the concluding clause and simply confuses matters. *Signing* is the much clearer choice.

DELIVER

5.14   It serves no purpose to refer to delivery in the concluding clause. The concluding clause introduces the signatures, and delivery—transfer of possession of the signed contract—happens after signing. And more to the point, delivery isn't required for a contract to be enforceable, other than a contract under seal (see 5.48–.56) or, under English law, a deed (see 5.58). For more on delivery, see 13.277.

Which Tense to Use

5.15   Contracts aren't treated as an after-the-fact historical record. That's why it would be unorthodox to use in the concluding clause *the parties signed*. Instead, it's appropriate to have the contract speak as of the moment of signing. You accomplish that by using the present progressive—*the parties are signing*. The concluding clause is a statement in anticipation of a transitional event—a comparable sentence would be *I'm giving this package to Sylvia to mail*—so the sense of duration normally associated with the progressive doesn't apply.

5.16   The traditional choice would be the present perfect (*have signed* or *have caused to be signed*), but it suggest that the action was completed at some point in the past.

5.17   If you use *the parties are signing*, consistency would require that you revise the standard statement of fact *This agreement has been validly executed by Acme* to read *This agreement is being validly signed by Acme*. (Whether such a statement of fact serves any purpose is a separate question.)

Using an *As Of* Date in the Concluding Clause

5.18   Many concluding clauses refer to the contract as being signed *as of* the date in the introductory clause, whether or not that date is an *as of* date (see 2.35). This manual recommends that you not use *as of* in association with a date in the introductory clause or in the concluding clause. Failing that, if you use or omit *as of* in one, do the same in the other.

Traditional Concluding Clauses

5.19   Traditional concluding clauses differ from those recommended in this manual. Here's a representative example of a traditional concluding clause that refers to a date stated in the introductory clause:

> IN WITNESS WHEREOF, the parties hereto, intending to be legally bound, have by their proper and duly authorized officers duly executed and delivered these presents as of the day and year first above written.

5.20   Traditional concluding clauses feature several shortcomings, besides those addressed in 5.8–.17.

REFERRING TO AUTHORIZATION

5.21   The body of the contract is a more sensible place than the concluding clause for statements of fact regarding authorization. But more generally, if you're concerned whether the individual signing for the other party is authorized, having the contract state that they're authorized should provide no reassurance. Instead, ask for confirmation, for example a board resolution.

5.22   A party might nevertheless want to refer to authorization in the concluding clause not because it's concerned whether the individual signing on behalf of the other party is authorized, but because it wants to remind its business people they shouldn't sign the contract unless they've been authorized to do so. Any such reminder would be more noticeable if placed in the signature blocks (see 5.34).

5.23   Some traditional concluding clauses contain the following, or a variant: *Each individual signing for an entity hereby personally warrants his or her legal authority to bind that entity.* Aside from the peculiar wording, attempting to establish a remedy against a signer if they're found not to have authority would seem a low priority. (For a comparable notation used under signature blocks, see 5.36.)

INTENDING TO BE LEGALLY BOUND

5.24   Under U.S. law the phrase *intending to be legally bound* is pointless: it isn't a requirement for enforceability of a contract that the parties have, or express in writing, an intent to be legally bound. (But see 2.186.) In England, an intention to be legally bound is at least formally required to form a valid contract. But a presumption that commercial agreements are intended to be legally binding, together with other evidentiary rules, means that generally it's not required that one show that intention, including by means of a statement in the contract to that effect.

5.25   Arguably the phrase *intending to be legally bound* could serve to remind parties that contracts are legally binding. That might be relevant for consumer contracts, but not for business contracts.

ACCEPTING THE TERMS OF THE AGREEMENT

5.26   Some traditional concluding clauses state that by signing, the parties are accepting the terms of the agreement. That's unnecessary, for the same reason that the phrase *intending to be legally bound* is unnecessary (see 5.24–.25): signing a contract is sufficient to indicate assent.

ARCHAISMS

5.27   Traditional concluding clauses are a reliable source of archaisms: *IN WITNESS WHEREOF* is a translation of the Latin *cuius rei testimonium* and means "in testimony of which" (regarding this sort of archaism generally, see 2.138); *these presents* is an archaic alternative to *this agreement*; and the phrase *the day and year first above written* is long-winded and imprecise. A standard alternative, *set forth above*, is also imprecise.

Avoiding Signature-Page Mix-Ups

5.28   If the parties to a contract are also parties to one or more other contracts and the concluding clause uses only *this agreement*, confusion might arise as to which contract a signature page belongs to. You can avoid that by referring in the concluding clause to the type of agreement involved instead of using *this agreement*. (For another solution, see 5.73.)

THE SIGNATURE BLOCKS

5.29   As shown in sample 8 and sample 9, the concluding clause is followed by a signature block for each party. A signature block consists of a party's name accompanied by a signature line. Don't use the name of a company division that will be performing under the contract: the division shouldn't be party to the contract (see 2.81–.82).

Format

5.30   If the party is a legal entity and not an individual, place the entity's name in all capitals above the signature line. Don't state above the entity name the defined term used for that name in the contract, and don't note after the entity name the entity's jurisdiction of organization—doing so just adds clutter, because that information is readily available elsewhere.

5.31   Be cautious about including two or more entity names above a signature line, to indicate that one person is signing on behalf of more than one entity. Under the laws of the U.S. states, all that's required is a manifestation of assent, so a multientity signature block might work, but it would be clearer to have a separate signature block for each entity. Under English law, a separate signature block is required for each company: section 44(6) of the Companies Act 2006 says, "Where a document is to be signed by a person on behalf of more than one company, it is not duly signed by that person for the purposes of this section unless he signs it separately in each capacity."

SAMPLE 9 ■ **CONCLUDING CLAUSE AND SIGNATURE BLOCKS, SIGNATURES DATED (USING** *MSCD* **HANDING-INDENT ENUMERATION SCHEME)**

14   **Effectiveness and Date**

This agreement will become effective when all parties have signed it. The date of this agreement will be the date this agreement is signed by the last party to sign it (as indicated by the date associated with that party's signature).

Each party is signing this agreement on the date stated opposite that party's signature.

MICKELGATE SYSTEMS, INC.

Date: _____ 2017   By: _____

Benjamin Green
Chief Executive Officer

WHARRAM CORPORATION

Date: _____ 2017   By: _____

Laura Black
President

5.32   Place *By:* next to the signature line to indicate that the individual signing is signing as a representative and not in their personal capacity.

5.33   Note the name and title of the person signing on behalf of a party under the signature in lowercase letters with initial capitals. If they are signing in a particular capacity, say so. For example, an individual might be signing as trustee of the party (see 2.78). If you don't know who will be signing, use *Name:* and *Title:*. If you do know, include that person's name and title (instead of, rather than next to, *Name:* and *Title:*), to spare someone having to write them in by hand.

5.34   If a legal-entity party wants to remind whoever's signing the contract on its behalf to obtain management approval (see 5.20), that could be accomplished by including the notation *and authorized signatory* (alternatively, *and authorized signer*) after that person's name and title in the legal entity's signature block.

5.35   For various possible reasons, a company might have two persons sign a contract on its behalf:

- It might be a function of risk management, the idea being that having two people sign the contract would make less likely entry into a contract that's inconsistent with company policies.

- The company's organizational documents might require that two people sign contracts on behalf of the company.

- The other party might insist that two officers sign on behalf of the company, to allow the other party to benefit from a statutory presumption of authority. For example, California Corporation Code § 313 states that if a contract is signed on behalf of a corporation by two officers holding positions specified in the statute, the contract isn't invalided as to the corporation by any lack of authority of the signing officers unless the other party knew that the signing officers had no authority.

- The contract might not be valid unless two people sign it. For example, English law provides that under various circumstances, a contract will not be valid unless two people sign it on behalf of a company.

5.36   A feature of Canadian and other non-U.S. contracts is use, under a signature block, of the notation *I have authority to bind* [*the Corporation*], with the notation using the defined term for that entity's name. It's not clear that that approach is an improvement over other ways of addressing authorization (see 5.21–.22), except that it might facilitate recording a contract in jurisdictions that require a statement of the signer's authority. (For a comparable notation in the concluding clause, see 5.23.)

5.37   If the signer for a legal-entity party is itself an entity and not an individual, as is often the case when a party is a partnership or a limited liability company, a signature block within a signature block is required; see for example the signature block for Jarrow Holdings LLC in sample 8.

5.38   If the party is an individual, place their name under the signature line in capital letters to distinguish it from the name of any individual signing on behalf of an entity. If there's any risk of confusion, add *in his* [or *her*] *own capacity* after the person's name. As with entity signature blocks (see 5.30), don't state above an individual's signature block the defined term used for that individual's name in the contract.

5.39   If you want each person signing to note the date they signed (see 5.5), place to one side of each signature line (as in sample 9), or directly underneath, the notation *Date:* followed by the date, leaving one or more elements blank to be filled in by the signer, as necessary.

5.40   Signature blocks are usually aligned one above the other on the right-hand side of the page, as in sample 8 and sample 9. To save space, you can place them side by side. In contracts with dated signatures, that would require moving each date line from the left side of the page to underneath its corresponding signature and associated information.

5.41   In England, an alternative arrangement for signature blocks persists: the signature-block information is collected on the left side of the page, on perhaps three lines, with to the right of that a vertical line of closing parentheses, one directly above the other, running down the middle of the page. That line of parentheses is the word-processing equivalent of what it replaces—a single curly bracket. The signature goes in the space to the right of the line of brackets. Don't use this arrangement: it doesn't make it clear what a signer is to do. If the information on the left contains a blank for the signer's printed name, don't be surprised if the signer signs in that blank and assumes that their work is done.

Read before Signing

5.42   Some contracts include above a signature block, or above all signature blocks, the notation *Read before signing*, usually in all capitals. (This is a rare instance of use of the imperative mood in a contract; see 3.124.)

This notation might be preceded by *Important* or *Caution*, with or without an exclamation point. Such notations are unobjectionable for contracts that have as a party an individual who might not be represented by counsel; otherwise, they would seem pointless.

Dealing with Undated Signatures

5.43   A recurring nuisance in exchanging signature pages containing dated signatures is that sometimes a party forgets to date their signature. An alternative to asking that party to submit another signature page, this time with a dated signature, would be to add the following to the provision recommended in 5.6:

> If a party signs this agreement but fails to date their signature, the date the other party receives the signing party's signature will be deemed to be the date the signing party signed this agreement.

5.44   And here's a version for a contract with more than two parties:

> If a party signs this agreement but fails to date their signature, the date [the Company] receives the signing party's signature will be deemed to be the date the signing party signed this agreement.

5.45   You would have to designate one party by name in the version for more than two parties, because the other parties might receive the signing party's signature on different dates. Note also the singular *their* in both versions (see 17.15–.17). Change it to *its* for a contract with only entities as parties.

5.46   If you receive an undated signature and the contract contains the language in 5.43 or 5.44, write the relevant date by hand in the blank next to the signature, with the notation *Determined in accordance with* the relevant section, and send the signature pages as so annotated to the one or more other parties.

Parties with Limited Roles

5.47   One can be party to a contract for only certain provisions. If you elect to highlight in the introductory clause a party's limited role in that contract (see 2.61), do so in that party's signature block too, by adding the phrase *with respect to only* [*specified provisions*]. That phrase, with an initial capital and a colon at the end, could go above the party's name in the signature block or, preceded by a comma at the end of the party's name, immediately below the party's name. The latter approach is slightly more economical.

Seals and Deeds

BACKGROUND

5.48   In medieval England, a seal—consisting of wax attached to a writing and bearing an impression—served as a marker to identify the parties to an agreement, and sealing was one formality required for a binding contract. For corporate seals, sealing wax gave way to an embossed impression.

5.49   As literacy increased, signatures slowly replaced seals as identifying markers. And the value of seals as a device for formally validating contracts dwindled as requirements regarding what is a seal were relaxed. By judicial decision or statute, the presence of the word *seal* near the signature—even on a preprinted form—has been enough to make a contract one under seal. The same applies to use of the phrase *locus sigilli*—meaning "the place of the seal"—or its abbreviation *L.S.* Some courts have found that a recital to the effect that the parties consider the document sealed is sufficient to make it sealed, even if no seal is present—hence the formula *signed, sealed, and delivered.*

5.50   These indicia of sealing are still in use, but the requirements for a contract under seal depend on the jurisdiction, and the standards can seem arbitrary. For example, under Delaware law the word "seal" must be affixed next to the signature lines—it's not enough for the concluding clause to refer to the contract being under seal. See *Sunrise Ventures, LLC v. Rehoboth Canal Ventures, LLC*, No. 4119-VCS, 2010 WL 975581 (Del. Ch. 4 Mar. 2010).

5.51   In the U.S. states, whether or not a contract is under seal can have implications in three contexts.

5.52   First, a sealed contract is binding absent consideration, or at least sealing creates a rebuttable presumption of consideration. But if under the law of a state a contract is at risk of being held unenforceable for lack of consideration, making the contract one under seal probably wouldn't be the clearest fix, even if the law governing the contract acknowledges the distinction between sealed and unsealed instruments. For alternative fixes, see 2.183–.184.

5.53   Second, sealing might affect the statute of limitations that applies to a contract, in that more than 20 U.S. jurisdictions acknowledge contracts under seal in their statutes of limitations. See 3-10 *Corbin on Contracts* § 10.18[H]. For example, Delaware has a 20-year statute of limitations for actions brought on contracts "under seal," as compared with the three-year statute of limitations for ordinary contracts.

5.54   And third, presence of a corporate seal on a contract can affect authorization. For example, section 107 of the New York Business Corporation Law says, "The presence of the corporate seal on a written instrument purporting to be executed by authority of a domestic or foreign corporation shall be prima facie evidence that the instrument was so executed." So for a contract governed by New York law, presence of a corporate seal would shift the burden of proof to whoever would argue that the person signing for that entity lacked authority. But it's not clear that this law has encouraged use of corporate seals.

5.55   The problem with attributing significance to a legal formality such as sealing contracts is that the significance to be attributed isn't evident from the nature of the formality, hence the arbitrary nature of the caselaw regarding the requirements for a contract under seal (see 5.50). Instead of requiring contract parties to go through a formality to achieve an unrelated legal effect on the need for consideration or the duration of a statute of limitations, it would be simpler to have the contract achieve that legal effect explicitly.

5.56   Furthermore, compared with a wax seal, what currently passes for sealing can't reasonably be considered conclusive evidence that a party intended the sealed instrument to contain an enforceable promise. And it wouldn't be reasonable to expect someone signing a contract to pay attention to or understand such obscure notations. That explains why more than half the U.S. states have abolished the distinction between sealed and unsealed instruments, and why section 2-203 of the Uniform Commercial Code has abolished the distinction for sales of goods. Even those states that haven't abolished the distinction altogether have modified it sufficiently so that a seal has little lingering vitality.

DEEDS

5.57   Signing formalities have a role to play in common-law jurisdictions outside the United States.

5.58   In England, the question is whether a contract is "under hand" or is a "deed." As with a contract under seal, the legal implications of whether a contract is a deed relate to consideration and to limitations periods. But use of a seal is now mostly no longer relevant. Instead, for a document to be a deed, it must be described as a deed or state that it is "executed as a deed," it must be signed by the appropriate one or more persons, it must be witnessed, and it must be "delivered" (in other words, the party signing the document must show, by words or by conduct, that it intends to be bound by the deed). The formalities are sufficiently complex that an entire book is devoted to describing them. See Mark Anderson & Victor Warner, *Execution of Documents* (3d ed. 2015). It seems unhelpful to have formalities play such a significant role in allowing contract parties to achieve unrelated substantive ends.

5.59   Australia recognizes the distinction between deeds and other contracts, and an Australian court opinion highlights the problem with such formalities. In *400 George Street (Qld) Pty Ltd and Ors v. BG International Ltd* [2010] QSC 66, the Queensland Supreme Court addressed whether a lease that was "executed as a deed" was in fact a deed. The court concluded that it was not a deed, citing a list of factors, one of which was that the lease used as a heading for the recitals "Background" rather than "Recitals." It's preposterous that such an ostensibly benign choice could have such nonobvious ramifications, but the greater the role of formalities in contract law, the greater the risk of such outcomes.

OTHER JURISDICTIONS

5.60   In some other jurisdictions, the corporate seal plays an important role. For example, in China, contracts are by law binding on a company if a representative signs the contract or if the company's corporate seal is applied to the contract. Some commentators recommend doing both, to reduce the possibility of arguments over authority. And the general practice in Russia is for parties to sign contracts and apply the corporate seal.

5.61   If by law a contract won't be enforceable unless signing formalities are observed, or if you would derive a legal advantage from observing signing formalities, then provide for the appropriate formalities. If that involves applying a corporate seal next to party signatures, consider placing the notation *Corporate seal here*, or some similar notation, next to each signature block as a reminder.

5.62   Otherwise, eliminate from your contracts all references to sealing and other irrelevant signing formalities.

Witnessing Signatures

5.63   By law, signatures to certain contracts must be witnessed. For example, statutes in at least some U.S. states require that anyone taking out a mortgage sign the mortgage document in the presence of witnesses. Also, contract signatures are often witnessed even if it's not required by law, presumably to preclude any claim that the signature to a contract is not that of the person named in the signature block. In most business contexts, this isn't likely to be a concern.

5.64   If you wish to provide for a signature to be witnessed, place a signature block for the witness, preceded by the notation *Witness:*, next to the signature block of the signature being witnessed. An alternative notation is *Attest:*—a witness "attests" to a signature—but its meaning would be obscure to many readers.

Notarizing Signatures

5.65   By law, signatures to certain contracts must be notarized—attested to by a notary public. For example, under Colorado law signatures to an independent contractor agreement must be notarized. See Colo. Rev. Stat. Ann. § 8-40-202. And under the laws of some states the grantor's signature on a deed to real property must be notarized. But it's commonplace for contracts to require that signatures be notarized even if it's not required by law. As with witnessed signatures (see 5.63), presumably the aim is to avoid any dispute as to the identity of a person signing a contract.

5.66   Generally, having a contract signature notarized in the United States involves having the person who signed declare to the notary that they freely signed the contract—that's known as an "acknowledgment." The notary then adds next to that person's signature a "certificate of acknowledgment" confirming that acknowledgment occurred.

5.67   The formalities involved in having a signature notarized depend on the jurisdiction. In Louisiana and civil-law countries, notaries perform a broader range of duties than do U.S. notaries public.

Signing a Contract Electronically

5.68   It's becoming commonplace for parties to sign a contract electronically, using an electronic process associated with the contract. (This is different from scanning your signature to create an electronic "signature stamp.") Electronic signatures generally include the date of signing.

5.69 If signing a contract electronically is optional rather than mandatory, retain the standard concluding clause (see 5.4) and dated signature blocks (see 5.39), and the boilerplate language recommended in 5.6. But if signing electronically is mandatory, it would make sense to dispense with the signature blocks and use this form of concluding clause: *Each party is signing this agreement electronically on the date stated in that party's electronic signature.*

Having Legal Counsel Sign

5.70 An unusual aspect of settlement agreements is that sometimes they contain, under the notation *APPROVED AS TO FORM AND CONTENT*, signature blocks for legal counsel to the parties. It seems odd to have attorneys formally approve a settlement agreement. It's the parties who are agreeing to settle—they don't need, and shouldn't seek, attorney approval. If the aim is to show that the parties had the advice of attorneys, it would make more sense to have the parties state as much in the settlement agreement.

CONSENTS

5.71 The signature blocks of a contract might be followed by a consent—referred to as such or as an "acknowledgment"—in which nonparties consent to something provided for in the contract. A contract restructuring Acme's indebtedness to Widgetco might contain, after the signature blocks, a consent signed by guarantors of Acme's debt. Strictly speaking, such a consent might be unnecessary, because guarantees usually provide that the underlying debt may be modified without the guarantor's consent.

BLANK SPACE AFTER THE BODY
OF THE CONTRACT

5.72 When a page break would otherwise cause the concluding clause and the signature blocks to be spread over two pages, it's neater to make sure that they stay together on a single page. But this can put the concluding clause at the top of a page, with the previous page occupied by the end of the body of the contract followed by an expanse of blank space. This can also occur when the concluding clause and signature blocks are kept on a separate page so a signer can sign in advance and not have that signature page rendered obsolete by later revisions. (Take care that this practice doesn't result in someone signing a contract without being aware of the most recent changes.) Either way, such blank space might be disconcerting to the reader, so you might want to add this notation after the end of the body of the contract: *[SIGNATURE PAGE FOLLOWS]*.

GIVING THE SIGNATURE PAGE AN IDENTIFYING NOTATION

5.73   As an alternative to the approach suggested in 5.28, you can avoid the risk of misidentifying a signature page by stating at the bottom of the signature page the type of agreement involved, including as necessary the date and one or more party names: *[Signature page to Acme Corporation credit agreement dated 17 July 2017]*.

5.74   A bottom-of-the-page notation is particularly useful when the signature blocks occupy more than one page, so you wouldn't have the benefit of the concluding clause to identify any signature pages other than the first.

ATTACHMENTS

Kinds of Attachments

5.75   Contracts feature two kinds of attachments, those that consist of stand-alone documents and those that consist of information that could have been included in the body of the contract but instead was moved to an attachment. It's helpful to use different terms to describe the two kinds of attachment.

5.76   In the United States, the prevailing but not universal convention is to use *exhibits* for attachments consisting of stand-alone documents and *schedules* for attachments containing information. This manual follows that convention. Other jurisdictions might use different terminology. For example, the convention in Australian is to use *annexure* instead of *exhibit*.

5.77   Instead of *exhibit* or *schedule* you can use *appendix, annex,* or *attachment*, which are generic terms for attachments.

5.78   If a contract has only a few attachments, don't feel you have to observe the distinction between exhibits and schedules—it can be awkward to refer to, say, three exhibits and one schedule rather than simply four exhibits or four attachments.

Placement of Attachments

5.79   In a contract that contains both schedules and exhibits, reader convenience suggests putting the schedules before the exhibits: the body of the contract and the schedules constitute two parts of a single text, and readers are likely to flip to the schedules more often than to the exhibits.

5.80   In the United States, the convention is to place schedules and exhibits after the signatures, but other jurisdictions might observe different conventions. For example, in Australia it's standard practice to place the signature pages after the schedules but before the exhibits (or annexures, to use the Australian term), perhaps as a way of acknowledging that the body of the contract and the schedules constitute a single text. But that makes for an abrupt transition between the body of the contract and the schedules and makes it harder to find the signature page.

References to Attachments

5.81   When referring to an attachment, don't use *hereto*, as in *a copy of which is attached as exhibit B hereto*—it's unnecessary to do so, because it would be unreasonable to think that the attachment is an attachment to some other contract.

5.82   Drafters often emphasize references to attachments, but it serves no purpose to do so—readers generally don't seek out references to attachments. (Regarding what text to emphasize, see 16.18.) And it's pointless to put the enumeration in quotation marks, as in *exhibit "A"*.

5.83   Don't use initial capitals in contract references to attachments, as in *as stated in Schedule 4.2*. Instead, follow the recommended practice in general writing and use all-lowercase letters in referring to attachments, as in *as stated in schedule 4.2* (see 17.34).

Enumerating Attachments

5.84   Enumerating attachments serves two functions. First, the number or letter used in referring to a particular attachment tells readers where they can expect to find it among the schedules or exhibits.

5.85   Enumerating attachments can also tell readers where in the body of the contract they could find at least one reference to that attachment. That could be useful for a reader who goes to an attachment and wants to return to the related provision but doesn't recall the section number.

5.86   When a contract is divided into articles and so uses the multiple-numeration system for section numbers (see 4.16), you can have attachment enumeration serve both functions by using for each schedule and exhibit the number of the section that refers to it. If more than one section refers to a particular schedule or exhibit, use the number of the section with the primary reference.

5.87   Even if a contract isn't divided into articles and so doesn't use the multiple-numeration system, you could still enumerate schedules and exhibits using section numbers. But that could cause reader miscues: A reader who consults a schedule and notes that it's schedule 10 wouldn't be able to tell whether the schedules were keyed to section numbers or simply numbered consecutively. Figuring the system out might require flipping through the contract. Furthermore, someone who encounters in the body of the contract a reference to schedule 10 wouldn't be able to tell from that alone whether it comes after schedule 9 or might come after a schedule bearing a lower, nonconsecutive number.

5.88   This confusion would also occur if in a contract not divided into articles you were to enumerate schedules and exhibits with consecutive numbers. Using consecutive letters (*A, B, C*) instead would prevent miscues of this sort.

5.89   There are other advantages and disadvantages to the different systems of enumerating attachments. If you use section numbers, you wouldn't have to renumber attachments if a new attachment is inserted for a section. But if a new section is inserted, that would change the section number used for each attachment that follows (in a contract not divided into articles) or each attachment that follows in that article (in a contract divided into articles). On the other hand, if you use consecutively numbered attachments, adding a new attachment would require renumbering those that follow. But attachments are usually compiled after the contract has been finalized, so these considerations shouldn't weigh heavily. Also, using section numbers for attachments means you wouldn't know from looking at a list of attachments whether one was missing. But that too wouldn't seem a compelling factor.

5.90   In contracts divided into articles, you could use a hybrid system for enumerating attachments, with schedules using section numbers and exhibits using consecutive letters. A hybrid system would have the advantage of preventing confusion between, say, schedule 3.2 and exhibit 3.2. As it is, exhibits aren't often keyed to multiple-numeration section numbers. You could also use a hybrid system for enumerating attachments in contracts not divided into articles, with schedules using consecutive numbers and exhibits using consecutive letters. That would prevent confusion between, say, attachment 1 and exhibit 1, if that's a concern.

Exhibits

5.91   An exhibit is a stand-alone document. It can be a document that's currently in effect, such as the organizational documents of Target Co. attached as exhibits to an acquisition agreement. Or it can be a document that's to be effective after signing, such as an ancillary contract to be entered into at the closing of the transaction provided for in the attaching contract. For example, someone selling all the stock of their company might require as a condition to the sale that at closing they and the company enter into an employment agreement in the form attached as an exhibit to the stock purchase agreement.

5.92   When in the body of the contract you refer to a form of document attached as an exhibit, use *in the form of exhibit A* rather than the more long-winded *in the form attached as exhibit A hereto*. An exhibit is by definition attached, so *attached* is unnecessary.

Schedules

5.93   Schedules consist of materials that could be included in the body of the contract but instead have been moved to after the signature blocks.

DISCLOSURE SCHEDULES

5.94   One kind of schedule is that containing factual information, such as details of ongoing litigation or lists of contracts; such schedules are often called "disclosure schedules." Link each disclosure schedule to the contract provision to which it relates (usually a statement of fact) by indicating in that provision that *stated in schedule X* are all instances of the thing at issue (or that *schedule X contains a list* of all such instances).

Alternatively, indicate that other than as stated in the schedule there are no such instances; this approach is generally used when the thing at issue is either undesirable or present in limited quantities.

5.95 Disclosure schedules are used for four reasons. First, the information in schedules is often sufficiently voluminous that it would be awkward to include it in the body of the contract.

5.96 Second, it's often the case that the party responsible for collecting factual information isn't the party whose attorneys are drafting the contract, so it simplifies matters to present that information separately.

5.97 Third, even if the party collecting the information is also the party responsible for drafting, collecting information about a company's operations involves a different process, perhaps a different time frame, and usually different personnel than does drafting and negotiating the contract.

5.98 And fourth, if the information to be disclosed to the other side is sensitive, putting it in a set of schedules can help minimize the risk of wider disclosure, as schedules are routinely omitted from drafts circulated for review. Also, Item 601(b)(2) of Regulation S-K under the U.S. Securities Act of 1933 allows schedules to merger agreements to be omitted from filing and disclosure, unless they contain information material to an investment decision and that information isn't otherwise disclosed in the agreement or the disclosure document.

5.99 If a section refers to information on a schedule but it's later determined that no such information is required, it's preferable to delete the reference to that schedule rather than force readers to flip to a schedule page that states *None* or *Not applicable*.

5.100 Put in the body of the contract, not on a cover sheet to the disclosure schedules, provisions governing the effect of disclosure schedules. They're provisions like any other, so the best place for them is the body of the contract. (See also 5.101.)

PLACING CONTRACT SECTIONS IN SCHEDULES

5.101 Don't place contract sections in a schedule, as doing so makes it less convenient to refer to them. In particular, don't place contentious provisions in a schedule to "bury" them (see 4.89). And don't shunt ostensibly routine provisions into schedules; they would be sufficiently out of the way if placed at the end of the body of the contract.

5.102 But if you wish to incorporate into a negotiated contract standardized provisions that aren't subject to negotiation, sometimes the simplest course is to relegate them to a schedule. In effect, you're "frontloading" not only the provisions subject to negotiation but also the signature blocks (see 4.96). Also, if a contract is sufficiently long and complex, some drafters prefer to place the definition section in a schedule that you can pull out and review side by side with the rest of the contract. (But see 6.95–.97 regarding placement of the definition section.) And if any deal terms—such as pricing information—are particularly sensitive, some drafters place them in a schedule to minimize the risk of wider disclosure (see 5.98).

IN, NOT *ON*

5.103   It's worthwhile to make a principled decision regarding even minor issues, for example whether to say *in schedule X* or *on schedule X*. Since *in* works in all circumstances, it's the better choice.

5.104   For referring to information stated in a work, use of the preposition *on* is generally limited to references to a particular page—*the information stated on page 43*. That's understandable, because a page is a single surface. Otherwise, use *in*—*the information stated in* [*section 4.3*] [*chapter 6*].

5.105   As in the case of a section, a schedule might occupy one page, but it could just as well occupy more than one page. It would be odd to adjust one's prepositions based on how long a schedule is. Because *in* works no matter how long the schedule, it's the better choice.

Attachments as Part of a Contract

5.106   Although many drafters assume otherwise, generally it's unnecessary to state explicitly that attachments to a contract constitute part of that contract. Any attachment to a contract would be mentioned in the body of the contract, and that reference by itself would be all that's required to bring the attachment within the scope of the contract.

5.107   So omit anything that seeks to make attachments part of the contract. Here are some examples:

> Schedule A constitutes a part of this agreement.

> All exhibits referenced in this agreement are made a part of this agreement.

> All exhibits and schedules annexed hereto are expressly made a part of this agreement as though fully set forth herein.

> This agreement (including any exhibits and schedules hereto) constitutes the entire agreement among the parties hereto.

5.108   See 2.127 and 13.388 for two other techniques that drafters use, unnecessarily, to make attachments part of the contract.

5.109   But make an exception for contracts with self-contained sets of provisions placed in schedules. Contracts with a "master" agreement structure (see 4.98) can feature such schedules. Because the body of the contract doesn't otherwise mention those schedules, to make them part of the contract it's necessary to state in the body of the contract that the schedules constitute part of the contract.

Virtual Attachments

5.110   Sometimes it's useful to make an ancillary document part of a contract without physically attaching it. This manual uses the term "virtual attachment" to describe any such ancillary document. An employment agreement might include as a virtual attachment the company's employee handbook; a commercial contract might include as a virtual attachment a web page containing general terms.

MAKING VIRTUAL ATTACHMENTS PART OF A CONTRACT

5.111   To make sure that a court considers a virtual attachment to be part of a contract, say that the virtual attachment is part of the contract.

5.112   Don't say that the contract is *subject to* the virtual attachment, as a court might hold that *subject to* fails to adequately express an intention to be bound by the virtual attachment. See *Affinity Internet, Inc. v. Consolidated Credit Counseling Services, Inc.*, 920 So. 2d 1286 (Fla. Dist. Ct. App. 2006). And don't simply say that the virtual attachment can be found on a specified web page. See *Manasher v. NECC Telecom*, No. 06-10749, 2007 WL 2713845 (E.D. Mich. 18 Sept. 2007).

5.113   Also, be cautious about using definitions to bring a virtual attachment within the scope of a contract:

> **"Support Services"** means Product support services described in the description of support services provided at the Acme Licenses website (http://www.acme.com/licenses) at any given time.

5.114   Acme's counsel might think this a low-key way to introduce Acme's ability to unilaterally amend a virtual attachment (see 5.115), but it's sufficiently wishy-washy that one could imagine a court holding that the description of support services doesn't in fact constitute part of the contract.

AMENDING VIRTUAL ATTACHMENTS

5.115   A contentious issue relating to virtual attachments is whether a party may unilaterally amend a virtual attachment. A related issue is whether one party must notify the other of any such amendment, and if so, how. Discussion of these issues is beyond the scope of this manual.

CHAPTER **6**

DEFINED TERMS

6.1   A contract usually contains terms for which it provides definitions. Those terms are called "defined terms." Definitions of defined terms are either autonomous (see 6.28) or integrated (see 6.61).

PURPOSE

6.2   A defined term makes a contract easier to read by allowing the drafter to use throughout the contract the shorter defined term instead of the longer definition. It also ensures that whatever is defined is expressed consistently throughout the contract.

THE NATURE OF DEFINED TERMS

6.3   Defined terms are almost always nouns—both common (*employee*) and proper (*Smith*)—and noun phrases (*material adverse change*), although occasionally one sees a verb (*transfer*) or even a prepositional phrase (*to Acme's knowledge*).

6.4   If the defined term is a common noun, use the singular form when defining it, unless it's simpler to use the plural form, see, for example, how the term *the Hastings Parties* is defined in sample 1. Defining a term in the singular and using it in the plural, or vice versa, wouldn't confuse a reasonable reader, so no purpose would be served by addressing this practice in an internal rule of interpretation (see 15.22). And nothing is gained by using both the singular and plural form when defining a term, as in *"Note" and "Notes" mean* ... and as in *each a "Member" and, collectively, the "Members"*.

6.5   Don't use as alternative defined terms both a word or phrase and an initialism or abbreviation, as in *"Customer Service Request" or "CSR" means* ... . Simplicity favors using one or the other; choosing between them involves balancing readability and concision.

6.6   To allow the reader to recognize defined terms, use initial capitals to distinguish defined terms from words for which the contract doesn't provide a definition. Do so even if the defined term is a routine one such as *Person* or *Subsidiary*. Don't use anything more emphatic—bold, italics, or all capitals—every time you use a defined term, because it's distracting.

6.7   Don't make exceptions to using initial capitals to distinguish defined terms. If a contract contains many instances of a defined term, that can make the contract harder to read (see 6.51), but not using initial capitals in stating that defined term could confuse readers. A better fix would be to find a way to omit that defined term.

6.8   Provide definitions for all initialisms, even those that are widely known, for example *SEC*, meaning the U.S. Securities and Exchange Commission. Contract drafting is most efficient when you apply an approach consistently—it complicates matters if the drafter makes judgment calls regarding whether the meaning of a particular initialism is obvious. And if drafters dispense with particular definitions, at some point you can expect reader confusion, either because a contract might have a broader readership than expected or because the drafter had an expansive notion of what terms have an obvious meaning.

ABBREVIATIONS AS DEFINED TERMS

6.9   Using abbreviations as defined terms offers economy. You can use acronyms or initialisms. According to *The Chicago Manual of Style*, at 10.2, "The word *acronym* refers to terms based on the initial letters of their various elements and read as single words (AIDS, laser, NASA, scuba)," whereas "*initialism* refers to terms read as a series of letters (IRS, NBA, XML)." *ERISA* is an example of an acronym one often sees in contracts; *SEC* is an example of an initialism.

6.10   When an abbreviation follows an indefinite article (in other words, acts as a common noun, not a proper noun), whether you use *a* or *an* as the indefinite article is determined by how the first syllable is sounded.

6.11   Consider the defined term *SOW* (meaning a statement of work issued under the contract in question). If treated as an acronym, it's likely that *SOW* would be sounded so it rhymes with *now* (as opposed to rhyming with *doe*). It seems unpromising to use as an important contract term a homophone for the word for a female pig, but some people do use *SOW* as an acronym. In that case, it would begin with a consonant sound, so you'd say *a SOW*. If it's treated as an initialism, it would begin with the same vowel sound as *egg*. It follows that you'd say *an SOW*.

6.12   When used to excess, acronyms and initialisms can turn contracts into alphabet soup. See 2.102, 2.128, and 9.79.

SELECTING DEFINED TERMS

6.13   If you wish to create a defined term to express a particular meaning and it's conventional to use a particular defined term—such as *Business Day, the Code, GAAP, Indemnifiable Losses*—to express that meaning or something close to it, use the conventional defined term. Contract drafting favors predictability over novelty.

6.14   If you use a conventional defined term but you give it a definition that's unorthodox, alert the reader to that by modifying the defined term appropriately. For example, instead of *Net Operating Income* use *Adjusted Net Operating Income*.

6.15   If you need to create a defined term for a definition that's unique to a particular transaction, use a term that's concise yet informative. Your choice of defined term will in part depend on what's required to distinguish it from other defined terms used in that contract. The term *the Property* might work as the defined term for a property in Acmetown if that property is the only property involved in the transaction. If other properties are involved, you must be more specific and use as the defined term, say, *the Acmetown Property.* If the other properties include other Acmetown properties, *the 144 Ninth Street Acmetown Property* would be your best choice. The need to distinguish a defined term from other defined terms in a contract can require a defined term that's a bit of a mouthful, such as *the PLM/Whitman Excluded Asset Proceeds.*

6.16   See 2.90–.123 regarding selecting defined terms for party names.

CIRCULAR DEFINITIONS

6.17   Dictionaries shouldn't use in a definition the term being defined, as that constitutes a form of circular definition. For example, it would be unhelpful for a dictionary definition of *chair* to include the word *chair.* But that doesn't apply to contract definitions. In a contract, a defined term simply serves as a convenient substitute for the definition, and only for that contract. So repeating a contract defined term in the definition is unobjectionable. An example: *"Trademark" means a registered trademark or service mark or any trademark or service mark that is the subject of any application, registration, or renewal.*

6.18   But contract definitions are prone to a different form of circular definition, in which concept A is defined in terms of concept B and the definition of concept B refers either directly or indirectly to the definition of concept A. An example would be defining an oak as a tree that grows from an acorn and defining an acorn as a nut produced by an oak.

6.19   These contract definitions are circular:

> **"Bonus Date"** means a date on which Acme determines that a Bonus Period concludes.
>
> **"Bonus Period"** means a period that commences on a date determined by Acme and concludes on a Bonus Date.

6.20   Their combined effect is to make the first definition read as follows:

> **"Bonus Date"** means a date on which Acme determines that a period that commences on a date determined by Acme and that concludes on a Bonus Date concludes.

6.21   And to make the second definition read as follows:

> **"Bonus Period"** means a period that commences on a date determined by Acme and concludes on a date on which Acme determines that a Bonus Period concludes.

6.22   So a Bonus Date is a date of unknown significance, and a Bonus Period is a period of unknown significance. Because in each case the defined term is in effect also in the definition, you're left chasing from one definition to the other, looking for meaning. The fix is to anchor one definition to some external reality.

6.23   Here's another example of circular definitions:

> "**Licensed Products**" means products that are within one or more claims of the Licensed Patents.

> "**Licensed Patents**" means any patents owned by the Licensor that claim any aspect of the Licensed Products.

OVERLAPPING DEFINITIONS

6.24   Be alert to the possibility of overlapping definitions. For example, if a contract uses the defined terms *Licensor*, *Software*, and *Licensor Software*, a reader who encounters *Licensor Software* away from its definition might mistakenly think that it's a combination of the defined terms *Licensor* and *Software* and not its own defined term.

6.25   And if a contract uses the defined terms *Control* (relating to the power to direct management) and *Change of Control* (relating to ownership of securities), a reader might mistakenly think that the defined term *Change of Control* incorporates the defined term *Control*, or wonder whether it does.

6.26   It might be difficult to come up with alternatives to *Control* and *Change of Control*, but usually it should be possible to choose defined terms that eliminate any overlap.

TYPES OF DEFINITIONS

6.27   This manual calls definitions either "autonomous" or "integrated," depending on how a definition is linked to its defined term.

Autonomous Definitions

6.28   An autonomous definition is linked to its defined term by a "definitional verb." The definition, definitional verb, and defined term together constitute a sentence, but for simplicity this manual uses the term "autonomous definition" also to refer to the entire sentence.

STRUCTURE

6.29   In autonomous definitions, the defined term can be placed after the definition, as in *Any such transfer is referred to in this agreement as a "Permitted Transfer."* But it's more economical to place the defined term before the definition, as in *"Exchange Act" means the Securities Exchange Act of 1934.* (Using an integrated definition might be even more economical.)

6.30   In an autonomous definition, don't put the definite article *the* or the indefinite article *a* (or *an*) before the defined term. And it adds clutter to put *The term* before the defined term.

6.31   At the front of a single autonomous definition, add the phrase *In this agreement*, followed by a comma. Before a set of autonomous definitions, whether "on site" or in a definition section (see 6.33), say *In this agreement, the following definitions apply,* followed by a colon. It's more efficient than wordier alternatives, such as *For purposes of this agreement, the following terms have the following meanings.*

6.32   In a set of autonomous definitions, state each autonomous definition as a separate paragraph, without a first-line indent (see 16.55). Don't add any additional text at the end of a paragraph constituting an autonomous definition. Put any set of autonomous definitions in alphabetical order. Don't enumerate them—it wastes space and distracts the reader, because alphabetical order by itself is enough of an organizing framework. And don't put a semicolon instead of a period at the end of autonomous definitions: it makes more sense to treat each autonomous definition as a sentence.

PLACEMENT

6.33   A single autonomous definition can be placed "on site" (see 6.88), either with other text in a section or subsection or, if it's more than a couple of lines long, in its own subsection. Alternatively, it can be placed in a definition section (see 6.87).

6.34   A set of autonomous definitions can constitute the entire definition section or it can be placed on site, in its own subsection.

6.35   Autonomous definitions placed on site should follow, in a section, right after the provisions that use the terms being defined. Placing definitions before the provisions that use the defined terms would cause readers to wonder why they're being provided the definitions. Placing definitions later in a section, separated by unrelated text from the provisions that use the defined terms, would force readers to work harder to consult the definitions.

EMPHASIS

6.36   Place in quotation marks and emphasize in bold a defined term linked to an autonomous definition—using quotation marks in this context is consistent with standard English, and using both conventions makes autonomous definitions easier to spot. Don't bold the quotation marks. (This manual follows that convention for the samples and the indented examples of contract text, but in examples incorporated in regular paragraphs, any terms being defined aren't stated in bold, to avoid distracting the reader.)

6.37 If the definition gives the entire meaning of the defined term (in other words, if the definition is "full"), use *means* as the definitional verb.

6.38 Don't use *mean* as the definitional verb:

> "**Products**" *mean* [read *means*] the MegaSonic motors listed in exhibit A.

6.39 Drafters who use *mean* do so on the assumption that because the defined term is defined in the plural, the verb should be plural too. But that misconstrues the function of the defined term in an autonomous definition: the definition says what the word or phrase means, not what each individual element means.

6.40 An "enlarging" definition, which expresses only part of the intended meaning, uses *includes* as the definitional verb, and a "limiting" definition, which excludes something from the meaning of the defined term, uses *does not include*. Enlarging and limiting definitions can create mischief, because they don't state the full scope of the definition. For example, protracted litigation in the United States over "Bratz" dolls concerned in part whether the defined term "inventions," as used in the employment agreement between Mattel and one of the litigants, included ideas. The definition of "inventions" was an enlarging definition, because it used as the definitional verb "includes, but is not limited to"—hence the potential for dispute. See *Mattel, Inc. v. MGA Entertainment, Inc.*, 616 F.3d 904, 909 (9th Cir. 2010).

6.41 Sometimes it's useful to combine a full definition with an enlarging definition or a limiting definition, or both: *W means X* [*and includes Y*] [*but does not include Z*] [*and includes Y but does not include Z*]. That avoids the uncertainty inherent in using enlarging and limiting definitions on their own. (For two contexts where it would be appropriate to use a full definition with a limiting definition, see 8.118 and 9.133.)

6.42 Don't use *means and includes*—as a matter of logic, it's not feasible to express complete and incomplete meanings simultaneously. And don't use *includes only*, which is equivalent to *means* but wordier and less clear.

6.43 Don't use a dash instead of a definitional verb, as in *"ERISA"—the Employee Retirement Income Security Act of 1974*, because a dash is less precise than a definitional verb. The same goes for using a colon instead of a definitional verb.

6.44 Use the definitional verb in the present tense, since definitional sentences are language of policy (see 3.307 and example [8-4]). No duty is being expressed, so don't use *shall mean* instead of *means* (see 3.308).

THE PART OF SPEECH OF THE DEFINED TERM

6.45 If the definitional verb is *means, includes*, or *does not include*, the part of speech of the defined term should match that of the definition, whether verb, adjective, noun, or other. Otherwise, use *refers to*.

6.46 If the part of speech of the defined term doesn't match that of the definition, usually it's because the defined term is stated in more than one form, each one a different part of speech, as in *"Register", "Registered", and "Registration" refer to a registration effected by preparing and filing a registration statement under the 1933 Act … .*

6.47   Another way to define different forms of a defined term is to handle each separately. Here are two ways to do that if the different forms are identical, which would be the case with the noun and verb forms of *Control* and *Transfer*:

> "[**Defined Term**]" means, when used as a noun, [first definition], and when used as a verb, [second definition].

> "[**Defined Term**]" when used as a noun means [definition]. "[**Defined Term**]" when used as a verb has a corresponding meaning.

6.48   Omit from these examples the references to the parts of speech if the different forms of a defined term aren't identical, which would be the case with the noun *Commercialization* and the verb *Commercialize*.

6.49   Yet another option would be to have an internal rule of interpretation (see 15.2) do the work:

> If a term is defined as one part of speech (for example, a noun), it will have a corresponding meaning when used as another part of speech (for example, a verb).

6.50   But if an undefined related form of a word that is used as a defined term occurs in the same contract, this principle of interpretation could have unexpected consequences. It would be safer to state explicitly what the defined terms are.

6.51   Defining different forms of a defined term can add to a contract many instances of that defined term in its different forms. That can make a contract harder to read. If you have an alternative to defining different forms of a defined term, take advantage of it.

"STUFFED" DEFINITIONS

6.52   Don't "stuff" or "load" autonomous definitions by including in them language better placed elsewhere.

6.53   One way to stuff a definition is to include in it language that couldn't constitute part of the definition proper. A symptom of that is use of *shall*, *must*, *may*, or *will* in an autonomous definition. So don't tack on to the definition of *Acme Financial Statements* the clause *which Acme shall deliver no later than three months after the end of each Acme fiscal year*. Instead, state that deadline elsewhere as language of obligation.

6.54   Here's another example of a stuffed autonomous definition:

> "**Alternative Clearing System**" means any clearing system designated by the Company and approved by the Trustee (any such approval not to be unreasonably withheld or delayed).

6.55   In this case, the stuffing isn't only the prohibition imposed on the trustee but also the requirement that the trustee have approved the company's choice of clearing system. It would be clearer to address these issues in a substantive provision. One symptom of a stuffed definition is repetition in the substantive provisions of elements in the definition. In this case, some references to *Alternative Clearing System* in the substantive provisions were accompanied by duplicative references to trustee approval.

6.56   Here's a third example:

> "**Committee**" means the Acme stock option committee composed of two or more members of the board of directors, which committee will be responsible for administering the Plan.

6.57   It would be preferable to limit the definition of *Committee* to "the Acme stock option committee" and address the makeup of the committee and its function in a substantive provision.

6.58   Stuffed definitions can pervade a contract if the drafter misguidedly thinks that it's best for the operative provisions to appear simple yet be full of defined terms. The complexity is swept into definitions stuffed to the point of bursting. That imposes on the reader the awkward task of unpacking the complexity.

OTHER MISUSE OF AUTONOMOUS DEFINITIONS

6.59   Don't include an integrated definition (see 6.61) within an autonomous definition, as in *"Effective Date" means the date on which the Registration Statement is declared effective by the Securities and Exchange Commission (the "SEC")*. Doing so makes integrated definitions longer and harder to read. Also, a reader wouldn't necessarily think to look in an autonomous definition for the definition of another term. It would be clearer to define the term *the SEC* elsewhere and use just the defined term in the autonomous definition.

6.60   Regarding using an autonomous definition to bring a virtual attachment within the scope of a contract, see 5.113–.114. And consider using *however referred to* as a way to avoid including many examples in an autonomous definition (see 1.50).

Integrated Definitions

6.61   The alternative to autonomous definitions (see 6.28) is "integrated" definitions.

STRUCTURE

6.62   Whereas an autonomous definition is a separate sentence, an integrated definition is part of a sentence included with the substantive provisions of a contract, with the defined term following the definition and in parentheses. An example: *Since 1 January 2017, Dynaco has filed with the SEC all reports, proxy statements, forms, and other documents it has been required by law to file with the SEC (those documents, the "Dynaco SEC Documents")*. This manual refers to such language in parentheses as a "defined-term parenthetical."

6.63   If you put the defined-term parenthetical at the end of a list of items and syntactic ambiguity (see 12.1) makes it unclear which items constitute the definition, consider prefacing the list with *the following* plus a colon and putting the defined-term parenthetical before the colon. That would make the definition *the following*, which is equivalent to the list of items.

6.64   Don't introduce the defined term using a traditional word or phrase such as *hereafter* or *hereinafter referred to as*. Such introductory text is redundant, because the parentheses and the emphasis used (see 6.68) signal that a term is being defined.

6.65   In contrast to autonomous definitions (see 6.28), include in a defined-term parenthetical the definite article *the* or the indefinite article *a* (or *an*), as appropriate. An article isn't necessary unless the defined term is a common noun (see 6.3). You can omit the article from a common noun that's a party-name defined term, although this manual recommends that you use an article (see 2.106). And if you do use the article with a party-name defined term, signal as much (for the benefit of anyone who'll be negotiating or revising the contract) by including the article in the defined-term parenthetical too.

6.66   It's awkward to put a defined-term parenthetical after a possessive, as in *If a customer's (a "Terminating Customer") contract with Acme terminates … .* The result is that the definition and the defined term aren't grammatically equivalent. Another example: *If Acme, Inc.'s and its affiliates' ("Acme") privacy practices … .* (For another problem with that definition, see 2.95.)

6.67   Don't put a defined-term parenthetical in a section heading. And don't put another set of parentheses within a defined-term parenthetical.

EMPHASIS

6.68   Place in quotation marks and state in bold any defined term that's being defined in a defined-term parenthetical. Don't bold the quotation marks. In general writing you can do without the quotation marks (see *The Chicago Manual of Style*, at 10.3), but use them in contracts so the conventions used for both autonomous and integrated definitions are consistent (see 6.36). To avoid distracting the reader, in this manual the terms defined in examples incorporated in regular paragraphs (as opposed to the samples and the indented examples of contract text) aren't stated in bold.

6.69   Follow standard practice and exclude the definite article *the* and the indefinite article *a* (or *an*), if present, from the quotation marks. One could put the article within the quotation marks, because it constitutes part of the defined term, but it makes sense to put within the quotation marks only what's specific to that defined term.

WHERE TO PLACE A DEFINED-TERM PARENTHETICAL

6.70   The principal source of confusion regarding integrated definitions is where to place the defined-term parenthetical and what it should consist of.

6.71 Don't place the defined-term parenthetical in the middle of the definition, as in each of the following examples. Instead, put it at the end. In each example, the mislocated text is shown in strikethrough and the text in italics shows the preferred location.

> The Company's board of directors has received a written opinion ~~(the "Fairness Opinion")~~ of the Financial Advisor stating that the proposed consideration to be received by the holders of Shares in connection with the Offer and the Merger is fair from a financial point of view to the holders of Shares *(that opinion, the "Fairness Opinion")*.

> The Company will have an irrevocable and exclusive option ~~(the "Repurchase Option")~~, for a period of 90 days from the Termination Date, to repurchase some or all of the Unvested Restricted Shares at the Repurchase Price *(that option, the "Repurchase Option")*.

> This amendment is effective on the first date ~~(the "Effective Date")~~ on which all the following conditions are satisfied *(that date, the "Effective Date")*: … .

> No later than 120 days after the Closing, the Company shall file with the SEC a registration statement on Form S-1 ~~(the "New Registration Statement")~~ registering for resale all Registrable Securities *(that registration statement, the "New Registration Statement")*.

> Acme shall maintain confidential all information it obtains from Widgetco ~~(the "Confidential Information")~~ in the course of providing services under this agreement *(that information, the "Confidential Information")*.

6.72 Usually, mid-definition defined-term parentheticals are merely awkward, but sometimes they can change meaning. Take this example:

> Schedule 3.12 contains an accurate list of all agreements, oral or written ~~("Contracts")~~, to which Dynaco is a party *(each such agreement, a "Contract")*.

6.73 As originally positioned, the defined term encompasses all agreements regardless of the identity of the parties. That might be appropriate in another contract, but in this case the drafter had intended that the defined term would encompass only Dynaco's agreements.

6.74 Don't place the defined term beyond the definition, as in these examples:

> The lease for Blackacre *(the "Lease")* must be substantially in the form of exhibit B ~~(the "Lease")~~.

> The purchase price for the Shares *(the "Purchase Price")* is $3 million ~~(the "Purchase Price")~~.

6.75 Regarding where to place the defined-term parenthetical when creating the defined term for a party name, see 2.94.

CLARIFYING THE SCOPE OF THE DEFINITION

6.76 If it might be unclear how far back an integrated definition goes, include in the defined-term parenthetical, just before the defined term, a reference to the pertinent noun in the definition: *that litigation, the "Acme Litigation"; those documents, the "Dynaco SEC Documents"; each such consent, a "Required*

Consent". This manual refers to this technique as "clarifying the scope" of a definition. It's featured in the examples in 6.71–.72.

6.77   If a definition consists of one or more of a set of enumerated clauses, make that clear in the defined-term parenthetical: *(the litigation listed in clauses (1) through (4) of this section 4(b), the "Acme Litigation")*.

COLLECTIVELY

6.78   If an integrated definition encompasses an entire string of nouns, you can help make that clear by adding the word *collectively* to the defined-term parenthetical, just before the defined term and after any language clarifying the scope of the definition (see 6.76): ... *relating to the confidential affairs of the Company, the Parent, and their respective subsidiaries and affiliates (collectively, the "Acme Entities")*.

BOOSTING A DEFINED TERM

6.79   You can supplement an integrated definition and thereby change the meaning conveyed by the defined term by adding language—generally using *together with*—to the defined-term parenthetical, just before the defined term and just after any language clarifying the scope of the definition (see 6.76) and the word *collectively* (see 6.78), if used. This manual refers to this practice as "boosting" a defined term. In this example, the boosting language is in italics:

> ... the Companies' officers, directors, financial advisors, accountants, attorneys, and other Affiliates (collectively, *together with the Company*, the **"Company Group"**).

6.80   For an example of inappropriate use of boosting, see 2.95.

STACKING DEFINED TERMS

6.81   You can define more than one term within a defined-term parenthetical by separating the defined terms with a semicolon and clarifying the scope of each (see 6.76): *Parent, Sub, and Target are party to a merger agreement dated 3 October 2016 providing for acquisition of Target by Parent by means of a merger of Sub into Target (that agreement, the "Merger Agreement"; that merger, the "Merger")*. This manual refers to this practice as "stacking" defined terms.

6.82   Stacking more than two defined terms is cumbersome: *Roe desires to sell to Jones 5,000 shares of common stock, par value $.01 per share, of Acme Corporation, a Delaware corporation ("Acme"; that common stock, the "Common Stock"; those shares, the "Shares")*. Instead, restructure the provision to define one or more terms separately.

6.83   You can boost (see 6.79) the second defined term in a stacked set: *(the "Endorsement Agreement"; together with the PSB Purchase Agreement and the RCO Purchase Agreement, the "Continuing Agreements")*.

MATCHING THE PARTS OF SPEECH

6.84   As with autonomous definitions (see 6.45), in integrated definitions the part of speech of the defined term should match that of the definition. Mismatch occurs more with integrated definitions than with autonomous definitions.

6.85   Here's an example of such a mismatch: *At the Effective Time, Merger Sub will merge into Acme (the "Merger").* It's not clear what the definition is, because the preceding sentence uses the verb *merge* whereas the defined term is a noun. You can fix this by adding transition language before the defined term. In this case, revise the defined-term parenthetical to read as follows: *(the merger thus effected, the "Merger").* That makes the definition of *Merger* a combination of the preceding sentence and the transition language. But perhaps curing a particular mismatch is best accomplished by restructuring the provision or defining the term elsewhere.

WHICH TYPE OF DEFINITION TO USE

6.86   How to present a definition is in part a function of how long it is. If a definition is relatively succinct, it's probably more efficient to present it as an integrated definition rather than as an autonomous definition, to save space and avoid disrupting the reading process unnecessarily. The longer the definition, the more likely it is that it would be best to present it as an autonomous definition, to avoid clogging up the related provision. Another factor in determining which type of definition to use is whether the best place for a definition is "on site" or in a definition section, an issue discussed immediately below.

THE DEFINITION SECTION

6.87   A definition can be placed in a definition section, which lists autonomous definitions in alphabetical order by defined term. Use the heading *Definitions*, and not *Glossary*, which is less informative. In longer documents, the definition section can constitute an entire article, and in particularly lengthy contracts it can be many pages long. (Regarding language to introduce the autonomous definitions in a definition section, see 6.31.)

Versus Defining Terms On Site

6.88   Alternatively, you can create a defined term "on site" by placing the definition, in the form of an integrated or autonomous definition, with a provision that uses the related defined term. An on-site autonomous definition can simply be a sentence among others in a section or subsection, or it can be placed in a separate subsection, either on its own or with other autonomous definitions (see 6.33–.34). Either way, the autonomous definition should come right after the provision that uses the defined term—placing it before would likely puzzle readers (see 6.35).

6.89   Drafters have traditionally favored placing definitions in definition sections. That has the disadvantage of forcing any reader who encounters an unfamiliar defined term to turn to the definition section to read the definition of that term. From there, the reader might have to consult the definition of one or more other defined terms in the definition section before resuming reading. In a document with many, or complex, defined terms, this flipping back and forth can disrupt one's reading.

6.90   But the definition section serves a purpose, in that it reduces clutter that would otherwise be caused by defining on site a term that readers likely know the meaning of. So deciding which terms can be placed in a definition section involves assessing the extent to which they can be understood independently of their definition.

6.91   Readers can be counted on to know the meaning of initialisms of relevant government agencies (for example, in the United States, *the SEC* and *the IRS*), relevant statutes (for example, in the United States, *ERISA*), and a basic business term such as *GAAP*, meaning "generally accepted accounting principles."

6.92   Somewhat less inherently comprehensible are defined terms with definitions that can vary somewhat from transaction to transaction— defined terms such as *Affiliate*, *Lien*, *Government Authority*, *Business Day*, and *Subsidiary*. To know the exact meaning of such a defined term you would need to read the definition, but the defined term on its own gives a good general sense of its meaning. It's unlikely that your understanding of the provisions in which such a defined term occurs would be meaningfully compromised if you haven't yet read the definition.

6.93   At the other end of the spectrum are defined terms such as *Equity Infusion* or *Excess Insurance Proceeds*—defined terms with a definition that is unique to the transaction, so the defined term can't be understood without consulting the definition.

6.94   Define in the definition section terms in the first category (6.91) and second category (6.92), so they don't unnecessarily clutter up the text. Define on-site terms in the third category (6.93), so they're readily accessible to the reader.

Where to Place the Definition Section

6.95   The definition section has traditionally been placed at the beginning of the body of the contract. This is inconsistent with the notion that provisions that are more important should come first (see 4.84). Readers generally turn first to the deal provisions rather than slogging through the definitions, and those who tackle the definitions head-on would likely need to reread them when they encounter, often many pages later, the provisions using the defined terms.

6.96   If you pare the definition section down to terms that are inherently familiar, no justification remains for keeping it at the beginning of the body of the contract, since readers would need to refer to it only to fine-tune their understanding. You can safely move a pared-down definition section toward the back of the contract, to the boilerplate. When purged of terms best defined on site, the definition section might be slight enough to consist of a single section rather than an entire article. In fact, it might be slight enough for you to dispense with a definition section entirely and define on site those few defined terms that would otherwise have been defined in the definition section.

6.97   It's best not to place the definition section in an attachment (see 5.101). Offering readers the convenience of being able to pull out the definition section and read it side by side with the rest of the contract is trivial compared with putting on site, with the relevant provisions, the definitions that readers would need to consult.

The Two-Column Definition Section

6.98   In contracts drafted in Commonwealth countries, the definition section is commonly presented in two columns, with the defined terms in the first column and the definitions in the second column. This manual recommends not using a two-column format for the definition section.

6.99   The rationale for the two-column format is that keeping the defined term apart from the rest of the definition makes it easier to scan through the defined terms and find the one you're looking for. (If you use a paragraph structure and the definition is more than one line long, the defined term will have text immediately below it.)

6.100   One version of the two-column format omits the definitional verb, making it implicit that *means* is the connection between the first column and the second column. But that precludes using other definitional verbs, including *refers to* (see 6.45).

6.101   If you use the definitional verb with the two-column format, whatever nominal advantage is presented by stating the defined term free of any surrounding text is offset by the awkwardness of chopping a sentence in two.

6.102   The two-column definition section is consistent with an approach to layout that places undue emphasis on breaking up text (see 4.73).

CROSS-REFERENCES TO DEFINITIONS

6.103   Cross-referencing in general is discussed in 4.100–.114, but it also applies to definitions.

The Index of Definitions

6.104   Definition sections have traditionally been used to provide, besides definitions, cross-references to sections where other terms are defined. But definition sections aren't suited to this task. The cross-references are rather cumbersome (the typical format is *"Material Permits" has the meaning given that term in section 3.4*). And because the cross-references are interspersed with autonomous definitions and occur throughout the definition section, it's likely that any reader consulting the definition section to see where a particular term is defined would have to flip through some pages.

6.105   A more efficient vehicle for helping readers quickly find their way around definitions is an index of definitions that lists the defined terms in two columns in alphabetical order and indicates the page where the definition of each term is located. (A page number is more useful than a section number, because readers told the page on which a section occurs would be able to turn to it more quickly than they would if they were given just the section number. Also, sections routinely occupy more than one page.)

6.106   The conventional term for such indexes is "index of defined terms." But seeing as they don't state the page number of each page where a defined term is used, "index of definitions" is a more accurate term.

6.107   Place an index of definitions after the table of contents (see 2.217). If a contract is too short to warrant a table of contents, you can assume that it's also too short to warrant an index of definitions.

6.108   You could instead place an index of definitions at the end of a definition section and include only those terms defined on site. But such an index would be less accessible and less useful than a comprehensive index of definitions placed after the table of contents, so this option is perhaps best reserved for those times when you want to use an index of definitions even though the contract doesn't have a table of contents.

6.109   Generate an index of definitions using Microsoft Word's indexing feature. As with any word-processing function that uses field codes, ensuring that an index of definitions remains accurate through the drafting and negotiating process usually requires that one person retain control of the draft (see 4.113).

Referring to the Definition Section

6.110   If a definition section is located someplace other than at the beginning of the body of the contract (see 6.95), the first section of the contract sometimes states that all or some defined terms are defined in a specified section, namely the definition section. Such provisions run counter to the principle that more-important provisions should come before less-important provisions (see 4.84). And such a provision would serve little purpose if, as recommended in 6.91, the definition section contains only definitions of terms with inherently familiar meanings. Omit such provisions and instead include in longer contracts an index of definitions.

If a Defined Term Is Used Before It Is Defined

6.111   Convention has it that a defined term should be defined where it's first used, so the reader doesn't have to flip pages looking for the definition. But in contracts that follow that convention, sometimes a defined term is used upstream of the definition, perhaps because the first use of that defined term is an incidental one. And sometimes revisions to a contract result in a defined term being inserted upstream of its definition and it's not thought worthwhile to relocate the definition. In such situations it's commonplace to add in parentheses, after the first use of the defined term, the unhelpfully imprecise *as defined below*, the more precise *as defined in section X*, or some variant.

6.112   The problem with this approach is that it assumes that readers start at the top of the contract and work their way methodically through to the end. Instead, it's likely that most readers skim through the text and focus on whichever provisions are of interest to them.

6.113   This has two implications. First, defining a term when it's first used doesn't necessarily help readers. Unless it makes more sense to define it in a definition section (see 6.91), define a term on site, right after the provision that makes the most extensive use of that defined term (see 6.88).

6.114   Second, parenthetical cross-references to where a term is defined are of little value. For readers jumping from one provision to another, it would be a matter of chance whether any such parentheticals happen to be of use. Also, it's tedious to have to check drafts to ensure that every defined term that precedes its definition is given a cross-reference the first time it's used. One could include many more such cross-reference parentheticals, but they would clog up the contract. Instead, in general drop such cross-references in favor of an index of definitions, if appropriate (see 6.104), using them only when, in the absence of an index of definitions, a defined term stranded in a far corner of the contract might have a reader wondering where it's defined.

USE DEFINED TERMS EFFICIENTLY

6.115   Don't create a defined term if you don't use it after having defined it. And usually it's not worthwhile to create a defined term if you use it only once or twice. Defined terms make prose harder to read, and creating a defined term adds clutter, so create a defined term only if the efficiencies it offers more than offset the drawbacks.

6.116   But a concept might be sufficiently complex that the only sensible course is to state it separately as an autonomous definition—even if it's only used once—rather than working it into a provision.

6.117   Also, if in revising a template contract for a transaction you delete all but one or two instances of a defined term, it might not be worthwhile to go back and eliminate that defined term on grounds of insufficient use.

6.118   Be alert to provisions that don't reflect the full meaning of a defined term. For example, in a reference to *Change in Control of the Company*, the words *of the Company* would be redundant if, as is usually the case, *Change of Control* is defined with respect to the Company.

LOOKING TO DICTIONARIES FOR DEFINITIONS

6.119   Some contracts tell readers to consult a dictionary. Here are two examples:

> [T]erms not defined in this agreement have the meaning ordinarily ascribed to them in the Oxford English Dictionary (Second Edition).

> All words, unless otherwise specifically defined in this agreement, have their ordinary meanings as set forth in any dictionary of American English in common usage; there are no secret or code words.

6.120   But seeking to attribute meaning to basic words divorced of any context is unpromising.

6.121   Some contracts that state that a dictionary is to be used to determine the meaning of specific terms:

> The Employee shall not make any disparaging comments, whether oral, written or via any web-based or social media vehicle, to anyone about Acme, any of its executives or employees, or its products or services, as the term "disparage" and "disparaging" is set forth in any dictionary of English or of law.

6.122   It's hard to imagine a court willingly limiting itself to what a dictionary says regarding the meaning of a legal term of art like *disparage*.

SOURCES OF UNCERTAIN MEANING IN CONTRACT LANGUAGE

7.1   Confusing contract language leads to uncertain meaning, and uncertain meaning can lead to disputes. This chapter provides an introduction to the different kinds of uncertain meaning in contract language, in particular ambiguity and vagueness.

7.2   Chapter 1 considers the characteristics of optimal contract language. This chapter 7 might seem the reverse image of chapter 1, with deviation from the characteristics of optimal contract language creating the different kinds of uncertain meaning. But the connection is less clear cut than that. Some of the characteristics of optimal contract language—notably omitting archaisms—relate primarily to making contract prose easier to read rather than avoiding uncertain meaning. And not all sources of uncertain meaning are a function of suboptimal contract language. For example, two separate provisions in a contract might be models of clarity, but if they conflict, the result is uncertain meaning.

7.3   Uncertain meaning in contract language arises from five sources—ambiguity, failure to be sufficiently specific, mistake, conflict, failure to address an issue, and vagueness. The first four are pernicious, whereas the last—vagueness—is an essential drafting tool when used with restraint.

7.4   Courts tend to attribute all instances of uncertain meaning to ambiguity—witness how *Black's Law Dictionary* defines *ambiguity* in part as "Doubtfulness or uncertainty of meaning or intention, as in a contractual term or statutory provision." But the sources of uncertainty operate differently from each other. Lump them together and you risk misunderstanding them.

AMBIGUITY

7.5   For linguists, text is ambiguous if it's capable of conveying two or more inconsistent meanings. If some who read a contract provision think it means one thing and others think it means something else, that provision is ambiguous.

7.6   Some who work with contracts are partial to "creative ambiguity"—the practice of deliberately including in a contract an ambiguous provision, with the aim of permitting the client to invoke, after signing, the hidden, alternative meaning if doing so would offer an advantage.

7.7   But such gamesmanship seems antithetical to a successful contract relationship, and it might violate lawyer ethics rules. And if the other side thinks a provision means one thing, and you're aware of that and do nothing to suggest that the provision means anything else, then a court might hold that that precludes you from arguing that the provision means something else. See, e.g., *United Rentals, Inc. v. RAM Holdings Inc.*, 937 A.2d 810, 836 (Del. Ch. 2007) (invoking "the forthright negotiator principle," namely that "a court may consider the subjective understanding of one party that has been objectively manifested and is known or should be known by the other party").

7.8   Different kinds of ambiguity occur in contracts. Some are addressed elsewhere in this manual:

- for discussion of ambiguity in references to time, see chapter 10

- for discussion of the ambiguity this manual considers under the rubric "the part versus the whole," see chapter 11

- for discussion of syntactic ambiguity, which arises principally out of the order in which words and phrases are used and how they relate to each other, see chapter 12

- for ambiguity associated with language of discretion, see 3.201–.214

7.9   Three other kinds of ambiguity are discussed in the following sections.

Lexical Ambiguity

7.10   Lexical ambiguity occurs when a word has more than one meaning. One form of lexical ambiguity is homonymy, which occurs when words have identical forms but unrelated meanings. An example is *bank*, which might mean a financial institution or the bank of a river. Given the unrelated meanings, homonymy is unlikely to cause to confusion—the context allows readers to determine which meaning is intended. That's particularly the case in the limited and stylized context of contracts.

7.11   The other kind of lexical ambiguity, polysemy, occurs when a word has lexical senses that relate to the same basic meaning of the word as it occurs in different contexts. To expand on the example above, *bank* can mean a financial institution or a building that houses a financial institution. Those meanings are complementary.

7.12   Lexical ambiguity occurs in some words and phrases that are standard in contracts, for example *represents* (see 3.374), *best efforts* (see chapter 8), *material* (see 9.7–.23), *year* (see 10.92), and *willful* (see 13.896). Another example is *foreclosure*: does it refer to foreclosure proceedings or to a foreclosure sale? See *Provident Bank v. Tennessee Farmers Mutual Insurance Co.*, 234 F. App'x 393 (6th Cir. 2007) (holding that it was unclear whether the term *foreclosure* referred to foreclosure proceedings or to a foreclosure sale).

7.13   To eliminate lexical ambiguity, make clear which meaning you have in mind, either by stating that meaning instead of using the ambiguous word or phrase or by using a defined term. For routine instances of lexical ambiguity, applying the fix should be routine too. But it can require imagination to spot lexical ambiguity in words and phrases that don't occur routinely in contracts.

Antecedent Ambiguity

7.14   In the sentence *John is late because he overslept*, the antecedent of *he* is *John* (assuming that the broader context doesn't suggest an alternative, such as John's father). Confusion can arise if it's not clear what the antecedent is of a given element. For example, in *John read Bill's email, and he is furious*, the antecedent of *he* could be either *John* or *Bill*.

7.15   This kind of ambiguity arises in contracts. For example, in *Loso v. Loso*, 31 A.3d 830, 831, 832–33 (Conn. App. Ct. 2011), the following contract language was at issue:

> The defendant agrees to pay for one-half the cost of Sarah's college educational expenses for a four year degree net of scholarships or grants subject to the limitation that said cost shall not exceed the tuition for a full-time residential student at UCONN-Storrs.

7.16   Was the defendant's liability capped at half the tuition for a full-time residential student at UCONN-Storrs (the meaning sought by the defendant), or was it capped at the full amount of that tuition? In other words, was the antecedent of "said cost" "one-half the cost" or "the cost" of Sarah's expenses? Disagreeing with the lower court, the appellate court held that the defendant's liability was capped at the full amount of the tuition. Furthermore, it said that the language was "clear and unambiguous"—a debatable assessment.

7.17   The drafter should have made the intended meaning clear enough to preclude a fight. Here's how the provision at issue could have been drafted to achieve the meaning sought by the defendant:

> The defendant shall pay half the cost of Sarah's college educational expenses for a four-year degree net of any scholarships and grants, up to an amount equal to half the tuition for a full-time residential student at UCONN-Storrs.

7.18   Another case involving antecedent ambiguity is *Trustees of First Union Real Estate Equity & Mortgage Investments v. Mandell*, 987 F.2d 1286 (7th Cir. 1993). Here's the language at issue (emphasis added):

> Tenant shall pay, from time to time, to Landlord as additional rent fifty percent (50%) of any and all percentage rent which S.S. Kresge Company, or its successor or assigns, pays to Tenant under their lease for part or all of the Demised Premises during the initial term and *any period thereof*, promptly after Tenant receives such percentage rent payments.

7.19   The question was whether "any period thereof" referred to "initial term" or "their lease".

7.20   Another relevant Seventh Circuit case is *Tompkins v. Central Laborers' Pension Fund*, 712 F.3d 995 (7th Cir. 2013). In the contract provision at issue in that case, it was not clear what the phrase "For such" referred to.

7.21   And an English case, *Rainy Sky S. A. and others v. Kookmin Bank* [2011] UKSC 50, involved uncertainty over what was the antecedent of "such sums" in the phrase "all such sums due to you under the contract."

7.22   As with all forms of ambiguity, the only solution is to be aware of the sources of such ambiguity and, when alternatives present themselves, to be clear which antecedent you're referring to. It's perhaps no coincidence that three of the four examples of antecedent ambiguity cited above involve archaisms—*said* (see 13.720), *thereof* (see 13.349), and *such* used instead of *those* (see 13.768). It's more challenging to spot antecedent ambiguity if you're wading through a fog of traditional contract language.

Contract-Reference Ambiguity

7.23   Ambiguity can arise in how a contract refers to itself. For example, does the word *hereunder* in a section apply just to that section or to the entire contract? See *Medicis Pharmaceutical Corp. v. Anacor Pharmaceuticals, Inc.*, No. CV 8095-VCP, 2013 WL 4509652 (Del. Ch. 12 Aug. 2013); *Weichert Co. of Maryland, Inc. v. Faust*, 419 Md. 306 (2011).

7.24   The same sort of confusion can be prompted by use of *herein*. See *Karmely v. Wertheimer*, 737 F.3d 197, 209–11 (2d Cir. 2013); *Bayerische Landesbank, New York Branch v. Aladdin Capital Management LLC*, 692 F.3d 42 (2d Cir. 2012). And *hereinbelow*. See *Dean St. Capital Advisors, LLC v. Otoka Energy Corp.*, No. 15-CV-824 (RJS), 2016 WL 413124, at *1 (S.D.N.Y. 1 Feb. 2016).

7.25   It isn't only *here-* words that pose a risk of contract-reference ambiguity. You can create comparable confusion by pointing above or below in a contract. The phrase *except as provided below* resulted in a dispute over what was being referred to. See *In re Lehman Bros. Holdings Inc.*, 513 F. App'x 75, 77 (2d Cir. 2013). So did *the foregoing*. See *Karmely v. Wertheimer*, 737 F.3d 197, 211 (2d Cir. 2013). It's easy to imagine the phrase *as aforesaid* creating comparable confusion. Say instead *in accordance with section X* or *as stated in section X.*

7.26   The word *hereunder* can cause this kind of confusion too, besides confusion over whether you're referring to an entire contract or just a part (see 7.23). In *Yosemite Insurance Co. v. Nationwide Mutual Insurance Co.*, No. 16 CIV. 5290 (PAE), 2016 WL 6684246 (S.D.N.Y. 10 Nov. 2016), an arbitration panel had held that *hereunder* referred not to the entire reinsurance contract but instead to the two articles below the provision in question. The arbitration panel in effect decided that the *-under* in *hereunder* meant not *by operation of* but instead meant *below.* So *hereunder* has the potential to create two kinds of confusion.

7.27   The fix for contract-reference ambiguity is straightforward. First, never use *here-* words (see 13.349). And second, instead of using *above* and *below* to refer to other parts of a contract, refer to specific sections (see 4.105).

FAILURE TO BE SUFFICIENTLY SPECIFIC

7.28 If a word or phrase in a contract turns out to have been too general, the parties might end up fighting over which more specific meaning had been intended.

7.29 For example, a dispute over alimony involved the meaning of the phrase *on a full-time basis*. See *In re C.P.Y.*, 364 S.W.3d 411 (Tex. App. 2012). The husband had to pay the wife alimony until, among other events, she returned to work "on a full-time basis." The wife got work as a contract attorney, so the husband sought an order declaring that he no longer had to pay alimony. The court held that the phrase "full-time basis" is ambiguous, but it would be more accurate to say that it was insufficiently specific, in that it can be uncertain in several respects what *on a full-time basis* means. How many hours a day and days per week must you work for work to be full-time? How long must that level of work be maintained? Must someone be an employee to work full-time, or can you be a consultant? Does volunteer work count?

7.30 Here are some other disputes involving a failure to be sufficiently specific:

- *Mosser Constructions, Inc. v. Travelers Indemnity Co.*, 430 F. App'x 417 (6th Cir. 2011) (considering whether "subcontractor" means any supplier to a contractor or something more)

- *Graev v. Graev*, 898 N.E.2d 909 (N.Y. 2008) (holding that the word "cohabitation" as used in a separation agreement did not have a plain meaning and that relevant factors might include whether those living together engaged in sexual relations or commingled their finances)

- *Jones v. Francis Drilling Fluids*, 613 F. Supp. 2d 858 (S.D. Tex. 2008) (considering whether the word "offshore," in connection with an oil rig, refers to a location in the Gulf of Mexico or in inland waters, and holding that it could convey either meaning)

7.31 See also discussion of the phrases *close of business* (see 10.34) and *moral turpitude* (see 13.528).

7.32 A failure to be sufficiently specific might be a function of changing circumstances rather than a drafting glitch. For example, *Richey v. Metaxpert LLC*, 407 F. App'x 198 (9th Cir. 2010), involved a dispute between a company and an employee who had agreed that he wouldn't compete with the company "in the computer gaming business" for two years after leaving the company. After he left the company, the employee started designing software for smartphone games. At issue in the dispute was whether the word *computer* included smartphones. The year the employee signed his contract was also the year the iPhone was launched, so perhaps one can't fault the drafter of that contract for not having anticipated the smartphone boom.

MISTAKE

7.33 Uncertainty of meaning can also arise if the parties are mistaken as to the facts and the contract reflects that mistake. A famous instance of such a mistake is found in the English case *Raffles v. Wichelhaus*, 159 Eng. Rep. 375 (Ex. 1864). The contract provided for purchase of cotton from a ship named "Peerless" that was to depart from Bombay. It transpired that two ships named "Peerless" were to depart from Bombay a couple of months apart—the buyer had one ship in mind, the seller the other.

7.34 The term *latent ambiguity* has been used to describe such situations. For example, *Black's Law Dictionary* defines latent ambiguity as "An ambiguity that does not readily appear in the language of a document, but instead arises from a collateral matter once the document's terms are applied or executed," and it alludes to *Raffles v. Wichelhaus*. But the contract text at issue in *Raffles v. Wichelhaus* doesn't present alternative meanings, so it's unhelpful to attribute the confusion to ambiguity. Judicial fondness for the phrase *latent ambiguity* perhaps arises from euphonious contrast with the phrase *patent ambiguity* (namely actual ambiguity).

CONFLICT

7.35 Conflict occurs when two or more components of a contract aren't compatible. It can be caused by careless repetition (see 1.62), for example when the words and digits used to state a number don't match (see 14.1–.16).

7.36 Entire provisions can conflict. For example, *United Rentals, Inc. v. RAM Holdings, Inc.*, 937 A.2d 810 (Del. Ch. 2007), a high-profile case involving an abortive acquisition, involved conflict between two provisions on remedies. See Kenneth A. Adams, *Merger Pacts: Contract Drafting, Cerberus Litigation*, New York Law Journal, 19 Feb. 2008.

FAILURE TO ADDRESS AN ISSUE

7.37 Uncertainty can occur if by oversight a drafter fails to address an issue that should have been addressed. That's different from the parties electing not to address an issue to facilitate their reaching agreement.

7.38 Consider *Sabatini v. Roybal*, 150 N.M. 478 (Ct. App. 2011), which addressed use of the phrase "private garage" in a contract. The lower court had held that for a restriction on building, "private garage" meant a garage capable of holding no more than a reasonable number of vehicles for use by a single family, rather than the 100-foot-by-50-foot structure built by the Roybals.

7.39 After noting that the phrase "private garage" was ambiguous, the court of appeals reversed, holding that the Roybals' garage complied with the restrictive covenant, as (1) the garage was used to store the Roybals' vehicles and was not available for use by the public and (2) the phrase "private garage" didn't incorporate any limits on size.

7.40   But "private garage" isn't ambiguous: it doesn't present alternative meanings. Instead, it's clear that the garage wasn't to be used by the public, but the drafter overlooked another issue likely to arise in a Santa Fe, New Mexico, subdivision—whether there was a limit on the size of the garage.

7.41   Avoiding this sort of uncertainty is more challenging than is avoiding the sorts of uncertainty discussed above, in that instead of eliminating that which is problematic, you have to figure out what's missing.

VAGUENESS

7.42   Vague words used in contracts include the adjectives *reasonable*, *prompt*, *material*, *negligent*, *satisfactory*, and *substantial* (among many others) and the related adverbs. With vagueness, whether a given standard has been met is a function of the circumstances. For example, how fast a contract party must act to comply with an obligation to do something promptly is a function of what would be reasonable under the circumstances. There's no specific deadline.

7.43   So with vagueness comes the possibility of dispute. A contract party under an obligation to do something promptly might act fast enough that no one could reasonably say they hadn't acted promptly. But the longer they take, the greater the likelihood of the other party deciding that they hadn't acted promptly.

7.44   That being the case, it would seem sensible to be specific instead of vague, for example by saying *no later than five days after*. But drafters use vagueness if lack of control (over the future; over someone else's conduct) means that a precise standard wouldn't make sense. For example, if a provision requiring reimbursement of legal expenses would apply to a broad range of litigation, from the trivial to the catastrophic, it might make sense to express a cap not as a specific amount but instead by referring to *reasonable legal expenses*—a vague standard.

7.45   Vagueness might also be expedient if addressing an issue precisely would make negotiations longer or more contentious than one or both parties want.

7.46   Different vague words might pose different challenges. For example, in a given context the time constraints might be clear-cut enough that there's little room for dispute over what's required for a party to act promptly. By contrast, a provision subject to a *substantial* standard might leave the parties wondering at what point along a spectrum from nothing to everything something has to be before it's substantial.

Limiting the Risk in Vagueness

7.47   Vagueness in a contract can be more risky or less, depending on how it's used.

7.48   It would be prudent to use vagueness only if not too much is at stake and the context is sufficiently commonplace that the parties and any court would have a basis for determining what would be reasonable in the circumstances.

7.49   It would also make sense to reduce the scope of vagueness. For how to do that when using the phrase *reasonable efforts*, see 8.88, 8.117.

Gradations of Vagueness

7.50   The notion of gradations in vagueness is unhelpful. It's on display in how people understand the phrases *negligent, grossly negligent, reckless,* and *wanton* (see 13.561–.577). But perhaps the biggest misconception regarding gradations of vagueness is the notion of a spectrum of standards featuring the word *efforts*. See 8.18–.33.

7.51   But in the appropriate context, it's possible to subdivide coherently a spectrum of vagueness. See the distinction this manual draws between *material* and *nontrivial* (see 9.17–.23).

BLURRED BOUNDARIES

7.52   Instead of being distinct, the categories of uncertain meaning can blend into each other.

7.53   The difference between lexical ambiguity (see 7.10) and failure to be sufficiently specific (see 7.28) is one of degree. The former involves established alternative meanings; the latter involves a broader range of alternative meanings. The one can shade into the other.

7.54   Similarly, the distinction between failing to be sufficiently specific about an issue and failing to address it at all is one of degree.

7.55   And contract usages can be both vague and ambiguous. Given the confusion over ostensible gradations in *efforts* standards, the phrase *best efforts* can be considered not only vague but also ambiguous (see 8.18–.27). So can the word *material* (see 9.7).

REASONABLE EFFORTS AND ITS VARIANTS

CONFUSION OVER *EFFORTS* (AND *ENDEAVOURS*)

8.1   There's widespread confusion over phrases using the word *efforts* (and in England and Australia, *endeavours*). This chapter considers the function of *efforts* standards, the variety of *efforts* standards, what people who work with contracts believe about *efforts* standards, how *efforts* standards evolved, and what caselaw says.

8.2   This manual recommends that of the different *efforts* standards, you use only *reasonable efforts*. Doing so allows *efforts* standards to serve their intended function, and it eliminates a potential source of confusion. The notion that different *efforts* standards impose obligations of different levels of onerousness is an illusion. But that's only part of what's involved in using *efforts* standards effectively. See 8.84–.122 for all this manual's recommendations regarding *efforts* standards.

THE FUNCTION OF *EFFORTS* STANDARDS

8.3   When accomplishing a specific goal isn't entirely within Acme's control, Acme should be reluctant to enter into a contract that imposes on Acme an unqualified obligation to accomplish that goal—doing so would pose undue risk of liability for nonperformance. The parties might instead agree to use *reasonable efforts*, or some other *efforts* standard, to express that obligation. All provisions using *efforts* standards are vague—complying with a given *efforts* obligation is a function of the circumstances (see 7.42).

8.4   Contracts use *efforts* standards in connection with many different obligations, such as an obligation to cause a securities registration statement to become effective by a certain time, an obligation to obtain consents required for closing, or an obligation to promote sales of a product.

8.5   *Efforts* standards are also used as a matter of expediency, if the parties don't want to spend time negotiating precise guidelines or decide it would be too contentious to do so.

8.6   This chapter addresses only explicit *efforts* standards. They're different from an *efforts* standard that a court imposes even though the contract appears to impose an unqualified obligation, or that a court implies in the absence of an explicit obligation.

A VARIETY OF *EFFORTS* STANDARDS

8.7 Drafters use a bewildering variety of *efforts* standards and alternatives to *efforts* standards. This section identifies the principal variants. Those discussed in 8.8–.12 are summarized in figure 4.

8.8 In the United States, it's conventional to use *efforts*, but in England and Australia *endeavours* is favored over *efforts*. One even encounters the Americanized version—*endeavors*. Both are also used in the singular, *effort* and *endeavour*. Although this section refers primarily to *efforts* (and *effort*), the alternatives described apply equally to *endeavours* (and *endeavor*).

8.9 Drafters use a broad assortment of adjectives in *efforts* provisions. Those used most frequently are *best efforts* and *reasonable efforts*, with *good-faith efforts* lagging behind. On the U.S. Securities and Exchange Commission's EDGAR system, one sees a bewildering variety of other adjectives used to create eccentric *efforts* standards: *extraordinary, utmost, substantial, persistent, good, diligent, prompt, business,* and perhaps others. Adjectives are often combined in twos (*reasonable best efforts*) and even threes (*best good-faith reasonable efforts*).

8.10 And there's the adverb *commercially*. It's used most often with *reasonable*, but you also see it with *best* and *good-faith*, although that doesn't make sense: one describes something as being *commercially reasonable*, but not *commercially best* or *commercially good-faith*.

8.11 The determiner *all* can be used with *efforts*, usually with an adjective (as in *all reasonable efforts*), but sometimes on its own (*all efforts*). The determiner *every* is always used with *effort*, sometimes on its own (*every effort*), and sometimes with one of the usual adjectives (*every reasonable effort*).

8.12 Adding to the variety is the range of verbs used: *make, exercise, exert, expend, undertake,* and *use*. You can also add a pronoun: *her, his, its,* or *their*.

FIGURE 4 ■ THE COMPONENTS OF *EFFORTS* PROVISIONS IN TRADITIONAL CONTRACT DRAFTING

VERB	DETERMINER	PRONOUN	ADVERB	ADJECTIVE (ONE OR MORE)	NOUN
make *exercise* *exert*	*all*	*her* *his* *its*	*commercially*	*best* *reasonable* *good-faith*	*efforts* *endeavours*
expend *undertake* *use*	*every*	*their*			*effort* *endeavour*

▨ Optional

8.13   An alternative to adjectives is to place a modifier after *efforts*, as in *efforts that are reasonable, efforts in good faith*, and *efforts that are consistent with the Servicing Standard*.

8.14   Drafters also use alternatives to *efforts* provisions that rely on an adjective (for example, *utmost*), an adverb (for example, *aggressively*), an adverb phrase (*to the best of its ability, to the extent it is able to do so*), or a verb (*endeavor, seek, strive, try*). And instead of requiring that a party use reasonable efforts to stop something, some contracts state that the party *shall not negligently permit* the act in question. These alternatives simply add to the confusion.

WHAT PEOPLE THINK *EFFORTS* STANDARDS MEAN

8.15   Anecdotal evidence suggests that many who work with contracts believe that *best efforts* obligations are more onerous than *reasonable efforts* obligations. The distinction is often expressed like this: *reasonable efforts* requires only what is reasonable in the context, whereas *best efforts* requires that you do everything you can to comply with the obligation, even if you bankrupt yourself. People are less certain of the implications of other *efforts* standards.

8.16   Commentators chime in on this. You can find blog posts confidently asserting distinctions among *efforts* standards. For example, that *best efforts* is equivalent to *all reasonable efforts*, which is more onerous than *commercially reasonable efforts*, which in turn is more onerous than *reasonable efforts*.

8.17   In an example of the no-smoke-without-fire school of contract interpretation (see p. xxxviii), judges and those who work with contracts are prone to suggesting that if people believe that different *efforts* standards are onerous to differing degrees, there must be something to that notion.

WHAT *EFFORTS* STANDARDS ACTUALLY MEAN

8.18   Suggesting that different *efforts* standards are onerous to different degrees requires ignoring English usage, contract law, and how *efforts* standards have evolved. What follows might seem professorial, but it crucially supplies what has been missing from discussion of *efforts* standards— actual evidence.

Best Efforts Is Not More Onerous Than *Reasonable Efforts*

HOW *EFFORTS* STANDARDS HAVE EVOLVED

8.19   The precursor of *efforts* is *endeavour*, both singular and plural, in the phrase *to do one's endeavour(s)*. *The Oxford English Dictionary* offers as the definition "to exert oneself to the uttermost; to do all one can (in a cause or to an end)," and notes that the phrase is archaic. It offers quotations using *to do one's endeavor(s)* from around 1500 to 1873.

8.20   In the same entry, *The Oxford English Dictionary* also offers quotations featuring variants of the phrase using the word *best*. One is a line from Shakespeare's *Merchant of Venice*, "My best endeuours shall be done heerein."

8.21   The simplest explanation of this use of the word *best* is that it's a rhetorical flourish that doesn't change meaning, just as adding the word *best* to *It's in your interests* (*It's in your best interests*), *to my knowledge* (*to the best of my knowledge*), and *use your judgment* (*use your best judgment*) doesn't change their meaning. Instead, use of the word *best* simply signals a measure of formality. It's consistent with this interpretation that in the entry for *to do one's endeavour(s)*, *The Oxford English Dictionary* doesn't distinguish quotations that use *best* from those that do not and doesn't comment on use of *best* in some quotations but not in others.

8.22   As for the level of exertion inherent in *to do one's endeavour(s)*, look to how modern equivalents are understood. If a 56-year-old man—a lawyer with no heroic sporting deeds in his past—says, "In the 2017 Garden City Turkey Trot, I'll do my best to improve on my 2016 time," he's not committing himself to hiring a running coach, strength coach, nutritionist, and physiotherapist and embarking on a full-time regimen involving high-altitude training, bariatric chambers, cutting-edge footwear, and the like. Instead, he's telling himself and anyone else idly listening that considering his age, physique, family obligations, work commitments, and his other interests, he'll try hard. Expressions of an intention to do one's utmost, however they're worded, make sense only if the speaker and listeners assume a level of effort that's reasonable, considering the circumstances.

8.23   According to a Google Ngram of *best endeavours* and *reasonable endeavours* showing the frequency with which those phrases occur in Google's British-English corpus of digitized books between 1800 and 2000, use of *best endeavours* rose to a peak around 1820 then gradually decreased. By contrast, *reasonable endeavours* is essentially absent from the Ngram until after 1980, when the frequency with which it appears starts creeping up. But even by 2000, *best endeavours* still occurs about ten times as often as *reasonable endeavours*.

8.24   The links to Google Books in that Ngram suggest that whereas *best endeavours* occurs in a variety of publications, *reasonable endeavours* occurs primarily in legal and governmental publications. It has never been used in everyday English. It appears that *reasonable endeavours* developed as an alternative to *best endeavours*, but one that conveys the same meaning. The most plausible explanation is that because lawyers are prone to literal-minded hairsplitting, writers of legal texts thought it appropriate to come up with an alternative to *best endeavours*. Presumably the aim was to avoid the suggestion, prompted by the dictionary definition of *best* as "exceeding all others," that *best endeavours* requires endeavours that are somehow better than other endeavours.

8.25   A Google Ngram of occurrence of *best efforts* and *reasonable efforts* in Google's American-English corpus shows use of *best efforts* gradually increasing over the two hundred years covered by the Ngram, much as *best efforts* increases in the British-English corpus. But *reasonable efforts* is essentially absent for the first fifty years and thereafter increases only very gradually until 1960, after which it increases markedly. But in 2000, *best efforts* still occurs four times as often as *reasonable efforts*. (Images of the two Ngrams described in 8.23–.25 and *The Oxford English Dictionary*'s definition of *to do one's endeavour(s)* are available at Kenneth A. Adams, *Distinguishing Between "Efforts" Standard Makes No Sense*, Adams on Contract Drafting (4 Apr. 2017), http://www.adamsdrafting.com/distinguishing-between-different-efforts-standards-makes-no-sense/.)

8.26   The principal difference between the British-English Ngram and the American-English Ngram is decreasing use of *best endeavours* in the former and increase use of *best efforts* in the latter. That's presumably a function of *endeavours* becoming less popular and *efforts* becoming more popular, something evident from an Ngram comparing the fortunes of those two words (see 8.91).

8.27   So *best endeavours* and *best efforts* are the only phrases used in everyday English, and they make sense only if understood as connoting conduct that is reasonable in the circumstances. *Reasonable endeavours, reasonable efforts*, and other variants have never been used in everyday English and are best understood as alternatives to *best endeavours* and *best efforts* introduced by the legal profession, to avoid having the idiomatic meaning of those phrases disregarded by literal-minded judges and lawyers.

IN CONTRACTS, MORE THAN REASONABLE IS UNREASONABLE

8.28   There's another reason why it doesn't make sense to suggest that a *best efforts* obligation is more onerous than a *reasonable efforts* obligation. If that were the case, then anyone under an obligation to use *best efforts* would be at risk of having to act more than reasonably—in other words, unreasonably—to comply with that obligation. Nothing in contract law suggests a standard requiring that one act unreasonably to comply with an obligation: contracts default to reasonableness in the absence of specificity. Furthermore, one would have no basis for determining at what point a *best efforts* obligation had been complied with—just how unreasonably would one have to act to meet that standard?

OBJECTIVE-VERSUS-SUBJECTIVE DOESN'T MAKE SENSE

8.29   Some who work with contracts think that *reasonable efforts* is an objective standard and *best efforts* a subjective standard, or vice versa. *Objective* refers to that which anyone can, in principle, observe. *Subjective* is a function of an individual's own particular viewpoint and traits. The first problem with tying *reasonable efforts* and *best efforts* to *objective* and *subjective* is that nothing in the labels *best efforts* and *reasonable efforts* suggests a distinction analogous to the distinction between *objective* and *subjective*.

8.30   But beyond that, whether someone has expended sufficient efforts is a function of the circumstances—in other words, objective reality. There's no basis for leaving it to a party under an *efforts* obligation to determine whether it felt it had done enough and having courts bound by that determination, no matter how divorced from reality.

All Doesn't Affect Meaning

8.31   In *all reasonable efforts*, the word *all* is a rhetorical flourish that does not affect meaning—it's used to the same effect in phrases such as *all due respect* and *all deliberate speed*.

8.32   Furthermore, must a party under an obligation to use *all reasonable efforts* take every action that might contribute to achieving the goal, as long as each action is reasonable? It would be nonsensical to suggest that under an *all reasonable efforts* standard you don't consider the task as a whole. After all, if you're asked to move a mountain of sand from one place to another using only a pair of tweezers, each act of moving a few grains of sand could readily be accomplished, but the task as a whole would nevertheless be unreasonable.

Commercially Doesn't Affect Meaning

8.33   There's no basis for saying that adding *commercially* to *reasonable efforts* affects its meaning—because *efforts* standards are vague (see 8.3), they take into account the circumstances of the transaction.

Reasonable Efforts Doesn't Require Moderation

8.34   One meaning of *reasonable* is "moderate"—getting a reasonable amount of exercise usually wouldn't extend to running a marathon. So if you want to impress on the other side that you expect it to do its utmost to sell widgets, *reasonable* can seem lacking, and the notion of *efforts* standards that are more onerous can be seductive.

8.35   But that's not a real concern, because a *reasonable efforts* standard takes circumstances into account (see 8.22). Nothing prevents a given set of circumstances from requiring that a reasonable person charged with performing a task act with urgency or commit considerable resources.

CASELAW AND THE UCC ON THE MEANING OF DIFFERENT *EFFORTS* STANDARDS

8.36   So as a matter of English usage, contract law, and how *efforts* standards have evolved, the notion that different *efforts* standards express different meanings is unworkable, and nothing a court says can change that. If courts elect to jump off an *efforts* cliff, don't follow them.

8.37   But those who work with contracts should be aware of the caselaw on *efforts* standards. It can affect how others approach *efforts* standards, and it relates to issues other than whether a reasonableness standard or some other standard applies.

U.S. Caselaw

8.38   To the credit of U.S. courts, they have largely avoided falling prey to the same misconception as those who work with contracts—the notion that different *efforts* standards express different meanings.

THE MEANING OF *BEST EFFORTS*

8.39   U.S. courts haven't required that a party under a duty to use best efforts to accomplish a specific goal make every conceivable effort to do so, regardless of the detriment to it. See, e.g., *Coady Corp. v. Toyota Motor Distributors, Inc.*, 361 F.3d 50, 59 (1st Cir. 2004) ("'Best efforts' … cannot mean everything possible under the sun … ."); *Triple-A Baseball Club Associates v. Northeastern Baseball, Inc.*, 832 F.2d 214, 228 (1st Cir. 1987) ("We have found no cases, and none have been cited, holding that 'best efforts' means every conceivable effort."); *Bloor v. Falstaff Brewing Corp.*, 601 F.2d 609, 614 (2d Cir. 1979) ("The requirement that a party use its best efforts necessarily does not prevent the party from giving reasonable consideration to its own interests.").

8.40   Different courts have used different terminology in attempting to articulate what *best efforts* does mean. Some have held that the appropriate standard is one of good faith, a standard grounded in honesty and fairness. See *Triple-A Baseball Club Associates*, 832 F.2d at 225 ("We have been unable to find any case in which a court found … that a party acted in good faith but did not use its best efforts."); *Soroof Trading Development Co. v. GE Fuel Cell Systems, LLC*, 842 F. Supp. 2d 502, 511 (S.D.N.Y. 2012) (holding that a *best efforts* provision imposes an obligation to act with good faith in light of one's own capabilities); *Bloor*, 601 F.2d at 614 (*best efforts* imposes an obligation to act with good faith in light of one's own capabilities); *Western Geophysical Co. of America v. Bolt Associates, Inc.*, 584 F.2d 1164, 1171 (2d Cir. 1978) (an obligation to use best efforts can be met by "active exploitation in good faith").

8.41   But some cases have held that the standard is higher than that of good faith. See *Martin v. Monumental Life Insurance Co.*, 240 F.3d 223, 234 (3rd Cir. 2001) ("Precedent treats 'best efforts' as a form of good faith and sound business judgment."); *Satellite Broadcasting Cable, Inc. v. Telefonica De Espana, S.A.*, 807 F. Supp. 210, 217 (D.P.R. 1992) (the net effect of the *best efforts* provision at issue was "to expand extra-contractual damages beyond a mere good faith requirement"); *Kroboth v. Brent*, 215 A.D.2d 813, 814 (N.Y. App. Div. 1995) ("'[B]est efforts' requires more than 'good faith,' which is an implied covenant in all contracts … .").

8.42   Other cases have held that the appropriate standard is one of diligence. See *National Data Payment Systems, Inc. v. Meridian Bank*, 212 F.3d 849, 854 (3d Cir. 2000); *T.S.I. Holdings, Inc. v. Jenkins*, 924 P.2d 1239, 1250 (Kan. 1996).

8.43   Still other cases have invoked reasonableness. See, e.g., *Corporate Lodging Consultants, Inc. v. Bombardier Aerospace Corp.*, No. 03-1467-WEB, 2005 WL 1153606, at *6 (D. Kan. 11 May 2005) ("Best efforts docs not mean perfection and expectations are only justifiable if they are reasonable.");

Coady Corp., 361 F.3d at 59 ("'Best efforts' is implicitly qualified by a reasonableness test ... ."); *Kroboth*, 215 A.D.2d at 814 ("'Best efforts' requires that plaintiffs pursue all reasonable methods ... .").

8.44 And some courts have acknowledged that *best efforts* and *reasonable efforts* mean the same thing. See, e.g., *Stewart v. O'Neill*, 225 F. Supp. 2d 6, 14 (D.C. Cir. 2002) (stating that "the agency was obligated to use its best efforts—that is, all reasonable efforts—to comply with all terms of the settlement agreement"); *Soroof Trading Development Co.*, 842 F. Supp. at 511 (holding that New York courts use the term *reasonable efforts* interchangeably with *best efforts*); see also *Trecom Business Systems, Inc. v. Prasad*, 980 F. Supp. 770, 774 n.1 (D.N.J. 1997) (in a case involving an implied rather than express duty, referring to the distinction between *best efforts* and *reasonable efforts* as "merely an issue of semantics").

8.45 It appears that only two courts have suggested that one can distinguish between *best efforts* and *reasonable efforts*. See *In re Chateaugay Corp.*, 198 B.R. 848, 854 (S.D.N.Y. 1996); *Krinsky v. Long Beach Wings*, LLC, No. B148698, 2002 WL 31124659, at *8 (Cal. Ct. App. 26 Sept. 2002). But in neither case does the court provide a coherent rationale for its position.

8.46 So U.S. courts have overwhelmingly rejected—either explicitly or by adopting an alternative interpretation—the notion that *best efforts* represents a more onerous standard than *reasonable efforts*.

8.47 Don't attribute any particular significance to the fact that courts use different buzzwords—*diligence, good faith, reasonableness*—in describing what *best efforts* does mean. That's a predictable result of courts seeking to explain a vague phrase by using other vague words and phrases.

A DELAWARE DISSENT

8.48 In his dissent in *Williams Companies, Inc. v. Energy Transfer Equity, L.P.*, No. 330, 2016, 2017 WL 1090912, at *9 (Del. 23 Mar. 2017), Chief Justice Strine observed that a particular obligation to use *commercially reasonable efforts* was "an affirmative covenant and a comparatively strong one." In a footnote supporting this proposition, he cites a 2001 edition of a treatise as stating that a *best efforts* obligation can require a party to take "extreme measures" and a *commercially reasonable efforts* obligation is "a strong, but slightly more limited, alternative." See Kenneth A. Adams, *"Efforts" Provisions and the Delaware Supreme Court's Opinion in the ETE-Williams Dispute*, Adams on Contract Drafting (3 Apr. 2017), http://www.adamsdrafting.com/delaware-supreme-court-opinion-ete-williams-dispute/.

8.49 The Chief Justice's observation regarding *efforts* provisions is inconsistent with the evidence (see 8.18–.28). And he cites no supporting caselaw—no meaningful caselaw to that effect exists. His dissent doesn't create binding precedent, but it muddies the waters, because what readers will take away from it is that one *efforts* obligation can be more onerous than another.

THE MEANING OF *REASONABLE EFFORTS*

8.50   Although it's the meaning of *best efforts* that has most perplexed those who work with contracts, *reasonable efforts* has potential for mischief. Consider two New York cases.

8.51   In *Rex Med. L.P. v. Angiotech Pharmaceuticals* (US), 754 F. Supp. 2d 616 (S.D.N.Y. 2010), the court was of the view that in determining whether a party has complied with an obligation to use commercially reasonable efforts to achieve an objective, its financial hardship was irrelevant—that was an argument that the party in question should, in the memorable words of the court, "save for a bankruptcy court." By contrast, in *MBIA Ins. v. Patriarch Partners VIII*, 950 F. Supp. 2d 568 (S.D.N.Y. 2013), the court held that acting in a commercially reasonable manner "does not require a party to act against its own business interests."

8.52   It make no sense to attempt to determine the reasonableness of a party's actions without considering its financial resources. Once you eliminate the need for a rational relationship between efforts expended and the return on those efforts, anything that leads to progress toward achieving the objective becomes mandatory, no matter what it costs.

8.53   But the role of the contract drafter isn't to complain about how a court was irrational in interpreting a contract. And although the approach of the court in *Rex Med* appears to be something of an anomaly, other courts might adopt a similar approach. So the task facing anyone drafting or reviewing a contract is to word *reasonable efforts* provisions to limit the scope for extreme interpretations.

ENFORCEABILITY OF *EFFORTS* PROVISIONS

8.54   Courts in most U.S. jurisdictions have held that *efforts* provisions are enforceable. The principal exception is Illinois courts, which have held that a promise to use best efforts is too vague to be binding if the parties fail to articulate what performance the phrase requires. See *Kraftco Corp. v. Kolbus*, 274 N.E.2d 153, 156 (Ill. App. Ct. 1971).

8.55   But some U.S. courts have held unenforceable an unlikely subset of *efforts* provisions, namely an obligation to use "best efforts" to agree. See, e.g., *Pinnacle Books, Inc. v. Harlequin Enterprises Ltd.*, 519 F. Supp. 118, 121–22 (S.D.N.Y. 1981). And at least one English case has held likewise regarding an obligation to use "reasonable endeavours" to agree. See *Phillips Petroleum Co. UK Ltd. v. Enron Europe Ltd.* [1997] CLC 329. By contrast, in *Denil v. DeBoer, Inc.*, 650 F.3d 635 (7th Cir. 2011), the U.S. Court of Appeals for the Seventh Circuit held that an obligation to use "best efforts" to reach agreement is equivalent to an obligation to negotiate in good faith. So if you want to include in a contract a provision making some arrangement contingent on future agreement, using a good-faith standard rather than an *efforts* standard would reduce the risk of a court holding that the provision is unenforceable.

8.56   Sometimes you can't avoid the uncertainty that goes with making contract relations contingent on future agreement. But if you incorporate the notion of future agreement as a way of putting off negotiations—as was the case in the dispute in *Denil*—you risk dispute.

WHETHER A PARTY HAS MADE REASONABLE EFFORTS

8.57 Because *reasonable efforts* is vague, determining whether a party has complied with a *reasonable efforts* obligation depends, as with all *efforts* standards, on the circumstances of the case, with all the uncertainty that entails. See *Martin*, 240 F.3d at 233 ("'Best efforts' depends on the factual circumstances surrounding an agreement."); *Triple-A Baseball Club Associates*, 832 F.2d at 225 (stating that *best efforts* "cannot be defined in terms of a fixed formula; it varies with the facts and the field of law involved").

8.58 So anyone inclined to include a *reasonable efforts* standard in a contract would benefit from understanding how courts have determined whether a party has in fact made reasonable efforts.

STANDARD FOR MEASURING PERFORMANCE

8.59 In *Kevin M. Ehringer Enterprises, Inc. v. McData Services Corp.*, 646 F.3d 321 (5th Cir. 2011), the U.S. Court of Appeals for the Fifth Circuit, applying Texas law, held that McData's promise to use "best efforts" to promote, market, and sell products during the three-year term wasn't an enforceable promise and so couldn't support a fraudulent-inducement claim. According to the court, that's because "a best efforts contract must set some kind of goal or guideline against which best efforts may be measured."

8.60 Another Fifth Circuit case applying Texas Law, *Herrmann Holdings Ltd. v. Lucent Technologies Inc.*, 302 F.3d 552 (5th Cir. 2002), involved "best efforts" provisions that required the defendant to file a registration statement and cause it to become effective "as promptly as practicable" and "in the most expeditious manner practicable." The court held that the latter two phrases established an objective goal, rendering the "best efforts" provision enforceable.

8.61 These two cases highlight that imposing on Acme an obligation to use reasonable efforts to sell widgets doesn't make sense unless you indicate how many widgets it must sell, and how quickly. And that imposing on Acme a *reasonable efforts* obligation to file a registration statement doesn't make sense unless you include an indication of how soon Acme has to file it. For an obligation to use reasonable efforts, always incorporate a standard for measuring performance. A vague standard—for example, one using *promptly*—would be sufficient.

IDENTIFYING A BENCHMARK

8.62 Determining whether a party has complied with an obligation to use reasonable efforts is facilitated if the efforts made can be compared against a benchmark. Courts have used different benchmarks:

- *Past performance*. See *Bloor v. Falstaff Brewing Corp.*, 601 F.2d 609, 614

(2d Cir. 1979) (in assessing compliance with a provision requiring the purchaser of assets relating to Ballantine beer to "use its best efforts to promote and maintain a high volume of sales," the court considered, among other things, sales figures over several years).

- *Promises made during contract negotiations for guidance on what efforts had been expected.* See *Stone v. Caroselli*, 653 P.2d 754, 757 (Colo. Ct. App. 1982) (stating that testimony by manufacturers as to distributors' promise during negotiations to "hit the road" to promote the product was admissible to explain the distributors' implied duty to use best efforts). But see *Olympia Hotels Corp. v. Johnson Wax Development Corp.*, 908 F.2d 1363, 1373 (7th Cir. 1990) ("The contract contains an integration clause, and the district judge was correct that the parol evidence rule forbade inquiry into precontractual discussions or agreements concerning the meaning of best efforts.").

- *Industry practice.* See *Zilg v. Prentice-Hall Inc.*, 717 F.2d 671, 681 (2d Cir. 1983) (noting that plaintiff's expert testified that "[defendant's] efforts were 'perfectly adequate,' although they were 'routine' and [defendant] 'did not follow through as they might'"); *First Union National Bank v. Steele Software Systems Corp.*, 838 A.2d 404, 448 (Md. Ct. Spec. App. 2003) (stating that in determining whether an obligation to use best efforts had been satisfied, the jury was entitled to consider such things as "the standard in the industry regarding similar contracts between banks and their settlement service vendors").

- *Efforts used by the promisor in connection with other contracts imposing an* efforts *standard.* See *Olympia Hotels Corp.*, 908 F.2d at 1373 (holding that if the promisor has similar contracts with other promisees, "'best efforts' means the efforts the promisor has employed in those parallel contracts where the adequacy of his efforts have not been questioned").

- *How the promisor would have acted if the promisor and promisee had been united in the same entity.* See *Petroleum Marketing Corp. v. Metropolitan Petroleum Corp.*, 151 A.2d 616, 619 (Pa. 1959) (in a case involving a promise by the buyers of a business to use best efforts to collect all accounts receivable on the books of the business on the closing date, the court noted that the parties had accepted that the buyers had had the duty to "use such efforts as it would have been prudent to use in their own behalf if they had owned the receivables, or such efforts as it would have been prudent for the [sellers] to use if they had retained possession of them").

8.63   Absent any such benchmark, a requirement that a promisor use reasonable efforts to accomplish a contract goal would likely be balanced against the broader constraints faced by the promisor in conducting the business that is the subject of the contract. See *Martin v. Monumental Life Insurance Co.*, 240 F.3d 223, 235 (3rd Cir. 2001) (holding that in agreeing to use best efforts, defendant did not compromise its right to exercise sound business judgment). Without this balancing, the promisor could be forced to expend resources at a level that renders the contract uneconomic.

NARROWLY DIRECTED EFFORTS

8.64 A situation that poses a risk of a court holding that a promisor had to make what might seem like disproportionate efforts arises when an *efforts* provision applies only to a discrete aspect of a business relationship. That makes it perhaps less obvious that one is to consider the required efforts in a broader context. For example, one court suggested, in dicta, that a party that undertook to use best efforts to take all actions necessary on its part to permit consummation of a merger might have to divest a subsidiary if that was necessary to obtain regulatory approval. See *Carteret Bancorp v. Home Group, Inc.*, No. 9380, 1988 Del Ch. LEXIS 2, at *20–21 (Del. Ch. 13 Jan. 1988).

English Caselaw

8.65 In *Rhodia International Holdings Ltd v. Huntsman International LLC* [2007] EWHC 292 (Comm), the court held as follows:

> As a matter of language and business common sense, untrammelled by authority, one would surely conclude that ["best endeavours" and "reasonable endeavours" did not mean the same thing]. This is because there may be a number of reasonable courses which could be taken in a given situation to achieve a particular aim. An obligation to use reasonable endeavours to achieve the aim probably only requires a party to take one reasonable course, not all of them, whereas an obligation to use best endeavours probably requires a party to take all the reasonable courses he can.

8.66 Use of the words "surely" and "probably" is wishful thinking—the court's reasoning is inconsistent with the evidence (see 8.18–.28, 8.31–.32).

8.67 And in *UBH (Mechanical Services) Ltd v. Standard Life Assurance Co.* T.L.R., 13 Nov. 1986 (Q.B.), the court suggested, contrary to English usage (see 8.31–.32), that "the phrase 'all reasonable endeavours' is probably a middle position somewhere between the other two, implying something more than reasonable endeavours but less than best endeavours." For a more recent English case to the same effect, see *Hiscox Syndicates v. Pinnacle Limited* [2008] EWHC 145 (Ch). See also *Astor Management AG v. Atalaya Mining plc* [2017] EWHC 425, at para. 67 (Comm) (referring to "judging whether the endeavours used were 'reasonable', or whether there were other steps which it was reasonable to take so that it cannot be said that 'all reasonable endeavours' have been used").

8.68 These cases are symptomatic of an English approach to contract interpretation that prizes spurious distinctions over plain meaning. (For similarly problematic English caselaw relating to *represents and warrants*, see 3.405.)

8.69 In *Jet2.com Ltd v. Blackpool Airport Ltd* [2012] EWCA Civ 417, which involved a dispute over what an airport operator had to do to comply with a *best endeavours* obligation, the English Court of Appeal displayed a more logical approach. In its opinion, it didn't discuss gradations of *endeavours* provisions, even though the contract used both *best endeavours* and *all reasonable endeavours*. The court said that the "natural meaning of ['all reasonable endeavours'] is that [the appellant] would do *its best* to ensure that charges made for ground services would support Jet2's low-cost pricing model." (Emphasis added.) That suggests a willingness to equate *best* with *reasonable* in this context. The court also noted that the litigants had agreed that the two *endeavours* standards "meant the same thing."

8.70   Perhaps the *Jet2.com* case is a sign that there's hope for a return to a more rational approach to *endeavours* provisions in England. But judging by the analyses offered by law firms, many English lawyers appear to endorse the notion that different *endeavours* provisions express varying degrees of onerousness.

Canadian Caselaw

8.71   The leading Canadian case on *best efforts* is an opinion of the British Columbia Supreme Court, *Atmospheric Diving Systems Inc. v. International Hard Suits Inc.* (1994), 89 B.C.L.R. (2d) 356 (S.C.). Here are the first two points of its seven-point digest of the relevant caselaw:

1.   "Best efforts" imposes a higher obligation than a "reasonable effort".

2.   "Best efforts" means taking, in good faith, all reasonable steps to achieve the objective, carrying the process to its logical conclusion and leaving no stone unturned.

8.72   So a *best efforts* obligation represents a more onerous standard than does *reasonable efforts* … but to comply with that obligation, all that's required is that you act reasonably! The court's first two points are incompatible, so the ostensible distinction collapses. But that hasn't stopped courts from citing it as precedent. See, e.g., *Diamond Robinson Building Ltd. v. Conn*, 2010 BCSC 76. And Canadian law firms continue mentioning it in earnest misinformation on *efforts* standards.

8.73   Another legacy of *Atmospheric Diving Systems* is the tendency of Canadian lawyers to invoke "leaving no stone unturned" to explain what *best efforts* means. It's silly to think a metaphor can reduce the uncertainty inherent in vagueness.

Other Caselaw

8.74   In *Hospital Products Ltd. v. United States Surgical Corp.* (1984), 156 CLR 41, at 64, the High Court of Australia stated sensibly that "an obligation to use 'best endeavours' does not require the person who undertakes the obligation to go beyond the bounds of reason; he is required to do all he reasonably can in the circumstances to achieve the contractual object, but no more." But the urge to create an unwarranted distinction is strong: in *Waters Lane v. Sweeney* [2007] NSWCA 200, the New South Wales Court of Appeal noted, but did not follow, a distinction offered by the trial court.

8.75 In *KS Energy Services Ltd v. BR Energy (M) Sdn Bhd* [2014] SGCA 16, the Singapore Court of Appeal considered the implications of an obligation to use "all reasonable endeavours." The court surveyed relevant caselaw in Singapore, England, and Australia. To its credit, the court held that "we do not find it useful to distinguish an 'all reasonable endeavours' obligation from a 'best endeavours' obligation." But the court also held that "We accept that an 'all reasonable endeavours' obligation is ordinarily more onerous than a 'reasonable endeavours' obligation." That doesn't make sense (see 8.31–.32, 8.67).

Misleading Commentary on Caselaw

8.76 In the United States, those who work with contracts are confused about *efforts* standards, but courts have dealt with them sensibly. Ideally, commentators would act as a bridge between the two constituencies, explaining to those who work with contracts that the ostensible distinctions between *efforts* standards are an illusion. But unfortunately, much of the commentary on *efforts* standards is ill-informed.

8.77 For example, according to *Garner's Dictionary of Legal Usage*, at 108, "[T]he majority view is for courts to consider *best efforts* as imposing a higher standard than *reasonable efforts*. But others treat the two as synonyms." That's woefully inaccurate.

8.78 The entry continues:

> Perhaps the safest course is, when possible, to use a *best-efforts* provision when insisting on an opposite number's performance— and to use a *reasonable-efforts* provision for one's own client's performance. Yet the phrases are fuzzy, the judicial decisions irreconcilable, and the effects admittedly uncertain.

8.79 So with a shrug, *Garner's Dictionary of Legal Usage* leaves its readers to figure out for themselves how to handle *efforts* standards.

8.80 *Efforts* misinformation has even appeared in the news. For example, Gretchen Morgensen, *After Merger, Two Competing Drugs and Billion-Dollar Questions*, N.Y. Times, 13 Nov. 2015, says this:

> Under the agreement, Sanofi would make "diligent efforts" to shepherd Lemtrada through the F.D.A. approval process and promote it as it would any drug. This set out a higher standard than Sanofi would have faced under an agreement to make only a "reasonable effort" with the drug.

8.81 That might accurately reflect the conventional wisdom in some circles, but it doesn't accurately reflect the caselaw or how the English language works.

The Uniform Commercial Code

8.82 The drafters of article 2 of the Uniform Commercial Code evidently saw no distinction between *best efforts* and *reasonable efforts*. Section 2-306(2) states as follows regarding implied obligations:

> A lawful agreement by either the seller or the buyer for exclu
> dealing in the kind of goods concerned imposes unless othe₁
> agreed an obligation by the seller to use best efforts to supply the
> goods and by the buyer to use best efforts to promote their sale.

8.83   Official Comment 5 to section 2-306(2) says that subsection (2) makes explicit the commercial rule under which parties "are held to have impliedly, even when not expressly, bound themselves to use reasonable diligence as well as good faith in their performance of the contract." Whatever might have been intended by equating *best efforts* with reasonableness, diligence, and good faith in this manner, doing so precludes, for purposes of article 2, using *best efforts* as a more onerous standard than *reasonable efforts*.

HOW TO DRAFT *EFFORTS* PROVISIONS

8.84   *Efforts* provisions are a source of confusion and uncertainty, but those who draft or review contracts can cut through the fog with *efforts* provisions that aren't susceptible to misinterpretation.

Whenever Possible, Be Precise Instead of Vague

8.85   *Efforts* standards are vague, and as such they can lead to a dispute (see 7.42) and unpredictable outcomes at trial (see 8.50–.53). Ideally, use *efforts* provisions only if justified by a party's lack of control (see 7.44). Avoid using *efforts* provisions as an expedient alternative to being specific (see 7.45).

Use Only *Reasonable Efforts*

8.86   Although it's clear from the evidence that there's no basis for claiming *reasonable efforts, best efforts, and other efforts standards* require anything other than what is reasonable, judges (depending on the jurisdiction) and those who work with contracts will doubtless continue to seek to distinguish the two by claiming that a party under an obligation to use *best efforts* must be willing to take extraordinary measures (see 8.15–.17). So using *efforts* standards other than *reasonable efforts* will always entail a significant risk of confusion, and you can't rely on them to deliver what many think they promise. To avoid that, use only *reasonable efforts*.

8.87   You could use something more colloquial, such as *shall try*, but the concept of *efforts* is entrenched in contracts. In a precedent-driven part of a conservative profession, it's best not to try to teach old dogs new tricks unless the benefits are meaningful.

8.88   To reduce the vagueness inherent in a *reasonable efforts* obligation, make it an unqualified obligation of the party in question to perform in addition tasks that are related to the desired goal and that the party does have control over. For example, you could supplement an obligation that Acme use reasonable efforts to obtain a permit by requiring that by a specified date Acme apply for the permit.

8.89   If the other side of a transaction balks at using *reasonable efforts*, tell them that the notion that *best efforts* is more onerous than *reasonable efforts* is mistaken and that caselaw doesn't support it (in the United States) or is confusing (elsewhere). If the other side nevertheless insists on *best efforts* and your client wishes to do the deal, consider telling the other side that your client is prepared to sign but doesn't accept their view of the implications of *best efforts* and is prepared to litigate if that ever becomes an issue.

8.90   You might be tempted to use *best efforts* in a contract because the other side isn't aware of the U.S. caselaw on *best efforts* and as a result might exert itself more than it would have if the contract had contained a reasonable efforts standard. But it would be more conducive to healthy contract relations if you sought a meeting of the minds.

Consider Using *Reasonable Efforts* Instead of *Reasonable Endeavours*

8.91   Those who use *endeavours* instead of *efforts*—they're mostly in England and Australia—should consider joining the rest of the world in using *efforts*. The word *endeavours* is dated. A Google Ngram of use of *efforts* and *endeavours* in Google's British-English corpus of digitized books shows that despite some ups and downs, use of *efforts* in 1950 was essentially where it was in 1800, but from 1950 to 2000 it experienced an upswing. By contrast, although in 1800 *endeavours* was used only slightly less frequently than *efforts*, from 1800 to 2000 *endeavours* experienced a long decline that suggests it's headed for oblivion. The modern choice is *efforts*.

8.92   In a newsletter available online in 2014, one English law firm said this:

> Also, please note that the majority of English case law looks at the interpretation of phrases using "endeavours" rather than "efforts". Consequently, for greater certainty of interpretation of such terms, it is better to frame obligations under English law as requiring the use of "endeavours" rather than "efforts".

8.93   That's unnecessarily timid. Although English caselaw on *endeavours* is misguided (see 8.65–.70), nothing suggests that English courts would consider that use of *efforts* instead of *endeavours* has substantive implications.

Set Standards for Measuring Performance

8.94   Consistent with caselaw on the subject (see 8.59), state in *efforts* provisions how performance is to be measured. For example, don't just say *Acme shall manufacture widgets*—state the timeframe for performing. You could state a period of time (*one year*), or you could just use *promptly* (see 8.60).

8.95   Find a way to express what volume of widgets Acme must manufacture to comply with the obligation. But it wouldn't make sense to express it as a number of widgets—if you could do that, you wouldn't need to use an *efforts* provision.

8.96   Similarly, courts can be unrealistic in saying that *efforts* provisions must include guidelines. For example, New York caselaw refers to the need for "a clear set of guidelines against which to measure a party's best efforts" to enforce such a provision. See *TPTCC NY v. Radiation Therapy Services*, 784 F. Supp. 2d 485, 506–07 (S.D.N.Y. 2011), quoting *Mocca Lounge v. Misak*, 94 A.D.2d 761, 763 (N.Y. App. Div. 1983). Again, it doesn't make sense to expect drafters to offer much in the way of guidelines for interpreting *reasonable efforts* provisions: the whole point of *reasonable efforts* provisions is that drafters use them when they can't or don't want to be specific.

8.97 Understand how other provisions might affect a court's notions of what performance is expected under an *efforts* provision. Suppose you've prepared a contract that imposes on Acme an obligation to use reasonable efforts to sell widgets. If you leave it at that, a fight could arise at any time over whether Acme has used reasonable efforts.

8.98 You could add to the contract a provision saying that you may terminate if Acme doesn't reach stated sales targets. That would give you an exit that you wouldn't have to fight over. But the trade-off is that if Acme achieves those targets, you might well have a harder time convincing a court that Acme hasn't used reasonable efforts, even though the one isn't necessarily related to the other. After all, it could be that unexpected market conditions mean that Acme reached those targets easily, and since doing so it has twiddled its thumbs. But you couldn't blame a court for assuming that any target you set for termination constitutes your minimum notion of acceptable performance by Acme.

8.99 And for two reasons, using sales targets in a termination provision wouldn't eliminate the need for a *reasonable efforts* obligation. First, you would retain the possibility of an action for breach, even if it might be challenging to recover if Acme meets the targets. Second, and more importantly, retaining a *reasonable efforts* obligation would give you a basis for terminating the contract for breach (depending on how the termination provisions are worded) instead of having to wait until Acme fails to meet the targets.

Eliminate Clutter and Inconsistency

8.100 Of the verbs used with *efforts* (see 8.12), the best option is *use*. If contracts filed with the U.S. Securities and Exchange Commission are at all representative, *use* is the most popular option. Using *make* would be more colloquial, but no one would mistake for colloquial English provisions using the phrase *reasonable efforts*, and there's no point pretending otherwise.

8.101 Omit *all* (see 8.11, 8.31–.32), and don't use a pronoun (see 8.12).

8.102 Instead of *every effort* (see 8.12), use *efforts* in the plural. Consistency favors using only one or the other, and *efforts* is the more widely used.

8.103 Some contracts require a party to use efforts to accomplish something *to the extent possible* (or words to that effect). That notion is redundant, because it's implicit in an *efforts* provision that the party under the obligation might be unable to comply, even after making the required effort. The phrase can be deleted, as in this example:

> Acme shall use reasonable efforts to cancel or mitigate, ~~to the extent possible,~~ each obligation that would cause Acme to incur expenses ... .

8.104 Don't refer to good faith or diligence in a *reasonable efforts* provision, as in *Each party shall use reasonable efforts, undertaken diligently and in good faith, to obtain all Consents before Closing.* Mixing different standards would only muddy the waters. And don't place the modifier after *efforts* in any other way (see 8.13).

Don't Use More than One *Efforts* Standard in a Contract

8.105 Because the notion that different *efforts* standards convey different meanings is unworkable, using two or more different *efforts* standards in a single contract invites confusion. But it's routine for contracts to have multiple *efforts* standards.

8.106 Usually it's the result of promiscuous copy-and-pasting without taking the trouble to make sure everything is consistent. A sign of that is when you have not only multiple *efforts* standards but also inconsistent ancillary usages, notably the verb used (see 8.12), whether pronouns are used (see 8.12), and whether *all* is used (see 8.11).

8.107 But sometimes it's clear that the drafter intended to invoke different efforts standards. Here are two examples of that:

> Guarantors shall use reasonable best efforts to file, and shall use commercially reasonable efforts to have become effective ... .

> Each party shall use best efforts, and in no event less than reasonable efforts, to ensure that the confidentiality of the other party's Confidential Information will be maintained ... .

8.108 Regarding the first example, a judge asked to interpret it should treat it as an example of mistake, whatever the drafter thought they were doing. The second example is nonsense: *and in no event* is for adding a precise standard after a vague one; it's not for adding another vague standard after a vague one.

Defining *Reasonable Efforts*

8.109 Even though the phrase *reasonable efforts* doesn't pose the same risk of confusion as *best efforts*, consider using it as a defined term. Doing so might assist a court and might help the parties better understand the implications of using *reasonable efforts*. And in the definition the parties could fine-tune their understanding of what *reasonable efforts* means.

THE CORE DEFINITION

8.110 A definition of *reasonable efforts* should specify what the core meaning is—it will necessarily be vague—and specify anything that's to be excluded from the definition. Here is the recommended core definition:

> "**Reasonable Efforts**" means, regarding conduct by a party, the efforts that a reasonable person in the position of that party would use to engage in that conduct competently and promptly.

8.111   For a definition to apply in all contexts, it must reflect that *reasonable efforts* isn't used exclusively in obligations—it could also be used in a conditional clause (*If Acme fails to use reasonable efforts …*) or even in a statement of fact (*Acme states that it has used reasonable efforts …*).

8.112   Use of *reasonable efforts* isn't just about getting something done competently and promptly. It might not even relate to accomplishing a specific task. Instead, it might be a matter of maintaining a status, or stopping something from happening. It would make sense to elucidate in the *reasonable efforts* provision the parties' expectations regarding the activity in question.

8.113   The parties might want to specify that what *reasonable efforts* means is to be determined by reference to the party in question's past practice or the practice in a particular industry. That could be accomplished by tacking on to the end of the core definition *consistent with its past practice* or, say, *consistent with the practice of comparable pharmaceuticals companies regarding pharmaceutical products of comparable market potential*. That might spare a court from having to come up with a suitable benchmark (see 8.62).

8.114   Otherwise, the core definition could be customized to reflect that, for example, *reasonable efforts* is used only in obligations, or that all instances of *reasonable efforts* apply to only one party.

8.115   Sometimes a definition of *reasonable efforts* will specify actions that a party must take for its efforts to constitute reasonable efforts. For example, when in a registration rights agreement an issuer is required to use reasonable efforts to cause a registration statement to become effective as soon as practicable after filing, the contract typically uses as a definition of *reasonable efforts* something like this:

> "**Reasonable Efforts**" means, among other things, that the Company shall submit to the SEC, within two business days after the Company learns that no review of a particular Registration Statement will be made by the staff of the SEC or that the staff has no further comments on the Registration Statement, as the case may be, a request for acceleration of effectiveness of the Registration Statement to a time and date not later than 48 hours after submission of that request.

8.116   Don't use such definitions: A *reasonable efforts* standard captures what the parties can't or don't want to address in detail when they enter into the contract (see 8.3–.5). If you're able to express in an absolute obligation something that a party must accomplish, state it as a freestanding obligation rather than in a definition of *reasonable efforts*. And more generally, don't use in autonomous definitions language of obligation and other language suited to substantive provisions (see 6.53).

CARVE-OUTS

8.117   Because the principal concern of a party subject to a *reasonable efforts* standard would be to avoid having to take actions out of proportion to the benefits to it under the contract (see 8.50–.53), it's likely that negotiations regarding the definition of *reasonable efforts* would mostly concern carve-outs, which specify what's excluded from the definition.

8.118   One issue is the language used to introduce carve-outs. Often a definition will place the carve-outs in a proviso: *provided, however, that an obligation to use Reasonable Efforts under this agreement does not require the promisor to … .* But given the shortcomings of the traditional proviso (see 13.665), a clearer and more economical way to introduce carve-outs in definitions is by using *but does not include* (see 6.41).

8.119   Because carve-outs are intended to provide certainty to offset the vagueness of the core definition, they should be specific. For example, one could exclude from the definition of *reasonable efforts* any one or more of the following (revising the wording to include any defined terms):

- incurring expenses [in excess of $X individually and $Y in the aggregate] other than as provided in this agreement

- incurring liabilities

- changing that party's business strategy

- disposing of significant assets of that party

- taking actions that would violate any law or order to which that party is subject

- taking actions that would imperil that party's existence or solvency

- initiating any litigation or arbitration

8.120   Some commonly used carve-outs would likely fall outside the scope of *reasonable efforts* anyway, but a party might nevertheless wish to make doubly sure of avoiding any dispute over what kind of efforts are required. Here's an example of such a carve-out:

- taking actions that would, individually or in the aggregate, result in a material adverse change in that party

ADD-INS

8.121   If you have in mind that complying with a given *reasonable efforts* obligation might require conduct that goes beyond what would be considered reasonable, you could say as much by supplementing a definition, or the provision itself, with something like the following, which takes an extreme approach that is broadly consistent with what many think *best efforts* means:

> Acme acknowledges that the money that a reasonable person in Acme's position would be willing to expend on, and the personnel that a reasonable person in Acme's position would be willing to devote to, complying with its obligations under this section 11 are unlimited.

8.122   But don't be surprised if the other side reacts adversely.

MATERIAL AND MATERIAL ADVERSE CHANGE

MATERIAL

9.1 An important drafting tool is the adjective *material*, as in *Widgetco is not party to any material litigation*. Drafters use it, and the adverb *materially* (as in *at a price materially below Fair Market Value*), to narrow an otherwise overly broad provision so it covers only what really matters. Whether something is material depends on the circumstances—*material* and *materially* are vague words (see 7.42).

9.2 The word *material* features in the phrase *material adverse change*, or *MAC*. (The phrase *material adverse effect*, or *MAE*, is used to convey essentially the same meaning; see 9.69–.77.) MAC provisions are always a focus of attention, particularly when uncertain economic conditions prompt deal parties, and the business and legal communities as a whole, to consider anew on what basis a MAC provision would allow a party to get out of a deal.

Vagueness

9.3 In *TSC Industries, Inc. v. Northway, Inc.*, 426 U.S. 438 (1976), the U.S. Supreme Court articulated what material means in securities fraud cases: "An omitted fact is material if there is a substantial likelihood that a reasonable shareholder would consider it important in deciding how to vote." (In this chapter, this meaning is called the "affects-a-decision" meaning.)

9.4 The influence of that decision can be seen in *Black's Law Dictionary*, which gives as one meaning of *material* "Of such a nature that knowledge of the item would affect a person's decision-making." The affects-a-decision meaning has also been embraced in cases addressing suppression of evidence in criminal matters and a variety of other fields, as well as in Delaware Court of Chancery opinions on materiality in a merger-and-acquisitions (M&A) context, including *IBP, Inc. v. Tyson Foods, Inc.*, 789 A.2d 14 (Del. Ch. 2001). In an M&A context, and from the buyer's perspective, this meaning of *material* refers to information that would have caused the buyer not to enter into the agreement or would cause the buyer not to want to close the transaction. The standard is a high one—think "deal-breaker."

9.5   But the affects-a-decision meaning is inescapably vague. The *TSC Industries* definition uses three vague words (*substantial*, *reasonable*, and *important*).

9.6   Lawyers apparently think that if you add enough words, you can escape vagueness. That much is suggested by the wordy but still vague definitions of *material* offered by regulatory bodies. See Emily Chasan, *Definition of Materiality Depends Who You Ask*, Wall St. Journal, 3 Nov. 2015.

A Source of Ambiguity

9.7   According to *Black's Law Dictionary*, another meaning of *material* is "significant"—in other words, important enough to merit attention. This meaning encompasses a broader range of significance than the affects-a-decision meaning—in this sense of the word, for something to be material to a contract party, it would simply have to be of more than trivial significance.

9.8   In a particular provision, such as the statement of fact *Acme's financial records contain no material inaccuracies*, either meaning could conceivably be intended. So *material* is not only vague, it's ambiguous, although that isn't the case with *material* when used in the phrase *material adverse change* (see 9.16, 9.88).

9.9   This ambiguity could cause confusion. For example, a buyer and its counsel might assume that any nontrivial nondisclosure regarding a statement of fact containing a qualification using *material* would render that statement of fact inaccurate. By contrast, a court might hold that for purposes of that statement of fact, *material* conveys the affects-a-decision meaning. That could result in the buyer not being entitled to indemnification for nondisclosure regarding a statement of fact qualified using *material* unless it were to meet the high standard associated with that meaning.

How *Material* Is Used

9.10   Given that cases addressing materiality invariably invoke the affects-a-decision meaning, one might ask whether the ambiguity inherent in *material* is theoretical and of no practical significance. But lawyers use the word *material* so liberally in drafts and in negotiation as to make it unlikely that each time they do so they have in mind a deal-breaker level of significance. Two pieces of evidence suggest that regardless of the caselaw, in many contexts drafters do in fact have in mind the important-enough-to-merit-attention meaning when they use the word *material*.

9.11   First, attributing the affects-a-decision meaning to the word *material* would often strip a provision of much of its utility. Consider this statement of fact: *There is no material litigation pending against the Company*. If in this statement of fact *material* were given the affects-a-decision meaning, it would be inaccurate only if litigation were pending against the Company and it were sufficiently significant that it would affect the buyer's decision whether to go ahead with the transaction. But one suspects that that's not what the buyer had in mind—that instead it would want to be compensated for any losses it incurs due to any nontrivial pending litigation that it hadn't been informed of. For the statement of fact to convey that meaning, *material* would have to mean "important enough to merit attention."

9.12   Consider also this example: *A credit agreement requires the lender to deliver certain forms unless doing so would result in the imposition on the Lender of any additional material legal or regulatory burdens, any additional material out-of-pocket costs not indemnified hereunder, or be otherwise materially disadvantageous to the Lender.* It's unlikely in this case that the lender thought it would be reimbursed only if the burdens, costs, and disadvantages imposed on the lender were sufficiently significant that it wouldn't have made the loan if it had known about them.

9.13   And the phrase *material breach* could mean different things depending on where it occurs in a contract. In the statement of fact *Widgetco is not in material breach of any Excelsior Contract*, the drafter might well have intended that only trivial breaches would render it inaccurate. By contrast, for the termination provision *Widgetco may terminate this agreement on material breach by Acme of any its obligations under this agreement*, it's likely that the drafter had in mind the affects-a-decision meaning of *material*.

9.14   The second piece of evidence suggesting that drafters do in fact have in mind the important-enough-to-merit-attention meaning of *material* is that in some contexts one cannot, as a matter of semantics, say that *material* conveys the affects-a-decision meaning.

9.15   Consider this statement of fact: *The Seller is not in breach of any material contract to which it is party.* The focus of this statement of fact is breach of the contracts, not the contracts themselves. It wouldn't make sense to modify the phrase *contract to which it is party* (as opposed to the word *breach*) with the word *material* if it were meant to convey the affects-a-decision meaning. In this context, *material* could only mean "important enough to merit attention."

9.16   Courts and practitioners appear to accept that in the phrase *material adverse change*, the word *material* conveys the affects-a-decision meaning—any party invoking a MAC provision would need to make a strong showing (see 9.4). But in any other context, either meaning of *material* could conceivably be the one intended. Although the context might suggest that one or the other meaning is intended, from a semantics perspective one cannot know for sure, because agreements invariably fail to specify which meaning is intended. For example, in the phrase *material inaccuracy*, it's not clear how significant an inaccuracy must be in order for it to be material.

Avoiding Ambiguity

9.17   As described in 9.7–.9, drafters use *material* not only to express the affects-a-decision meaning but also to express the important-enough-to-merit-attention meaning. That can create confusion.

9.18   Because courts attribute the affects-a-decision meaning to *material*, that can be considered the safe meaning—it would be counterproductive to look for another word to express that meaning. Instead, the sensible thing to do would be to look for another word to express the meaning "important enough to merit attention."

9.19 The obvious candidate for that is *significant.* There's precedent for according *significant* the important-enough-to-merit-attention meaning: In connection with guidance on evaluating internal controls, the U.S. Securities and Exchange Commission has defined the term "significant deficiency" to mean a deficiency "that is less severe than a material weakness, yet important enough to merit attention by those responsible for oversight of the registrant's financial reporting." See SEC Release No. 33-8829.

9.20 But colloquially, *significant* can be used to suggest a greater level of importance—*That was a significant achievement!* So it's not a safe choice.

9.21 Previous editions of this manual recommended using *significant* as a defined term. Now this manual recommends using instead the word *nontrivial.* It's a little awkward, but that's more than offset by how it makes it clear that the standard can be triggered by something at the less important end of the spectrum of importance: anything more than trivial is nontrivial.

9.22 *Nontrivial* is vague, so it's possible to have differences of opinion as to whether something is nontrivial. But because it relates to the less-important end of the spectrum, not much would be at stake. Given that its meaning is relatively clear and given that serious fights over what *nontrivial* means are unlikely, no purpose would be served treating it as a defined term.

9.23 *Trivial* can be useful too—*Acme's financial records contain no inaccuracies other than trivial inaccuracies.*

Defining *Material*

9.24 Using *nontrivial* to express the meaning "important enough to merit attention" reduces the risk of ambiguity. But the risk of confusion remains, because some readers might not know that courts attribute the affects-a-decision meaning to *material*.

9.25 The surest way to avoid that confusion would be to use *material* as a defined term and define it to make explicit that it expresses the affects-a-decision meaning. You would also need to make clear whose perspective applies for determining materiality. In *IBP, Inc. v. Tyson Foods, Inc.*, 789 A.2d 14 (Del. Ch. 2001), the court considered materiality from the perspective of the "reasonable acquiror"; for this approach to apply in any context, one would need to refer to the perspective of a reasonable person in the position of the party in question. (A more conventional alternative would be simply to say, for example, *from the Buyer's perspective*, but it's preferable to make it clear that the standard isn't a subjective one—you wouldn't adopt the perspective of an unreasonable buyer.)

9.26 You might find it useful to also define *materially*. As a matter of logic, it's the most appropriate choice to use in the bringdown condition (see 9.52) instead of the phrase *material adverse change* (see 9.56).

9.27   Exactly how you would define *material* would depend on the context and on which parties are covered by the definition. This definition of *material* would apply to the buyer in an M&A transaction:

> ### Definition of "Material" and "Materially" (Applies to the Buyer)
>
> "**Material**" and "**Materially**" refer to a level of significance that would have affected any decision of a reasonable person in the Buyer's position regarding whether to enter into this agreement or would affect any decision of a reasonable person in the Buyer's position regarding whether to consummate the transaction contemplated by this agreement.

9.28   By referring to entry into the agreement and consummation of the transaction, the definition addresses circumstances relating to the periods before and after signing.

9.29   It's commonplace for both the seller and the buyer to be subject to provisions containing a materiality standard. For example, if in a contract the bringdown condition to the buyer's obligations is subject to a materiality standard, often the bringdown condition to the seller's obligations will likewise incorporate a materiality standard (see 9.53). In such contexts, the definition of *Materially* (and *Material* too) would need to apply to all parties:

> ### Definition of "Material" and "Materially" (Applies to More Than One Party)
>
> "**Material**" and "**Materially**" refer, regarding a given Person, to a level of significance that would have affected any decision of a reasonable person in that Person's position regarding whether to enter into this agreement or would affect any decision of a reasonable person in that Person's position regarding whether to consummate the transaction contemplated by this agreement.

9.30   It's not the current practice to treat *material* as a defined term, and this manual doesn't suggest that it should become standard to do so. But it might be appropriate for a particular transaction.

Limiting Qualifications Relating to Significance

9.31   A buyer that wishes to close a transaction without delay might be amenable to having a statement of fact be subject to a qualification using *material* or *nontrivial* if the alternative would be having the seller devote an inordinate amount of time to compiling a schedule of exceptions. Beyond that, whether to make a statement of fact or a condition subject to such a qualification is essentially a function of the respective bargaining power of the parties.

9.32   But some statements of fact are rarely subject to qualifications relating to significance, either because they are too straightforward to be anything other than unqualified or because the matters being represented are sufficiently fundamental that the buyer is unwilling to accept any inaccuracies. Such statements of fact include statements of fact as to organization, capitalization, and authority to enter into the transaction.

9.33   Of the two standards, qualifications using *nontrivial* seem the less useful. Determining whether an issue merits the buyer's attention is prone to arbitrariness, given the low threshold involved. A party could reasonably claim that if it's willing to go to court to recover damages it claims arose from inaccuracy of a statement of fact subject to a qualification using *nontrivial*, then by definition the inaccuracy was nontrivial.

9.34   So consider using bright-line alternatives to a qualification using *nontrivial*. Instead of having a party make a statement of fact as to absence of *breach of any nontrivial agreement to which the Seller is party*, you could refer to absence of *breach of any agreement to which Acme is party listed in schedule 2.4*. And rather than having a party make a statement of fact as to absence of *any pending nontrivial litigation*, consider referring to absence of litigation over a stated dollar amount or seeking injunctive relief. (Using quantitative guidelines in this manner to replace materiality is different from using quantitative guidelines in defining MAC; see 9.91.)

9.35   And in some contexts you might decide to dispense with a qualification using *nontrivial* and do without any substitute. For example, rather than imposing on Acme a duty to notify Widgetco of changes that merit attention in an agreement that Acme has entered into with a nonparty, it would be simpler to impose an unqualified obligation if it's unlikely that the agreement would be amended sufficiently extensively, and sufficiently often, to render that obligation burdensome. So in this instance, a significance qualification would accomplish nothing other than to add an unnecessary element of uncertainty.

9.36   And more generally, in a transaction that provides for a delayed closing and indemnification, the seller might be willing to omit from its statements of fact some or all qualifications relating to significance—whether using *material*, *nontrivial*, or more precise alternatives—if you incorporate a materiality qualification in the seller's bringdown condition (see 9.45), using *materially* (see 9.27), and specify in the indemnification provisions that indemnification doesn't apply until indemnifiable losses have reached a specified amount—in other words, if you establish a "basket," whether of the "threshold" or "deductible" variety. Doing so should eliminate any concern on the part of the seller that giving an unqualified statement of fact could result in the transaction not closing due to a relatively minor inaccuracy, or result in that party's incurring indemnification liability for a relatively minor inaccuracy.

9.37   A seller might want to retain qualifications relating to significance in any statements of fact that it expects would otherwise likely be inaccurate when made at closing, but it should be able instead to address that concern by negotiating an appropriate basket.

Which Noun to Modify

9.38   A statement of fact might contain only one noun that could be modified by *material*, as in example [1] below. But a statement of fact might contain two such nouns, raising the question whether for qualifying the statement of fact by materiality you should modify one or the other noun, as in [2] and [2a], or both, as in [2b]. It would make the most sense to modify the noun that's the focus of the statement of fact. The focus of example [2] and its variants is contract defaults, not the contracts themselves, so it would make the most sense to have *material* modify *default*, as in [2].

[1]   Schedule 4.8 lists each material contract to which the Seller is party.

[2]   The Seller is not in material default under any contract to which it is party.

[2a]   The Seller is not in default under any material contract to which it is party.

[2b]   The Seller is not in material default under any material contract to which it is party.

9.39   By contrast, example [2a] would seem both overinclusive and underinclusive—it would be rendered inaccurate by any default under any of the contracts in question, no matter how trivial, but wouldn't be rendered inaccurate by default under a contract that doesn't meet the high level of significance inherent in *material*, no matter how serious the consequences of that default. And [2b] would be underinclusive—it would seem unhelpful to exclude from the scope of the statement of fact, just because they involve contracts other than material contracts, defaults that would otherwise fall within the definition of *material*.

MATERIAL ADVERSE CHANGE

9.40   MAC provisions raise many subtle drafting issues. These issues fall into two categories: those relating to using MAC provisions and—since MAC is generally used as a defined term—those relating to how MAC is defined. (If all that you are looking for is a basic definition of MAC, see 9.80.)

Using *Material Adverse Change*

WHERE *MAC* PROVISIONS ARE USED

9.41   MAC provisions are used in different parts of a contract. They occur most commonly in statements of fact, where they can be used in two ways.

9.42   First, a party can make a statement of fact regarding nonoccurrence of a MAC since a specified date—*Since 31 December 2016, no MAC has occurred.* (This chapter uses the term "absolute MAC provision" to mean any provision that in this manner addresses directly nonoccurrence of a MAC. Regarding an expanded form of absolute MAC provision, see 9.68.)

9.43   A buyer might want to rephrase an absolute MAC statement of fact as follows to ensure that it also encompasses adverse changes that are only material when considered in the aggregate—*Since 31 December 2016, no events or circumstances have occurred that constitute, individually or in the aggregate, a MAC.* But in this context a court should be willing to aggregate adverse changes even without explicit contract language to that effect. The absolute MAE and the definition of MAE at issue in the *IBP* case didn't explicitly provide for aggregation of adverse changes, yet the court didn't dispute the defendant's assertion that a combination of factors can amount to an MAE. See *IBP*, 789 A.2d at 65 (noting that "taken together, Tyson claims that it is virtually indisputable that the combination of these factors amounts to a Material Adverse Effect").

9.44 Second, a MAC provision can modify a statement of fact as to some aspect of a party's operations to indicate the absence of anything leading to a MAC. The modification is in the negative when the noun or noun phrase being modified—in the following example, *inaccuracies*—is in the negative: *Acme's financial records contain no inaccuracies except for inaccuracies that would not reasonably be expected to result in a MAC.* The modification is in the affirmative when the negative is expressed elsewhere in the statement of fact: *Acme is not* [or *No Seller is*] *party to any litigation that would reasonably be expected to result in a MAC.* (This chapter calls a "modifying" MAC provision any MAC provision that modifies a statement of fact in this manner.) Adding *individually or in the aggregate* would aggregate, for determining materiality, instances of the thing in question, but using a mass noun (*litigation*) or a plural count noun (*inaccuracies*) should be sufficient to accomplish that.

9.45 MACs also occur in closing conditions. Any statement of fact containing a MAC provision could, with a suitable introduction, serve as a condition: *The Buyer's obligation to consummate at the Closing the transactions contemplated by this agreement is subject to satisfaction, or waiver by the Buyer, of the following conditions at or before the Closing: … that since 31 December 2016, a MAC has not occurred; that Acme is not party to any litigation that would reasonably be expected to result in a MAC … .* It would, however, be redundant to repeat in the closing conditions any statements of fact made in that contract, since it's standard practice to require as a closing condition that the statements of fact be accurate on the closing date as well as on the signing date. This "bringdown" of the statements of fact would allow the party relying on the statements of fact to avoid its obligations under the contract if a statement of fact is inaccurate at closing. (The bringdown condition is discussed further at 9.51–.57.)

9.46 A MAC provision could be incorporated as a condition rather than as a statement of fact, but it would afford better protection if drafted as a statement of fact: although an unsatisfied condition would allow a party to walk, an inaccurate statement of fact could also result in that party's having a cause of action for damages or a claim for indemnification.

9.47 MAC provisions are also found in parts of a contract other than the statements of fact and conditions. For example, a contract might impose on Acme an obligation to promptly notify Widgetco of any MAC. And a contract governing an ongoing relationship between the parties, such as a license agreement, might give a party the right to terminate upon occurrence of a MAC affecting the other party. Similarly, a credit agreement might provide that occurrence of a MAC affecting the borrower constitutes an event of default.

9.48 An alternative to a modifying MAC provision is simply to use the word *material* on its own. For example, the modifying MAC statement of fact in 9.44 could be rephrased as *Acme's financial records contain no material inaccuracies*. If Widgetco is concerned that an inaccuracy in an Acme statement of fact could adversely affect Acme's fortunes, then in the interest of precision it would be best to use MAC to qualify that statement of fact, even though a court might hold that *material* by itself in effect conveys the same meaning. But if Widgetco is instead concerned about a potential inaccuracy directly affecting Widgetco—if, for example, the statement of fact is in an asset purchase agreement and concerns an Acme asset that is of little significance to Acme but is central to Widgetco's plans—it would be best to stick with *material*.

9.49 But not all provisions using *material* can be turned into MAC provisions. A statement of fact as to absence of any *breach of any material contract to which Acme is party* cannot, as a matter of semantics, be restructured to use a MAC provision instead (see 9.15).

9.50 In some contexts—for example, in a statement of fact stating that a party *has made no material change in any method of accounting or accounting practice*— it's likely that the drafter is seeking to convey a level of significance below that associated with MAC provisions (see 9.88). In that case, it would be best to restructure the provision to use *nontrivial* (see 9.21) as opposed to a MAC provision or to eliminate any significance qualification (see 9.34).

THE BRINGDOWN CONDITION

9.51 A bringdown condition (including the introductory language) could be phrased like this:

> The Buyer's obligation to consummate the transaction contemplated by this agreement is subject to satisfaction of the following conditions: … that the statements of fact made by the Seller in article 2 were accurate on the date of this agreement and are accurate at Closing;

9.52 But usually the seller succeeds in having the buyer's bringdown condition be subject to a materiality qualification. Often that's accomplished by having the condition require that the statements of fact be *accurate in all material respects*, but *materially accurate* is a more concise way of expressing the same concept:

> that individually and in the aggregate, the statements of fact made by the Seller in article 2 were materially accurate on the date of this agreement and are materially accurate at Closing;

9.53 You could elect to use *materially* as a defined term (see 9.26). If you do and, as is often the case, the bringdown condition to the buyer's obligations and the bringdown condition to the seller's obligations both incorporate a materiality standard, *materially* would have to be defined to apply to all parties (see 9.29). That in turn would require that each bringdown condition make it clear from whose perspective materiality is determined:

> that from the Buyer's perspective, individually and in the aggregate the statements of fact made by the Seller in article 2 were Materially accurate on the date of this agreement and are Materially accurate at Closing;

9.54 If a bringdown condition incorporates a materiality qualification, it would be to the buyer's benefit to have it include the phrase *individually and in the aggregate*, so materiality is determined by considering not only the extent to which each statement of fact is inaccurate but also the cumulative effect of all inaccuracies. Arguably that could be accomplished by saying just *in the aggregate*, but using the longer phrase makes it clearer what is intended.

9.55 If you omit *individually and in the aggregate*, the bringdown condition should refer to *each statement of fact made by the Seller*—that would make it clear that the cumulative effect of all inaccuracies has no effect on materiality.

9.56 A materiality qualification incorporated in a bringdown condition is often phrased using MAC. But it's illogical to think in terms of a statement-of-fact inaccuracy resulting in a MAC, given that the only consequence of an inaccurate seller statement of fact would be that the buyer is entitled not to close or has a claim for indemnification. It's the facts underlying a statement-of-fact inaccuracy, rather than the inaccuracy itself, that could result in a MAC.

9.57 The materiality qualification in a bringdown condition can be subject to carve-outs if the buyer is reluctant to have the materiality qualification apply across the board. A statement of fact often included in such carve-outs is the seller's statement of fact regarding its capitalization. This sort of carve-out would only make sense if the statement of fact itself did not include a materiality qualification. More generally, it's not clear that such carve-outs accomplish much, given that the notion of the buyer refusing to close because of an immaterial inaccuracy seems unpromising, whatever the statement of fact.

DOUBLE MATERIALITY

9.58 Another issue related to materiality is "double materiality." It ostensibly arises when a materiality qualification is included in the bringdown condition to one party's obligation to close and in one or more statements of fact of the other party. The concern is apparently that if the bringdown condition to the buyer's obligation to close incorporates a materiality qualification, then to determine whether that condition has been satisfied you apply a discount to the accuracy required for a given seller statement of fact to be accurate. If a seller statement of fact itself includes a materiality qualification, the same discount is also applied to the statement of fact, so that the level of accuracy required to satisfy the bringdown condition is further reduced. The buyer could be required to close even if a seller statement of fact was on the date of the agreement, or is at closing, materially inaccurate.

9.59 It's common practice for drafters to seek to neutralize double materiality. To do so, either they incorporate in the bringdown condition a materiality qualification regarding only those statements of fact that do not themselves contain a materiality qualification, or for the bringdown condition they strip out materiality qualifications from those statements of fact that have them and apply instead a materiality qualification across the board.

9.60   But such contortions are unnecessary. If *material* conveys the affects-a-decision meaning (see 9.3), then materiality qualifications are not in fact equivalent to an across-the-board discount on accuracy, and materiality on materiality isn't equivalent to a discount on a discount. Instead, for determining both accuracy of a statement of fact subject to a materiality qualification and satisfaction of a bringdown condition subject to a materiality qualification, one would consider the same external standard—whether the statement-of-fact inaccuracy would have affected the buyer's decision to enter into the contract or would affect the buyer's decision to consummate the transaction. Because the same standard applies in both contexts, for determining satisfaction of the bringdown condition it's irrelevant whether the statement of fact too contains a materiality qualification.

9.61   So the notion of double materiality is based on a misunderstanding of how materiality operates. Not surprisingly, caselaw makes no mention of double materiality—it's a figment of practitioner imagination.

9.62   Because courts don't recognize double materiality, attempting to neutralize it would seem to put a party in no worse a position than would have been the case had the issue been ignored. But the verbiage needed to address double materiality adds useless clutter. And if parties spend time negotiating double-materiality language, that's time wasted. Furthermore, assuming that double materiality is a valid concept requires a skewed view of materiality. On balance, disregarding double materiality seems the more efficient option.

9.63   Including the following novel provision could help remove double materiality as a negotiation issue:

> **Double Materiality.** The parties acknowledge that regardless of whether any court recognizes it for other contracts, the contract-interpretation concept known as "double materiality" does not apply to this agreement, so the level of statement-of-fact inaccuracy permitted by the materiality qualification to which section X [the bringdown condition] is subject will not be affected by a materiality qualification to which a statement of fact is subject.

USE OF VERBS IN MAC PROVISIONS

9.64   A modifying MAC provision (see 9.44) addresses the possibility of future MACs, so it might seem natural to use *will* in expressing it: *Acme's financial records contain no inaccuracies except for inaccuracies that will not result in a MAC.* Using *will* in this statement of fact would mean that the statement of fact would be inaccurate only if a MAC were to materialize before closing or if it were to become apparent before closing that a MAC is certain to occur in the future.

9.65   A party to whom such a statement of fact is made would generally want it phrased in such a way that if the party identifies a problem with the potential to lead to a MAC, it could avoid its obligations under the contract or recover damages caused by the inaccurate statement of fact. This could be achieved by using *could*, as in *could* [or *could not*] *result in a MAC*. This formulation is very favorable to the party not making the statement of fact. Assume that Acme makes this statement of fact: *Acme's financial records contain no inaccuracies except for inaccuracies that could not result in a MAC*. To say that an inaccuracy could not result in a MAC is to say that no matter how the future might develop, no possible alternative course of events could lead to a MAC occurring. If, after signing, it were discovered that Acme's financial records contain an inaccuracy that might result in a MAC, that discovery would in theory render the statement of fact inaccurate, no matter how remote the possibility of a MAC's actually occurring.

9.66   So your best bet would be to use instead the formulation *would* [or *would not*] *reasonably be expected to result in a MAC*, meaning that a reasonable person would (or would not) expect the subject of the statement of fact to result in a MAC. In this context, *expect* means "regard as likely to happen," but it's not clear what *likely* means, so don't expect to establish with mathematical certainly what level of likelihood that conveys (see 13.496).

9.67   Other alternatives are available, such as *could* [or *could not*] *reasonably be expected* or *would* [or *would not*] *result in a MAC*, but they offer no advantages.

9.68   For an absolute MAC statement of fact (see 9.42), the present perfect—*no MAC has occurred*—is the appropriate tense. That's because such statements of fact address MACs that have occurred. But it would be advantageous to the party that has the benefit of an absolute MAC provision if it were extended to cover, in the manner of a modifying MAC provision, the possibility of future MACs. This can be easily achieved by grafting a modifying MAC provision onto any absolute MAC provision: *Since 31 December 2016, there has not occurred any MAC or any events or circumstances that would reasonably be expected to result in a MAC*. This sort of modifying MAC provision supplements any modifying MAC provisions in statements of fact addressing specific aspects of the operations of the party making the statement of fact. Using the plural nouns *events* and *circumstances* should make it unnecessary to add *individually or in the aggregate*; see 9.44.

WHETHER TO USE MAC OR MAE AS THE DEFINED TERM

9.69   The defined term MAE is used as an alternative to the defined term MAC. In absolute provisions one can say that since a specified date *no MAE has occurred*, but MAC works better   it sounds a little odd to refer to an *effect*, as opposed to a *change*, as not having occurred since a specified date.

9.70   Some drafters attempt to cure this awkwardness by inserting transitional language—for example, *there has been no change, event, or condition that has resulted in a MAE*. This sort of fix is more than just wordy—it also suggests that it's not enough to show that an MAE has occurred. Instead, you have to show that something has caused an MAE. Such a cause-and-effect scenario not only doesn't make sense, it potentially reduces the buyer's protection.

9.71   For example, in the purchase agreement at issue in *Great Lakes Chemical Corp. v. Pharmacia Corp.*, 788 A.2d 544, 557 (Del. Ch. 2001), the seller, Pharmacia, stated that since the baseline date "there has been no change in the business of the Company which would have a Material Adverse Effect." It would have been simpler to have the statement of fact say instead that *no MAC has occurred*. Perhaps the drafter, having opted to use MAE, thought it odd to have the statement of fact say *there has been no MAE* and so shoehorned in the additional language. The additional language had the potential to be detrimental to the buyer, in that it could be interpreted as meaning that what falls within the scope of the absolute MAE provision is not any MAE, but only a subset of all MAEs, namely those caused by a change in the Company's business. This raised the possibility of the seller's claiming that the absolute MAE provision covers only internal changes at the seller, rather than external market changes and problems at other companies. This is what the seller claimed in a motion for summary judgment made by the seller in response to a breach-of-contract claim brought by the buyer. The court denied the seller's motion but noted that the seller might ultimately prevail on this theory at trial. The seller might have made the same argument even if the absolute provision had been drafted as recommended in 9.42, but it would probably have had a harder time doing so.

9.72   An agreement might use both MAC and MAE. There are two reasons for this practice (a third is described in 9.85).

9.73   First, a drafter might want to use the terms interchangeably. One way to accomplish this would be to provide a full definition for one term, then piggyback off that definition for the other definition by specifying that MAC *means a change that has* a MAE. Another way would be to create a twofer definition: *"Material Adverse Change" and "Material Adverse Effect" mean any material adverse change or material adverse effect in … .* There is some value to each approach, because drafters cannot always be relied on to keep track of which defined term they are using. (For example, sometimes the text of a section entitled "No Material Adverse Effect" will refer to MAC.) But rather than providing a safety net for imprecision, it's better to be precise.

9.74   Second, a drafter might want to use in modifying provisions a broader definition of MAC than is used in an absolute statement of fact in the same contract; because one defined term cannot have two definitions, the drafter uses MAC as the defined term for one definition and MAE for the other. For example, credit agreements often use MAC for the absolute statement of fact and MAE for modifying provisions, with MAE being defined more broadly than MAC because it incorporates any material adverse effect on the rights of the agent or any lender under the loan documents or on the borrower's ability to perform its obligations under the loan documents (see 9.99). Presumably, the reason for this is that since in the absolute statement of fact the focus is more on past adverse changes, the impact on rights and obligations under the loan documents is less relevant.

9.75   But using both MAC and MAE as defined terms in this manner is potentially confusing and generally should be unnecessary, since the broader definition should work equally well in all contexts.

9.76   Given that usually you should be able to make do with one defined term, you have a choice between MAC and MAE. Because MAC is better suited to absolute statements of fact (see 9.69) and should work as well as MAE in all other contexts, MAC is the better term to use.

9.77   One encounters in the literature on MAC provisions the suggestion that there is a substantive basis for distinguishing between MAC and MAE. That's not the case.

THE BASELINE DATE

9.78   An absolute MAC statement of fact must specify the baseline date, which is the date from which the statement of fact runs. Common baseline dates include the date the agreement was signed and the date of the most recent audited, or most recent unaudited, financial statements. Given a choice between using as a baseline date the date of audited or the date of unaudited financial statements, a buyer will generally prefer to use the date of audited financial statements, because they provide a more reliable picture of the target. One can also use other dates as the baseline date. For example, in the case of an unaudited startup company, the date of formation would be an appropriate baseline date. And a lender might want the borrower's absolute MAC statement of fact to use the date when the lender issued the financing commitment.

Defining *Material Adverse Change*

9.79   Drafters generally provide a definition for MAC and use it as a defined term. Doing so allows you to specify precisely what's meant by MAC but without burdening readers by requiring them to wade through the entire definition every time the contract refers to MAC. And it allows you to ensure that the concept is expressed consistently throughout the contract (see 6.2). You could use the initialism MAC as the defined term, but it's preferable that you spell it out—the fewer acronyms and initialisms in a contract the better, because they make a contract harder to read (see 2.128). This chapter uses the initialism so as not to use the entire phrase repeatedly.

9.80   Here's the basic definition recommended by this manual (although you also have the option of using *material* as a defined term; see 9.27):

> **"Material Adverse Change"** means any material adverse change in the business, results of operations, assets, liabilities, or financial condition of the Seller, as determined from the perspective of a reasonable person in the Buyer's position.

9.81   The remainder of this chapter will explain the basis for this definition.

CHANGE VERSUS EXPECTATION OF CHANGE

9.82   When defining MAC, a drafter must decide whether a MAC should be defined as a material adverse change in something, as any event or circumstance that would reasonably be expected to result in a material adverse change in something, or as both.

9.83   The first approach is the better one. If the definition incorporates the *would reasonably be expected* formula, the drafter should omit it from the MAC provisions themselves, since it would be redundant and potentially confusing to have it present at both levels. (Regarding its use in absolute and modifying MAC provisions, see 9.44, 9.66, and 9.68.) But a MAC provision from which this formula has been omitted (*Acme's financial records contain no inaccuracies except for inaccuracies that do not constitute a MAC*) presents its own problems: relegating to the definition the concept of likelihood conveyed by the *would reasonably be expected* formula would suggest to readers who have not studied the definition that the MAC provisions are concerned solely with current, rather than future, adverse changes. This probably explains why many drafters who use the *would reasonably be expected* formula in the definition of MAC also use it, however incongruously, in the MAC provisions themselves.

9.84   Similar redundancy occurs when a drafter uses the *would reasonably be expected* formula, including a reference to *events*, or *events* and *circumstances*, in the definition of MAC and also refers to *events*, or *events* and *circumstances*, in a MAC provision.

9.85   Often when a drafter incorporates the *would reasonably be expected* formula in the MAC definition, the drafter created the defined term expressly for use in absolute provisions, with the defined term MAE (defined without the *would reasonably be expected* formula) being used in modifying provisions. (The relationship between these two defined terms is discussed in 9.69–.77.) Presumably drafters do this because it's not immediately obvious to them how to fit the *would reasonably be expected* formula into absolute provisions. But it's easily done (see 9.68).

NO TAUTOLOGY IN USING *MATERIAL ADVERSE CHANGE* IN THE DEFINITION OF *MAC*

9.86   Using the phrase *material adverse change* in the definition of MAC doesn't entail circularity or tautology—in contracts it's commonplace for a definition to include the term being defined (see 6.17).

USING NOUNS BESIDES *CHANGE* IN THE DEFINITION OF *MAC*

9.87   Instead of referring to material adverse change, often the definition of MAC will state that MAC means *any change, effect, development, or circumstance materially adverse to … ,* or some variant. The extra language is superfluous and is evidence of lawyers' appetite for redundancy (see 1.37). It's clearer and more concise simply to state that MAC means *any material adverse change in … .*

9.88 The *adverse change* part of *material adverse change* means, evidently enough, a change for the worse. As regards *material*, courts and practitioners appear to accept that when used in MAC, *material* conveys the affects-a-decision meaning. Any court would likely echo the *IBP* court in requiring that a party "make a strong showing" when invoking a MAC provision. See *IBP*, 789 A.2d at 68. Using *material* as a defined term would allow you to avoid any confusion on that score (see 9.24).

9.89 If you elect to use a definition of *Material* that applies to more than one party (see 9.29), then not only in the bringdown condition (see 9.53) but also in the definition of MAC you would need to specify from whose perspective materiality is determined:

> **"Material Adverse Change"** means, from the perspective of the Buyer, any Material adverse change in the business, results of operations, assets, liabilities, or financial condition of the Seller.

9.90 If you elect not to use in the definition of MAC the defined term *Material*, you would need to make it clear in the definition of MAC whose perspective applies for determining materiality. That's what the definition in 9.80 does.

QUANTITATIVE GUIDELINES

9.91 To relieve courts of any responsibility for determining whether a given adverse change is material, parties sometimes include in a contract quantitative guidelines regarding what constitutes a MAC. Sometimes a quantitative guideline provides the exclusive basis for determining whether an adverse change is a MAC, as when a purchase agreement defines MAC as *a material adverse change in the business, results of operations, assets, liabilities, or financial condition of Acme in an amount equal to $6.5 million or more*. Alternatively, quantitative guidelines can supplement a conventional definition of MAC.

9.92 But such an approach presents four problems:

9.93 First, adverse changes could conceivably be measured by means of several quantitative indicia. Setting a threshold for all possible indicia would seem impractical, and addressing only a limited number could be arbitrary.

9.94 Second, establishing one or more numerical thresholds for materiality can complicate the negotiation process.

9.95 Third, if the quantitative indicia are illustrative rather than exclusive, adding them to the definition of MAC would increase the risk that a court wouldn't consider to be a MAC a change that doesn't resemble the examples.

9.96 And fourth, MAC provisions are intended to capture the unknown. If a party is able to articulate a concern sufficiently to be able to quantify it, it follows that the concern would be better addressed somewhere other than in the definition of MAC.

9.97 Given these concerns, it's not surprising that quantitative guidelines are little used. But an aggressive buyer, or one with ample bargaining power, might nonetheless want to have one or more favorable quantitative guidelines in the definition of MAC to make it easier for the buyer to invoke a MAC provision.

A MATERIAL ADVERSE CHANGE IN WHAT?

9.98 Defining MAC requires that you determine what needs to experience a material adverse change for a MAC to occur; in the following discussion, this is called the "field of change."

9.99 When representing a buyer acquiring a company, an appropriate field of change would consist of *the business, results of operations, assets, liabilities, or financial condition* of the target, but the exact formulation depends on the type of transaction involved. For example, if the acquisition is in the form of an asset purchase, you might want to formulate the definition so it covers a MAC in the assets being acquired. Sometimes the field of change can be unusually broad. For example, credit agreements often define MAE to include—instead of, in addition to, or as an alternative to a more traditional field of change—any material adverse effect on the rights of the agent or any lender under the loan documents or the ability of the borrower to perform its obligations under the loan documents. And in merger agreements it's commonplace to include within the field of change any event that results in a material adverse change in the ability of one or more parties to complete the merger.

9.100 The word *liabilities* can mean financial obligations required to be disclosed on a balance sheet. It can also mean, more broadly, any legal responsibility to another—*liabilities* in this sense would include contract obligations or an obligation to remediate environmental contamination. For the recommended field of change, the broader sense is intended. It would be cumbersome to attempt to eliminate this ambiguity with a more explicit field of change, but if a contract uses the defined term *Liabilities* elsewhere (for example, in indemnification provisions) to convey the broader meaning, that defined term could be used in the field of change.

9.101 If when a deal is signed the target is planning to enter into a new line of business, the buyer's counsel might want to have the field of change refer to *the business (as it is currently being conducted or as Target currently proposes to conduct it)*. (Changes that adversely affect the target's plans to enter into a new line of business might well fall within the scope of *prospects*, but as discussed in 9.114, a buyer would be better off excluding *prospects* from the field of change. Since such changes would likely not be covered if, as recommended in 9.114, one were to incorporate *prospects* by the "back door," it would be appropriate to address such changes separately (see 9.116).) If the target's plans to enter into a new line of business are sufficiently developed, a more precise alternative to appending a parenthetical to *the business* and relying on an absolute MAC statement of fact or condition would be to have statements of fact or conditions that address circumstances relating to the proposed expansion.

9.102 You can find surplusage in the field of change. For example, excluded from the field of change recommended above are *properties, operations,* and *capitalization.* Little is to be gained by including both *assets* and *properties,* and *operations* (as opposed to *results of operations*) should fall within the scope of *business*—otherwise, one might wonder what, if anything, *business* means. Regarding *capitalization,* it's an ambiguous word that could refer either to the number and type of shares outstanding or to the "market capitalization," or value, of those shares. If the former meaning is intended, it isn't clear what an adverse change would consist of; if the latter meaning is intended, the parties would be advised to address explicitly, in exchange-ratio provisions or elsewhere, the impact on their deal of changes in stock price. In any event, only rarely does *capitalization* feature in the field of change. Don't assume that changes in stock price would come within the scope of a standard field of change that excludes *capitalization*—it's far from clear that it would.

9.103 Many definitions include *condition (financial or otherwise),* but you can use instead just *financial condition,* because whatever might fall within the scope of *otherwise* would be covered by the other elements in the recommended field of change.

9.104 One could argue that the standard elements of the field of change other than *business* are also surplusage, in that any adverse change to the results of operations, assets, liabilities, or financial condition of Acme (to use the elements of the recommended field) would fall within the scope of Acme's business. But in *Pine State Creamery Co. v. Land-O-Sun Dairies, Inc.,* No. 5:96-CV-170-BO, 1997 U.S. Dist. LEXIS 22035, at *9 (E.D.N.C. 22 Dec. 1997), the district court held that the operating profits and losses of Pine State did not fall within the scope of a condition requiring that "there shall not have occurred any material adverse change in the Business." "Business" was defined to mean a dairy processing plant and wholesale dairy distribution system. Although in overturning that decision the U.S. Court of Appeals for the Fourth Circuit stated that "Pine State's financial activities are fairly included within the term 'Business,'" *Pine State Creamery Co. v. Land-O-Sun Dairies, Inc.,* No. 98-2441, 1999 U.S. App. LEXIS 31529, at *10 n.1 (4th Cir. 2 Dec. 1999), other courts might be inclined to narrowly interpret a field of change consisting solely of *the business.* Accordingly, it would be prudent to sacrifice some economy in the field of change.

9.105 Even if you use a broad field of change, a court could hold that a development doesn't constitute a MAC because it doesn't constitute change falling within the field of change. There's mixed caselaw on whether industry-wide or general factors over which a party had only partial control (such as market share) or no control (such as the availability or price of one or more commodities) constitute a MAC. In cases such as *Borders v. KRLB, Inc.,* 727 S.W.2d 357, 358 (Tex. App. 1987), and *Pittsburgh Coke & Chemical Co. v. Bollo,* 421 F. Supp. 908, 930 (E.D.N.Y. 1976), the court held that such change didn't constitute a MAC. On the other hand, in *IBP* the court declined to "preclude industry-wide or general factors from constituting a Material Adverse Effect"—if the target, IBP, had wanted to exclude the factors, "IBP should have bargained for it." *IBP,* 789 A.2d at 66.

9.106   So if a party wants to ensure that it could walk away from a deal if a MAC is caused by one or more specific industry-wide or general developments, it had best incorporate that concept in the contract.

9.107   One way to make clear that certain changes constitute material adverse changes falling within the field of change would be to list them at the end of the MAC definition, preceded by *including*. But for reasons explained in 9.131, it would be best to address those concerns in a statement of fact, condition (either directly or by bringdown of the statements of fact), or other provision.

PROSPECTS

9.108   A recurring topic in negotiations is whether to include *prospects* in the field of change. The buyer wants it included—the future of the business, it says, is a legitimate concern, because the buyer is acquiring the business to operate it in the future. The seller wants it excluded—it's willing, it says, to stand behind how the business is currently being operated, but risks relating to future operations are the buyer's concern. More often than not the seller wins this battle.

9.109   But generally little thought is given to what *prospects* means and what the implications are of including it in, or excluding it from, the field of change.

9.110   In everyday usage, *prospects* means "chances or opportunities for success." The term is not often defined in contracts, but when it is, this is often the definition used: *"Prospects" means, at any time, results of future operations that are reasonably foreseeable based on facts and circumstances in existence at that time.*

9.111   Here's an example of the effect of including *prospects* in the field of change: If one of Acme's competitors secures an alternative source of raw materials that would allow it to produce goods more cheaply, that development could be said to have an adverse effect on Acme's prospects if it appears that Acme would likely be forced to reduce its profit margins. And an adverse effect on prospects could be predicated not only on the occurrence, preclosing, of an event likely to have an adverse effect on Acme's business, but also on the preclosing likelihood of such an event occurring sometime in the future. Such a circumstance was at issue in *Pacheco* and *Goodman*, discussed immediately below.

9.112   The question arises how *prospects* relates to the other standard elements of the field of change. Arguably, material adverse change in a company's prospects constitutes a material adverse change in the company's current business condition, so a change in the company's prospects would allow one to say a MAC has occurred even if *prospects* is absent from the field of change. But in the two cases bearing on the meaning of *prospects*, the courts rejected this argument. See *Pacheco v. Cambridge Technology Partners (Massachusetts), Inc.*, 85 F. Supp. 2d 69 (D. Mass. 2000), and *Goodman Manufacturing Co. v. Raytheon Co.*, No. 98 Civ. 2774(LAP), 1999 WL 681382 (S.D.N.Y. 31 Aug. 1999).

9.113 But you can effectively render *prospects* superfluous. As stated in 9.44, 9.66, and 9.68, if you represent a party that has the benefit of MAC provisions in a contract, then your best course would be to use in any modifying MAC provisions the formula *would* [or *would not*] *reasonably be expected to result in a MAC* and to tack on to any absolute MAC provision the phrase *or any event or circumstance that would reasonably be expected to result in a MAC.* Determining how likely it is that an event or circumstance will cause a MAC requires that one make a reasonable assessment, based on facts and circumstances in existence at the time, of how the business would operate, both in the presence and in the absence of the event or circumstance in question. This analysis is largely identical to the analysis required to determine whether something constitutes a material adverse change in results of future operations that are reasonably foreseeable based on facts and circumstances in existence at that time—in other words, *prospects* as the term is commonly defined.

9.114 Given that the two approaches serve essentially the same purpose, omitting *prospects* from the field of change and instead (1) using consistently the formula *would* [or *would not*] *reasonably be expected to result in a MAC* and (2) expanding as suggested any absolute MAC provisions should afford protection equivalent to *prospects* to the party that would benefit from the MAC provisions while sparing it—with luck—the skirmishing that parties commonly engage in over whether to include *prospects* in the field of change. This approach has been called incorporating *prospects* by the "back door." There is, however, no caselaw on point.

9.115 But in two contexts, a drafter might be reluctant to dispense with *prospects*. First, *Pacheco* is precedent for the notion that if a company is likely to fail to meet its publicly announced financial projections, that constitutes a material adverse change in the company's prospects. Some might think it rash to lose the benefit of that precedent by relying on the back-door approach. But relying on a court to follow *Pacheco* presents risks of its own; if you represent a buyer that wants to be certain that it can walk if it appears that the target will fail to meet its projections, your safest bet would be to make it a condition to closing that there exists no event or circumstance reasonably expected to result in the target failing to meet any publicly announced financial projections.

9.116 Second, what if a buyer learns before closing that the anticipated expansion of the target, Acme, into a new line of business has been stymied? If the definition of MAC includes *prospects*, a court might well consider that such an adverse development falls within the scope of the absolute MAC statement of fact in the purchase agreement. If by contrast the contract sought to incorporate *prospects* by the back door, it's not clear that a court would find that a MAC had occurred: under the back-door approach, the absolute MAC statement of fact would encompass future changes to Acme's current business but not necessarily future changes to a business that Acme had yet to engage in (in this case, the failure of a line of business to materialize). But don't rely on *prospects* to address in a MAC provision a target's knowledge of adverse developments about a proposed expansion. Instead, your best bet would be either to refer in the field of change to *the business (as it is currently being conducted and as Acme currently* *proposes to conduct it)* or, if the plans to enter into a new line of business are sufficiently developed, to include statements of fact or conditions that address circumstances relating to the proposed expansion (see 9.101).

9.117　As a general matter a party with specific concerns that might fall within the scope of *prospects*, either directly or through the back door, would be advised to also address them in statements of fact, conditions, or termination provisions.

WHOSE MATERIAL ADVERSE CHANGE?

9.118　If the definition of MAC is meant to encompass only adverse changes to a single company, make that clear by referring to, for example, *a material adverse change in … of the Seller*.

9.119　MAC definitions are often drafted to cover an entity and some or all of its subsidiaries, using *taken as a whole*. Sometimes a party's parent entity is included, and in merger agreements MAC is sometimes defined to include an adverse change to the surviving entity. A MAC definition can also cover several parties on one side of a deal, such as all borrowers under a credit agreement together with their subsidiaries and, perhaps, any guarantors.

9.120　An agreement might contain some MAC provisions that can be invoked by Acme against Widgetco, and others that can be invoked by Widgetco against Acme. (Whether the target in an acquisition should seek the protection of MAC provisions would depend on the consideration to be paid. If the buyer were paying cash, the target would normally forgo such protection. If the buyer were paying with its own stock, whether the target would benefit from the protection of MAC provisions would depend on the exchange ratio and whether the agreement incorporates other mechanisms to address major changes in the buyer's business.)

9.121　When both sides of a deal have the benefit of MAC provisions, any MAC provision should state which party that MAC provision applies to. It would be simplest to refer to *a Seller MAC* rather than, say, *a MAC of* [or *in*] *the Seller*.

9.122　You could define MAC generically so it applies to more than one party. Here's a generic definition that uses the defined term *Material*:

> **"Material Adverse Change"** means, regarding any Person, any Material adverse change in the business, results of operations, assets, liabilities, or financial condition of that Person.

9.123　And here's a generic definition that doesn't use the defined term *Material*:

> **"Material Adverse Change"** means, regarding any Person, any material adverse change in the business, results of operations, assets, liabilities, or financial condition of that Person, as determined by a reasonable person in the position of any party having the benefit of that provision.

9.124　But it would be clearer to give each side its own comprehensive MAC-defined term, such as *Buyer MAC* and *Seller MAC*. This approach would allow you to create customized definitions of MAC that take into account the parties' differing roles in the transaction and any differences in negotiating leverage.

9.125 If both sides to a transaction have the benefit of MAC provisions and the generic definition or the customized definitions (as applicable) use the defined term *Material*, you would need to use the generic definition of *Material* (see 9.29).

9.126 Finally, if a definition of MAC applies to only one party, take care not to use that defined term in a MAC provision that applies to another party.

AGGREGATING INSTANCES OF CHANGE

9.127 As discussed in 9.43, 9.44, 9.54, and 9.68, for determining occurrence of a MAC, a MAC provision can raise for the drafter whether events or circumstances should be considered individually or should be considered individually and in the aggregate.

9.128 Occasionally one finds aggregation addressed in the definition of MAC. A simple way to accomplish this would be by modifying the recommended form of definition as follows:

> **"Material Adverse Change"** means any adverse change in the business, results of operations, assets, liabilities, or financial condition of the Seller that is material, as determined from the perspective of a reasonable person in the Buyer's position, when considered individually or together with each other such adverse change.

9.129 But this sort of definition is awkward. It aims to lump together all adverse changes, of whatever kind, for determining whether a MAC has occurred. It's clear enough how this definition would affect an absolute MAC provision, which looks at MACs that have already occurred, but it wouldn't seem to make sense for a modifying MAC statement of fact. For example, if Acme states that its financial records contain no inaccuracies except for inaccuracies that would not reasonably be expected to result in a MAC, and a dispute arises regarding an inaccuracy, the inquiry would be whether at signing or closing (as applicable) it would have been reasonable to expect that inaccuracy to result in a MAC. Since that inquiry would look to the possibility of future adverse change, it's unclear what other adverse changes could be aggregated with any adverse change that one could reasonably expect to be caused by that inaccuracy in the financial records.

9.130 The expanded absolute MAC provision recommended in 9.68 offers a better way to ensure broad-based aggregation of adverse changes.

INCLUSIONS AND CARVE-OUTS

9.131 Given that, as described in 9.105, some courts have held that a MAC provision was not triggered by an adverse change in a matter over which the seller had only partial control or no control, any buyer that wants to be able to get out of a deal on such grounds had best specify as much in the agreement. Furthermore, a buyer might have in mind some other circumstances that it wants to be sure would constitute MACs. One way to make clear that certain changes constitute material adverse changes coming within the field of change would be to list them out at the end of the MAC definition, preceded by *including*. But it would be best not to include in the definition of MAC examples of changes that would fall within the definition, because doing so would increase the risk that a court would not consider to be a MAC a change that does not resemble the examples (see 13.371). You would avoid this risk by instead incorporating nonoccurrence of any of those changes in statements of fact, conditions to closing, or termination provisions, as appropriate.

9.132   It has become commonplace to exclude from the definition of MAC, by means of "carve-outs," specific adverse changes. And carve-outs can themselves be subject to carve-outs. Carve-outs don't relate to historical facts, but instead are worded generally to cover the stated circumstances, whatever the time frame. There are many possible carve-outs; here are some common ones:

- any change affecting economic or financial conditions generally (global, national, or regional, as applicable)

- any change affecting the party's industry as a whole (it can be specified that this carve-out does not apply if those conditions disproportionately affect the party in question)

- any change caused by announcement of the transaction or any related transaction (this carve-out can be general or limited to changes related to specific aspects of the party's operations, such as loss of customer orders or employee attrition; note that this carve-out could increase the buyer's risk as to whether it could successfully invoke a MAC provision, because it might be unclear whether a particular adverse effect was caused by announcement of the transaction)

- any change in a party's stock price or trading volume (in most contexts a carve-out for changes in stock price would probably be unnecessary, since it isn't clear that a drop in stock price would fall within the scope of a field of change that doesn't include capitalization (see 9.102), but the cautious drafter might want to avoid any possibility of confusion on the subject by including this carve-out)

- strikes or other labor disruptions

- any failure to meet analysts' or internal earnings estimates

- any action contemplated by the agreement or taken at the buyer's request

- any action required by law

9.133   You can introduce carve-outs by stating that MAC *means any material adverse change in ... other than* [or *except for* or *but does not include*] *any of the following, either alone or in combination ... .*

9.134   Any time you represent an acquisition target, you must decide the extent of the carve-outs that you wish to seek. One factor in your decision would presumably be the parties' relative bargaining power. A second factor would be the nature of your client's business. Carve-outs are associated with technology deals because they address the distinctive characteristics of technology companies, such as unusually short product cycles, intense competition, and the importance of qualified personnel. These characteristics are not unique to technology companies. For example, in any industry in which personnel represent an important component of a company's assets, announcing the deal might result in target personnel leaving. A third factor would be the deal-making practices at the time.

9.135   A restrained position for seller's counsel to take would be to propose carving out adverse changes in the economy or in the industry in question as well as adverse changes attributable to the deal or announcement of the deal. But in negotiating carve-outs, bear in mind that not including a carve-out for a particular circumstance when defining MAC doesn't necessarily mean that a court would hold that occurrence of that circumstance resulted in a MAC.

HOW *MAC* PROVISIONS RELATE TO OTHER PROVISIONS

9.136   Whether a plaintiff convinces a court that a MAC has occurred under an agreement can be influenced by what is, or isn't, included in the other provisions of that agreement.

9.137   For one thing, caselaw shows that a court might use the narrow scope of a statement of fact or condition to conclude that a MAC had not occurred. In *Gordon v. Dolin*, 434 N.E.2d 341, 348–49 (Ill. App. Ct. 1982), the buyer of a manufacturing plant claimed that the absolute MAC statement of fact in the purchase agreement had been triggered by the decision of the seller's principal customer to shift part of its business to a new supplier. It was a condition to closing that before the closing date the seller not have received "actual notice" from any customer that the customer intended to stop purchasing any products from the seller or intended to reduce the quantity of products purchased; the seller had not in fact received actual notice. The court held that the buyer could not rely on the absolute MAC statement of fact, because the narrower condition "modified and limited" the absolute MAC statement of fact: "Where a contract contains both general and specific provisions relating to the same subject, the specific provision is controlling."

9.138   One could conclude from this case that the buyer's MAC claim would have succeeded had the contract not contained the condition regarding customer purchases. But a court might consider that if a contract doesn't address a given topic, then that topic could not have been material to the deal. In *Northern Heel Corp. v. Compo Industries, Inc.*, 851 F.2d 456, 465–66 (1st Cir. 1988), the court, affirming a lower court, found meritless defendant Compo's claim that a downturn in daily shoe production constituted inaccuracy of certain statements of fact in the purchase agreement, including an absolute MAC statement of fact. One reason for the court's decision was the absence of a statement of fact about daily shoe production: "Had the parties deemed average daily production important ('material' to the deal), surely an appropriate reference would have been included. But, it was not."

9.139   The lesson to draw from this is that when drafting a contract, ideally include—and express as broadly as possible—provisions addressing any issue that might conceivably form the basis for a claim by your client or provide grounds to walk. With luck, your client would then need to rely on an absolute MAC provision only in disputes relating to matters that were not foreseeable when the contract was signed.

REFERENCES TO TIME

10.1   In a contract, a reference to time could serve one of four functions:

10.2   First, it could give a date to something, as in *the financial statements dated 31 December 2016*.

10.3   Second, it could specify a point in time, as in *Roe became an Acme employee on 23 March 2016*.

10.4   Third, it could specify a period of time that begins or ends at a stated point in time and has a stated duration, as in *Roe was an Acme employee for two years starting 23 March 2014*, and *Acme may exercise the Option during a 90-day period starting 1 July 2018*. Paired points in time are equivalent to a period of time beginning or ending at a point in time, and the former can with varying degrees of awkwardness be restated as the latter, and vice versa. The preceding examples of periods of time can be restated as *Roe was an Acme employee from 23 March 2014 to 23 March 2016* and *Acme may exercise the Option from 1 July 2018 to 28 September 2018*.

10.5   And fourth, it could apportion a quantity per unit of time, as in *Acme shall pay Doe an annual salary of $250,000* and *Acme shall not exercise the Option more than twice a year*.

10.6   This chapter considers in turn issues raised by each of these four functions.

DATES

10.7   A date is a numbered day in a month, usually stated with the month and the year (*23 April 2018*). In other words, a date is the designation used for a given day, to anchor that day in time. Dates can also be referred to indirectly. For example, *the date of this agreement* refers to the date used to fix when the contract was signed (see 2.30).

Format

10.8   To state dates, this manual uses the format *1 January 2018*. One reason is that this format—the day-month-year format—is used in most of the world. The format generally used in the United States is *January 1, 2018*—the month-day-year format—but the United States is the only country in which that format predominates. And even in the United States, there are important exceptions. For example, the U.S. military uses the day-month-year format, and that's the format used in U.S. passports.

10.9   Furthermore, the month-day-year format is awkward. In terms of logic, it has the disadvantage of putting the middle value at the front. Also, it requires a comma after the one or more digits representing the day, to set them apart from the digits representing the year, and another comma after the year (unless the date is used as an adjective). Those commas add clutter to prose. (A date would nevertheless be followed by a comma if the date comes at the end of introductory matter: *Since 30 January 2017, Acme has not … .*)

10.10   For a book geared to an international readership, it doesn't make sense to use an awkward format that's widely used in only one country. That's why this manual joins, for example, *Garner's Modern English Usage* in using the day-month-year format.

10.11   The drawbacks to using the month-day-year format in this manual apply equally to contract drafting. Drafters based in the United States should consider switching to the day-month-year format. It creates no confusion, it streamlines your prose, and it would result in greater consistency internationally. And if it's good enough for the U.S. military and the U.S. State Department, it should be good enough for those reading your contract.

10.12   Because all-digit dates generally aren't used in books or in contracts, the confusion that results from mixing all-digit dates that use different formats isn't relevant for this discussion.

10.13   Last, it's eccentric to add *A.D.*, short for *Anno Domini* (meaning *in the year of the Lord*), before the year.

Date and Day

10.14   *Day* is a generic unit of time. (See 10.72.) If you're referring to a day without anchoring it in time, use the word *day*. But drafters are prone to using the word *date* in this context:

> Those values may be determined on either (1) the *date* [*read* day] of purchase or (2) the *date* [*read* day] the person became a director, whichever value is greater.

> … plus interest from the beginning of the *date* [*read* day] the disputed payment was originally due through the *date* [*read* day] before the *date* [*read* day] of payment.

10.15   It follows that it would make sense to use *closing day* to refer to the day a closing would take place. But instances of *closing date* greatly outnumber *closing day*. Because overuse of *date* couldn't result in confusion, it would be pedantic to insist that *day* be used instead.

The Date That Is

10.16   The phrase *the date that is*—as in *before the date that is, after the date that is, no later than the date that is,* and so on—is almost always clutter:

> If the Exchange Offer is not completed … *on or before the date that is* [*read* by] 270 days after the Closing Date … .

> … and in no event later than ~~the date that is~~ 60 days after the closing of the merger with Everbright Solar, Inc.

> Each Letter of Credit will expire on the earlier of (1) ~~the date that is~~ one year after the date of the issuance of such Letter of Credit … .

10.17   The phrase is appropriate only in the definition of a defined term that uses the word *date*:

> "**LIBOR Determination Date**" means (1) with respect to the initial Interest Accrual Period, *the date that is* two LIBOR Business Days before the Closing Date … .

The Date Notified

10.18   Here's an example of use of the phrase *the date notified*:

> "**First Hand Date**" means *the date notified* by ABC to XYZ upon which the first hand of poker is played for real money on the Platform.

10.19   The phrase forms part of a passive-voice construction. To put the above example in the active voice, you would say **the date ABC notified to XYZ*. That's ungrammatical (hence the asterisk): you notify someone, you don't notify a date. That's masked somewhat when you use the passive voice, but it's still a problem.

10.20   Say instead *the date that ABC specifies by notice to XYZ*. And more generally, don't use *the date notified*.

POINTS IN TIME

10.21   Drafters generally fix a point in time by reference to a date (such as 24 *January 2017*, or *the date of this agreement*) or other day (*the Closing Day*). You can also specify an anniversary of a date (see 13.26); the concept of an anniversary is equivalent to a forward-looking period of years (see 10.62).

Prepositions Used to Refer to a Day

10.22   *On* is the preposition used to express something happening by reference to a date (*The Option will expire on 9 April 2019*) or other day (*The Option will expire on the Closing Day*).

10.23   If a point in time comes at the beginning or end of a period of time, it can be unclear whether the day in question is to be excluded (in other words, is "exclusive") or is to be included (is "inclusive") for determining exactly when that point in time occurs.

10.24   Each of the following examples uses one of the prepositions most often used to denote a beginning point in time; next to it is a short assessment of the caselaw addressing whether that preposition is inclusive or exclusive.

Acme may exercise the Option *from* 9 April 2018.	Most courts have held that *from* is exclusive, but some have held that it's inclusive.
Acme may exercise the Option *after* 9 April 2018.	Most courts have held that *after* is exclusive, but some have held that it's inclusive.
Acme may exercise the Option *starting* 9 April 2018.	A court would likely hold that *starting* is inclusive.
The Option Period commences *on* 9 April 2018.	A court would likely hold that in this context *on* is inclusive.

10.25 And each of the following examples uses one of the prepositions most often used to denote an ending point in time:

Acme may exercise the Option *until* 9 April 2019.	Some courts have held that *until* is inclusive, others that it's exclusive.
Acme may exercise the Option *to* 9 April 2019.	Some courts have held that *to* is inclusive, others that it's exclusive.
The Option Period will end *on* 9 April 2019.	A court would likely hold that in this context *on* is inclusive.
Acme may exercise the Option *before* 9 April 2019.	A court would likely hold that *before* is exclusive.
Acme may exercise the Option *through* 9 April 2019.	A court would likely hold that *through* is inclusive.
If Acme exercises the Option *by* 9 April 2018, ...	Some courts have held that *by* is inclusive, others that it's exclusive.

10.26 *Between* links beginning and ending points in time; most courts consider *between* to be exclusive at both ends. Pairing *from* and *to*, as in *from 1 February 2017 to 30 April 2017*, and *after* and *before*, as in *after 1 February 2017 and before 30 April 2017*, can serve the same purpose, but subject to whatever ambiguity afflicts the individual prepositions.

10.27 Although U.S. caselaw relating to some prepositions provides a good indication of whether a court would treat it as exclusive or inclusive, the caselaw relating to other prepositions is less clear-cut. And a court could always hold that based on the circumstances, a preposition that most courts have considered exclusive is inclusive (or vice versa).

10.28 Even if the caselaw regarding the effect of a particular preposition is mostly consistent, that doesn't mean that the parties to a contract had that effect in mind. If anything, the potential for confusion caused by prepositions is perhaps greater than is suggested by the caselaw.

When in a Day a Point in Time Occurs

10.29   Even if it's certain on which day a stated point in time is to occur, there remains the question of when on that day it is to occur. In this context *day* means the 24 hours from one midnight to the next, so a beginning point in time could occur at midnight at the beginning of the day in question (if it's inclusive) or at the end of the day in question (if it's exclusive), and an ending point in time could occur at midnight at the end of the day in question (if it's inclusive) or at the beginning of the day in question (if it's exclusive). Or a party might decide that it had in mind some other time of day (see 10.34). As such, referring to a point in time by reference to a day is an example of failure to be sufficiently specific (see 7.28).

10.30   Instead of simply tolerating the uncertainty inherent in references to points in time, you can make it explicit whether the date for a point in time is inclusive or exclusive. One way to accomplish that would be to say as much, as in *Acme may exercise the Option any time from 1 February 2017, inclusive, to 30 April 2017, exclusive*, although that's legalistic.

10.31   Or you could say *from the beginning of 15 April 2017 to the end of 30 April 2017*, but references to the beginning or end of a day could be understood as referring to business hours rather than a day of 24 hours.

10.32   Another alternative would be to include in contracts a section specifying how references to time are to be interpreted, but to be comprehensive— and it should be comprehensive—such a section would have to be lengthy. (For a fragment of such a provision, see 15.16.)

Stating the Time of Day

10.33   A clearer way to avoid uncertainty in referring to a point in time is to state a time of day for each beginning and ending point in time.

10.34   It's best to state the time of day directly—*the Option expires at 2:00 p.m. on 25 September 2017*. You could refer to it indirectly, as in *the Option expires at the close of business on 25 September 2017*, with the exact time to be determined by reference to the practice of the business in question. But *close of business* can cause dispute. See *Lehman Brothers International (Europe) v. ExxonMobil Financial Services BV* [2016] EWHC 2699 (Comm) (opinion of the High Court of Justice of England and Wales); *Re Electron Holdings; McCann v. Halpin* [2013] IEHC 495 (opinion of the High Court of Ireland). The same applies to *opening of business*.

10.35   The simplest time of day to use in beginning or ending points in time is midnight. It's simplest to deal in entire days. And because most businesses are closed at midnight, using *midnight* to specify a point in time reduces the likelihood of dispute over when a notice or payment was received.

10.36   But don't refer to midnight, or noon for that matter, as *12:00 a.m.* or *12:00 p.m.* Just as noon isn't part of either the 12 *ante meridiem* (before noon) hours or the 12 *post meridiem* (after noon) hours, but represents the boundary between the two, midnight is the boundary between any set of *post meridiem* hours and the following set of *ante meridiem* hours.

10.37   Although simply referring to noon avoids any confusion as to which day is intended—each day has only one noon—referring to midnight raises the issue whether you're referring to the midnight that marks the beginning of the day question or the midnight that marks its end. There's a convention that *midnight of 15 August* refers to the midnight that follows 15 August, but it's not clear that it has been universally accepted or that the parties to a contract know of it.

10.38   One way that drafters address this ambiguity is by moving forward by one minute to 12:01 a.m. any midnight point in time that begins a period in time and by moving back by one minute to 11:59 p.m. any midnight point in time that ends a period of time, but that's a clumsy way around the problem. An overly subtle variant is to specify that the beginning point in time occurs at one minute before 12:01 a.m. and the ending point in time occurs at one minute after 11:59 p.m. A simpler solution would be to refer to *midnight at the beginning* [or *end*] *of* the date in question. (For another explanation of use of *12:01 a.m.* and *11:59 p.m.*, see 10.42.)

TIME OF DAY AS A BOUNDARY BETWEEN PERIODS OF TIME

10.39   A time of day isn't a period of time. Instead, it's a boundary between the period of time that comes before and the period of time that comes after.

10.40   So if a contract states that a deadline is midnight at the end of a given day, the deadline will pass once the last second of the 11:00 p.m. hour expires and the first second of the next hour begins. Midnight is the boundary between those two seconds.

10.41   It seems that some drafters aren't convinced of that. For example, included in contracts filed on the U.S. Securities and Exchange Commission's EDGAR system are plenty of contracts that use *5:01 p.m.* to state a point in time. The implication is that when you state a time of day, you're referring to a minute-long period of time, so *5:00 p.m.* constitutes a period of time that isn't over until *5:01 p.m.*

10.42   That suggests that although drafters might use *12:01 a.m.* and *11:59 p.m.* to avoid the ambiguity in *midnight* (see 10.38), it's likely that some who use *12:01 a.m.* and *11:59 p.m.* are doing so because they think that a time of day refers to a minute-long period of time.

10.43   There's no sign that this potential for confusion has caused fights, with a contract party claiming that it should have been given an extra minute. And there's no simple way to draft around this misconception—you'd have to include an internal rule of interpretation (see chapter 15) that says, in effect, a time of day is a boundary between periods of time. It would be silly to indulge the misconception by stating a time of day in hours, minutes, and seconds (for example, *17:00:00*), presumably so that the period of time ostensibly at issue is one second rather than one minute. So instead, be on the lookout for the misconception, a potential sign of which is a draft that states a time of day that is a minute more or less than what you'd expect.

USING *AT* TO STATE A DEADLINE

10.44   Because a time of day marks the boundary between blocks of time and occupies no time itself, it's impossible for something to take place *at* a point in time. Instead, it will take place before or after, or it will straddle the point in time. It follows that providing in a contract for an act to occur at a specified time is to invite confusion, as it's not clear how much time before or after that time the party in question has to perform the act.

10.45   A court might conclude that for something to happen at a specified time, it's sufficient that it happen in the minute after that point in time. See, e.g., a Canadian case, *Bradscot (MCL) Ltd. v. Hamilton-Wentworth Catholic District School Board* [1999] 42 O.R.3d 723 (O.C.A.). But it would be reckless to build this uncertainty into a contract, so don't use *at* to state a deadline. Use instead a beginning point in time (see 10.24) or an ending point in time (see 10.25).

HOW TO STATE A TIME OF DAY

10.46   Use digits, not words, to state the time of day—say *5:30 p.m.*, not *five thirty p.m.* And don't use both words and digits, as in *five thirty (5:30) p.m.* (Regarding using words and digits to state numbers generally, see 14.1.)

10.47   Don't include *o'clock* when stating a time of day, as in *2:00 o'clock p.m.*

10.48   The abbreviations *a.m.* and *p.m.* can instead be stated in capitals, in which case periods are unnecessary—*5:30 PM*. In book publishing it would be standard to use small capitals, but that would be unnecessarily fussy for contracts.

10.49   In jurisdictions that use the 24-hour system, it would be appropriate to use that system in contracts—*17:30* instead of *5:30 p.m.* But don't state time in hours, minutes, and seconds (*17:30:00*) unless extraordinary circumstances require it.

TIME ZONES

10.50   If a contract is between parties based in different time zones, or if a contract contemplates business being transacted across time zones, specify in any reference to the time of day which time zone is to be used for determining when that time of day has come.

10.51   You could accomplish that by stating the applicable time zone, but doing so poses three minor problems relating to daylight saving time. Daylight saving time—also known as "summer time"—is the convention of adjusting clocks forward in spring, so that afternoons have more daylight and mornings have less, and then adjusting them backward in autumn. The time when daylight saving time is not in effect is known as "standard time."

10.52   First, it's commonplace for drafters to forget to take into account daylight saving time and when it applies. And many people are unaware that the initialisms PST, MST, CST, and EST refer to standard time and so shouldn't, strictly speaking, be used for references to time on days when daylight saving time is in effect. As a result, many drafters use incorrect time-zone designations—for example Pacific Standard Time rather than Pacific Daylight Time, as in *1:00 p.m. PST* [read *PDT*] *on 5 July 2017*.

10.53 Second, within a given time zone some jurisdictions might observe daylight saving time and others might not. For example, in the Mountain Time Zone, Colorado observes daylight saving time, but not Arizona (except for the Navajo Nation), meaning that in the notation *1:00 p.m. MDT on 5 July 2017*, the time-zone designation would be correct if you're referring to time in Colorado but incorrect if you're referring to time in most parts of Arizona.

10.54 And third, if you're specifying the time of day on a day that could occur any time during the year—as in *Acme shall cause Product Support personnel to be on call from 6:00 a.m. to 6:00 p.m. PST each Business Day*—it would arguably be preferable to use instead the neutral, albeit informal, designation *PT*, given that on some days Pacific Standard Time would be observed and on the other days Pacific Daylight Time.

10.55 A simple way to avoid such annoyances and any potential uncertainty is to refer to time in a city, presumably one with some bearing on the transaction—*6:00 p.m., New York time*. You could elect to do so by means of an internal rule of interpretation; see 15.7. It can be safer to refer to time in a city than in a state, as some states are in more than one time zone.

Prepositions to Use to Refer to Occurrence of an Event

10.56 Prepositions used to refer to a day (see 10.22) can also be used to express something happening on occurrence of an event (for example, *sale of the Acme Assets*). So can *upon*.

10.57 In this context, *upon* and *on* express the meaning "on the occasion of" or "when (something) occurs." This use of *upon* and *on* can cause confusion.

10.58 Use of *upon* or *on* doesn't pose a problem when language of policy is used to express something that happens automatically on occurrence of an event (*The Option will expire upon sale of the Acme Assets*). But with language of discretion (*Acme may exercise the Option upon sale of the Acme Assets*) or language of obligation (*Acme shall vacate the Premises upon sale of the Acme Assets*), the question arises how long after occurrence of the event you have to take the action specified.

10.59 This issue arose in *IPE Asset Management, LLC v. Fairview Block & Supply Corp.*, 999 N.Y.S.2d 465 (App. Div. 2014). The contract at issue stated that upon expiration of a 15-month period after closing, the buyer could elect to sell the property back to the seller. The closing took place on 30 June 2005; in November 2010 and again in December 2010 the buyer notified the seller that it wished to sell the property back to the seller. The buyer argued that the contract gave it an open-ended option; the seller argued that the plaintiffs could exercise the option only during "a reasonable time" after the 15-month period had expired. The appeals court held that the language was ambiguous.

10.60 To avoid this confusion, state a period for taking the action in question, using something other than *upon*—for example, *If during the 30 days after* *that 15-month period the Buyer notifies the Seller that it wishes to sell the Property back to the Seller … .*

PERIODS OF TIME

10.61   A period of time can run either forward or backward from a point in time.

Forward-Looking Periods of Time

10.62   A forward-looking period of time is usually indicated by *from, following,* or *after* (as in *Smith may exercise the Option during the ten days from his receipt of* [or *following his receipt of* or *after he receives*] *the Option Notice*). To determine the ending date of a forward-looking period of time using any of these prepositions, the convention is that you leave out the day from which you are counting and include the last day of the specified period, unless it's clear that the period must consist of a certain number of entire days, in which case both the first and last days are excluded, or unless it's clear that the parties intend that the first day be included. Applying this convention to the preceding example, if Smith receives the Option Notice on 1 January, the first day of the ten-day period is 2 January and Smith must exercise the Option before midnight at the end of 11 January. This convention is generally recognized by courts, so usually contracts aren't explicit as to how the ending date of a forward-looking period of time is to be determined. But to avoid any uncertainty, be explicit.

10.63   If you know the beginning and end points of a forward-looking period of time, it would be clearer to express it by paired points in time, because that would render irrelevant having to determine when the forward-looking period ends.

Backward-Looking Periods of Time

10.64   A backward-looking period of time is usually indicated by *before* (as in *Acme may exercise the Option during the ten days before the Exclusivity Period expires*) and *prior to.* (Regarding *prior to,* see 17.19.) To determine when a backward-looking period of time begins, the convention is that you count one of the terminal days and don't count the other. Using the preceding example, if the Exclusivity Period expires 31 December, then 30 December is the first day before expiration, 21 December is the tenth day before expiration, and the first day that Acme may exercise the Option is 21 December. As with forward-looking periods of time (see 10.62), making it explicit how the beginning date of a backward-looking period of time is to be determined would eliminate any uncertainty.

10.65   Backward-looking periods of time are often used to specify the minimum notice that must be given in a certain situation, as in *Smith shall provide Jones with at least* [or *no fewer than*] *ten days' prior notice of any Proposed Transfer.* (Regarding *prior notice,* see 13.585.) Many courts have held that in this context too the general rule applies—you count one of the terminal days but not the other. But other courts have held that requiring at least a certain number of days' (or weeks' or months') advance notice means that those days (or weeks or months) must be "clear" or "entire" days, so you must exclude both the first and last terminal days. Consider how these differing approaches would play out using the preceding example, with 31 December being the date of the Proposed Transfer: Using the exclude-one-day approach, 21 December, the tenth day before 31 December, would be the last day on which notice could validly be given. Using the exclude-both-days approach, 20 December, the eleventh day before 31 December, would be the last day on which notice could validly be given.

10.66   Given the divided caselaw on minimum-notice provisions, it would be best to eliminate the ambiguity in such provisions, at least to avoid confusing contract parties and their lawyers. Besides being explicit about how to calculate the beginning date (see 10.64), you could accomplish that by denoting a minimum-notice period in *entire days*, *entire* being a term that occurs in the caselaw. The term *clear* occurs more frequently in caselaw, but it might be less evident what *clear* means.

Don't Use Confusing Points in Time

10.67   To determine a period of time, don't use a point in time that could result in the parties arguing when, or whether, the point in time occurred. For example, using as a point in time *final resolution of any disputes* raises the question what *final resolution* means.

Don't Use *Within*

10.68   It's best not to use *within*: depending on the context, it can denote a period of time that is both forward- and backward-looking, a fact that might escape a party and its lawyers. For example, if a contract provides that *to validly exercise the Option, Acme must submit an Option Notice to Widgetco within seven days of the first anniversary of this agreement*, that could be interpreted as meaning that Acme may exercise the Option no more than seven days before and no more than seven days after the anniversary, or the drafter might have thought it meant one or the other. It would be best to make the intended meaning explicit.

10.69   In a given context it might be apparent that the period of time could only run forward, as in *to validly exercise the Option, Acme must submit an Option Notice to Widgetco within seven days of receiving a Sale Notice*, but it would be clearer to use instead *no later than seven days after it receives a Sale Notice*. That's because instead of presenting the reader with the ambiguity caused by *within*, then resolving it, it would be clearer to avoid the ambiguity.

10.70   Under California law, the word *within* is particularly awkward when used in leases. For exercising a lease option to purchase, it has been held that *within 30 days prior to* means *during the 30 days before*, but for options to renew leases, California courts have decided that *within 30 days prior to* means *at least 30 days before*. See *Wilson v. Gentile*, 10 Cal. Rptr. 2d 713 (Ct. App. 1992). It's bizarre to attribute a different meaning to a phrase depending on the kind of contract it occurs in—instead of using *within X days prior to*, express more clearly the meaning you intend.

Which Unit of Time to Use

10.71   Drafting a provision referring to a period of time requires determining not only when the period begins or ends and how long it lasts, but also what unit of time to state it in.

10.72   The smallest unit is the day. Often it's preferable to denote periods of time in *business days* rather than simply *days*. (A business day is usually defined in contracts to mean any day other than a weekend or a public holiday in a specified jurisdiction, or any day that banks generally are, or a named bank is, open for business.) Denoting a period of time in business days gives the parties a better sense of the working days available to take a specified action. It would also ensure that the last day is a business day, which would make it more feasible for a party to act at the last minute. Similarly, denoting in business days a period for giving notice would ensure that the last day is a business day; this could be significant if the contract also provides—as is often the case—that notice given on a day other than a business day is not effective until the next business day.

10.73   On the other hand, using simply *days* makes it easier to quickly determine without a calendar when the period begins or ends, as applicable. It's unnecessary, and potentially confusing, to use *calendar days* instead of *days*.

10.74   And don't use the awkward *nonbusiness day*. Instead, say *a day other than a business day*.

10.75   You can also state periods of time in months. It's a generally accepted convention that a period of a month counting forward from a date ends at midnight at the beginning of the corresponding day of the following month, the day from which one is counting having been excluded. If next month doesn't have a corresponding day, the period ends on the last day of that month; in other words, a period of a month counting from 31 March ends on 30 April. Because one can quickly determine without referring to a calendar the end date of a period denoted in months, it can simplify matters to denote in months periods of time of longer than, say, 90 days.

10.76   You can denote periods of time in weeks, but doing so provides no advantages over using days or months. In fact, it's simpler to determine the end date of a period of time if it's denoted in months rather than weeks. In this context, *week* is generally defined as a space of any seven consecutive days, whatever the starting point, rather than seven successive days beginning with the day traditionally fixed as the first day of the week, whether it be Sunday or Monday.

10.77   A period of time can also last one or more years, in which case it runs through the day before the relevant anniversary of the first day included.

10.78   Some drafters are reluctant to express periods of time in months or years for fear that a court will construe *month* to mean one of the 12 months of the year, starting on the first day of that month, or *year* to mean 12 consecutive months starting 1 January. Because a period of time is measured from a stated beginning or ending point, this isn't a valid concern. (But see 10.92–.98.)

10.79   The prefixes *bi-* and *semi-* are confusing. *Bimonthly* means "occurring every two months," and *semimonthly* means "occurring twice a month." *Biweekly* and *semiweekly* reflect the same distinction. But *biannual* and *semiannual* both mean "occurring twice a year," although some dictionaries also have *biannual* meaning the same thing as *biennial*, namely "occurring every two years." To avoid this confusion, use instead *twice a week/month/year* and *every two weeks/months/years*.

One Year and a Day

10.80   One encounters in lending documents provisions in which a lender agrees not to commence bankruptcy proceedings against the borrower until *one [or a] year and a day* after the borrower has repaid the specified debt. That's because section 547 of the U.S. Bankruptcy Code permits the trustee or debtor-in-possession to avoid certain preferential transfers, and one element of a preferential transfer is that the transfer must have occurred between 90 days and one year before the petition was filed if at the time of the transfer the creditor was an insider.

10.81   But it would be sufficient to say instead *no sooner than one year* after. If the debt was repaid on 1 January 2017, one year after that would be 2 January 2018, assuming you exclude the day from which the year is being counted, as is standard (see 10.62). One year before that day would be 2 January 2017, assuming again that you exclude the day from which you're counting. It follows that repayment on 1 January 2017 would be more than a year before the day the petition was filed.

10.82   The origin of *one year and a day* perhaps lies in the rhetorical flourish it offers, one that's on display in *forever and a day*, meaning "for a very long time." If the *and a day* construct made sense, you would see it used routinely, and with *month* too. You don't.

Using *On* to Denote a Day-Long Period of Time

10.83   A period of time need not be anchored to a stated beginning or ending point in time in one context—when an act or event must take place *on* a specified date. In that case, the period of time is the 24 hours of the day in question, and no beginning or ending point in time need be explicitly stated—they are midnight at the beginning and end of that day, respectively. A reference to an event that is to occur on a given day can be supplemented by adding a beginning or ending time of day, or both (see 10.33).

Using a Time of Day for the End of a Period of Time

10.84   Consider the following: *If the Buyer delivers a Claim Notice to the Seller before 2:00 p.m. on the date that is 20 Business Days after the Closing … .*

10.85   Because that sentence conveys two possible meanings, it's not clear how long the buyer has to deliver a claim notice. The first possible meaning is that the condition would be satisfied if the notice were delivered anytime during the 20 business days up to 2:00 p.m. on the 20th business day.

To convey that meaning, say instead *If the Buyer delivers a Claim Notice to the Seller between the Closing and 2:00 p.m. 20 Business Days after the Closing … .*

10.86   The second possible meaning is that the condition would be satisfied if the notice were delivered before 2:00 p.m. on the 20th business day, whereas delivery on any of the preceding 19 business days would not satisfy the condition. To express that meaning, say instead *If the Buyer delivers a Claim Notice to the Seller on the 20th Business Day after the Closing, before 2:00 p.m. … .*

Confusion Resulting from Referring to a Point in Time Instead of a Period in Time

10.87   If a contract refers to, for example, *the Revenues as of the 24-Month Revenue Measurement Point*, don't be surprised if a fight ensues over whether that reference is to revenues for only the second 12-month period or for both 12-month periods. When referring to a figure that pertains to a period of time, refer to that period of time, not to the point in time marking the end of that period.

During the Period

10.88   Usually there's a better alternative to *during the period* (and *during a period*) for establishing a period of time:

> … ~~*during the period*~~ from the relevant Early Termination Date to the date for payment determined under section 6(d).

> *During the period that* [read *While*] the Warrant is outstanding, the Company shall … .

> … by reason of the Employee's separation from service *during a period in which* [read *while*] the Employee is a Specified Employee … .

10.89   But nothing is wrong with, for example, *during that period*, or *during the period specified in*, or *during the period for calculating the Exercise Price*—they're used not to establish a period but instead to refer to a period stated elsewhere in the contract or in another document.

Will Have Plus a Period of Time

10.90   Stating that a party *will have* a period of time to do something can result in confusion as to whether what is being expressed is an obligation or a condition. Consider this sentence: *After termination, Acme will have 60 days to return to Widgetco any Confidential Information in Acme's possession.* The drafter presumably intended it to function as an obligation, so it would be better to express it as such: *No later than 60 days after termination, Acme shall return to Widgetco any Confidential Information in Acme's possession* (see 3.72). Now consider this sentence: *After termination, Acme will have 60 days to exercise the Option by notice to Widgetco.* The drafter presumably intended it to function as a condition, so it would be better to express it as such (see 3.356): *To validly exercise the Option, Acme must no later than 60 days after termination notify Widgetco that it is doing so.*

APPORTIONING QUANTITIES PER UNIT OF TIME

10.91   When apportioning quantities per unit of time (as in *Acme shall pay Doe an annual salary of $250,000*), two issues arise. First, the alternative meanings of the unit of time used. And second, how to deal with any short period at the beginning or end of the contract.

The Possible Meanings of Certain Units of Time

10.92   When apportioning quantities per unit of time (as opposed to stating periods of time; see 10.78), the word *year* can be ambiguous, in that it could mean a year from the date of the agreement and each subsequent anniversary, or it could mean the 12-month period from any 1 January. In this context, most courts have held that *year* means the 12-month period from 1 January.

10.93   In this context, the same ambiguity afflicts *month*, in that *month* can mean the period from one day to midnight at the beginning of the corresponding day of the following month (see 10.75), but it can also mean one of any of the 12 months of the year.

10.94   It would be best to avoid this ambiguity by stating what *year* or *month* means. You could do so by using a more specific alternative to *month* or *year* consistent with the alternative meanings given in 10.92 and 10.93. Or you could use a defined term, although it would make sense to do so only if you use the term several times (see 6.115).

10.95   U.S. caselaw suggests that using the term *calendar year* would make it more likely that a court interprets *year* to mean the period from 1 January through 31 December. On the other hand, it's not the clearest usage— that there's caselaw regarding what it means suggests as much. The term *civil year* means the same thing as *calendar year*, but if anything it's less familiar.

10.96   Some contracts say that the meaning of *year* (and *month*) is to be determined according to the Gregorian calendar—the most widely used civil calendar—but that does nothing to resolve which meaning of *year* applies.

10.97   U.S. caselaw suggests that for apportioning quantities per unit of time, as opposed to measuring a period of time, a U.S. court would likely hold that *calendar month* refers to one of the months of the year. But it's not the clearest way to express that meaning. English courts are inclined to treat *calendar month* as meaning the period from a given day to the beginning of the corresponding day of the following month. That inconsistency confirms the potential for confusion.

10.98   You can use *day* when apportioning quantities per unit of time, but it's rare that parties need to apportion quantities daily. As regards using *week*, the ambiguity that afflicts *year* and *month* would be aggravated: not only could *week* mean any seven consecutive days or seven consecutive days beginning with the day traditionally fixed as the first day of the week, it's also unclear what that tradition is. If you wish to apportion quantities by the week, specify what *week* means.

Handling Short Periods

10.99   If in apportioning quantities per unit of time you use *year* to mean the 12-month period beginning any 1 January or use *month* to mean one of the 12 months of the year beginning with the first day of each month, it might be necessary to state how the parties are to treat any short period between the date of the agreement and the beginning of the next month or year, as well as any short period between the end of the last complete month or year and the date of termination. If instead the meaning of *month* or *year* is keyed to the date of the agreement, one is still faced with the possibility of an ending short period.

10.100   It might be sufficient to say that any short period is to be handled by prorating the number or amount—such as the number of vacation days to which an employee is entitled—that applies in the case of a complete month or year; you would probably also need to provide for rounding up, down, or to the nearest whole number. (Regarding rounding, see 14.53.)

10.101   If the number or amount apportioned to a period is expressed as a percentage of a performance or other index—as is the case when Roe's bonus is based on her employer's annual gross revenue—it might be appropriate to provide that if there is a short period, the percentage will be of that portion of the index that applies to the short period rather than of a pro-rata portion of the entire period. Doing so in the case of Roe would result in Roe receiving the stated percentage of gross revenue for the short period between her starting work and 1 January of the next year, rather than the stated percentage of a pro-rata portion of gross revenue for the entire year. This approach might produce an unfair result; for example, giving Roe the stated percentage of gross revenue for a short period consisting of the last two months of the year would be particularly favorable to Roe if her employer is a retailer that collects the bulk of its earnings during the holiday season. Also, it might be difficult or impossible to determine what portion of the index is attributable to the short period.

10.102   An alternative would be to use the entire index and prorate the percentage figure, but that might not make sense in the case of a performance bonus. For example, that approach would mean that Roe's first bonus would depend in part on how her employer's business performed during a period that preceded Roe becoming an employee. Also, if the short period comes at the end of the contract, it might not be reasonable to expect Roe to wait until after the end of the year in which she was terminated to receive any bonus to which she is entitled for the short period starting 1 January of that year.

10.103   Given these difficulties, it might be necessary to arrange for beginning and ending short periods.

Apportioning Units of Time

10.104   When what is being apportioned in a unit of time is one or more other units of time, that raises the question whether the units of time being apportioned have to constitute a single block of time.

10.105 Consider the following: *For two months each year the Employee shall work in Acme's Budapest office.* Leaving aside what *year* means (see 10.92), it's not clear whether to comply with this obligation the employee must spend one two-month block of time working in the Budapest office or instead can accumulate the required time during two or more visits to Budapest.

10.106 The simplest way to make it clear that an apportioned period of time must constitute a block of time is to use the word *consecutive*, as in *For two consecutive months each year*. (For that to work, the block of time would have to consist of more than one unit of time, so you would need to convert a reference to one month to *30 consecutive days*.) If that's not the intended meaning, make that clear. For example, you could say *Over the course of one or more visits, each no shorter than five business days, excluding travel days, the Employee shall work in Acme's Budapest office for two months of each year.*

OTHER STANDARDS FOR SPEED, FREQUENCY, AND DURATION

10.107 In addition to containing precise references to time, contracts also use vagueness to state when and how often actions are to take place. (For vagueness generally, see 7.42.)

Promptly, Immediately

10.108 For obligations and conditions, it's likely that in the minds of many drafters *immediately* requires speedier action than does *promptly*. Some caselaw supports that distinction. For example, the District Court for the Southern District of New York has said that *promptly* doesn't mean *immediately*, but rather within a reasonable time. See *Morgan Guaranty Trust Co. of New York v. Bay View Franchise Mortgage Acceptance Co.*, No. 00 CIV. 8613 (SAS), 2002 WL 818082 (S.D.N.Y. 30 Apr. 2002).

10.109 But this distinction disappears when you look more closely at it.

PROMPTLY

10.110 *The Oxford English Dictionary* defines *promptly* to mean "readily, quickly, directly, at once, without a moment's delay." And courts have uniformly held that promptness is a function of circumstances. Here are three representative cases:

- *State v. Chesson*, 948 So. 2d 566, 568 (Ala. Civ. App. 2006) (stating that the term "promptly" has been construed to mean within a reasonable time in light of all the circumstances).

- *Doe Fund, Inc. v. Royal Indemnity Co.*, 825 N.Y.S.2d 450, 451 (App. Div. 2006) ("[W]hen an insurance policy requires notice of an occurrence or action be given promptly, that means within a reasonable time in view of all of the facts and circumstances.").

- *Buck v. Scalf*, No. M2002-00620-COA-R3-CV, 2003 WL 21170328, at *5 (Tenn. Ct. App. 20 May 2003) ("It has generally been held that the terms 'promptly' or 'prompt notice' mean that notice must be given within a reasonable time in view of all the facts and circumstances of the case.").

10.111   The tenth edition of *Black's Law Dictionary* doesn't contain an entry for *promptly*, but the sixth edition, published in 1990, does, saying that the meaning of *promptly* "depends largely on the facts in each case, for what is 'prompt' in one situation may not be considered such under other circumstances or conditions."

10.112   Given that the meaning of *promptly* depends on the circumstances, it follows that saying *as promptly as practicable* [or *possible*] adds nothing other than some unnecessary extra words.

IMMEDIATELY

10.113   *The Oxford English Dictionary* gives as the definition of *immediately* "Without any delay or lapse of time; instantly, directly, straightaway; at once." (*Immediately* has other meanings, including "without intermediary," as in *the immediately preceding Business Day*.)

10.114   The current edition of *Black's Law Dictionary* says that *immediate* means occurring without delay, and the sixth edition says that *immediately* means "without delay; directly; within a reasonable time under the circumstances of the case; promptly and with reasonable dispatch."

10.115   So just in terms of dictionary definitions, *immediately* looks very much like *promptly*. And this similarity becomes more pronounced when you look at the caselaw, which indicates that just like *promptly*, *immediately* is subject to a reasonableness standard. Here are some representative cases:

- *Dwoskin v. Rollins, Inc.*, 634 F.2d 285, 294 n.6 (5th Cir. 1981) ("[S]everal Georgia cases arising in a variety of contexts suggest that immediate delivery means performance with reasonable diligence concerning the circumstances.")

- *Continental Savings Association v. U.S. Fidelity and Guaranty Co.*, 762 F.2d 1239, 1243 (5th Cir. 1985) ("Under Texas law, similar phrases, such as 'as soon as practicable' or 'immediately,' require only that notice be given within a reasonable time in light of the circumstances involved.")

- *Briggs Ave LLC v. Insurance Corp. of Hannover*, No. 05 Civ. 4212 (GEL), 2006 WL 1517606, at *5 n.3 (S.D.N.Y. 30 May 2006) ("In any event, there is little or no functional difference between terms like 'immediately' or 'as soon as practicable'; whatever language a policy uses to limit the time for notice, the touchstone is always the same, reasonableness under the circumstances.")

- *Martinez v. District 1199J National Union of Hospital & Health Care Employees*, 280 F. Supp. 2d 342, 353 (D.N.J. 2003) ("The Court finds that 'immediately prior' means that a reasonable amount of time would pass between eligibility for health coverage with the Fund and the start of unemployment.")

- *Sunshine Textile Services, Inc. v. American Employers' Insurance Co.*, No. 4:CV-95-0699, 1997 U.S. Dist. LEXIS 22904, at *7 (M.D. Pa. 12 May 1997) ("The requirement of notice 'as soon as practicable' or 'immediately' both prescribe notice within a reasonable amount of time under the circumstances after learning of the occurrence, taking into account the exercise of due diligence.")

10.116 In *Morgan Guaranty* (see 10.108), the court said that *promptly* doesn't mean *immediately*, but rather within a reasonable time. But that was a case construing *promptly*, not *immediately*, so it's of no real value as support for the proposition that *immediately* isn't subject to a reasonableness standard.

10.117 And plenty of cases use the phrase *immediately or within a reasonable time*, suggesting that *immediately* isn't subject to a reasonableness standard, but those cases don't address the meaning of *immediately* either.

THE SEMANTICS

10.118 The net effect is that for contract drafting, *promptly* and *immediately* mean the same thing. The same goes for the adjectives *prompt* and *immediate*.

10.119 In idiomatic usage, *immediately* can mean "instantly"—*I didn't hear what John said, but Mathilde immediately turned and walked away. Immediately* can also be used when some time would be required—*the U.S. Navy immediately began work on a new aircraft carrier.*

10.120 As for *promptly*, it conveys a sense that some time would be required. *Promptly* can mean "instantly," but only if you're aiming for a slightly droll effect—*I didn't hear what John said, but Mathilde promptly turned and walked away.*

10.121 So *immediately* conveys a slightly broader meaning than *promptly*. But the instantaneous sense of *immediately* works best when you're describing events that have occurred, particularly simple cause-and-effect scenarios. To regulate conduct—as in contracts—it's problematic, because business affairs manifestly don't lend themselves to instant responses. You must always consider what the circumstances reasonably permit.

10.122 The notion that *immediately* requires speedier action than does *promptly* is reminiscent of the ostensible distinction between *best efforts* and *reasonable efforts* (see 8.18–.27). In both cases, an untenable distinction lives on due to the failure of drafters to appreciate how a reasonableness standard limits the reach of the seemingly more onerous standard.

RECOMMENDATION

10.123 Because *immediately* seems to promise more than it can deliver, omit it from your contracts for stating obligations and conditions. Use *promptly* instead.

10.124 One exception would be if you're seeking to express a real sense of urgency, as in *If the Service Provider detects any unauthorized use of a User's account, the Service Provider shall suspend that account immediately.* But even in such contexts, assume that anyone under an obligation to act immediately isn't required to act instantaneously.

10.125   Don't include both *promptly* and *immediately* in a contract. To do so is to invite a disgruntled party to argue for gradations of meaning where none had been intended.

10.126   It would be pointless to indulge in synonyms such as *as soon as practicable*, *expeditiously*, the stale and officious *forthwith*, and *right away*. Similarly, don't use *without undue delay*—by using *promptly* you express the intended meaning positively instead of negatively and save two words in the process. But in a contract governed by German law, it might be appropriate to use *without undue delay* as a convenient English equivalent to the German legal term *unverzüglich*.

10.127   If future circumstances are predictable enough for you to specify an absolute time limit rather than a vague one, do so—it would allow you to reduce the uncertainty in your contract (see 7.42). Or you could combine a vague and absolute limit—*promptly, but not later than X days after … .*

At Any Time

10.128   If a contract uses *may* to grant Acme discretion to take a particular action, then absent any indication to the contrary Acme would be free to take that action whenever it wishes. It follows that *at any time* should generally be redundant in language of discretion:

> Any Lender may at any time assign or pledge to a Federal Reserve Bank all or any portion of that Lender's rights under this agreement and any Term Notes issued to it.

10.129   But if an instance of language of discretion is particularly important, a drafter might nevertheless find it prudent to use *at any time* to preclude any argument on the issue.

10.130   Don't use *at any time* in language of obligation—nothing is gained by saying *Each party shall at any time before the Effective Time* as opposed to *Each party shall before the Effective Time*. The same applies to use of *at any time* in conditional clauses, except see 3.322.

From Time to Time and On One or More Occasions

10.131   To make it explicit that a right isn't a one-time-only right, use *on one or more occasions* instead of *from time to time*.

10.132   In language of discretion, the phrase *from time to time* is used to mean, in essence, "on one or more occasions." In theory, *from time to time* makes it clear, with respect to a given right, that a party isn't limited to exercising that right just once.

10.133   That might not be an issue. For one thing, repeated exercise of a right isn't possible in the case of a right that by its nature can be exercised only once, as in *Acme may terminate this agreement in the following circumstances*. And if a right allows a party to engage in an ongoing process, it would be odd to state that the party may exercise that right on one or more occasions. For example, if a contract says *Acme may sell Widgets to any Person outside* *the Territory*, you couldn't reasonably claim that Acme had exhausted that right after having sold a single lot of widgets.

10.134 But that leaves instances in which a party is granted a right to take a specified action and nothing in the provision suggests how often the right may be exercised.

10.135 You might be willing to assume that absent any language indicating otherwise, a right may be exercised multiple times. Or it might be clear, as a matter of industry practice, that the right isn't a one-time-only right, so it would be odd to say so explicitly:

> The Maker may ~~on one or more occasions~~ prepay all or any portion of the Principal or Interest of this Note to the Holder without premium or penalty.

10.136 But the safest approach is to make it explicit that the right isn't a one-time-only right, to avoid giving a desperate litigant even a weak argument to make. In such contexts, *from time to time* isn't the ideal phrase. It means "once in a while," and although a party could conceivably exercise a right periodically, it might instead exercise it, for example, twice in quick succession. Both alternatives are better captured by the phrase *on one or more occasions*:

> The Bank may *from time to time* [read *on one or more occasions*] adjust the Advance Rate based on changes in its collection experience regarding Accounts or other factors relating to the Accounts or other Collateral.

10.137 By extension, if you wish to make it clear in language of obligation or in a conditional clause that the action in question could be taken on one or more occasions, use that phrase and not *from time to time*.

At All Times

10.138 You shouldn't need to use *at all times*, but the reasons for that depend on the context.

10.139 If you state an ongoing obligation (*The Debtor shall maintain at its principal place of business all records relating to the Collateral*), usually the obligation applies at all times without your having to say so.

10.140 But that isn't necessarily always the case. Consider this example: *Parent shall take all actions necessary to ensure that the Payment Fund includes cash sufficient to satisfy the Parent's obligation to pay the Merger Consideration.* One could argue that the account need contain the cash only when it's time to pay the Merger Consideration. If you want to make it clear that the account always has to contain the minimum amount, that's the word to use—*always*, not *at all times*.

10.141 And consider this statement of fact: *Acme has conducted its operations in compliance with … .* Someone looking for a fight could argue that it means that at some point, but not necessarily always, Acme's operation complied with the standard in question. The simplest fix for that isn't adding *at all times*. Instead, state a time period. For example, *since 1 January 2017*.

So Long As

10.142   In everyday English, the phrase *so long as* means "on condition that". As in, *You may go to the movies, so long as Juanita goes too.* It's used to convey that meaning in contracts too, but it would be simpler and clearer to use *if* instead:

> After the redemption date, interest will cease to accrue on Notes called for redemption *so long as* [read *if*] the Company has deposited with the Paying Agent funds sufficient to pay … .

10.143   But *so long as* is also used to convey the meaning *for as long as*, or *while*, as in, *We'll be able to remain on the island so long as our water supplies last.* For contracts, *if* is the simplest and clearest choice to convey this meaning too:

> *So long as* [read *If*] the Indemnifying Party is conducting the defense of the Nonparty Claim in accordance with section 8.7(b), the Indemnifying Party will not be responsible for … .

Periodically

10.144   Don't use *periodically*, which means "at regular intervals" or just "from time to time." Instead, be specific. Consider this language of obligation:

> The Bank shall *periodically* provide the Client with a statement of account for each Account, identifying Assets held in the Accounts.

10.145   It would be clearer to omit *periodically* and instead state specific intervals, or have the bank provide a statement whenever the client asks for one.

10.146   And consider this language of discretion:

> The Trustees of the Trust may *periodically* review the commissions paid by the Portfolio to determine if the commissions paid over representative periods of time were reasonable in relation to the benefits to the Portfolio.

10.147   Presumably the idea is that the trustees would review commissions whenever they think it appropriate. The word *periodically* doesn't express that.

10.148   And if you want to express that things might change over time, you can do better than *periodically*:

> … and will be determined by the Agent in accordance with this agreement and the Agent's loan procedures *periodically* [read *then*] in effect … .

AVOIDING CONFUSION BY ADDING A TIME COMPONENT

10.149   When in a contract you refer to one or more things that pertain to a party (or anyone else, for that matter), make it clear whether you're referring to those one or more things at the time the contract is being signed or at some other time, to preclude the possibility of a fight over the intended meaning.

10.150 For example, a provision that applies to affiliates or subsidiaries of a party can cause confusion if it's not made clear whether it applies only to affiliates or subsidiaries in existence when the contract was signed, as opposed to when the provision is being applied. See *GTE Wireless, Inc. v. Cellexis International, Inc.*, 341 F.3d 1 (1st Cir. 2003) (regarding the meaning of *affiliates*); *Ellington v. EMI Music, Inc.*, 21 N.E.3d 1000 (N.Y. 2014) (same).

10.151 To avoid that kind of confusion, address the issue explicitly in the provision in question or in a related definition. The following definition shows in italics and in brackets language intended to make it clear that it applies at signing (the first addition) or at any time in the future:

> "**Subsidiary**" means, for a Person [*on the date of this agreement*] [*at a given time*], a … legal entity of which that Person or one of that Person's Subsidiaries … *then* owns … .

10.152 In *Alliantgroup, L.P. v. Solanji*, No. 01-12-00798-CV, 2014 WL 1089284, at *1 (Tex. App. 18 Mar. 2014), a similar dispute arose over the meaning of *client*. And in *Kia Motors Am., Inc. v. Glassman Oldsmobile Saab Hyundai, Inc.*, 706 F.3d 733 (6th Cir. 2013), the issue was whether *applicable law* referred to the law at the time the contract was signed or as in effect in the future. (See 13.54 regarding *as amended*.)

10.153 Also, see 3.458 for how it can be unclear whether a reference to *shares* means just shares owned on the date of the agreement or whether shares acquired later are also included. Again, it's best to make it clear which meaning is intended.

AMBIGUITY OF THE PART VERSUS THE WHOLE

11.1   Use of plural nouns and the words *and, or, every, each*, and *any* can cause ambiguity. In each case, the question is whether it is a single member of a group of two or more that's being referred to, or the entire group, so this manual uses the phrase "the part versus the whole" to refer to this sort of ambiguity. This chapter explores the sources of this kind of ambiguity and how to avoid it or eliminate it. The level of detail is justified, given the shifting complexity of the topic and the alternative meanings riding on subtle distinctions. So as not to introduce unhelpful complexity, the terminology used ignores some linguistics nuances.

11.2   To illustrate the analysis, this chapter contains numbered example sentences. (Chapter 12 also contains such example sentences.) Each such sentence that is ambiguous is followed by one or more italicized sentences that convey its alternative meanings, like this:

[0]   Each numbered example in regular text is either ambiguous or unambiguous.

[0a]   *Each numbered-and-lettered example in italics represents one of the possible meanings of the immediately preceding numbered example.*

WHETHER SINGULAR MEANS PLURAL

11.3   It can be unclear whether a reference in the singular also applies to the plural. The drafter might have omitted the plural to exclude the plural from the scope of the provision or because they hadn't spotted the issue or had assumed that the provision would include the plural anyway.

11.4   One example of this uncertainty was featured in *Coral Production Corp. v. Central Resources, Inc.*, 273 Neb. 379 (2007). The contract provision at issue stated that a preferential right to purchase certain oil and gas assets wouldn't apply if "substantially all of the assets and/or stock of the selling party is sold to a non-affiliated third party." The party seeking to invoke the preferential right contended that sale of the oil and gas assets didn't fall within that exception because the assets had been sold to more than one nonaffiliated person. The court found in favor of the party that had sold the assets, holding that the exception applied to sale to more than one person.

11.5   Similarly, *ION Geophysical Corp. v. Fletcher International, Ltd.*, No. CIV.A. 5050-VCP, 2010 WL 4378400 (Del. Ch. 5 Nov. 2010), concerned whether a party to a stock purchase agreement could issue more than one notice under a procedure that would allow that party, under certain circumstances, to increase the total number of common shares into which it could convert preferred shares. The provision in question used "notice" in the singular. After analyzing, none too convincingly, use of "notice" with the definite article *the* and the indefinite article *a*, the court held that the provision was unambiguous—the parties had intended that more than one notice could be issued.

11.6 But what the courts held in these disputes is less relevant than how the disputes could have been avoided. Whenever you're drafting a provision that refers to a thing or an unnamed person, consider whether you want that provision to apply (1) regardless of the number of things or persons, (2) only regarding one thing or person, or (3) only regarding more than one thing or person. More often than not, the first meaning is the one you'll want to convey. In that case, make it explicit. Whoever drafted the language at issue in *Coral Production* could have accomplished that by using the phrase *one or more*, as in "one or more non-affiliated persons." By contrast, to fix the language at issue in *ION Geophysical*, the drafter would have had to add another sentence.

11.7 Use the phrase *one or more* rather than the formula *X or Xs*—say *one or more widgets* instead of *the widget or widgets*.

11.8 Don't rely on an internal rule of interpretation to ensure that another provision in a contract applies regardless of the number of things or persons. Such provisions are clumsy (see 15.22), and you can't assume that such a provision would be enough to prevent a fight over singular versus plural. For example, the contract at issue in *Coral Production* featured just such an internal rule of interpretation.

The Role of *Any*

11.9 Consider the following:

> if Acme files a complaint with a government body

> if Acme files a complaint with any government body

11.10 Some might think that using *any* in the second example would ensure that the provision couldn't be read as applying only if Acme files a complaint with a single government body, as opposed to two or more government bodies. (If you think it unlikely that anyone would argue for the narrower interpretation, consider *Coral Production*; see 11.4.)

11.11 But *any* can't be counted on to accomplish that, because it could be taken to mean that the provision applies to any one member of the class in question (see 11.103). That's the meaning conveyed by the indefinite article *a*, so using instead *any* serves only, in some contexts, a minor rhetorical function.

11.12 If you want to convey the broader meaning, use *one or more*, as in *if Acme files a complaint with one or more government bodies*.

A Balanced Approach

11.13   You could go out of your way to make it clear that every provision that's phrased as applying to a single item also applies to more than one of that item, but the result would be ponderous prose. Compare the following two versions of the same provision, the first of which is worded to apply to single items and the second of which is worded to apply to one or more items:

> Acme shall not disclose to a Representative any information if doing so would cause Acme to breach a duty to another Person to keep that information confidential or would cause Acme to violate a law or an order of a Government Body.

> Acme shall not disclose to one or more Representatives any information if doing so would cause Acme to breach a duty to one or more other Persons to keep that information confidential or would cause Acme to violate one or more laws or orders of one or more Government Bodies.

11.14   The second version is sufficiently ponderous as to suggest that it's not feasible to make it explicit in each case that a provision that applies to one item also applies to more than one of that item. Instead, the more reader-friendly approach would be to use *one or more* intermittently, presumably in those contexts that pose a greater risk of dispute.

PLURAL NOUNS

11.15   Sentences containing plural nouns can be unambiguous—for example, *The Acme Subsidiaries are Delaware corporations.* But in many sentences a plural noun can engender ambiguity, with the nature and extent of the ambiguity being a function of context. In the following examples, adding *all of* to a plural noun—for example, saying *all of the Stockholders* rather than simply *the Stockholders*—wouldn't affect the analysis.

Subject Ambiguity

11.16   When a plural noun is the subject of a sentence that uses any category of contract language other than language of discretion, as in [1] below (which uses language of obligation), it can be unclear whether the persons or things constituting the subject are to act individually, as in [1a], or collectively, as in [1b], so the group is treated as one. Often when a contract requires that parties act collectively, an agent is appointed to act on their behalf. That precludes ambiguity of the sort exhibited by [1].

[1]   The Stockholders shall notify Acme.

[1a]   *Each Stockholder shall notify Acme.*

[1b]   *The Stockholders, acting collectively, shall notify Acme.*

11.17 When language of discretion is used, an additional meaning is possible. Imposing an obligation on each member of a group, as in [1a], has the same effect as imposing that obligation on all members of that group. By contrast, saying that the members of a group have discretion to take a given action could mean either (1) that any one member may take that action, regardless of whether any other member takes that action (see [2a]), or (2) that no member may take that action unless all members do (see [2b]).

[2] The Stockholders may notify Acme.

[2a] *One or more Stockholders may notify Acme.*

[2b] *The Stockholders may notify Acme, but only if they all do.*

[2c] *The Stockholders, acting collectively, may notify Acme.*

Direct-Object Ambiguity

11.18 When a plural noun is other than the subject of a sentence, the potential ambiguity is similar to the ambiguity that arises when a plural noun is the subject. See [3], in which the plural noun serves as the direct object. But when it doesn't make sense to distinguish between treating the persons or things constituting the direct object individually and treating them collectively, the potential number of meanings is reduced. For example, whereas [3b] is one of the possible meanings of [3] because giving a single notice could notify a group, no analogous meaning is possible in the case of [4].

[3] Acme shall notify the Stockholders.

[3a] *Acme shall notify each of the Stockholders.*

[3b] *Acme shall notify the Stockholders, considered collectively.*

[4] Acme *shall* sell the Shares.

11.19 As is the case when the plural noun is the subject of the sentence, the potential number of meanings in [3] increases when the sentence is expressed using language of discretion: when the members of the object group are considered individually rather than collectively, it's not clear whether the subject has discretion to act regarding all the members, as in [5a], or some or all of them, as in [5b]. The same ambiguity is present when one restates [4] using language of discretion (see [6]).

[5] Acme may notify the Stockholders.

[5a] *Acme may notify the Stockholders, but only if it notifies all of them.*

[5b] *Acme may notify one or more Stockholders.*

[5c] *Acme may notify the Stockholders, considered collectively.*

[6] Acme may sell the Shares.

[6a] *Acme may sell the Shares, but only if it sells all of them.*

[6b] *Acme may sell one or more Shares.*

Subject-and-Direct-Object Ambiguity

11.20   When both the subject and the direct object are plural nouns, it can be unclear whether the plural direct object relates to each member of the plural subject considered separately or to all members considered as a whole. In the case of [7], the question is whether each Stockholder is required to submit one questionnaire or more than one. Often it will be clear from the context which is the intended meaning.

[7]   The Stockholders shall promptly submit the completed questionnaires.

[7a]   *Each Stockholder shall promptly submit a completed questionnaire.*

[7b]   *Each Stockholder shall promptly submit the completed questionnaires.*

[7c]   *The Stockholders, acting collectively, shall promptly submit the completed questionnaires.*

AND

11.21   Related to the ambiguity caused by plural nouns is that engendered by nouns or adjectives linked by *and.*

11.22   *And* concerns a set in its totality. *We'll invite Kim, Pat, and Alex* entails inviting them all. See *The Cambridge Grammar of the English Language* (referred to in this chapter as *CGEL*), at 1293.

11.23   Often *and* is unambiguous, as in the sentence *Acme and Widgetco are Delaware corporations.* But *and* can engender ambiguity—it can convey that the members of a group are to be considered together but can also convey that they are to be considered together and separately. This has been acknowledged in the literature on drafting. See, e.g., F. Reed Dickerson, *The Fundamentals of Legal Drafting* (2d ed. 1986), at 105; *Garner's Dictionary of Legal Usage*, at 639. Furthermore, in contracts it can be unclear whether nouns linked by *and* are acting, or are being acted on, individually or collectively. (The latter kind of ambiguity also arises in connection with plural nouns; see 11.6.) Whether *and* is ambiguous, and in what way, depends on the grammatical context, something that the literature on drafting has not explored in any detail.

Subject Ambiguity

11.24   When contract parties linked by *and* constitute the subject of a sentence using any category of contract language other than language of discretion, as in [8] (which uses language of obligation), it can be unclear whether the persons or things constituting the subject are to be considered individually, as in [8a], or collectively, as in [8b]. (The ambiguity in [8] is analogous to that in [1].)

[8]   Able and Baker shall notify Acme.

[8a]   *Able and Baker shall each notify Acme.*

[8b]   *Able and Baker, acting collectively, shall notify Acme.*

11.25   Language of discretion causes greater ambiguity than does language of obligation. (The ambiguity in [9] is analogous to that in [2].)

> [9]   Able and Baker may notify Acme.
>
> [9a]   *Both Able and Baker, as opposed to just one or the other of them, may notify Acme.*
>
> [9b]   *Able or Baker, or both of them, may notify Acme.*
>
> [9c]   *Able and Baker, acting collectively, may notify Acme.*

Direct-Object Ambiguity

11.26   A similar range of potential meanings arises when parties linked by *and* are other than the subject of the sentence. See, for example, [10], in which nouns linked by *and* serve as direct objects. But when the persons or things constituting direct objects cannot be considered collectively, as in [11], the potential ambiguity is reduced.

> [10]   Acme shall notify Able and Baker.
>
> [10a]   *Acme shall notify both Able and Baker.*
>
> [10b]   *Acme shall notify Able and Baker, considered collectively.*
>
> [11]   Acme shall dissolve Subsidiary A and Subsidiary B.

11.27   As with [8], the number of potential meanings conveyed by [10] increases when it is expressed using language of discretion; when the members of the object group are considered individually rather than collectively, it's not clear whether the subject has discretion to act regarding all the members, as in [12a], or some or all of them, as in [12b]. The same ambiguity is present when one restates [11] using language of discretion; see [13].

> [12]   Acme may notify Able and Baker.
>
> [12a]   *Acme may notify both Able and Baker, as opposed to one or the other of them.*
>
> [12b]   *Acme may notify either Able or Baker, or both of them.*
>
> [12c]   *Acme may notify Able and Baker, considered collectively.*
>
> [13]   Acme may dissolve Subsidiary A and Subsidiary B.
>
> [13a]   *Acme may dissolve both Subsidiary A and Subsidiary B, as opposed to one or the other of them.*
>
> [13b]   *Acme may dissolve one or both of Subsidiary A and Subsidiary B.*

11.28   A range of ambiguity comparable to that in [12] and [13] arises when instead one uses language of prohibition, as in [14] and [15]. The more natural meaning of [14] and [15] is conveyed by [14a] and [15a], respectively. If you wish to convey the meaning in [14b] or [15b], you shouldn't rely on [14] or [15] to do so.

[14] Acme shall not notify Able and Baker.

[14a] *Acme shall not notify Able and shall not notify Baker.*

[14b] *Acme shall not notify both Able and Baker but may notify just one or the other of them.*

[14c] *Acme shall not notify Able and Baker, considered collectively.*

[15] Acme shall not dissolve Subsidiary A and Subsidiary B.

[15a] *Acme shall not dissolve Subsidiary A and shall not dissolve Subsidiary B.*

[15b] *Acme shall not dissolve both Subsidiary A and Subsidiary B but may dissolve one or the other of them.*

Subject-and-Direct-Object Ambiguity

11.29 Example [16] demonstrates the ambiguity found in [8], but in addition, it's unclear whether the *and*-coordination of the subjects is "distributive" (as in [16a]) or "joint" (as in [16b]). See *CGEL*, at 1282. In other words, it's unclear whether each of the subjects is to notify one or both of the objects. (Regarding *respectively*, as used in [16b], see 13.706.)

[16] Able and Baker shall notify Acme and Widgetco.

[16a] *Able and Baker shall each notify Acme and Widgetco.*

[16b] *Able and Baker shall notify Acme and Widgetco, respectively.*

[16c] *Able and Baker, acting collectively, shall notify Acme and Widgetco.*

Multiple Verb Phrases

11.30 A variant of the ambiguity present in [12] occurs when in language of discretion the subject and a single *may* are used with two verb phrases, as in [17]. Using *may* in each verb phrase, as in [17b], would make it clear that Acme's discretion is not limited to either selling assets and making capital expenditures or doing neither. Example [17c] accomplishes the same goal. When there are three or more verb phrases, it may be most efficient to express this meaning by stating that the subject *may do any one or more of the following.*

[17] Acme may sell assets and make capital expenditures.

[17a] *Acme may sell assets and make capital expenditures, but not just one or the other.*

[17b] *Acme may sell assets and may make capital expenditures.*

[17c] *Acme may sell assets or make capital expenditures, or it may do both.*

11.31 When the first verb phrase logically leads to the second, it is likely that the sense *together and not separately* is intended, as in [18].

[18] Parent may dissolve Sub and liquidate its assets.

Ambiguity of Direct Object Plus Objects of Preposition

11.32   When a direct object is accompanied by nouns separated by *and* that are functioning as objects of a preposition (in the case of [19], [20], and [21], the indirect objects *Echo* and *Foxtrot*), the ambiguity can be analogous to that exhibited in [10], [12], and [14].

[19]   Delta shall issue a promissory note to Echo and Foxtrot.

[19a]   *Delta shall issue a promissory note to each of Echo and Foxtrot.*

[19b]   *Delta shall issue a promissory note to Echo and Foxtrot jointly.*

[20]   Delta may issue a promissory note to Echo and Foxtrot.

[20a]   *Delta may issue a promissory note to each of Echo and Foxtrot, as opposed to just one or the other.*

[20b]   *Delta may issue a promissory note to Echo, to Foxtrot, or to each of them.*

[20c]   *Delta may issue a promissory note to Echo and Foxtrot jointly.*

[21]   Delta shall not issue a promissory note to Echo and Foxtrot.

[21a]   *Delta shall not issue a promissory note to each of Echo and Foxtrot, as opposed to just one or the other.*

[21b]   *Delta shall not issue a promissory note to Echo or Foxtrot.*

[21c]   *Delta shall not issue a promissory note to Echo and Foxtrot jointly.*

11.33   But when the objects of prepositions cannot be considered collectively, there is reduced scope for ambiguity. Because it would not be possible to construct a factory located in both California and Florida, the language of obligation in [22] is unambiguous and the language of discretion in [23] and language of prohibition in [24] exhibit fewer possible meanings than the analogous [20] and [21].

[22]   Acme shall construct a factory in California and Florida.

[23]   Acme may construct a factory in California and Florida.

[23a]   *Acme may construct a factory in California, in Florida, or in both states.*

[23b]   *Acme may construct a factory in both California and Florida, as opposed to in just one state or the other.*

[24]   Acme shall not construct a factory in California and Florida.

[24a]   *Acme shall not construct a factory in California or in Florida.*

[24b]   *Acme shall not construct a factory in both California and Florida, as opposed to in one or the other.*

The Effect of Adjectives

11.34   Another form of ambiguity associated with *and* is that which derives from (1) adjectives that modify a noun and are linked by *and* (as in *temporary and part-time employees*) and (2) nouns modified by adjectives and linked by *and* (as in *temporary employees and part-time employees*).

11.35   The ambiguity that arises in a provision using a plural noun modified by adjectives joined by *and* is a function of context and of the kind of contract language used. Below are two examples: [25] uses language of obligation and [26] uses language of discretion. Because [26] uses language of discretion, it exhibits a greater number of possible meanings than does [25] (see 11.17).

[25]   Tango shall terminate the employment of Acme's temporary and part-time employees.

[25a] *Tango shall terminate the employment of those Acme employees who are temporary and those Acme employees who are part-time.*

[25b] *Tango shall terminate the employment of those Acme employees who are both temporary and part-time.*

[26]   Tango may terminate the employment of Acme's temporary and part-time employees.

[26a] *Tango may terminate the employment of no fewer than all Acme employees who are temporary and no fewer than all Acme employees who are part-time. Tango shall not terminate all the employees in one group without also terminating all the employees in the other group.*

[26b] *Tango may terminate the employment of one or both of the following: (1) no fewer than all Acme employees who are temporary and (2) no fewer than all Acme employees who are part-time.*

[26c] *Tango may terminate the employment of (1) one or more Acme employees who are temporary and (2) one or more Acme employees who are part-time.*

[26d] *Tango may terminate the employment of no fewer than all Acme employees who are both temporary and part-time.*

[26e] *Tango may terminate the employment of one or more Acme employees who are both temporary and part-time.*

11.36   But in the case of an *and*-coordination featuring mutually exclusive attributes, ambiguity would be reduced. An example of mutually exclusive attributes is *full-time and part-time employee*—an employee cannot be both full-time and part-time simultaneously. Using that *and*-coordination in [25] would eliminate the ambiguity, because the meaning conveyed by [25b] wouldn't be possible, leaving as the only possible meaning that of [25a]. Using that *and*-coordination in [26] would have the same effect, eliminating [26d] and [26e] as possible meanings.

11.37   An alternative to having a noun modified by two or more adjectives is to repeat the noun with each adjective, as in *temporary employees and part-time employees*. Using that *and*-coordination in [25] and [26] would have the same effect as using an *and*-coordination featuring mutually exclusive attributes (see 11.36).

Every X and Y and *Each X and Y*

11.38   When *every* and *each* are used before two or more nouns linked by *and*, another kind of ambiguity results. In [27], the question arises whether every director and every officer is entitled to indemnification, or whether only persons who are both a director and an officer are entitled to indemnification. Context will often suggest the intended meaning; in the case of [27], the intended meaning is presumably that expressed in [27a] rather than that expressed in [27b].

[27]   Acme shall indemnify every director and officer of Widgetco.

[27a]   *Acme shall indemnify every director and every officer of Widgetco.*

[27b]   *Acme shall indemnify every person who is both a director and an officer of Widgetco.*

Adding Contingency to *And*

11.39   Drafters might find it helpful to acknowledge a contingent quality in one or more elements linked by *and*.

11.40   Consider *County of Du Page v. Illinois Labor Relations Board*, 231 Ill. 2d 593, 900 N.E.2d 1095 (2008). At issue was section 9(a-5) of the Illinois Public Labor Relations Act, which provides that as an alternative to an election, the Illinois Labor Relations Board may certify a union based on evidence showing that a majority of the employees wish to be represented by the union for the purposes of collective bargaining.

11.41   Section 9(a-5) provides in part as follows (emphasis added):

> If the parties to a dispute are without agreement on the means to ascertain the choice, if any, of employee organization as their representative, the Board shall ascertain the employees' choice of employee organization, on the basis of dues deduction authorization *and* other evidence, or, if necessary, by conducting an election.

11.42   An employer objected to certification of a union. Among other things, it argued that section 9(a-5) required the union to submit both evidence of authorization to deduct dues and some other evidence of majority support. The Illinois Labor Relations Board rejected this argument, but the appellate court vacated the Board's decision and remanded the matter to the Board for further proceedings.

11.43   On appeal, the Illinois Supreme Court reversed, holding "that the word 'and,' as used in the phrase 'dues deduction authorization and other evidence,' was intended by the legislature to mean 'or.'" In other words, the union wasn't required to submit evidence in addition to a dues checkoff card.

11.44   This protracted and unedifying litigation could have been avoided if the drafters had simply inserted the word *any* after *and*. That would have made it clear that the union wasn't required to submit additional evidence but instead had the option to do so.

11.45   Although this case involved the language of a statute, it applies equally to contracts. So, drafters, remember the utility of *and any*.

OR

11.46   *Or* indicates that the members of a set are alternatives. Whereas *We'll invite Kim, Pat, and Alex* (see 11.22) entails inviting all of them, *We'll invite Kim, Pat, or Alex* entails only that we'll invite (at least) one of them. See *CGEL*, at 1293–98.

11.47   The literature on drafting says that *or* can be "inclusive," with *A or B* conveying *A or B or both*, or "exclusive," with *A or B* conveying *A or B, but not both*. See F. Reed Dickerson, *The Fundamentals of Legal Drafting* 104 (2d ed. 1986); *Garner's Dictionary of Legal Usage*, at 639. But the literature on drafting hasn't explored this subject in any depth.

Background

11.48   By contrast with the ambiguity caused by plural nouns and the ambiguity caused by *and*, the ambiguity engendered by nouns or adjectives linked by *or* is not simply a function of context. One must also address a broader issue—the distinction between the exclusive *or* and the inclusive *or*.

11.49   According to *CGEL*, *or* is most characteristically used when the speaker believes that only one of the component propositions joined by *or* is true, and as a result *or* typically conveys the implicature that not all of the propositions are true. An implicature is a proposition that is implicitly conveyed rather than being explicitly said. It is not strictly part of the meaning of the sentence itself: as *CGEL* says, "*or* doesn't mean that only one of the alternatives is true."

11.50   *CGEL* explains the "not and" implicature of *or as follows:*

> In general we don't use the weaker of two terms if we could use the stronger—e.g. we don't generally say *'P or Q'* if we know *'P and Q'* to be true. If I know they appointed Kim and Pat to oversee the election, it will normally be inappropriate to say *They appointed Kim or Pat to oversee the election*, for this is likely to suggest that they appointed just one but that I don't know which of the two it was. Similarly, if I intend to invite Kim and Pat to dinner, it is normally misleading to say *I'll invite Kim or Pat to dinner*. The most likely reason for saying *'P or Q'* rather than *'P and Q'*, therefore, is that the latter would be false, which leads to the "not and" implicature. But that isn't the only reason for saying *'P or Q'*: it may be that I know that one or other of 'P' and 'Q' is true, but don't know whether both are … .

11.51   As an example of use of *or* when the speaker doesn't know whether both propositions are true, *CGEL* offers *Either the mailman hasn't arrived yet or there's no mail for us*, saying that this example "certainly does not rule out the case where the mailman is still on his way but has no mail for us."

11.52   And *CGEL* uses the example *They are obtainable at Coles or at Woolworths* to suggest that even a speaker who knows that both propositions are true might nevertheless use *or.* The reason for using *or* here even though the speaker could have said *and* is that it reflects that you have a choice as to which store you obtain them from.

11.53   *CGEL* points out that alternatives joined by *or* are often mutually exclusive, as in *He was born on Christmas Day 1950 or 1951.* In such contexts, our knowledge of the world allows us to rule out the possibility that both propositions are true.

11.54   Regarding confusion as to whether a given *or* is inclusive or exclusive, *CGEL* says that "the implicature can be made explicit in a *but*-coordinate: *He'll invite Kim or Pat, but not both*" and that "it can be cancelled in similar ways: *He'll invite Kim or Pat, perhaps both.*"

11.55   And *CGEL* says that *either* tends to strengthen the "not and" implicature:

> *I'll be seeing her on either Friday or Saturday* conveys somewhat more strongly than the version without *either* that I'll be seeing her on just one of those days. Exclusiveness nevertheless is still only an implicature: *They are obtainable at either Coles or Woolworths* emphasizes the choice but, like the version without *either*, could readily be used in a context where they are obtainable at both stores.

11.56   *CGEL* notes that "When a sub clausal *or*-coordination falls within the scope of a negative, it is equivalent to an *and*-coordination of negative clauses"—*I didn't like his mother or his father* means *I didn't like his mother and I didn't like his father.* (In negation, the distinction between the inclusive and exclusive *or* doesn't apply.) That's also the meaning derived from application of one of the pair of logic rules known as De Morgan's laws, the relevant rule being in effect *Not (A or B) = (Not A) and (Not B).* But *CGEL* goes on to note that "wide scope readings are possible as less likely interpretations." A less likely reading of the preceding example is *I didn't like his mother or his father, I liked them both.* Using a *neither ... nor* structure—*I liked neither his mother nor his father*—would preclude the possibility of such an alternative meaning. Another less-likely reading is *I didn't like his mother or his father, I can't remember which.*

As Applied to Contracts

11.57   In a contract, it might be that a given *or* could only be exclusive. One example is the *or* in *Parent shall incorporate Sub in Delaware or New York*—a company cannot be incorporated in more than one state simultaneously.

11.58   But regarding how the inclusive and exclusive *or* is manifested in contracts, consider [28], which is language of obligation. Maybe the drafter intended the *or* to be exclusive and didn't think of making the implicature explicit, as in [28a]. Alternatively, the drafter may have focused on expressing that Acme has a choice and didn't think of canceling the implicature, as in [28b]. (Regarding alternative ways of expressing *or both*, see 11.87.) Which is more likely would depend on the context. The same alternatives are present in other categories of contract language, except for language of prohibition; [29] is language of discretion.

[28]   Acme shall dissolve Subsidiary A or Subsidiary B.

[28a]   *Acme shall dissolve Subsidiary A or Subsidiary B but not both.*

[28b]   *Acme shall dissolve Subsidiary A or Subsidiary B or both.*

[29]   Acme may dissolve Subsidiary A or Subsidiary B.

[29a]   *Acme may dissolve Subsidiary A or Subsidiary B but not both.*

[29b]   *Acme may dissolve Subsidiary A or Subsidiary B or both.*

11.59   A drafter should seek to avoid having a court decide what a provision means. If you're looking for a particular *or* to be exclusive and an inclusive meaning is possible, you shouldn't rely on the "not and" implicature, whether or not bolstered by *either*, to ensure that the provision in question has the intended meaning. A court might be influenced by the presence of *either* to hold that a given *or* is exclusive. See, e.g., *Mintz v. Pazer*, No. 32842(U), 2014 N.Y. Misc. LEXIS 4827 (N.Y. Sup. Ct. 7 Nov. 2014). But winning a fight is a distant second-best to avoiding the fight.

11.60   And if you're looking for a particular *or* to be inclusive, you shouldn't assume that the context will be sufficient to override the "not and" implicature. Consider the case of *SouthTrust Bank v. Copeland One, L.L.C.*, 886 So. 2d 38 (Ala. 2003). Defendant SouthTrust operated an automated teller machine (ATM) at an Alabama mall. It did so under a lease with the landlord that provided as follows: "Tenant [SouthTrust] shall have the exclusive right during the term of this lease and any renewals to operate an ATM or any other type of banking facility on the Property." This caused litigation over whether the *or* in this provision was exclusive or inclusive. After deciding that the provision was ambiguous, the court construed it against the drafter, SouthTrust, holding that the *or* was exclusive.

11.61   So express explicitly the meaning intended: instead of [28] use either [28a] or [28b], and instead of [29] use either [29a] or [29b].

11.62   As explained in 11.56, the inclusive and exclusive *or* plays no role in language of prohibition. But there's uncertainty nevertheless: According to *CGEL*'s analysis, the more likely meaning of [30] is [30a]. Using *neither … nor*, as in [30b], conveys that meaning more economically. Another possible meaning is that the prohibition applies to only one or the other of Subsidiary A and Subsidiary B. That's articulated more clearly in [30c]. A third possible meaning is [30d]. It's unlikely that anyone would derive the meaning of [30d] from [30] without the benefit of the language of discretion in [30d], but it's conceivable that a disgruntled contract party might attempt such a leap. A fourth possible meaning is [30e], which is analogous to the example in 11.56, *I didn't like his mother <u>or</u> his father, I liked them both.* But no reader could derive the meaning of [30e] from [30] without stress on the *or* in [30] and the benefit of the second clause in [30e].

[30]   Acme shall not dissolve Subsidiary A or Subsidiary B.

[30a]   *Acme shall not dissolve Subsidiary A and shall not dissolve Subsidiary B.*

[30b] *Acme shall dissolve neither Subsidiary A nor Subsidiary B.*

[30c] *Acme shall not dissolve both Subsidiary A and Subsidiary B but may dissolve just one or the other of them.*

[30d] *Acme shall not dissolve just one or the other of Subsidiary A and Subsidiary B, but it may dissolve both.*

[30e] *Acme shall not dissolve just one or the other of Subsidiary A and Subsidiary B but shall instead dissolve both.*

11.63   Alternative meanings analogous to the possible meanings of [30] can be found in negation used in other contexts, for example in language of declaration (*Acme has not dissolved Subsidiary A or Subsidiary B*) and condition clauses (*If Acme has not dissolved Subsidiary A or Subsidiary B*).

11.64   As with use of *or* with other categories of contract language, be explicit which meaning is intended when using *or* in negation. For example, in one case the language at issue was equivalent to *You may not eat ice cream on Saturday or Sunday.* Although the more likely meaning is that you're not allowed to eat ice cream on both days, the court held that the prohibition applied only to one of the two days. See *Alloy Bellows & Precision Welding, Inc. v. Jason Cole*, No. 1:15CV494, 2016 WL 1618108, at *1 (N.D. Ohio 22 Apr. 2016). And it would be reckless for anyone to draft on the assumption that a court would invoke De Morgan's laws (see 11.56).

When One of a Series Linked by *Or* Is Modified by a Conditional Clause

11.65   In addition to uncertainty over whether a given *or* is exclusive or inclusive, ambiguity can also arise when one of a series of items linked by *or* is modified by a conditional clause.

11.66   Consider this example featuring two items linked by *or*:

[31] Charles will have dinner with Fred or, if she's in town, Nancy.

[31a] *Charles will have dinner with Fred or Nancy; if Nancy isn't in town, he'll have dinner with Fred.*

[31b] *Charles will have dinner with Nancy if she's in town; if she isn't, he'll have dinner with Fred.*

[32] Charles will have dinner with Nancy, if she's in town, or with Fred.

11.67   In [31], the second item (Nancy) is modified by a conditional clause. Examples [31a] and [31b] are the possible alternative meanings of [31], with [31a] perhaps being the more natural reading. Examples [31a] and [31b] are also the possible alternative meanings of [32], with [31b] perhaps being the more natural reading. The difference between [31] and [32] is that in [32], the conditional clause is associated with the first item.

11.68   The difference between [31a] and [31b] is that the more limited meaning of [31b] isn't derived from a strict reading of [31]; instead, the reader understands that it's implied. That reading is encouraged by the fact that Nancy's presence in town is referred to at all. If the choice were between Fred and Nancy, regardless of whether Nancy were in town, then it wouldn't be necessary to refer to Nancy's presence in town: if she were out of town, it would follow that Charles wouldn't be having dinner with her.

11.69   The analysis changes when more than two items are linked by *or*, as in these examples:

[33]   Charles will have dinner with Inga, Fred, or, if she's in town, Nancy.

[33a]   *If Nancy is in town, Charles will have dinner with Inga, Fred, or Nancy; if Nancy is out of town, Charles will have dinner with Inga or Fred.*

[33b]* *If Nancy is in town, Charles will have dinner with Nancy; if Nancy is out of town, Charles will have dinner with Inga or Fred.*

[34]   Charles will have dinner with Inga or Fred or, if she's in town, Nancy.

[34a]   *If Nancy is in town, Charles will have dinner with Inga, Fred, or Nancy; if Nancy is out of town, Charles will have dinner with Inga or Fred.*

[34b]   *If Nancy is in town, Charles will have dinner with Nancy; if Nancy is out of town, Charles will have dinner with Inga or Fred.*

11.70   Example [33a] conveys the same meaning as [33], perhaps more clearly. But most readers of [33] likely wouldn't conclude that it conveys the meaning of [33b], which is analogous to [31b] (hence the asterisk next to [33b]). That's because if dinner with Nancy were to take priority, you would expect the three names to be presented not in a group of three, as in [33], but in two groups, with Nancy by herself and Inga and Fred in a second group separated from Nancy by one *or*, with a second *or* between Inga and Fred, as in [34]. So [33] isn't subject to the same ambiguity as [31] and [32].

11.71   One of the two alternative meanings of [34] is [34b], which is the same as [33b]. If you wish to convey the meaning of [34b], you'd be advised to use the wording of [34b] rather than [34], to avoid also conveying the meaning of [34a].

11.72   Statute language analogous to [31] was at issue in *Brooks Capital Services, LLC v. 5151 Trabue Ltd.*, No. 10CVE-07-10386, 2012 Ohio App. LEXIS 3901 (27 Sept. 2012). A member of 5151 Trabue Ltd., a limited liability company (LLC) whose management had not been reserved to its members, fraudulently signed a promissory note and mortgage on behalf of the LLC. The question was whether those documents were valid under Ohio Rev. Code Ann. section 1705.35, which provides as follows:

> Instruments and documents providing for the acquisition, mortgage, or disposition of property of a limited liability company are valid and binding upon the company if the instruments or documents are executed by one or more members of the company or, if the management of the company has not been reserved to its members, by one or more of its managers.

11.73   The lender argued that under the statute, loan documents signed by one member bound the LLC; the LLC argued that they did not. The trial court granted summary judgment to the LLC; the Court of Appeals affirmed. In reaching its conclusion, the Court of Appeals said that "R.C. 1705.35 is ambiguous and susceptible of different interpretations." The dissent disagreed.

11.74   The Court of Appeals in effect held that the language at issue conveyed a meaning analogous to [33b]; the dissent was in effect of the view that it conveyed a meaning analogous to [33a]. In its analysis, the Court of Appeals distinguished the language at issue from Ohio Rev. Code Ann. section 1705.44, which features three items linked by *or*. The Court of Appeals in effect held that section 1705.44 conveyed a meaning analogous to [33a].

11.75   *Brooks Capital Services* involved statute language, but this kind of ambiguity is just as likely to occur in a contract. To avoid it, use unambiguous language—language analogous to the examples above in italics.

Plural Nouns

11.76   When nouns linked by *or* constitute the subject of a sentence, the number of potential meanings increases when the direct object is plural, as in [35], whatever the category of contract language. The added uncertainty relates to whether the items constituting the direct object are to be treated individually or as a group.

[35]   Able or Baker shall submit invoices to Charlie.

[35a]   *Able or Baker shall submit invoices to Charlie, with all invoices being submitted by Able and none by Baker, or vice versa.*

[35b]   *Able or Baker shall submit invoices to Charlie, with any invoice being submitted by Able or Baker individually and not by Able and Baker jointly.*

[35c]   *Able or Baker shall submit invoices to Charlie, with any invoice being submitted by Able or Baker individually or by Able and Baker jointly.*

11.77   The same issue arises when the direct object is plural and is accompanied by nouns separated by *or* that are functioning as objects of a preposition (in the case of [36], the indirect objects *Echo* and *Foxtrot*).

[36]   Delta shall issue promissory notes to Echo or Foxtrot.

[36a]   *Delta shall issue promissory notes to Echo or Foxtrot, with Echo being issued all the promissory notes and Foxtrot none of them, or vice versa.*

[36b]   *Delta shall issue promissory notes to Echo or Foxtrot, with any promissory note being issued to Echo or Foxtrot individually and not to Echo and Foxtrot jointly.*

[36c]   *Delta shall issue promissory notes to Echo or Foxtrot, with any promissory note being issued to Echo or Foxtrot individually or to Echo and Foxtrot jointly.*

11.78   And ambiguity arises when the nouns linked by *or* are plural. For example, in [37], which uses language of obligation, it's uncertain whether each group of fruit should be considered collectively. This ambiguity also arises in language of discretion.

[37]   Acme shall sell apples or oranges.

[37a]   *Acme shall sell apples and not oranges or shall sell oranges and not apples, without alternating from selling one to selling the other.*

[37b]   *Acme shall sell apples and not oranges or shall sell oranges and not apples, but it may as often as it wants alternate from selling one to selling the other.*

[37c]   *Acme shall sell apples or oranges and may sell both concurrently.*

The Effect of Adjectives

11.79   As with *and*, another form of ambiguity associated with *or* is that which derives from (1) adjectives that modify a noun and are linked by *or* (*temporary or part-time employees*) and (2) nouns modified by adjectives and linked by *or* (*temporary employees or part-time employees*).

CUMULATION OF ATTRIBUTES

11.80   But first, determining the meaning conveyed by adjectives in an *or*-coordination requires considering what this manual calls "cumulation of attributes." For example, [38] raises the question whether termination of an Acme employee who is both a temporary employee *and* a part-time employee would mean that Tango has complied with the obligation expressed in [38]. If [38] is understood as conveying the meaning of [38a], that would mean Tango has complied; if it's understood as conveying the meaning of [38b], that would mean Tango hasn't complied.

[38]   Tango shall terminate the employment of one Acme temporary or part-time employee.

[38a]   *Tango shall terminate the employment of one Acme employee who is temporary or part-time or both.*

[38b]   *Tango shall terminate the employment of one Acme employee who is temporary or part-time but not both.*

11.81   Stated more generally, the question raised by [38] is whether an *or*-coordination featuring attributes that aren't mutually exclusive applies to anything that combines those attributes. Cumulation of attributes arises in connection with not only adjectives but also adjectival phrases; see for example the sample language in 13.542. But it doesn't arise with *or*-coordination featuring mutually exclusive attributes, for example *full-time or part-time employee*—an employee cannot be both full-time and part-time simultaneously.

11.82   If a provision applies to anything exhibiting one of two or more attributes in an *or*-coordination, economy of hypothesis would suggest that it also applies to anything exhibiting any combination of those attributes. That presumption might be strong enough that it wouldn't be reasonable to describe the alternative meanings of [38] as rising to the level of ambiguity—it's hard to imagine why the parties would intend that terminating an Acme employee who is both temporary and part-time, as opposed to terminating an Acme employee who is one or the other, wouldn't represent compliance with that obligation. So if you wish to preclude cumulation of attributes, it would be reckless not to make that explicit by using language analogous to [38b].

11.83   Making it explicit that you can cumulate attributes would preclude a disgruntled contract party from arguing otherwise. Whether making that explicit is worthwhile involves balancing the added certainty against the cost, namely the extra effort involved in having the drafter articulate that you can cumulate attributes and having the reader digest it (see 11.145).

PLURAL NOUNS

11.84   Examples [39] and [36] demonstrate the ambiguity in a provision using a plural noun modified by adjectives joined by *or*. Just as [26] exhibits a greater number of possible meanings than does [25], use of language of discretion results in [40] exhibiting a greater number of possible meanings than does [39]. The variants of [39] and [40] don't reflect the alternative meanings relating to cumulation of attributes—each variant would give rise to two cumulation-of-attributes alternative meanings.

[39]   Tango shall terminate the employment of Acme's temporary or part-time employees.

[39a]   *Tango shall terminate the employment of those Acme employees who are temporary or those Acme employees who are part-time.*

[39b]   *Tango shall terminate the employment of all those Acme employees who are temporary and all those Acme employees who are part-time.*

[40]   Tango may terminate the employment of Acme's temporary or part-time employees.

[40a]   *Tango may terminate the employment of no fewer than all Acme employees who are temporary or no fewer than all Acme employees who are part-time.*

[40b]   *Tango may terminate the employment of one or more of those Acme employees who are temporary or one or more of those Acme employees who are part-time.*

[40c]   *Tango may terminate the employment of no fewer than all those Acme employees who are temporary and no fewer than all those Acme employees who are part-time, but Tango shall not terminate the employment of all the employees in one group without also terminating the employment of all the employees in the other group.*

[40d]   *Tango may terminate the employment of one or more of those Acme employees who are temporary and may terminate the employment of one or more of those Acme employees who are part-time.*

11.85   An alternative to having a plural noun modified by two or more adjectives would be to repeat the noun for each adjective, as in *temporary employees* *or part-time employees.* Using that *or*-coordination in [39] would eliminate the ambiguity, because the meaning conveyed by [39b] wouldn't be possible, leaving as the only possible meaning that of [39a]. Using that *or*-coordination in [40] would have the same effect, leaving only the two alternative meanings arising from use of language of discretion with plural nouns.

AND/OR

11.86   Since the mid-20th century, judges and legal-writing commentators have railed against use of *and/or* to convey the meaning of the inclusive *or* (see 11.47). But given all that ails traditional contract language, it seems that *and/or* has gotten more than its fair share of spittle-flecked invective. And *and/or* does have a specific meaning—*X and/or Y* means *X or Y or both.* One could conceivably use *Acme may dissolve Subsidiary A and/or Subsidiary B* as an alternative to [13b].

11.87   But *X or Y or both* is clearer than *X and/or Y.* (Depending on how *X* and *Y* are worded, it may be preferable to use the structure *one or both of X and Y,* or even *one or both of the following: X; and Y.*) Because *and/or* is less clear, that makes it more likely that a disgruntled contract party will attempt to use it as a stick in a dispute, even in a way that makes no sense. See, e.g., *Redmond v. Sirius International Insurance Corp.,* No. 12-CV-587, 2014 WL 1366185, at *1 (E.D. Wis. 7 Apr. 2014).

11.88   And here are three additional sources of *and/or* confusion: First, drafters sometimes use *and/or* when the only possible meaning is that conveyed by *or*: *Acme shall incorporate the Subsidiary in Delaware and/or New York.*

11.89   Second, it's confusing to use *and/or* in language of obligation or language of prohibition, with the obligation or prohibition in effect being stated two different ways. Instead of *Acme shall purchase Widget A and/or Widget B,* say *Acme shall purchase Widget A or Widget B and may purchase both.*

11.90   And third, if *and/or* is used to link more than two items, it would be unclear whether the *or* is inclusive or exclusive (see 11.58). In other words, *A, B, and/or C* could mean either *one or all of A, B, and C* or *one or more of A, B, and C.* One suspects that usually the latter meaning is intended.

11.91   So given these issues, don't use *and/or.* If you find that using *and/or* in a provision offers significant economy, that's a sign you should restructure the provision.

AND ... OR

11.92   When in any string of three nouns (as in [41]), verbs, adjectives, adverbs, or clauses the first and second are separated by *and* and the second and third are separated by *or,* or vice versa, the meaning varies depending on which conjunction "has scope over" the other. See *CGEL,* at 1279–80. In [41], either *or* has scope over *and* (with the choice being between Able and Baker on the one hand and Charlie on the other) or *and* has scope over *or* (with the choice being between Baker and Charlie).

[41]   Acme shall hire Able and Baker or Charlie.

[41a]   *Acme shall hire (1) Able and Baker or (2) Charlie.*

[41b]   *Acme shall hire either Able and Baker or Charlie.*

[41c]   *Acme shall hire Able and Baker, on the one hand, or Charlie, on the other hand.*

[41d]   *Acme shall hire (1) Able and (2) Baker or Charlie.*

[41e]   *Acme shall hire Able and either Baker or Charlie.*

[41f]   *Acme shall hire Able, on the one hand, and Baker or Charlie, on the other hand.*

11.93   Enumeration, as in [41a] and [41d], is the simplest way to eliminate this ambiguity. Alternatively, you could use *either* to mark the beginning of the first coordinate in an *or*-coordination, with [41b] as a variant of [41a] and [41e] as a variant of [41d]. A third solution is to use *on the one hand … on the other hand* (see 13.623), as in [41c] and [41f], and as in this example:

> any other transaction involving Parent or any Restricted Subsidiary, on the one hand, and Invest Bank or any of its Affiliates, on the other hand

11.94   For an example of legislation featuring this kind of ambiguity, see California Corporations Code § 313, which refers to the effect of a document "signed by the chairman of the board, the president *or* any vice president *and* the secretary, any assistant secretary, the chief financial officer or any assistant treasurer" of a corporation (emphasis added).

11.95   The question is, does the "or" have scope over the "and," or is it the other way around? If the "or" has scope over the "and," the document must be signed by (1) the chairman, (2) the president, or (3) both (A) any vice president and (B) one of the secretary, any assistant secretary, the chief financial officer, or any assistant treasurer. If the "and" has scope over the "or," the presumption of authority is established if the document is signed by (1) the chairman, the president, or any vice president and (2) the secretary, any assistant secretary, the chief financial officer, or any assistant treasurer. California courts have held that the latter meaning is the one intended (see *Snukal v. Flightways Manufacturing, Inc.*, 23 Cal. 4th 754, 3 P.3d 286 (2000)), but it would be preferable to have the statute preclude alternative meanings.

11.96   In *BL Partners Group, L.P. v. Interbroad, LLC*, No. 465 EDA 2016, 2017 WL 2591473 (Pa. Super. Ct. 15 June 2017), the language at issue was "In the event that Lessor's building is damaged by fire or other casualty *and* Lessor elects not to restore such building, *or* Lessor elects to demolish the building, Lessor may terminate the Lease … ." (Emphasis added.) May the lessor terminate if it elects to demolish the building regardless of the condition of the building, or must the building have been damaged by fire or other casualty? Here's a simplified version of the language at issue: *If A and B, or C, then D.* Confusion would have been avoided if it had been expressed as *If A and B, or if C, then D* (if the first meaning had been intended) or as *If A and either B or C, then D* (if the second meaning had been intended).

USING *AND* INSTEAD OF *OR*, AND VICE VERSA

11.97   Problems with *and* and *or* aren't limited to a given *and* or *or* conveying alternative possible meanings, or someone thinking it does. In addition, drafters sometimes use *and* when it would make sense to use *or* instead. Or they do the converse.

11.98   Just such a problem arose in 2014 in connection with a series of transactions that freed the gambling company Caesars Entertainment from having to guarantee a portion of the debt of its subsidiary Caesars Entertainment Operating Co., thereby causing bondholders substantial losses.

11.99   The language at issue—in an indenture—said "the Parent Guarantee shall terminate … upon" the operating company's (1) no longer being a wholly owned subsidiary, (2) merging into another company, *and* (3) paying off or defeasing all its debts. Upon occurrence of the first of the three events, Caesars Entertainment declared that the guarantee had been terminated. In litigation, the bondholders claimed that all three conditions had to be satisfied. But it would make no sense to require that all three conditions be satisfied. So this use of *and* would seem to be a mistake.

11.100   Using just *or* works when occurrence of only one of the specified alternatives is feasible or desirable. But if you want to avoid having someone argue that occurrence of more than one of the specified alternatives precludes operation of the provision in question, then put the phrase *one or more of the following* before the specified alternatives and put *and* after the next-to-last alternative.

EVERY, EACH, ALL, AND *ANY*

11.101   *Every* is used to refer to all the individual members of a set without exception. *All* is used to refer to the totality of members. And *each* means every one of two or more people or things, regarded and identified separately. The meaning of these words overlaps.

11.102   In certain contexts, one can use without risk of ambiguity *every* and *each* (see [42]) and also *all* (see [42a]). But if you use language of discretion, *every* and *each* become ambiguous, as in [43], and so does *all*, as in [43a]. (If the noun is a mass noun, for example flour, instead of a count noun (vehicle), the ambiguity afflicts equivalents to *all*, for example *the entire*.)

[42]   Acme shall purchase [every] [each] vehicle included in the Roe Assets.

[42a]   Acme shall purchase all vehicles included in the Roe Assets.

[43]   Acme may purchase [every] [each] vehicle included in the Roe Assets.

[43a]   Acme may purchase all vehicles included in the Roe Assets.

[43b]   *Acme may purchase no fewer than all vehicles included in the Roe Assets.*

[43c]   *Acme may purchase one or more of the vehicles included in the Roe Assets.*

11.103   *Any* exhibits similar ambiguity, except that it manifests itself in language of obligation (see [44]). Analogous to using *any* in [44] to convey the meaning of [44a] is how *any* is used in the sentence *Take the name of any person who comes through the door*: the speaker presumably had in mind that *any* means "every," with the added implication that no one might come through the door. And analogous to use of *any* in [44] to convey the meaning of [44b] is how it's used in *Pick any card*—the reasonable interpretation is that one is being invited to pick a single card. By contrast, with language of discretion (see [45]) the question is whether the drafter intended *any* to mean "one," as in [45a], or "one or more," as in [45b].

[44]   Acme shall purchase any vehicle included in the Roe Assets.

[44a]   *Acme shall purchase no fewer than all vehicles included in the Roe Assets.*

[44b]   *Acme shall purchase one of the vehicles included in the Roe Assets.*

[45]   Acme may purchase any vehicle included in the Roe Assets.

[45a]   *Acme may purchase only one of the vehicles included in the Roe Assets.*

[45b]   *Acme may purchase one or more of the vehicles included in the Roe Assets.*

11.104   *Every*, *each*, *all*, and *any* are also ambiguous in a sentence expressing failure or inability. Examples [46] (regarding *every*, *each*, and *any*) and [46a] (regarding *all*) are examples of such a sentence; both could have the meaning of either [46b] or [46c].

[46]   "Disability" means the Employee's inability to perform [every] [each] [any] duty under this agreement.

[46a]   "Disability" means the Employee's inability to perform all duties under this agreement.

[46b]   *"Disability" means the Employee's ability to perform no duties under this agreement.*

[46c]   *"Disability" means the Employee's inability to perform one or more duties under this agreement.*

11.105   A dispute involving *all* used in the context of failure or inability is featured in the opinion of the Chancery Division of the High Court of Justice of England and Wales in *Dooba Developments Ltd v. McLagan Investments Ltd* [2016] EWHC 2944 (Ch).

11.106   Dooba Developments Ltd and McLagan Investments Ltd (referred to as "Asda" in the proceedings) entered into a contract for purchase of land that was to be the site of an Asda Superstore. The contract was subject to satisfaction of four conditions relating to planning permission and consent to undertake highway works in developing the site.

11.107   Asda rescinded the contract because Dooba had failed to satisfy the four conditions by the stipulated date (the "Longstop Date"). Dooba sought a declaration that Asda's notice of rescission was invalid and that the agreement had become unconditional. Asda then applied for summary judgment, claiming (1) that there was no real prospect of Dooba establishing that one of the conditions—the one relating to highway construction—had been satisfied by the Longstop Date and (2) that for rescission, it was sufficient that one or more conditions remained unsatisfied at the Longstop Date.

11.108   Here's the language at issue (emphasis added):

> Without prejudice to the provisions of paragraph 3 *if all of the Conditions have not been discharged* in accordance with this Schedule by the Longstop Date, then either Asda or Dooba may rescind this Agreement by giving to the other not less than ten working days written notice to that effect.

11.109   The initial hearings were before a master of the Chancery Division. Asda prevailed on both points. Dooba appealed against the master's decision on the second issue. Invoking "strict Boolean logic," the deputy High Court judge accepted Dooba's argument that the right arose only if all four conditions had not been satisfied by the Longstop Date.

11.110   The judge's analysis conflicts with the analysis in *CGEL*, at 359, of *All of the meat wasn't fresh*:

i a. [*Not all* of the meat] was fresh.≡ b.[*Some* of the meat] was_n't_ fresh.

ii a. [*All* of the meat] was_n't_ fresh. ≡ b.[*None* of the meat] was fresh.

In [ia] *all* is within the scope of the negation ("It is not the case that all of the meat was fresh"), while in [ib] *some* has scope over the negative ("Some of the meat had the property that it wasn't fresh"). In abstraction from prosody, the clause *All of the meat wasn't fresh* is ambiguous with respect to scope. In one interpretation the negative has scope over the quantifier ([*All of the meat*] was_n't_ fresh), making it simply an alternant of [ia]; this is the kind of interpretation we have in the proverb *All that glitters is not gold*. In a second interpretation, the one indicated in the notation in [iia], *all* has scope over the negative ("All of the meat had the property of not being fresh"); this is equivalent to [iib]. Examples like *All of the meat wasn't fresh* are relatively infrequent: it is much more common to use one or other of the unambiguous equivalents, [ia] or [iib].

11.111   So this case serves as a reminder that you cannot expect courts to make sense of this kind of ambiguity unaided.

A CASE STUDY

11.112   The nuances of ambiguity of the part versus the whole are sufficiently intricate that one could sympathize with anyone who would rather ignore the topic. But because this kind of ambiguity creates confusion in practitioners, clients, and judges, drafters ignore it at their peril.

11.113   A noteworthy example of that is the opinion by the U.S. Court of Appeals for the Third Circuit in *Meyer v. CUNA Mutual Insurance Society*, 648 F.3d 154 (3d Cir. 2011). Because its flawed analysis caused the court to find ambiguity in an insurance policy—a kind of contract—where a reasonable reader would have found none, the court decided the case incorrectly.

This case offers general lessons in how to handle ambiguity of the part versus the whole.

Background

11.114 Plaintiff Meyer, a railroad employee, purchased a credit disability insurance policy from defendant CUNA Mutual Group in connection with Meyer's purchase of a car with financing provided by a credit union. Under the policy, CUNA would make car-loan payments on Meyer's behalf if he were deemed disabled. After Meyer injured himself on the job, CUNA made his car payments for approximately three years, then notified Meyer that it would stop the payments: Meyer no longer met the definition of "Total Disability," as stated in CUNA's policy, because Meyer's doctors had determined that he could return to work in some capacity.

11.115 Here's how "Total Disability" was defined in the policy:

> during the first 12 consecutive months of disability means that a member is not able to perform substantially all of the duties of his occupation on the date his disability commenced because of a medically determined sickness or accidental bodily injury. After the first 12 consecutive months of disability, the definition changes and requires the member to be unable to perform any of the duties of his occupation or any occupation for which he is reasonably qualified by education, training or experience.

11.116 Meyer responded to CUNA's stopping payments on the car by filing a class action with the District Court for the Western District of Pennsylvania. He argued that the policy language was unambiguous and meant that after the first 12 consecutive months, he qualified as totally disabled if he could show either that (1) he was unable to perform the duties of his occupation or (2) he was unable to perform the duties of any occupation for which he was reasonably qualified by education, training, or experience. By contrast, CUNA argued that for the post-12-month period, the "any occupation" standard applied.

11.117 The district court granted Meyer's motion for partial summary judgment, holding that the definition of the term "Total Disability" was ambiguous and so should be construed in favor of Meyer. CUNA appealed; the Third Circuit affirmed.

The Third Circuit's Analysis

11.118 In its opinion, the Third Circuit noted that contract language is ambiguous when it's reasonably susceptible of being understood in different ways; that ambiguous language in an insurance policy should be construed against the insurance company; and that words in an insurance policy "should be construed in their natural, plain and ordinary sense."

11.119 After considering the dictionary definition of *or* and citing two cases, the court concluded that "The commonly used and understood definition of 'or' suggests an alternative between two or more choices." In other words, the *or* was, to use the court's terminology, disjunctive rather than conjunctive. The court found unpersuasive the caselaw cited by CUNA to support its interpretation. The court noted that its conclusion that Meyer's interpretation was reasonable was bolstered by the fact that CUNA could have avoided any ambiguity by using the word *and* instead of *or* to convey that it indeed intended a conjunctive meaning. The court summarized its position as follows: "Based on our analysis of a plain reading of the language and common, disjunctive meaning of the word 'or,' we find that Meyer's interpretation is not unreasonable."

11.120   The court declined to accept arguments to the effect that CUNA's interpretation was consistent with the relevant Pennsylvania statute and industry practice. It also rejected, because the "substantially all" standard of the first half of the definition differed from the "any" standard of the second half, the argument that the meaning sought by Meyer would result in the same standard applying to both the first 12 months and the following period.

11.121   But the court noted a "potential contextual defect" that arises from attributing a disjunctive meaning to the *or* in question—it renders meaningless the second part of the provision relating to the period after the first 12 months. That caused the court to conclude that the definition is ambiguous and that CUNA's interpretation too was reasonable. But the court held that due to Pennsylvania's policy of construing against the insurer any ambiguities in an insurance policy, the meaning claimed by Meyer was the one that applied.

What Are the Possible Meanings?

11.122   So the Third Circuit accepted Meyer's argument that the definition applied to him because he could not perform any of the duties of his occupation—all that was required for him to fall within the scope of the definition was that his inability apply to one of the alternatives presented.

11.123   But the court's reasoning is deficient in how it determined the possible alternative meanings and which should apply. The approach taken by the Third Circuit is broadly comparable to that taken by other courts, but that doesn't make it any less mistaken. In relying on the dictionary definition of *or* and caselaw that was essentially irrelevant, the Third Circuit failed to consider unavoidable nuances of the English language. A broader analysis is required, one that recognizes that the ambiguity associated with *or* is a complex issue of English usage rather than a narrow legal question.

11.124   As a first step in such an analysis, let's consider the possible alternative meanings. Here's the relevant portion of the definition (emphasis added):

> [a member is] unable to perform any of the duties of his occupation *or* any occupation for which he is reasonably qualified by education, training or experience.

11.125   But by analogy with [30a], a natural interpretation of the language at issue in *Meyer* is the following:

> [a member is] unable to perform any of the duties of his occupation and [a member is] unable to perform any of the duties of any occupation for which he is reasonably qualified by education, training or experience.

11.126   That is the meaning advocated by CUNA. The only other possible meaning is that advanced by Meyer, which is analogous to [30c]. (Because negation is inherent *in unable* rather than achieved by using *not*, a meaning analogous to [30d] isn't possible.)

Is CUNA's Meaning Reasonable?

11.127   That the language at issue gives rise to two alternative meanings isn't enough to make it ambiguous. For that to be the case, each alternative meaning would have to be reasonable. Given that *CGEL* acknowledges the reading giving rise to the meaning advanced by CUNA (see 11.56), any court should hold that that meaning is a reasonable one.

11.128   But the Third Circuit pointed to use of "any occupation" in the language at issue rather than "any other occupation" as an argument against CUNA's interpretation.

11.129   Reading the phrase conjunctively, one could argue that inclusion of continued coverage if a member cannot perform "any of the duties of his occupation" is redundant or unnecessary if "duties of any occupation … for which he is reasonably qualified" includes the member's own occupation.

11.130   The court was correct—omitting *other* does render superfluous the reference to "his occupation," and drafters should aim to avoid redundancy. But omission of *other* doesn't leap out at the reader—in everyday English it's commonplace to link with *or* a reference to a member of a class and a reference to the entire class, without carving out that member—for example, *I can't eat ice cream or any dairy products*. (In speech, you would stress the *any*.)

11.131   And more importantly, that overlap is benign—the meaning conveyed by the whole is unaffected. So the court had no basis for hinting that omission of *other* brings into question whether the language at issue conveys CUNA's meaning.

Is Meyer's Meaning Reasonable?

11.132   By contrast, Meyer's meaning is problematic—if you assume that the *or* is disjunctive, the remainder of the definition is rendered superfluous.

11.133   Understanding how this plays out requires first considering a second potential ambiguity in the definition of "Total Disability"—the alternative meanings conveyed by the word *any*, which can mean one of several items, or all of them (see 11.103).

11.134   The word *any* occurs twice in the language at issue. The phrase "any of the duties of his occupation" could be taken to mean *one of* the member's duties, but the context makes it clear that the intended meaning is *all* duties—the standard for the first 12 months refers to substantially all duties, and it's clear that the intention was to make the standard for the following period more onerous.

11.135   The second instance of *any* occurs in the phrase "any occupation for which he is reasonably qualified." This could be taken to mean "one of the occupations for which he is reasonably qualified." But that would suggest that inability to perform the duties of a single occupation—say, truck driver—would be enough to satisfy the second part of the standard relating to the post-12-month period. The member's ability to perform any number of other occupations would be irrelevant. But it would be nonsensical to allow the member to meet the requirements for total disability simply by finding a single occupation that the member cannot perform the duties of. Instead, the phrase makes sense only if it's understood as referring to all occupations for which the member is qualified.

11.136   With that in mind, if you accept that the language at issue conveys Meyer's meaning, a member who cannot perform any of the duties of his former occupation wouldn't have to worry about establishing that no suitable occupation remained available to him. The court said as much:

> If he cannot perform any of the duties of his occupation, construing 'or' disjunctively, he is qualified for coverage, and there is no need to move to the second part of the clause—whether he can perform the duties of any occupation for which he is qualified—to determine coverage.

11.137   And the court noted that the second part of the language at issue is similarly superfluous if the member can perform any of the duties of his former occupation:

> If, on the other hand, an insured can perform one or more tasks of his former occupation, he is not qualified for coverage and there is no need to look to the second part of the clause because he has already failed to qualify for coverage—his own occupation is a subset of any occupation for which he is qualified.

11.138   So accepting Meyer's meaning requires that you disregard the second part of the language at issue. As a matter of contract interpretation, that's deeply problematic, particularly when compared to the benign overlap in CUNA's meaning caused by the absence of *other*. If the meaning you seek to apply to a provision renders redundant half that provision, the only possible conclusion is that the meaning doesn't make sense—that it's unreasonable.

11.139   The court noted that "Courts should not distort the meaning of the language or strain to find an ambiguity," but that's what the Third Circuit did in nevertheless endorsing Meyer's meaning. It blithely dismissed the problem as a "potential contextual defect," offering in support of its disregard of the redundancy only one case, one that has only the most remote bearing on the issue.

Mixing Analyses of Different Meanings

11.140   The court capped its flawed analysis by concluding that the redundancy inherent in accepting Meyer's meaning "does lead us to find that the phrase is capable of being understood in more than one sense and that a conjunctive interpretation is also reasonable." That doesn't make sense. When weighing the reasonableness of alternative possible meanings, you consider them independently. The defects in one possible meaning go only to its reasonableness—they don't bolster the reasonableness of the other possible meaning. The conclusion that follows from the redundancy required by Meyer's meaning is that Meyer's meaning is unreasonable, not that CUNA's meaning is somehow made more palatable.

11.141 Similarly, it didn't make sense for the court to conclude that reasonableness of Meyer's meaning was bolstered by the court's mistaken view that CUNA could have avoided any ambiguity by using the word *and* instead of *or*. Again, the ostensible weakness of one alternative meaning doesn't bolster the reasonableness of another alternative meaning.

PRACTICAL CONSIDERATIONS

11.142 The Third Circuit's analysis of the provision at issue in *Meyer* has lessons to offer drafters.

The Risks

11.143 *Meyer* serves as a reminder that if you draft contracts, it would be reckless of you not to be alert to ambiguity of the part versus the whole. Unless you're attuned to it, the odds are that you'll be oblivious to alternative possible meanings unless they cause a dispute.

11.144 And *Meyer* is one of many cases in which judges have shown themselves ill-equipped to analyze issues relating to ambiguity of the part versus the whole. The judge in *Meyer* instead relied on a dictionary definition, something judges are increasingly doing. See Adam Liptak, *Justices Turning More Frequently to Dictionary, and Not Just for Big Words*, N.Y. Times, 13 June 2011, at A11. That's usually a poor substitute for the semantic acuity required to rigorously parse confusing contract language. So don't expect judges to be equipped to sort out in a sensible manner any part-versus-the-whole mess you create.

Whether to Eliminate Alternative Meanings

11.145 The court's opinion in *Meyer* serves as a reminder that drafters should consider how far to go in seeking to avoid ambiguity of the part versus the whole.

11.146 Alternative meanings caused by *or* and *and* are virtually inescapable in contract language. Consider two components of the definition of "Total Disability" that weren't at issue in *Meyer*. The definition refers to "a medically determined sickness or accidental bodily injury." Does disability due to sickness *and* injury not fall within the definition? And consider the reference to "any occupation for which he is reasonably qualified by education, training or experience." Does that mean that if the member is qualified because of some combination of education, training, and experience, it would be irrelevant for purposes of the definition?

11.147   You could revise contract language to eliminate the possibility of alternative meanings, but that would make it more wordy. If any alternative meanings aren't reasonable, you could elect to leave the language as is, because the limited risk of ambiguity doesn't warrant the extra verbiage. For example, it would be outlandish to revise the definition of "Total Disability" to rule out the possible meanings suggested in the immediately preceding paragraph.

11.148   But you cannot expect courts to be equipped to determine whether the alternative meanings of a given provision are reasonable and so cause ambiguity—after all, the court in *Meyer* wasn't. If an alternative meaning appears unreasonable but could cause mischief if misconstrued by a court, the cautious drafter should consider redrafting that provision to eliminate the alternative meaning. The meaning attributed by Meyer to the language at issue in his dispute perhaps represents just such an alternative meaning.

11.149   Examples [47] and [48] involve the sort of judgment calls required when determining whether to eliminate possible alternative meanings. Each example expresses two possible meanings, but anyone inclined to recommend that a drafter restructure them to eliminate one of those meanings should consider two factors. First, of the two possible meanings of each example, one is clearly the more natural, namely [47a] and [48a]. Second, given the extra verbiage required to avoid ambiguity, prose stylists would likely steer clear of [47a] and [48a]. Whether to eliminate a possible meaning involves a balancing—whether conscious or not—of expediency and risk, and in a particular contract expediency might well trump risk.

[47]   The Seller has complied with all laws applicable to the Business and the Acquired Assets.

[47a]   *The Seller has complied with all laws applicable to the Business and all laws applicable to the Acquired Assets.*

[47b]   *The Seller has complied with each law applicable to both the Business and the Acquired Assets.*

[48]   The Seller has complied with all laws applicable to the Business or the Acquired Assets.

[48a]   *The Seller has complied with each law applicable to the Business or the Acquired Assets.*

[48b]   *The Seller has complied with all laws applicable to the Business or all laws applicable to the Acquired Assets.*

11.150   Incidentally, note how [47a] and [48a] convey the same meaning. That happens when alternative meanings arise in a provision whether you use *and* or *or* and the most likely meaning using *and* is identical to the most likely meaning using *or*. This adds an ironic twist to analysis of alternative meanings associated with *and* and *or*.

Drafting to Avoid Alternative Meanings

11.151   *Meyer* also offers a lesson to companies seeking to put their contract process on a more efficient footing. It's ironic that the language at issue was compiled as part of an effort by CUNA to make its policies easier to read. Besides the three sets of alternative meanings included in, and omission of the word *other* from, the second sentence of the definition, the definition as a whole isn't a model of clarity.

11.152   The following version eliminates the alternative meanings and restores the missing *other*.

> due to sickness or accidental bodily injury, as determined by a physician, (1) the member is unable to perform substantially all the duties of the member's occupation (applies only during the first 12 consecutive months of that disability) and (2) the member is able to perform none of the duties of the member's occupation and each other occupation for which the member is reasonably qualified by education, training, or experience (applies thereafter).

11.153   It's often the case that instead of requiring just targeted adjustments of the sort discussed in this chapter, eliminating alternative part-versus-the-whole meanings becomes part of broader redrafting.

12

SYNTACTIC AMBIGUITY

12.1   Syntactic ambiguity arises principally out of the order in which words and phrases appear and how they relate to each other grammatically. (See 3.318 for an explanation of the conventions used in the numbered example sentences in this chapter.) It features regularly in litigation—more frequently than, say, the ambiguity of the part versus the whole (see chapter 11).

MODIFIERS

12.2   A modifier is a word or phrase that changes the meaning of a word or phrase to which it is grammatically related. Modifiers can lead to ambiguity in various ways.

Modifiers Preceding or Trailing Two or More Nouns

PRECEDING MODIFIERS

12.3   It's often unclear whether a modifier that precedes two or more nouns modifies all the nouns or only the first. For example, in [1] *children's* could modify just *apparel*, or it could modify all three nouns. If the former is the intended meaning, using enumeration, as in [1a], would eliminate the ambiguity. So would using semicolons, as in [1b], although that's more subtle than using enumeration.

> [1]   Acme may sell in the Stores only children's apparel, accessories, and footwear.

> [1a]   *Acme may sell in the Stores only (1) children's apparel, (2) accessories, and (3) footwear.*

> [1b]   *Acme may sell in the Stores only the following: children's apparel; accessories; and footwear.*

> [1c]   *Acme may sell in the Stores only accessories, footwear, and children's apparel.*

> [1d]   *Acme may sell in the Stores only children's apparel, children's accessories, and children's footwear.*

> [1e]   *Acme may sell in the Stores only the following items for children: apparel, accessories, and footwear.*

12.4   Another way to avoid ambiguity when you intend that a preceding modifier modify only one of a series of nouns would be to put that noun last, as in [1c]. If instead the modifier modifies all the nouns, you could repeat it before each noun, as in [1d], or perhaps you could be more economical, as in [1e].

12.5   *Regency Commercial Associates, LLC v. Lopax, Inc.*, 869 N.E.2d 310 (Ill. App. Ct. 4 May 2007), provides a good example of how a preceding modifier can create ambiguity leading to a dispute. Here's the contract provision at issue: "any fast food … restaurant or restaurant facility whose principal food product is chicken on the bone, boneless chicken or chicken sandwiches." The question was whether the preceding modifier, "fast food," modified just "restaurant" or modified both "restaurant" and "restaurant facility."

12.6   *In re Mobilactive Media, LLC*, No. CIV.A. 5725-VCP, 2013 WL 297950, at *1 (Del. Ch. 25 Jan. 2013), offers another example. The language at issue was "interactive video programming and advertising content." One party wanted it interpreted to mean *interactive video programming and interactive advertising content*; the other sought the meaning *interactive video programming and interactive video advertising content*. (A third possible meaning is *advertising content and interactive video programming*, but neither party sought that meaning.)

TRAILING MODIFIERS

12.7   Similarly, it's often unclear whether a clause that follows two or more nouns (a "trailing" modifier) modifies all the nouns or only the last one. In [2], it's not clear whether the $500,000 limit applies to just capital expenditures or to debt and capital expenditures.

[2]   Acme shall not incur any debt or make any capital expenditure in excess of $500,000.

[2a]   *Acme shall not do any of the following: incur any debt; or make any capital expenditure in excess of $500,000.*

[2b]   *Acme shall not do any of the following:*

   (1)   incur any debt; or

   (2)   make any capital expenditure

   in excess of $500,000.

[2c]   *Acme shall not make any capital expenditure in excess of $500,000 or incur any debt.*

[2d]   *Acme shall not incur any debt in excess of $500,000 or make any capital expenditure in excess of $500,000.*

12.8   Enumeration by itself cannot rectify the ambiguity caused by a trailing modifier, since the trailing modifier would not be isolated in one enumerated clause—nothing would preclude a reader from assuming that it modifies all the enumerated clauses, not just the final one.

12.9   If a trailing modifier modifies just the last noun, you can make that clear using semicolons, as in [2a], although as with [1b], that's not as clear as it might be. If it modifies all nouns, you'd need to add tabulation too, as in [2b]. But tabulation mainly makes clauses that are relatively lengthy and complex easier to read by breaking them out (see 4.41). Tabulating short clauses might eliminate ambiguity, but it doesn't make them easier to read and can be a waste of space. Furthermore, if the trailing modifier modifies each of the nouns, tabulation would result in the trailing modifier being positioned flush left underneath the tabulated clauses, as in [2b]. Such "dangling" text is awkward (see 4.44).

12.10   If you intend that a trailing modifier modify only one of a series of nouns, another way to avoid ambiguity would be to put that noun first, as in [2c]. If instead you intend that the modifier modify all the nouns, repeating the trailing modifier after each noun, as in [2d], would make that clear.

12.11   *Anderson v. Hess Corp.*, 649 F.3d 891 (8th Cir. 2011), involved a dispute caused by a trailing modifier. In the mineral leases at issue, the phrase "drilling or reworking operations" occurred several times. In this context, is "drilling" a noun, or is it an adjective modifying "operations"? In other words, the question posed was, according to the court, "whether the term 'engaged in drilling or reworking operations' included 'drilling operations' and 'reworking operations,' or 'drilling' and 'reworking operations'." This was a significant distinction, because to engage in drilling you would have to actually drill into the ground, whereas "drilling operations" could include activities other than drilling.

12.12   This instance of syntactic ambiguity generated a couple of years' worth of litigation. That could have been avoided had the drafter referred to "drilling operations or reworking operations" or "reworking operations or drilling," depending on which meaning was intended.

12.13   When faced with ambiguity caused by a trailing modifier, a court might apply the "rule of the last antecedent," which is an arbitrary rule of interpretation that states that a qualifying phrase is to be applied to the word or phrase immediately preceding it and shouldn't be interpreted as modifying others more remote. (See 3.443.) Don't assume that a court would apply the rule of the last antecedent to interpret an ambiguity in your favor. The rule of the last antecedent "has little weight or value." Joseph Kimble, *The Doctrine of the Last Antecedent, the Example in* Barnhart, *Why Both Are Weak, and How Textualism Postures*, 16 Scribes J. Legal Writing 5 (2015). And even if a court were to rule in your favor, winning a fight is a distant second to avoiding the fight. Instead, eliminate the ambiguity.

PRECEDING AND TRAILING MODIFIERS

12.14   When sets of nouns are modified by both preceding and trailing modifiers, four meanings are possible; [3] is a simple example of this. If the intention is that the trailing modifier *qualified to do business in New York* not modify the first noun phrase *Delaware corporations*, the simplest way to make that clear would be to switch the order of the noun phrases, as has been done in [3a] and [3b]; if the opposite is intended, the simplest way to avoid ambiguity on that score would be to repeat the trailing modifier, as in [3c] and [3d]. These changes also eliminate the ambiguity caused by the preceding modifier *Delaware*. In [3a] and [3c] *Delaware* modifies *LLCs* and *corporations*; that's made clear by repeating the adjective *Delaware*. In [3b] and [3d] it does not; that's made clear by switching the order of the noun phrases.

[3]   Delaware corporations and LLCs qualified to do business in New York

[3a]   *Delaware LLCs qualified to do business in New York and Delaware corporations*

[3b]   *LLCs qualified to do business in New York and Delaware corporations*

[3c]   *Delaware corporations qualified to do business in New York and Delaware LLCs qualified to do business in New York*

[3d]   *LLCs qualified to do business in New York and Delaware corporations qualified to do business in New York*

12.15 Ambiguity caused by a trailing modifier was one issue raised in *United Rentals, Inc. v. RAM Holdings, Inc.*, 937 A.2d 810, 813 (Del. Ch. 2007), a case about a $6.6 billion transaction that failed to close. The contract at issue contained this:

> ... and in no event shall the Company seek equitable relief or seek to recover any money damages in excess of such amount from [the RAM entities and related entities].

12.16 The plaintiff, United Rentals, argued that the trailing modifier "in excess of such amount" modified not only the phrase "seek to recover any money damages" but also went farther back up the sentence and modified the phrase "seek equitable relief." The defendants argued that that interpretation was unreasonable. From a drafting perspective, what matters is not which meaning is the more likely but that meaning was disputed at all.

Modifiers Occurring between Two or More Nouns

12.17 When a modifier follows one noun in a string of nouns, as in [4], it can be unclear whether the subsequent nouns are incorporated in the modifier or are grammatically equivalent to the noun that precedes the modifier. This ambiguity can be remedied in various ways. You could use enumeration, as in [4a] and [4b]. Or you could enclose the modifier in parentheses, as in [4c] and [4d] (see 13.632). Or, if the intent is to have the modifier not incorporate any of the nouns that follow, you could move the modifier and the noun it modifies to the end of the string of nouns, as in [4e], although that's less clear than the other alternatives, given the potential for confusion inherent in trailing modifiers (see 12.7). You could also use tabulation, but as explained in 12.9, that approach isn't recommended.

[4]   Widgetco shall sell to Acme the Roe Assets, excluding the Smith Assets, the Jones Assets, and the Doe Assets.

[4a]   *Widgetco shall sell to Acme (1) the Roe Assets, excluding the Smith Assets, (2) the Jones Assets, and (3) the Doe Assets.*

[4b]   *Widgetco shall sell to Acme the Roe Assets, excluding (1) the Smith Assets, (2) the Jones Assets, and (3) the Doe Assets.*

[4c]   *Widgetco shall sell to Acme the Roe Assets (excluding the Smith Assets), the Jones Assets, and the Doe Assets.*

[4d]   *Widgetco shall sell to Acme the Roe Assets (excluding the Smith Assets, the Jones Assets, and the Doe Assets).*

[4e]   *Widgetco shall sell to Acme the Jones Assets, the Doe Assets, and the Roe Assets, excluding the Smith Assets.*

Squinting Modifiers

12.18   A modifier is described as "squinting" if it's not clear whether it modifies what comes before or what comes after. In [5], *within 10 days* could refer to the time by which Acme must reject any Asset or the time by which the Seller must reimburse Acme. Although placing a comma before the modifier, as in [5a], or after the modifier, as in [5b], would signal which meaning was intended, it can be risky to rely only on a comma to avoid ambiguity (see 12.74–.75). It would be clearer to resolve the ambiguity by moving the modifier; in [5c], the modifier occurs twice, in revised form, to convey both possible meanings.

[5]   If Acme rejects any Asset within 10 days the Seller shall reimburse Acme that portion of the Purchase Price allocated to that Asset.

[5a]   *If Acme rejects any Asset within 10 days, the Seller shall reimburse Acme that portion of the Purchase Price allocated to that Asset.*

[5b]   *If Acme rejects any Asset, within 10 days the Seller shall reimburse Acme that portion of the Purchase Price allocated to that Asset.*

[5c]   *If no later than 10 days after the Closing Acme rejects any Asset, the Seller shall no later than 10 days after receiving the notice of rejection reimburse Acme that portion of the Purchase Price allocated to that Asset.*

12.19   Because they require particularly clumsy drafting, squinting modifiers are rare in contracts.

Modifiers of Uncertain Length

12.20   Ambiguity can also arise when it's unclear whether a modifier incorporates a following relative clause. In [6], the modifier could be either *not constituting a Product* or *not constituting a Product that …* . The simplest way to eliminate the ambiguity would be to place the modifier in a conditional clause, as in [6a] and [6b]. (The intended meaning is that in [6a].)

[6]   Acme may sell at any Store any item of apparel not constituting a Product that Widgetco has at any time during the previous 12 months sold at any of the stores that Widgetco operates.

[6a]   *Acme may sell at any Store any item of apparel, on condition that it does not constitute a Product that Widgetco has at any time during the previous 12 months sold at any of the stores that Widgetco operates.*

[6b]   *Acme may sell at any Store any item of apparel that Widgetco has at any time during the previous 12 months sold at any of the stores that Widgetco operates, on condition that the item does not constitute a Product.*

Poorly Placed Modifiers

12.21   An objective reading of [7] would suggest that the modifier *no later than five Business Days after the closing of the related sale* relates to when Galactic must designate an account. The drafter had in fact intended that the modifier indicate the timing for delivery of the Proceeds; that would have been better accomplished by moving to the front of the sentence a slightly revised version of the modifier, as in [7a].

> [7]   The Sellers shall deliver the Proceeds to Galactic by wire transfer of immediately available funds to an account designated by Galactic no later than five Business Days after the closing of the related sale.

> [7a]   *No later than five Business Days after the closing of a sale, the Sellers shall deliver the Proceeds of that sale to Galactic by wire transfer of immediately available funds to an account designated by Galactic.*

12.22   A similar problem afflicts [8]: an objective reading would suggest that the modifier *that is in Acme's possession* modifies *a motor vehicle included in the Assets*. The intention had in fact been that it would modify *every certificate of title*. Repositioning the modifier, as in [8a], would have made that clearer.

> [8]   Acme has provided Widgetco with a copy of every certificate of title relating to a motor vehicle included in the Assets that is in Acme's possession.

> [8a]   *Acme has provided Widgetco with a copy of every certificate of title that is in Acme's possession relating to a motor vehicle included in the Assets.*

Opening and Closing Modifiers

12.23   Analogous to the ambiguity caused by modifiers that precede or trail two or more nouns (see 12.3–.16) is the ambiguity that can result when a phrase begins or ends a sentence containing two or more other elements, as in [9] and [9a]: it can be unclear whether the phrase that begins or ends the sentence modifies one or both of the other elements.

12.24   If in [9] and [9a] the adverbial phrase *other than in the Ordinary Course of Business* modifies both of the verb clauses in the remainder of the sentence, and if both verb clauses have the same subject, the simplest course would be to combine the verb clauses and place the adverbial phrase in front of the resulting clause, as in [9b]. (Placing the adverbial phrase at the end would not eliminate the ambiguity.) If the adverbial phrase relates to the first verb clause but not the second, place the adverbial phrase after the first verb clause and before the second, as in [9c]. If the adverbial phrase relates to the second verb clause but not the first, reverse the order of the verb clauses and place the adverbial phrase after what had been the second verb clause and is now the first, as in [9d].

> [9]   Other than in the Ordinary Course of Business, Acme shall not incur debt and Acme shall not make any capital expenditures.

> [9a]   Acme shall not incur debt and Acme shall not make any capital expenditures, other than in the Ordinary Course of Business.

[9b]   *Other than in the Ordinary Course of Business, Acme shall not incur debt or make any capital expenditures.*

[9c]   *Acme shall not incur debt other than in the Ordinary Course of Business or make any capital expenditures.*

[9d]   *Acme shall not make any capital expenditures other than in the Ordinary Course of Business or incur any debt.*

12.25   To resolve ambiguity caused by a closing modifier, a court might invoke the flimsy rule of interpretation known as the rule of the last antecedent (see 12.13). In this context, the shortcomings of the rule of the last antecedent are exacerbated by a related rule of interpretation, what this manual calls "the comma test under the rule of the last antecedent." It holds that if in a sentence a series of nouns, noun phrases, or clauses is followed by a modifier and the modifier is preceded by a comma, the modifier applies to the entire series, not just the final element in the series. This principle conflicts with English usage, so it should be abandoned. See Kenneth A. Adams, *Bamboozled by a Comma: The Second Circuit's Misdiagnosis of Ambiguity in* American International Group, Inc. v. Bank of America Corp., 16 Scribes J. Legal Writing 45 (2014–15). It would be beyond reckless to rely on the rule of the last antecedent, including the comma test, as an alternative to drafting clearly. Instead, fix the ambiguity.

12.26   The comma test was apparently invoked in a dispute between two Canadian companies. In 2002, the cable unit of Rogers Communications Inc., a telecommunications company, entered into a contract with Aliant Inc. in which Aliant agreed to string Rogers cable lines across utility poles for an annual fee per pole. In 2005, Aliant informed Rogers that it wished to terminate the contract and increase its rates. Rogers objected, on the grounds that the contract couldn't be terminated until after the first five-year term. Aliant disagreed, claiming that the agreement could be terminated at any time on one year's notice.

12.27   The contract between the parties had been drafted by Canadian regulators. Here's the language at issue:

> Subject to the termination provisions of this Agreement, this Agreement shall be effective from the date it is made and shall continue in force for a period of five (5) years from the date it is made, and thereafter for successive five (5) year terms, unless and until terminated by one year prior notice in writing by either party.

12.28   The dispute concerned whether the closing modifier—the phrase "unless and until terminated by one year prior notice in writing by either party"—modified both preceding clauses or just the immediately preceding clause.

12.29   The dispute reached the Canadian Radio-television and Tele-communications Commission. Echoing an argument offered by Aliant, the Commission noted that based on "the rules of punctuation," the presence of a comma immediately before the word "unless" meant that the closing modifier modified both preceding clauses. That initially led the Commission to side with Aliant in concluding that under the contract Aliant could terminate on one year's notice during the initial five-year term. In invoking that comma, it's likely that the Commission was relying on the comma test under the rule of the last antecedent.

12.30 The Commission's finding made the news, with headlines such as *The Comma That Costs 1 Million Dollars (Canadian)*. The author of this manual, acting as expert witness for Rogers Communications, submitted an affidavit to the Commission stating that the presence of a comma could not reasonably be used to resolve the ambiguity created by the closing modifier. Regarding the possible significance of the two commas in the language at issue, see 12.37.

12.31 On appeal, the Commission found in favor of Rogers without revisiting the question of punctuation. Instead, it decided that the dispute should be governed by the French-language version of the contract, which provided for a markedly different, and more sensible, arrangement than that in the English-language version, namely that the contract would automatically renew for additional five-year terms unless at least one year before renewal either party notifies the other that it doesn't want to renew. The arrangement in the English version doesn't make sense: being able to terminate at any time by giving one year's notice renders illusory the notion of a fixed term. It appears that the language at issue was the result of poor translation of the French version of the contract.

Closing Modifiers with Offsetting Commas

12.32 A subset of closing modifiers is a closing modifier that a drafter seeks to link with one or both of two preceding components by using offsetting commas. Omitting one or both offsetting commas from a sentence can affect its meaning.

12.33 For example, if the commas in [11] are included, *of the Asset that is the subject of the Claim* is semantically linked to *the Redemptive Value*; without the commas, it could be linked to *as of the Cut-off Date*.

> [11]   Acme shall pay Roe 100% of the Redemptive Value [,] as of the Cut-off Date [,] of the Asset that is the subject of the Claim.

12.34 In [12], the commas make it clear that the sentence addresses expenses incurred in redeeming the Excluded Assets; if you omit the commas, it could be read as addressing only expenses incurred in redeeming any Grantor's interest in the Excluded Assets.

> [12]   Alpha shall promptly reimburse BCSC any expenses incurred by BCSC in redeeming [,] or protecting any Grantor's interest in [,] the Excluded Assets.

12.35 If you include the comma in brackets, the security interest granted in [13] covers only the inventory that Roe sold to Acme; if you omit the comma, the security interest covers all inventory.

> [13]   Acme grants Roe a security interest in all Acme inventory, including but not limited to all agricultural chemicals, fertilizers, and fertilizer materials [,] that Roe sold to Acme.

12.36   It's best to avoid drafting a provision so that much depends on how presence or absence of a comma is interpreted—commas are too easily misunderstood or ignored (see 12.74–.75). For example, in *Shelby County State Bank v. Van Diest Supply Co.*, 303 F.3d 832 (7th Cir. 2002), the court, in interpreting language analogous to [13], ignored the absence of a comma and held that the security interest covered only a subset of all inventory.

12.37   Furthermore, if what comes before the first comma of a pair of ostensibly offsetting commas can stand on its own, as opposed to requiring what follows the second offsetting comma for completion (as with [12]), that makes it debatable whether the commas are, in fact, offsetting. The language at issue in the dispute between Rogers and Aliant (see 12.27) features two commas. They could be considered offsetting commas linking to the initial five-year period the right to terminate on giving one year's notice. But one could equally argue that the commas are independent, with each serving its own syntactic function, so that there's nothing to link the closing modifier to what precedes the first comma. This type of ambiguity is another reason to be wary of commas (see 12.74–.75).

ONE WAY TO ELIMINATE POTENTIAL OFFSETTING-COMMA CONFUSION

12.38   Consider the offsetting commas in this example:

> The Vendor will not be liable to Acme or any Buyer, and neither Acme nor any Buyer will be liable to the Vendor, for any damages that are not a reasonably foreseeable consequence of breach.

12.39   The offsetting commas indicate that the closing modifier *for any damages …* modifies both *The Vendor will not …* and *neither Acme nor any Buyer will … .* But someone might be willing to argue the point and claim that the Vendor isn't liable to Acme or any Buyer, period. (These potential alternative meanings are analogous to the ambiguity noted in 12.27–.28.)

12.40   And as is, this sentence could cause a reader miscue—you might not realize that the opening phrase isn't self-contained until after you encounter the second comma and what follows. So it would be clearer to revise this sentence to read as follows:

> The Vendor will not be liable to Acme or any Buyer for, and neither Acme nor any Buyer will be liable to the Vendor for, any damages that are not a reasonably foreseeable consequence of breach.

12.41   By moving *for* before each comma—in effect subdividing a single prepositional phrase, namely *for any damages …*—you make it clear that in both instances something is yet to come. That makes life easier for the reader and eliminates any possibility of confusion.

12.42   You could eliminate the potential confusion in other ways, for example by using two separate sentences. But depending on the context, the economy offered by an offsetting-commas structure might make it more efficient to tweak that structure instead of scrapping it in favor of a different approach.

THAT AND *WHICH*

Background

12.43   Good drafting, like good writing, requires that you distinguish between restrictive clauses and nonrestrictive clauses. Authorities on general English usage recommend using *that* for restrictive clauses and comma-*which* for nonrestrictive clauses.

12.44   In the sentence *The cakes that George baked were delicious*, the clause *that George baked* is restrictive, because it gives essential information about the preceding noun (*cakes*) to distinguish it from similar items with which it might be confused (cakes baked by someone else).

12.45   By contrast, in the sentence *The cakes, which George baked, were delicious*, the clause *which George baked* is nonrestrictive, because it gives us supplemental information that doesn't further delimit the meaning of the preceding noun; we are being told that not only are the cakes delicious, it so happens that George baked them. Use of *which* and the offsetting commas tells us that the clause constitutes an aside.

Current Usage

12.46   Many drafters don't observe a clear distinction between *that* and *which*. In contracts, *which* is often used instead of *that* in restrictive clauses:

> There is no fact known to any Credit Agreement Party or any of its Subsidiaries *which* [read *that*] has had, or could reasonably be expected to have, a Material Adverse Effect.

12.47   Sometimes comma-*which* is used instead of *that*:

> In the case of an assignment to a *Purchasing Lender, which* [read *Purchasing Lender that*] is an Affiliate of the assigning Lender, that assignment will be effective between that Lender and its Affiliate … .

12.48   And sometimes *which* is used instead of *that* and is preceded by the closing comma of a subordinate clause, which makes the restrictive clause look even more like a nonrestrictive clause:

> **"Pension Plan"** means any Employee Benefit Plan, other than a *Multiemployer Plan, which* [read *Multiemployer Plan, that*] is subject to the provisions of Title IV of ERISA or section 412 of the Code … .

12.49   In the case of nonrestrictive clauses, the comma is sometimes inappropriately dropped before *which* (*that* cannot be used instead of *which* in nonrestrictive clauses):

> All outstanding promissory notes issued by the Borrower to the Existing Lenders under the Existing Credit Agreement must be promptly returned to the Administrative *Agent which* [read *Agent, which*] shall forward them to the Borrower for cancellation.

12.50   Inconsistent use of *that* and *which* in restrictive and nonrestrictive clauses can cause ambiguity. In [10], the clause *which are subject to section 4.3* could be a restrictive clause using *which* instead of *that*; were that the case, the intent would not have been that the clause constitute an aside, but instead that it limit the scope of the exception. [10a] uses *that* instead of *which*, to make it clear that one is dealing with a restrictive clause. If the clause were instead a nonrestrictive clause with a comma missing in front of *which*, the exception would apply to *all Assumed Contracts*, and the clause would essentially serve as a cross-reference. [10b] inserts a comma in front of *which*, to make it clearer that one is dealing with a nonrestrictive clause.

> [10]   This section 4.7 applies to all Contracts other than Assumed Contracts which are subject to section 4.3.

> [10a]   *This section 4.7 applies to all Contracts other than Assumed Contracts that are subject to section 4.3.*

> [10b]   *This section 4.7 applies to all Contracts other than Assumed Contracts, which are subject to section 4.3.*

12.51   And inconsistent usage also means that a court might not take a given usage at face value. For example, in *AIU Insurance Co. v. Robert Plan Corp.*, 836 N.Y.S.2d 483 (Sup. Ct. 2006), the court concluded that a comma-*which* in the contract provision at issue was restrictive, even though, as the court acknowledged, authorities recommend that comma-*which* be used to introduce a nonrestrictive clause.

Recommendation

12.52   For two reasons, it's best not to use nonrestrictive clauses in contracts.

12.53   First, the *AIU Insurance* case suggests that even if you use *that* for restrictive clauses and comma-*which* for nonrestrictive clauses, your drafting wouldn't be immune from the confusion between restrictive and nonrestrictive clauses. That's because any nonrestrictive clause risks being construed as a restrictive clause, as happened in *AIU Insurance*. By contrast, it would seem less likely that a restrictive clause would be construed as a nonrestrictive clause.

12.54   Second, and more importantly, a nonrestrictive clause typically gives supplemental, nonessential information. Contract prose isn't the place for nonessential asides—either tackle an issue head-on or omit it entirely.

12.55   And use *that* rather than *which* in restrictive clauses. If you were to use *which*, all that would distinguish a restrictive clause from a nonrestrictive clause is the presence or absence of a comma. That's asking for trouble (see 12.74–.75).

12.56   But in some contexts using *that* rather than *which* in a restrictive clause might not be enough to avoid confusion. For example, even as revised, the definition in 12.48 could cause confusion over whether *that* modifies *any Employee Benefit Plan* or *a Multiemployer Plan*, because all that points to *that* modifying *any Employee Benefit Plan* is the comma before *that*. The simplest way to make it clearer that that is the intended meaning would be to put parentheses around *other than a Multiemployer Plan* (see 13.632).

THE SERIAL COMMA

12.57 When the last two elements in a series of three or more are joined by a conjunction (*and* or *or*), a comma used immediately before the conjunction is known as a serial comma or Oxford comma.

12.58 In American English, use of the serial comma is standard except in journalistic writing; *The Chicago Manual of Style*, at 6.19, strongly recommends using the serial comma. But in British English it's standard to do without the serial comma. This manual recommends using the serial comma to avoid the ambiguity described in this section.

Inadvertent Combined Elements

12.59 One kind of ambiguity that can result from omitting the serial comma is that the reader might be uncertain whether the last two elements in the series constitute a combined element. Consider this sentence: *John ordered the following flavors of ice cream: chocolate, vanilla, strawberry, chocolate chip* [,] *and cherry.* Without the serial comma, the reader might wonder whether chocolate chip and cherry were two separate flavors or one mixed flavor. If it were a mixed flavor, normally you would expect an *and* before *chocolate*, but its omission could be due to the rhetorical device known as *asyndeton*. A serial comma makes it clear that they're separate flavors.

12.60 And consider this sentence: *John ordered the following flavors of ice cream: chocolate, vanilla, strawberry, raspberry and chocolate chip* [,] *and cherry.* Without the serial comma, the reader might wonder whether the combined flavor is raspberry and chocolate chip or is chocolate chip and cherry; the serial comma makes it clear that it's the former.

Inadvertent Apposition

12.61 Omitting the serial comma can also result in the reader seeing apposition—two noun phrases side by side, with one defining the other—where no apposition had been intended.

12.62 Consider this book dedication: *To my parents, Ayn Rand* [,] *and God.* With the serial comma, the dedication tells the reader that the book is dedicated three ways. Without the serial comma, the reader could think either that the book is dedicated three ways or that the book is dedicated to the writer's parents, who happen to be Ayn Rand and God. The latter meaning is obviously ludicrous, but change the elements and real confusion could result.

12.63 But the serial comma can also create ambiguity. Consider this adjusted version of the dedication: *To my mother, Ayn Rand* [,] *and God.* With the serial comma, the reader could understand the dedication as meaning either that the book is dedicated three ways or that the book is dedicated to the writer's mother, who happens to be Ayn Rand, and to God. Omitting the serial comma makes the latter meaning less likely. That's why *Garner's Modern English Usage*, at 748, is mistaken in saying that "omitting the final comma may cause ambiguities, whereas including it never will."

12.64   The confusion discussed in 12.62 features in *Telenor Mobile Communications AS v. Storm LLC*, 587 F. Supp. 2d 594, 605–08 (S.D.N.Y. 2008). At issue was the following definition of "control" in a shareholders agreement:

> [C]ontrol (including, with its correlative meanings, "controlled by" and "under common control with") shall mean, with respect to any Person, the possession, directly or indirectly, of power to direct or cause the direction of management or policies (*whether through ownership of securities or partnership or other ownership interests, by contract or otherwise*) of a Person.

12.65   The litigants offered alternative meanings for what's in the second set of parentheses (in italics). One argued that "by contract or otherwise" referred to the sources of ownership rights. The other argued that what's in the parentheses listed the three sources of "power to direct or cause the direction of management or policies."

12.66   The language at issue is ambiguous because the "or" before "otherwise" can link either two or three alternatives. In the first interpretation, these are the two alternatives:

> [1]   by contract
>
> [2]   otherwise

12.67   In the second interpretation, these are the three alternatives:

> [1]   through ownership of securities or partnership or other ownership interests
>
> [2]   by contract
>
> [3]   otherwise

12.68   The court held that the latter meaning was the more reasonable one, but it noted that including a serial comma before "or otherwise" would have made that clearer.

Inadvertent Object of Preposition

12.69   *O'Connor v. Oakhurst Dairy*, No. 16-1901, 2017 WL 957195 (1st Cir. 13 Mar. 2017) involved yet another kind of confusion that can be caused by absence of a serial comma.

12.70   The dispute was over whether truck drivers were entitled to overtime pay. The statute at issue specified that overtime pay doesn't apply to the following:

> The canning, processing, preserving, freezing, drying, marketing, storing, packing for shipment or distribution of: (1) Agricultural produce; (2) Meat and fish products; and (3) Perishable foods.

12.71   Here are the alternative interpretations offered by the litigants:

> The canning, processing, preserving, freezing, drying, marketing, storing, packing for shipment [,] or distribution of … .
>
> The canning, processing, preserving, freezing, drying, marketing, storing, [or] packing for shipment or distribution of … .

12.72   Under the first interpretation, "distribution" is exempt from overtime; the dairy isn't required to pay the truck drivers extra. Under the second interpretation, only "packing for distribution" is exempt; the dairy must pay. Use of a serial comma would have made it clearer that the first meaning was the one intended. As it was, absence of a serial comma allowed one side to argue that both "shipment" and "packing" were objects of the preposition "for". Absence of an *or* before "packing" was attributed to asyndeton (see 12.59).

Staying Out of Trouble

12.73   For the drafter, it might appear that the simplest way to stay out of trouble would be to always use the serial comma in a list of three or more items, while watching for circumstances in which a serial comma creates ambiguity rather than resolves it. If using a serial comma is inconsistent with the intended meaning, then make whatever adjustments are required to express that meaning.

12.74   But *O'Connor* demonstrates that that isn't necessarily the safest choice. Litigants can't be counted on to understand commas. It's easy to imagine a disgruntled contract party thinking that if all that stands between them and a satisfactory outcome is something as insubstantial as a comma, it could be argued out of existence, just as in *O'Connor* one side argued that absence of an *or* was insignificant.

12.75   Judges can't be counted on to understand commas either. For example, in *Medfusion, Inc. v. Allscripts Healthcare Solutions, Inc.*, No. 14 CVS 5192, 2015 WL 1455680 (N.C. Super. 31 Mar. 2015), the court misunderstood the significance of a serial comma. See Kenneth A. Adams, *The North Carolina Business Court and the Serial Comma: It's Not Pretty*, Adams on Contract Drafting (1 June 2015), http://www.adamsdrafting.com/the-north-carolina-business-court-and-the-serial-comma/. For other instances of judicial understanding of commas being called into question, see 12.25, 12.36, 12.51.

12.76   So don't rely on a comma. It would be safer instead or in addition to use some other way to eliminate ambiguity. What technique you use depends on which meaning is intended and what the context permits. For example, in the language at issue in *O'Connor*, putting parentheses around "for shipment" would have made it clear that "packing" wasn't an object of the preposition "for" (see 13.632). Or reordering the elements might have worked (see 12.3). With the *O'Connor* language, it would have been awkward to use semicolons or enumeration (see 12.3) or tabulation (see 12.7), but those techniques might work in other contexts.

AVOIDING SYNTACTIC AMBIGUITY BY RESTRUCTURING

12.77   In each of the previous examples in this chapter, the ambiguous example is followed by examples that incorporate the minimum changes necessary to avoid ambiguity. But sometimes instead of making the best of an awkward structure, it would be best to start afresh.

12.78   Consider this example:

> Upon occurrence of a Change in Law or a Force Majeure Event that adversely affects the Seller's performance under this agreement, the Buyer and the Seller shall negotiate in good faith whether to issue a change order addressing the effect of those circumstances and the terms of any such change order.

12.79   It raises the question whether the obligation is triggered by "occurrence of a Change in Law" or by "occurrence of a Change in Law … that adversely affects the Seller's performance under this agreement." Assume that the intended meaning is the latter. If you aim to retain the current wording, the only way to eliminate the ambiguity would be to repeat "that adversely affects the Seller's performance under this agreement," which would be awkward.

12.80   Instead, eliminate the abstract noun "occurrence":

> If a Change in Law or a Force Majeure Event adversely affects the Seller's performance under this agreement, the Buyer and the Seller shall negotiate in good faith whether to issue a change order addressing the effect of those circumstances and the terms of any such change order.

12.81   That way, you avoid syntactic ambiguity and as a bonus end up with a sentence that is three words shorter instead of nine words longer.

SELECTED USAGES

ACTION OR PROCEEDING

13.1   It's commonplace for drafters to use the phrase *action or proceeding*, as in *any legal action or proceeding arising out of this agreement.*

13.2   But *proceeding* encompasses *action*. For example, *Black's Law Dictionary*, quoting an 1899 source, notes that *proceeding* "is more comprehensive than the word 'action,'" and 1A *Corpus Juris Secundum* Actions § 22 says "The term 'proceeding' is broader than the word 'action.'"

13.3   So nothing is gained by using *action or proceeding* rather than simply *proceeding.*

ACTIVELY

13.4   *Actively* is the opposite of *passively*. As such, *actively* would seem redundant when used with a verb structure that connotes activity:

> Liens for taxes not yet delinquent or which are being *actively* contested in good faith … .

> The Company … is *actively* taking steps to ensure that it will be in compliance with other provisions of the Sarbanes-Oxley Act … .

13.5   If by using *actively* you're trying to distinguish between different levels of activity, instead be explicit. For example, if you want a provision not to apply to an employee if the employee is on some kind of leave, make that explicit instead of relying on the phrase *while actively employed.*

ACTUAL, ACTUALLY

13.6   The word *actual* has a role to play in contracts when it's used to draw a contrast with some other attribute, as in *any actual or alleged damage* and *their actual or potential adverse impact.* Or when a word arguably has some other, non-actual meaning.

13.7   But *actual* can serve as padding, in which case you eliminate it:

> permits in Seller's ~~actual~~ physical possession

> a copy of the ~~actual~~ proposed Lease

once *actual* statements for the month of Closing become available

before the *actual* taxes and special assessments payable during such year are known

in each case for the *actual* number of days elapsed

13.8 As for *actually*, in everyday English it means *in fact* and signals difference of opinion or disagreement over facts. Contracts aren't for debating, so generally *actually* has no place in contract prose. Eliminate it from each of these examples:

The Company shall pay or reimburse all Expenses *actually and* reasonably incurred by Indemnitee in connection with that subrogation.

... equal to the product of (1) the amount of cash dividends per share *actually* paid by the Company on the outstanding Common Stock ... .

... had the increase with respect to issuance of such rights, options, or warrants been made on the basis of delivery of only the number of shares of Common Stock *actually* delivered.

... if that Person has the right to then acquire or obtain from the Company any Registrable Securities, whether or not that acquisition has *actually* been effected.

AFFIRMATIVELY, AFFIRMATIVE

13.9 Contracts would be better off without *affirmatively* and *affirmative*.

unless the Employee *affirmatively* elects otherwise; ... .

... the Company's board of directors has *affirmatively* publicly recommended to the Company's shareholders that ... .

The Recipient hereby *affirmatively* consents to ... .

13.10 As for *affirmative*, it's mostly used with *vote*:

The Fund may act by the *affirmative* vote of a majority of the outstanding shares of the Fund.

13.11 Presumably the function of *affirmative* is to make it clear that it's not sufficient that the combined votes for and against constitute a majority of the outstanding shares—that instead the votes in favor must constitute a majority of outstanding shares. But if that's the case, it would be clearer to say so, like this:

The Fund may act by vote of the shareholders in which a majority of the outstanding shares vote in favor of the action.

13.12 *Affirmative* is also redundant in the phrase *affirmative action*, unless you're referring to employment or higher-education admissions policies:

The Company will not be required to take any *affirmative* action to cause delivery of Restricted Shares to comply with any such law.

13.13   And you can always do better than *Affirmative Covenants* as a heading, particularly because *covenant* is archaic (see 3.166). *Certain Obligations* would be an improvement.

ALLONGE

13.14   Don't use the term of art *allonge*.

13.15   According to *Black's Law Dictionary*, *allonge* means "A slip of paper sometimes attached to a negotiable instrument for the purpose of receiving further indorsements when the original paper is filled with indorsements." (An indorsement transfers or guarantees a negotiable instrument or acknowledges payment.) *Black's Law Dictionary* gives 1859 as the date of earliest usage, so *allonge* is a relative newcomer. It's obscure and studiously foppish; *indorsement supplement, indorsement addendum,* or *indorsement certificate* are clearer alternatives.

13.16   A further problem with *allonge* is that it has come to have another meaning: you see it used instead of *amendment* in promissory notes, as in the title *FIRST ALLONGE TO PROMISSORY NOTE*. Use *amendment* instead. (This other use is an example of how the meaning of obscure terms of art can drift. Another example of that is *attorn*; see 13.93.)

ALSO, IN ADDITION

13.17   Be restrained in using *also* and *in addition*. Contract provisions on discrete topics should be able to stand on their own.

AMONG OTHER THINGS

13.18   The phrase *among other things* is benign when it's used to refer to something treated fully elsewhere—for example, in the same contract (see the first example below) or in another contract (see the example under it).

> Attached as appendix A is an amended and restated schedule B to the Subadvisory Agreement stating, *among other things*, the fee that the Adviser will pay the Subadviser with respect to … .

> The Borrowers, the Administrative Agent, and the Lenders have agreed to enter into the Floorplan Credit Agreement, subject to, *among other things*, a condition that the parties amend and restate the Existing Guaranty Agreement as provided in this agreement; and … .

13.19   But *among other things* can also be used in an open-ended way, leaving the reader to wonder what it adds to the contract.

13.20   Sometimes it's equivalent to *includes* or *including*. In that case, in the interest of consistent terminology (see 1.63), use instead whichever word applies. For example, instead of *"Reasonable Efforts" means, among other* *things, … ,* say *"Reasonable Efforts" includes … .* (But see 6.40 regarding the risks of using *includes* as the definitional verb.)

13.21 *Among other things* is also used to signal that only the items specified are relevant. If that's the case, you don't need to allude to unspecified other items:

> Each Letter of Credit must~~, among other things,~~ (1) provide for payment of … and (2) have an expiration date of not later than … .

13.22 There's no good reason to use the Latinism equivalent of *among other things, inter alia* (see 13.492).

AMONGST, WHILST

13.23 Pick the simplest and clearest usages and stick with them, even with everyday words. So use *among* instead of *amongst.*

13.24 *Garner's Modern English Usage* says that in American English, *amongst* is an archaism and is "pretentious at best," but that it's "more common and more tolerable in [British English], where it doesn't suggest affectation." But a Google Ngram of use of *among* and *amongst* in two hundred years' of digitized British-English books shows that in England, *among* has consistently been more popular than *amongst.* So it even makes sense for English drafters to use *among* and not *amongst.*

13.25 The same analysis applies to use of *whilst*—use *while* instead.

ANNIVERSARY

13.26 *Anniversary* means a day that marks occurrence of an event on that date in a previous year, but it's also used informally to mark a milestone in months or even weeks. The latter use of *anniversary* is routine in contracts, and eliminating it results in prose that's not only more logical but also more concise. Here's an example:

> The Company shall redeem this debenture in 24 equal installments of principal and accrued interest monthly beginning ~~on the one-month anniversary following~~ [*read* one month after] the First Closing Date.

13.27 Silly but nonetheless commonplace is *12-month anniversary,* as in *ending on the 12-month anniversary of the Termination Date.* Because 12 months make a year, the phrase *12-month is* superfluous.

ANNUAL MEETING

13.28 It's generally accepted that an annual meeting doesn't have to take place on the same day every year. So what does *annual meeting* mean? The notion that *annual meeting* should mean roughly 365 days apart is vague: how many days can you add or subtract before your meeting no longer qualifies as annual? The meaning of *annual meeting* was at issue in *Airgas, Inc. v. Air Products & Chemicals, Inc.*, 8 A.3d 1182 (Del. 2010).

13.29   Avoiding this uncertainty would require being more specific. You could, for example, specify that a meeting qualifies as the annual meeting for a given year if it's held anytime in that year.

ANYONE

13.30   If a provision encompasses anyone, consider using that word—*anyone*, as in *If anyone commences an involuntary case against the Company*. It's more concise than always using instead *any person or entity* or *any Person*. But don't use it in a sensitive context, as there's little relevant caselaw.

APPLICABLE

13.31   The adjective *applicable* is used in contracts in three ways.

Applicable Plus Noun

13.32   Sometimes *applicable* is used before a noun; in this context, it means "whichever is relevant." It's possible to use *applicable* appropriately in this manner:

> The Company shall provide the Employee with pension and welfare benefits and group employee benefits such as sick leave, vacation, group disability, and health, life, and accident insurance, and any similar indirect compensation offered generally to the Company's executive personnel, subject in each case to the terms of the *applicable* benefit plan or program.

13.33   But often, as in the three examples that follow, *applicable* should be omitted. That's because it inappropriately suggests that the provision applies to a subset of a whole, whereas in fact it applies to the whole. In particular, the *applicable* in *applicable law* is redundant: if a law doesn't apply to you, then you're not violating it.

> Recipient shall pay all ~~applicable~~ taxes incurred in connection with the Consultant's performance of services under this agreement.

> Conveyance of the Mortgage Notes and the Mortgages by the Company under this agreement is not subject to the bulk transfer laws of any ~~applicable~~ jurisdiction.

> Acme's execution and delivery of this agreement and performance of its obligations under this agreement do not violate any ~~applicable~~ law.

13.34   And often *applicable* is used where greater precision is called for:

> The Company shall pay the Employee a bonus of $33,000 not later than 30 days after each of the first three anniversaries of the Commencement Date, *on condition that the Employee is employed by the Company on the applicable anniversary* [read *except that the Company will not be required*

> *to make a payment with respect to a given anniversary if the Employee is then no longer employed by the Company*].

The Verb *To Be* Plus *Applicable*

13.35 *Applicable* is also used with the verb *to be*. Generally, you would be better off instead using the verb *apply*, as in the following examples. If you have a choice, it's better to use verbs rather than adjectives or abstract nouns (see 17.7).

> The provisions of this section 7.2 will *be applicable* [read *apply*] solely to work that the Tenant performs, or causes to be performed, before the Commencement Date.

> Any such modification or revocation … will not *be applicable* [read *apply*] to investment transactions to which the Advisor has committed the Company before the date the Advisor receives that notice.

As Applicable

13.36 The phrase *as applicable* is unobjectionable. It's equivalent to, but a little more succinct than, the phrase *as the case may be* (see 13.74):

> The terms of this warrant will apply to the shares of stock and other securities and property received on exercise of this warrant after consummation of that reorganization, consolidation, or merger or the effective date of dissolution following any such transfer, *as applicable*.

ARISING OUT OF OR RELATING TO

Implications

13.37 The phrase *arising out of or relating to* is a fixture of contracts, but there's a better alternative.

13.38 The phrase appears in dispute-resolution provisions (notably governing-law provisions, forum-selection provisions, and arbitration provisions), which often state that they cover all matters *arising out of or relating to* the contract in question. For example, the American Arbitration Association's standard arbitration clause refers to "Any controversy or claim arising out of or relating to this contract." The phrase also features in provisions that seek to limit liability.

13.39 Here's the concern that use of the phrase is intended to address:

13.40 If the parties to a transaction get into a dispute, they might bring against each other claims based on the contract between them or, instead or in addition, other kinds of claim: a tort claim, such as a claim for misrepresentation; a claim challenging a patent; or a claim authorized by statute.

13.41 Contracts offer predictability in business transactions. It follows that drafters would likely be inclined to arrange matters so a contract's provisions cover all possible disputes, not just those grounded in contract. (Whether that's in fact a good idea would depend on the circumstances.) And it's not surprising that drafters should avail themselves of *arising out of or relating to*, as *arising out of* expresses a narrower meaning than does *relating to*. Think of how one arises out of one's parents but is related to a broader group of people.

13.42   But is *arising out of or relating to* the best way to articulate this intended meaning? In a passage relating to drafting arbitration provisions, Morton Moskin, *Commercial Contracts: Strategies for Drafting and Negotiating* § 5.04[D][1] (2012) (citations omitted), summarizes the entrenched conventional wisdom regarding *arising out of or relating to*:

> It is essential that an arbitration clause cover precisely the subject matter that the parties intend to be submitted to arbitration. In most contracts that provide for arbitration, the parties intend that all disputes arising out of or relating to the contract be subject to arbitration, and in the United States the phrase "arising out or relating to" has become the model for broad arbitration clauses. Also effective is the phrase "in connection with." By using a more limited description—e.g., one which covers only disputes "arising out of" the contract, and not those "relating to" the contract—the parties create the risk that a court will conclude that the parties did not intend the clause to be broad and, in particular, intended to exclude tort claims, which may be considered to "relate to" the contract but not to "arise out of" the contract.

13.43   It would indeed be a good idea to state precisely the types of claims that are to be submitted to arbitration. But instead of precision, *arising out of or relating to* uses two vague standards that offer little predictability regarding what falls within the scope of the provision.

13.44   In particular, invoking the broader *relating to* standard could result in a party being unpleasantly surprised by the consequences of something unexpectedly falling within the scope of a provision. Imagine that in drafting a contract you provide that California law will govern all disputes *arising out of* it, since you know that from your perspective, California law would treat more favorably a key issue under the contract. But you also provided that California law will govern all disputes *relating to* the contract. Thereafter, you find yourself embroiled in a tangential dispute you hadn't anticipated, and you certainly didn't check the pros and cons of having that dispute governed by California law. In such a context, *relating to* could represent a roll of the dice.

13.45   For a case in which a party unsuccessfully argued that a dispute didn't fall within the scope of an arbitration provision that used *related to*, see *In re TFT-LCD (Flat Panel) Antitrust Litigation*, No. M 07-1827 SI, 2011 WL 2650689 (N.D. Cal. 6 July 2011).

An Alternative Approach

13.46   If you want to bring a broad but predictable set of claims within the scope of a provision, it would make sense to focus not on the contract but instead on the activities that the parties will be engaging in as part of the transaction contemplated by the contract. That would allow you to dispense with *or relating to*, as you wouldn't need to make the leap from contract claims to other claims—any claim, whatever its nature, would have to arise out of activities the parties engage in under the contract.

13.47 You could articulate this meaning by using *arising out of the subject matter of this agreement*, but you would be trading one kind of vagueness for another—there's no shortage of litigation regarding what *the subject matter of this agreement* means in a given contract. You would be better off instead saying what the subject matter of the contract is.

13.48 For example, if you're dealing with a confidentiality agreement, you could say *any disputes arising out of this agreement or the Recipient's handling, disclosure, or use of any Confidential Information.*

13.49 And if you want to make sure that a fee-shifting provision in a limited-liability-company operating agreement would apply to proceedings seeking dissolution, then instead of referring to "any action or proceeding brought to enforce any provision of this Agreement," say *any dispute arising out of this agreement, ownership of any Interest, or management or operations of the Company.* Regarding the dispute over the scope of the narrower alternative, see *Henderson v. Henderson Investment Properties, L.L.C.,* 148 Idaho 638, 227 P.3d 568 (2010).

13.50 This approach allows you to articulate clearly the intended meaning. Instead of establishing an overly narrow set—the contract—and relying on a vague standard to reach beyond it, you establish the relevant set—activities under the contract.

13.51 Plenty of courts have assessed the meaning of *arising out of or relating to,* but that hasn't served to make it any less vague. You can count on it continuing to blindside contract parties and their lawyers.

13.52 Some courts don't require broad language to hold that tort claims fall within a contract's dispute-resolution provisions. Scc, e.g., *Maynard v. BTI Group, Inc.,* 157 Cal. Rptr. 3d 148, 154 (Ct. App. 2013) (holding that a contract reference to "any dispute" included tort claims). But it's far better to be explicit than to rely on confusing contract language and hope that your dispute lands in front of a court with an expansive view of what claims are covered.

13.53 If in fact you want to limit the scope of a dispute-resolution provision to claims arising under the contract, it would be reckless to assume that using only *arising out of* would accomplish that. Instead, include a provision excluding extracontractual liability.

AS AMENDED

13.54 The phrase *as amended* can be used in a contract to modify references to statutes or to other contracts, as in *Acme shall comply with the Securities Act.* It's standard practice for drafters to tack on *as amended* after each such reference, the idea being to ensure that at any time compliance is measured against the statute or contract as it is then in effect.

13.55   But adding *as amended* serves no purpose: compliance with a statute or contract could be measured against the statute or contract only as it is then in effect, even without *as amended*.

13.56   If in a contract dated 3 November 2017 you say that since 1 January 2015 Acme has complied with the Securities Act, it would be unreasonable to interpret that to mean that throughout that period Acme complied with the Securities Act not as then in effect but as in effect in 1933 or on the date of the contract. You can't comply with a version of a statute that no longer exists or a version that has yet to exist.

13.57   And if in that same contract you say "Acme shall comply with the Securities Act," it would be unreasonable to interpret that to mean that thereafter complying with the Securities Act as in effect in 1933 or on the date of the contract, regardless of any later amendments, would constitute compliance with that obligation. Again, you can't comply with a version of a statute that no longer exists.

13.58   But a contract might also refer to a statute or another contract not regarding compliance but instead regarding an element of that statute or contract.

13.59   For example, a contract might refer to a term as it is defined in a statute or other contract. If the intent is to freeze the definition as it is on the date of the agreement, then refer to the statute or the other agreement *as in effect on the date of this agreement*. If the intent is to incorporate any future amendments to the definition, then refer to the statute or the other agreement *as then in effect*. If that leaves room for confusion, be more specific; for example, *as in effect on exercise of the Option*. (Simply saying *as amended* wouldn't specify what point in time you're referring to. And if the statute or contract hadn't been amended at the time in question, *as amended* wouldn't make sense.)

13.60   So when in a contract you're referring to an element of a statute or another contract, make it clear whether you're referring to the statute or the other contract as in effect on the date of the contract you're drafting or as in effect whenever that provision applies. But when referring to compliance with a statute or another contract, don't tack on *as amended*.

AS CONSIDERATION

13.61   In addition to featuring in the traditional recital of consideration (see 2.166), the word *consideration* is used in the body of the contract, particularly in language effecting a release. There are better alternatives.

13.62   Here are examples of *consideration* used in release language:

> As additional *consideration* for the assignment made under this agreement, the Assignee hereby releases the Assignor ... .

> In *consideration* of the payments made and benefits provided under this agreement, and except for any claims the Executive has under

> this agreement, the Executive (on behalf of himself and his personal representatives) hereby releases the Company ... .

> As further *consideration* for the amendments, consents, and waivers in this agreement, each Borrower hereby releases the Agent and each Lender ... .

> In exchange for the above-referenced *consideration*, the Employee hereby releases ... .

13.63   Consideration references in the body of the contract raise two issues. First, whether a contract calls something consideration is unrelated to whether as a matter of law it actually is consideration (see 2.173). So saying in the body of the contract that something is consideration accomplishes nothing other than adding a pointless legalism.

13.64   And second, the bargained-for exchange that constitutes consideration usually consists of more than single tit-for-tat promises. Instead, one party exchanges a parcel of promises in exchange for the other party's parcel of promises. Why single out one promise in particular as being supported by consideration?

13.65   It's likely that drafters allude to consideration in release language because often it's an add-on to the deal. Because releases can seem free-standing, drafters are inclined to reiterate the notion of consideration to tie the release to the deal. To accomplish that using the word *consideration*, the simplest alternative would be the phrase *in consideration*, which is used colloquially; it expresses the notion of exchange. But it would be even simpler and clearer to say that the release is *in exchange for* a specified action or promise by the party being released, omitting any mention of consideration.

AS LIQUIDATED DAMAGES AND NOT AS A PENALTY

13.66   The phrase *as liquidated damages and not as a penalty* occurs in provisions in which the parties, instead of having actual damages determined in a dispute, specify what damages a party is to pay on breach of a particular obligation. But it's formulaic—it would be better to address the underlying issue more clearly.

13.67   24 *Williston on Contracts* § 65:1 (footnotes omitted) provides some background:

> Under the fundamental principle of freedom of contract, the parties to a contract have a broad right to stipulate in their agreement the amount of damages recoverable in the event of a breach, and the courts will generally enforce such an agreement, so long as the amount agreed upon is not unconscionable, is not determined to be an illegal penalty, and is not otherwise violative of public policy.

13.68   But if the parties say that a given payment constitutes liquidated damages and not a penalty, doesn't that settle it? Apparently not. According to the

Restatement (Second) of Contracts § 356 cmt. c (1981), "Neither the parties' actual intention as to its validity nor their characterization of the term as one for liquidated damages or a penalty is significant in determining whether the term is valid."

13.69   But it doesn't follow that instead of saying "Acme shall pay Widgetco $3 million, as liquidated damages and not as a penalty," you might as well just say "Acme shall pay Widgetco $3 million." That's because courts have given varying weight to the language used by the parties. See, e.g., *Ludlow Valve Manufacturing Co. v. City of Chicago*, 181 Ill. App. 388 (1913), in which the court said, "The fact that parties fix a sum to be paid in case of a breach of the contract and call that sum 'liquidated damages' is not conclusive, but is one of the circumstances tending to prove the actual intent of the parties." (Recent Illinois cases have cited *Ludlow*, so it's still good law.)

13.70   Because at least some courts pay attention to how a contract characterizes a payment to be made on breach of an obligation, include that sort of characterization when providing for liquidated damages in a contract.

13.71   But do more than just trot out *as liquidated damages and not as a penalty*. It's sufficiently rote and terse as to be jargon. Because drafters and their clients don't give it much thought, courts would be entitled not to pay much attention to it either.

13.72   Here's a more meaningful way of saying that liquidated damages don't constitute a penalty:

> Acme acknowledges that the actual damages likely to result from breach by Acme of its obligations under this section X are difficult to estimate on the date of this agreement and would be difficult for Widgetco to prove. The parties intend that Acme's payment of the Liquidated Damages Amount would compensate Widgetco for any such breach. They do not intend for it be a penalty for any such breach.

13.73   It would also be helpful to explain why actual damages are difficult to estimate.

AS THE CASE MAY BE

13.74   When in a contract a sentence provides for alternative courses of action, often one or more sentences that follow address the consequences. When the contract is signed, it won't be known which of the alternative courses of action will be relevant, so those sentences must track the alternative scenarios. But they must make it clear that whichever choice is made regarding the initial sentence, that choice will flow through to the sentences that follow. That's the function of *as applicable* (see 13.36) and *whichever applies*, and it's also the function of *as the case may be*:

> Able shall transfer the Shares to Baker or Charlie no later than 31 March 2018. No later than five days after that transfer, Baker or Charlie, *as the case may be,* shall enter into a noncompetition agreement with Widgetco in the form of exhibit A.

13.75 But generally you can convey the required meaning more economically than by using *as the case may be*. For example, in the above example one could refer to *the transferee* instead of *Baker or Charlie, as the case may be*.

13.76 And often *as the case may be* is misused, in that it's tacked on to an expression of simple alternatives:

> "Date of Termination" means the date on which a Covered Change in Control Termination or Covered Termination Prior to a Change in Control occurs, ~~as the case may be~~.

AT LEAST ONE OF X AND Y

13.77 Use only *at least one of X and Y*. Don't use *or*. Or you could say instead *one or more of X and Y*. Unfortunately, that recommendation requires detailed explication. That's because in a well-known case, *SuperGuide Corp. v. DirecTV Enterprises, Inc.*, 358 F.3d 870 (Fed. Cir. 2004), the U.S. Court of Appeals for the Federal Circuit (the only appellate-level court with the jurisdiction to hear appeals in patent cases) botched its analysis of *at least one of X and Y*.

The Court's Analysis

13.78 Here's part of the language at issue, from a patent claim:

> An online television program schedule system comprising:
>
> first means for storing at least one of a desired program start time, a desired program end time, a desired program service, and a desired program type; ... .

13.79 Does this refer to storing at least one unit within each of the four categories, or storing at least one category?

13.80 Here's what the court said (footnotes and citations omitted):

> In interpreting this phrase, the district court concluded that the term "a desired," which precedes "at least one of," is repeated for each category and because the final category in the criteria list is introduced by "and a desired," the list is conjunctive. The court also concluded that accepting SuperGuide's position that "at least one of" refers only to one category of the criteria would contradict the purpose of the invention as described in the written description, as depicted in Figure 4a and recited in claim 1. Thus, the court construed the phrase "at least one of ... and" as meaning "at least one of each desired criterion; that is, at least one of a desired program start time, a desired program end time, a desired program service and a desired program type. The phrase does not mean one or more of the desired criteria but at a minimum one category thereof."
>
> On appeal, SuperGuide contends that the claim phrase "at least one of" unambiguously requires the selection and storage of one

or more of the four listed criteria (start time, end time, service channel, or type) and does not require storing all four criteria. …

DirecTV counters that the district court's construction is supported by the patentee's use of the conjunctive word "and" and by the grammatical rule requiring that the phrase "at least one of" be applied to each category in the list. …

…

We agree with DirecTV. The phrase "at least one of" precedes a series of categories of criteria, and the patentee used the term "and" to separate the categories of criteria, which connotes a conjunctive list. A common treatise on grammar teaches that "an article of [sic] a preposition applying to all the members of the series must either be used only before the first term or else be repeated before each term." William Strunk, Jr. & E.B. White, *The Elements of Style* 27 (4th ed. 2000). Thus, "[i]n spring, summer, or winter" means "in spring, in summer, or in winter." Applying this grammatical principle here, the phrase "at least one of" modifies each member of the list, i.e., each category in the list. Therefore, the district court correctly interpreted this phrase as requiring that the user select at least one value for each category; that is, at least one of a desired program start time, a desired program end time, a desired program service, and a desired program type.

13.81   The court also suggested that the outcome would have been different if the language at issue had used as a conjunction *or* instead of *and*. Specifically, in footnote 10 the court said, "SuperGuide does not articulate its argument that 'at least one of' means 'one or more of the four listed criteria' without using the term 'or' to separate the four listed categories." It then noted that an earlier Federal Circuit decision had interpreted a claim constructed as "at least one of A, B, or C" as covering only A, only B, only C, or any combination of the three.

Critique

13.82   The court's analysis makes no sense. First, the passage from *The Elements of Style* is irrelevant. It simply states that as a matter of writing style it would be awkward to say *in spring, summer, or in winter* instead of one of the two alternatives the court quoted. It has nothing to do with identifying ambiguity.

13.83   And second, there's no question that the phrase "at least one of" modifies each member of the list, as the court says. That's not the issue. Instead, the issue is whether "one of" refers to an item within a category or to the category itself.

13.84   So the "Therefore" that begins the final sentence of the extract above is unearned—nothing has been demonstrated.

13.85   The meaning suggested by SuperGuide is the more natural reading, but it's conceivable that a not-particularly-skilled drafter might have worded it that way even if they had intended to express the DirecTV meaning.

So one could imagine a court holding that the language at issue conveys the *SuperGuide* meaning or holding that it's ambiguous. The one conclusion that's implausible is the one the court arrived at—that the language at issue conveys unambiguously the meaning sought by DirecTV.

13.86 Also problematic is the court's suggestion that the outcome would have been different if the language at issue had used *or* instead of *and*. That too makes no sense. For one thing, as described above, the possible alternative meanings of the language at issue don't arise from use of *and*.

13.87 Furthermore, *and* is actually the logical choice. Consider the following simple examples, in which *at least one of X and Y* is used with just units not categories:

[1]   at least one of Tom, Dick, and Harry

[1a]   *at least one of Tom, Dick, or Harry

13.88 The reference is to at least one of a group, making *and* the appropriate choice, as in [1]. Using *or* instead would suggest that one is referring to at least one out of one of the three. That doesn't make sense. Option 1[a] is ungrammatical—hence the asterisk. (For discussion of this issue regarding an analogous usage, *the earlier of X and Y*, see 13.809.)

Recommendation

13.89 Beyond the ramifications for the litigants, the court's opinion in *SuperGuide* is unfortunate. Specifically, it has set an unhelpful precedent by suggesting that the outcome would have been different if the language at issue had used as a conjunction *or* instead of *and*.

13.90 Although it's a patent case, it wouldn't be surprising if a court considering the phrase in the context of a contract dispute were to consult *SuperGuide*, given that the *SuperGuide* court claimed that its holding was based on "the plain and ordinary meaning of the disputed language." And anecdotal evidence indicates that some drafters have concluded, based on *SuperGuide*, that one should always use *or* after *at least one of*.

13.91 Instead, courts and those who work with contracts should ignore *SuperGuide* and do as follows: Use only *at least one of X and Y*. Don't use *or*. To avoid problems, pay attention to how you use this phrase. If you're referring to units, as in [1], there's nothing to consider—the meaning is clear, and furthermore *SuperGuide* doesn't apply. If you use it in relation to categories, make it explicit that you're referring to categories, as in [2] (the meaning sought by SuperGuide). If you use it in relation to units within categories, make it explicit that you're referring to units, and furthermore make it clear whether you're referring to units in all the categories, as in [3] (the meaning sought by DirecTV), or fewer than all, as in [4].

[2]   at least one of the following categories: nuts, bolts, and screws

[3]   at least one unit in each of the following categories: nuts, bolts, and screws

[4]   at least one unit in [at least] one of the following categories: nuts, bolts, and screws

13.92   You can convey the same meaning as *at least one of X and Y* by saying *one or more of X and Y*. The same analysis applies to both formulations, but the latter has the advantage of being simpler.

ATTORN

13.93   *Attorn* is a term of art, but it's unnecessary. Here's how *Garner's Dictionary of Legal Usage*, at 95, defines the related noun:

> **attornment** has two analogous senses, the first relating to personal property and the second relating to land. It may mean either (1) "an act by a bailee in possession of goods on behalf of one person acknowledging that he will hold the goods on behalf of someone else" ... ; or (2) a person's agreement to hold land as the tenant of someone other than the original landlord; a tenant's act of recognizing that rent is to be paid to a different person. Both senses are used in [British English] and [American English].

13.94   Although in the United States real-estate lawyers are familiar with *attorn*, it's likely to befuddle anyone else. Some terms of art add unnecessary complexity (see 1.7). *Attorn* is an example of such a term of art—in a provision effecting an attornment, the word *attorn* simply expresses consent. Use that word instead:

> Tenant shall *attorn* [read *consent*] to any party's succeeding to the Landlord's interest in the Premises, whether by purchase, foreclosure, deed in lieu of foreclosure, power of sale, or otherwise, at that party's request, and shall execute any agreements confirming *that attornment* [read *the Tenant's consent*] as that party reasonably requests.

13.95   If nevertheless you feel you must refer to attornment, use *Attornment* as a section heading.

13.96   Interestingly, in Canada the word *attorn* is also used in connection with consent to a court having personal jurisdiction. In addition to occurring in legislation and court opinions, it appears in contracts:

> The parties to this agreement hereby *attorn* to the nonexclusive jurisdiction of the courts of the Province of Quebec.

> Lender hereby irrevocably *attorns* to the nonexclusive jurisdiction of the courts of the Provinces of Ontario regarding all matters arising out of this power of attorney.

13.97   As with other uses of *attorn*, the problem with this use of *attorn* is that the meaning sought to be conveyed has nothing to do with the doctrinal connotations of *attorn*. Here too, all that's being conveyed is consent.

13.98   Canadian use of *attorn* in this context highlights two additional problems. First, some Canadian commentary suggests that consenting by contract to the jurisdiction of specified courts doesn't constitute attornment. A term of art can be used inadvertently in contexts that are inconsistent with doctrinal subtleties attached to the word, and this use of *attorn* might be an example of that.

13.99   Second, Canadians use *attorn* in a way that drafters in no other jurisdiction do. The result is pointless inconsistency that might create confusion in cross-border transactions.

AUTOMATICALLY

13.100   For contract drafting, *automatically* is often dispensable.

13.101   For example, eliminating *automatically* from each of the following examples wouldn't affect its meaning, as it would nevertheless be clear that the example doesn't involve action by the parties. (A drafter might be inclined to use instead *immediately* in the second and third examples, but even without *immediately*, the reasonable reader would conclude that the result in question would occur all at once.)

> ... and restrictions on any such awards will ~~automatically~~ lapse at midnight at the beginning of the Date of Termination ... .

> ... when that restriction is lifted, that property will ~~automatically~~ become part of the Collateral ... .

> On occurrence of a Change of Control, all unvested SARs will ~~automatically~~ vest ...

13.102   But in other contexts *automatically* has a role to play. Consider this example:

> ... and each 1 January thereafter, this agreement will be [automatically] extended for one additional year unless not later than ... .

13.103   This example is in the passive voice, and the most likely candidate for the missing *by*-agent (see 3.12) is *the parties*. Without *automatically*, this example could conceivably be understood as suggesting that action by the parties would be required for the term of the agreement to be extended. Adding *automatically* would make it clear that's not the case.

13.104   Sometimes *automatically* is inappropriate because it suggests that action will take place, whereas a legal fiction is being established. Legal fictions are best expressed using *deem* (see 13.216):

> ... the distribution terms and Acme's other rights to that payment or benefit *will be automatically* [read *will be deemed to have been*] modified to conform to the tax law requirements to ensure that constructive receipt does not occur.

BASIS (INCLUDING *TIMELY*)

13.105   Be careful how you use the word *basis*. As noted in *Garner's Modern English Usage*, it "often signals verbosity in adverbial constructions."

13.106   So instead of *on a daily basis*, try *daily*, as in "Interest will accrue *on a daily basis* [read *daily*]." In other words, use *daily* as an adverb rather than as an adjective. Analogous fixes would take care of *on a weekly basis, on a regular* *basis*, and other such phrases. And if you can't simply omit *on an ongoing basis*, address timing specifically.

13.107   The same applies to *on a pro-rata basis*, as in "Those shares will be allocated *on a pro-rata basis* [read *pro rata*] to the Remaining Holders."

13.108   In *on a timely basis*, *in a timely manner*, and *in a timely fashion*, the word *timely* is an adjective. But in American English *timely* can also be an adverb, so in the interest of concision, you would be better off replacing those phrases with *timely*, as in "a material adverse effect on the Company's ability to *perform on a timely basis* [read *timely perform*] its obligations under any Transaction Document." (*Garner's Dictionary of Legal Usage*, at 895, notes that "This adverbial use of *timely* is archaic in [British English].")

13.109   Sometimes eliminating *basis* requires a bigger fix, as in this example: "Acme shall not enter into any transaction with any Affiliate *unless that transaction is made on an arm's-length basis and* [read *other than an arm's-length transaction that*] has been approved by a majority of the disinterested directors of the Company."

BECAUSE

13.110   Contracts regulate conduct rather than explicate, so drafters should have little need for the word *because* in the body of the contract (see 1.57). But *because* does occur in conditional clauses, to express the concept *If X because of Y, then Z*. That raises the possibility of a dispute: does Y have to be the sole cause of X, or is it enough that Y was one of several factors contributing to X?

13.111   That's an issue that the U.S. Supreme Court addressed in *Gross v. FBL Financial Services, Inc.*, 557 U.S. 167 (2009), holding that a statute's requirement that an adverse employment action be taken "because of" age meant that a plaintiff must prove that age was the "but-for" cause of the employer's adverse decision.

13.112   So whenever you use *because* in a contract, consider being specific regarding the type of causation required.

BELIEF

13.113   It docsn't make sense to state categorically in a contract the legal implications of facts as they exist on the date of the agreement. Instead, it would be up to a court to decide what those implications are—the best a party could do is give its opinion. In such contexts, it's preferable to use belief to qualify that statement of fact, as in *The parties believe this agreement complies with the requirements of section 409A of the IRS Code.*

13.114   But it's routine for drafters to present legal opinions as statements of fact. Examples include statements regarding topics also covered by standard legal opinions delivered at closing—formation, existence, enforceability of obligations, no violations of law, and other matters.

13.115 Such statements don't assert facts within the knowledge of the party making the statement. Instead, they allocate risk. Although often it would go against long-established convention, it would be clearer, but not necessarily more convenient, to qualify those statements of fact using belief, supplemented by provisions addressing indemnification, termination fees, or another risk-allocation mechanism.

BETWEEN OR AMONG

13.116 Some contracts refer to agreements or some other activity *between or among* the parties, as in *all prior understandings and agreements, whether oral or written, between or among the parties.*

13.117 This usage is presumably prompted by the conventional wisdom that one speaks of a contract as being *between* the parties if there are only two parties and *among* the parties if there are more than two. As noted in 2.49 in connection with the introductory clause, there's no basis in English usage for this distinction. If the concern is that using *between* in referring to agreements of the three or more parties to a contract would cover only agreements between any two of the parties, that could be resolved by saying *agreements between two or more of the parties.*

13.118 But thanks to copy-and-paste, be prepared to find *between or among* in contracts between only two parties, where it would be irrelevant.

BOOKS AND RECORDS

13.119 In the standard phrase *books and records*, the word *books* is redundant.

13.120 *Books* could mean corporate books, which *Black's Law Dictionary* defines as "Written records of a corporation's activities and business transactions." Or it could mean books of account, also known as shop books, which *Black's* defines as "Records of original entry maintained in the usual course of business by a shopkeeper, trader, or other businessperson."

13.121 *Black's* doesn't offer a definition of *records*. But for our purposes, all that matters is that the *Black's* definitions in the previous paragraph lead with the word *records*—books are an example of records. That's why in the phrase *books and records*, the word *books* is redundant.

13.122 If you want to capture the narrower, accounting-related meaning of *books*, you could use *accounting records* (the term used in the UK Companies Act 2006) or *financial records*. Using a narrower term might spare a contract party an unpleasant surprise when the other party asks to audit many types of records.

13.123 Some drafters might be inclined to leave the phrase *books and records* as is, because it features in the Delaware General Corporation Law (particularly in section 220, which addresses the rights of a shareholder to inspect the "books and records" of the corporation), as well as in other statutes. But the vast majority of contract references to "books and records" are unrelated to use of the phrase in statutes. And even if a statute reference to "books and records" were related to a contract, that's no reason to parrot the statute's mushy terminology. If an explicit link to the statute is required, you would be better off saying something like "in accordance with" the statute in question.

BUY, PURCHASE

13.124   The verb *purchase* is used in contracts more often than the verb *buy*. Given that simpler words generally are better, why not use *buy* instead of *purchase*? Here's what that would look like:

> Acme hereby *purchases* [read *buys*] the Shares ... .

13.125   But aside from ingrained habit, an obstacle to making this change might be the noun form of *buy*:

> *The buying* of the Shares ... .

13.126   The gerund *buying* is awkward. By contrast, the noun *purchase* doesn't pose this problem. And the past participle *bought* is more awkward than *purchased*.

13.127   References to a fundamental concept in a contract are easier to read if you use related verb and noun forms to express that concept. It follows that the brevity of the verb *buy* is more than offset by the awkwardness of *bought* and the noun form of *buy*. Use the verb *purchase*. (For a similar analysis regarding the verb *end*, see 13.257.)

BYLAWS

13.128   *Bylaws* is spelled both with and without a hyphen. For example, *Black's Law Dictionary* gives a definition for *bylaw* but notes that it's sometimes spelled *by-law*.

13.129   It appears that *bylaws* is gaining the upper hand. For example, the 1915 edition of *Robert's Rules of Order Revised* uses *by-laws*, but the current edition of *Robert's Rules of Order Newly Revised* uses *bylaws*. And although its predecessor used *by-laws*, the Massachusetts Business Corporation Act, effective 2004, uses *bylaws*. So use *bylaws*.

13.130   But according to *Garner's Modern English Usage*, both the spelling and the sense of *bylaw* differ on the two sides of the Atlantic:

> In [American English], *bylaws* are most commonly a corporation's administrative provisions that are either attached to the articles of incorporation or kept privately. In [British English], *bylaws* are regulations made by a local authority or corporation, such as a town or a railway.
>
> The spelling without the *-e-* is preferred in [American English]. Though etymologically inferior, *byelaw* (sometimes hyphenated) is common in [British English].

CERTAIN

13.131   In addition to featuring in the archaism *that certain* (see 13.808), the word *certain*—meaning "not named or described, though definite and perhaps known"—is sometimes used inappropriately to refer to a subset of a whole. Here's one example: *certain assets* [read *the assets*] *listed in schedule B.* Here's another: *Executive may provide certain services* [read *provide services*] *to Acme, if provision of those services does not … .*

CERTIFY

13.132   The verb *certify* is commonplace in contracts, as in this sentence: *At the Seller's request, the Customer shall certify in writing to the Seller that the Customer has complied with these requirements.*

13.133   But in such contexts, *certify* isn't the best choice. *Black's Law Dictionary* gives as a definition of *certify* "To attest as being true or as meeting certain criteria." That certainly fits, but *certify* implies a level of formality that isn't necessary in this context—it suggests use of a certificate, which *Black's Law Dictionary* defines as "A document in which a fact is formally attested."

13.134   In the example above, the Customer should be able to comply with the obligation in question by sending a one-sentence letter stating that it has done whatever was required. That could be expressed by saying *the Customer shall notify the Seller that … .* And if the agreement has a notices provision that says that notices must be in writing, you wouldn't need to specify that this particular notice must be in writing.

CHANGE IN CONTROL, CHANGE OF CONTROL

13.135   The phrases *change in control* and *change of control* are equally acceptable, and searches on the U.S. Securities and Exchange Commission's EDGAR system and on Google suggest that they're used with similar frequency. But to facilitate copying and pasting between contracts, pick one phrase and stick with it.

CLOSING

13.136   Drafters get to make small decisions as well as big ones. One such small decision is whether to use the definite article *the* with the word *closing*, as in this example:

> … under a contract to take effect on or before [the] Closing.

13.137   Although many drafters would omit *the* from this example, it would be better to retain it. To explain why, this section considers use of the word *closing* in contracts.

Gerundial Noun

13.138   A gerund is a noun formed by taking a verb and adding the suffix *-ing*. A gerund can act like a noun—in which case it's known as a gerundial noun—or it can act more like a verb.

13.139   The word *closing* can mean the moment a transaction is consummated. That's how it's used in this example:

> The financial statements of Company to be prepared after the Agreement Date and prior to the Closing (A) will be true, accurate, and complete in all material respects … .

13.140   In this context, *Closing* acts like a noun in three respects. First, it begins with the definite article *the*. Definite articles usually come before nouns. Second, in this context *Closing* could be modified by an adjective, for example *first*, instead of by an adverb. Adjectives usually modify nouns. And third, because *Closing* is a defined term meaning the closing of the transaction contemplated by the agreement in question, the object of *the Closing* in effect is the prepositional phrase *of the transaction contemplated by this agreement*. The phrase is headed by the preposition *of*; prepositional phrases that start with *of* usually follow nouns.

Other Forms

13.141   In the sentence *Closing deals is hard work*, the word *closing* is part of the gerund phrase *closing deals*. (This use of *closing* isn't one you would expect to find in contracts.)

13.142   In this context, *closing* refers to a process, not a moment dividing the time before the deal and the time after the deal. As such, it differs from the gerundial-noun example in 13.139, in that in this example *closing* acts as verb in two respects. First, in this example, *closing* could be modified by an adverb, for example *quickly*, not an adjective. And the object, *deals*, comes right after the gerund, just like it would after an ordinary verb, not inside a prepositional phrase like the one starting with *of* in the previous example.

13.143   In contracts, *closing* is also used as a present participle (as in, *if the Qualified Preferred Equity Investment is closing concurrently with the Permitted Direct Assumption*) and as an attributive noun (as in, *the average closing price for a single Share*).

Making the Right Choice

13.144   What drafters should take away from this is that when *closing* is used to mean the moment a transaction is consummated, it's acting as a gerundial noun—use it with the definite article *the*. That's the case with use of *closing* in the example in 13.139.

13.145   Omitting *the* from that example would suggest that *closing* is being used as a verb and refers to the process of consummating a transaction. That doesn't make sense. It would also raise the question, Closing what?

13.146 Omitting *the* in this context makes the prose a tiny bit awkward, although it wouldn't result in confusion. But if you're the one doing the drafting, you might as well get this use of *closing* right.

COGNIZANT

13.147 *Cognizant* is a formal word meaning knowledgeable of something, especially through personal experience. It's sometimes used in contracts, but you can usually dispense with it, as in this example:

> The Contributor acknowledges that an investment in the Securities involves substantial risk and the Contributor is *fully cognizant of and understands* [read *aware of*] all of the risk factors related to the Securities.

13.148 *Cognizant* is also used in an inelegant term of art in federal contracting: *cognizant agency*. It's defined by statute, so it's the appropriate term to use if you want to invoke the arrangement provided for by statute. But be on the lookout for the phrase *cognizant agency* used inappropriately when the intended meaning is simply *relevant*.

COMPETITIVE

13.149 The word *competitive* is routinely misused in contracts. That's not surprising, given that it's routinely misused in legal and business writing generally.

13.150 *Competitive* means (1) "of, involving, or based on competition" and (2) "likely to succeed in competition." In the following provision, *competitive* is used to express the first meaning:

> The Executive acknowledges the highly *competitive* nature of the Company's business.

13.151 And in this provision, it's used, albeit awkwardly, to express the second meaning:

> The Customer shall give VEM every opportunity to be included on Approved Vendor Lists for materials and components that VEM can supply, and if VEM is *competitive* with other suppliers with respect to reasonable and unbiased criteria for acceptance established by the Customer, the Customer shall include VEM on those Approved Vendor Lists.

13.152 But *competitive* is also used in contexts where the adjective *competing* or the verb *to compete* would be a better fit:

> In this agreement, the term "**Competitive** [read **Competing**] **Business**" means any business that is similar to or *competitive* [read *competes*] with the business of the Company for which Executive has had direct responsibility.

COMPLETE AND ACCURATE

13.153   Generally, you should be able to do without some or all of *complete and accurate*.

13.154   For purposes of an obligation to compile data, it's hard to imagine that data could be accurate without being complete—that, for example, a court might accept the argument that a database containing names of only half of Acme's customers is accurate because the information provided for each of those customers is accurate.

13.155   So you should be able to dispense with *complete*:

> Excelsior shall maintain ~~complete and~~ accurate books of account.

> The Servicer shall maintain ~~complete and~~ accurate records pertaining to each Contract to enable it to comply with this agreement.

13.156   But if possible, dispense with both *accurate* and *complete*. For example, instead of saying *Acme shall maintain an accurate database containing the following customer information*, say *Acme shall maintain a database that lists for all customers the following information*. Inherent in that obligation is the requirement that the information be accurate, even if you don't use the word *accurate*.

13.157   *Accurate* wouldn't encompass *complete* in a provision that seeks to confirm that the data in question satisfy some requirement stated in the agreement:

> All information that Acme has furnished to Widgetco under section 5 is *complete and accurate.*

13.158   But more to the point, the section 5 referred to in the previous example presumably states that Acme must provide Widgetco with certain information. It would be more economical to address adequacy of that information by referring to Acme's compliance with section 5:

> Acme has complied with its obligations under section 5.

13.159   When you're referring to copies of something, you could safely do without both elements of *accurate* and *complete*. After all, *copy* means "a full reproduction." If Acme gives you a photocopy of its certificate of incorporation but omits page 6, Acme would be hard pressed to claim it had given you a copy. If that makes you nervous, it would make more sense to retain *complete* and dispense with *accurate*.

13.160   But it would be unproductive to eliminate one element from *complete and accurate* and then find yourself in a fight over whether the remainder is in fact as comprehensive as you think it is. So first determine whether you can dispense entirely with *complete and accurate*. If you decide it would be prudent to retain at least one element, consider retaining the entire phrase. Unlike some other redundant synonyms, the only drawback to *complete and accurate* is two superfluous words. That's a small price to pay for not risking a fight.

CONSEQUENTIAL DAMAGES

13.161 Here's a representative example of a provision excluding certain types of damages:

> Neither party will be responsible or held liable for any consequential, special, or incidental losses or damages.

13.162 Sellers routinely ask for such provisions, and buyers routinely accept including them. But many lawyers and their clients have an uncertain grasp of what such provisions are meant to accomplish. As explained in this section, there are better alternatives.

Terminology

13.163 Even absent any limitation, for a nonbreaching party to recover damages for losses caused by breach of a contract, generally those losses must be a reasonably foreseeable consequence of the breach. Contract damages aren't intended to compensate parties for remote losses.

13.164 Understanding the implications of excluding certain types of damages by reference to that baseline is challenging. The terms of art used are, to varying degrees, difficult to define clearly, given that each term expresses a vague standard and given the inconsistent guidance provided by the wealth of related caselaw in different jurisdictions. Here's a rough guide:

13.165 *Direct damages.* These are damages that one would reasonably expect to arise from the breach in question, without considering any special circumstances of the nonbreaching party; also known as "general" damages.

13.166 *Incidental damages.* These are expenses incurred by a buyer on rejection of nonconforming goods delivered by the seller in breach of contract, or by a seller on wrongful rejection by a buyer of conforming goods delivered by the seller to the buyer.

13.167 *Consequential damages.* These are losses sustained by the nonbreaching party that are attributable to any special circumstances of the nonbreaching party that the parties knew of when they entered into the contract; in other words, consequential damages encompass all contractually recoverable damages that are neither direct nor incidental damages; also known as "special" damages.

13.168 It's clear what consequential damages don't do: they don't compensate a buyer for remote or speculative losses, which shouldn't even constitute losses. But many people are unaware of that. Here's what Glenn D. West & Sara G. Duran, *Reassessing the "Consequences" of Consequential Damage Waivers in Acquisition Agreements*, 63 Business Lawyer 777, 783–84 (2008) [referred to below as *West & Duran*], says on that subject (footnotes omitted):

> [T]o define "consequential damages" as those losses that are so remote that they were beyond the contemplation of the parties at the time they entered into the contract is to define consequential damages as losses for which the law does not allow recovery in

contract, regardless of any provision excluding such damages. Yet, many sellers purport to require waivers of consequential damages because they believe consequential damages relate to losses beyond those that the breaching party would have ordinarily and reasonably foreseen or contemplated.

The rules limiting all contractual damages to those that are "natural, probable, and reasonably foreseeable" impose a judicially created "rule of reasonableness" that generally limits the extent to which any damages, including consequential damages, may be awarded for breach of contract. As a result, even in the absence of a contractual waiver of consequential damages, this standard of reasonableness creates limits on the extent of the non-breaching party's recovery for losses that the breaching party did not otherwise specifically agree to bear.

Problems

13.169 Given that background, excluding certain types of damages can be unhelpful for five reasons. First, many of those seeking to exclude certain types of damages assume incorrectly that otherwise the nonbreaching party could recover remote damages.

13.170 Second, the terms of art used in language excluding consequential damages are ill-understood and so are conducive to dispute.

13.171 Third, it can be arbitrary to exclude certain types of damages recoverable under the contract but not others.

13.172 Fourth, some provisions pile on the exclusions in a way that makes no sense. For example, one product offered in October 2011 by Rocket Lawyer, a mass-market seller of contract templates, was a confidentiality agreement that included a provision excluding liability for "direct, indirect, special, or consequential damages." But "special" and "consequential" are generally treated as synonyms by courts. And if a contract excludes both "direct" and "indirect" damages, that could lead to a fight over whether all damages are excluded or whether the contract is void. See *Innovate Technology Solutions, L.P. v. Youngsoft, Inc.*, 418 S.W.3d 148, 151 (Tex. App. 2013).

13.173 And fifth, if the recipient discloses confidential information other than as provided in a confidentiality agreement, any damages that the disclosing party suffers would likely consist of consequential damages, so excluding consequential damages would deprive the disclosing party of a meaningful remedy.

Alternatives

13.174 As stated in *West & Duran*, at 781, "While sellers have legitimate concerns over their potential liability for breach ... , there are other means of addressing those concerns without the use of terms that have such uncertain meanings." Given the problems with conventional provisions excluding damages, drafters should consider instead addressing the seller's concerns directly. Here's an example:

> Neither party will be liable for breach-of-contract damages that the breaching party could not reasonably have foreseen at the time of breach.

13.175 *West & Duran*, at 806, in effect endorses this approach: "Instead of waiving 'consequential' damages, buyers should seek waivers of 'remote' or 'speculative' damages." This provision simply states what a court would likely conclude anyway, but it serves a purpose, because many sellers don't understand that a buyer is entitled to only those damages that are foreseeable.

13.176 If that doesn't satisfy the seller—it wants to exclude some otherwise recoverable damages—you could put an absolute cap on damages as an alternative to engaging in the arbitrary and uncertain exercise of excluding certain types of damages.

13.177 If nevertheless you want to limit certain types of damages, consider that it would be simpler to describe what damages are included rather than those that are excluded. In the case of sale of goods, presumably you would articulate, without using those terms of art, expectancy damages (the value of the thing promised less the value of the thing delivered) and the difference between the cost of cover (purchase of substitute goods) and the contract price, with perhaps a cap built in.

13.178 If you also, or instead, want to exclude certain types of damages, it would be best not to use the phrase *consequential damages*, given the widespread confusion regarding what it actually means. And from the seller's perspective, it's risky to rely on excluding consequential damages, as courts are prone to holding that elements of damages that the seller might have intended to exclude are in fact direct rather than consequential. See, for example, two English cases, *GB Gas Holdings Ltd v. Accenture (UK) Ltd* [2009] EWHC 2734 (Comm) and *McCain Foods (GB) Ltd v. Eco-Tec (Europe) Ltd* [2011] EWHC 66.

13.179 So consider being specific about what you're excluding. Don't use legal terms of art; instead, refer to whatever types of damages are of concern. (But see 13.181 regarding problems with excluding lost profits.) Whatever types of damages you include, think through the implications. To get a sense of what that might involve, *West & Duran*, at 795–804, explores two hypothetical situations and the different types of damages involved.

13.180 Finally, a buyer might be more willing to live with a limited range of damages if it's entitled to liquidated damages.

Lost Profits

13.181 Excluding lost profits can be problematic. For example, in *Biotronik A.G. v. Conor Medsystems Ireland, Ltd.*, 11 N.E.3d 676 (N.Y. 2014), the court held that the lost profits sought by a distributor constituted general damages (also known as direct damages) that were recoverable under the liability-limiting provision at issue; they weren't consequential damages. One judge dissented, with two others concurring. See also *Luminara Worldwide*,

LLC v. Liown Electronics Co., No. 14-cv-03103-SRN-FLN, 2017 WL 1064887, at *5 (D. Minn. 27 Feb. 2017) (holding that because of the nature of the transaction, lost profits arising during the term of the contract were properly considered direct damages).

13.182   So even *lost profits*, which would seem less slippery than *consequential damages*, is still tricky. Here are the implications for the contract drafter:

13.183   If your liability-limiting provision refers to consequential damages and doesn't mention lost profits, whether a court would conclude that lost profits constitute consequential damages would depend on the context, and different judges might reach different conclusions.

13.184   If your liability-limiting provision says that consequential damages include lost profits, in a dispute a court might decide that the lost profits at issue are general damages and so don't constitute lost profits that fall within the scope of the liability-limiting provision.

13.185   If your liability-limiting provision refers to lost profits without mentioning consequential damages, that seems arbitrary—it doesn't reflect that lost profits have different implications in different contexts.

13.186   So disputes over lost profits always have the potential to create confusion, however you address, or don't address, the issue. That's one more reason for considering alternatives to the traditional liability-limiting provision.

CONTINUOUSLY, CONTINUOUS

13.187   Generally, the word *continuously* is redundant. That's because unless you specify otherwise, a provision will apply continuously:

> The Company ... shall use reasonable efforts to keep the Registration Statement, with respect to each Holder, ~~continuously~~ effective under the Securities Act until the earlier to occur of ... .

> The Borrower (and each applicable Credit Party) shall ... diligently ~~and continuously~~ enforce the material obligations of the ground lessor or other obligor thereunder; ... .

13.188   In some contexts, the fix might be alternative wording:

> "Cash Equivalents" means ... (5) shares of any money market mutual fund that (A) ~~has~~ [read *keeps*] substantially all of its assets invested ~~continuously~~ in the types of investments referred to in clauses (1) and (2) above, ...

13.189   Another drawback with *continuously* is that it could be understood as suggesting nonstop, every-minute-of-the-day activity. That usually doesn't make sense, as in these examples:

> ... then the Issuer will have an additional 90 days to cure that default, on condition that the Issuer diligently ~~and continuously~~ pursues that cure; ... .

> ... the Advisor shall ... supervise ~~continuously~~ the investment program of the Trust and the composition of its investment portfolio; ... .

13.190 But one can find examples where circumstances make it appropriate to emphasize that something is nonstop, as in *made available to both parties electronically via a continuously "on" data link*. Even in this context, *constant* or, indeed, *nonstop* would be a better choice.

13.191 The adjective *continuous* shares the same shortcomings as *continuously*:

> … including a requirement that the Participant remain ~~continuously~~ employed or provide ~~continuous~~ services for a specified period of time … .

13.192 One exception is use of *continuous* in the securities term of art *continuous offering*:

> On or before the Filing Date, the Company shall prepare and file with the Commission the Initial Registration Statement covering resale of all Registrable Securities for a resale offering to be made on a *continuous* basis.

CONTRACTUAL

13.193 The adjective *contractual*, meaning "of, pertaining to, or secured by a contract," is an awkward mouthful. It's nevertheless routine to see it in contracts.

13.194 Instead of, for example, *contractual terms* and *contractual obligations*, say *contract terms* and *contract obligations*.

13.195 And rather than referring to *contractual instruments* or *contractual arrangements*, just say *contracts*.

COSTS AND EXPENSES

13.196 The couplet *costs and expenses* occurs routinely in contracts, as in the following example:

> If an action is instituted to collect this Note, the Company shall pay all *costs and expenses*, including reasonable attorneys' fees and costs, incurred in connection with that action.

13.197 *Black's Law Dictionary* says that *expense* means "An expenditure of money, time, labor, or resources to accomplish a result; esp., a business expenditure chargeable against revenue for a specific period." By contrast, it defines *costs* more narrowly as "The charges or fees taxed by the court, such as filing fees, jury fees, courthouse fees, and reporter fees."

13.198 In other words, costs are a type of expense. The couplet *costs and expenses* is analogous, semantically, to *trousers and clothing*—you can do without one of the two elements. Refer instead to *court costs, other litigation costs, and any other expenses* (or some variant), or drop *costs* and use only *expenses*.

COUPLED WITH AN INTEREST

13.199   It's commonplace for a power of attorney to use the phase *coupled with an interest* to describe the nature of that power. Often *coupled with an interest* is used with *irrevocable*, as in *This power of attorney is coupled with an interest and will be irrevocable for the term of this agreement and thereafter as long as any of the Obligations remain outstanding.*

13.200   It's likely that many drafters who use *coupled with an interest* don't know what it means. This section offers an explanation and suggests how to help readers understand what it means.

13.201   According to 3 *Am. Jur. 2d* Agency § 56 (2017), "Where the authority or power of an agent is coupled with an interest, it is not revocable by the act, condition, or death of the principal before the expiration of the interest unless there is some agreement to the contrary between the parties."

13.202   But "[i]n order for a power to be irrevocable because it is coupled with an interest, the interest must be in the subject matter of the power and not in the proceeds which will arise from the exercise of the power." 3 *Am. Jur. 2d* Agency § 58. For example, in one case the court held that death of the principal terminated the authority of a real-estate agent to sell on commission, because the authority wasn't a power coupled with an interest in the property on which the power was to operate. See *Crowe v. Trickey*, 204 U.S. 228, 240 (1907). (For further such cases, see M.T. Brunner, Annotation, *What Constitutes Power Coupled with Interest Within Rule as to Termination of Agency*, 28 A.L.R.2d 1243 § 2 (1953).)

13.203   In many powers of attorney, the drafter might well have given no thought whether the agent had an interest in the subject matter.

13.204   Furthermore, to determine whether an interest exists that makes a power irrevocable, courts look at the parties' entire agreement and the circumstances of their relationship. The terminology used by the parties isn't controlling—just saying that a power is coupled with an interest doesn't make it so. 3 *Am. Jur. 2d* Agency § 58; 28 A.L.R.2d 1243 § 2[c].

13.205   It isn't a viable alternative simply to say that the power will survive the death of the principal. Unless a power is coupled with an interest, as a matter of law it will cease at the principal's death, even if the power contains a specific provision to the contrary. 3 *Am. Jur. 2d* Agency § 49.

13.206   So before saying that a power of attorney is coupled with an interest, ask yourself whether you want the power to last beyond the death or incompetence of the principal. If you don't, dispense with *coupled with an interest*—simply saying that the power is irrevocable would serve your purpose.

13.207   If you do want the power to survive beyond the death or incompetence of the principal, ask yourself whether the agent has an interest in the subject matter of the power. If the agent does not, *coupled with an interest* likely won't do you any good.

13.208 If the agent does have an interest in the subject matter of the power, consider making the power of attorney clearer by adding this instead of one of the standard formulas:

> [The principal] acknowledges that this power of attorney is coupled with an interest, in that the agent has an interest in [refer to whatever is the subject of the power]. As a result, in addition to any other consequences under law, this power is irrevocable and will survive [the principal's] death or incompetence.

13.209 By adding explication to the term of art, this provision makes it clear that whether the power is coupled with an interest is a matter of law rather than something that can be agreed to by the parties. It would also ensure that the parties understand the implications of the power's being coupled with an interest. This approach is at odds with the principle that you should never say the same thing twice in a contract (see 1.62), but the benefits outweigh that concern.

CURING BREACH

Generally

13.210 Contracts often allow parties to cure their breach of an obligation. (UK contracts use the term *remediable breach*.) But the concept of curing breach is overused.

13.211 Here's an example of a provision—it's an element of a definition of "Seller Default"—that provides for cure:

> the Seller breaches any obligation under this agreement and, if that breach is capable of being cured, fails to cure that breach in the 30 days after the Buyer notifies the Seller of that breach, except that if that breach is amenable to cure but not within 30 days and the Seller is using reasonable efforts to cure that breach promptly, that breach will not constitute a Seller Default if the Seller continues to use reasonable efforts to cure it and cures it no later than 90 days after the Buyer notifies the Seller of that breach; ... .

13.212 What does it mean to cure a breach? And when is a breach amendable to cure? Here are three scenarios:

- Alpha is under an obligation to deliver artwork by 1 May. The artwork is destroyed in a fire while in Alpha's possession.

- Bravo is under an obligation not to transfer certain shares. Bravo nevertheless transfers the shares. Bravo buys back the shares.

- Charlie is under an obligation to deliver certain equipment by 1 September. Charlie fails to meet that deadline.

13.213 The first and second scenarios aren't amenable to cure, because the artwork was destroyed and the shares were transferred—you can't unbreak an egg. Provisions allowing for cure can explicitly exclude such scenarios by covering only breaches capable of being cured. That's what the example in 13.211 does.

13.214 The third scenario would presumably be amenable to cure—you would give Charlie more time. But it's not as if curing the default makes things better, in the original sense of the word *cure*. Instead, you would simply be changing the rules. More to the point, the parties to a contract commit to perform. Why give a party across-the-board permission to breach? The example in 13.211 seems particularly indulgent. It's also relevant that in at least some jurisdictions, the law provides a measure of protection against claims for what constitutes minimal breach. Consider providing for cure only in contexts where it seems appropriate. One such context might be payment: if Acme fails to make a payment, Widgetco might not be risking much by giving Acme a few days to get its act together and make the payment.

Amenable to Cure

13.215 The example in 13.211 uses the phrase *amenable to cure*. Breaches are also described using the phrase *capable of being cured*, but that seems as awkward as saying that a mountain is capable of being climbed. Use instead *amenable to cure*.

DEEM

13.216 In contracts, *deem* means to treat a thing as that which it is not or might not be, or as possessing certain qualities it does not or might not possess. In other words, it's used to create a legal fiction.

13.217 In contracts, *deem* is generally used in the passive and almost always with *shall*, as in *Any notice shall be deemed to have been received on delivery*. Because no duty is being imposed, it's inappropriate to use *shall* with *deem*—it fails the *has a duty* test (see 3.74). Instead, *deem* is used with language of policy. Because *deem* applies to future events, use *deem* with *will* (see 3.307): *Any notice will be deemed to have been received on delivery*.

13.218 You could use *deem* in the active rather than passive voice—*The parties will deem any notice to have been received on delivery*. But that would be inconsistent with how language of policy works: it operates automatically, without the parties being involved.

13.219 It muddies the waters to use *deem* in a provision that doesn't establish a legal fiction:

> Any violation of the restrictions stated in this section 4.2 by any officer or director of Acme or any investment banker, attorney, or other advisor or representative of Acme will be ~~deemed to be~~ a breach by Acme of this section 4.2.

> The date of exercise will be ~~deemed to be~~ the date on which the Company receives notice of exercise.

Making a Release Automatic

13.220 You can make a release automatic by using *deem* instead of language of obligation: instead of saying *If X, Acme shall release Widgetco*, say *If X, Acme will be deemed to have released Widgetco*. The release happens automatically, without Acme's being requiring to do anything.

13.221 Making a release automatic can simplify matters for the released party. Consider *Management Strategies, Inc. v. Housing Authority of City of New Haven*, No. X06 CV 07 5007102 S, 2009 WL 1958170 (Conn. Super. Ct. 2 June 2009): The plaintiff and the defendant were party to a contract under which the plaintiff had to release the defendant from liability. The plaintiff never issued the release, even though the defendant had satisfied the conditions. The plaintiff objected to the defendant's motion for summary judgment, claiming that because the plaintiff hadn't released the defendant, the defendant wasn't entitled to summary judgment. Sensibly enough, the court held that the plaintiff couldn't base its claim on its own failure to issue a release it had been required to issue under the contract. From a drafting perspective, if the release had been automatic, the plaintiff would have been precluded from making its argument.

13.222 And more generally, making a release automatic would spare the released party having to follow up with the releasing party to obtain a copy of the document effecting the release.

DEFAULT

13.223 Provisions regarding default can be awkward in two respects. This section recommends two fixes: First, in the paired defined terms *Default* and *Event of Default*, replace *Default* with *Potential Default*. And second, instead of describing an event of default as *continuing*, consider referring to *cure*.

Default or Event of Default

13.224 The phrase *default or event of default* is a fixture of loan agreements and other contracts for financial transactions. Usually *default* and *event of default* are used as defined terms. *Event of Default* is straightforward enough—it's defined to mean anything a bank wouldn't want to have happen to its borrowers.

13.225 A problem might not become an event of default until notice has been given or a cure period has run. It's standard for loan agreements to use for such latent events of default the defined term *Default*, with the following definition, or a variant:

> "**Default**" means any event that with notice or passage of time, or both, would constitute an Event of Default.

13.226 A default might trigger lesser remedies. For example, the lender might have the right to refuse to make additional advances.

13.227 But a defined term should give the reader some sense of the definition. Considering the defined terms *Default* and *Event of Default* without consulting the definitions, one might wonder whether they mean the same thing.

13.228   That's presumably why instead of *Default* some contracts use the defined term *Potential Event of Default*—it reflects the definition better. To simplify matters further, shorten *Event of Default* to *Default* and *Potential Event of Default* to *Potential Default*.

13.229   Another possible alternative to *Default* is *Incipient Event of Default*, but *incipient*, meaning "beginning to develop," suggests a gradual process toward becoming an event of default, whereas something either is or is not an event of default.

Has Occurred and Is Continuing

13.230   A contract might refer to remedies that are triggered by an event of default. It might also make it a condition to performance by one party that an event of default (and potential event of default) of the other party not have occurred. In the latter context, contracts often use the phrase *has occurred and is continuing*:

> The obligation of Lenders to make any Loan is subject to the further satisfaction or waiver of each of the following conditions: … (c) no Potential Event of Default or Event of Default *has occurred and is continuing* as of the date that Loan is made.

13.231   Use of *is continuing* poses two problems. First, as a matter of semantics, *is continuing* makes sense regarding a status but not regarding an event. If a lawsuit is pending against Acme, it would be appropriate to say that pendency of that lawsuit "is continuing." By contrast, it would be odd to say that the fact that someone has filed a lawsuit against Acme "is continuing"—an event happens, then it's over. To avoid that awkwardness, phrase events of default in terms of status rather than events. But that won't always be possible. For example, if equipment is destroyed, it wouldn't make sense to describe destruction of that equipment as "continuing."

13.232   And second, if a statement of fact is inaccurate, it's inaccurate at signing or closing; it doesn't make sense to say that the inaccuracy "is continuing" (see 3.434). So *is continuing* doesn't work with an event of default triggered by an inaccurate statement of fact.

13.233   For conditions to performance, it would make sense to refer to events of default in a way that takes these distinctions into account. In this regard, the notion of curing defaults is more versatile than the phrase *is continuing*: you can refer to whether something is amenable to cure, whereas there's no equally convenient way to express that something is capable of continuing. Here's the extract in 13.230, revised to use *cure*:

> The obligation of Lenders to make any Loan is subject to the further satisfaction or waiver of each of the following conditions: … (c) no Potential Event of Default or Event of Default *has occurred and, if it is amenable to cure, has not been cured* as of the date that Loan is made.

13.234 But that formulation leaves open to discussion whether a given event of default is amenable to cure. Regarding *cure* generally, see 13.210.

DIRECTLY

13.235 The word *directly* is used in contracts to say that a party may do something, or is prohibited from doing something, directly or indirectly. But usually there's a clearer alternative:

> To facilitate redemption of Shares by shareholders *directly* [read *through the Company*] or through dealers ... .

> ... and are owned by the Company, *directly or through* [read *or its*] subsidiaries, free and clear of any security interest, mortgage, pledge, lien, encumbrance or claim.

13.236 And *directly* on its own can be redundant. That's because unless the context suggests otherwise, a direct connection is implicit:

> Acme shall pay *directly to* the landlord all rent due under this lease ... .

> In her capacity as chief executive officer of the Company, Ms. Lopez shall report *directly* to the board of directors.

> ... to deliver the certificates for the purchased Shares *directly* to that broker or dealer to complete the sale; ... .

> The Company shall reimburse Maxim *directly* out of the proceeds of the Placement.

13.237 Furthermore, in everyday English *directly* can also connote urgency, as in *In an emergency, go directly to the assembly point.* To avoid confusion regarding which meaning is intended, use *promptly* or perhaps *immediately* instead of *directly* if you wish to express urgency (see 10.108).

DISCLAIM

13.238 A disclaimer is a renunciation of one's legal right or claim or a repudiation of another's right or claim. And the verb *disclaim* has the corresponding meaning.

13.239 But when a party disclaims something (usually warranties), generally a simpler and clearer alternative is available:

> The Agent Parties *expressly disclaim liability* [read will not be liable] for errors or omissions in the Communications.

> The Seller *disclaims* [read is not making] any warranty of merchantability or fitness for a particular purpose in connection with the Buyer's purchase of units of any Product under this agreement.

13.240 It's relevant that section 2-316 of the Uniform Commercial Code refers to what's required to "exclude or modify" warranties. It doesn't use *disclaim* or *disclaimer*.

DUE OR TO BECOME DUE

13.241   The phrase *due or to become due* is standard, but it's also awkwardly archaic. Make it clearer:

> ... any payments ~~due or to become due~~ [*read* that are then due or that become due] in respect of that Collateral ... .

DULY

13.242   According to *Black's Law Dictionary*, *duly* is an adverb meaning "In a proper manner; in accordance with legal requirements." But usually the verb or verb phrase that *duly* modifies itself incorporates the notion of "in a proper manner," making *duly* redundant.

13.243   Consider this example, which features two sentences, each using *duly*:

> The execution, delivery, and performance by that party of this agreement have been *duly* and validly authorized by all necessary corporate or similar proceedings (including approval by the board of directors and, if necessary, shareholders). This agreement has been *duly* executed and delivered by that party and constitutes the legal, valid, and binding obligation of that party enforceable against that party in accordance with its terms.

13.244   If something has been authorized, then necessarily it was properly authorized. If the appropriate procedures hadn't been followed, then no authorization would have been granted. Similarly, if, say, an imposter signs on behalf of a party, it follows that the contract won't have been signed by that party.

13.245   That's why *Garner's Dictionary of Legal Usage*, at 301, says, regarding *duly authorized*, "Because *authorize* denotes the giving of actual or official power, *duly* (i.e., 'properly') is usually unnecessary. Likewise, *duly* is almost always redundant in phrases such as *duly signed*."

13.246   Here's another example:

> Notices and all other communications provided for in this agreement ... will be deemed to have been *duly* given when delivered or mailed by certified or registered mail, return receipt requested, postage prepaid, addressed to the respective addresses set forth below: ... .

13.247   The *duly* is redundant—because the provision specifies what's required to give notice under the contract, it follows that any notice that complies with those requirements will have been properly given.

13.248   But *duly* can also be used to allude to a broader range of concerns. For example, "An opinion that a company has been 'duly incorporated' means that the incorporators complied with all requirements in effect at the time of incorporation for the company to be incorporated under the applicable corporation statute and that government officials took the steps required by that statute to bring the company into existence as a corporation." Scott T. FitzGibbon, Donald W. Glazer & Steven O. Weise, *Glazer & FitzGibbon on Legal Opinions* § 6.2 (3d ed. 2008 & Supp. 2012).

Because in this context *duly incorporated* constitutes shorthand for a parcel of issues, the word *incorporated* can't by itself express the notion of "in a proper manner," so the word *duly* isn't redundant.

13.249 The same applies to the phrase *duly organized*. Both *duly incorporated* and *duly organized* feature in contracts as well as in legal opinions.

13.250 So if *duly* occurs in a term of art with broader substantive implications, leave *duly* alone. But outside of those contexts, *duly* is usually redundant.

13.251 As in the first example above, *duly* is often paired with the equally unnecessary *validly*. In contracts, redundancy loves company.

DURING ... EMPLOYMENT

13.252 In *Mattel, Inc. v. MGA Entertainment, Inc.*, 616 F.3d 904, 912 (9th Cir. 2010), the court considered the ambiguity inherent in having a provision in an employment contract apply during the "employment" of that employee:

> The phrase "at any time during my employment" is ambiguous. It could easily refer to the entire calendar period Bryant worked for Mattel, including nights and weekends. But it can also be read more narrowly to encompass only those inventions created during work hours ("during my employment"), possibly including lunch and coffee breaks ("at any time").

13.253 So instead of saying *during Roe's employment*, be more specific.

DURING THE TERM OF THIS AGREEMENT

13.254 *During the term of this agreement* is usually redundant. The default rule is that contract provisions that address party actions apply only during the term of the contract. So if you use *during the term of this agreement* to modify language of obligation, discretion, or prohibition, you're stating the obvious. In the interest of concision, you would be better off omitting it:

> During the term of this agreement, the [read The] Company shall pay Jones an automobile expense allowance of $1,000 per month, grossed up for income tax purposes, and shall reimburse Jones for all gasoline and maintenance expenses that he incurs in operating his automobile.

13.255 But if you're deviating from the default rule, *during the term of this agreement* might be necessary for specifying duration:

> During the term of this agreement and for five years thereafter, the Recipient shall not, and shall cause each of its Representatives not to, disclose any Confidential Information except as contemplated in this agreement.

13.256 Some drafters use the phrase *during continuance of this agreement* instead of *during the term of this agreement*. In general usage, the meanings of *continuance* include "duration," so the word is apt. But it's also awkward. Furthermore, when used as a legal term, its usual meaning is "postponement; the adjournment or deferring of a trial or other proceeding until a future date." So don't use *continuance* in contracts to convey the meaning "duration."

END

13.257   The verb *terminate* is used in contracts more often than the verb *end*. Given that simpler words are generally better, why not use *end* instead of *terminate*? Here's what that would look like:

> This agreement will *terminate* [read *end*] on 29 October 2019.
>
> Acme may *terminate* [read *end*] this agreement if … .

13.258   But aside from ingrained habit, an obstacle to making this change might be the noun forms of *end*:

> [*At the end of*] [*At the ending of*] this agreement … .

13.259   A reader might initially think that *at the end of this agreement* refers to the back of the contract. And the gerund *ending* is awkward. By contrast, *termination* poses no such problem.

13.260   References to a fundamental concept in a contract are easier to read if you use related verb and noun forms to express that concept. So the brevity of the verb *end* is more than offset by the awkwardness of the noun forms of *end*. Use the verb *terminate*. (For a similar analysis regarding the verb *buy*, see 13.124.)

13.261   Regarding *termination* and *expiration*, see 13.783.

ESPECIALLY, PARTICULARLY, IN PARTICULAR

13.262   It's best not to use the word *especially* in contracts:

> If the scope of work of a Work Order changes, *especially* the estimated timelines, then the applicable Work Order may be amended as provided in this section 5.3(a).
>
> Executive's obligations under article 3 and article 4 of this agreement (*especially* those relating to confidentiality, noncompetition, and nonsolicitation) will continue after his employment with the Company is ended, regardless of the nature or reason for his termination.
>
> The Sellers acknowledge that disclosure of confidential information to others, *especially* the Company's existing and potential competitors, would cause substantial harm to the Company.

13.263   The problem with *especially* is that it's used to indicate that something is particularly important. Necessarily, that suggests that everything else is less important. That could effect how a contract is interpreted. The same goes for *particularly* and *in particular*.

13.264   If you want to make sure that something falls within the scope of a provision, you could accomplish that in ways that are more neutral than by using *especially, particularly*, or *in particular*—for example, through disciplined use of *including* (see 13.354).

13.265   Drafters also use *especially* to mean "specifically," as in *a separate committee created especially for this purpose*. Using instead *specifically* would be a better choice.

ETC.

13.266   *Etc.* is casual, so it's unsuited to the limited and stylized world of contract prose. But more to the point, *etc.* is either redundant, in which case you should delete it, or it's not redundant, in which case it's potentially hazardous and you should delete it.

13.267   *Etc.* is redundant when it's tacked on to a list of items already identified as examples. We know that the list isn't exclusive, so the *etc.* adds nothing. An example:

> … tangible property (including computers, laptops, pagers, *etc.*) … .

13.268   But in the following examples, the items listed aren't examples of a class, so *etc.* indicates that the provision applies to more than the items listed:

> Tenant acknowledges that portions of the Project may be under construction following Tenant's occupancy of the Premises, and that such construction may result in levels of noise, dust, obstruction of access, *etc.* that are in excess of that present in a fully constructed project.

> The Bank shall follow the established procedures and controls to identify exceptions, tolerance breaches, *etc.* and to research and resolve or escalate any pricing inaccuracies; … .

13.269   Presumably a court would rely on a judicial rule of interpretation to limit any additional items to ones that are comparable to the listed items. But a drafter should be alert to that. Ideally, you would specify a class and nothing else or you would make the list exhaustive. If neither is possible, then use *including* instead (see 13.354).

ET SEQ.

13.270   If a contract refers to a statute, don't use *et seq.* when stating the first section of the relevant enacted legislation. Even better, don't state the section at all—the name of the statute is sufficient.

13.271   Here's how *Black's Law Dictionary* defines *et seq.*

> **et seq.** (et **sek**) *abbr* [Latin *et sequens* "and the following one," *et sequentes* (masc.) "and the following ones," or *et sequentia* (neuter) "and the following ones"] (18c) And those (pages or sections) that follow <11 USCA §§ 101 et seq.>.

13.272   Not only is *et seq.* old-fashioned, it also contributes to adding indigestible text—sometimes a lot of it—to a contract. Here's an example (with *et seq.* in bold and italics to make it stand out, although some drafters like to acknowledge its Latin roots by stating it italics in contracts):

> ... including but not limited to any claims under (1) the Age Discrimination in Employment Act, 29 U.S.C. § 621 ***et seq.***, Title VII of the Civil Rights Act of 1964, 42 U.S.C. § 2000e ***et seq.***, the Americans With Disabilities Act of 1990, 42 U.S.C. § 12101 ***et seq.***, the Family and Medical Leave Act, 29 U.S.C. § 2601 ***et seq.***, the Worker Adjustment and Retraining Notification Act ("WARN"), 29 U.S.C. § 2101 ***et seq.***, the Massachusetts Fair Employment Practices Act, M.G.L. c.151B, § 1 ***et seq.*** (or any equivalent in the State of New York), the Massachusetts Civil Rights Act, M.G.L. c.12, §§ 11H and 11I, the Massachusetts Equal Rights Act, M.G.L. c.93, § 102 and M.G.L. c.214, § 1C, the Massachusetts Labor and Industries Act, M.G.L. c.149, § 1 ***et seq.***, and the Massachusetts Privacy Act, M.G.L. c.214, § 1B (or any equivalents in the State of New York), the Fair Credit Reporting Act, 15 U.S.C. § 1681 ***et seq.*** and the Employee Retirement Income Security Act of 1974 ("ERISA"), 29 U.S.C. § 1001 ***et seq.***, all as amended ("**Claims**").

13.273   Instead just say, for example, *the Worker Adjustment and Retraining Notification Act*, without saying where it's codified. It's not as if there are two WARN Acts.

EXECUTE AND DELIVER

13.274   The phrase *execute and deliver* (and *execution and delivery*) is a fixture in contracts, as in *The Borrower shall from time to time execute and deliver to the Bank, at the request of the Bank, all Financing Statements and other documents that the Bank requests.* (Regarding use of *execute* and *deliver* in the concluding clause, see 5.9–.14.) And an opinion regarding execution and delivery is a standard element of legal opinions.

13.275   But it's not clear what one accomplishes by using *execute* rather than *sign*, particularly as different authorities offer differing definitions of *execute* (see 5.10–.11).

13.276   *Deliver* is also problematic. Scott T. FitzGibbon, Donald W. Glazer & Steven O. Weise, *Glazer and FitzGibbon on Legal Opinions* § 9.5 (3d ed. 2008 & Supp. 2012), says as follows:

> Historically, delivery by one party to an agreement to the other has been effected by its physically handing over a signed counterpart of the agreement to a representative of the other party. Today, transactions often are closed electronically, and, when they are, few, if any, documents are physically delivered. Whatever form delivery takes, an opinion that the company has "duly delivered" the agreement means that the company, having duly authorized and executed the agreement, delivered the agreement in a manner that under applicable law ... had the effect of making the agreement a binding obligation of the company.

13.277 This would suggest that delivery is required for an effective contract. But although one of the requirements of a contract under seal is delivery, that's not the case with other kinds of contracts. Here's what 1-2 *Corbin on Contracts* § 2.11 (footnotes omitted) says regarding "informal" contracts, in other words contracts not under seal:

> All that is necessary to the creation of an informal contract, however, whether reduced to writing or not, is an expression of assent in any form. The writing itself is not necessary, if put in writing, a signature is not necessary. Even if in writing and signed, a delivery is not necessary. It is an expression of assent that is required. Delivery of a writing may be sufficient evidence of such an assent. Words of assent are sufficient, and conduct other than delivery may also be sufficient.

13.278 Given that signing a contract and handing the signed copy to the other party isn't the only way to indicate assent, in certain contexts it would seem simpler just to refer to entry into the agreement in question:

> The Company has all requisite corporate power and authority to *execute and deliver* [read *enter into*] this agreement.

13.279 On the other hand, if Acme is under an obligation to enter into a given contract or sign some ancillary document, or if its entry into a given contract constitutes a condition, the surest way to verify that it has performed that obligation, or to verify that the condition has been satisfied, would be to have Acme sign the contract or document and deliver a signed copy. So in that context, it would make sense to refer to signature and delivery. (Be prepared to have someone insist on using *execute* rather than *sign*.)

FAILS TO

13.280 The phrase *fails to* (and its variants) is standard in contracts, but often it's used in a context that doesn't involve failure. And it's never necessary to invoke failure. So usually it's best to use *does not* or some other alternative.

13.281 Some examples:

> … and CRISPR ~~*fails to*~~ [read *does not*] bring any such action or proceeding with respect to infringement in the Tracr Field within … .

> If such Dissenting Stockholder withdraws its demand for appraisal or ~~*fails to*~~ [read *does not*] perfect or otherwise loses or waives its right of appraisal … .

> … or inducing others ~~*to fail to*~~ [read *not to*] cooperate … .

> The Indemnifying Party will not be relieved of its obligation to indemnify the Indemnified Party with respect to that claim ~~*if the Indemnified Party fails to timely deliver*~~ [read *unless the Indemnified Party timely delivers*] the Indemnity Notice … .

FAITHFULLY

13.282   No point is served in using *faithfully* and comparable adverbs in provisions stating the standard of performance expected of an employee.

13.283   An employment agreement for a high-level employee will usually say that the employee is obligated to perform duties specified by the chief executive officer (or, in the case of the chief executive officer, by the board of directors), is obligated to work full-time, and can be fired for specific transgressions. Beyond that, whether the employee is a success will depend on the employee's expertise, judgment, imagination, and experience. Unless you come up with quantifiable targets, you can't capture those intangibles in a contract.

13.284   But drafters can't resist trying. That's why they use *faithfully*, usually along with comparable adverbs (*diligently*, *competently*, *industriously*, and others):

> Executive shall devote her best efforts and sufficient business time and attention to the business and affairs of the Company and shall diligently, *faithfully*, and competently perform her duties and responsibilities hereunder; ... .

> During the Employment Term, Executive shall ... (2) use Executive's best efforts to perform *faithfully* and efficiently Executive's duties hereunder ... .

> Executive shall be a loyal executive and shall at all times *faithfully*, industriously, and to the best of his ability, experience, and talents perform all duties required of him ... .

13.285   But it's unlikely that a court would consider that working hard but not having that reflected in the company's performance would constitute breach of a standard of performance that uses one or more of those adverbs. And whether an employer can bring a claim against an employee for failing to be faithful in performing their duties would depend on the law of agency, not on whether the word *faithfully* is used in the employee's contract.

13.286   So instead of the empty gesture of using *faithfully* and the like to express the standard of performance expected of an employee, be as specific as possible regarding an employee's duties.

FAX

13.287   As between *fax*, *facsimile*, *telefacsimile*, and *telecopier*, your best bet is *fax*, for both the machine and that which it transmits.

13.288   *Garner's Modern English Usage* says that *fax* "is now all but universal, in the face of which *facsimile transmission* is an instant archaism—and a trifle pompous at that," and that *fax* "is now perfectly appropriate even in formal contexts."

13.289   *Telecopier* is a brand name, so don't use it to refer to all makes of machine. And don't write *fax* in all capitals—it's not an acronym.

13.290   The fax machine is heading toward obsolescence, but you can expect that contracts will continue to refer to faxing for a good long while. After all, Telex appears to be all but dead as a means of communication, but plenty of contracts still refer to giving notice by Telex.

FIXED FEE

13.291   When in a contract you want to specify the amount of a fee to be paid, it's redundant to use the phrase *flat fee* or *fixed fee*:

> The Bank shall pay AZ Financial ~~a fixed fee of~~ $37,500, plus reimbursable expenses, preparing and delivering the original appraisal report.

> DigitalGlobe shall pay the Consultant ~~a fixed fee of~~ $10,000 per month for up to 15 hours per month of the Consultant's time.

13.292   Those phrases make sense only if you're referring generally to a kind of payment, rather than a specific fee:

> At the Landlord's option, the Tenant shall pay that fee as either a fixed fee or an hourly fee that takes into account the time expended by the Landlord's agents and representatives in supervising the Tenant's construction.

FOR ANY REASON OR NO REASON

13.293   The phrase *for any reason or no reason* is commonly used in employment contracts between a company and an at-will employee. Even though the point of at-will employment is to allow the company to terminate the employee whenever it wants, a company might want to enter into an employment contract with an at-will employee to address matters such as confidentiality, severance, and ownership of intellectual property. In such a contract, it would make sense also to address employment status, and language relating to at-will employment is routinely supplemented to state that the company may terminate the employee "for any reason or no reason."

13.294   But terminating a contract for no reason doesn't make sense—when someone terminates a contract, there's always a reason. If Acme fires Roe, it might be because Roe has proved ineffectual; because Roe behaved inappropriately at the Christmas party; because Acme's chief executive officer wants to hire the chief executive officer's cousin instead; because Acme's chief executive officer doesn't like Roe's hairstyle.

13.295   Furthermore, *any reason* doesn't imply that the company must have a good reason, so *any reason* on its own is sufficiently comprehensive.

13.296   In referring to termination for no reason, the drafter might be attempting to avoid having to explain why it had terminated the employee. It would be better to address that issue directly by having the contract state that the company won't be required to provide an explanation. (A company might in fact be required by law to provide an explanation.)

13.297   Don't assume that using either or both of *for any reason* and *for no reason* in referring to termination would mean that the employee has in effect waived the benefit of the implied duty of good faith (see 3.225). A more promising approach would be to have the employee acknowledge factors that the company wouldn't be required to consider if it decides to terminate the employee. (For a different example of this approach, see 3.248.)

13.298   More generally, *for any reason or no reason* is used in other kinds of contracts instead of *at its sole discretion* (see 3.224) as a way to attempt, unhelpfully, to circumvent the implied duty of good faith.

13.299   Regarding use of *for any reason or no reason* as an alternative to the phrase *termination for convenience*, see 13.805.

FORCE AND EFFECT

13.300   The phrase *force and effect* is widely used in contracts, in *no force and* [or *or*] *effect* and *the same force and effect* but mostly in *full force and effect*:

> If Doe does not sign and return this agreement by 15 February 2018, the offer of Severance Benefits will be deemed withdrawn and this agreement will be of *no force and effect*.

> … each of the obligations in the Credit Agreement and the other Loan Documents is hereby reaffirmed with *the same force and effect* as if each were separately stated herein and made as of the date hereof;

> … the obligations of the Borrower under this section 3 will remain in *full force and effect* until … .

13.301   But *force* is redundant—omit it from the phrase.

13.302   *Garner's Dictionary of Legal Usage*, at 370, suggests that "the emphasis gained by *force and effect* may justify use of the phrase, more likely in drafting (contracts and statutes) than in judicial opinions." But that misconstrues the nature of contract language—it doesn't aim to persuade anyone of anything (see 1.57), so that sort of emphasis has no place in a contract.

FORMAL, FORMALLY

13.303   In these examples, the world *formal* is redundant:

> Unless ~~formal~~ pleadings are waived by agreement among the parties and the referee … .

> … without the necessity of commencing a foreclosure action with respect to this Mortgage, making ~~formal~~ demand for the Rents, obtaining the appointment of a receiver, or taking any other affirmative action … .

> All arbitrators … must have a ~~formal~~ financial/accounting, engineering, or legal education.

13.304 The same goes for the word *formally in these examples*:

> Lender may conclusively rely on that certificate until ~~formally~~ advised by a like certificate of any changes therein.

> ... under valid contracts of license, sale, or service that have been ~~formally~~ awarded to a Borrower ... .

> ... nothing herein will require the Purchaser, in connection with the receipt of any regulatory approval, to agree to ... litigate or ~~formally~~ contest any proceedings relating to any regulatory approval process in connection with the Contemplated Transactions.

13.305 Such uses of *formal* and *formally* are puzzling—they suggest that what matters isn't just the thing involved or the action taken but also unspecified procedures. If you have such procedures in mind, make them explicit.

FORM AND SUBSTANCE

13.306 In contracts, the phrase *form and substance* refers to documents to be delivered, as in *an opinion of counsel in form and substance satisfactory to the Buyer*. As with most couplets, it adds nothing more than a rhetorical flourish.

13.307 *Form* arguably relates solely to the appearance of a document. If that's the case, *form* should be omitted. And if *form* means something more than that, then it would tread on the toes of *substance* and, as such, should be omitted.

13.308 One could say *in substance satisfactory to the Buyer*, but why not omit *in substance*, too? Saying *an opinion of counsel satisfactory to the Buyer* is sufficiently all-encompassing. (Regarding *satisfactory* generally, see 13.722.)

13.309 If you want to avoid any preclosing haggling, it would be best to attach the document in question as an exhibit. The contract would say that the document delivered has to be in the form of that exhibit or, if you want to build in some flexibility, in a form substantially similar to that exhibit. But if the document relates to some future transaction the terms of which are as yet unknown, it might not be feasible to attach the document as an exhibit.

FOR THE AVOIDANCE OF DOUBT

13.310 Don't use *for the avoidance of doubt*.

13.311 Drafters use this phrase to introduce language that ostensibly clarifies the preceding language, usually by indicating that something either falls within or is excluded from the scope of the preceding language.

13.312 But used in that manner, *for the avoidance of doubt* is merely a filler—what follows has to be able to stand on its own, as in this example:

> This arbitration agreement applies to all matters relating to this agreement, the RSU Agreement, and the Executive's employment with the Company,

including disputes about the validity, interpretation, or effect of this agreement, or alleged violations of it, any payments due hereunder or thereunder, and all claims arising out of any alleged discrimination, harassment, or retaliation. *For the avoidance of doubt, this* [read *This*] arbitration agreement does not apply to any dispute under the Indemnification Agreement.

13.313 When *for the avoidance of doubt* is used in this manner in a definition, restructure the definition as a single sentence, as in this example:

"Insider Shares" means all shares of Company common stock owned by an Insider immediately before the Company's *IPO. For the avoidance of doubt, Insider Shares will not include* [read *IPO and excludes*] any IPO Shares purchased by Insiders in connection with or after the Company's IPO.

13.314 But *for the avoidance of doubt* is sometimes used, unhelpfully, to state the blindingly obvious. The immediately preceding example is an example of that—it might be best to strike the second sentence.

13.315 Sometimes *for the avoidance of doubt* is doubly pointless, in that the language that follows doesn't refer to something that comes within or is excluded from the scope of the preceding language:

Nothing in this agreement gives to any Person other than the parties and their successors, the Owner Trustee, any separate trustee or co-trustee appointed under section 6.10 of the Indenture, the Note Insurer, the Swap Counterparty, and the Noteholders any benefit or any legal or equitable right, remedy, or claim under this agreement. *For the avoidance of doubt, the* [read *The*] Owner Trustee, the Note Insurer, and the Swap Counterparty are third-party beneficiaries of this agreement and are entitled to the rights and benefits under this agreement and may enforce the provisions of this agreement as if they were a party to it.

13.316 Drafters also use *for the avoidance of doubt* as an inferior alternative to having a party acknowledge a fact:

For the avoidance of doubt, [read *The Seller acknowledges that*] Invest Bank has implemented reasonable policies and procedures, taking into consideration the nature of its business, to ensure that individuals making investment decisions would not violate laws prohibiting trading on the basis of material nonpublic information.

13.317 And *for the avoidance of doubt* is also used as a form of rhetorical emphasis (see 1.58). Just as rhetorical emphasis generally is unhelpful, so is this use of *for the avoidance of doubt*:

For the avoidance of doubt, nothing [read *Nothing*] in this agreement gives Acme any rights to any of Pharmaco's compounds or methods of compound synthesis, including the Pharmaco Product, the Pharmaco Technology, any Patent Rights owned, licensed, or controlled by Pharmaco, or any Pharmaco Confidential Information.

The Executive will be responsible for paying any tax and employee's national insurance contributions imposed by any taxation authority in respect of any of the payments and benefits provided under this agreement (other than ~~*for the avoidance of doubt*~~ any tax or employee's national insurance contributions deducted or withheld by the Company in paying the sums to the Executive).

13.318 But even without the benefit of these examples, it's clear enough from the awkward buried verb *avoidance* (see 17.7) that *for the avoidance of doubt* is problematic.

13.319 The phrase *for clarity* raises the same issues.

FRAUD AND INTENTIONAL MISREPRESENTATION

13.320 It's commonplace in mergers-and-acquisitions contracts for claims of fraud or intentional misrepresentation to be included in exceptions to limits on indemnification. But how does fraud relate to intentional misrepresentation?

13.321 26 *Williston on Contracts* § 69:2 (footnotes omitted) defines fraud as "a deception deliberately practiced in order to unfairly secure gain or advantage, the hallmarks of which are misrepresentation and deceit, though affirmative misrepresentation is not required, as concealment or even silence can under certain circumstances constitute fraud."

13.322 Because intentional misrepresentation would seem equivalent to "misrepresentation and deceit," intentional misrepresentation would seem to constitute fraud. That much is confirmed by the *Restatement (Second) of Torts* § 526, which states that "misrepresentation is fraudulent if the maker (a) knows or believes that the matter is not as he represents it to be, (b) does not have the confidence in the accuracy of his representation that he states or implies, or (c) knows that he does not have the basis for his representation that he states or implies."

13.323 But given the cases cited in *Williston* to the effect that fraud can arise not only through misrepresentation but also concealment, it would seem that intentional misrepresentation is only one kind of fraud. That suggests that for contracts, it would be more economical and less confusing simply to refer to fraud and omit any reference to intentional misrepresentation, unless for some reason you wish to convey the narrower meaning.

13.324 On the other hand, the elements of a claim for misrepresentation are different from the elements of a claim for fraud. That might lead a court to treat a reference to fraud not as an umbrella term that covers various kinds of claims but instead as a reference to a kind of claim, one distinct from a claim for intentional misrepresentation. So referring to both fraud and intentional misrepresentation would seem the safer approach.

13.325 But as with terms of art generally (see 1.7), the exact meaning attributed to the terms "fraud" and "intentional misrepresentation" would likely be unclear to many readers. And that meaning would likely vary depending on the jurisdiction.

13.326 So rather than using terms of art, it would be clearer to focus on the underlying conduct: an alternative to "any claim for fraud or intentional misrepresentation" would be "any claim that the Indemnifying Party intentionally supplied one or more Indemnified Parties with information that the Indemnifying Party knew [or should have known] was inaccurate or any claim that the Indemnifying Party intentionally withheld information from one or more Indemnified Parties."

13.327   This language uses more words, and it's novel. But a drafter might conclude that that's a modest price to pay for greater clarity.

FROM THE BEGINNING OF TIME

13.328   A picturesque fixture of release language is *from the beginning of time*, as in *Jones hereby releases Acme from any claims … arising from the beginning of time to the date of this agreement.* A comparable phrase is *from the beginning of the world.*

13.329   Besides being quaint, this language is redundant. If you agree to release all claims against Acme, that indeed means all claims, as opposed to just those claims that arose in the past year, or the past century, or some other limited period.

13.330   See 13.398 regarding *until/to the end of time* and *until/to the end of the world.*

FULL-TIME

13.331   Using in a contract the adjective *full-time* regarding work is an invitation to uncertainty. See, e.g., *In re C.P.Y.*, 364 S.W.3d 411 (Tex. App. 2012) (considering the meaning of a provision in a divorce decree requiring payment of alimony until the ex-wife "returns to work on a full time basis"). It raises three issues:

13.332   First, what is the minimum amount of work, in hours per day and days per week, required for work to be full-time work?

13.333   Second, for how long must that level of work be maintained for that work to be full-time work? One day? One week? More?

13.334   And third, must someone be employed to be engaged in full-time work? What about volunteer work? What if the person is an independent contractor?

13.335   So to avoid confusion, be more specific than *full-time.*

GUARANTEE, GUARANTY

13.336   Here's what *Garner's Dictionary of Legal Usage*, at 399, says regarding the difference between *guaranty* and *guarantee*, both pertaining to a promise to answer for payment of a debt or performance of a duty on failure of another:

> The distinction in [British English] was formerly that *guarantee* is the verb, *guaranty* the noun. Yet *guarantee* is now commonly used

as both noun and verb in both [American English] and [British English] … .

In practice, *guarantee*, n., is the usual term, seen often, for example, in the context of consumer warranties or other assurances of quality or performance. *Guaranty*, by contrast, is now used primarily in financial and banking contexts in the sense "a promise to answer for the debt of another." *Guaranty* is now rarely seen in nonlegal writing, whether in [British English] or [American English]. Some legal writers prefer *guaranty* in all noun senses.

Guaranty was formerly used as a verb but is now obsolete as a variant of *guarantee*, vb.

13.337 *The New Fowler's Modern English Usage* 343 (R. W. Burchfield ed., 3d revised ed. 2004) offers what appears to be a simple rule:

> **guarantee, guaranty.** 'Fears of choosing the wrong one of these two forms are natural, but needless. As things now are, *-ee* is never wrong where either is possible' (Fowler, 1926). The advice is still sound.

13.338 Review of a small sample of contracts filed on the U.S. Securities and Exchange Commission's EDGAR system suggests that there's a roughly even split between *guaranty* and *guarantee* used as nouns, but that in a finance context—namely in credit agreements—*guaranty* is indeed the preferred form of the noun. But even in a finance context *guarantee* is used as a noun roughly a quarter of the time, so if in all contexts you use *guarantee* as both noun and verb, you would have plenty of company. And it would have the advantage of simplicity—to insist on a distinction between the noun forms *guaranty* and *guarantee* is to invite continued confusion.

13.339 So in all circumstances use *guarantee* as a verb and noun.

13.340 Don't use *guarantee* as a counterpart of *guarantor*—in other words, to mean a person to whom a guarantee is given. That's asking for confusion, given the primary meaning of *guarantee*.

GUARANTEE (THE VERB) AS TERM OF ART

13.341 Here's how *Black's Law Dictionary* defines the verb *guarantee*:

> **guarantee**, *vb.* (18c) **1.** To assume a suretyship obligation; to agree to answer for a debt or default. **2.** To promise that a contract or legal act will be duly carried out. **3.** To give security to.

13.342 When the verb *guarantee* is used in a contract (and is followed not by a *that*-clause but by a noun, which is usually the case; see 13.346), its complete meaning derives not from the word itself but from the context—in other words, exactly what the party in question is guaranteeing.

13.343   Consider this example:

> The New Borrower hereby guarantees payment and performance when due, whether at stated maturity, by acceleration, or otherwise, of all Obligations.

13.344   If you consider *hereby guarantees* in isolation, it simply conveys the meaning "will be liable for," as does *indemnifies* (see 13.439). What the New Borrower is liable for is spelled out in the rest of the sentence.

13.345   So the verb *guarantee* is an example of an unnecessary term of art (see 1.11) that could be replaced by a much simpler phrase. Whether that's feasible is a function of inertia and expediency, not semantics.

GUARANTEES THAT

13.346   Here are two ways to create a guarantee:

> Acme *guarantees that* Widgetco will comply with its obligations under this agreement.

> Acme *guarantees* Widgetco's compliance with its obligations under this agreement.

13.347   The first alternative—*guarantees that*—is seldom used, perhaps because in everyday English it can express exuberant wishful thinking: *I guarantee that Accrington Stanley will defeat Spennymoor United!* But consider using it to create a guarantee—whereas in the second alternative *guarantees* is followed by an abstract noun (*compliance*), *guarantees that* is followed by a verb, resulting in prose that's clearer and more concise (see 17.7).

13.348   *Guarantees that* is also used in throat-clearing (see 3.25).

HERE- AND THERE- WORDS

13.349   Use of *here-* words (such as *hereby*, *herein*, and *hereof*) and their *there-* counterparts is a hallmark of legalese. One problem is that *here-* words cause ambiguity (see 7.23–.24, 7.26). Beyond that, *here-* and *there-* words add an archaic and legalistic tone to prose.

13.350   So never use *here-* words, except for *hereby* in language of performance (see 3.35). For example, instead of *herein*, use *in this agreement.* Use *there-* words only to avoid awkward or long-winded repetition, as in "the first supplemental indenture dated 25 October 2016 between Acme and Big Bancorp and any amendments *thereto.*" Even in that example, you could say instead "any amendments *to it,*" although for most drafters that would take some getting used to. (Regarding use of *hereof* in cross-references, see 4.105; regarding *therefor*, see 13.817. Regarding a related internal rule of interpretation, see 15.15.)

IN ACCORDANCE WITH, ACCORDING TO

13.351   *Garner's Modern English Usage* says that *according to* "means (1) 'depending on'; (2) 'as explained or reported by (a person)'; or (3) 'in accordance with.'" It's used in contracts to convey the last of these meanings, as in *Any dispute must be resolved by arbitration according to the procedures stated in this section 12.10.*

13.352   By contrast, *in accordance with* doesn't have alternative meanings, so it's preferable to use *in accordance with* rather than *according to* to convey that meaning—that would spare readers from having to select from among alternative meanings. But don't use either phrase if *under* would do.

INCLUDING, INCLUDES

13.353   It's standard practice to add *without limitation* or *but not limited to* after *including,* and *without limitation* or *but is not limited to* after *includes.* (You also see wordier variants, two being *including without limiting the generality of the foregoing* (see 13.898) and *including without implication of limitation.*) But these additions are more trouble than they're worth, and they can't be counted on to accomplish the intended purpose. What's required is a more nuanced approach to use of *including* and *includes.*

A Source of Uncertainty

13.354   Here's how *Black's Law Dictionary* defines *include*: "To contain as a part of something. The participle *including* typically indicates a partial list <the plaintiff asserted five tort claims, including slander and libel>." In interpreting contracts and statutes, courts have routinely held that *including* or *includes* introduces an illustrative list. See, e.g., *Federal Land Bank of St. Paul v. Bismarck Lumber Co.,* 314 U.S. 95, 99–100 (U.S. 1941) ("[T]he term 'including' is not one of all-embracing definition, but connotes simply an illustrative application of the general principle."). Texas has even adopted this meaning in the context of statutory construction. Tex. Gov't Code Ann. § 311.005(13).

13.355   But a drafter might ill-advisedly use *including* or *includes* to introduce what could only be an exhaustive list, or might use an overbroad noun before *includes* or *including,* so that the list that follows better expresses the intent of the parties.

13.356   That's presumably why many courts have accepted that *including* and *includes* can also introduce an exhaustive list, or a list that limits the scope of the preceding general noun or noun phrase—in other words, that they can convey a restrictive meaning. Some courts have explicitly acknowledged that possibility. See, e.g., *Muller v. Automobile Club of Southern California,* 61 Cal. App. 4th 431, 444 (1998) (noting that the word *includes* "creates an ambiguity"). Others do so by saying that *including* or *includes* ordinarily conveys the illustrative meaning, the implication being that a restrictive meaning is possible. See, e.g., *DIRECTV, Inc. v. Crespin,* 224 F. App'x 741, 748 (10th Cir. 2007) (referring to "the normal use of 'include' as introducing an illustrative—and non-exclusive—list"); *Auer v. Commonwealth*, 621 S.E.2d 140, 144 (Va. Ct. App. 2005) ("Generally speaking, the word 'include' implies that the provided list of parts or components is not exhaustive and, thus, not exclusive."). The "typically" in the *Black's Law Dictionary* definition (see 13.354) serves the same function.

13.357   Furthermore, courts have been willing to hold that *including* or *includes* is restrictive. See, e.g., *Frame v. Nehls*, 550 N.W.2d 739, 742 (Mich. 1996) (holding that a statute that provides that definition of child custody dispute "includes" two types of proceedings limits child custody disputes to those two types of proceedings).

13.358   Some courts have even suggested that the restrictive meaning is the principal or only meaning. See, e.g., *Department of Treasury of Indiana v. Muessel*, 32 N.E.2d 596, 598 (Ind. 1941) (stating that ordinary use of the word *including* "is as a term of limitation"); *Application of Central Airlines*, 185 P.2d 919 (Okla. 1947) (holding, regarding use of the word *including*, that "if the lawmakers had intended the general words to be used in their unrestricted sense they would have made no mention of the particular classes").

An Unhelpful Fix

13.359   Due to this uncertainty regarding the meaning of *including* and *includes*, regrettably it's now standard practice for drafters to use the phrases *including without limitation* and *including but not limited to* (and their equivalents using *includes*) with the aim of making it clear that the unrestricted meaning applies.

13.360   Caselaw offers a measure of support. See, e.g., *Jackson v. O'Leary*, 689 F. Supp. 846, 849 (N.D. Ill. 1988) (describing "including, but not limited to" as "the classic language of totally unrestricted (and hence totally discretionary) standards"); *Coast Oyster Co. v. Perluss*, 32 Cal. Rptr. 740, 746 (Ct. App. 1963) (noting use of the phrases "includes, but is not limited to" and "including, but not limited to," as opposed to "includes," to make it clear that the intent was to enlarge and not to limit); *Matter of Estate of Meyer*, 668 N.E.2d 263, 265 (Ind. Ct. App. 1996) ("If he had intended to use the word 'including' as a term of enlargement rather than a term of limitation, [the testator] could have modified 'including' with the phrase 'but not in limitation of the foregoing.'")

13.361   But there are two problems with using this approach to make it clear that the unrestricted meaning applies.

13.362   First, given that the illustrative meaning of *including* and *includes* is the primary meaning, usually the extra verbiage would be redundant. That's presumably why *Black's Law Dictionary* states that *including without limitation* and *including but not limited to* "mean the same thing" as *including*. And at least one court has noted this potential for redundancy. See *St. Paul Mercury Insurance Co. v. Lexington Insurance Co.*, 78 F.3d 202, 206–07 (5th Cir. 1996) (stating that the word "including" "is generally given an expansive reading, even without the additional if not redundant language of 'without limitation'"). So for drafters, it's a nuisance to have to tack on the extra verbiage every time you use *including* or *includes*, and for the reader it's annoying to encounter at every turn. Using an internal rule of interpretation (see 15.18) would allow you to eliminate much of the clutter, but in effect you would still be applying by rote extra language that would be redundant in most contexts.

13.363   And second, courts are willing to hold that *including* or *includes* is restrictive even when so modified, so you can't assume that the extra verbiage would ensure that a court attributes an illustrative meaning to *including* or *includes*.

13.364   For example, in *Shelby County State Bank v. Van Diest Supply Co.*, 303 F.3d 832 (7th Cir. 2002), the court disregarded the phrase *but not limited to* in holding that an item falls within the scope of the preceding noun only if it falls within one of the items in the list following *including*:

> [I]t would be bizarre as a commercial matter to claim a lien in everything, and then to describe in detail only a smaller part of that whole. This is not to say that there is no use for descriptive clauses of inclusion, so as to make clear the kind of entities that ought to be included. But if all goods of any kind are to be included, why mention only a few? A court required to give "reasonable and effective meaning to all terms" must shy away from finding that a significant phrase (like the lengthy description of chemicals and fertilizers we have here) is nothing but surplusage. [Citations omitted.]

13.365   And in *Horse Cave State Bank v. Nolin Production Credit Ass'n*, 672 S.W.2d 66 (Ky. Ct. App. 1984), the court held that a list following "including but not limited to" limited the scope of the preceding noun phrase:

> [Appellee's] description does not merely state that it covers 'all farm machinery' without more. Rather, the description includes the qualifying language 'including but not limited to tractor, plow, and disc.' The qualifying language gave appellant and other persons notice that [appellee's] financing statement was intended to cover any tractor, plow, and disc owned by the debtor as well as all *similar* farm machinery." [Emphasis added.]

13.366   See also *In re Clark*, 910 A.2d 1198, 1200 (N.H. 2006) ("When the legislature uses the phrase 'including, but not limited to' in a statute, the application of that statute is limited to the types of items therein particularized."); *Holy Angels Academy v. Hartford Insurance Group*, 487 N.Y.S.2d 1005 (Sup. Ct. 1985) (holding that use of *including but not limited to* did not preclude application of the rule of interpretation known as *ejusdem generis*, which has it that general words, when combined with specific items or examples, apply only to things of the same kind or class as the specific things).

13.367   That some courts disregard *but not limited to* shouldn't come as a surprise. A court handling a contract dispute will want to determine the meaning intended by the drafter. In the process, it might elect to disregard any language unrelated to that. Given that it's routine for drafters reflexively to add *without limitation* or *but not limited to* to each instance of *including* (and *without limitation* or *but is not limited to* to each instance of *includes*), a court could conclude that such phrases are essentially meaningless.

Avoiding Uncertainty

13.368   How to avoid having a court give a restrictive meaning to an *including* or *includes* that you had intended to be illustrative depends, first, on the nature of the general word that precedes *including* or *includes*.

13.369   If you're relying on the general word to convey its everyday meaning, don't follow it with a list of obvious examples of that noun or noun phrase—by saying *fruit, including oranges, lemons, and grapefruit*, you invite a court to conclude that *fruit* consists of only citrus fruits, and not melons or bananas. Eliminating such lists shouldn't pose a problem. Everyone knows that oranges, lemons, and grapefruit are fruit.

13.370   Instead, if you're relying on the general word to convey its everyday meaning, use *includes* or *including* only to make it clear that the preceding noun in fact includes something that otherwise might not fall within its scope—*fruit, including tomatoes*. (Are tomatoes a fruit or a vegetable? Your answer might depend on whether you're a botanist or a cook.) Doing so leaves little possibility for mischief—because *tomatoes* lurks at the margins of *fruit*, a court couldn't reasonably conclude that *fruit* in fact means only tomatoes or tomato-like produce. (This manual refers to this as using an enlarging item after *including*; see 13.385.)

13.371   You might nevertheless feel compelled to include as an example an obvious member of the general word—*fruit, including oranges*. (Perhaps oranges play a particular important role in a client's business.) Although it would look rather odd, given that oranges are so obviously fruit, a court might have a hard time restricting the meaning of *fruit* if only a single specific item is named. (For a better way to convey this meaning, see 13.377.) But the more items you add, the greater the risk of a court applying a restrictive meaning to *including* or *includes*.

13.372   Instead of relying on the general word that precedes *including* or *includes* to convey its everyday meaning, you might be relying on it to convey a specialized meaning. Perhaps it's a meaning that differs from the everyday meaning of that noun. Or perhaps the noun is a creation of the contract (such as *excluded liabilities*) and so has no everyday meaning. Either way, your best bet would be not to use *including* or *includes*, as the meaning of the noun wouldn't be clear enough for a court to assess whether an illustrative or restrictive meaning of *including* or *includes* had been intended. Instead, provide an exhaustive list, perhaps in the form of a definition, with the noun constituting the defined term.

13.373   In any event, the first step to avoiding uncertainty over *including* or *includes* is to select your general word with care. The more specific you make it, the less mischief *including* or *includes* can cause. And you might be able to do without them entirely.

Putting the General Word at the End

13.374 You could reverse the order—instead of a general word followed by specific items, with *including* as the link, you could have the specific items lead, with the general word bringing up the rear. In other words, instead of *fruit, including oranges, lemons, and grapefruit,* you could say *oranges, lemons, grapefruit, and other fruit.* But generally, doing so wouldn't serve any useful purpose.

13.375 That's because if you want *fruit* to include melons and bananas, putting the general word last would likely increase the risk of a court holding that *fruit* does not express that meaning. Most courts are willing to apply to a list of items followed by a catchall phrase (as opposed to a general word followed by specific items) the rule of interpretation known as *ejusdem generis.* It holds that when a general word or phrase follows a list of specifics, the general word or phrase includes only items of the same class as those listed.

13.376 More to the point, it's best to avoid the uncertainty that comes with using with a general word a limited list of obvious members of the general word, regardless of where the list is placed in relation to the general word. Such a list can be understood as an invitation to limit the scope of the general word.

13.377 But if the client's needs leave you with no choice but to include a list of obvious members of the class, putting the general word last can provide a more convenient way to do so. To block any implication that the specific items limit the general word, you can adjust the general word, as in *oranges, lemons, grapefruit, and other fruit, whether or not citrus.* If you were trying to convey the same meaning using *including* (see 13.371), a comparable adjustment would be clumsier—*citrus and noncitrus fruit, including oranges, lemons, and grapefruit.* And if oranges, lemons, and grapefruit loom so large for your client, it's appropriate to lead with them.

Commentary in Favor of *But Not Limited To*

13.378 Bryan Garner, the lexicographer and authority on legal writing, has been vocal about the merits of supplementing *including.* On Twitter and on his blog, Garner has recommended that to ensure that *including* isn't interpreted as introducing an exhaustive list, *including* should be defined to mean *including but not limited to.* See Bryan A. Garner (@BryanAGarner), Twitter (20 Aug. 2015), https://twitter.com/bryanagarner/status/634425867372879872; Bryan A. Garner, *LawProse Lesson #226: "including but not limited to",* LawProse Blog (2 Sept. 2015), http://www.lawprose.org/lawprose-lesson-226-including-but-not-limited-to/.

13.379 According to Garner, such an internal rule of interpretation would in effect preclude the phrase *fruit, including oranges, lemons, and grapefruit* from being interpreted so that *fruit* means only oranges, lemons, and grapefruit. Using the internal principle also allows you to "rigorously avoid the cumbersome phrasing each time you want to introduce examples."

13.380   But elsewhere, Garner says that the phrases *including but not limited to, including without limitation,* and *including without limiting the generality of the foregoing* serve a different function: they're "intended to defeat three canons of construction: *expressio unius est exclusion alterius* ('to express one thing is to exclude the other'), *noscitur a sociis* ('it is known by its associates'), and *ejusdem generis* ('of the same class or nature')." *Garner's Dictionary of Legal Usage,* at 439–40.

13.381   Without considering whether, and how, each of those three judicial rules of interpretation relates to this issue, it's clear that Garner has in mind avoiding, for example, having the phrase *fruit, including oranges, lemons, and grapefruit* interpreted so that *fruit* means only fruit similar to those listed, namely citrus fruit.

13.382   It's easy to reconcile Garner's conflicting rationales: the internal rule of interpretation could logically be intended to preclude attributing any limiting effect to items following *including,* whether that limiting effect consists of interpreting those items to be an exhaustive list or requiring the class in question to consist only of items similar to the listed items.

13.383   But courts have been willing to ignore *including but not limited to* (see 13.364–.367), so it follows that they would be willing to ignore the related internal principle. In the blog post mentioned in 13.378, Garner seems to reject this, saying, "Will judges take such a definition seriously? Generally, yes. I defy anyone to produce a case in which this definition hasn't worked, so that *including* defined in this way has nevertheless been held to introduce an exhaustive listing."

13.384   This manual won't take Garner up on his challenge, as it seems unlikely that a court would deem a list exhaustive even if it's introduced as not being limited. More relevant are those cases in which courts endorse the notion that a group followed by a list of items introduced by *including but not limited to* is limited to items similar to the listed items. That interpretation is less limiting than holding that a list is exhaustive, but it's nevertheless limiting, and in a way that drafters relying on *including but not limited to* might not expect. So because it ignores the real threat, Garner's challenge is too narrow to be meaningful. He offers no reason for this manual to change its recommendation that instead of adding to *including* and *includes,* you use them in a more targeted way.

Related Problematic Usages

13.385   Use of *for example* to introduce a specific list after a general word raises the same issues as does use of *including,* except that it wouldn't work to use an enlarging item (see 13.370) after *for example.* In other words, it would be a little odd to say *fruit, for example tomatoes.* Because this manual recommends not using *including* in contracts to list obvious examples of a general word (see 13.369), it follows that it also recommends not using *for example* before a list of items. That applies also to the abbreviated Latinism *e.g.* (*exempli gratia*). But *for example* can introduce illustrative scenarios. It could, for instance, be used to introduce an example of how a formula might operate.

13.386 The phrase *including with limitation* occurs just often enough to make one wonder whether instead of being a mistake, it's a misguided attempt to say "consisting of." Either way, don't use it.

13.387 A related oddity is *excluding without limitation*. It suggests that not only is a specified item being excluded from a class, so is other unspecified stuff. It has the potential to be pointless (*fruit, excluding without limitation bicycles*) or perplexing (*fruit, excluding without limitation apples*), but never useful. It features in particularly bloated traditional drafting, so it's likely that while blundering around in the fog, the drafters never noticed that *excluding without limitation* makes no sense.

INCORPORATED BY REFERENCE

13.388 Because the concept of incorporation by reference is often misapplied in contracts, and because on those occasions when it is used appropriately there are clearer ways of expressing the concept, don't use the phrase *incorporated by reference* in a contract.

13.389 Sometimes a contract will provide, in referring to a particular exhibit or schedule, that the exhibit or schedule is *incorporated herein by reference*. (A wordier take: *is incorporated by this reference and made a part of this agreement*.) Or it might state, *All of the schedules and exhibits attached to this agreement are deemed incorporated herein by reference*. But if under a contract Acme is required to send notices to the stockholders at the addresses in schedule 3.1, that reference is enough to bring schedule 3.1 within the scope of the contract. Incorporation by reference accomplishes nothing.

13.390 Comparable to this usage is stating in one contract that another contract is being incorporated into it when the only reason for so stating is that both contracts represent separate components of one transaction. For example: *This note is entered into in accordance with a pledge and security agreement between the Borrower and the Lender dated the date of this agreement, which pledge and security agreement is incorporated herein by reference in its entirety*. The interplay between the constituent components of a transaction would be spelled out in the contracts, rendering redundant the notion of incorporation by reference.

13.391 Just because one contract is subject to a provision in another contract doesn't mean that the provision must be incorporated by reference:

> Recourse to and the liability of any past, present, or future partner of the Borrower is limited as provided in section 9.12 of the Credit Agreement ~~and the provisions of that section are hereby incorporated by reference~~.

13.392 And don't incorporate recitals by reference into the body of the contract (see 2.154).

13.393 But incorporation by reference is appropriate to describe the act of importing into an agreement, without repeating them, provisions from a separate agreement. For example, if Baker is purchasing assets from Able and reselling them to Charlie, the purchase agreement between Baker and Charlie might incorporate by reference, as if Baker were making them in that agreement, all statements of fact made by Able in the purchase agreement between Able and Baker. But instead of using the jargon *incorporated by reference,* it would be simpler and more concise to describe what is actually happening: *Baker hereby makes to Charlie, as if they were in this agreement, all statements of fact made by Able to Baker in the Able–Baker Purchase Agreement.* (In that regard, see the discussion of *mutatis mutandis* at 13.546.)

INDEFINITELY, PERPETUALLY

13.394   In contracts, the word *indefinitely* is used to convey two different meanings. One meaning is "without limit," the implication being that although a limit hasn't been specified, one could be specified at some point.

> Acme may terminate this agreement upon giving 30 days' notice to Widgetco if Acme discontinues or *indefinitely* suspends development of the Product.

13.395   But *indefinitely* is also used to convey the meaning "perpetually." The word *perpetually* itself conveys that meaning more clearly, in that there's nothing that isn't definite about forever:

> During the term of this agreement and *indefinitely* [read *perpetually*] thereafter … .

13.396   If the notion of "perpetually," however articulated, is followed by *until,* you can dispense with the notion of "perpetually":

> Participant acknowledges that the Securities must be held ~~indefinitely~~ until they are registered under the Securities Act or an exemption from registration is available.

13.397   And it doesn't make sense to perpetually (or forever) release someone. You release someone once—you don't keep on releasing them. (Regarding using *irrevocably* in a release, see 3.43.)

13.398   As alternatives to *perpetually, forever* has an unfortunate fairy-tale quality to it, *until/to the end of time* and *until/to the end of the world* even more so.

INDEMNIFY

Function

13.399   If a party makes an inaccurate statement of fact in a contract or breaches a contract obligation, the counterparty will have remedies available. In common-law jurisdictions, it can bring a claim for damages under the contract or in tort.

13.400   But it might benefit contract parties to address in their contract how specified claims are to be handled. That's the function served by indemnification provisions. The potential benefits are described below.

INDEMNIFICATION CAN BENEFIT A PARTY BRINGING A CLAIM

13.401 *Bring In Deep Pockets.* A party with limited resources wouldn't be a promising target for a lawsuit seeking common-law remedies. In an indemnification provision, a party could arrange for someone more substantial—typically a parent company—to be responsible for any liabilities of the other party.

13.402 *Recover for Disclosed Liabilities.* If a party has disclosed a problem—for example, environmental contamination—the other party couldn't base a common-law cause of action on that problem, given that it had been disclosed. An indemnification provision would allow the nondisclosing party to arrange for the disclosing party to compensate it if the disclosed problem causes the nondisclosing party to incur losses or liabilities.

13.403 *Recover for External Events or Circumstances.* Indemnification provides one way to allocate risk for occurrence or nonoccurrence of an event or circumstance that isn't entirely under the control of the indemnifying party, for example whether a government agency issues a permit.

13.404 *Recover for Losses Caused by Nonparties.* If Acme incurs losses or liabilities due to a claim by a nonparty that's related to the subject matter of the contract—for example, purchased assets—but that isn't due to the counterparty's having breached an obligation or having made an inaccurate statement of fact, Acme couldn't bring a claim against the other party to the contract unless the other party had agreed to provide indemnification for any such losses or liabilities.

13.405 *Ensure Losses Aren't Covered by a Provision Excluding Certain Types of Damages.* Seeking to be indemnified for losses incurred due to nonparty claims constitutes a claim under the contract. That would make it difficult for the indemnifying party to argue that those losses constitute consequential damages or some other kind of excluded damages (see 13.161).

13.406 *Recover Attorneys' Fees and Expenses.* In litigation in the United States seeking common-law remedies, it's the norm that the plaintiff isn't entitled to recover attorneys' fees and expenses. Indemnification provisions could specify otherwise. (That could also be achieved by a separate contract provision outside of indemnification.)

INDEMNIFICATION CAN BENEFIT A PARTY SUBJECT TO A CLAIM

13.407 *Can Provide for a Cap.* Common-law remedies aren't subject to a cap on liability. In indemnification provisions, the parties can agree to cap indemnification liability.

13.408 *Can Provide for Shorter Time Limits.* A plaintiff could seek common-law remedies until the statute of limitations expires. In indemnification provisions, the parties could agree to shorter time limits for bringing claims. (Depending on that jurisdiction, that could also be achieved by a separate contract provision outside of indemnification.)

13.409 *Can Provide for a Basket.* A plaintiff could bring a common-law claim for a relatively trifling amount. In indemnification provisions, the parties could agree on a minimum that would have to be reached before indemnification kicks in—in other words, a "basket," whether of the "threshold" or "deductible" variety.

INDEMNIFICATION ADDS PREDICTABILITY

13.410   In indemnification provisions, the parties can specify procedures to be followed if a party brings a claim for indemnification. That makes for greater predictability than simply leaving such matters to litigation. But predictability is assured only if indemnification is the exclusive remedy for such claims.

WHEN YOU CAN DO WITHOUT INDEMNIFICATION

13.411   If you're not worried about gaining access to deeper pockets; if you don't need to address the consequences of disclosed liabilities; or if your being subject to nonparty claims isn't a major concern (either because they're a remote possibility or because any claims would likely be for modest amounts), then indemnification would probably be more trouble than it's worth. Remedies otherwise available would likely address your needs, so including indemnification provisions in your contract would add a lot of words for little benefit.

13.412   And if your main concern is allowing the prevailing party in a dispute to recover attorneys' fees (see 13.652), you could address that issue outside of indemnification provisions.

13.413   So before you provide for indemnification in a contract, ask yourself whether the claims that might arise justify lumbering the contract with full-blown indemnification provisions.

WHAT KINDS OF CLAIMS

13.414   The discussion above anticipates that indemnification provisions can—but don't have to—cover claims between the parties as well as nonparty claims against one or other party. Many practitioners think that indemnification provisions serve primarily, or exclusively, to address nonparty claims.

13.415   Whatever the historical practice, it's now unexceptional to have indemnification cover claims between the parties. In fact, it's standard in mergers-and-acquisitions transactions. And in defining *indemnify*, *Black's Law Dictionary* refers to reimbursing another for "a loss suffered because of a third party's or *one's own* act or default" (emphasis added).

13.416   But if you want indemnification to cover claims between the parties, make that clear in the indemnification provisions themselves or risk getting into a fight over it. For an example of a court holding, for debatable reasons, that an indemnification provision covered just nonparty claims, see the opinion of the Alberta Supreme Court, Appellate Division, in *Mobil Oil Canada Ltd. v. Beta Well Service Ltd.* (1974), 43 D.L.R. (3d) 745 (A.B.C.A.). For an example of a court holding that an indemnification provision covered claims between the parties, see *Hot Rods, LLC v. Northrop Grumman Systems Corp.*, 242 Cal. App. 4th 1166, 1179 (2015). See also *NevadaCare,*

Inc. v. Department of Human Services, 783 N.W.2d 459, 470 (Iowa 2010), reh'g denied (22 June 2010) ("Currently, there is a split of authority as to whether an indemnification provision applies to claims between the parties to the agreement or only to third-party claims.").

Say *Shall Indemnify*, Not *Hereby Indemnifies*

13.417 *Black's Law Dictionary* says that *indemnify* means both "To reimburse (another) for a loss suffered because of a third party's or one's own act or default" and "To promise to reimburse (another) for such a loss." So *indemnify* can be used in both language of obligation (*Acme shall indemnify Widgetco*) and language of performance (*Acme hereby indemnifies Widgetco*). Review of an informal sample of contracts filed by public companies on the U.S. Securities and Exchange Commission's EDGAR system suggests that drafters greatly prefer *indemnify* as language of obligation rather than language of performance.

13.418 Although both usages are adequate to accomplish the intended purpose, there's value to uniformity, so hasten the demise of *hereby indemnifies* by using only *shall indemnify*. What doesn't make sense is combining the two—*hereby indemnifies and shall keep indemnified*.

Don't Use *Indemnify and Hold Harmless*

13.419 It's commonplace for drafters to use the phrase *indemnify and hold harmless* (or *save harmless*). Use instead just *indemnify*—it's clearer and more concise.

MEANING

13.420 *Black's Law Dictionary* treats *indemnify* and *hold harmless* as synonyms. It defines *hold harmless* as follows: "To absolve (another party) from any responsibility for damage or other liability arising from the transaction; INDEMNIFY." (For the *Black's Law Dictionary* definition of *indemnify*, see 13.417.) *Garner's Dictionary of Legal Usage*, at 443–44, collects other dictionary definitions to the same effect, concluding that "The evidence is overwhelming that *indemnify* and *hold harmless* are perfectly synonymous."

13.421 Some courts have come to the same conclusion, notably the Delaware Court of Chancery. In *Majkowski v. American Imaging Management, LLC*, 913 A.2d 572, 588–89 (Del. Ch. 2006), then-Vice Chancellor Strine suggested that many transactional lawyers would be quite surprised to learn that by adding *hold harmless* to *indemnify* they had been creating additional rights. He continued, "As a result of traditional usage, the phrase 'indemnify and hold harmless' just naturally rolls off the tongue (and out of the word processors) of American commercial lawyers. The two terms almost always go together. Indeed, modern authorities confirm that 'hold harmless' has little, if any, different meaning than the word 'indemnify.'" See also *Paniaguas v. Aldon Companies, Inc.*, No. 2:04-CV-468-PRC, 2006 WL 2788585 (N.D. Ind. 26 Sept. 2006) (holding that *hold harmless* is synonymous with *indemnify*); *Consult Urban Renewal Development Corp. v. T.R. Arnold & Associates, Inc.*, No. CIV A 06-1684 WJM, 2007 WL 1175742 (D.N.J. 19 Apr. 2007) (same); *In re Marriage of Ginsberg*, 750 N.W.2d 520,

522 (Iowa 2008) (same); *Loscher v. Hudson*, 182 P.3d 25, 33 (Kan. Ct. App. 2008) ("[A] hold harmless provision in a separation agreement is the same as an indemnity agreement.").

13.422   But some commentators have seen fit to endorse a distinction between *indemnify* and *hold harmless*. For example, David Mellinkoff, *Mellinkoff's Dictionary of American Legal Usage* 286 (1992), says that *"hold harmless* is understood to protect another against the risk of loss as well as actual loss." It goes on to say that *indemnify* is sometimes used as a synonym of *hold harmless*, but that *indemnify* can also mean "reimburse for any damage," a narrower meaning than that of *hold harmless*.

13.423   Some courts have done likewise. For example, in *United States v. Contract Management, Inc.*, 912 F.2d 1045, 1048 (9th Cir. 1990), the Ninth Circuit Court of Appeals noted in dicta that "the terms 'indemnify' and 'hold harmless' refer to slightly different legal remedies." And in *Queen Villas Homeowners Ass'n v. TCB Property Management*, 56 Cal. Rptr. 3d 528, 534 (Ct. App. 2007), the court fabricated a distinction—that *indemnify* is an "offensive" right allowing an indemnified party to seek indemnification whereas *hold harmless* is a "defensive" right allowing an indemnified party not to be bothered by the other party's seeking indemnification itself.

13.424   And in the Canadian case *Stewart Title Guarantee Company v. Zeppieri*, [2009] O.J. No. 322 (S.C.J.), the Ontario Superior Court of Justice held, without providing any support, that "the contractual obligation to save harmless, in my view, is broader than that of indemnification," in that someone having the benefit of a *hold harmless* provision "should never have to put his hand in his pocket in respect of a claim" covered by that provision.

ELIMINATING RISK

13.425   So the redundancy in the phrase *indemnify and hold harmless* is risky, in that a disgruntled contract party might seek to have unintended meaning attributed to *hold harmless*. And relying on the rule of interpretation that every word in a contract is to be given effect, a court might decide that *indemnify* and *hold harmless* express different meanings.

13.426   To stay out of trouble, never use *hold harmless*. Using just *indemnify* is no obstacle to saying whatever you want to say.

13.427   The basic issue regarding the coverage provided by indemnification is whether you're indemnified just for those losses you've paid for, or whether the indemnifying party must also step in when you've incurred a liability that you're being asked to pay. That distinction is what Mellinkoff (see 13.422) and the court in *Stewart Title* (see 13.424) allude to in attributing a broad meaning to *hold harmless*. But relying on *hold harmless* to ensure that an indemnified party is covered in both contexts is to shirk a drafter's responsibility to articulate meaning clearly.

13.428   To ensure that indemnification covers both contexts, impose on Acme the obligation to indemnify Widgetco against both losses and liabilities. *Black's Law Dictionary* defines *loss* in part as "the disappearance or diminution of value, usu. in an unexpected or relatively unpredictable way," and it defines *liability* in part as "A financial or pecuniary obligation." If you address both those concepts, Acme would be indemnifying Widgetco against both actual loss and risk of loss. It would be redundant to have Acme also hold Widgetco harmless, whatever that might mean.

13.429 But instead of simply alluding to losses and liabilities, indemnification provisions should be more explicit. A defined term—"Indemnifiable Losses" or some variant—should be used to specify exactly what losses and liabilities are covered. For example, including judgments as one element would help make it clear that an indemnified party isn't required to pay a court judgment before having it covered by indemnification. And provisions specifying indemnification procedures (see 13.431) should address, among other things, payment of litigation expenses.

Don't Use *Shall Indemnify and Keep Indemnified*

13.430 A variant of *shall indemnify* is *shall indemnify and keep indemnified.* Don't use it—it serves no discernable purpose. For a similar hybrid, see 13.418.

Defend Is Inadequate

13.431 Drafters routinely add *defend* to *indemnify and hold harmless*, but that doesn't begin to address how defense of nonparty claims is to be handled. See, e.g., *Fillip v. Centerstone Linen Services*, LLC, No. CIV.A. 8712-ML, 2014 WL 793123, at *4 (Del. Ch. 27 Feb. 2014) (holding that "an obligation to defend is not the equivalent of an obligation to advance defense costs"). To avoid uncertainty and the possibility of dispute, address that explicitly in provisions governing indemnification procedures. How to do that is beyond the scope of this manual, but one resource is Kenneth A. Adams, *My Indemnification Language*, Adams on Contract Drafting (13 Aug. 2013), http://www.adamsdrafting.com/my-indemnification-language/.

Prepositions

USE A SINGLE PREPOSITION

13.432 You could use *indemnify* with *for*, *from*, or *against*. Which you choose depends in part on what follows the preposition.

13.433 Courts have relied on prepositions in holding that an indemnification provision doesn't cover claims between the parties. See *Jacobson v. Crown Zellerbach Corp.*, 539 P.2d 641 (Or. 1975) (holding that if the parties had intended indemnification to cover claims between the parties, the provision in question would have read "For any claim," not "From any claim"); see also *Cecil Lawter Real Estate School, Inc. v. Town & Country Shopping Center Co.*, 694 P.2d 815 (Ariz. Ct. App. 1984) (citing *Jacobson* in holding that because the provision in question read "from and against all loss," it covered only nonparty claims).

13.434 But that sort of mischief happens only when the drafter fails to express key indemnification issues. Address them clearly and your choice of preposition becomes irrelevant.

DON'T USE MULTIPLE PREPOSITIONS

13.435   The triplet *for, from, and against* occurs in indemnification language. Perhaps the three prepositions were originally linked to *indemnify, hold harmless, and defend* (in whatever order):

> The New Operators shall indemnify, defend, and hold harmless the Owners for, from, and against any liability … .

13.436   That linking of triplets would appear to owe as much rhetorical grandeur as to semantics. For example, *against, from, and against* would be a legitimate alternative, but it doesn't have had the same flair as *for, from, and against*.

13.437   That use of *for, from, and against* was driven by rhetorical appeal rather than substance would explain why nowadays there's no clear link between a specific verb and a specific preposition. Instead, the number of verbs is routinely different from the number of prepositions:

> … defend, save, indemnify, and hold CIG Financial harmless for, from, and against any and all liabilities … [*four verbs, three prepositions*]

> … hold Seller harmless from and indemnify Seller for, from, and against any and all claims … [*two verbs, three prepositions*]

> … indemnify, defend, and hold harmless the other party and its affiliates, parent companies, subsidiaries, and their respective directors, officers, and employees, from any and all claims … [*three verbs, one preposition*]

13.438   This manual recommends using just *indemnify* (see 13.419), thereby rendering multiple prepositions redundant.

Indemnify as a Term of Art

13.439   Many contracts professionals are skittish about assuming indemnification obligations, particularly in commercial contracts. The concern is that a claim for indemnification provides the claimant advantages not available to a breach-of-contract claimant.

13.440   More specifically, some courts and commentators believe that whereas in a breach-of-contract claim the court determines how much to compensate a nonbreaching party for nonperformance by the breaching party, an obligation to indemnify (particularly if unrelated to an underlying breach of a contract) actually constitutes an obligation to pay an amount of money if certain specified events occur and as such isn't subject to the rule-of-reasonableness standards to which breach-of-contract claims are subject. See Glenn D. West & Sara G. Duran, *Reassessing the "Consequences" of Consequential Damage Waivers in Acquisition Agreements*, 63 Business Lawyer 777, 785–88 (2008).

13.441   It's not clear how much of an issue this is, and whether it can be drafted around. But the aversion to indemnification is real, and any drafter who encounters it should consider using terminology that's less loaded than *indemnify*. The likeliest candidate is the formulation *Acme will be liable to Widgetco for*. You can make that switch because *indemnify* is a term of art fraught with doctrinal implications that are irrelevant for establishing contract relations (see 1.7).

INDENTURE

13.442   Here's how *Black's Law Dictionary* defines *indenture*: "A formal written instrument made by two or more parties with different interests, traditionally having the edges serrated, or indented, in a zigzag fashion to reduce the possibility of forgery and to distinguish it from a deed poll."

13.443   Contracts are no longer given serrated edges, but the word *indenture* has survived in the terms *bond indenture*, *debenture indenture*, and *trust indenture*.

13.444   So *indenture* is simply a synonym of *contract* now used to refer to a limited group of contracts. One could just as well refer to a *bond agreement* or *trust agreement*, and such a change would be unobjectionable. All that *indenture* has going for it is tradition. It doesn't create any problems, but don't attach any significance to it.

IN OTHER WORDS

13.445   If you use the phrase *in other words* in a contract, you're acknowledging that you failed to state the concept in question clearly enough the first time around. Get it right the first time and you won't need *in other words*.

13.446   The abbreviated Latinism *i.e.* (*id est*, meaning *that is*) is roughly equivalent to *in other words*, so don't use *i.e.* or *that is* either. The same goes for *namely* and the archaic *to wit*.

INURE

13.447   Obscure wording is often a reliable sign that a provision is expendable. An example of that is use of the word *inure*. (The variant spelling *enure* is popular in Canada.) It means to take effect, to come into use. It features in the phrase *inures to the benefit*, which is a fixture in contracts.

13.448   It's used as a wordy alternative to the verb *benefits*. Here's an example from a credit agreement:

> The Borrower hereby acknowledges that the issuance of Letters of Credit for the account of Subsidiaries *inures to the benefit of* [read *benefits*] the Borrower ... .

13.449   But apart from this general use of *inures to the benefit*, the phrase occurs primarily in two contexts. You find it in the pointless "successors and assigns" provision. See Kenneth A. Adams, *It's Time to Get Rid of the "Successors and Assigns" Provision*, The Advocate, June/July 2013, at 30. It's also used in trademark license agreements, as well as in other kinds of contracts that include the grant of a trademark license. Here's an example:

> The parties intend that any and all goodwill in the Mark arising from the Licensee's use of the Fund Names will *inure solely to the benefit* of the Licensor.

13.450   Although some trademark lawyers are convinced that in this context the phrase serves a valuable function, in fact it's either redundant or an inferior alternative to directly addressing the issue in question. See Kenneth A. Adams, Inures to the Benefit *and Trademark Licensing*, 105 Trademark Reporter 944 (2015).

IT BEING UNDERSTOOD

13.451   Don't use *it being understood*. There's always a better alternative.

13.452   Usually *it being understood* serves the same function as *for the avoidance of doubt* (see 13.310), in that it introduces language that seeks to clarify or supplement preceding language. The appropriate fix depends on the context. It might involve deleting *it being understood* and performing whatever additional minor surgery is required to carve out what follows as a separate sentence:

> Except to the extent that Advances are deemed to be loans, no Seller has any material outstanding loan to any Person Related to the ~~Business, it being understood that~~ [read Business. *For purposes of the immediately preceding sentence,*] obligations to reimburse employees for relocation, business, travel, entertainment, or similar expenses incurred in the Ordinary Course of Business do not constitute loans.

13.453   In the following example, the entire parenthetical beginning *it being understood* can safely be deleted, because the *If* that begins the sentence is all that's required to convey discretion.

> If the Company maintains employee benefit plans (including pension, profit-sharing, disability, accident, medical, life insurance, and hospitalization plans) ~~(it being understood that the Company may but shall not be obligated to do so)~~, the Executive will be entitled to participate therein in accordance with the Company's regular practices with respect to similarly situated senior executives.

13.454   Sometimes *it being understood* is used to insert, in parentheses, one provision in the middle of another. That makes for a particularly disjointed provision:

> If all of the Equity Interests of any Pledgor owned by the Borrower or any of its Subsidiaries are sold to a Person other than a Credit Party in a transaction permitted under the Credit Agreement, then that Pledgor will be released as a Pledgor under this agreement without any further action hereunder (*it being understood* that the sale of all of the Equity Interests in any Person that owns, directly or indirectly, all of the Equity Interests in any Pledgor will be deemed to be a sale of all of the Equity Interests in that Pledgor for purposes of this section), and the Pledgee is authorized and directed to execute and deliver such instruments of release as are reasonably satisfactory to it.

13.455   The phrase *it being understood* can also be used to express the same meaning as *acknowledge* (see 3.436)—that the party in question doesn't have first-hand knowledge of a fact but instead is accepting as accurate that fact as asserted by another party. If that's the intended meaning, then use *acknowledge*, as it's the simpler and clearer alternative:

> If any of the Collateral is in the possession of a warehouseman or bailee, the Borrowing Agent shall promptly notify the Bank and, upon request of the Bank, the Borrowers shall use reasonable efforts to obtain promptly a Collateral Access Agreement, ~~it being understood and agreed, however,~~ [read. *The Borrower acknowledges*] that failure to obtain a Collateral Access Agreement might (in accordance with clause (c) of the definition of Eligible Inventory) result in decreased availability under the Borrowing Base.

JOINDER

13.456   In lending and corporate transactions, *joinder* has come to mean a document by which someone becomes party to an existing contract:

> ... the Company shall cause each such Permitted Subsidiary to become party to the Guaranty by signing a *joinder* to the Guaranty reasonably satisfactory to the Required Holders.

13.457   Or you could use *joinder agreement*:

> ... will become a Holder under this agreement by signing a joinder agreement in which it agrees to become subject to the terms of this agreement.

13.458   This use of *joinder* represents an extension of the original meaning. (*Black's Law Dictionary* defines *joinder* as "The uniting of parties or claims in a single lawsuit.") There's no reason not to coin a new meaning for a word if it serves a purpose, but it seems unnecessarily legalistic to repurpose an unrelated legal term of art instead of coming up with simpler, clearer terminology.

13.459   An alternative term used to convey the same meaning is *accession agreement*. But that too uses borrowed terminology: *Black's Law Dictionary* defines *accession* in part as "A method by which a country that is not among a treaty's original signatories becomes a party to it."

13.460   The contract in question is in effect an *amendment*, so it would be simplest to call it that. And the extract in 13.457 could be adjusted to read as follows:

> ... will become a Holder under this agreement by signing an amendment to this agreement to that effect.

JOINT AND SEVERAL

13.461   The implications of the phrase *joint and several* are different from what the conventional wisdom suggests. There are clearer ways to address the related issues.

Theory

13.462   The concepts *joint* and *several* refer to liability, but for contracts, authorities refer to such liability as arising out of promises. For example, here's what 12 *Williston on Contracts* § 36:1 (footnotes omitted) says:

> Copromisors are liable jointly if all of them have promised the entire performance of the contract. The effect of a joint obligation is that each joint promisor is liable for the whole performance jointly assumed ... .
>
> ...
>
> A several obligation, by contrast, has the effect of creating two separate liabilities on a single contract. Thus, when a several obligation is entered into by two or more parties in one instrument, it is the same as though each has executed separate instruments. Under these circumstances, each party is bound separately for the performance which it promises and is not bound jointly with anyone else.
>
> Finally, a joint and several contract is a contract made by the promisee with each promisor and a joint contract made with all the promisors, so that parties having a joint and several obligation are bound jointly as one party, and also severally as separate parties at the same time.

13.463   Here's an example of a joint obligation: *A and B shall pay C $100*. And here's an example of several obligations: *A shall pay C $50, and B shall pay C $50*. You don't have to use the word *joint* to create joint obligations or the word *several* to create several obligations.

13.464   As regards a joint and several obligation, the *Restatement (Second) of Contracts* § 289 (1981) says, "The standard modern form to create duties which are both joint and several is 'We jointly and severally promise,' but any equivalent words will do as well."

13.465   But making an obligation joint and several doesn't affect what can be recovered. Regarding joint obligations, the *Restatement* says, "A and B owe $100 to C jointly, and C obtains a judgment against A and B for $100. Execution may be levied wholly on the property of either A or B, or partially on the property of each." That wouldn't change if you made the obligation joint and several.

13.466   Furthermore, the *Restatement* says, "A and B severally promise to pay C the same $100. C may obtain scparate judgments against each for $100, and may levy execution under either judgment until $100 is collected." So C is covered to the same extent, whether the obligation is joint or several.

Practice

13.467   Transactional lawyers use the terms *joint, several,* and *joint and several* primarily regarding liability, not obligations. That makes sense—if those terms ultimately relate to liability, why not couch them in those terms, rather than in terms of obligations?

13.468 But the substantive redundancy inherent in *joint and several* and in *several* is equally manifest when you speak in terms of liability, with one important exception: *several liability* is sometimes given a meaning that's narrower than the usual meaning, in that it's used, by means of the phrase *several but not joint*, to refer to apportioning liability among holders of ownership interests in an entity in proportion to their respective ownership interests. But given the broader meaning of *several*, it risks confusion to use it also to convey that narrower meaning.

Procedural Implications

13.469 The literature acknowledges the substantive irrelevance of any distinction between *joint* and *several*: the *Restatement (Second) of Contracts* § 288 says that "the distinction between 'joint' and 'several' duties is primarily remedial and procedural."

13.470 The procedural distinction is that if A and B are only jointly liable and not severally liable, failure to join both A and B in a suit for recovery might subject you to dismissal, or at least protracted argument over the issue. If A and B are severally liable, you can proceed against one without the other.

What Should the Drafter Do?

13.471 So the word *joint* is subsumed by *several*—if you're able to go after each obligor separately, you can also go after them all. So nothing is accomplished by using the phrase *joint and several*. And one can improve on the archaic *several* (meaning "separate").

13.472 It follows that although the phrase *joint and several* is a fixture in contracts and is accepted without question by, for example, *Garner's Dictionary of Legal Usage*, at 493, it's a mess. Here's a clearer way to express the concept:

> Acme may elect to recover from any one or more Widgetco Entities the full amount of any collective liability of the Widgetco Entities under this agreement, and Acme may bring one or more separate actions against any one or more Widgetco Entities regarding any such liability.

13.473 And instead of using *several but not joint*, here's how to convey more clearly that liability is to be shared pro rata among holders of ownership interests and that the claimant may proceed against the holders separately:

> Acme may recover from each Shareholder a proportion of any collective liability of the Shareholders under this agreement equal to the proportion of all Shares then outstanding represented by the Shares then owned by that Shareholder. Acme may bring one or more separate actions against any one or more Shareholders regarding any such liability.

Relevance of Statutes

13.474 An added wrinkle is that, as noted in the *Restatement (Second) of Contracts* § 289, "statutes in a sizable number of jurisdictions provide that joint promises have the effect of creating joint and several duties, and statutes in others create a presumption of joint and several duties either in all cases or where all promisors receive a benefit from the consideration." So those statutes would allow you to capture the concept of *several* without having to articulate any liability, or any obligation, as several, whether by using that word or otherwise.

13.475   But drafters might not be inclined to explore the implications of such statutes. And it can sometimes be helpful to make clear to the parties what the law provides. So expressing the *several* concept as proposed in 13.473 wouldn't hurt, even if *several* would be read into a contract by statute.

KNOWLEDGE

13.476   This section considers why one would want to qualify a statement of fact to reflect a party's knowledge. It also contains the components for creating a definition of *knowledge*.

The Function of Knowledge Qualifications

13.477   A party making a statement of fact (known in traditional contract language as a representation, or a warranty, or both; see 3.374) can "qualify" it regarding knowledge: *To the Seller's knowledge, the Seller is not in violation of any Environmental Laws*. The effect of such a qualification is that the party making the statement isn't claiming that it's accurate. Instead, the party is stating that it isn't aware of anything suggesting that the statement is inaccurate.

13.478   A party should consider including a knowledge qualification in a statement of fact if that party is not in a position to determine whether the statement is accurate, usually because the statement refers to matters that might be hidden (such as environmental contamination) or are under the control of others (such as threatened litigation).

13.479   Who bears the risk of unknown problems is a function of risk allocation. The party making the statement would likely argue that it would be unfair to insist that it make a statement of fact if it has no way of knowing whether the statement is accurate. By contrast, the other party would likely argue that as between the parties, the party making the statement should bear the risk of the unknown.

13.480   Certain statements of fact—such as statements regarding threatened litigation—almost invariably include a knowledge limitation. Others—such as a company's statement regarding its capitalization—never do, because they relate to matters over which the party making the statement has control. In the case of yet others—such as statements regarding violations of environmental laws—there is no fixed practice. If including a knowledge qualification in a given statement would not be standard practice, getting the other party to accept that qualification might require that the party making the statement either have superior bargaining power or be willing to make concessions elsewhere in the contract.

13.481   In phrasing a knowledge qualification, don't refer to *the best of* someone's knowledge. For one thing, it adds nothing, because *to the best of Acme's* *knowledge* means exactly the same thing as *to Acme's knowledge*. In this context, the word *best* adds nothing more than a rhetorical flourish (see 8.21), and using *the best of* could lead a reader to assume incorrectly that it implies an obligation to investigate (see 13.488) or some sort of heightened level of knowledge.

13.482 And don't use the couplet *knowledge and belief*. It's a meaningless exercise in redundancy (see 1.37) that a disgruntled contract party might seek to invest with meaning.

Defining *Knowledge*

13.483 Consider using *knowledge* as a defined term. Doing so would allow you to address two issues that otherwise would be subject to uncertainty: whose knowledge would be relevant and whether those one or more persons are under a duty to investigate.

13.484 If the term is to be used regarding a single party that is a legal entity, you would use the form of autonomous definition in [1]. If it is to be used regarding more than one party, you would define the term using the form of autonomous definition in [1a], which should be revised appropriately if the parties are all individuals or all entities.

[1]   "**Acme's Knowledge**" refers to what [*specify whose knowledge applies; see* [2] *and its variants*] [*insert level of knowledge; see* [3] *and its variants*].

[1a]   "**Knowledge**" refers, regarding any Person, to (1) what that Person (if that Person is an individual) [*insert level of knowledge; see* [3] *and its variants*] or (2) what [*specify whose knowledge applies; see* [2] *and its variants*] (if that Person is not an individual) [*insert level of knowledge; see* [3] *and its variants*].

[2]   John Doe

[2a]   [Acme's] [that Person's] executive officers [(as defined in rule 405 of the Securities Act)]

[2b]   [Acme's] [that Person's] directors and executive officers

[2c]   [Acme's] [that Person's] directors, officers, and any other persons having supervisory or management responsibilities regarding [Acme's] [that Person's] operations

[2d]   directors and officers of [Acme and any Acme Subsidiary] [that Person and any of its Subsidiaries] and any other person having supervisory or management responsibilities regarding the operations of [Acme or any Acme Subsidiary] [that Person or any of its Subsidiaries]

[2e]   [Acme's] [that Person's] shareholders, directors, officers, and other employees

[2f]   the shareholders, directors, officers, and other employees of [Acme and any Acme subsidiary] [that Person and any of its Subsidiaries]

[3]   know[s], with no requirement to investigate

[3a]   know[s] or should have known, after inquiring with [Acme's employees] [that Person's employees] [employees of the Acme Plant]

[3b]   know[s] or should have known, after reasonable investigation

13.485   If the party making the statement of fact is an entity and not an individual, whose knowledge would be relevant for determining the accuracy of a statement containing a knowledge qualification? The party making the statement would want to limit the number of people whose knowledge would be relevant, whereas the other party would want to specify as broad a group as possible. Example [2] and its variants demonstrate some possibilities, from limited to broader.

13.486   The reference in [2a] to rule 405 would reduce the likelihood of disagreement regarding who is an executive officer, but it should be used in a contract only if the party benefiting from the knowledge qualification is a U.S. public company.

13.487   A company selling a subsidiary or division would face the question of whose knowledge is relevant for statements regarding the business being sold. Managers of the business being sold would be the most knowledgeable, but the seller could be concerned that if the managers remain with the business being sold, they might be pressured into determining that they had, in fact, known that a given statement was inaccurate, or might come to that conclusion themselves in their eagerness to ingratiate themselves with their new employer. So the seller might prefer to omit from the definition of *Knowledge* officers involved in the business being sold, something the buyer would resist.

13.488   In addition to the question of whose knowledge is relevant, a definition of *Knowledge* should address whether it means actual knowledge (as [3]) or knowledge after some level of investigation. A more limited alternative to the reasonable-investigation standard stated in [3b] is a standard based on inquiry of a specified group of employees, as in [3a]. Both [3a] and [3b] use *know[s] or should have known* to make it clear that if no investigation takes place, the standard will be one of constructive knowledge. (Avoid, as being unclear, references to *reasonable knowledge*.)

Don't Use *Is Unaware Of*

13.489   Consider this example using *is unaware of*, followed by a version using *knowledge*:

... the Company *is unaware of* any facts that would form a reasonable basis for any such claim.

... to the Company's *knowledge*, no facts exist that would form a reasonable basis for any such claim.

13.490   It would be reckless to assume that one could create in a contract a meaningful distinction between absence of knowledge and knowledge of absence. Use *knowledge*—it's widely used, unlike *is unaware of*, and the different ways it can be defined make it more versatile.

LATINISMS

13.491 Many contracts filed by public companies on the U.S. Securities and Exchange Commission's EDGAR system contain one or more of these words and phrases derived from Latin:

- ab initio
- allocatur
- bona fide
- contra proferentem
- de facto
- de jure
- de minimis
- de novo
- ejusdem generis
- ex gratia
- ex parte
- in personam
- in rem
- inter alia (see 13.22)

- ipso facto
- mala fides
- mutatis mutandis (see 13.546)
- nunc pro tunc
- pacta sunt servanda
- parens patriae
- pari passu
- per diem
- prima facie
- pro tanto
- qui tam
- res judicata
- sui generis
- ultra vires

13.492 Some Latinisms have become so ingrained that they can now be accepted as English—for example, *pro rata*, *status quo*, and *vice versa*. Contracts would be clearer if all remaining Latinisms, including those in the above list, were omitted. Instead, express the intended meaning in standard English. (See 13.266 regarding *etc.*; see 13.270–.273 regarding *et seq.*)

LEGAL FEES INSTEAD OF *ATTORNEYS' FEES*

13.493 The problem with the phrase *attorneys' fees* isn't where to put the apostrophe. (Yes, it's best to place it after the *s*, to spare one getting into fights over whether it refers to fees of just one attorney.) Instead, the problem is the word *attorney*, which in the United States is an unnecessarily formal alternative to *lawyer*.

13.494 What to use instead? The obvious alternative is *lawyers' fees*, but *legal fees* is preferable—it doesn't require an apostrophe, it would cover paralegal fees too, and it should be acceptable outside the United States, regardless of how legal professionals are referred to in a given jurisdiction.

LIKELY

13.495   The word *likely* is used routinely in contracts: *As used herein, the term "Disability" means a physical or mental incapacity or disability that has rendered, or is likely to render, the Executive unable to perform … .* But *likely* is a slippery word. In certain contexts one can't avoid using *likely*, but you should be aware of the uncertainties.

13.496   First, consider what *likely* isn't—it isn't vague. Vague words such as *promptly* and *material* require that you assess circumstances from the perspective of a reasonable person (see 7.42). By contrast, *likely* is an expression of the degree of probability that something will occur. As such, likelihood isn't a function of reasonableness.

13.497   But it's not clear what *likely* means. Here's what *Garner's Dictionary of Legal Usage*, at 545, says:

> **likely** has different shades of meaning. Most often it indicates a degree of probability greater than five on a scale of one to ten… . But it may also refer to a degree of possibility that is less than five on that same scale.

13.498   One indication that *likely* doesn't have a set meaning is how *likely* relates to *probable*, a word that exhibits the same characteristics. Consider the following:

> "Although the term 'likely' connotes something more than a mere possibility, it also connotes something less than a probability or reasonable certainty." *State v. Green*, 18 Ohio App. 3d 69, 72, 480 N.E.2d 1128, 1132 (1984).

> "Probable and likely are synonyms." *Anderson v. Bell*, 303 S.W.2d 93, 98 (Mo. 1957).

13.499   If two courts can reach different conclusions regarding how *likely* relates to *probable*, that suggests that you can't rely on any court to have a clear idea what one or the other word means. You could get around that by instead referring to a percentage probability: *a physical or mental incapacity or disability that has rendered, or is likely to render* [read *has a probability of greater than 50% of rendering*], *the Executive unable to perform.*

13.500   Even if you assume that it's clear what *likely* means, a further problem is that although referring to a mathematical degree of probability is appropriate when you're rolling dice or playing cards, it's hard to see how it would be relevant for contract provisions. Arguments over likelihood quickly become meaningless once you move from one or other end of the spectrum of probability into the middle. For example, it's hard to see how one could have a meaningful debate over whether an event has a 49% or a 51% chance of occurring.

13.501   And don't say *reasonably likely*—nothing is accomplished by adding vagueness to a degree of probability.

LOOK TO

13.502   Consider use of *look to* in these examples:

> The Tenant shall *look to* the provider of the Tenant's insurance for coverage for loss of the Tenant's use of the Premises and any other related losses or damages incurred by the Tenant during any reconstruction period.

> … and those Holders will thereafter be entitled to *look to* the Issuer only as general creditors for payment thereof (unless otherwise provided by law); … .

13.503   *Look to* seems oddly colloquial, but the bigger issue is what's really at stake. Consider *The Holder shall look to only the Issuer for payment on this note*. It's phrased as language of obligation, but presumably whoever this provision is intended to benefit—let's assume it's the issuer's parent— doesn't actually care whether the holder looks to anyone for payment. A clearer way to express what underlies this provision would be to use language of policy—*Only the Issuer will be liable for payment on this note*. But it would be even clearer to say *Parent will not be liable for payment on this note*.

13.504   So instead of saying *A shall look to only B for X*, consider saying instead *C will not be liable for X*. But if the set of C consists of more than one member, consider saying *Only B will be liable for X*.

LUMP SUM

13.505   In construction and some other fields, the term *lump sum* can have a specialized meaning. But *lump-sum payment* is also used generally as a clumsy alternative to *single payment*. In that case, if a contract specifies when a payment is to be made, the benefits of specifying that the payment should be a lump-sum (or single) payment are marginal. Consider this example:

> No later than 60 days after the Company has Sufficient Funds, it shall pay all Deferred Portions to the Executive [*in a single lump-sum payment*], subject to the usual withholding.

13.506   Given that the company could wait 60 days to pay what it owes the executive, it wouldn't benefit the executive to prevent the company from paying the executive in installments over the course of the 60 days, in the unlikely event it wished to do so.

13.507   And if a contract specifies the day that a payment is to be made, no purpose would be served by specifying that it should be made in a single payment, unless you wish to protect against the possibility of the payment being made in installments on that one day:

> … the Company shall pay the Executive an additional amount equal to 12 times the monthly rate of the Executive's Base Salary on the Date of Termination, which amount the Company shall pay ~~in one lump-sum payment~~ on the 30th day after the Date of Termination (or the first business day thereafter if the 30th day is not a business day).

MERELY, MERE

13.508   The word *merely* has a dismissive quality that makes it unsuited to contract language.

13.509   Depending on the context, the fix for *merely* in contracts might be simply to delete it or to use *just* or *only* instead:

> ... and any advice given by any Purchaser or any of their respective representatives or agents in connection with the Transaction Documents and the transactions contemplated thereby is ~~merely~~ incidental to the Purchasers' purchase of the Securities.

> ... as if those limitations applied to the Participant's entire Vested Interest and not ~~merely~~ [read *only to*] amounts contributed under Code Section 401(k).

13.510   And the same applies to the adjective *mere*:

> ... except that the term "Participate In" does not include ~~mere~~ ownership of less than 5% of the stock of a publicly held corporation ... .

> ... and the Plan constitutes ~~a mere~~ [read *only a*] promise by the Company to make benefit payments in the future.

13.511   Regarding use of *mere* and *merely* in referring to categories of contract language, see 3.3.

MONEY—STATING AMOUNTS OF

13.512   Stating amounts of money in a contract raises several issues.

Use Only Digits

13.513   This manual recommends generally using words for numbers up to ten and digits thereafter (see 14.13–.15), but to state amounts of money use only digits: in a contract it would be odd to use a mix of words (*nine dollars*) and digits (*$12*).

13.514   For the same reason that they use words and digits in stating numbers generally (see 14.1), it's commonplace for drafters to use words and digits when stating amounts of money: *Acme shall pay Widgetco One Million Dollars ($1,000,000).* Don't do that.

Decimal Fractions

13.515   *The Chicago Manual of Style*, at 9.20, says that when stating amounts of money you should use zeros after a decimal point only when fractional amounts appear in the same context. In other words, say *$2* rather than *$2.00*, unless the provision in question also refers to, for example, *$3.78* and *$12.93*. And it's redundant to add *and 00/100 dollars* after an even number of dollars.

13.516 If you're stating less than a whole unit of currency, put a zero before the decimal point, as in *$0.32*. You could conceivably say instead *32¢*, but it would be a nuisance to have the convention you use depend on whether the amount is less than a dollar.

13.517 Some countries use a comma rather than a decimal point to express fractional amounts. And whereas in the United States and the United Kingdom a comma is used as a thousands separator, as in *1,234,567*, other countries follow other conventions. Pick the conventions you think most appropriate and apply them consistently.

Very Large Amounts

13.518 It's commonplace for drafters to use a mixture of words and digits to express large amounts of money: *$4.4 billion*; *$3 million*. This approach can make amounts of money easier to read, particularly if a provision includes several large amounts. But don't switch to a mixture of words and digits if other numbers in the same context use all digits. And don't go beyond two decimal points to express fractional amounts.

13.519 In the United States, *billion* means 1,000,000,000 (one thousand millions), but in Germany and many other non-English-speaking regions, *billion* means one million millions; the U.S. *trillion* equals the German *billion*. Great Britain has been shifting from the German system to the U.S. system. If in an international transaction confusion might arise regarding the meaning of *billion*, use only digits to state amounts of one thousand million units or more of the currency in question.

Currencies

13.520 A reference to an amount of money would have to specify the currency. You can accomplish that by using a currency sign or by using the three-letter currency code specified for that currency in ISO 4217, the list established by the International Organization for Standardization. For example, the currency sign for the Euro is €; the currency code is *EUR*. And the currency sign for the Norwegian Kroner is *Kr*; the currency code is *NOK*. Which choice is preferable is a matter of custom. Don't use both a currency sign and a currency code when stating a given amount of money.

13.521 Some currency signs are shared by many currencies, and you can make it clear which currency you're referring to by supplementing the currency sign. For example, the dollar sign (*$*) is used for currencies in many countries other than the United States, principally those using currencies denominated in dollars (including Australia, Brunei, and Canada) or pesos (including Argentina, Chile, and Mexico). If a contract between parties from different countries refers to a currency that uses the dollar sign, using a currency code or a suitably modified currency sign, such as *A$* for Australian dollars and *Mex$* for Mexican pesos, would make it clear which currency is being referred to.

13.522 Always put a space between the currency code and the number: *EUR 2,400,000*. If a currency sign consists of one or more letters, put a space between the currency sign (in this case, Swiss francs) and the number: *SFr. 334,583*. But if the currency sign consists of a symbol, don't use a space, even if you add one or more letters in front of the symbol: *C$655,000*.

13.523   In many countries, especially those in the English-speaking world, the practice is to place the currency sign before the amount. In other countries, it's placed after the amount. Pick the convention you think most appropriate and apply it consistently.

13.524   Another way to make it clear what currency is being referred to is to use an autonomous definition such as *"Dollars" and "$" mean United States dollars and "A$" means Australian dollars*. You would define the word *dollars* only if you use both words and digits to express a dollar amount. This manual recommends that you not do so (see 13.513).

13.525   You could conceivably use an autonomous definition as an excuse not to supplement a multicurrency sign. You could, for example, use a simple dollar sign in referring to Australian dollars and use the autonomous definition *"$" means Australian dollars*. But it would be preferable to use *A$* every time you state an amount of money, as that by itself should be enough to inform most readers what currency is being referred to.

MORAL TURPITUDE

13.526   The phrase *moral turpitude* is insufficiently specific (see 7.28), so don't use it. This section explains the nature of the problem and suggests an alternative approach.

Background

13.527   *Black's Law Dictionary* defines *moral turpitude* in part as "Conduct that is contrary to justice, honesty, or morality." It also quotes 50 *Am. Jur. 2d* Libel and Slander § 165, at 454 (1995):

> Moral turpitude means, in general, shameful wickedness—so extreme a departure from ordinary standards of honest, good morals, justice, or ethics as to be shocking to the moral sense of the community. It has also been defined as an act of baseness, vileness, or depravity in the private and social duties which one person owes to another, or to society in general, contrary to the accepted and customary rule of right and duty between people.

13.528   For all its heavy-breathing pomposity, this definition is no more enlightening than the more succinct *Black's Law Dictionary* definition.

13.529   That explains how in *Marmolejo-Campos v. Gonzales*, 503 F.3d 922 (9th Cir. 2007), the court concluded that driving drunk isn't an act of moral turpitude, but driving drunk without a license is. It also explains why one judge felt the need to offer a lengthy dissenting opinion.

13.530   Despite its shortcomings, the phrase *moral turpitude* is a fixture in contracts—such as employment agreements, consulting agreements, and employee benefit plans—where it routinely features as one of the grounds for termination for cause:

> the Executive's admission or conviction of, or plea of nolo contendere to, a felony or of any crime involving *moral turpitude*, fraud, embezzlement, theft or misrepresentation; ... .

13.531 It also serves other functions. For example, in a loan agreement the lender might require the borrower to state that no person associated with the borrower has been convicted of a crime involving moral turpitude.

13.532 Coming up with an alternative for termination provisions requires that one consider more generally termination provisions that feature *moral turpitude*. This manual calls such provisions "termination-for-crime provisions."

13.533 Termination-for-crime provisions allow a party to terminate if another party has been involved in a crime. But they feature several possible elements, each of which can be structured in different ways. Each element is considered below.

What Crime?

13.534 The crime triggering the right to terminate might be expressed in one or more of the following ways:

- *crime* (preferable to the bureaucratic "criminal offense")

- *felony* or the equivalent *crime punishable by death or imprisonment in excess of one year* (includes murder, rape, kidnapping, grand theft, arson, fraud, and other major crimes; but the term *felony* isn't recognized in civil-law jurisdictions, most non-U.S. common-law jurisdictions, and even some U.S. states, for example New Jersey, and in those states where it is recognized, its meaning might vary from state to state)

- *misdemeanor* (more serious misdemeanors include theft, prostitution, public intoxication, simple assault, disorderly conduct, trespass, vandalism; less serious ones involve only fines and no social stigma and include parking and minor traffic offenses, late payment of fees, and building code violations; the term *misdemeanor* poses the same problem as *felony*)

Involving What Offense?

13.535 Sometimes the kind of crime is modified by an adjectival phrase providing further information regarding the nature of the offense. This is where *moral turpitude* comes in, along with several other labels that drafters are fond of stringing together:

- moral turpitude
- dishonesty
- deceit
- misrepresentation
- theft

- fraud

- embezzlement

13.536 Alternatively, in an employment or similar agreement you could refer to the crime as being *related to the Employee's employment.*

Other Criteria?

13.537 It can help to tack one or more other criteria on to the kind of crime. Here are three examples of carve-outs to crimes that would trigger the right to terminate:

- a crime for which a fine or other noncustodial penalty is imposed

- a crime that does not relate to driving while intoxicated or driving under the influence

- a crime that does not relate to services performed under the agreement

At What Stage?

13.538 At what point in the criminal process does the right to terminate kick in? Here's the spectrum, from earlier in the crime to later:

- *when Doe commits the crime* (but before any proceedings, it wouldn't be known whether Doe had committed a crime)

- *when Doe is arrested for the crime* (but only with more serious crimes is the suspect arrested)

- *when Doe is indicted for the crime* (but only with more serious crimes is the suspect indicted, and in many jurisdictions indictment is not the only way of charging a suspect)

- *when Doe is charged with the crime* (this would apply to all crimes)

- *when Doe is convicted of the crime or pleads guilty or no contest to the crime* (given the often protracted nature of criminal proceedings when anything other than a minor crime is involved, using this standard might, from the terminating party's perspective, unduly delay the right to terminate)

Which Jurisdiction?

13.539 If you use terminology that might vary by jurisdiction, you would need to refer to a particular jurisdiction, to avoid any argument about what, for example, *felony* means. For example, you might say *constituting a felony in the jurisdiction in which the crime is committed.*

Doubling Up?

13.540 A drafter might want to refer to two or more kinds of crime in a termination-for-crime provision. For example, the right to terminate could arise on conviction of a felony or conviction of a crime involving dishonesty.

13.541 One could complicate matters further by referring to a different procedural posture for each crime—for example, conviction for a felony and indictment for a felony involving dishonesty or fraud.

Recommendation

13.542 One could cobble together a truly complicated termination-for-crime provision out of the above parameters. Keep it simple, unless you have a good reason to make it more complicated. Here's a reasonable pro-employer termination-for-crime provision to use in an employment agreement (but see 11.81 for an issue regarding how it's worded):

> ... the Employee is charged with a crime that (1) is punishable by a custodial penalty, instead of or in addition to a fine or other noncustodial penalty, or (2) is related to the Employee's employment; ... .

13.543 For the reasons noted above, it would be best to avoid formal labels in referring to the kind of crime. And if the offense doesn't merit jail time, it shouldn't be of undue concern, unless the conduct relates directly to the employee's job. Furthermore, a company wouldn't want to be compelled to keep someone as an employee until they had been convicted or pleaded guilty. It's possible that the charges might be dismissed, but that eventuality could be addressed elsewhere in the contract.

13.544 An employment agreement might also include a broader provision allowing the company to terminate if the employee engages in conduct that the employee knew, or that a reasonable person in the position of the employee would have known, would have or would reasonably be expected to have a material adverse effect on the business or reputation of the company or any of its directors, officers, employees, or affiliates.

13.545 But whatever language you use, omit *moral turpitude*.

MUTATIS MUTANDIS

13.546 When a drafter incorporates into a contract, by reference, provisions from a separate agreement (see 13.393), it's sometimes necessary to adjust those provisions to reflect that, for example, the parties to one contract are different from the parties to the other contract. Such adjustments can be explicit:

> The terms of the Master Lease are hereby made part of this agreement, as if they were in this agreement, except that (1) each reference to "Lease" will be deemed a reference to "Sublease" and (2) each reference to "Landlord" and "Tenant" will be deemed a reference to "Sublandlord" and "Subtenant," respectively.

13.547   But sometimes incorporating by reference can require, in addition to any explicit major adjustments, minor adjustments to individual provisions. For example, if a guarantor, a Delaware limited-liability company, is required to make in a guaranty the statements of fact that the borrower, a New York corporation, is making in a credit agreement, the statements of fact regarding organization and authority would have to be adjusted to reflect, at a minimum, the difference in jurisdiction and form of entity. Since it would be time-consuming to note each such adjustment, it's conventional to accomplish this instead in one fell swoop with the Latin phrase *mutatis mutandis*, meaning literally "with those things having been changed that need to be changed":

> Each Guarantor hereby makes to the Lender, as if they were in this agreement, *mutatis mutandis*, each of the statements of fact made by the Borrower in the Loan Agreement.

13.548   But a phrase such as *together with any necessary conforming changes* would convey the same meaning more clearly. Generally, it's best to keep contracts free of Latinisms (see 13.492).

MUTUAL, MUTUALLY

13.549   In contracts as in general usage, the words *mutual* and *mutually* are prone to misuse.

13.550   The principal meaning of the adjective *mutual* is "reciprocal" or "directed by each toward the other or others," as in *Their relationship was characterized by mutual mistrust.* When in a contract *mutual* is used to convey this meaning, it often modifies *agreement*, as in *"Product" means any product whose promotion and detailing is assigned to Acme by mutual agreement with Pharmaco.* In this context *mutual* is redundant, as reciprocity is inherent in the notion of agreement.

13.551   Also commonplace are references to *mutual consent*, as in *This agreement may be amended at any time by mutual consent of the parties.* It would be preferable to use *by the mutual exchange of written consents*, but better yet would be simply stating that to be effective, an amendment must be in writing and signed by both parties (see 3.467).

13.552   Another meaning of *mutual* is "pertaining to both parties." Stating in a set of recitals that the parties want to take a given action *for their mutual benefit* is an example of appropriate use of *mutual*—a wordy alternative would be *for the benefit of each of them*. Combining the two, as in *for the mutual benefit of each of them*, would result in redundancy.

13.553   Like *mutual*, the adverb *mutually* can be used to convey reciprocity. Here's an example of appropriate use of *mutually* in a contract to express that meaning: *Merger Sub and the Company shall issue mutually acceptable press releases announcing the signing of this agreement.*

13.554   Often *mutually* is used with the verb *agree*, as in *such other date as the parties mutually agree.* It is also used to modify the adjective *agreeable*, as in *Any public announcement must be in a form mutually agreeable to the Company* *and Parent.* In both cases, *mutually* is redundant, for the same reason that *mutual* is superfluous in *mutual agreement* (see 13.550).

13.555 *Mutually* is sometimes mistakenly used instead of *jointly*, as in *a nationally recognized independent public accounting firm mutually* [read *jointly*] *selected by the Stockholders' Representatives and Acme.*

NEGLIGENCE, GROSS NEGLIGENCE

13.556 The way *negligence, gross negligence,* and related terminology is used in contracts is confusing. This section explains why and offers recommendations.

How the Terms Are Used

13.557 The terms *negligence* and *gross negligence* appear frequently in contracts. They're used in two ways.

13.558 First, provisions featuring gross negligence or featuring both negligence and gross negligence can be used as a sword—to terminate a contract, as grounds for being indemnified by the other party, or to circumvent a waiver of liability or cap on indemnification benefiting the other party.

13.559 And second, such provisions can be used as a shield—in a provision releasing a party from liability for its own negligence or for its own negligence and gross negligence.

13.560 Courts in many jurisdictions have held that advance releases of liability in cases of gross negligence are unenforceable as against public policy. See, e.g., *City of Santa Barbara v. Superior Court,* 161 P.3d 1095 (Cal. 2007) (California); *Sommer v. Federal Signal Corp.,* 79 N.Y.2d 540 (1992) (New York). Releases of liability that use a negligence standard, as well as the other kinds of provisions (whether featuring just negligence or both negligence and gross negligence), are presumably enforceable.

Confused Terminology

13.561 In general usage, *negligence* means "carelessness." But it's likely a court interpreting a contract provision that uses the term *negligence* will treat it as referring to the tort of negligence, which is grounded in, to use the *Black's Law Dictionary* definition, "The failure to exercise the standard of care that a reasonably prudent person would have exercised in a similar situation."

13.562 *Gross negligence* is a tort term of art. Like *negligence,* it's vague, so determining whether a party's conduct has been negligent or grossly negligent depends on the circumstances (see 7.42). But beyond that, *gross negligence* has no settled meaning.

13.563 For example, in *Sommer,* 79 N.Y.2d at 554, the New York Court of Appeals held that gross negligence must "smack of intentional wrongdoing" and that it is conduct that "evinces a reckless indifference to the rights of others." By contrast, in *City of Santa Barbara,* 161 P.3d at 1099, the California Supreme Court, quoting a 1941 case, held that gross negligence "long has been defined in California and other jurisdictions as either a 'want of even scant care' or 'an extreme departure from the ordinary standard of conduct.'"

13.564   The *Sommer* and *City of Santa Barbara* standards might seem broadly compatible, but in *City of Santa Barbara*, 161 P.3d at 1099 n.4, the court said, "By contrast, 'wanton' or 'reckless' misconduct (or 'willful and wanton negligence') describes conduct by a person who may have no intent to cause harm, but who intentionally performs an act so unreasonable and dangerous that he or she knows or should know it is highly probable that harm will result." Because the *Sommer* standard invokes recklessness, the *Sommer* standard seems to require greater misconduct than does the *City of Santa Barbara* standard. So courts from two states have given a different meaning to the term *gross negligence*.

13.565   Considering the caselaw more generally, *gross negligence* "is a nebulous term that is defined in a multitude of ways, depending on the legal context and the jurisdiction." 57A *Am. Jur. 2d* Negligence § 227 (2017). Consistent with the distinction between the *Sommer* and *City of Santa Barbara* definitions, some jurisdictions distinguish between gross negligence and willful, wanton, or reckless conduct, whereas other jurisdictions treat those terms as being the same or substantially the same. See 57A *Am. Jur. 2d* Negligence § 231, § 232.

13.566   Confusing matters still further is the notion that "the word *wanton* usually denotes a greater degree of culpability than *reckless*." *Garner's Dictionary of Legal Usage*, at 936.

13.567   This chaos is in part the result of attempts by courts to demarcate distinct levels of misconduct on what is a slippery slope of vagueness, with differences measured in degrees rather than absolutes (see 7.50). One gets the sense that courts resort to an affected vocabulary, such as "smack of" (*Sommer*) and "scant" (*City of Santa Barbara*), to help cut through that slipperiness, but to no avail.

13.568   Given this state of affairs, it's not surprising that many jurisdictions, among them Pennsylvania, don't recognize degrees of negligence. "The view taken is that negligence, whatever epithet is given to characterize it, is the failure to exercise the care and skill which the situation demands, and that it is more accurate to call it simply 'negligence' than to attempt expressions of degrees of negligence." 57A *Am. Jur. 2d* Negligence § 219.

13.569   The law of a non-U.S. jurisdiction might recognize negligence and—less likely—gross negligence, or it might use a different analytical framework.

Recommendations

13.570   Given the confusion described above, here are eight recommendations regarding how to express degrees of misconduct in a contract. First, the meaning of negligence is relatively consistent across U.S. jurisdictions, so using it in contracts doesn't involve undue uncertainty.

13.571   Second, unless you're in a position to research the tort law of each jurisdiction relevant to contracts you draft and negotiate, it would be safer not to use the term *gross negligence*, as its meaning changes from jurisdiction to jurisdiction.

13.572   Third, if you want to use a term for misconduct that goes beyond negligence, use *recklessness*, or the adjective *reckless*, or the adverb *recklessly*, instead of *gross negligence* and related forms. Given that assessing misconduct depends entirely on the circumstances and involves differences of degree, it would be pointless to agonize over whether to choose another standard more or less exacting than *recklessness*. In particular, it's unrealistic to think that in contracts one could usefully distinguish between *reckless conduct* and *wanton conduct*. It's a safe bet that many contract readers don't know what *wanton* means and that the remainder would assume, sensibly enough, that *wanton* is an annoying legalism that means pretty much the same thing as *reckless*. But if you use *reckless*, bear in mind that in those jurisdictions that don't recognize degrees of negligence, a negligence standard might apply.

13.573   Fourth, use *intentional* (and *intentionally*) instead of *willful* (and *willfully*) (see 13.896).

13.574   Fifth, make it clear that whatever one or more labels you use, they relate not to the party's action but to the consequences of the party's action—that makes more sense. It's possible to act intentionally without intending to cause damages. If Fred throws a ball—an intentional act— and unintentionally breaks a window, it would be illogical to accuse him of intentional misconduct, as opposed to acting negligently or recklessly.

13.575   Sixth, adjust to reflect the governing law. If it's the law of a jurisdiction that doesn't recognize concepts used in the United States, don't insist on incorporating those concepts in the contract.

13.576   Seventh, don't define *recklessness* or any other form of the word. It means … recklessness. Defining it would just clog up the contract with verbiage without adding certainty. *Recklessness* is a vague standard—if you invoke vagueness, you have to accept that it comes with a measure of uncertainty.

13.577   And eighth, consider not using tort-based standards in a contract in connection with performance under that contract. Acme decides that some aspect of its contract with Widgetco no longer makes business sense, so it elects not to perform. Widgetco has a remedy under the contract for that nonperformance—why add a tort-based remedy? In particular, if a cap on indemnification contains a carve-out for recklessness or intentional misconduct and the indemnification covers Widgetco for Acme's failure to comply with obligations under the contract, the carve-out could interfere with the limit on indemnification. Such a carve-out would make more sense in the case of, for example, indemnification of Widgetco for losses relating to Acme's relations with nonparties.

A Sample Provision

13.578   How do these recommendations play out in practice? Here are "before" and "after" versions of a sample provision:

Before

The Processor shall not be liable to any party hereto or any other person for any action or failure to act under or in connection with this Agreement except to the extent such conduct constitutes its own willful misconduct or gross negligence.

After

The Processor will not be liable to any party or nonparty for damages arising from an act or failure to act on its part in connection with its performance under this agreement, except to the extent that as a result of its reckless disregard for the consequences of that act or failure to act, or its intentionally causing those consequences, the Processor causes the party or nonparty to suffer damages.

NO LATER [OR *EARLIER, MORE,* OR *LESS*] THAN

13.579   To be consistent in your contract usages, you have to make decisions big and small. Here's a small one: which to use, *no later than* or *not later than?*

13.580   Here's what the "Ask the Editor" feature of the website for Merriam-Webster's *Learner's Dictionary* had to say:

> [T]here are differences in the way these two expressions are used. *No later than* is used more often than *not later than*, and it is less formal. *Not later than* is used mostly in formal documents, such as rulebooks, government laws, and academic papers.

13.581   So use only *no later than.* Given the choice between more-formal and less-formal, it makes sense to choose less-formal—contracts are formal enough as it is without adding formality unnecessarily. An unscientific sample of contracts filed on the U.S. Securities and Exchange Commission's EDGAR system during a 60-day period found that contracts using *no later than* were half again as numerous as contracts using *not later than*, so this recommendation would seem already to reflect the majority usage.

13.582   Likewise, say *no earlier than* and *no more than. Garner's Modern English Usage*, at 628, says that *no more than* "is the more natural idiom—and historically by far the more common one." *Not more than* occurs in three times as many contracts filed on EDGAR during the 60-day period referred to in 13.581 than does *no more than*, but that's no reason to favor *not more than.*

13.583   But it doesn't follow that one should also use *no less than* instead of *not less than*. Here's what *Garner's Modern English Usage*, at 628, says:

> *No less* connotes surprise <he weighs no less than 300 pounds>. The phrasing in the example expresses astonishment that he weighs so much. *Not less* is more clinical and dispassionate <he weighs not less than 300 pounds>. That example states matter-of-factly that he weighs at least that much and maybe more.

13.584 That perhaps explains why on EDGAR during the 60-day period referred to in 13.581, contracts using *not less than* were more than three times as numerous as contracts using *no less than*. Make an exception in this context and use *not less than*.

NOTICE

Notice and Prior Notice

13.585 The noun *notice* is ambiguous; consider using the verb *notify* instead. This section explains why.

13.586 *The Oxford English Dictionary* gives as one definition of *notice* "an intimation by one of the parties to an agreement that it is to terminate at a specified time, *esp.* with reference to quitting a house, lodgings, or employment." So you can announce, "I've given notice at work!" and have it be understood as meaning that you told your boss that in ten days (or some other interval) you would no longer be working there.

13.587 But *The Oxford English Dictionary* says that the phrase *to give notice* also simply means to convey information. So *to give notice* can convey two contrasting meanings—in one, information is given before the event in question, whereas in the other information is given afterward.

13.588 So the sentence *Acme shall provide Doe with notice of any change of address* is ambiguous. One reading is that if Acme were to change its address and then inform Doe of the new address, it would have complied with the obligation. In other words, *to provide notice* can mean *to notify*. You could make this clear by modifying the verb *provide* with an adverb or adverbial phrase, such as *promptly* or *in no later than ten days*, or by modifying the noun *notice* with the adjective *prompt*.

13.589 But if instead you modify the noun *notice* with the adjectival phrase *ten days'*, the natural reading becomes that Acme is required to inform Doe in advance that it will subsequently be changing its address. In other words, in this context *to provide notice* conveys the meaning of the first *Oxford English Dictionary* definition mentioned above. It wouldn't be reasonable to conclude that Acme would be complying with its obligation if it were to notify Doe of the change of address after it had occurred.

13.590 That being the case, nothing would be served by referring to *ten days' prior* (or *advance*) notice rather than *ten days' notice*. But given the two possible meanings of *to give notice* and the subtleties involved in distinguishing them, it's understandable that for contracts, drafters should want to tack on *prior* to reinforce that information is to be given before the event in question.

13.591 But when considering alternative usages, often you can sidestep debate, and that's the case here. *Notice* is an abstract noun—a "buried verb" (see 17.7). Replacing buried verbs with verbs results in prose that's more concise, and in this case doing so would allow you to avoid the ambiguity inherent in *to provide notice*.

13.592   Consider the following alternative versions—one using *notice*, the other *notify*—of two sentences conveying the different meanings of *to provide notice*. The versions using *notify* represent an improvement.

1. *Using Buried Verb*

   Acme shall provide Doe with prompt notice of any change of address.

   Using Strong Verb

   Acme shall promptly notify Doe if it changes its address.

2. *Using Buried Verb*

   Acme shall provide Doe with at least ten days' prior notice of any change of address.

   Using Strong Verb

   Acme shall notify Doe at least ten days in advance if Acme changes its address.

Termination with Prior Notice

13.593   A contract might require that a party give notice when terminating. For example:

> Acme may terminate this agreement [upon] [by giving] [with] 60 days' prior notice to Widgetco.

13.594   It would make sense for the contract to terminate 60 days after Acme notifies Widgetco. But *upon* and *by giving* suggest that termination happens when you give notice, not after the notice period elapses. And *with* isn't clear either way.

13.595   Another issue arises if a party may give prior notice after a given date or event:

> After X, Acme may terminate this agreement [upon] [with] [by giving] 60 days' prior notice to Widgetco.

13.596   Even if you assume that termination occurs after the period elapses, it's unclear whether the date restriction applies just to termination or also to giving notice. May Acme give notice before the specified date?

13.597   Neither issue arises if you express termination with prior notice as follows:

> If [after Y] Acme notifies Widgetco that Acme is terminating this agreement in accordance with this section 4, this agreement will terminate 60 days after the day Widgetco receives that notice.

Notice—Using an Apostrophe with Periods of Time

13.598   When referring to someone's giving prior notice (see 13.590), follow the recommended usage and use an apostrophe with the associated period of time, as in *one week's* notice and *five days'* notice.

NOTWITHSTANDING, SUBJECT TO, EXCEPT AS PROVIDED IN

Notwithstanding

13.599   In the sentence "Notwithstanding section 3.2, Acme may own 1% or less of a publicly traded company," *notwithstanding* means "in spite of" or "despite" and indicates that although the subject matter of section 3.2 overlaps with that of the quoted sentence, the quoted sentence should be read and interpreted as if section 3.2 did not exist.

[handwritten margin note: JFF: good to use when trumping entirety]

13.600   In addition, drafters begin a provision with *notwithstanding anything in this agreement to the contrary* if they want that provision to prevail over any other provision in the agreement that might overlap with it. *Notwithstanding the foregoing* serves the same function, but only regarding text that precedes the provision in question.

13.601   There are good reasons not to use *notwithstanding*. For one thing, *notwithstanding* operates remotely on the provisions it prevails over; readers could accept at face value a given contract provision, unaware that it is undercut by a *notwithstanding* in a different provision.

13.602   Furthermore, although a *notwithstanding* clause that refers to a particular section at least warns readers what is being undercut, one that encompasses the entire agreement leaves to the reader the often awkward task of determining which provisions are affected. The answer might be none: some drafters throw in *notwithstanding anything in this agreement to the contrary* just in case, to inoculate particularly significant provisions against the possibility of conflict with other provisions.

13.603   And although *notwithstanding the foregoing* might seem relatively benign, in that the provision that's undercut would seem to be close at hand, *the foregoing* could conceivably refer to the previous sentence, to the entirety of the preceding part of the body of the contract, or to something in between (see 7.25).

13.604   Aside from these shortcomings, you can create even greater confusion with *notwithstanding* if a contract contains conflicting provisions and each of the provisions is accompanied by a *notwithstanding* clause to the effect that that provision prevails over all other provisions in the contract. For an example of that, see *Schepisi v. Roberts*, 111 A.D.3d 506, 974 N.Y.S.2d 446 (2013). *[handwritten check mark]*

13.605   A usage note: some think that *notwithstanding* should come at the end of the phrase in question, not at the front. According to *Garner's Dictionary of Legal Usage*, at 615, that's not so:

> The question that literalist drafters ask is, What doesn't withstand what else? Are the limitations of § 3.5 "not withstanding" (i.e., subordinated to) the present section or is the present section "not withstanding" (subordinated to) § 3.5? Because the former is the correct reading, some believe that *notwithstanding* should be sent to the end of the phrase in which it appears: *The limitations contained in § 3.5 notwithstanding*, as opposed to *Notwithstanding the limitations contained in § 3.5.*

But that literalist argument is very much in vain, as the *OED* attests with a 14th-century example of *notwithstanding* as a prepositional sentence-starter. This usage has been constant from the 1300s to the present day. In fact, the construction with *notwithstanding* after the noun first appeared more than a century later, and has never been as frequent.

Subject To

13.606   There's an alternative to *notwithstanding*. Section 4 of a contract requires that Acme pay the purchase price to Jones, whereas section 5 requires that Acme pay $10,000 of the purchase price to a nonparty, Smith, if the closing occurs after a specified date. Instead of prefacing the latter provision with *Notwithstanding section 4*, it would be much clearer to qualify the former provision with *Subject to section 5*. Using *subject to* allows you to signal to the reader that a provision is undercut by another provision, and the reader doesn't have the burden of spotting a *notwithstanding* elsewhere in the contract. And if you use *subject to*, nothing would be gained by also using *notwithstanding*.

13.607   But even drafters who normally use *subject to* sometimes have use for *notwithstanding*. When you're proposing a change to the other side's draft that would undercut one or more other provisions, using *notwithstanding* rather than *subject to* would allow you to make only one change, instead of adding the undercutting provision and adding a cross-reference to it, using *subject to*, in the one or more provisions being undercut. That might prove useful, particularly if you're making a last-minute change.

13.608   Key language of performance (*Acme hereby grants Pharmaco a license*) and key language of obligation (*the parties shall cause Cyberco to merge into Dynamix Corp.*) is often preceded by *Subject to the terms of this agreement*. This phrase can be superfluous, as the rights and obligations of the parties to a contract are determined by considering the contract as a whole rather than each provision in isolation. If, for example, a party grants an option in one section and states in one or more other sections the exercise price and the exercise period, it doesn't follow that the grant should be made "subject to the terms" of that contract. It would be inconceivable for the party granted the option to claim that there is no exercise price or that the option is exercisable indefinitely.

13.609   When using *subject to*, generally it's best to be specific regarding which provision is doing the undercutting. But when a key obligation—for example, the obligation to cause Cyberco to merge into Dynamix Corp.— is subject to satisfaction of certain conditions and the right of one or more parties to terminate the agreement in certain circumstances, it's generally simpler to state at the outset that the obligation is *Subject to the terms of this agreement* rather than specify at greater length the sections containing those conditions and termination rights.

Except as Provided In

13.610 An alternative to stating that a provision ~~is subject to~~ a given section is to say *except as provided in* that section. *Except as provided in* is the narrower of the two phrases: it indicates that ~~the other~~ provision is an exception, whereas if section 8 is subject to section 9, that could mean that section 9 is an exception to what is provided in section 8, but it could also mean that section 9 supplements section 8 in any number of ways. For example, section 9 could impose a condition to a right provided for in section 8. By extension, *except as otherwise provided in this agreement* is narrower than *subject to the terms of this agreement*.

Confusing Interplay

13.611 Besides the issue of how to express most clearly that one provision prevails over one or more other provisions, you also have to express clearly the nature of the interplay between the provisions. For an example of a dispute caused by failure to do just that, see *BDC Finance L.L.C. v. Barclays Bank PLC*, 974 N.Y.S.2d 39 (App. Div. 2013); see also Kenneth A. Adams, *A New Case Involving "Notwithstanding"*, Adams on Contract Drafting (28 Oct. 2013), http://www.adamsdrafting.com/a-new-case-involving-notwithstanding/ (discussing *BDC Finance L.L.C.*).

Eliminating Nullified Provisions

13.612 It's evidently common practice in negotiating mergers-and-acquisitions contracts that when you add new language that nullifies language in the previous draft, you retain the nullified language and signal its relationship to the new by means of *subject to* (in the nullified language) or *notwithstanding* (in the new language). Or you tack on provisos (see 13.663). Presumably that's felt to be more diplomatic than proposing to delete language offered by the other side.

13.613 That approach might help you get the deal done, but leaving in nullified language can result in a party claiming that the ostensibly nullified language still has life in it. That's what led to litigation over the abortive acquisition of United Rentals, Inc., by acquisition vehicles controlled by funds and accounts affiliated with Cerberus Capital Management, L.P., the private-equity buyout firm. See *United Rentals, Inc. v. RAM Holdings, Inc.*, 937 A.2d 810 (Del. Ch. 2007); see also Kenneth A. Adams, *Merger Pacts: Contract Drafting, Cerberus Litigation*, New York Law Journal, 19 Feb. 2008.

NOVATION

13.614 It's standard for an amendment to a loan agreement to contain a provision stating that entry into the amendment "does not effect a novation" of the obligations under the loan agreement.

13.615 *Novation* is a term of art (see 1.7), and many readers of contracts won't know what it means. Here's how *novation* is defined in *Black's Law Dictionary*: "The act of substituting for an old obligation a new one that either replaces an existing obligation with a new obligation or replaces an original party with a new party."

13.616 Instead of saying that an amendment "does not effect a novation," it would be clearer to say it "will not result in any of the Obligations being replaced." Or if you think that it's important to retain the word *novation*, you could combine the two approaches: "does not effect a novation of the Obligations, in that it will not result in any of the Obligations being replaced."

ONLY

13.617 Here's what *Garner's Modern English Usage* says about *only*:

> *Only* is perhaps the most frequently misplaced of all English words. Its best placement is precisely before the words intended to be limited. The more words separating *only* from its correct position, the more awkward the sentence; and such a separation can lead to ambiguities ... . Yet the strong tendency in [American English] is to stick *only* right before the verb or verb phrase regardless of the illogic ... .

13.618 This is the case in contracts. Consider this example (emphasis added):

> The Tenant may *only* move furniture, fixtures, and equipment into and out of the Premises during nonbusiness hours unless Landlord gives approval otherwise.

13.619 So the tenant may only to move furniture, fixtures, and equipment in the specified manner. That's all the tenant is allowed to do—the tenant is precluded from also making breakfast, going to work, taking a shower ... . That's obviously a ludicrously literal reading, but one can imagine contexts in which that sort of reading might be less ludicrous but equally unintended.

13.620 So move *only* farther back in the sentence:

> The Tenant may move furniture, fixtures, and equipment into and out of the Premises *only* during nonbusiness hours unless Landlord gives approval otherwise.

13.621 Here's another example:

> When a Termination Event has occurred and is continuing, the Seller shall ~~only~~ exercise its rights and remedies under the Purchase Agreement [read *only*] in accordance with the instructions of the Agent.

ON THE ONE HAND ... ON THE OTHER HAND

13.622 The construction *on the one hand ... on the other hand* bifurcates a list of three or more items. And it does so in two ways.

To Indicate Which Conjunction Has Scope Over the Other

13.623 When in a string of three nouns, verbs, adjectives, or adverbs the first and second are separated by *and* and the second and third are separated by *or*, or vice versa, the meaning varies depending on which conjunction "has scope over" the other. One way to clarify that ambiguity is to use *on the one hand … on the other hand*. That's discussed at 11.92–.93.

To Divide a List into Two Categories

13.624 *On the one hand … on the other hand* is also used to divide between two categories a list of three or more items using *and* as the only conjunction. In sample [1] below, it's not clear to which category B belongs—debtor or creditor? That's made clear in samples [1a] and [1b]. You could instead use enumeration to remedy the confusion, as in sample [1c], but *on the one hand … on the other hand* seems the simpler option.

[1] the relationship between A and B and C is that of debtor and creditor

[1a] *the relationship between A, on the one hand, and B and C, on the other hand, is that of debtor and creditor*

[1b] *the relationship between A and B, on the one hand, and C, on the other hand, is that of debtor and creditor*

[1c] *the relationship between (1) A and B and (2) C is that of debtor and creditor*

Used Unnecessarily

13.625 But more often than not *on the one hand … on the other hand* is used when it's not needed—in other words, it's used even when a list doesn't need to be bifurcated.

13.626 For example, it's sometimes used with a list containing only two items, as in the following examples. As there's no risk of confusion, it should be omitted.

> The relative fault of the indemnifying party ~~on the one hand~~ and the indemnified party ~~on the other hand~~ is to be determined by reference to … .

> Each of Parent~~, on the one hand,~~ and the Stockholders' Representative, ~~on the other hand,~~ shall cooperate with each other in preparing the 2017 Income Statement.

13.627 But what if one of the two items is plural? Here are two examples:

> The Sellers, *on the one hand*, and the Purchaser, *on the other hand,* are each responsible for paying half the Transfer Taxes arising out of the transactions contemplated by this agreement.

> … in such proportion as is appropriate to reflect the relative benefits and the relative fault of the Company, *on the one hand,* and the Placement Agents, *on the other hand,* in connection with the statements or omissions that resulted in those losses, damages, or liabilities.

13.628 In this context, *on the one hand … on the other hand* is presumably used to indicate that the members of the plural item are acting together. It would be clearer and more economical to say as much (making sure to place the plural item first, to avoid any syntactic ambiguity):

> The Sellers (considered collectively) and the Purchaser are each responsible for paying half the Transfer Taxes arising out of the transactions contemplated by this agreement.

> … in such proportion as is appropriate to reflect the relative benefits and the relative fault of the Placement Agents (considered collectively) and the Company in connection with the statements or omissions that resulted in those losses, damages, or liabilities.

13.629   And *on the one hand … on the other hand* is sometimes used with a list of three or more items even though there's no need to bifurcate those items. For example:

> ~~The Corporate Taxpayer and the Partnerships, on the one hand, and the applicable Limited Partner, on the other hand,~~ [read *The Corporate Taxpayer, the Partnerships, and the applicable Limited Partner*] acknowledge that, as a result of an Exchange, the Corporate Taxpayer's basis in the applicable Original Assets will be increased by the excess, if any, of … .

13.630   Similarly, one sometimes sees *on the one hand … on the other hand* used to group three or more parties to a transaction, just as drafters used to use *party of the first part … party of the second part* (see 2.115). But this practice is unnecessary:

> This asset purchase agreement is dated 6 August 2017 and is between ABLE CORPORATION, a Delaware corporation (the "**Buyer**"), ~~on the one hand, and~~ BAKER MERCHANDISING LLC, an Ohio limited liability company (the "**Seller**"), CHARLIE ENTERTAINMENT, INC., a Florida corporation ("**Charlie**"), and DAVID DELTA, as trustee of the David Delta Trust (the "**Trustee**"; together with Charlie, the "**Members**")~~, on the other hand~~.

13.631   It's preferable not to indicate in the introductory clause who is performing what role—that's what the recitals are for (see 2.84).

PARENTHESES

Function

13.632   In regular prose, parentheses (round brackets, like those enclosing these words) are used to offset text that constitutes an explanation or aside. The limited and stylized prose of contracts isn't the place for explanations and asides, so drafters should have no reason to use parentheses to serve that function. But parentheses represent one way to eliminate syntactic ambiguity (see 12.17, 12.56, 12.76). They're also used with enumeration (see 4.28, 4.45) and to create a defined term after an integrated definition (see 6.62).

13.633   And if you need to express that two different arrangements apply in different circumstances, maybe the most convenient way to express those different circumstances is by using paired sets of parentheses. (For an example of that, see the proposed language in 11.152.)

Parentheses Within Words

13.634 Don't use parentheses within a single word. For example, don't tack *(s)* onto the singular form of a noun to convey that a situation might involve one or more than one of the item in question. (A particularly awkward variant is *beneficiar(y/ies)*.) Instead, say *one or more* (see 11.6, 11.13):

> Parent shall cause to be filed *a registration statement(s)* [read *one or more registration statements*] on Form S-3

> ... upon the surrender of *the certificate(s)* [read *one or more certificates*] previously representing those shares ... .

13.635 More elaborate are *(sub)licensee*, *(sub)contractor*, and *(self)insured*. Whatever they offer in economy is more than offset by their awkwardness.

13.636 And there are better ways to achieve gender-neutral drafting than *(s)he* (see 17.11).

PARTY AS AN ADJECTIVE

13.637 *Party* is often used in a noun phrase, as in "Acme is *a party* to a confidentiality agreement with Widgetco" and "Acme and Widgetco are *parties* to a confidentiality agreement." Be more concise and use it as an adjective, as in "Acme is *party* to a confidentiality agreement with Widgetco" and "Acme and Widgetco are *party* to a confidentiality agreement."

PERCENTAGES

13.638 Some drafters use *100%* when it would be simpler to omit it or use *all* or some other alternative:

> The Guarantor proposes to distribute to its shareholders ~~*100% of the*~~ [read all] outstanding shares of the Company's common stock.

> ... a Series A Warrant registered in the name of that Purchaser to purchase up to a number of Ordinary Shares equal to ~~*100% of the*~~ [read *the number of*] Shares issuable to the Purchaser on the Closing Date.

> The XYZ Shareholders own 100 shares of common stock, no par value, ~~*being 100% of the presently*~~ [read *and those are the only XYZ Shares currently*] issued and outstanding SKM Shares.

> ... the Loans are secured by Cash and Cash Equivalents in an amount not less than ~~*100% of*~~ the principal amount of the Loans plus interest to accrue through the Special Arrangement Period ... .

> ... an Issuing Bank will not be required to issue, amend, or increase any Letter of Credit unless it is satisfied that the related exposure will be ~~*100%*~~ [read *fully*] covered by the Commitments of the non-Defaulting Lenders ... .

13.639 Similarly, simplicity favors using *half* rather than *50%*, as in "*50% of* [read *half*] the shares" and "*50% of* [read *half*] the members of the Company's board of directors." If you can, do without the preposition *of*—don't say *half of the shares*.

13.640   But it makes sense to use *100%* and *50%* to refer to a numerical value in a provision that includes one or more other percentages: … *with a target award-date value of 100% of the Base Salary and a maximum award value of 150% of the Base Salary, subject to … .*

13.641   Fractions other than half (for example, *one-quarter, one-fifth*) offer no advantage over percentages, as they're more cumbersome. The exception is fractions that would require a recurring decimal to be expressed in percentages, for example *one-third* and *two-sevenths*.

PERSONAL DELIVERY

13.642   It's confusing to use *personal delivery* in a notices provision in a contract. Does *personal* relate to the person doing the delivering? If so, does it mean that the party giving the notice has to be the one to deliver it, rather than, say, FedEx? After all, one says, "I delivered it personally," meaning that the speaker was the one who delivered the item.

13.643   Or does *personal* relate to the recipient? If so, does complying with the provision require that notice be handed to the recipient? What if it's placed before the recipient? What if the recipient is in the next room? And so on.

13.644   The meaning of "deliver it personally" was at issue in the English case *Ener-G Holdings plc v. Hormell* [2012] EWCA Civ 1059 (31 July 2012). The court decided that the best interpretation was that "personally" referred to the recipient, so that complying with the provision required that notice be handed to the recipient.

13.645   To avoid this sort of confusion, don't use in a contract *personal delivery* or *deliver … personally*. Instead, provide for delivery to a person at a specified address by specified means (by national transportation company, by registered mail, by hand, or otherwise) and specify when notice will be deemed to have been received.

PERSONNEL

13.646   Some use personnel as a synonym for employees. Others use it to include others, perhaps even companies. Here's a definition that does that:

> "**Personnel**" means the Affiliates, officers, directors, employees, agents, contractors, consultants, vendors, invitees, and representatives of a party and that party's Affiliates.

13.647   The broader definition isn't necessarily anomalous. For example, *Black's Law Dictionary* gives as a definition of *personnel*, "Collectively, the people who work in a company, organization, or military force." One can work in a company without being an employee.

13.648   If some contracts define *personnel* to mean more than employees, it's conceivable that in other contracts drafters use *personnel* to convey that broader meaning but without using it as a defined term. You have the potential for a fight over the meaning of *personnel*. That's not an unlikely notion, given that people have litigated whether a court-appointed receiver qualifies as court personnel.

13.649   And *personnel* has another strike against it—it's a plural noun with no singular form, and there's no other singular noun applying to an individual member of the set it denotes.

13.650   So if you mean employees, use *employees*. If you mean employees and other representatives, create and use the defined term *Representative*. If the group in question includes more than employees and representatives, you could use the defined term *Personnel*, but consider whether you need such an unwieldy group.

PREVAILING PARTY

13.651   A standard piece of boilerplate is a provision stating that the "prevailing party" (or "successful party") in a dispute may recover costs.

13.652   In the United States, generally attorneys' fees aren't recoverable in a commercial contract dispute unless provided for by statute or contract. So if in a transaction you want to recover attorneys' fees and other expenses, say so in the contract.

13.653   But one problem with such provisions is that the meaning of *prevailing party* has "spawned a great deal of litigation." Robert L. Rossi, 1 *Attorneys' Fees* § 6:8 (3d ed. 2012). If the plaintiff voluntarily dismisses its action, has the defendant prevailed? If a party's case has been dismissed for want of jurisdiction, has the other party prevailed? What if both a complaint and a counterclaim have been dismissed? If the plaintiff has recovered on its complaint against the defendant and the defendant has recovered on its counterclaim against the plaintiff, is the prevailing party the one in whose favor a net judgment was entered, or are both parties entitled to recover? Is a decision required, or can you prevail in a settlement or consent decree? Is a money judgment required, or do equitable remedies qualify? And to be the prevailing party in a dispute, do you have to succeed on all issues, or just some? Those are only a few of the uncertainties.

13.654   You could attempt to be specific regarding what determines whether a party has prevailed. There are three main ways to do so. First, a party is the prevailing party if it secures a judgment or any kind of dismissal. That has the benefit of being clear-cut, but it would allow a party to recover fees even after failing to prevail on most of its claims.

13.655   Second, a party is the prevailing party if it gets substantially what it had sought. That has fairness in its favor, but given its vagueness, a court would likely have to decide this.

13.656   And third, a party is the prevailing party if it's the net winner, regardless of what it had sought. So if Party A wins one claim out of 20 and recovers

$10 and Party B wins its one claim and gets $9, Party A is the net winner. It's not clear whether that's fair.

13.657   Given all the potential issues, and given that determining the prevailing party is such a fact-specific inquiry, the risks of setting rules in advance might outweigh the potential benefits.

13.658   Cal. Civil Code § 1717(b)(1) contains a definition of *prevailing party* for claims under a contract. That definition is mandatory and cannot be altered or avoided by contract. See, e.g., *Exxess Electronixx v. Heger Realty Corp.*, 75 Cal. Rptr. 2d 376, 383 (Ct. App. 1998).

PRODUCT, UNITS OF THE PRODUCT

13.659   The word *product* is ambiguous—it can mean either a product line or individual samples of a product line. Using the defined term *Product* for the former meaning and referring to *units of the Product* for the latter would eliminate any confusion.

PROPRIETARY

13.660   The word *proprietary* is overused in contracts. In particular, it's unhelpful to use *proprietary* in defining the term *Confidential Information*.

13.661   *Black's Law Dictionary* defines *proprietary* in part as follows: "1. Of, relating to, or involving a proprietor <the licensee's proprietary rights>. 2. Of, relating to, or holding as property <the software designer sought to protect its proprietary data>." So information can be proprietary but not confidential.

13.662   It follows that if *Confidential Information* is defined to mean proprietary information, or is defined to mean information that is proprietary or confidential, information that isn't confidential would, unhelpfully, fall within the scope of the definition. If *Confidential Information* is defined to mean information that is both proprietary *and* confidential, that would exclude information that isn't proprietary but is nevertheless information that a disclosing party might want to keep confidential, for example information disclosed to it by someone else under a confidentiality agreement.

PROVIDED THAT

13.663   A traditional component of legal drafting is the proviso, which consists of a provision introduced by *provided that* and set off from the preceding clause by a comma or semicolon. In contracts, provisos are often introduced with a semicolon and *provided, however, that*, with *provided* and *however* underlined for emphasis. In the case of a proviso that immediately follows another proviso, the formula used is *provided further, however, that* or something similar.

13.664 The problems with *provided that* go beyond the archaic trappings of the traditional proviso. In this context, *provided that* is a truncation of the "term of enactment" *it is provided that.* Into the 19th century, *provided that* was used to introduce statutory provisions. But *provided* is also a conjunction meaning *if* or *on condition that*—"I'll let you go to the party, provided you take a taxi home." Maybe this everyday use of *provided* dulls modern drafters to the fact that as currently used in contracts, *provided that* essentially continues to serve its original function: it's used to introduce not only conditions to the main clause but also limitations and exceptions to the main clause, as well as new provisions that can be considered independently of the main clause. In other words, using *provided that* is an imprecise way to signal the relationship between two conjoined contract provisions.

13.665 For an example of how using *provided that* in a contract can lead to dispute, see *Jacobsen v. Katzer*, 535 F.3d 1373 (Fed. Cir. 2008). This case involved a copyright license that granted users the right to use software, "provided that [the user] insert a prominent notice in each changed file stating how and when [the user] changed that file, and provided that [the user] do at least ONE of the following: … ." The defendants took none of the actions specified in the *provided that* language, so the licensor sued. The question was whether that failure meant that the defendants' use of the software fell outside the scope of the license or whether it represented breach of the license. The lower court held that the *provided that* language didn't limit the license grant. The Federal Circuit disagreed, holding that the *provided that* language stated conditions to effectiveness of the license. The wrong lesson to take from this case is that you should use *provided that* to state a condition. Instead, it would be best to avoid confusion, with the attendant risk of litigation, by steering clear of *provided that*.

avoid, but limit to mean except

13.666 A more precise alternative to *provided that* is always available. Below are sample provisos, one for each category of meaning drafters seek to convey with provisos. In each, the clearer alternative to the italicized text incorporating *provided that* is noted in italics in the brackets that immediately follow.

Exception

When issued in accordance with this agreement, the Warrant Shares will be validly issued, fully paid, and nonassessable, and will be free of any *Liens; provided, however, that* [read *Liens, except that*] the Warrant Shares may be subject to restrictions on transfer under state and federal securities laws.

Limitation

The Closing must take place at the offices of the Purchaser's counsel promptly after the date of this *agreement; provided, however, that the Closing must occur* [read *agreement, and in any event*] no later than 1 December 2017, at 5:00 p.m. New York time, unless the parties agree to another date.

Condition

Acme shall reimburse the Consultant all reasonable expenses the Consultant incurs in performing services under this *agreement; provided, however, that the Consultant shall obtain* [read *agreement, on condition that the Consultant obtain*] Acme's written consent before incurring any such expense in excess of $200.

Addition

"**Purchase Period**" means the ten-day period following the end of each calendar *quarter; provided, however, that the Purchase Period shall include any other periods* [read *quarter and any other periods*] the Committee designates.

PROVISION

13.667   The word *provision is* used to describe something in a contract, but without being specific. You can use *provision* in a contract, usually in the plural. Here are two examples:

> … any additional shares of Common Stock issued and issuable in connection with any antidilution *provisions* in the Notes or the Warrants … .

> … or the consent of whose Holders is required for any waiver of compliance with certain *provisions* of this Indenture … .

13.668   But usually it's redundant:

> … in accordance with ~~the provisions of~~ this section 4.1.1 … .

> … if the Borrower timely complies with ~~each of the provisions in~~ section 4.2.

> … as amended in accordance with ~~the provisions of~~ the Deposit Agreement … .

13.669   The redundant *provision* also occurs in the silly *terms and provisions*, which is presumably used by those enamored of *terms and conditions* (see 13.807):

> … be bound by ~~the terms and provisions of~~ the Intercreditor Agreement … .

> *All terms and provisions of the* [read *The*] Purchase Agreement and the other Transaction Documents will remain in effect.

13.670   *Provisions* used in section and article headings? You can always do better:

> ~~Other Interpretive Provisions~~ [read Interpretation]

> Definitions ~~and Other Definitional Provisions~~

> ~~Patent Provisions~~ [read Patents]

> ~~Certain Provisions Relating to~~ Limited Liability Company and Limited Partnership Interests.

REASONABLE, REASONABLY

13.671   Reasonableness is expressed in contracts by means of the adjective *reasonable* and the adverb *reasonably*. How they're used can raise some subtle issues.

13.672   *Black's Law Dictionary* defines *reasonable* in part as "Fair, proper, or moderate under the circumstances." So determining whether someone has acted reasonably requires an objective inquiry—you consider the circumstances, not the actor's intent.

13.673   That's the meaning of *reasonable* as it's used in, for example, *a reasonable fee* and *in reasonable detail*. But it conveys a different meaning in, for example, *to the reasonable satisfaction of Acme*, in that *reasonable* doesn't refer to reasonableness of the satisfaction. Instead, *to the reasonable satisfaction of Acme* means *to the satisfaction of Acme, determined from the perspective of a reasonable person in Acme's position*. It would be clearer to say it that way.

13.674   When *reasonably* modifies a verb, as in *reasonably requests* and *reasonably determines*, the word *reasonably* can be paraphrased as "in a reasonable manner." But when *reasonably* modifies a verb it can be redundant, depending on the verb. For example, *reasonably* is redundant in *Acme shall cooperate reasonably with Widgetco*, as reasonableness is inherent in the notion of parties cooperating.

13.675   When it's used to modify anything other than a verb, *reasonably* is problematic.

13.676   It's redundant when used to modify the adverb *promptly*, in that promptness is determined based on what is reasonable considering the circumstances (see 10.110). The same applies to using *reasonably* to modify other adverbs.

13.677   As regards using *reasonably* to modify adjectives, it's redundant in the phrase *reasonably likely*—reasonableness has nothing to do with an expression of likelihood.

13.678   When *reasonably* is used to modify other adjectives, for example *satisfactory* or *necessary*, the word *reasonably* doesn't refer to reasonableness of the satisfaction, or of the necessity. Instead, as with *reasonable satisfaction* (see 13.673), *reasonably satisfactory* means *satisfactory, as determined from the perspective of a reasonable person in Acme's position*. And it would be clearer to say it that way. Courts would likely attribute that meaning to *satisfactory* regardless (see 13.722), but making that explicit would eliminate a potential source of dispute.

REASONABLENESS AND GOOD FAITH

13.679   When should you use a reasonableness standard and when should you use a good-faith standard? And does it make sense to use both in a provision?

Whether to Use a Reasonableness Standard or a Good-Faith Standard

13.680   Generally, it would benefit a contract party to have a reasonableness standard rather than a good-faith standard apply to a counterparty's conduct. A reasonableness standard can be imposed not only by using *reasonable* and *reasonably* but also by using words such as *appropriate*.

13.681   A reasonableness standard is objective—what would a reasonable person have done in the circumstances? By contrast, a good-faith standard is subjective—did the party in question think it was acting reasonably, regardless of whether it was when viewed from the perspective of a reasonable person? It wouldn't be in a party's interest to give the other party room to act unreasonably but in good faith. That's why, for example, it makes sense to refer to *reasonable efforts* rather than *good-faith efforts*. But if your client is the one subject to a given provision, you might prefer a good-faith standard.

13.682   But a good-faith standard is the appropriate choice if a party is taking a position—for example, contesting something (*taxes that are being contested in good faith*), claiming that something happened, or filing a complaint. Using *good faith* confirms that the party's public position matches its actual state of mind.

13.683   And use *good faith* to qualify an obligation to negotiate—you can't be forced to agree to something just because a reasonable person in your position would have done so (see 8.55).

13.684   When you're referring to a party's actual state of mind, *good faith* is redundant. For example, the phrase *good-faith belief* doesn't make sense—if you believe something, necessarily you believe it in good faith. But when a reasonableness standard is used with *believes* and *satisfactory* and other words usually associated with a state of mind, what is being referred to is not the state of mind of a party but the state of mind of a reasonable person in the position of that party (see 13.722–.723).

13.685   In jurisdictions that recognize the implied duty of good faith (see 3.225), it wouldn't be necessary to make it explicit that a good-faith standard applies in a given context—it's what would apply by default in the absence of another standard. But it can be helpful to remind the parties that that's the case, and doing so might eliminate a potential source of dispute.

13.686   The difference between a reasonableness standard and a good-faith standard can be more apparent than real. Often it's impossible to determine what a contract party was thinking in taking an action—either you have no evidence on that score, or the evidence you have is self-serving. So courts often decide whether a party acted in good faith by considering how others have behaved in similar circumstances—by in effect applying a reasonableness standard. That might be relevant if the other side balks at being subject to a reasonableness standard.

Using Both Standards Together

13.687   What about using both a reasonableness standard and a good-faith standard in one provision? Usually that wouldn't make sense—if a party meets the more exacting reasonableness standard, what would be the point of invoking good faith? It follows that drafters using phrases such as *reasonable good-faith efforts* and *reasonable good-faith judgment* are indulging in redundancy.

13.688 But in a given context you might want to be sure not just that a party is conducting itself reasonably but also that it's not acting under a pretext. For example, if a party is contesting taxes (see 13.682), one issue is whether it's taking appropriate steps to do so; another is whether it's using the process as a pretext to create delay. You could address both concerns by referring to taxes being contested "in good faith by appropriate proceedings."

REGARD SHALL BE HAD TO

13.689 The phrase *regard shall be had to* doesn't occur often in contracts, but it's clumsy enough—passive voice, *shall* that fails the *has a duty* test (see 3.74)—to be worth pointing out. Two examples:

> In computing the majority when a poll is demanded, *regard shall be had to* the number of votes to which each Member is entitled by the Articles.

> In determining the rights of the US$ Note Trustee to additional remuneration following an Event of Default, *regard shall be had to* any amounts paid to the US$ Note Trustee following an event described in section 12.3(b).

13.690 It's not amenable to a quick fix. One approach would be to use the active voice and *take into account, consider,* or *include.*

REMEDIATE

13.691 In contracts and elsewhere, it's standard to use the word *remediation* in connection with cleanup or treatment of environmental contamination. It's also standard to use the verb *remediate* to refer to the act of remediation.

13.692 According to *Garner's Modern English Usage,* "*remediate,* a back-formation from *remediation,* is either a needless variant of *remedy* or a piece of gobbledygook." But in environmental circles, *remediation* has acquired a specialized meaning, and the verb *remediate* evokes that specialized meaning. To insist that drafters instead use the verb *remedy* to convey that meaning is to fight an uphill battle.

13.693 Furthermore, the remedy for environmental contamination could consist of cleanup, a monetary award, a civil or criminal penalty, or injunctive relief. Using *remediate* instead of *remedy* in connection with cleanup or treatment makes it clear which meaning is intended.

REMIT, REMITTANCE

13.694 *Black's Law Dictionary* gives as one definition of *remit* "To transmit (as money) <upon receiving the demand letter, she promptly remitted the amount due>." And here's how it defines *remittance*: "1. A sum of money sent to another as payment for goods or services. 2. An instrument (such as a check) used for sending money. 3. The action or process of sending money to another person or place."

13.695   *Remit* and *remittance* are old-fashioned choices to express these meanings in a contract. More straightforward are *pay* and *payment*, as in these examples:

> Upon Substantial Completion of each System, Owner shall *remit to* [read *pay*] Contractor half the amount retained with respect to that System.

> ... an amount as that Lender or the Administrative Agent, as applicable, determines to be the proportion of the refunded amount as will leave it, after that *remittance* [read *payment*], in no better or worse position than it would have been if ... .

13.696   Some contexts might require using instead *transfer* or *refund* (in both cases, the verb or the noun).

13.697   And if you can replace the abstract noun *remittance* with the verb *pay* (see 17.7), so much the better:

> *If legal restrictions prevent the prompt remittance of* [read *If by law Acme is prevented from paying promptly*] any royalties with respect to any country in the Territory where the Product is sold ... .

RESPECTIVE, RESPECTIVELY

13.698   More often than not, *respective* and *respectively* are misused when used in contracts. Such misuse is unlikely to result in any dispute, but it doesn't do the reader any favors.

Respective

13.699   *Respective* means "as relates individually to each of two or more persons or things," as in *George and Hannah drove their respective cars home*. It indicates that the components of one group are to be considered separately in pairing them with one or more components of another group.

13.700   Here's an example of *respective* used appropriately in a contract:

> "**Eligible Party**" means a party other than Acme, Widgetco, or any of their *respective* Affiliates.

13.701   But it's easy to find examples of the extraneous *respective*. Sometimes *in question* would work better:

> Each employee's election to participate made in accordance with the provisions of section 4.2 will remain in effect for the one-year period that begins on the first day of the ~~respective~~ Class Year [read *in question*] and ends on the last day of that Class Year.

13.702   At other times, *respective* is inappropriately used with a construction in the singular:

> Each of the Trustee and the Company states that it has the full right and power and has been duly authorized to enter into this agreement and to perform its ~~respective~~ obligations as contemplated hereunder.

> On or before the Effective Date, each of the Private Investors shall deliver to the Escrow Agent certificates representing that Private Investor's ~~respective~~ Escrow Founder Units.

> All selling security holders and the Company shall bear the expenses of the underwriter pro rata in proportion to the ~~respective~~ dollar amount of securities each is selling in such offering.

13.703 Sometimes *any* should have been used rather than *the respective*, in that no pairing is involved:

> "**Release Date**" means *the respective dates* [read *any date*] on which the Founder Units, Sponsor Warrants, Co-Investment Units, and Aftermarket Shares are disbursed from escrow in accordance with section 3 of the Securities Escrow Agreement.

13.704 And you might be able to eliminate *respective* by making the groups singular:

> *All capitalized terms that are* [read *Each capitalized term*] used but not defined in this SOW *have the respective meanings given to them* [read *has the meaning given to it*] in the Purchase Agreement.

13.705 Even if *respective* works, you might have choices. The first of the following alternatives uses *respective*. The second, also using *respective*, is slightly more concise than the first, and significantly more concise than the third, which doesn't use *respective*. If the tenant were an individual and the landlord an entity, the pronoun "its" in the second version wouldn't work, making the first version the best option.

> The Tenant and the Landlord shall cause their respective casualty policies to contain a provision allowing the foregoing waiver of claims.

> The Tenant and the Landlord shall each cause its casualty policies to contain … .

> The Tenant shall cause the Tenant's, and the Landlord shall cause the Landlord's, casualty policies to contain … .

Respectively

13.706 *Respectively* means "in regard to each of two or more, in the order named." It indicates that each item in a list earlier in a sentence is to be paired with its counterpart in a list that follows and contains an equal number of items, as in *The first and second prizes went to Marie and Frank, respectively.* (The list earlier in the sentence and the list associated with *respectively* should both use *and* rather than *or*.)

13.707 Here are two examples of appropriate use of *respectively* in a contract:

> Each Newco1 Director and Newco2 Director will have one vote on all matters requiring the approval or action of the Newco1 Board and the Newco2 Board, *respectively*.

> Smith and Jones will be responsible for paying one-third and two-thirds, *respectively*, of any Additional Tax.

13.708   But *respectively* is redundant if there's no preceding list to echo, as in these examples:

> … if Tenant fails to provide Landlord with the financial statements or the estoppel certificates within the time periods referenced in sections 23.16 and 23.17~~, respectively~~.

> *Company and Put Grantor, respectively, state that each party has been represented by that party's* [read The *Company and the Put Grantor each states that it has been represented by*] legal counsel regarding all aspects of this agreement.

> The Executive is employed by [read *each of*] XYZ, the Company, and the Bank *in senior executive capacities, respectively* [read *in a senior executive capacity*].

> Owner and Tenant are ~~*respectively*~~ signing this agreement on the date stated in the introductory clause.

RIGHTFULLY, RIGHTFUL

13.709   The word *rightfully* occurs routinely in contracts, most often in one of the standard exceptions to the definition of *Confidential Information* in a confidentiality agreement: … *information that the Licensee rightfully obtains from any person that has the right to transfer or disclose that information.* The word *rightful* is used less often.

13.710   The problem with *rightfully* and *rightful* is that they're imprecise. *Rightful* means "having a just or legally established claim; held by right or just claim." But neither *rightfully* nor *rightful* gives the reader any sense of the basis for the entitlement.

13.711   For example, regarding use of *rightfully* in the exclusion from the definition of *Confidential Information*, it's not clear whether *rightfully* means that the recipient must not have received the information in question from someone who is under an obligation of confidentiality not to disclose that information, or whether it means that the recipient must not have somehow broken the law to get that information, or whether it's meant to convey both of those meanings.

13.712   So consider whether you can replace *rightfully* and *rightful* with a clearer alternative. The same applies to *wrongfully* and *wrongful*.

RIGHT, TITLE, AND INTEREST

13.713   *Right, title, and interest* is a bloated legalism, with the three nouns serving primarily to make legal prose suitably sonorous. That the three elements are invariably kept in the same order is a sign that they serve as incantation.

13.714   *Garner's Dictionary of Legal Usage*, at 788–89, offers this analysis:

> **right, title, and interest.** This phrase, one of the classic triplets of the legal idiom, is the traditional language for conveying a

quitclaim interest. … Technically, only one of the three words is necessary, as the broad meaning of *interest* includes the others: though you can have an *interest* without having *title* and perhaps without a given *right*, you cannot have *title* or a *right* without having an *interest*.

13.715 It's easy enough to find caselaw to that effect. Here are two examples:

> In common parlance the word "interest" is broader and more comprehensive than the word "title," and its definition in a narrowed sense by lexicographers as any right in the nature of property less than title indicates that the terms are not considered synonymous. *In re Baldwin's Estate*, 134 P.2d 259, 263 (Cal. 1943).

> In the context of property law, a "right" is a "legally enforceable claim of one person against another, that the other shall do a given act or shall not do a given act," and an interest "generically … include[s] varying aggregates of rights, privileges, powers and immunities and distributively … mean[s] any one of them." *Dennison v. North Dakota Department of Human Services*, 640 N.W.2d 447, 453 (N.D. 2002).

13.716 You might think that there's no point in being adventurous and tinkering with *right, title, and interest*. But if you take that deferential approach with *right, title, and interest*, you'll likely do the same with other usages, and your contracts will suffer.

13.717 Furthermore, the phrase might have its roots in conveying a quitclaim interest, but it can now be found in all sorts of contracts. It has gotten annoying. *Right, title, and interest* occurs in enough different contexts that this manual won't offer a blanket rule. Instead, consider using only *interest*; if you decided that *interest* alone is inadequate, then add only whatever is necessary address to whatever you think *interest* alone doesn't cover.

13.718 If your concern is that having Acme transfer its interest in an asset might leave Acme with something, you could address that by having Acme acknowledge that after the transfer, Acme would be left with nothing relating to the asset.

SAID USED AS A POINTING WORD

13.719 It remains commonplace for drafters to use *said* instead of one of the "pointing words" *this, that, these,* and *those*. An example: *If the Executive contests in good faith whether he was properly terminated for "Cause," the Executive and the Company shall immediately refer said* [read *that*] *dispute to arbitration in accordance with section 15*. This usage is one of the hallmarks of legalese, and it contributes nothing to drafting other than an annoyingly legalistic tone.

13.720 This use of *said* is related to misuse of *such* (see 13.767). In the following extract, the drafter could have used *said* instead of *such,* and vice versa, but it would have been best to use *that* instead: *if for a period of 12 consecutive* *months a majority of the board of Borrower or any Guarantor is no longer composed of individuals who were members of said* [read *that*] *board on the first day of such* [read *that*] *period.*

SAME USED AS A PRONOUN

13.721   To use *same* as a pronoun is to pontificate. Often one can simply use instead a more conventional pronoun—*it, its, them, they, their*—or repeat the noun in question, perhaps with a suitable "pointing word" (see 13.719). At other times more extensive revisions are required. Some examples follow; in each, the recommended alternative to the italicized text incorporating *same* is noted in brackets.

> The Company shall furnish to the Lender promptly after *the same* [read *they*] become publicly available copies of all periodic and other reports, proxy statements, and other materials filed by the Company with the Securities and Exchange Commission.

> The Company shall pay its Indebtedness and other obligations, including Tax liabilities, before *the same* [read *they*] become delinquent or in default.

> Regarding any Loans made by it under this agreement, each Agent in its individual capacity and not as Agent will have the same rights and powers as any other Lender and may exercise *the same* [read *those rights and powers*] as though it were not an Agent.

> Any notice given under this agreement that is delivered by mail will be deemed received *upon the depositing of the same in the U.S. mail* [read *when it is deposited in the U.S. mail*].

SATISFACTORY

13.722   If you say that something has to be *satisfactory to Acme*, the standard might be an objective one, in that it would be met if a reasonable person in Acme's position would be satisfied. Alternatively, it could mean that Acme actually has to be satisfied, subject only to the implied duty of good faith—the standard is a subjective one. The result is ambiguity. Courts prefer the former meaning; see 2-5 *Corbin on Contracts* § 5.33; 13 *Williston on Contracts* § 38:22.

13.723   Saying instead *reasonably satisfactory to Acme* is a succinct way of making it clear to the parties, and to any court, that the objective meaning is intended. To make it clear that the subjective meaning is intended, drafters customarily say *satisfactory to Acme at its discretion* (or a variant; see 3.228–.232). But strictly speaking, that doesn't go to the meaning of *satisfactory.* The following formula is wordier but explicit: *satisfactory to Acme, with Acme's satisfaction in this instance being a function of whether Acme is actually satisfied (subject to any implied duty of good faith), rather than whether a reasonable person in Acme's position would be satisfied.* It's hard to imagine any counterparty accepting such a standard.

SHAREHOLDER OR *STOCKHOLDER*?

13.724 Many lawyers think that it's necessary to use *stockholder* rather than *shareholder*—in contracts and elsewhere—if the corporation in question was formed under Delaware law. Insisting on this distinction would seem odd, in that *stockholder* and *shareholder* are synonyms meaning, of course, a holder of shares of stock of a corporation.

13.725 Presumably no one is under any illusion that which term you use in a contract could affect a party's rights. More likely, the distinction derives from wanting to show good manners by conforming to local custom. But in this case, local custom is far from clear-cut, as both terms are used in the Delaware General Corporation Law and in Delaware caselaw. And treatises on Delaware corporate law use the terms interchangeably. So for all purposes, including contract drafting, you may with a clear conscience use either *stockholder* or *shareholder* when referring to a holder of shares of stock of a Delaware corporation.

SHAREHOLDERS AGREEMENT

13.726 What should you call an agreement between shareholders? This manual recommends using *shareholders agreement*, but each of the three following alternatives is defensible:

- *shareholders' agreement* (plural plus apostrophe)

- *shareholder agreement* (singular, no apostrophe-*s*)

- *shareholders agreement* (plural without the apostrophe)

13.727 *Shareholders' agreement*, conveying the meaning "agreement of the shareholders," is perhaps the most traditional option. It would be unobjectionable but for the apostrophe—because an apostrophe in a contract title is a rarity, it's always at risk of being dropped.

13.728 *Shareholder agreement* is analogous to *shareholder meeting*, which is a standard alternative to *shareholders' meeting*. But judging by contracts filed on the U.S. Securities and Exchange Commission's EDGAR system, this alternative is used about half as often as alternatives featuring the plural *shareholders*, with or without the apostrophe.

13.729 In *shareholders agreement*, the word *shareholders* is an attributive noun, answering the question "What kind of?" as opposed to "Whose is it?" *Shareholders agreement* is analogous to *carpenters union* and *homeowners association*. It has the advantage of using the plural—it's better to choose the more popular option if there's no drawback to doing so—without the nuisance of the apostrophe.

13.730 Obviously the same alternatives apply if you use the word *stockholder* instead of *shareholder*; see 13.724.

SIGNATORY

13.731   The word *signatory* is ambiguous. *Black's Law Dictionary* defines *signatory* as "A person or entity that signs a document, personally or through an agent, and thereby becomes a party to an agreement." But it's also used to mean someone who physically signs a contract, whether as a party or on behalf of a party.

13.732   To avoid reader miscues, use instead *party* to convey the former meaning and *individual signing this agreement for Acme* to convey the latter meaning. Don't say instead *on behalf of Acme*, as that could be understood as referring to only an agent, not an Acme officer.

13.733   But when it's used in a signature block (see 5.34), it's clear that *signatory* refers to the individual signing. In that context, this manual suggests as an alternative the word *signer*. Throughout this manual *signer* is used to convey that meaning, because it's the simpler word.

SILENT ON

13.734   The phrase *silent on* is sometimes used in contracts to state that the contract doesn't address a given topic, as in *This agreement is silent on the law that governs disputes arising out of this agreement*.

13.735   There can be value, for both negotiation and interpretation, to being explicit that the parties have elected not to address a given issue. But it would be simpler to say *This agreement does not address* the issue in question.

SOLE, EXCLUSIVE

Sole, Exclusive in Licensing

13.736   In licensing circles, it's widely accepted that a *sole* license is different from an *exclusive* license. In a sole license, the licensor is obligated not to grant any additional licenses but retains the right to practice the licensed subject matter; in an exclusive license, only the licensee has the right to practice the licensed subject matter. See *Drafting License Agreements* § 1.02 (Michael A. Epstein and Frank L. Politano eds., 4th ed. 2012).

13.737   But in using *sole* and *exclusive* to convey those meanings, drafters are using jargon that isn't comprehensible to the uninitiated. That likely includes some clients.

13.738   Furthermore, for two reasons the distinction isn't as clear as it seems. First, a sole license could also be understood to mean not that the licensor retains the right to practice the licensed subject matter, but that prior licenses granted are preserved. See Roger M. Milgrim, *Milgrim on Licensing* § 15.33 (2012). And second, the confusing phrase *sole and exclusive* (see 13.741) is used widely in contracts generally, and one sees instances of *sole and exclusive* used in granting language in different kinds of licenses. That muddies the notion of distinct meanings for *sole* and *exclusive*.

13.739 Another way to express the meaning of *sole* described in 13.736 is *exclusive (except as to the Licensor)*. But it would be clearer still to state in a separate sentence that the licensor retains the right to practice the licensed subject matter. See Robert A. Matthews, Jr., 1 *Annotated Patent Digest* § 9:59 (2015).

13.740 The term *coexclusive* is used by some as an alternative to *sole*. See, e.g., R. Gwen Peterson, *Patent Licensing Considerations*, Ass'n of Corp. Counsel (27 Aug. 2013). But that could cause confusion over whether the licensor may name an additional licensee.

Sole and Exclusive

13.741 Drafters can always do better than use the phrase *sole and exclusive*, with its inherent redundancy.

13.742 Instead of *sole and exclusive remedy*, you could say *sole remedy* or *only remedy*. In a forum-selection provision, say *exclusive jurisdiction* rather than *sole and exclusive jurisdiction*. Or more significant surgery might be required: Instead of saying that all interests in something are *the sole and exclusive property* of Acme, say that Acme *owns* all those interests. And saying that Widgetco may do something *at its sole and exclusive option* raises issues similar to those raised by *at its sole discretion* (see 3.224) and *from time to time* (see 10.131).

13.743 For granting a license, the problem with *sole and exclusive* goes beyond redundancy (see 13.736).

SOLICIT

13.744 The word *solicit*, meaning "to entice," can be used awkwardly in no-solicit provisions in confidentiality agreements.

13.745 Here's one way it's used: *The Recipient shall not hire or solicit any of the Disclosing Party's employees*. But that raises the question, solicit them for what? Usually referring to soliciting without specifying a purpose suggests prostitution, or going door to door for contributions. Obviously, that's not the meaning intended in no-solicit provisions.

13.746 That explains use of the phrase *solicit to employ*. But usually when *solicit* is followed by a verb, the verb pertains to an activity to be undertaken by the person being solicited—*I solicited him to be our sponsor*. So *solicit to employ* is awkward.

13.747 For optimal clarity, you would have to say something like *The Recipient shall not solicit employees of the Disclosing Party to accept employment with the Recipient*. That's wordy. Use instead *solicit to be hired*. It too is rather awkward, but at least it's concise and is consistent with how *solicit* is usually used.

SPECIFIC

13.748   When it occurs in contracts (besides its use in the phrase *specific performance*), more often than not the word *specific* serves no purpose. The drafter would have done well to omit *specific* from each of these examples, making other adjustments as necessary:

> The written decision must (1) state ~~specific~~ reasons for such decision, (2) ~~provide specific reference~~ [read *refer*] to the ~~specific~~ Plan provisions on which the decision is based, ...

> If any one or more provisions of this section is for any reason held invalid or unenforceable, *it is the specific intent of the parties* [read *the parties intend*] that those provisions will be modified to the minimum extent necessary to make them or their application valid and enforceable.

> The Company and the Purchasers acknowledge that irreparable damage would occur if any of the provisions of this agreement or the other Transaction Documents are not performed in accordance with their ~~specific~~ terms or are otherwise breached.

> No such employees shall admit any person (Tenant or otherwise) to any office without ~~specific~~ instructions from Landlord.

13.749   In the following examples it would have been better to replace *specific* with a different word:

> ... but the Company may provide such indemnification or advancement of Expenses in *specific* [read *individual*] cases if the Company's board of directors finds it to be appropriate; ... .

> ... other than those statements of fact that expressly relate solely to a *specific* [read *specified*] earlier date, ...

13.750   So if you're tempted to use *specific*, try omitting it. If that doesn't work, consider whether a different word would work better.

SPOUSE

13.751   Instead of referring to the wife or husband of a contract party, it simplifies drafting to use *spouse*. It works whether the party in question is a woman or a man, and it works whether the individual to whom that party is married is a woman or a man.

SUBROGATION

13.752   The noun *subrogation* and the verb *subrogate* are terms of art. In contract provisions that relate to just the parties, use instead simpler alternatives. (Regarding unnecessary terms of art generally, see 1.11–.15.)

13.753   Here's the *Black's Law Dictionary* definition of *subrogation*:

> **subrogation** (səb-rə-**gay**-shən) *n.* (15c) **1.** The substitution of one party for another whose debt the party pays, entitling the paying

party to rights, remedies, or securities that would otherwise belong to the debtor. ... **2.** The equitable remedy by which such a substitution takes place. **3.** The principle under which an insurer that has paid a loss under an insurance policy is entitled to all the rights and remedies belonging to the insured against a third party with respect to any loss covered by the policy.

13.754 And here's an example of how to eliminate a reference to subrogation contained in a provision that addresses an aspect of the relations between the parties and doesn't involve nonparties:

> ... Acme *will not be entitled to be subrogated to* [read *hereby waives*] any of the rights of the Administrative Agent or any Bank against Capitalco or any guarantee or right of offset held by the Administrative Agent or any Bank for payment of the Capitalco Obligations ... .

13.755 Changing subrogation terminology in provisions specifying requirements for insurance is more challenging. It would involve presenting an insurance company with novel terminology. That might cause delay and uncertainty—the insurance industry has its own way of doing things and relies on specialized terminology. Even techniques suggested elsewhere in this manual for combining terms of art with clearer alternatives (see 13.208, 13.890) risk complicating matters. It might be best to leave well enough alone.

SUCH AS

13.756 *Such as* is ambiguous—it might be unclear whether the clause it introduces reduces the scope of the class represented by the preceding noun. This can cause contract disputes.

13.757 Consider this sentence:

> Richard collects books about painters such as Botticelli and Donatello.

13.758 Given the general nature of this class (*painters*) and the narrowness of the items in the *such as* phrase (two Italian painters of the early Renaissance), the reasonable reader would assume that Richard doesn't collect books about all painters but instead collects books about painters comparable to those listed. So the *such as* phrase reduces the scope of the noun *painters*—it's acting like a restrictive clause. (For more about restrictive and nonrestrictive clauses, see 12.43–.45.)

13.759 The alternative would be for the nouns in the *such as* phrase simply to be examples of the class represented by the preceding noun. That would result in the *such as* phrase acting like a nonrestrictive clause. Regarding the sample sentence above, that could be accomplished either by narrowing the class represented by the preceding noun (see the first example below) or by including a broader range of nouns in the *such as* phrase (see the second example below):

> Richard collects books about Renaissance painters, such as Botticelli and Donatello.

Richard collects books about painters, such as Botticelli, Gustav Klimt, J.M.W. Turner, and Andy Warhol.

13.760   Placing a comma before the *such as* phrase, as in the two preceding examples, would make the *such as* phrase nonrestrictive.

13.761   Nonrestrictive use of a *such as* phrase makes sense only if the meaning or scope of the class represented by the preceding noun might otherwise be unclear to the reader. That's why the last of the above examples is rather odd—the class represented by the noun *painters* is so vast as to make the examples provided unnecessary.

13.762   But a bigger problem is that a reader might be uncertain whether a given *such as* phrase is intended to be restrictive or nonrestrictive. For example, it might have been intended that the *such as* phrase in the second of the three above examples be restrictive—maybe the meaning sought to be conveyed is not that Richard collects books about all Renaissance painters but instead that he collects books about Italian painters of the early Renaissance. It would be rash to rely on a comma to ensure that a given *such as* phrase is read as being nonrestrictive.

13.763   *Lawler Manufacturing Co. v. Bradley Corp.*, 280 F. App'x 951 (Fed. Cir. 2008), provides an example of a contract dispute caused by confusion regarding a *such as* phrase. The contract provided that a specified patent royalty rate would apply "[i]f a Licensed Unit is invoiced or shipped in combination in another product such as an emergency shower or eyewash." The question before the court was whether the *such as* phrase reduced the scope of the noun in question, "product"—in other words, whether the *such as* phrase was restrictive or nonrestrictive. The court reversed the lower court, holding that the *such as* phrase was restrictive—that the royalty rate in question didn't apply to all products but only to products similar to those included in the *such as* phrase.

13.764   Given the general nature of the preceding noun ("products"), the narrowness of the nouns included in the *such as* phrase, and the absence of a comma before *such as*, the court's holding was a reasonable one—the language at issue resembles the first of the three examples above.

13.765   But the contract language was sufficiently confusing that it not only caused protracted litigation, it also prompted a dissent by one judge of the U.S. Court of Appeals for the Federal Circuit, who thought that the *such as* phrase was nonrestrictive.

13.766   Given the potential for confusion, don't use *such as*. Instead, be precise in describing the class in question. If there's any risk of uncertainty regarding the boundaries of the class, resolve that uncertainty by using *including* in the manner recommended in 13.368–.373.

SUCH USED AS A POINTING WORD

13.767   It's appropriate to use *such* in conjunction with a noun phrase echoing an antecedent noun phrase if *such* conveys the meaning "of this kind." In this context, *such* is often prefaced by *any* or *no*, as in "The Escrow Agent shall give written notice of any *such* deposit to the Purchaser and the Sellers" and "No *such* default or breach now exists."

13.768   But drafters often use *such* instead of the "pointing words" *this*, *that*, *these*, and *those*. This usage goes against the principle that in drafting you shouldn't use one word to convey different meanings (see 1.64), and it also alienates nonlawyers. Below are examples of this usage, with the recommended alternatives to *such* noted in brackets.

> "**Affiliate**" means, regarding any Person, any other Person controlling, controlled by, or under common control with *such* [read *that*] Person.

> Widgetco shall complete its review within ten days. If Widgetco does not within *such* [read *that*] ten-day period notify the Licensee, in writing, of its disapproval and the reasons for *such* [read *its*] disapproval, the Licensee may publish the Licensed Work.

> Acme has purchased all shares of Widgetco common stock held by the Widgetco stockholders listed in schedule A and has received from each of *such* [read *those*] stockholders a certificate representing its shares of Widgetco common stock.

13.769   Sometimes the pointing word *that* is preceded by the *that* of a *that*-clause. If *that that* seems awkward, you can replace the pointing word *that* with *the*, as there would be no risk of confusion:

> The Manager will not be liable to the Company or to any Member for any loss or damage sustained by the Company or any Member except to the extent *that that* [read *that the*] loss or damage is the result of the Manager's gross negligence, willful misconduct, or breach of this agreement.

SUFFER

13.770   In contracts, the verb *suffer* can be used intransitively and transitively. The former is silly, the latter annoying.

Intransitive

13.771   First, the intransitive use of *suffer*. When used to mean "to submit to or be forced to endure," *suffer* is unobjectionable: *I suffer from chronic insomnia.* But it's a bit much when used in contracts to mean "undergo, experience." Usually the simplest fix is to use *incur* instead. But because *suffer* is used with abstract nouns (for examples, *losses*), sometimes your best bet is to use an adjective instead:

> The Executive acknowledges that if he were to divert this information and the relationships to a competitor, ~~the Company would suffer irreparable harm to its business and goodwill~~ [read *the Company's business and goodwill would be irreparably harmed*] in an amount that cannot be readily quantified.

Transitive

13.772   *Suffer* is used transitively to mean "to allow, especially by reason of indifference." It's pompous and archaic. Usually the simplest fix is using *permit* instead:

> The Borrower Representative shall not, and shall not permit any of its Subsidiaries to, create, incur, assume, or *suffer* [read *permit*] to exist any Lien on any of its assets.

SURVIVAL

13.773   The concept of "survival" crops up in contracts in three ways, and in each of those contexts it's either unnecessary or inferior to an alternative approach. Each context is discussed below.

Survival of Claims

13.774   A contract might specify that any claims that arise before termination will survive termination. Here's an example:

> **Survival of Claims.** Termination of this agreement will not relieve either party of any claims against it that arise under this agreement before the agreement is terminated.

13.775   Such provisions state the obvious—terminating a contract because of breach doesn't preclude the injured party from filing a claim for damages. See, e.g., 2 E. Allan Farnsworth, *Farnsworth on Contracts* § 8.15 (3d ed. 2012) ("If the injured party chooses to terminate the contract, it is said to treat the breach as total. The injured party's claim for damages for total breach takes the place of its remaining substantive rights under the contract.").

13.776   Reflecting settled law in a contract can be helpful, because the parties won't necessarily know what the law is. But in drafting business contracts, it's appropriate to assume that the reader understands basic principles of contract law, as it would be a nuisance to have to restate them in each contract. That claims survive is one such principle.

Survival of Provisions

13.777   The default rule is that performance under a contract ends with the contract. That's why it's unnecessary to tack onto contract provisions the phrase *during the term of this agreement* (see 13.254).

13.778   But what if you want an obligation—for example, Acme's obligation to keep certain information confidential—to continue after the contract terminates? You could state in the contract that the provision in question will survive termination of the contract, but it's clearer and simpler to build duration into obligation, for example by saying *during the term of this agreement and for five years thereafter* (see 13.255).

13.779   Sometimes a contract will state that the dispute-resolution provisions and other boilerplate survive termination. That's unnecessary—after the agreement terminates, a party may bring a claim in accordance with the boilerplate, subject to whatever limits the law provides.

Survival of Statements of Fact

13.780   Invariably, the principal language of obligation used in indemnification provisions (such as *The Seller shall indemnify the Buyer Indemnitees against all Indemnifiable Losses arising out of ...*) doesn't specify a time frame for that obligation. As such, it's an exception to the notion, described in 13.778, that you should be explicit if you want an obligation to continue after an agreement terminates.

13.781   One can do without a time frame in this context because when you can bring a claim for indemnification should be addressed elsewhere in indemnification provisions. Usually, an agreement will speak in terms of how long the indemnifying party's statements of fact survive. It's commonplace for most statements of fact in a contract to survive for a limited time (often one year), whereas others survive until the applicable statutes of limitations expire and still others survive indefinitely.

13.782   Although it's standard to refer in this manner to survival of statements of fact (traditionally known as *representations and warranties*; see 3.374), it's unhelpful to do so. You should resort to such legal jargon in a contract only if no clearer alternative presents itself. And referring to survival of statements of fact addresses only one of the potential bases of a claim for indemnification—for example, it doesn't put time limits on when you can bring a claim for indemnification for breach by the indemnifying party of any of its obligations. That's why it's preferable instead to address this topic directly, and more broadly, in a section entitled *Time Limitations*. See *GRT, Inc. v. Marathon GTF Technology, Ltd.*, No. CIV.A. 5571-CS, 2011 WL 2682898, at *14 n.79 (Del. Ch. 11 July 2011) (noting that the approach to survival of statements of fact recommended in this manual is different from the traditional approach).

TERMINATION, EXPIRATION

What to Use in Termination Provisions

13.783   Some might take issue with this sentence: *This agreement terminates on 23 August 2019.* They might argue that termination entails one or more parties' ending a contract sooner than it otherwise would have ended, and that in this case the correct word to use is *expires.*

13.784   It's certainly easy to find contract language suggesting that expiration (*expiry* in British English) isn't a form of termination. For example: *All such charges and expenses shall be promptly settled between the parties at the Closing or upon termination or expiration of further proceedings under this agreement.* If expiration is a form of termination, logic would require omitting "or expiration."

13.785   But just because drafters are partial to a distinction between *termination* and *expiration* (and between the verbs *terminate* and *expire*) doesn't mean that a distinction is necessary, or even helpful.

13.786   One can readily find in legal reference works instances of *terminate* and *termination* used to refer to different means by which a contract comes to an end. For example, compare 17A *Am. Jur. 2d* Contracts § 519 (2017) ("Where a contract specifies the period of its duration, it terminates on the expiration of such period.") and 17A *Am. Jur. 2d* Contracts § 527 (2017) ("An oral contract may be modified or terminated orally.")

13.787   This understanding of the relationship between termination and expiration can be found outside the realm of contracts. For example, the heading of 4 *N.Y. Jur. 2d* Appellate Review § 651 (2017) is "Expiration or other termination of order appealed from." Again, expiration is just one form of termination. The definitions of *termination* and *terminate* in *Black's Law Dictionary* are consistent with termination including expiration. *Termination* is defined as "The act of ending something" and "The end of something in time or existence." In other words, termination is both something you do and something that can simply happen. To the same effect, *terminate* is defined as meaning "To put an end to; to bring to an end" and "To end; to conclude."

13.788   Furthermore, using *terminates* in termination provisions instead of *expires* is unobjectionable, in that there's no possible confusion regarding the meaning of *This agreement terminates on 23 August 2019.*

13.789   But why not use *expires* in termination provisions instead of *terminates*? Because not only would it be unnecessary to do so, it would also lumber you with having to use elsewhere in the contract more ponderous constructions, such as *When this agreement expires or is terminated* [or *otherwise terminates*] rather than just *When this agreement terminates.* If you don't do so, the result can be confusion leading to a dispute. See *Hamden v. Total Car Franchising Corp.*, No. 7:12-CV-00003, 2012 WL 3255598 (W.D. Va. 7 Aug. 2012). The same can happen if in one contract you don't track the references to "expiration" and "termination" in another contract. See, e.g., *Holtzman Interests 23, L.L.C. v. FFC Sugarloaf, L.L.C.*, No. 298430, 2012 WL 468257 (Mich. Ct. App. 14 Feb. 2012).

13.790   And don't use *terminates and expires*, as in *This agreement will terminate and expire upon cessation of commercial operation of the Plant.* It exhibits either inconsistency or redundancy, depending on the meaning attributed to *terminates.*

Referring to Termination Provisions

13.791   But if you use *terminates* to refer to any means by which a contract comes to an end, you have to be careful how you refer to the termination provisions.

13.792   If you refer in a contract to *termination of this agreement* and the contract uses the verb *terminate* in referring to both the end of the term and a party bringing the contract to an end, a reasonable reader would conclude that you're referring to any form of termination. But if the term of a contract is stated using the noun *term*, as in *The term of this agreement is three years from the date of this agreement*, the fact that the contract doesn't use the verb *terminate* in stating the term would give a disgruntled contract party room to argue that end of the term represents expiration of the contract rather than termination. So if the contract doesn't use the verb *terminate* in stating the term, refer explicitly to both the end of the term and the parties bringing the contract to an end if you intend the provision to encompass both kinds of termination; also referring to any relevant sections of the contract would be clearer still. Being explicit in that manner would be beneficial even if the contract does use the verb *terminate* to express the end of the term—the reader wouldn't have to check the terminology used in the termination provisions to understand what *termination* means.

13.793 If you say *if this agreement terminates*, that could be understood as applying only to termination by operation of the contract without party action. If that's what you intend, make that clear by referring to the one or more sections that provide for termination without party action.

13.794 If you say *if this agreement is terminated*, that could be understood as applying only to termination by one or more parties. If that's what you intend, it would be clearer to use the active voice (*if either party terminates this agreement*) rather than the passive voice with missing *by*-agent (see 3.12). The same meaning would be conveyed by *termination of this agreement by either party*. Also referring to any relevant sections would be clearer still.

TERMINATION FOR CONVENIENCE

The Implications of *Termination for Convenience*

13.795 The phrase *termination for convenience* is somewhat misleading. It occurs in different types of agreements that provide for ongoing performance. Here's an example from a services agreement:

> **Termination by PhoneCo for Convenience.** Commencing one year after the Effective Date, PhoneCo may terminate for convenience this agreement, the Services performed at any Site, and any one or more Statements of Work by giving at least 90 days' prior written notice to the Provider.

13.796 *Termination for convenience* would seem to be a euphemism for termination for any reason at all. The phrase originates in government contracts and refers to the government's right to terminate a contract without breaching the contract, on condition that the decision to terminate isn't an abuse of discretion and wasn't made in bad faith. But the phrase has come into more general use, perhaps because it sounds less threatening than *termination for any reason* and rolls off the tongue more readily.

13.797 You can see this in the way some drafters use it as a section heading but lay out the harsh reality in the body of the section:

> **Termination for Convenience.** Either party may terminate this agreement, for any reason or for no reason, upon not less than 45 days' prior written

> notice to the other party delivered in accordance with section 11.1 stating that party's intention to terminate this agreement.

13.798   But Acme might want to terminate its agreement with Widgetco for any number of reasons. Maybe it found it could get better terms elsewhere. Maybe it decided to stop selling widgets. Maybe it became embroiled in litigation with Widgetco. *Convenience* seems a pallid word to capture all those reasons.

13.799   And more to the point, an imaginative (or desperate) litigator might argue that Acme could terminate for convenience only if its agreement with Widgetco imposed some sort of burden, and that the prospect of a better deal elsewhere wasn't a sufficient reason.

13.800   So *termination for convenience* is problematic. For what it's worth, an informal survey of contracts filed on the U.S. Securities and Exchange Commission's EDGAR system suggests that contracts using the phrase *termination* [or *terminate*] *for any reason* outnumber by a wide margin those that use the phrase *termination* [or *terminate*] *for convenience*.

Alternative Language

13.801   The following provision demonstrates the full range of language you could use instead of *termination for convenience*:

> Acme may terminate this agreement [at any time] [for any reason] [or for no reason] by giving the Vendor at least 30 days' prior notice.

13.802   What about the first two bracketed elements? If you say that Acme may terminate at any time, that carries with it the implication that Acme may terminate for any reason. If you say that Acme may terminate for any reason, that carries with it the implication that Acme may terminate at any time. Is the implication strong enough that you can use one of these two elements and not the other? What about dispensing with both of them?

13.803   It would be best to use *for any reason,* as that's the most important concept. The associated implication that Acme may terminate whenever it wants is sufficiently strong to allow one to dispense with *at any time*. In language of discretion, a party should be free to take the action in question whenever it wishes, absent any indication to the contrary, so generally *at any time* should be redundant; see 10.128. And dispensing with both elements would be rash, even though one could readily make the argument that if a provision doesn't impose any limitations on reasons for termination, one wouldn't need any reason. Three extra words is a small price to pay for being categorical.

13.804   But if you're drafting an agreement that provides for termination for cause, instead of *termination for any reason* you could use *termination without cause*, in the interest of symmetry.

13.805   You shouldn't have any qualms about eliminating *or for no reason* (see 13.294). Businesses act rationally or irrationally, prudently or imprudently, competently or incompetently. What they don't do is act entirely at random.

13.806 As for a section heading, if *Termination for Any Reason* seems too stark, you could try *Unrestricted Termination*. Alternatively, you could avoid trumpeting the issue in a section heading by instead grouping termination provisions according to who has the right to terminate—for example, by using the section headings *Buyer Termination*, *Seller Termination*, and *Buyer or Seller Termination*.

TERMS AND CONDITIONS

13.807 The phrase *terms and conditions* is a fixture in commercial contracts. Sometimes *exceptions* is tacked on the end. But a condition is a kind of term, as is an exception. It would be more concise just to say *terms*.

THAT CERTAIN

13.808 Using *that certain* when referring to an agreement is an archaism. Use *a* (or *an*) instead: *Acme and Big Bancorp are party to that certain* [read *a*] *credit agreement dated 12 August 2017.*

THE EARLIER [OR *LATER*, *GREATER*, OR *LESSER*] OF X AND Y

13.809 It's commonplace for a contract to provide for selection of the earlier or later, or greater or lesser, of two alternatives. (When three or more items are involved, refer to the earliest or latest, or greatest or least, of those alternatives.) Which conjunction should you use between the alternatives? The following example uses *and*:

> Acme shall retain any records of the Business transferred to Acme under this agreement until the later of (1) expiration of the applicable tax statute of limitations, including any extensions, and (2) the seventh anniversary of the Closing Date.

13.810 Many drafters would use *or*, presumably because when you select one item from a group, *or* is usually the appropriate conjunction to use, as in *You may select A, B, or C*. But the logical choice is *and*, in that one is selecting one item from a group of two or more. Using *or* would require that one select, say, the greater of each item considered individually, which wouldn't make sense.

13.811 *Garner's Dictionary of Legal Usage*, at 517, reaches a different conclusion:

> **later of [date] or [date]; later of [date] and [date].** Drafters frequently debate whether the proper conjunction in this phrase is *or* or *and*. The better idiomatic choice is *or*—nine of every ten lawyers believing it is the proper choice.

> True, *and* has logic on its side. … But the wording with *and* sounds as pedantic—and as wrong—as *a number of people was there*.

13.812   This assessment is problematic in several respects. First, selecting contract usages by following the herd is deeply unpromising. Second, it seems unlikely that "nine of every ten lawyers" is a real statistic. Third, the comparison with *a number of people was there* is comparing apples and oranges and as such is unhelpful. Fourth, this manual thinks that *and* sounds just fine. And fifth—and most importantly—contracts are not the place to sacrifice logic for flimsy notions of what sounds right. Contract parties have gotten into costly and embarrassing disputes over *and* and *or* (see 11.98). If you find yourself on the wrong side of logic in such a dispute, you'll likely regret it.

13.813   To use *or* appropriately in the preceding examples, you would need to rephrase them using *whichever is*. The first example so rephrased:

> Acme shall retain any business records of the Business transferred to Acme under this agreement until (1) expiration of the applicable tax statute of limitations, including any extensions, or (2) the seventh anniversary of the Closing Date, whichever is later.

13.814   Because it places at the end of the sentence the basis for selecting between the items being compared, the formula *whichever is* is best reserved for when the description of those items is relatively succinct.

THERE CAN BE NO ASSURANCE THAT

13.815   The phrase *there can be no assurance that* has made its way from securities offerings into contracts:

> *There can be no assurance that* the Owner will receive that notice in time to enable the Owner to instruct the Depositary before the Instruction Cutoff Date.

13.816   Beginning a sentence with *there* plus verb inflicts on the sentence a fake subject and fake verb (see 17.24). And the notion of one party giving the other no assurances that something will happen doesn't fit in any of the categories of contract language. Instead, have whoever would benefit acknowledge that whatever it is might not come to pass:

> The Owner *acknowledges that* the Owner might not receive that notice in time to enable the Owner to instruct the Depositary before the Instruction Cutoff Date.

THEREFOR

13.817   Unless using a *here-* or *there-* word affords economy, it's best to be explicit regarding what's being referred to (see 13.349). But in the case of *therefor*, you can simply delete the word if it's clear from the context what's being referred to:

A Participant required to sell any Depositary Receipts in accordance with this section 6(b) will be entitled to receive in exchange ~~therefor~~ the purchase price per Depositary Receipt received by the Majority Institutional Investors with respect to their Depositary Receipts in that transaction ... .

13.818 If you elect to use *therefor*, don't be surprised if people attempt to change it to *therefore*.

THING

13.819 A drafter who uses in a contract *any thing* or *all things* is presumably referring to either one or more acts or pieces of property. It would be preferable to refer to them as such rather than using, instead or in addition, the word *thing*.

THIRD PARTY

13.820 Don't use *third party*. This section explains why.

13.821 Parties entering into a contract were once divided into classes, or "parts." Generally the owner or seller was referred to as *the party of the first part* and the buyer was referred to as *the party of the second part*. This cumbersome and confusing usage has become a rarity (see 2.115–.116).

13.822 More common is a usage that it gave rise to—using the term *third party* in a contract to denote any individual or entity that is not a party to that contract. It would be for the best if this usage, too, were dropped: because the word *party* is now used as a general term for one who has entered into a contract (see 2.111), it's anomalous to use that word as part of a term meaning just the opposite. Also, the designation *third* makes no particular sense, given that contracts often have more than two parties.

13.823 *Person* (defined to mean an individual or an entity) is a suitable alternative to *third party* when there's no need to exclude the parties to the contract from the scope of a provision: *"Lien" means, in the case of securities, any purchase option, call, or similar right of a third party* [read *any Person*] *regarding those securities.*

13.824 You can use *any Person other than a party* when you need an alternative to *third party* that excludes parties: *Confidential Information does not include any information that ... was subsequently lawfully disclosed to the receiving party by a third party* [read *by a Person other than a party, on condition that that Person was*] *not under a duty to keep that information confidential.* Even simpler would be *nonparty*.

13.825 *Third party* is sometimes used as a defined term or as part of a defined term such as *Third-Party Claims*. A clearer alternative would be *Nonparty*.

13.826 But in contract drafting you can't dispense entirely with the term *third party*, given that it features in terms of art such as *third-party beneficiary* and in legislation.

THROUGHOUT THE UNIVERSE

13.827   The phrase *throughout the universe* is used in rights-granting language:

> Client shall have the sole and exclusive right *throughout the universe* in perpetuity to use and exploit all or any part of the Properties and all or any part of any material contained therein or prepared therefor, whether or not used therein, in any format or version, by any means and in any media, whether now known or hereafter developed.

13.828   If whoever's being granted rights has no prospect of using them in space (in satellites or otherwise), *worldwide* would be a more sober alternative.

TIME IS OF THE ESSENCE

13.829   A fixture of contract language is the phrase *time is of the essence*. But it's formulaic; you can express any underlying issue more clearly.

13.830   According to *Black's Law Dictionary*, *of the essence* means "so important that if the requirement is not met, the promisor will be held to have breached the contract and a rescission by the promisee will be justified."

13.831   It's used in provisions such as this: *Tenant's surrender of the Surrender Premises on the Surrender Date is of the essence*. But that doesn't mean that it's a good idea to use *of the essence*. Because *of the essence* is jargon, you can't expect readers to know what you're trying to say when you use *of the essence*. It would be clearer to use instead a termination provision to express the intended meaning. If appropriate, you could supplement it by having the parties acknowledge that breach of specified sections constitute material breach.

13.832   But *of the essence* occurs mostly in the phrase *time is of the essence*. The meaning attributed to *time is of the essence* in *Garner's Dictionary of Legal Usage*, at 895, reflects the conventional wisdom among practitioners: "When a contractual stipulation relating to the time of performance is 'of the essence' of a contract, a party's failure to meet that stipulation automatically justifies the other party's rescinding the contract—no matter how trivial the failure."

13.833   Drafters use the phrase because courts tend to hold that late performance isn't grounds for termination unless the purpose of the contract or the circumstances surrounding it indicate that the parties intended for that to be the case. See *Am. Jur. 2d*. Contracts § 594 (2017). But for various reasons, *time is of the essence* isn't up to the task.

13.834   First, the phrase is generally used in a provision stating—the exact wording varies—that *Time is of the essence of this agreement*. This formula is too general: "A contract may contain many promises for sundry performances, varying in amount and importance. A general provision that 'time is of the essence' should not apply to all of the promises for performance." 8-37 *Corbin on Contracts* § 37.3.

13.835 Second, even if it happens to be clear what performance the phrase applies to, the phrase is silent regarding the consequences of untimely performance.

13.836 Third, you see *time is of the essence* provisions even in contracts that use liquidated-damages provisions and express termination provisions to specify the consequences of delay. As 8-37 *Corbin on Contracts* § 37.3 says, "The provision 'time is of the essence' may be inserted in a contract without any realization of its significance. Other terms contained in the agreement, interpreted in the light of the conduct of the parties, may show that the provision has no legal effect."

13.837 And fourth, although termination for any tardiness may make sense in some contexts, in other contexts—for example, in a construction project—a missed deadline might occur after substantial performance, and allowing the other party to terminate could result in unjust enrichment. A common-law judge might or might not be troubled by that unfairness, but it would likely create problems in civil-law jurisdictions, which frown on rescinding a contract based on trivial nonperformance.

13.838 So it's unsurprising that courts have proved willing to ignore *time is of the essence* provisions because you can't assume that the parties to a contract understood and agreed on the ostensible meaning of the phrase.

13.839 For example, the *Restatement (Second) of Contracts* § 242, comment d. (1981), says that "stock phrases such as 'time is of the essence'" do not necessarily have the effect of making failure to timely perform grounds for discharge, although such phrases "are to be considered along with other circumstances in determining the effect of delay."

13.840 To make it clearer that a deadline is important and what the consequences are of failing to meet the deadline, it would be best to address the issue explicitly. Assume that you represent the buyer in an acquisition and the draft acquisition agreement specifies that either party can terminate if the transaction hasn't closed by a specified date—the "drop-dead date." You want to make sure that a court wouldn't grant the seller any leeway if the buyer terminates because the transaction hasn't closed by the drop-dead date and the seller sues, claiming that a missing consent in fact materialized a day later and that the buyer should have been willing to close. A clearer alternative to saying that time is of the essence regarding the drop-dead-date provision would be to include this:

> The parties acknowledge that due to [describe time constraints on the parties], if a party wishes to terminate this contract in accordance with section X [the drop-dead-date provision], that party will not be required to give the other party any time beyond the Drop-Dead Date to allow that party to satisfy any condition or perform any obligation under this agreement.

TOGETHER WITH, AS WELL AS

13.841 Outside of its use in "boosting" defined terms (see 6.79), the phrase *together with* can sometimes be replaced with a single word. That word might be *and*:

> "Hotel" means the Site *together with* [read *and*] the Buildings.

13.842 In other contexts, it's *with*:

> The Advisor shall send the Report to the Stockholders ~~together~~ with an explanation of … .

13.843 Or it might be *plus*:

> If the Advisor is found not to be entitled to indemnification, the Advisor shall repay the Company the advanced funds *together with* [read *plus*] interest].

13.844 The same range of fixes can be applied to *as well as*. Economy in contract drafting resides in small adjustments as well as large.

TO THE EXTENT PERMITTED BY LAW

13.845 If conduct contemplated in a contract might, depending on the circumstances, result in a party's breaking the law, make that clear by using the phrase *to the extent permitted by law*, as in *To the extent permitted by law, Acme* [*shall*] [*may*] *incinerate the Excess Materials*. If Acme were to break the law, including that phrase would make it difficult for Acme to argue that its unlawful activity doesn't provide Widgetco with grounds for terminating the contract or bringing against Acme a claim for damages under the contract. It would also signal to nonparties, particularly government agencies, that the parties were aware that Acme's conduct was subject to legal restrictions.

13.846 But the phrase serves a different function in language of performance. Consider this example: *To the extent permitted by law, each party hereby waives its right to a trial by jury*. It has been recommended that you use *to the extent permitted by law* in this context because "there are instances when jury trial waivers are not enforceable as a matter of law. This clause would preserve the effectiveness of the jury trial waiver as between the parties in instances where the law does not prohibit waiver." *Negotiating and Drafting Contract Boilerplate* 155 (Tina L. Stark ed., 2003). But if the governing law doesn't prohibit waiver, you would have no need for *to the extent permitted by law*. And if it does prohibit waiver, the phrase would be equally irrelevant. Instead, in this context *to the extent permitted by law* simply tells the parties that depending on the law of the forum in any dispute, the waiver might or might not be enforceable.

13.847 If the phrase is used with the intent that it signal to a court that the parties are willing to have an unenforceable provision modified to the extent necessary to make it enforceable, it would be clearer and more standard to use a severability provision to convey that meaning.

TRADEMARKS—REFERENCES TO

13.848 Sometimes in commercial agreements, each reference to a registered trademark is stated in all capital letters, with the registration symbol "®" appended, as in *PLAXICOL®*. But using all capitals and the registration symbol at every turn distracts readers and doesn't help protect trademark rights. To make your contracts more readable, drop the registration symbol. And in trademark license agreements or other agreements relating to rights in a trademark, use all capitals when referring to that trademark by name. But if a trademark simply identifies particular goods or services, use initial capitals.

13.849 If your client has strict rules about how its trademarks are to be referred to, you'll need to follow those rules, even to the detriment of readability. But judicious use of defined terms might allow you to minimize the effect on readability.

13.850 The remainder of this section explains what underlies these recommendations.

All Capitals or Initial Capitals?

13.851 Treatises on trademark law recommend that when using a trademark, you distinguish it from the surrounding text so that the public will recognize it as a trademark. In this regard, Anne LaLonde & Jerome Gilson, 1-2 *Gilson on Trademarks* § 2.02 (2017), states as part of a "Checklist for Preventing Loss of Distinctiveness" that "the mark owner should display the mark prominently and use a distinctive type face, solid capital letters or, at the very least, capitalization of the first letter." Similarly, Siegrun D. Kane, *Kane on Trademark Law* § 5:2.1 (2016) says that to distinguish trademarks from ordinary descriptive or generic terms, they should be set off from surrounding text, and that this can be accomplished, among other ways, by using all caps or initial caps.

13.852 In so recommending, those treatises don't distinguish between types of use, but it makes sense to do so. When considering how trademarks should be shown in contract text, bear in mind that any public dissemination of commercial agreements is purely incidental. Compared with text on pill bottles, in promotional materials, or in advertising, contract text couldn't reasonably be considered a potential source of loss of distinctiveness. So the typographic convention you use in a contract to refer to a trademark wouldn't jeopardize rights in that trademark. As a matter of trademark law, nothing is gained by stating in all capitals contract references to a trademark.

13.853 But that doesn't mean that it's always pointless to use all capitals in contract references to trademarks. In trademark license agreements and other agreements relating to trademark rights, trademarks are referred to purely in their capacity as trademarks. By contrast, other kinds of contracts refer to trademarks in their capacity as labels for particular goods or services. For example, in an agreement providing for purchase of vials of Tamiflu vaccine, the trademark "Tamiflu" simply identifies the vaccine—that it's a trademark is incidental.

13.854   So in trademark license agreements and other agreements relating to trademark rights, the extra emphasis provided by all capitals helps distinguish references to trademarks as trademarks from the descriptive function of trademark references in other kinds of agreements. And when a trademark reference doesn't relate to rights in that trademark, nothing is gained by using all capitals, so you can give it the initial capital befitting a proper noun.

Registration Symbol or No Registration Symbol?

13.855   The owner of a registered trademark doesn't have to use with its trademark the registration symbol "®" or some other statutory notice (such as the words "Registered in U.S. Patent and Trademark Office") to be entitled to protect that trademark from unauthorized use. But to recover damages and profits in a suit for infringement under the Lanham Act, a trademark owner must be able to show either that it had used the registration symbol or other statutory notice or that the defendant had actual notice that the owner had registered the mark. (See 15 U.S.C. § 1111.) And using a statutory notice is another way to protect against loss of distinctiveness.

13.856   So Anne Lalonde & Jerome Gilson, 1 *Gilson on Trademarks* § 2.02 (2017), states, in the checklist mentioned in 13.851, that "the trademark owner should indicate the legal status of the mark wherever it appears." Other authorities acknowledge, however, that doing so can drive a reader batty. For example, the International Trademark Association says, "Generally, it is not necessary to mark every occurrence of a trademark in an advertisement or other promotional materials but, at a minimum, this identification should occur at least once in each piece of printed matter, either the first time the mark is used or with the most prominent use of the mark."

13.857   But if trademark protection were the only concern, drafters could, for two reasons, drop from their contracts registration symbols and other statutory notices.

13.858   First, as mentioned in 13.852, commercial agreements aren't disseminated publicly, so there's no risk of loss of distinctiveness.

13.859   And second, it's unlikely that a contract party would need to rely on its use of statutory notice in a contract to be entitled to recovery under the Lanham Act. Any trademark license agreement or other agreement relating to trademark rights would state explicitly that the one or more trademarks in question are indeed trademarks, so appending a statutory notice to each trademark reference would be redundant. And regarding other kinds of agreements, if Acme enters into a contract with a drug company to buy quantities of a drug, Acme couldn't rationally argue that because the registration symbol isn't appended to references to the drug in the contract, it didn't know that the drug's name was a registered trademark. A court should find that Acme had actual notice, given that the registration symbol had been prominently displayed in all public materials relating to the drug.

13.860   And if a trademark owner were concerned about unauthorized use of its trademarks by a party to one of its contracts, it should address that explicitly in the contract instead of relying on appending statutory notice to references to its trademarks.

13.861   Given these considerations, it's not surprising that the registration symbol is rarely used in contracts.

Relationship to Trademark Guidelines

13.862   It's commonplace for company trademark guidelines to mandate that all capitals and the registration symbol be used in every reference to one of the company's trademarks. Such rules couldn't coexist with this manual's recommendation that in contract references to trademarks you use initial capitals and drop the registration symbol.

13.863   One way around this, short of making the trademark guidelines less rigid, would be to use a defined term instead of repeatedly using all capitals and a registration symbol in referring to a given trademark. In a trademark license agreement, you might use the defined term *the Licensed Mark*; in a commercial agreement, you might use the defined term *the Product*.

UNLESS AND UNTIL

13.864   *Unless and until* is an expression that weakens the expectation (conveyed by *until* alone) that the condition in the clause will be realized. In everyday English, you use *unless and until* if you expect or hope that the condition will be satisfied (as suggested by *until*) but want to signal to the reader or listener, by means of *unless*, that it might not be.

13.865   That sort of rhetorical nuance is useful in speech or in narrative or persuasive writing, but not in the more rigid world of contract drafting— use instead *unless* by itself.

UNLESS THE CONTEXT OTHERWISE REQUIRES

13.866   The phrase *unless the context otherwise requires* (a variant uses *requires otherwise*) is used in provisions such as these:

> *Unless the context otherwise requires*, capitalized terms used in this agreement have the following meanings.

> *Unless the context otherwise requires*, references to the "Company" will be deemed to refer to the Company and its Subsidiaries.

> Each of the statements of fact of the Loan Parties contained in this agreement (and all corresponding definitions) are made after giving effect to the Transactions, *unless the context otherwise requires*.

13.867   It would be best to eliminate *unless the context otherwise requires*, as it adds uncertainty that a litigator might be able to take advantage of. If in a contract you want to deviate from some across-the-board convention, be specific about it.

UNLESS THE PARTIES AGREE OTHERWISE

13.868   Generally, the phrase *unless the parties agree otherwise* is redundant. As a matter of contract law, the parties could agree to waive, amend, or delete any provision in a contract, regardless of whether that contract says that they may. But it would be appropriate to use *unless the parties agree otherwise* if a party thinks that it would facilitate negotiation of a given provision if everyone were reminded that the parties might at some later point agree on a different arrangement.

UTMOST

13.869   In a phrase such as *with the utmost dispatch*, the adjective *utmost* is used as an idiosyncratic alternative to *reasonable efforts* (see 8.9). But it's also used to qualify standards of care—*utmost good faith, utmost care, utmost diligence*. Because those standards are based on what would be reasonable in the circumstances, *utmost* adds nothing other than rhetorical emphasis (see 1.59). If you have something specific in mind, express it clearly. Otherwise, omit *utmost*, in this context and everywhere else.

VERY

13.870   The word *very* occurs infrequently in contracts. That's not surprising, since for contracts, *very* isn't a meaningful indication of magnitude—the reader has no way of knowing where *very* falls on the spectrum from nothing to everything. The same applies to *extremely* and *highly*.

VIRGULE, ALSO KNOWN AS THE FORWARD SLASH

13.871   Here's what *Garner's Modern English Usage*, at 754, has to say about the virgule, also known as the forward slash:

> Some writers use [the virgule] to mean "per" <50 words/minute>. Others use it to mean "or" <and/or> or "and" <every employee/ independent contractor must complete form XJ42A>. Still others use it to indicate a vague disjunction, in which it's not quite an *or* <the novel/novella distinction>… . In all these uses, there's almost always a better choice than the virgule. Use it as a last resort.

13.872   So the virgule isn't conducive to clarity—don't use it in contracts other than to state a fraction. (See 11.86 regarding *and/or*.)

VOLUNTARILY, INVOLUNTARILY

13.873 Depending on the context, the words *voluntarily* and *involuntarily* might not make sense. Some examples:

> … until that employee's employment with the Company has been voluntarily or involuntarily terminated for at least six months … [The notion of voluntary termination is unorthodox. If this applies whether the employee quits or was fired, say that instead. Or *ceases to be an employee for any reason*.]

> … Restricted Shares may not be … encumbered, either voluntarily or involuntarily, until the restrictions have lapsed and the rights to the Shares have vested. [It doesn't make sense to prohibit someone from involuntarily encumbering shares, because that person wouldn't be the one doing the encumbering. If *involuntarily* is intended to address a legitimate issue, address it some other way. And deleting *involuntarily* renders *voluntarily* redundant.]

> … and hereby voluntarily releases and forever discharges Lender … [The word *voluntarily* is redundant, as there's no such thing as an involuntary release.]

> The Borrower may … voluntarily prepay Revolving Loans … [The word *voluntarily* is redundant, as there's no such thing as involuntarily prepaying a debt.]

13.874 Similarly, the word *freely* is usually redundant: *The Landlord may freely lease … .*

WARRANT, WARRANT CERTIFICATE, WARRANT AGREEMENT

13.875 A *warrant* is an instrument granting the holder a long-term option to buy shares at a fixed price. (See 13.879–.893 regarding the unrelated verb *to warrant* and noun *warranty*.)

13.876 A warrant is an intangible right, but it's evidenced by a document. Many drafters don't distinguish the two: contracts refer to *exercise of this warrant* (that is, the intangible right) and *surrender of this warrant* (in other words, the document evidencing that right). It would be clearer to observe the distinction.

13.877 What you call the piece of paper depends on who signs it. If it's signed by the issuer and the holder, call it a warrant agreement; if it's signed by the issuer only, call it a warrant certificate. Often you'll have a warrant agreement that provides for issuance of warrant certificates.

WARRANTY, THE VERB *WARRANT*

Background

13.878 As explained in 3.374–.411, it's pointless and confusing to use the phrase *represents and warrants* (and *representations and warranties*) in a contract. But in sales contracts it's standard to use *warrants* (and the noun *warranty*) on its own, without *represents* (and *representation*). But clearer and more concise choices are available.

Definition of *Warranty* and the Verb *Warrant*

13.879 *Warranty* is a term of art. Under common law, an express warranty is a seller's affirmation of fact to the buyer, as an inducement to sale, regarding the quality or quantity of goods, title, or restrictive covenants to real property. See Howard O. Hunter, *Modern Law of Contracts* § 9.5 (2017).

13.880 But section 2-303 of the Uniform Commercial Code says, "Any affirmation of fact or promise made by the seller to the buyer which relates to the goods and becomes part of the basis of the bargain creates an express warranty that the goods shall conform to the affirmation or promise." So under the UCC, a statement of fact can be a warranty (as is the case under common law) but so too can an obligation.

13.881 As for the verb *warrant, Black's Law Dictionary* simply says in part that it means "to promise or guarantee."

Using the Verb *Warrant* to Introduce a Statement of Fact

13.882 Considering definitions in isolation isn't helpful. Instead, to understand the role of the verb *warrant,* one needs to consider it in context.

13.883 In contracts, one function of *warrants* is to introduce statements of fact, either present facts (*The Vendor warrants that the Software conforms to the Specifications*) or future facts (*The Vendor warrants that during the six months following the date of this agreement, the Software will conform to the Specifications*).

13.884 Given that a statement doesn't need to be called a warranty to be a warranty (see 3.392), it follows that one doesn't need to use *warrants* with a statement of fact for that statement to be a warranty. So when used with a statement of fact, the sole function of *warrants* is the same as the function of *states*—to identify who is making the statement (see 3.371).

13.885 This manual recommends using *states* instead of *represents* to introduce a statement of fact (see 3.416). Consistency would seem to favor using *states* instead of *warrants,* too, when introducing a statement of fact. But before considering that, one must first address another issue relating to the kinds of statement of fact that are introduced using *warrants.*

13.886 More specifically, anyone making a statement of future facts couldn't be aware of those facts, because those facts wouldn't yet exist. Instead, a statement of future facts sets a benchmark against which warranty obligations will be measured. That's why statements of future facts introduced by *warrants* would logically be followed, although not necessarily immediately, by a statement of the remedy that applies if the statement of fact is inaccurate. It would be more logical, and more efficient, to combine the statement of fact and remedy into a single sentence, turning the statement of future facts into a conditional clause and the remedy into the matrix clause (see 3.317).

13.887 Here's an example:

> ### Statement of Fact Followed by Remedy
>
> The Vendor warrants that during the six months after the date of this agreement, the Equipment will conform to the Specifications. In the event of breach of the foregoing warranty, the Vendor shall modify or replace the Equipment.
>
> ### Conditional Clause and Matrix Clause
>
> If during the six months after the date of this agreement the Equipment fails to conform to the Specifications, the Vendor shall modify or replace the Equipment.

13.888 By contrast, statements of present facts (for example, *the Equipment is in good working order*) don't share the illogic of statements of future facts, so you could retain them. If you do, introduce them using the verb you use to introduce other statements of fact—the manual recommends using *states* (see 3.416). But as with statements of future facts, you could combine statement of fact and remedy into a single sentence, as in *If no later than 15 days after the date of this agreement the Buyer notifies the Seller that the Equipment is not in good working order, then … .* Doing so would eliminate the need for a verb to introduce the statement of fact. Whether it makes sense to do so depends on whether you're able to express all desired remedies in that sentence.

Don't Use the Verb *Warrant* to Introduce an Obligation

13.889 Don't use *warrants* to introduce obligations, as in *Acme warrants that it shall perform routine maintenance on the Hardware once every quarter*. It's an example of what this manual calls "throat-clearing" (see 3.25).

Using the Word *Warranty*

13.890 The noun *warranty* can be used to refer to provisions in an agreement (as in *The warranties in this section 5 will not apply if …*) and provisions absent from an agreement (as in *Acme makes no warranties, express or implied*). And even if you don't use *warrants* in a provision, it would be appropriate to give it the heading *Warranty* or *Warranties* if that's what the section consists of.

13.891 But whether a provision constitutes a warranty depends on its content, not on whether you've called it a warranty (see 3.391–.392). So although you might think all the warranties in a contract are to be found in the section with the heading *Warranties*, a court could hold that a statement of fact or obligation located elsewhere in the contract constitutes a warranty supporting an action for breach of warranty, even though the contract doesn't refer to it as a warranty.

13.892   Similarly, even if a contract calls a provision a warranty, a court could hold that it's a statement of fact supporting an action for misrepresentation.

WELL AND TRULY

13.893   The phrase *well and truly* is idiomatic English. It means *completely*: *We're well and truly lost.* This sort of lexical coupling has long served a rhetorical function. Another example is *high and mighty*.

13.894   *Well and truly* also features in contracts, but it's invariably redundant:

> ... if each of the Obligations is ~~well and truly~~ performed in accordance with the Loan Documents ... .

13.895   *Well and truly* has long featured in a different kind of legal document, oaths. That's presumably how *well and truly* has come to be used in contracts. Because oaths involve an element of theater, rhetorical emphasis isn't out of place in oaths. But it is out of place in contracts (see 1.58).

WILLFUL, WILLFULLY

13.896   As it's usually used in contracts, the word *willful*, as in *willful misconduct*, is not only vague but also ambiguous. It means "intentional," but drafters usually don't make it clear whether the focus is on the party's action or on the consequences of the party's action—it's possible to act intentionally without intending to cause damages (see 13.574). For a case that involved this ambiguity, see *Johnson & Johnson v. Guidant Corp.*, 525 F. Supp. 2d 336, 349–51 (S.D.N.Y. 2007).

13.897   Instead of *willful* or *willfully*, use *intentional* or *intentionally* (they're clearer words) and specify that the party's intent pertains to the consequences of its action (see 13.578 for an example of a provision that does that), unless given the context it makes more sense to have the party's intent pertain to its taking that action.

WITHOUT LIMITING THE GENERALITY
OF THE FOREGOING

13.898   Drafters use the phrase *without limiting the generality of the foregoing* to introduce one or more examples of a concept described in the immediately preceding language. But you should almost always be able to express the relationship between two blocks of text in less ponderous a manner.

13.899   One problem is that it's not necessarily clear what *the foregoing* refers to. (*Notwithstanding the foregoing* suffers from the same problem; see 13.603.) But the main problem with this phrase is that it's so ponderous.

13.900   A simple alternative would be *including,* which serves the same function (see 13.353). Not only is it shorter, it also allows you to express the same meaning in one sentence rather than two, thereby allowing you to eliminate further surplusage:

> Acme shall not make any claim or take any action adverse to Bolin GPL's ownership of or interest in *the Bolin Marks. Without limiting the generality of the foregoing, Lone Star shall not attempt to register* [read *the Bolin Marks, including registering*] any Bolin Mark or any mark confusingly similar thereto in any jurisdiction.

13.901   It would be redundant to use both *without limiting the generality of the foregoing* and *including*:

> If an Event of Default occurs, Mortgagee, in addition to any other rights, will have all rights granted a secured party on default under the Uniform Commercial Code, including ~~without limiting the generality of the foregoing~~ the right to take possession of the Collateral or any part thereof and to take such other measures as Mortgagee deems necessary to preserve the Collateral.

13.902   Another alternative would be to place the examples at the front and modify the general concept so that it becomes a catchall at the end:

> **Before**
>
> Each Credit Party is now and has always been in compliance with all Environmental and Safety Requirements. *Without limiting the generality of the foregoing*, each Credit Party has obtained and complied with, and is in compliance with, all permits, licenses, and other authorizations required under Environmental and Safety Requirements for occupation of its facilities and operation of its business.
>
> **After**
>
> Each Credit Party (1) has obtained and complied with, and is in compliance with, all permits, licenses, and other authorizations required under Environmental and Safety Requirements for occupation of its facilities and operation of its business and (2) is in compliance with all other Environmental and Safety Requirements.

13.903   And you can keep the general concept and the examples in separate sentences if you use *includes* (or *include*):

> **Before**
>
> The General Partner shall manage the business and affairs of the Partnership. *Without limiting the generality of the foregoing*, the General Partner shall do the following:
>
> **After**
>
> The General Partner shall manage the business and affairs of the Partnership. The General Partner's duties include the following:

13.904   Sometimes what follows *without limiting the generality of the foregoing* is in fact not an example of what precedes it. In such cases, simply eliminate the phrase:

> Each Note Purchaser and its advisors, if any, have been afforded the opportunity to ask questions of the Company and have received complete and satisfactory answers to any such inquiries. ~~Without limiting the generality of the foregoing, each~~ [read *Each*] Note Purchaser has also had the opportunity to obtain and to review the Company SEC Documents.

13.905   If the general concept and the examples are sufficiently unwieldy, it might make sense to use *without limiting the generality of the foregoing.* But that's unlikely to be the case.

13.906   A variant on *without limiting the generality of the foregoing* is *in furtherance of the foregoing.* Sometimes both phrases are conjoined, redundantly— *in furtherance of the foregoing and not in limitation thereof.* The same considerations apply to both phrases, so you should be able to do without *in furtherance of the foregoing.*

WITHOUT PREJUDICE

13.907   Contracts refer to claims being dismissed *with prejudice,* in other words in a way that finally disposes of a claim and bars any future action on that claim. That's unobjectionable.

13.908   But *without prejudice* is different. It too is a litigation term of art; it refers to disposing of a claim in a way that doesn't affect one's legal rights. But when used in contracts, *without prejudice* is usually unnecessarily legalistic. Use instead *does not affect* or *will not affect*:

> That right of setoff *is without prejudice and in addition to* [read *does not affect*] any other right to which the Holder is otherwise entitled under this Note.

> That resignation will *be without prejudice to* [read *will not affect*] the contract rights of the Trust.

WORKMANLIKE

13.909   The word *workmanlike* is a term of art. A dated and gender-specific term of art.

13.910   Construction law acknowledges an implied warranty of workmanlike performance. And *workmanlike* features in contracts:

> Borrower shall only use contractors … who generally have a good reputation for completing their work in a neat, prompt, and *workmanlike* manner … .

> All Tenant Improvements must be done in a first-class *workmanlike* manner.

13.911   Caselaw offers many definitions of *workmanlike.* For example, one court held that it means "doing the work in an ordinarily skilled manner as a skilled workman should do it." *J. W. Hancock Enterprises, Inc. v. Registrar of Contractors,* 617 P.2d 19, 22 (Ariz. 1980). Another held, "We define good and workmanlike as that quality of work performed by one who has the knowledge, training, or experience necessary for the successful practice of a trade or occupation and performed in a manner generally considered proficient by those capable of judging such work." *Melody Home Manufacturing Co. v. Barnes*, 741 S.W.2d 349, 354 (Tex. 1987). The wordiness of such definitions is a function of courts struggling, to no avail, to escape the clutches of vagueness.

13.912   A simpler alternative to *workmanlike* is *competent*. Unless you're referring to the implied warranty, consider using *competent* and *competently* instead. But it would be even better to be specific, because the more specific you are regarding the work expected of contractors, the less you have to rely on *workmanlike* or other vague alternatives.

NUMBERS AND FORMULAS

WORDS OR DIGITS

Why Words and Digits?

14.1 Many drafters use both words and digits when stating a number, placing the digits in parentheses: *six (6)*; *five thousand dollars ($5,000)*; *eighteen percent (18%)*; and so forth. This practice may have arisen because drafters noted that numbers expressed in digits are easier to read than numbers expressed in words but are more vulnerable to typographic errors than are numbers expressed in words. Such glitches do happen. For example, in a mortgage prepared in New York in 1986, the principal amount was erroneously stated as $92,885 rather than $92,885,000. The result was "a spate of litigation, hundreds of thousands of dollars in legal fees, millions of dollars in damages and an untold fortune in embarrassment." David Margolick, *At the Bar; How Three Missing Zeros Brought Red Faces and Cost Millions of Dollars*, N.Y. Times, 4 Oct. 1991.

14.2 In theory, combining both usages affords the immediacy of digits while providing insurance against a transposed or missing decimal point or one or more extra, missing, or incorrect digits. This insurance was rendered more effective by the judicial rule of interpretation that a number expressed in words controls in the case of conflict. The words-and-digits approach has doubtless saved the occasional contract party (and its lawyer) from the adverse consequences of a missing decimal point or other error involving digits, or would have done had it been used.

14.3 Another ostensible benefit to using words and digits is that digits can be hard to read in a fax, or a fax of a fax, or fifth-generation photocopy. But that's not compelling, now that few people send faxes anymore.

Problems

GENERALLY

14.4 Those benefits come at a prohibitive cost. It's tedious for the reader to encounter, at every turn, numbers expressed in both words and digits. And this belt-and-suspenders approach is faintly ludicrous when applied to all numbers throughout a contract, even though lower numbers are less susceptible than are higher numbers to a significant typographical error that goes undetected. For use of words and digits in, for example, *three (3) members of the board of directors* to be of any benefit, those drafting and reviewing the contract would have to be particularly inattentive.

14.5   And using both words and digits violates a cardinal rule of drafting—that you shouldn't say the same thing twice in a contract, because it introduces a potential source of inconsistency (see 1.62). Even if when you first state a words-and-digits number the words and digits are consistent, they might become inconsistent in the course of revising a draft. It's easy to see how that can happen—digits are more eye-catching than words, so you might change the digits but forget to change the words.

14.6   Because it's more likely that any inconsistency is due to changing digits and forgetting to change the words, rather than vice versa, application of the rule that words govern might result in a court choosing a meaning that's contrary to what the drafter had intended.

14.7   And using words and digits interferes with other usages in two minor but annoying ways. First, normally you would use a hyphen when a number is part of a phrasal adjective, as in *successive five-year periods*. If you use words and digits, retaining the hyphen would look decidedly odd: *successive five (5)-year periods*. The better choice would be to dispense with the hyphen, as in *successive five (5) year periods*, but that would still be less than ideal.

14.8   And when the words-and-digits approach is used in a block of text that includes integrated enumerated clauses, that can result in the reader mistakenly thinking, if only for a moment, that a single-digit in parentheses signals the presence of an enumerated clause.

14.9   So using words and digits is more of a problem than the issue it was intended to fix—digit mistakes.

STATING BIG NUMBERS

14.10   It might seem that using words and digits for the one big number in, for example, loan documentation would be less annoying than using words and digits for all numbers in a contract. But if anything, big numbers are more prone to words-and-digits inconsistency than are smaller numbers, because you're less likely to read the words component if it's several words long. And the consequences can be particularly unfortunate.

14.11   *Charles R. Tips Family Trust v. PB Commercial LLC*, 459 S.W.3d 147 (Tex. App. 2015), involved a dispute over a loan agreement and guaranty in which the principal amount was stated as "ONE MILLION SEVEN THOUSAND AND NO/100 ($1,700,000.00) DOLLARS." So the amount stated in words was $693,000 less than the amount stated in digits.

14.12   The Texas Court of Appeals held that the words prevailed over the digits—the principal amount of the loan was $1,007,000.00. By itself, that should come as no surprise, because courts generally accept the rule of interpretation that words prevail over digits. And the Uniform Commercial Code as enacted in Texas says that "[i]f an instrument contains contradictory terms, typewritten terms prevail over printed terms, handwritten terms prevail over both, and words prevail over numbers." But more disconcertingly, the court also refused to consider parol evidence that the borrowers allegedly received $1.7 million from the lender.

Using First Words, Then Digits

14.13   So instead of using words and digits, use words for whole numbers one through ten and use digits for numbers 11 and above. *Garner's Modern English Usage*, at 639, also recommends that approach, whereas *The Chicago Manual of Style*, at 9.2, recommends using words for whole numbers through 100. Because contracts prose is relatively numbers-heavy, this manual prefers an earlier transition.

14.14   The words-to-digits approach applies to ordinal numbers (*seventh*, *22nd*) as well as cardinal numbers. There are exceptions: use digits for whole numbers below 11 in lists of numbers; when numbers occur frequently in the text; in percentages; and in statements of amounts of money (see 13.513) and times of day. And use words for numbers 11 and over at the beginning of sentences. But which system you use is less important than ensuring that you don't distract the reader by being inconsistent.

14.15   Use just digits for the big number in a contract, although it can be appropriate to use a mix of words and digits to express very large amounts of money (see 13.518).

14.16   Using only digits does leave one prone to digit errors. The best fix for that? Proofreading.

Using Only Digits for All Numbers

14.17   In *Numbers: Figures or Words: A Convention Under the Spotlight*, 50 Clarity 32 (Nov. 2003), the Australian legal-writing commentator Robert Eagleson argues that in legal documents, all numbers should be stated in digits, and that "the convention that certain numbers must occur as words has a strong streak of irrationality about it."

14.18   This manual doesn't recommend adopting Eagleson's approach. For one thing, in everyday English it makes sense to shift from words to digits once numbers pass a certain point. Using digits is redolent of prose used in numbers-heavy fields, so numbers can seem intrusive, as in *We ordered only 1 pizza*. But stating larger numbers in digits makes them much easier to read. And with larger numbers, you're more likely to be in a numbers world.

14.19   It would be more efficient to use only digits to state numbers in contracts. And arguably, contracts prose is sufficiently numbers-heavy to justify using only digits. But shifting from traditional contract prose to something more modern requires accepting pervasive change. Instead of asking drafters to abandon an entrenched and relatively harmless general-writing usage, this manual focuses on change with greater implications. But you can elect to make this change yourselves.

FORMULAS

14.20   Contracts often include provisions that address how to calculate, post-signing, a given quantum, such as an interest rate, the number of surplus shares an investor may purchase, or the amount by which the exercise price of an option should be adjusted. Formulas can be expressed in ordinary contract prose or with mathematical equations.

Using Prose

SIMPLE FORMULAS

14.21 At their simplest, contract formulas involve only one kind of calculation, as in *Acme shall pay Roe an amount equal to X [plus] [minus] [multiplied by] [divided by] Y*. (Don't use a comma before *plus*, *minus*, *multiplied by*, or *divided by*. And when calculating an amount of money, insert the phrase *an amount equal to* before the calculation to reflect that money is fungible.) With such simple formulas, concision favors omitting any extra phrases referring to the end product of calculation, as in *an amount equal to the sum of X plus Y* and *an amount equal to the excess of X over* [insert *X minus*] *Y*. Such phrases have their uses in other contexts (see 14.27, 14.29, and 14.35).

14.22 A quantum can also be expressed as a percentage of a given amount, as in *an amount equal to 5% of the Overdue Amount*.

SPECIFYING THE ORDER OF OPERATIONS

14.23 With formulas involving only addition or only multiplication, you don't have to be concerned about the order in which to perform the operations. For example, the result of the calculation $2 + 3 + 4$ isn't affected by the order in which the numbers are added. This isn't the case when, for example, a formula combines addition and multiplication. The calculation $2 \times 3 + 4$ gives two different results, 10 or 14, depending on which operation you perform first. (Confusion regarding the order of operations is a specialized form of ambiguity and is analogous to the "squinting modifier"; see 12.18.)

14.24 In mathematics, the convention is that you first do all operations that lie inside parentheses, then do all multiplication and division, and finally do all addition and subtraction. So if in the calculation $2 \times 3 + 4$ the addition is to be performed first, it would be expressed as $2 \times (3 + 4)$. If the multiplication is to be performed first, the calculation could, according to mathematical convention, be left as is, but if the calculation were to be performed by someone unfamiliar with mathematical convention—by a lawyer, for example—it would be advisable to use parentheses in this calculation, too: $(2 \times 3) + 4$.

14.25 The order of operations also affects the result of a formula that includes both addition and subtraction. For example, if in the calculation $10 - 4 + 2$ the addition is to be performed first, it should be expressed as $10 - (4 + 2)$, with 4 as the result. If the subtraction is to be performed first, a convention to the effect that you proceed from left to right in performing additions and subtractions would allow you to do without parentheses. But you can't count on that convention being universally recognized, so the calculation should be expressed as $(10 - 4) + 2$, with 8 as the result.

14.26   When a mathematical formula is written in words, you can't use parentheses to specify the order of operations. Instead, two other mechanisms are available, and to avoid any chance of confusion, one or the other should be used whenever priority is to be given one or more operations.

14.27   One mechanism is use of the word *result* to isolate an operation from the rest of the formula. This is usually done by using the phrase *the result of* before the operation in question, as in this example (the three values that constitute the variables in the formula are shaded):

> After the Close of the Distribution, the number of shares of Parent Common Stock subject to a Nonconvertible Parent Option will equal the number of shares of Parent Common Stock that immediately before the Distribution Date are subject to that Nonconvertible Parent Option multiplied by **the result of** the Parent Stock Value divided by the Parent Opening Stock Value.

14.28   The phrase *the result of* indicates that it is the result of the operation that follows the phrase (rather than either variable in that operation) that is to be factored into the rest of the formula. But *the result of* doesn't indicate the nature of the following operation; that's conveyed by using X [*plus*] [*minus*] [*multiplied by*] [*divided by*] Y. (Don't use *and* to indicate addition.) Since it's open-ended, the phrase *the result of* eliminates ambiguity only if the operation that it relates to occurs at the end of a formula.

14.29   Instead of *the result of*, drafters often use *the* [*sum*] [*difference*] [*product*] [*quotient*] *of* with calculation by addition, subtraction, multiplication, and division, respectively. Because each of these terms conveys the operation being performed, it's standard to refer to, for example, *the quotient of X and Y*. But you can't count on readers knowing what these terms mean (other than *sum*), so you would instead need to refer to, for example, *the quotient of X divided by Y* or *the quotient obtained by dividing X by Y*. Because it would be tautological to do so, the phrase *the result of* represents a better alternative: it's simple and it applies to all calculations. But occasionally it's necessary to use one of the other phrases, to avoid repetition (see 14.35–.36).

14.30   There are yet further ways of expressing subtraction, but they should be avoided whatever the context. The phrase *the amount by which A exceeds B* is wordy; the phrase *the excess of A over B* could be confusing, since *A over B* could also be used to express a fraction; and *the difference between A and B* could also be confusing, since the difference between 5 and 7 could conceivably be either 2 or –2.

14.31   Another way the word *result* can be used to isolate an operation from the rest of the formula is by (1) placing at the front of the formula the operation that's to be isolated, (2) referring thereafter to the result of that operation, and (3) using in the formula the present participle form of the verb of calculation. The following formula represents the formula in 14.27 as revised to reflect this approach (again, the values that constitute the variables in the formula are shaded):

> After the Close of the Distribution, the number of shares of Parent Common Stock subject to a Nonconvertible Parent Option will be determined by dividing the Parent Stock Value by the Parent Opening Stock Value and

> multiplying *the result* by the number of shares of Parent Common Stock that immediately before the Distribution Date are subject to that Nonconvertible Parent Option.

14.32 A second way to avoid ambiguity is to use enumeration, as in this variant of the example in 14.27:

> After the Close of the Distribution, the number of shares of Parent Common Stock subject to a Nonconvertible Parent Option will equal (1) the number of shares of Parent Common Stock that immediately before the Distribution Date are subject to that Nonconvertible Parent Option multiplied by (2) the Parent Stock Value divided by the Parent Opening Stock Value.

14.33 Enumeration is equivalent to placing parentheses around each enumerated clause.

WHEN A FORMULA CONTAINS THREE OR MORE SEQUENTIAL OPERATIONS

14.34 In mathematical equations, you can have parentheses within parentheses— the result of one calculation features in a second calculation, the result of which features in a third calculation, and so on. The equivalent is found in contract formulas expressed in prose. The added complexity means that uncertainty regarding which operations come first is best addressed by using enumeration, as described in 14.32.

14.35 In this context, the phrase *the result of* is inadequate to make clear which operation comes first, but it nevertheless comes in handy. Consider this example:

> "**Eurodollar Rate**" means, regarding a Eurodollar Advance for the relevant Interest Period, (1) *the result of* (A) the Eurodollar Base Rate applicable to that Interest Period divided by (B) one minus the Reserve Requirement (expressed as a decimal) applicable to that Interest Period plus (2) the Applicable Margin.

14.36 In this example, the phrase *the result of* doesn't clarify the order of operations—that's accomplished by enumeration. But it does serve a different function. This formula is equivalent to parentheses within parentheses, with the enumeration *(1)* and *(A)* acting as the equivalent of two opening parentheses. In algebraic equations featuring parentheses within parentheses, the two opening or closing parentheses are located immediately next to each other. But inserting the phrase *the result of* between the enumerations makes it clearer to the reader how the elements of the formula relate to each other; it's best not to place enumerations next to each other without intervening text (see 14.29).

14.37 Here's an example of a formula that features the equivalent of two sets of double parentheses within a further set of parentheses:

> If there are any outstanding Closing Date Liabilities (other than the Identified Debt) or any outstanding Purchaser Claims at the time that the Seller wishes to transfer any Shares, the Seller may transfer only that number of Shares equal to (1) *the result of* (A) *the product of* (i) the aggregate number of Shares held by the Seller multiplied by (ii) the Stipulated Value minus (B) *the sum of* (i) the aggregate dollar amount of the outstanding Closing

Date Liabilities (other than the Identified Debt) plus (ii) the aggregate dollar amount of the Purchaser Claims divided by (2) the Stipulated Value.

14.38   Emphasized in bold are three instances of a filler phrase used to keep apart enumerations. Since using *the result of* three times would have made for confusion, two alternative phrases were also used, despite the tautology (see 14.29).

AN INSTANCE OF FORMULA AMBIGUITY

14.39   The English case *Chartbrook Limited v. Persimmon Homes Limited and others* [2009] UKHL 38 provides an example of formula ambiguity leading to dispute. The following language was at issue:

> 23.4% of the price achieved for each Residential Unit in excess of the Minimum Guaranteed Residential Unit Value less the Costs and Incentives.

14.40   It could be interpreted two ways:

Meaning 1

An amount equal to (1) 23.4% of the price achieved for each Residential Unit in excess of the Minimum Guaranteed Residential Unit Value minus (2) the Costs and Incentives.

Meaning 2

An amount equal to 23.4% of the result of (1) the price achieved for each Residential Unit in excess of the Minimum Guaranteed Residential Unit Value minus (2) the Costs and Incentives.

14.41   ("Costs and Incentives" was a label for a single value. If it had meant "Costs plus Incentives," that would have added to the mix an additional operation and additional alternative meanings.)

14.42   The House of Lords held that the first meaning was the appropriate one. If the drafter had used enumeration to express that meaning unambiguously, the parties would have been spared three levels of court review.

AN INSTANCE OF FORMULA MISTAKE

14.43   An opinion of the Quebec Superior Court offers an instance not of formula ambiguity but of mistake in ordering the operations. Here's the language that ended up in the contract:

> "Resort Operation Payment Amount" means the amount, if any, equal to the amount by which (a) 4.8 times Net Resort EBITDA during the Resort Operation Payment Calculation Period exceeds (b) $2,000,000;

14.44   Here's what it should have said:

> "Resort Operation Payment Amount" means the amount, if any, equal to 4.8 times the amount by which (a) Net Resort EBITDA during the Resort Operation Payment Calculation Period exceeds (b) $2,000,000.

14.45   The drafter's mistake was to put the words "the amount by which" before "4.8 times" instead of after. The result was that instead of owing nothing, her client (Intrawest, a developer and manager of ski and golf resorts) found itself subject to a claim for C$6,203,632. ✓. $0

14.46 Perhaps if this formula had been expressed as a mathematical equation (see 14.60) the drafter would have spotted the mistake.

FRACTIONS

14.47 A standard component of formulas, including contract formulas, is fractions. They are used when a pro-rata quantum is being calculated. The following sentence is a representative example of language used to express fractions in prose:

> Each Investor who elects to purchase Nonpurchased Units may purchase a number of Nonpurchased Units calculated by multiplying the number of Nonpurchased Units by a fraction the numerator of which is the maximum number of Units that Electing Investor has agreed to purchase under this agreement and the denominator of which is the maximum number of Units that all Electing Investors have agreed to purchase under this agreement.

14.48 A fraction could always be expressed more succinctly as the value of the numerator divided by the value of the denominator, but expressing a calculation as a fraction serves as a helpful signal that a number is being prorated. If a number is not being prorated, a fraction should not be used as an alternative to dividing one number by the other.

"EXPRESSED AS A PERCENTAGE"

14.49 Often a drafter will want to express the result of a calculation as a percentage. For example, it would be more comprehensible to speak in terms of a lender having an Aggregate Exposure Percentage of 22.45% rather than, say, an Aggregate Exposure Factor of 0.2245.

14.50 When a formula includes a fraction, the result can be converted to a percentage by referring, in the formula, to *a fraction, expressed as a percentage, the numerator of which ... .* One can also express as a percentage the result of a division calculation: *"Offeree Percentage" means, as to each offeree, the result, expressed as a percentage, of the total number of Common Stock Equivalents held by that offeree divided by the total number of Common Stock Equivalents.*

14.51 When specifying that a number is to be expressed as a percentage, drafters sometimes use a ratio: *"Aggregate Exposure Percentage" means, regarding any Lender at any time, the ratio, expressed as a percentage, of that Lender's Aggregate Exposure at that time to the Aggregate Exposure of all Lenders at that time.* It's simpler to use a division calculation instead.

14.52 Converting a number to a percentage requires that you multiply it by 100, and drafters sometimes state as much in a formula: *The Sale Percentage applicable to each Stockholder equals the result, multiplied by 100, of the aggregate number of Shares of the Majority Group proposed to be transferred in that Sale divided by the aggregate number of Shares held by the Majority Group.* But you don't need to be that specific, because "expressed as a percentage" is clear enough.

ROUNDING

14.53   When a contract contains a formula, it's generally a good idea to provide for rounding of the result.

14.54   What increment you use depends on what's being rounded; convention may play a part. Shares of stock are usually rounded to the nearest whole share; bank interest rates, by contrast, are often rounded to the nearest 1/100th of 1%. Rounding can also be expressed in terms of decimal places; lending documents routinely contain formulas that require calculation to up to nine decimal places.

14.55   Also specify whether amounts are to be rounded up to the nearest increment, rounded down to the nearest increment, or rounded up or down, whichever increment is nearest. Again, convention may play a part. For example, lenders tend to round interest rates up. Although there exists a convention that decimal numbers are rounded up or down, whichever is nearest, you can't count on that convention being recognized.

14.56   An issue relating to rounding up or down, whichever increment is nearest, is how to round an amount that's exactly halfway between increments. For example, if one is rounding up or down to the nearest cent, does one round $1.245 to $1.24 or $1.25? The convention in mathematics is to round up, but if you want to avoid confusion on the subject, specify how such amounts are to be treated.

14.57   Rounding can be addressed within a formula, for example by referring to *the result,* [*rounded up to the nearest whole share*] [*rounded down to the nearest cent*] [*rounded up or down, whichever is nearer, to three decimal places*], *of X multiplied by Y.* But if a contract contains several formulas, it might be efficient to address rounding in an internal rule of interpretation: *All calculations in* [*this agreement*] [*this section 2.4*] *are to the nearest cent (with $.005 being rounded upward) and to the nearest one-tenth of a share (with .05 of a share being rounded upward).*

14.58   Rounding can be awkward when a fixed number or quantity is allocated pro rata among a group. For example, a shareholders agreement might provide that the shares of a selling shareholder are to be allocated pro rata among those of the remaining shareholders who wish to purchase. If, when implementing this provision, you round up the shares allocated to each remaining shareholder, you risk having the remaining shareholders agree to buy more shares than are actually being sold; if you round down, you risk having shares left over; if you round up or down, whichever is nearest, you risk one or the other outcome. The best course is to round down; when the time comes to allocate shares, the purchasing shareholders would presumably be willing to have the numbers adjusted to include any selling shareholder's leftover shares.

TABULATION

14.59   To make it easier to read, you could tabulate the enumerated clauses included in a formula. (Regarding tabulating enumerated clauses, see 4.41.) But if a formula is sufficiently complex that it would benefit from tabulation, it's likely that it would benefit even more from being expressed as a mathematical equation (see 14.60).

Using Mathematical Equations

14.60 The more complex a formula is, the more likely it is that expressing it as a mathematical equation rather than in words would make it clearer.

14.61 For example, the formula in 14.37 would be easier to understand if expressed as this mathematical equation:

> If there are any outstanding Closing Date Liabilities (other than the Identified Debt) or any outstanding Purchaser Claims when the Seller wishes to transfer any Shares, the Seller may transfer a number of Shares no greater than the number of Shares calculated according to this formula:

$$X = \frac{(SS - SV) - (CDL + PC)}{SV}$$

> In this formula, the following applies:
>
> X = the number of shares that the Seller may transfer
>
> SS = the aggregate number of Shares held by the Seller
>
> SV = the Stipulated Value
>
> CDL = the aggregate dollar amount of the outstanding Closing Date Liabilities, other than the Identified Debt
>
> PC = the aggregate dollar amount of the Purchaser Claims

14.62 You shouldn't need to use the percent sign in mathematical equations, and doing so could cause confusion: $3 \div 4\%$ could conceivably mean either 75% (with the percent sign conveying "expressed as a percentage") or 0.75%. If you want a result to be expressed as a percentage (see 14.49), say so in the prose preamble to the equation.

14.63 If a mathematical equation is particularly complicated, it can be helpful to include in a schedule, as an illustration, a sample set of calculations.

CONSECUTIVE RANGES OF NUMBERS

Distinguishing between "Stepped Rates" and "Shifting Flat Rates"

14.64 When in a contract a quantity is determined by reference to another quantity—as when a royalty or commission is based on sales of widgets—the relationship can often be expressed by a simple formula. For example, a royalty can be expressed as a stated percentage of annual gross revenue from sale of widgets, or it can instead be expressed as a per-widget amount.

14.65 But parties might want a different formula to apply as the quantity being referred to changes. For example, Acme and Widgetco might want to provide that the royalty rate that Acme pays to Widgetco on sales of widgets will increase as the number of widgets that Acme sells increases. Specifically, they agree to the following royalty schedule, with the royalties based on a percentage of annual gross revenue from sale of widgets, the percentage increasing as revenue increases.

Annual Gross Revenue	Royalty
Not over $1 million	5%
Over $1 million but not over $2 million	6%
Over $2 million but not over $3 million	7%
Over $3 million but not over $4 million	8%
Over $4 million but not over $5 million	9%
Over $5 million	10%

14.66   But this schedule is ambiguous. If the annual gross revenue is $3.4 million, it's not clear from this schedule whether the 8% rate is applied to all gross revenue (this manual refers to such a rate as a "shifting flat rate") or only revenue over $3 million, with the lower rates being applied to the increments of revenue under $3 million (this manual refers to such a combined rate as a "stepped rate").

14.67   There are three ways to express the schedule in 14.65 as a stepped rate. One way would be as follows: *5% of the first million dollars of annual gross revenue; 6% of the next million dollars; 7% of the next million dollars; 8% of the next million dollars; 9% of the next million dollars; and 10% thereafter.* (This is the method used to express the "Lehman formula" used in calculating compensation for investment banking services.) Alternatively, a single range could be expressed as follows: *When the annual gross revenue from sale of widgets exceeds $1 million, the royalty rate on the next $1 million will be 6%.*

14.68   The second way to express a stepped rate would be to use instead the table below. This is perhaps the clearest alternative. (This method is used by the Internal Revenue Service to explain tax schedules.)

Annual Gross Revenue	Royalty
Not over $1 million	5% of the total amount
Over $1 million but not over $2 million	$5,000 plus 6% of the amount over $1 million
Over $2 million but not over $3 million	$11,000 plus 7% of the amount over $2 million
Over $3 million but not over $4 million	$18,000 plus 8% of the amount over $3 million
Over $4 million but not over $5 million	$26,000 plus 9% of the amount over $4 million
Over $5 million	$35,000 plus 10% of the amount over $5 million

14.69   The third way to express a stepped rate would be to so state in the preamble to the table: *The royalty percentage stated next to a given range of annual gross revenue will be used to calculate only royalties to be paid on revenue falling within that range.*

14.70   Conversely, if a given percentage does apply to all gross revenue—in other words, if the rate is a shifting flat rate—one way to make that clear would be to state as much in the preamble to the table: *The percentage stated next to the range of annual gross revenue within which falls the annual gross revenue for a given year will be used to calculate all royalties to be paid on that revenue as opposed to just royalties to be paid on revenue falling within the stated range.* It would not be clear enough to state, for example, that royalties are based on the "incremental rates" stated in the table.

14.71   A second and simpler way to express a shifting flat rate would be to add *of total gross annual revenue* after each percentage figure in the second column.

Gaps and Overlaps

14.72   When expressing consecutive ranges of numbers as described in 14.65, drafters sometimes create overlap. For example, if royalties are keyed to the number of widgets sold, if two of the ranges are "1–10 widgets" and "10–20 widgets," and if ten widgets are sold, it would not be clear which royalty rate applies. To avoid overlap, the two ranges should have been expressed as "1–10 widgets" and "11–20 widgets." If the contract provides for a shifting flat rate (see 14.66), more would be at stake than if it had provided for a stepped rate. In the former case, the rate to be applied to all widget sales would be at issue; in the latter case, the question would be the royalty rate that applies to the sale of the tenth widget.

14.73   Overlap can also occur when creating consecutive ranges of numbers that can be expressed to decimal places, such as dollar amounts, as in "from $1,000 to $2,000" and "from $2,000 to $3,000." You could fix this overlap in one of two ways. You could revise the ranges so one ends just before the other begins, as in "from $1,000.01 to $2,000" and "from $2,000.01 to $3,000." (Depending on the unit making up the ranges, it might be necessary to express to several decimal places one of the two numbers in a range.) Or you could use wording similar to that used in the tables in 14.65 and 14.68: "over $1,000 but not over $2,000" and "over $2,000 but not over $3,000." This would seem the simpler, and therefore better, alternative.

14.74   Revising the ranges to read "from $1,000 to $1,999" and "from $2,000 to $2,999" would create a different problem, namely a gap between two ranges, leaving unclear the range into which $1,999.01, $1,999.99, and any amount in between would fall. But such a gap is appropriate if the unit involved comes only in whole units. For example, because it doesn't make sense to speak of half a widget, there is no gap between the ranges in the last sentence of 14.72.

14.75   When consecutive ranges consist of dates rather than amounts, take care to avoid gaps and overlap due to the ambiguity inherent in many prepositions used in expressing dates (see 10.22).

.

INTERNAL RULES OF INTERPRETATION

15.1 In contract disputes, courts invoke rules of interpretation to attribute meaning to confusing or disputed contract language. Judicial rules of interpretation are generalized notions, pieced together by courts and commentators over time, about the most likely meaning that writers express, and readers derive, in a given context.

15.2 Some contracts include their own rules of interpretation—what this manual calls "internal" rules of interpretation. Each is stated in a separate section, or they're collected in one section, usually under the heading *Interpretation* or *Construction*.

15.3 This chapter contains tidied-up versions of common internal rules of interpretation, divided into three types. The first type is comparable to autonomous definitions: they apply a stated meaning to a particular kind of expression. This chapter considers only two examples; for another example, see 14.57. The second type states the obvious, or aims to accomplish something that a drafter could achieve more clearly or simply using other means. For another example, see 6.49–.50. And the third type overreaches in trying to create order; for another example, see 17.37. The first type might be useful; the second type you can do without; and you shouldn't rely on the third type.

15.4 Just as judicial rules of interpretation are problematic (for example, see 12.13 regarding the rule of the last antecedent), internal rules of interpretation usually aren't compelling. Generally, if you can't count on readers understanding basic usages in your contracts without help, something is amiss.

15.5 Internal rules of interpretation are different from autonomous definitions, but autonomous definitions are often included with internal rules. They should instead be placed in the definition section, if the contract has one.

15.6 Some internal rules of interpretation begin "Unless otherwise specified" or "Unless the context otherwise requires." The latter formulation undercuts the certainty that this sort of provision is meant to offer (see 13.866).

THESE MIGHT BE USEFUL

15.7   *All references to a time of day are references to the time in [location].* This provision would spare the drafter having to specify, after each reference to a time of day, which location or time zone would be used to determine when that time of day had come. This would be an issue only in a contract between parties based in different time zones or in a contract providing for business to be conducted across time zones (see 10.50). This provision would be of use only in contracts containing more than a couple of references to the time of day.

15.8   *If any date specified in this agreement as the only day, or the last day, for taking action falls on a day that is not a Business Day, then that action may be taken on the next Business Day.* This provision aims to avoid having a party's ability to act on a given day undercut because that day isn't a business day. It would be redundant in a contract that measures all periods of time in business days (see 10.72).

THESE ARE UNNECESSARY, OR SHOULD BE

15.9   *References in this agreement to articles, sections, exhibits, and schedules are references to articles, sections, exhibits, and schedules of this agreement.* This states the obvious (see 4.105, 5.106).

15.10   *The definitions in this agreement apply equally to both singular and plural forms of the terms defined.* This is intended to ensure that, for example, the definition of *Employee* applies to any reference to *Employees,* or that the definition of *Consents* applies to a reference to *any Consent.* But this would manifestly be the case even absent this provision. (For the same reason, defining terms in the singular and plural just adds clutter; see 6.4.)

15.11   *Any reference to an agreement means that agreement as amended, subject to any restrictions on amendment in that agreement.* This provision spares drafters having to add *as amended* after each reference to a contract. But given that adding *as amended* is unnecessary (see 13.54), this provision should be unnecessary too.

15.12   *Any reference to a statute or regulation means that statute or regulation as amended and any corresponding provisions of successor statutes and regulations.* This provision is analogous to the provision in 15.11, and equally unnecessary.

15.13   *The words "party" and "parties" refer only to a named party to this agreement.* This provision aims to preclude a court from concluding, regarding a contract provision specifying that no rights or remedies are being conferred on anyone other than the parties, that the term *parties* includes persons other than the named parties. But there's a more economical way to address that issue (see 2.113).

15.14   *A pronoun used in referring generally to any member of a class of persons, or persons and things, applies to each member of that class, whether of the masculine, feminine, or neuter gender.* This would allow a drafter to use gender-specific language in a contract without running the risk of a court holding that, for example, use of only masculine pronouns in that contract excludes corporations from the scope of certain provisions. But it would be unnecessary if you were to use gender-neutral drafting, which is always a good idea (see 17.11).

15.15   *The words "hereof," "herein," "hereunder," and "hereby" refer to this agreement as a whole and not to any particular provision of this agreement.* This doesn't accurately reflect use of *hereby* in language of performance (see 3.35). But more to the point, you shouldn't use *here-* words at all, except for *hereby* in language of performance (see 13.349–.350).

15.16   *For computing periods of time from a specified date to a later specified date, the word "from" means "from and including" and the words "to" and "until" each mean "to but excluding."* This provision is fine as far as it goes, but it addresses only a small part of the ambiguity inherent in references to time (see chapter 10). A provision resolving all sources of that ambiguity would be long and unwieldy. Instead of addressing a small part of the problem, you would do better to purge each reference of any ambiguity. That would require that you become familiar with the ways that references to time can be ambiguous.

THESE OVERREACH BY TRYING TO CREATE ORDER

15.17   *The headings in this agreement are provided for convenience only and do not affect its meaning.* This seeks to render insignificant any inconsistency between the heading given a contract provision and the substance of that provision (see 4.22). But if it's clear that because of careless drafting a heading doesn't match what's in the related provision, this provision would accomplish only what a court would likely do anyway. If it's arguable that a unique component of a heading reflects the intended scope of the related provision, then a court might ignore a headings-for-convenience provision. See, e.g., *Infrassure, Ltd. v. First Mutual Transportation Assurance Co.*, No. 16-306, 2016 WL 6775921, at *1 (2d Cir. 16 Nov. 2016). That makes this provision of questionable use to drafters.

15.18   *The words "including," "includes," and "include" are to be read as if they were followed by the phrase "without limitation."* For why this unhelpful, see 13.363, 13.379–.385.

15.19   *The word "or" is disjunctive; the word "and" is conjunctive;* also *The word "or" is not exclusive.* Given the subtle ways the ambiguity associated with *and* and *or* manifests itself (see chapter 11), these two provisions grossly oversimplify. For one thing, consider how, regarding *or*, they take opposite approaches.

15.20   *The word "will" is to be construed as having the same meaning as the word "shall."* This provision represents a hopeless attempt to resolve confusion over use of *will* and *shall* (see 3.72–.103).

15.21   *The word "shall" is used to express a mandatory duty; the word "may" is used to express discretion.* If as this manual recommends you use *shall* only to impose a duty on a party that's the subject of the sentence, you wouldn't need this, because courts generally hold that in a contract (as opposed to legislation), *shall* is mandatory (see 3.73). And those drafters who indulge in the traditional overuse of *shall* shouldn't use this provision, since it couldn't be applied to their drafting.

15.22   *The singular form of nouns and pronouns includes the plural, and vice versa.* Presumably what this provision is groping at is the notion that any reference to *a widget* should be construed to mean *one or more widgets*. If that's the meaning you wish to convey, then say *one or more widgets* rather than relying on this overbroad provision (see 11.6). And you shouldn't rely on this kind of internal principle to prevent a fight over singular versus plural (see 11.8).

15.23   *A reference to any Person is to be construed to include that Person's successors and assigns.* It would be more usual, and clearer, to address this with a provision specifying to what extent a party may transfer elements of its performance under the contract.

TYPOGRAPHY

16.1   Word-processing software has given drafters many options for making a contract more readable or, conversely, impenetrable. Here are some points to consider.

FONTS

The Usual Suspects

16.2   When it comes to choosing a font for contracts, drafters are conservative. Most contracts use one of a handful of fonts.

16.3   In recent decades, the overwhelming majority of contracts have used one of two fonts, namely 12-point Times New Roman, a serif font, and 10-point Arial, a sans serif font. (For an explanation of *serif* and *sans serif*, see 16.13.) Companies in technical fields used the latter; everyone else used the former. Both are shown in sample 10.

16.4   Despite its enduring popularity, Times New Roman is not a favorite of typography professionals. It was designed for use in a newspaper, so it has comparatively narrow characters. It works well in the short lines of newspaper columns, but in longer lines, compared with other fonts, Times New Roman can seem crowded and harder to read. *The Complete Manual of Typography*, at 70, says, "Times is probably used inappropriately more than any other typeface today."

16.5   Beyond that, Times New Roman suffers from overexposure. *Typography for Lawyers*, at 119, says, "When Times New Roman appears in a book, document, or advertisement, it connotes apathy ... . Times New Roman is not a font choice so much as the absence of a font choice, like the blackness of deep space is not a color." It goes on to say, "If you have a choice about using Times New Roman, **please stop**. You have plenty of better alternatives."

16.6   Arial too is unpopular in the typography community. *Typography for Lawyers*, at 80, says, "After 25 years as a system font, Arial has achieved a ubiquity that rivals Times New Roman. And like Times New Roman ... , Arial is permanently associated with the work of people who will never care about typography."

16.7   Two plausible alternatives are Calibri and Constantia (see sample 10), introduced by Microsoft in 2007. Calibri, a sans serif font, is the default font for body text in Office 2016; Constantia is a serif font. The Word

2016 default font for body text is 11-point Calibri. Both Calibri and Constantia were designed for screen reading; the loss of design details makes them less compelling in printed form. In its classification of system fonts, *Typography for Lawyers*, at 79, puts both Calibri and Constantia in "The B list: OK in limited doses."

SAMPLE 10 ■ TYPEFACES (USING *MSCD* FIRST-LINE-INDENT ENUMERATION SCHEME)

Calibri 11pt

3.7 **Financial Statements.** Vector has previously delivered to Holdings the audited consolidated balance sheet of Vector as of 31 December 2016 (the "**Balance Sheet**") and the related consolidated audited statements of income and cash flow for Vector for the year then ended. Those financial statements have been prepared in accordance with GAAP consistent with Vector's past practice (except as described in the notes thereto) and on that basis present fairly the financial position and the results of operations and cash flow of Vector at and as of 31 December 2016 and for the period referred to in those financial statements.

Times New Roman 12pt

3.7 **Financial Statements.** Vector has previously delivered to Holdings the audited consolidated balance sheet of Vector as of 31 December 2016 (the "**Balance Sheet**") and the related consolidated audited statements of income and cash flow for Vector for the year then ended. Those financial statements have been prepared in accordance with GAAP consistent with Vector's past practice (except as described in the notes thereto) and on that basis present fairly the financial position and the results of operations and cash flow of Vector at and as of 31 December 2016 and for the period referred to in those financial statements.

Arial 10pt

3.7 **Financial Statements.** Vector has previously delivered to Holdings the audited consolidated balance sheet of Vector as of 31 December 2016 (the "**Balance Sheet**") and the related consolidated audited statements of income and cash flow for Vector for the year then ended. Those financial statements have been prepared in accordance with GAAP consistent with Vector's past practice (except as described in the notes thereto) and on that basis present fairly the financial position and the results of operations and cash flow of Vector at and as of 31 December 2016 and for the period referred to in those financial statements.

Constantia 11pt

3.7   **Financial Statements.** Vector has previously delivered to Holdings the audited consolidated balance sheet of Vector as of 31 December 2016 (the "**Balance Sheet**") and the related consolidated audited statements of income and cash flow for Vector for the year then ended. Those financial statements have been prepared in accordance with GAAP consistent with Vector's past practice (except as described in the notes thereto) and on that basis present fairly the financial position and the results of operations and cash flow of Vector at and as of 31 December 2016 and for the period referred to in those financial statements.

16.8   The author of this manual switched from Times New Roman to Calibri. That's why the indented extracts of contract text throughout this manual are in Calibri, as are the samples and the redrafted version of the contract in the appendix. With its rounded ends and variation in line width, Calibri might be palatable to both Arial users and those who use Times New Roman.

Constraints on Choice

16.9   Drafters could be more adventurous in their choice of font. But understanding the options requires considering the constraints that come with sharing electronic documents.

16.10   If you pick a font that isn't recognized by someone else's computer, it will be displayed in some fallback font. That would interfere with, for example, exchanging signature pages. It might also interfere with negotiations, because the line breaks and page breaks in the recipient's version would likely be different from those in the sender's version. You could try to get around that by distributing only PDF files, but that's generally frowned upon by those who work with contracts.

16.11   So your best bet is to use system fonts—those already installed on your computer—as opposed to professional fonts you buy online and install. It's likely that those you send a document to will have them on their computer. You can't be sure of perfect visual fidelity, but that shouldn't be an issue when exchanging drafts of contracts.

16.12   But there are system fonts on Mac computers, system fonts on computers running Windows, and fonts installed with MS Office. If you want a font that works across all systems, your choice would be limited to a few fonts. But for exchanging drafts with law firms and company law departments, it's safe to assume that they have Microsoft Office installed on their computers. That would give you more fonts to choose from. Included would be Calibri and Constantia, but you could explore others. For example, included in the fonts that *Typography for Lawyers*, at 79, lists in "The A list: Generally tolerable" and "The B list: OK in limited doses" are several Word 2016 system fonts suitable for body text. If design considerations are important to you, you could experiment with system fonts without jeopardizing cross-system compatibility.

Serif and Sans Serif

16.13 Serifs are finishing flourishes at the ends of a character's main strokes. One way to categorize fonts is to distinguish those with serifs from those without, which are known as sans serif fonts.

16.14 It has long been assumed that serif fonts are easier to read than sans serif fonts. But studies have cast doubt on this assumption. *The Complete Manual of Typography*, at 68, says, "Bad typesetting and bad typeface design aside, the fact seems to be that the most readable typefaces are the ones you're accustomed to reading." That's why the author of this manual has no qualms about using Calibri, a sans serif font.

JUSTIFICATION

16.15 Justification refers to fitting text into the width of a column of type. You have a choice between "justified" margins and "ragged-right" margins (also known as "flush-left" margins). With justified margins, the margins are vertical on both left and right. With ragged-right margins, all lines begin flush with the left-hand margin but are allowed to end short of the right-hand margin, creating an irregular margin along the right side of the text column. (For an example of each, see sample 11.)

SAMPLE 11 ▪ JUSTIFICATION (USING *MSCD* FIRST-LINE-INDENT ENUMERATION SCHEME)

Ragged-Right Margin

3.7 **Financial Statements.** Vector has previously delivered to Holdings the audited consolidated balance sheet of Vector as of 31 December 2016 (the "**Balance Sheet**") and the related consolidated audited statements of income and cash flow for Vector for the year then ended. Those financial statements have been prepared in accordance with GAAP consistent with Vector's past practice (except as described in the notes thereto) and on that basis present fairly the financial position and the results of operations and cash flow of Vector at and as of 31 December 2016 and for the period referred to in those financial statements.

Justified Margins

3.7 **Financial Statements.** Vector has previously delivered to Holdings the audited consolidated balance sheet of Vector as of 31 December 2016 (the "**Balance Sheet**") and the related consolidated audited statements of income and cash flow for Vector for the year then ended. Those financial statements have been prepared in accordance with GAAP consistent with Vector's past practice (except as described in the notes thereto) and on that basis present fairly the financial position and the results of operations and cash flow of Vector at and as of 31 December 2016 and for the period referred to in those financial statements.

16.16 Most printed text, whether in books, magazines, or newspapers, uses justified margins. But using justified margins in word-processed documents, including contracts, makes them harder to read. According to typographers, that's because subtle word-spacing, letter-spacing, and hyphenation algorithms are needed to make justified text easy to read, and those in word-processing software aren't up to the task. Word-processed documents shouldn't have justified margins.

16.17   Those who favor using justified margins in word-processed documents will tell you that it looks "professional." But it's a phony professionalism, because it comes at the expense of readability, which should be the first priority of any kind of typesetting, including word processing.

EMPHASIS

16.18   You can make certain words, phrases, or paragraphs of a contract particularly conspicuous by using italics, bold, capital letters, underlining, or bold italics, or by putting a box around the text (see sample 12).

SAMPLE 12   ▪   **EMPHASIS (USING *MSCD* FIRST-LINE-INDENT ENUMERATION SCHEME)**

No Emphasis

  3.7   **Financial Statements.** Vector has previously delivered to Holdings the audited consolidated balance sheet of Vector as of 31 December 2016 (the "**Balance Sheet**") and the related consolidated audited statements of income and cash flow for Vector for the year then ended. Those financial statements have been prepared in accordance with GAAP consistent with Vector's past practice (except as described in the notes thereto) and on that basis present fairly the financial position and the results of operations and cash flow of Vector at and as of 31 December 2016 and for the period referred to in those financial statements.

All Capitals

  3.7   **FINANCIAL STATEMENTS.** VECTOR HAS PREVIOUSLY DELIVERED TO HOLDINGS THE AUDITED CONSOLIDATED BALANCE SHEET OF VECTOR AS OF 31 DECEMBER 2016 (THE "**BALANCE SHEET**") AND THE RELATED CONSOLIDATED AUDITED STATEMENTS OF INCOME AND CASH FLOW FOR VECTOR FOR THE YEAR THEN ENDED. THOSE FINANCIAL STATEMENTS HAVE BEEN PREPARED IN ACCORDANCE WITH GAAP CONSISTENT WITH VECTOR'S PAST PRACTICE (EXCEPT AS DESCRIBED IN THE NOTES THERETO) AND ON THAT BASIS PRESENT FAIRLY THE FINANCIAL POSITION AND THE RESULTS OF OPERATIONS AND CASH FLOW OF VECTOR AT AND AS OF 31 DECEMBER 2016 AND FOR THE PERIOD REFERRED TO IN THOSE FINANCIAL STATEMENTS.

Underlining

  3.7   <u>**Financial Statements.** Vector has previously delivered to Holdings the audited consolidated balance sheet of Vector as of 31 December 2016 (the "**Balance Sheet**") and the related consolidated audited statements of income and cash flow for Vector for the year then ended. Those financial statements have been prepared in accordance with GAAP consistent with Vector's past practice (except as described in the notes thereto) and on that basis present fairly the financial position and the results of operations and cash flow of Vector at and as of 31 December 2016 and for the period referred to in those financial statements.</u>

Italics

3.7   ***Financial Statements.*** *Vector has previously delivered to Holdings the audited consolidated balance sheet of Vector as of 31 December 2016 (the "**Balance Sheet**") and the related consolidated audited statements of income and cash flow for Vector for the year then ended. Those financial statements have been prepared in accordance with GAAP consistent with Vector's past practice (except as described in the notes thereto) and on that basis present fairly the financial position and the results of operations and cash flow of Vector at and as of 31 December 2016 and for the period referred to in those financial statements.*

Bold

3.7   **Financial Statements. Vector has previously delivered to Holdings the audited consolidated balance sheet of Vector as of 31 December 2016 (the "Balance Sheet") and the related consolidated audited statements of income and cash flow for Vector for the year then ended. Those financial statements have been prepared in accordance with GAAP consistent with Vector's past practice (except as described in the notes thereto) and on that basis present fairly the financial position and the results of operations and cash flow of Vector at and as of 31 December 2016 and for the period referred to in those financial statements.**

Bold Italics

3.7   ***Financial Statements. Vector has previously delivered to Holdings the audited consolidated balance sheet of Vector as of 31 December 2016 (the "Balance Sheet") and the related consolidated audited statements of income and cash flow for Vector for the year then ended. Those financial statements have been prepared in accordance with GAAP consistent with Vector's past practice (except as described in the notes thereto) and on that basis present fairly the financial position and the results of operations and cash flow of Vector at and as of 31 December 2016 and for the period referred to in those financial statements.***

Bold Italics with Border

3.7   ***Financial Statements. Vector has previously delivered to Holdings the audited consolidated balance sheet of Vector as of 31 December 2016 (the "Balance Sheet") and the related consolidated audited statements of income and cash flow for Vector for the year then ended. Those financial statements have been prepared in accordance with GAAP consistent with Vector's past practice (except as described in the notes thereto) and on that basis present fairly the financial position and the results of operations and cash flow of Vector at and as of 31 December 2016 and for the period referred to in those financial statements.***

Emphasizing Names and Article Headings

16.19   Use all capital letters to emphasize article headings, the names of the parties in the introductory clause, and the names of the parties in the signature blocks. Because the eye cannot easily differentiate characters that are all of a uniform size, capitalized text is harder to read —don't use it for continuous body text (see 16.29).

Emphasizing Section Headings and Defined Terms

16.20   Emphasize in bold all section headings (see 4.20) and each defined term when it's being defined (see 6.36, 6.68)—doing so helps readers find their way around a document.

16.21   Don't use underlining for emphasis. Underlining is a typewriter convention created to approximate common typographic effects that couldn't be achieved with a typewriter. Typographers don't like it. *The Complete Manual of Typography*, at 85, notes that in word-processing software, underlining is too close to the baseline, causing it to overlap descending letters—the effect is "not pretty, and you should avoid using it." *Typography for Lawyers*, at 74, says, "In a printed document, don't underline. Ever. It's ugly and makes text harder to read."

What Not to Emphasize

16.22   Don't emphasize cross-references and references to attachments—doing so doesn't help the reader. It might make it easier for the drafter to check cross-references and keep track of attachments, but drafter convenience shouldn't be at the expense of distracting the reader. And using Word's "find and replace" function is quicker and more reliable.

Emphasizing Provisions

WHAT TO EMPHASIZE

16.23   Unless a statute or caselaw requires it, or unless you're seeking to counterbalance a substantial disparity of bargaining power or sophistication between the parties, don't emphasize any part of the provisions themselves. It's appropriate to assume that sophisticated parties, or at least their lawyers, will read the entire contract and be able to assess the various provisions for themselves. And flagging a provision as particularly important necessarily involves downplaying the significance of others—an uncertain proposition, given that contract disputes routinely arise from ostensibly mundane aspects of a transaction.

16.24   Some statutes specify that certain statements must be in all capitals. See, e.g., Arizona Revised Statutes § 12-1366(A)(1). Others in effect do so by stating in all capitals text that must be included in a contract. See, e.g., Florida Statutes § 718.202(3); Oregon Revised Statutes § 93.040.

16.25   Other statutes say that certain statements must be "conspicuous." For example, section 2-316(2) of the Uniform Commercial Code (UCC) states that a disclaimer of the implied warranty of merchantability must be "conspicuous." And in *Dresser Industries, Inc. v. Page Petroleum, Inc.*, 853 S.W.2d 505, 509-11 (Tex. 1993), the Texas Supreme Court held that the UCC's standard for conspicuousness applies to a contract provision indemnifying a party for that party's own negligence.

16.26   Section 1-201(10) of the UCC says that "conspicuous" means "so written, displayed, or presented that a reasonable person against which it is to operate ought to have noticed it," and includes examples of the attributes of conspicuous terms.

16.27   But a provision doesn't necessarily have to be emphasized to be conspicuous. The court in *American General Finance, Inc. v. Bassett (In re Bassett)*, 285 F.3d 882, 887 (9th Cir. 2002), used the UCC's definition of "conspicuous" to construe a Bankruptcy Code requirement that a contract contain a "clear and conspicuous" statement. The court held that although the statement wasn't emphasized in the contract in question, it was conspicuous—it was the first sentence of a contract that took up less than one side of a page, and no aspect of formatting or appearance of the statement made it less visible or difficult to read.

16.28   In response to caselaw, many drafters emphasize waivers of jury trial. But the caselaw addressing whether waivers of jury trial must be emphasized is inconsistent. In New York, for example, a waiver of jury trial may be printed in the same size type as the rest of the contract, whereas courts in some other jurisdictions, in holding a waiver of jury trial to be enforceable, have noted that the waiver of jury trial was in bold or in all capitals. Unless you're able to do the necessary research, the cautious approach would be to make waivers of jury trial conspicuous regardless of the law governing the contract.

HOW TO EMPHASIZE IT

16.29   Most drafters use all capitals to emphasize an entire provision, but that's counterproductive—the reader is likely to skim over text in all capitals, because it's a chore to read (see 16.19). The prevalence of all capitals is a relic from typewriter days—the only easy way to emphasize text on a typewriter was to use all capitals. And depending on the context, text in all capitals might not even be conspicuous. As the court in *American General Finance, Inc.*, 285 F.3d at 886, noted, "Lawyers who think their caps lock keys are instant 'make conspicuous' buttons are deluded." See also *Broberg v. Guardian Life Insurance Co. of America*, 171 Cal. App. 4th 912, 922 (2009) (holding that disclaimers "buried in a sea of same-sized, capitalized print" might not be conspicuous). So unless a statute requires it (see 16.24), don't use all capitals to emphasize a provision.

16.30   Text emphasized in bold italics would be much easier to read. It's likely that text in bold italics would be conspicuous for purposes of the UCC, given that section 1-201(10) of the UCC specifies that "language in the body of a form is 'conspicuous' if it is in larger or other contrasting type or color."

16.31   You could also, or instead, place a border around a provision—section 1-201(10) of the UCC says that a term is conspicuous if it's "set off from surrounding text of the same size by symbols or other marks that call attention to the language."

16.32   When a contract states the legend that's to be placed on stock certificates, the legend is invariably stated in all capitals. Use regular text instead, both in the contract and on the stock certificates. If you want to make the legend more conspicuous, put a border around it, use bold italics for all or part of it, or do both.

16.33   Because the distinction between regular text and text in italics is too subtle, don't use italics for emphasis, except perhaps in amendments (see 18.20).

ACKNOWLEDGING THAT TEXT IS CONSPICUOUS

16.34   The lack of specific guidelines has resulted in drafters trying to establish by contract that certain text is in fact conspicuous:

ACME AND WIDGETCO ACKNOWLEDGE THAT THIS STATEMENT CONSTITUTES
CONSPICUOUS NOTICE.

16.35   But such statements are illogical. They might appear unobjectionable—if
a party subject to a contract provision acknowledges that it's conspicuous,
that might reassure a court that the party had in fact noticed that provision.
But invariably such acknowledgments are located in the provision at
issue. If that provision is inconspicuous, the acknowledgement would be
inconspicuous too. So the acknowledgement would be of value only if the
provision is conspicuous. That defeats the purpose of the acknowledgment.

RHETORICAL EMPHASIS THROUGH TYPOGRAPHY

16.36   Don't emphasize selected words in a provision for rhetorical emphasis—as
a way of saying "and we really mean it!" (For more on rhetorical emphasis,
see 1.58.) An example of that is the emphasized *not* in this example:

> The Licensor shall NOT indemnify, defend, or hold the Licensee harmless
> from and against any loss, cost, damage, liability, or expense (including
> reasonable legal fees) suffered or incurred by the Licensee in connection
> with any claim by any Person of infringement of any patent, copyright, or
> other intellectual property with respect to the Licensed Products.

FONT SIZE

16.37   Choice of font size, expressed in "points," depends in part on what
typeface you use. The standard choices have been 12 point for Times
New Roman and 10 point for Arial, except when used with a two-column
format (see 4.75).

16.38   Regarding the progressively larger Calibri point sizes on display in sample
13, 11-point Calibri is the Office 2016 and Word 2016 default for body
text. It's a safe choice, but you can experiment with other point sizes.

SAMPLE 13   ▪   FONT SIZE (USING *MSCD* FIRST-LINE-INDENT ENUMERATION SCHEME)

Calibri 10pt

3.7   **Financial Statements.** Vector has previously delivered to Holdings the
audited consolidated balance sheet of Vector as of 31 December 2016 (the "**Balance
Sheet**") and the related consolidated audited statements of income and cash flow for
Vector for the year then ended. Those financial statements have been prepared in
accordance with GAAP consistent with Vector's past practice (except as described in the
notes thereto) and on that basis present fairly the financial position and the results of
operations and cash flow of Vector at and as of 31 December 2016 and for the period
referred to in those financial statements.

Calibri 11pt

3.7   **Financial Statements.** Vector has previously delivered to Holdings the audited consolidated balance sheet of Vector as of 31 December 2016 (the "**Balance Sheet**") and the related consolidated audited statements of income and cash flow for Vector for the year then ended. Those financial statements have been prepared in accordance with GAAP consistent with Vector's past practice (except as described in the notes thereto) and on that basis present fairly the financial position and the results of operations and cash flow of Vector at and as of 31 December 2016 and for the period referred to in those financial statements.

Calibri 12pt

3.7   **Financial Statements.** Vector has previously delivered to Holdings the audited consolidated balance sheet of Vector as of 31 December 2016 (the "**Balance Sheet**") and the related consolidated audited statements of income and cash flow for Vector for the year then ended. Those financial statements have been prepared in accordance with GAAP consistent with Vector's past practice (except as described in the notes thereto) and on that basis present fairly the financial position and the results of operations and cash flow of Vector at and as of 31 December 2016 and for the period referred to in those financial statements.

Calibri 13pt

3.7   **Financial Statements.** Vector has previously delivered to Holdings the audited consolidated balance sheet of Vector as of 31 December 2016 (the "**Balance Sheet**") and the related consolidated audited statements of income and cash flow for Vector for the year then ended. Those financial statements have been prepared in accordance with GAAP consistent with Vector's past practice (except as described in the notes thereto) and on that basis present fairly the financial position and the results of operations and cash flow of Vector at and as of 31 December 2016 and for the period referred to in those financial statements.

CHARACTERS PER LINE

16.39   Some commentators recommend that the number of characters per line not exceed 70; others cite a considerably lower number. *Typography for Lawyers*, at 140, recommends a line length of 45 to 90 characters.

16.40 The more characters there are per line, the greater the risk that the reader will get lost in midline or in moving from one line to the next. A line of 11-point Calibri on letter-size paper with one-inch margins (the default page setup) contains between 85 and 95 characters. That's at the high end of, or in excess of, the recommended limits, although if you use ragged-right justification (see 16.15), the character count would be lower for those lines that don't reach the right margin.

16.41 If you would like to reduce the number of characters per line, the simplest way to do so would be to increase the left and right margins to 1.5 to 2 inches. *Typography for Lawyers*, at 141, recommends that you do so, saying that for proportional fonts, one-inch margins are too small. But keeping your blocks of text short (see 4.70) mitigates the high character count's adverse effect on readability. The author of this manual hasn't felt the need to increase his margins.

LINE SPACING

16.42 It has been standard to use single-spaced lines for contracts. Typewriters allowed for single-spacing or double-spacing, but word-processing software allows you to adjust line spacing in much smaller increments. Some find single-spaced text dense and hard to read, so you might want to experiment with adding extra space.

16.43 One option for setting line space in Word is "Multiple." *Typography for Lawyers*, at 138, recommends that you use a "Multiple" value of 1.03 to 1.24. In 2017, the default in Word is a "Multiple" setting of 1.08. Another popular "Multiple" setting is 1.15. Sample 14 shows three different line-spacing settings. The samples in this manual are based on Word documents with single-spacing.

SPACE AFTER PUNCTUATION

16.44 Use only one space, rather than two, after punctuation, whether it separates two sentences (periods, question marks, exclamation marks) or parts of a sentence (colons).

16.45 Using two spaces creates "rivers" of white space. It's inefficient, requiring an extra keystroke for every sentence. And it results in documents containing instances of three spaces or one space after a period and two spaces in the middle of a sentence.

16.46 This is standard advice. For example, *The Chicago Manual of Style*, at 2.9, says, "Like most publishers, Chicago advises leaving a single character space, not two spaces, between sentences and after colons used within a sentence." And *Typography for Lawyers*, at 44, says that use of one space "has the support of typography authorities and professional practice."

SAMPLE 14 ▪ **LINE SPACING (USING *MSCD* FIRST-LINE-INDENT ENUMERATION SCHEME)**

Single-Spacing

3.7 **Financial Statements.** Vector has previously delivered to Holdings the audited consolidated balance sheet of Vector as of 31 December 2016 (the "**Balance Sheet**") and the related consolidated audited statements of income and cash flow for Vector for the year then ended. Those financial statements have been prepared in accordance with GAAP consistent with Vector's past practice (except as described in the notes thereto) and on that basis present fairly the financial position and the results of operations and cash flow of Vector at and as of 31 December 2016 and for the period referred to in those financial statements.

Multiple Line Spacing at 1.08

3.7 **Financial Statements.** Vector has previously delivered to Holdings the audited consolidated balance sheet of Vector as of 31 December 2016 (the "**Balance Sheet**") and the related consolidated audited statements of income and cash flow for Vector for the year then ended. Those financial statements have been prepared in accordance with GAAP consistent with Vector's past practice (except as described in the notes thereto) and on that basis present fairly the financial position and the results of operations and cash flow of Vector at and as of 31 December 2016 and for the period referred to in those financial statements.

Multiple Line Spacing at 1.15

3.7 **Financial Statements.** Vector has previously delivered to Holdings the audited consolidated balance sheet of Vector as of 31 December 2016 (the "**Balance Sheet**") and the related consolidated audited statements of income and cash flow for Vector for the year then ended. Those financial statements have been prepared in accordance with GAAP consistent with Vector's past practice (except as described in the notes thereto) and on that basis present fairly the financial position and the results of operations and cash flow of Vector at and as of 31 December 2016 and for the period referred to in those financial statements.

"CURLY" AND "STRAIGHT" QUOTATION MARKS AND APOSTROPHES

16.47   "Curly" and "straight" quotation marks and apostrophes are of interest not so much from a typography perspective but because of what they can tell you about how a contract was drafted.

16.48   In most typefaces, curly quotation marks (also known as "curved" or "smart" quotation marks) look, to a greater or lesser extent, like small figures six and nine with the enclosed portions filled in. Straight quotation marks (also known as "dumb" quotation marks) point straight down. You can have double and single quotation marks, and single quotation marks do double duty as apostrophes.

16.49   Straight quotation marks were introduced on typewriters to reduce the number of keys on the keyboard, and they were retained for computer keyboards and character sets. But curly quotation marks are preferred in formal writing, so Microsoft Word provides an option under "AutoFormat As You Type" that allows you to replace straight quotation marks with curly quotation marks.

16.50   That option is set by default, so unless you deselect it, as you type quotation marks and apostrophes they will automatically be changed from straight to curly. But if you import into a document—whether from another Word document, the U.S. Securities and Exchange Commission's EDGAR system, or elsewhere—blocks of text containing straight quotation marks, those straight quotation marks will remain straight unless you change them. The converse can apply: if the "AutoFormat As You Type" option isn't selected, you can introduce curly quotation marks into a document in which you've typed straight quotation marks.

16.51   What's the significance of having both straight and curly quotation marks in a draft contract? It's messy typographically, but that's the least of it. When you send a contract to the other side for their review, you would like them to get the impression that you prepared it using contracts that have formed the basis for many transactions. But mixing straight and curly quotation marks is a hallmark of the sloppy copy-and-paste job. A savvy reviewer will pick up on that and will know to look for other, potentially more significant problems.

16.52   Make all your quotation marks curly, given that curly quotation marks are preferred for formal writing. If when you type quotation marks straight quotation marks appear, select the Word option that automatically turns your straight quotation marks into curly quotation marks as you type them. If your quotation marks are already curly, you know that this option has already been selected.

16.53   And to change to curly all instances of double straight quotation marks, use Word's "Find and Replace" function, typing a double quotation mark in both the "Find what" and "Replace with" boxes. Use the same process for single quotation marks.

FIRST-LINE INDENTS

16.54   One way to signal the start of a new paragraph is to indent the first line. Another way is to put space between paragraphs. Typography professionals recommend that you not use both techniques. For example, *Typography for Lawyers*, at 135, says, "First-line indents and space between paragraphs have the same relationship as belts and suspenders. You only need one to get the job done. Using both is a mistake. If you use a first-line indent on a paragraph, don't use space between. And vice versa."

16.55   That's why in the samples in this manual and in the redrafted version of the contract in the appendix, paragraphs without enumeration—the introductory clause, the recitals, the lead-in, the concluding clause, and autonomous definitions—don't use first-line indents. (That's a change from previous editions of this manual.)

16.56 The *MSCD* first-line-indent scheme requires first-line indents for sections (see 4.55) and subsections (see 4.58), but that's unrelated to presentation of unenumerated paragraphs.

DESIGN EMBELLISHMENTS

16.57 Most drafters, and most law firms and law departments, have a conservative, no-frills approach to document design—they're unlikely to have any interest in adjusting line spacing and margins or experimenting with different fonts.

16.58 But one can go well beyond that by adding further design elements: Different typefaces for headings. Different point sizes for headings. Color for headings. A horizontal line at the top of each section.

16.59 Law firms in Commonwealth countries are partial to adding such design elements to their contracts. This manual leaves it to readers to determine whether they wish to follow suit.

16.60 But it might be that design embellishments are less a function of ease of reading than of "selling"—catching and keeping a reader's attention in a time of short attention spans and endless distractions. Contracts aren't discretionary reading, so that selling function is less relevant. But it's not necessarily absent—for example, a company in a design business might want the document design of its contracts to be consistent with its image.

16.61 Any organization that wants to implement a sophisticated document design for its contracts should consider making it mandatory that drafters apply the design by using a numbering utility such as PayneGroup's Numbering Assistant (see 4.67). Using a more improvised approach isn't promising, in terms of the potential for erratic results and time wasted fiddling with the design elements.

DRAFTING AS WRITING

17.1   Contract prose may be limited and stylized, but clear and effective drafting nevertheless requires an understanding of general principles of good writing. This chapter considers those that are most relevant.

DON'T MAKE SENTENCES TOO LONG

17.2   In general, long sentences are harder to read than shorter ones. Although contract sentences will usually be longer—often much longer—than the 20 to 25 words recommended for general legal writing, whittle down those sentences that are unnecessarily long.

17.3   A sentence is too long if it strings together clauses that could stand on their own as separate sentences, or if it incorporates one or more unwieldy exceptions, qualifications, or conditions. If you can break such a sentence down into its constituent components and express, clearly and economically, how the components relate to each other, the sentence will be more readable.

17.4   Below is a 143-word sentence; below that is the same sentence, restructured as three sentences (149 words total). Although it's a few words longer, the "after" version takes much less of a toll on the reader than the "before" version. The first shaded portion in the "before" version constitutes the first sentence of the "after" version. The second shaded portion in the "before" version is an awkwardly positioned, passive-voice nonrestrictive clause; it forms the basis for the active-voice third sentence of the "after" version. The unshaded portion of the "before" version constitutes, with the addition of a brief introductory clause, the second sentence of the "after" version; it, like the first shaded portion, describes a consequence of default, but it can be turned into a separate sentence.

> **_Before_** If a Default described in section 8(f) occurs with respect to the Borrower, the Lenders' obligation to make Loans and the LC Issuer's obligation to issue Facility LCs will automatically terminate and the Obligations will immediately become due without any election or action on the part of the Administrative Agent, the LC Issuer, or any Lender and the Borrower will become unconditionally obligated, without any further notice or act, to pay to the Administrative Agent an amount in immediately available funds, which funds must be held in the Facility LC Collateral Account, equal to the difference of (1) the LC Obligations then outstanding minus (2) the amount then on deposit in the Facility LC Collateral Account that is free and clear of all rights and claims of third parties and has not been applied against the Obligations (that difference, the "Collateral Shortfall Amount").

> *After* If a Default described in section 8(f) occurs with respect to the Borrower, the Lenders' obligation to make Loans and the LC Issuer's obligation to issue Facility LCs will terminate and the Obligations will immediately become due without any election or action on the part of the Administrative Agent, the LC Issuer, or any Lender. Upon any such Default, the Borrower will become unconditionally obligated, without any further notice or act, to pay to the Administrative Agent an amount in immediately available funds equal to the difference of (1) the LC Obligations then outstanding minus (2) the amount then on deposit in the Facility LC Collateral Account that is free and clear of all rights and claims of third parties and has not been applied against the Obligations (that difference, the "Collateral Shortfall Amount"). The Administrative Agent shall hold the Collateral Shortfall Amount in the Facility LC Collateral Account.

17.5   It's standard practice to present lists—such as lists of items to be delivered at closing or lists of events of default—in long sentences made up of enumerated clauses. Tabulating the enumerated clauses breaks such sentences down into manageable portions.

KEEP SUBJECT, VERB, AND OBJECT CLOSE TOGETHER

17.6   A sentence is easier to understand if the subject, the verb, and the object (if any) are close together. Drafters often create unnecessary gaps between subject and verb or between verb and object. In the first example below, the gap is between the subject and the verb; in the second, it's between the verb and the object. Sometimes fixing this requires turning the intervening words into a separate sentence; at other times, as in the examples below, they can be shunted to the beginning or end of the sentence. (In the examples below, shading denotes the offending text and shows where it was moved.)

Gap	*No Gap*
Acme shall not without the prior written consent of Excelsior, which Excelsior shall not unreasonably withhold, transfer the Shares to any Person.	Acme shall not transfer the Shares to any Person without the prior written consent of Excelsior, which Excelsior shall not unreasonably withhold.
Acme shall deliver to Widgetco, no later than 15 days after each Quarterly Period, unless the Gross Revenue for that Quarterly Period is less than $1,000,000, a stock certificate representing those shares of Acme common stock that Acme is required to issue with respect to that Quarterly Period.	No later than 15 days after each Quarterly Period, unless the Gross Revenue for that Quarterly Period is less than $1,000,000, Acme shall deliver to Widgetco a stock certificate representing those shares of Acme common stock that Acme is required to issue with respect to that Quarterly Period.

DON'T BURY VERBS

17.7   Like other writers, contract drafters are prone to using abstract nouns at the expense of verbs. This practice has been variously described as using 'buried" verbs (the label this manual uses), using "zombie" nouns, and using "nominalizations" (itself an abstract noun). See *Garner's Modern English Usage*, at 983. Abstract nouns are the opposite of concrete nouns—they express things we can't feel, touch, see, hear, or taste.

17.8   Using buried verbs is a reliable way to write like a bureaucrat and clutter prose with prepositions and "weak" verbs, including *is* (see the fourth example in the table below) and *has* (see the eighth example). Using buried verbs also allows you to drop the *by*-agent (see 3.12), thereby obscuring who the actor is, as in the first example in the table below. The effect is comparable to use of the passive voice (see 3.13). That can force the reader to work harder and can create confusion.

17.9   Whenever possible, use instead "strong" verbs. The first five examples in the table below show two versions of sample language, one version using an abstract noun, the other using a verb. Adjectives can also act as buried verbs; in the sixth and seventh examples in the table below, an adjective is replaced with a verb. (The adjective in the seventh example makes that example a buried-actor policy; see 3.309.) This manual uses the label "buried verb" loosely—maybe the best alternative to an abstract noun is an adjective, as in the eighth example in the table below.

	Uses Abstract Noun (or Adjective)	*Uses Verb (or Adjective)*
1.	Immediately following issuance of the Notes, … .	Immediately after Acme issues the Notes, … .
2.	… all expenses the Bank incurs in connection with establishment and maintenance of the Deposit Account.	… all expenses the Bank incurs in establishing and maintaining the Deposit Account.
3.	Upon the failure of Smith to timely make the payment of the Purchase Price, … .	If Smith fails to timely pay the Purchase Price, … .
4.	If there is a merger or consolidation of Acme … .	If Acme merges or consolidates … .
5.	Jones shall promptly give notice to the other parties … .	Jones shall promptly notify the other parties … .
6.	If this section is violative of any law or public policy … .	If this section violates any law or public policy … .
7.	The Warrants are not redeemable by Acme.	Acme shall not redeem the Warrants.
8.	… for which the Redeemed Member has liability.	… for which the Redeemed Member is liable.

17.10   Because buried verbs allow you to drop the actor, they sometimes serve a purpose, just as use of the passive voice sometimes does (see 3.22). If several different parties might exercise a particular option, you could use the wordy *When any one or more Optionholders exercises the Option* to introduce the obligations triggered by exercising the option, but a better choice would be *Upon exercise of the Option*.

AVOID GENDER-SPECIFIC LANGUAGE

17.11   When a contract provision refers to a group of persons that includes, or might during the life of the contract include, one or more women and one or more men, it's best that you not use exclusively the masculine pronouns *he*, *his*, and *him* when referring generally to a member of that group. Such gender-specific language might offend, distract, or mislead readers—drafters can no longer assume that readers consider male pronouns to include persons of both genders when the reference is general. And gender-specific language simply seems old-fashioned now.

17.12   In addition, using only gender-specific pronouns when referring generically to a member of a group is jarring when the group includes one or more entities.

17.13   When you're dealing with a template or any other contract that's likely to be used as a model, gender-specific language would be a concern even if it happened to be appropriate for the transaction at hand: it would be a nuisance if, each time the contract were revised for a new transaction, the drafter might have to change the pronouns.

17.14   You can avoid in three ways using gender-specific language in contracts: instead of using only a masculine pronoun, (1) use a plural pronoun and make conforming changes elsewhere, (2) repeat the noun, or (3) use a feminine or neuter pronoun, or both, in addition to a masculine pronoun. Which solution works best depends on the context. Here's how these options play out in an example involving a member of a group of individuals:

Gender-specific version	Each Stockholder must surrender his stock certificates ... .
Gender-neutral version using plural noun	The Stockholders must surrender their stock certificates ... .
Gender-neutral version that repeats noun	Each Stockholder must surrender that Stockholder's stock certificate ... .
Gender-neutral version that uses both masculine and feminine pronouns, or masculine, singular, and neuter pronouns	Each Stockholder must surrender [his or her] [his, her, or its] stock certificates ... .

17.15   A fourth option is to use the singular *they* (and its related forms) as a gender-neutral third-person singular personal pronoun. For example:

Gender-neutral version using their *as singular personal pronoun*	Each Stockholder must surrender their stock certificate ... .

17.16   This usage has become increasingly accepted. See Ben Zimmer, *"They," the Singular Pronoun, Gets Popular*, Wall St. Journal, 10 Apr. 2015. This manual regards it as acceptable, but at least for now it's up to each drafter to decide whether they wish to embrace the singular *they*. For an example featuring the singular *their*, see 5.43, 5.44.

17.17   But don't use the singular *they* (and its related forms) for a member of a group composed only of entities—in that context, *it* (and its related forms) would be more suitable.

17.18   Finally, a general point regarding pronouns: if you use *it* (and related forms) in referring to an individual, don't be surprised if a court sees that as somehow significant, even though a copy-and-paste glitch might be the more likely explanation. See *Total Recall Technologies v. Luckey*, No. C 15-02281 WHA, 2016 WL 199796 (N.D. Cal. 19 Jan. 2016) (pointing to use of *its* in a contract reference to an individual as a factor suggesting that the individual intended the contract to benefit the general partnership of which he was partner).

DON'T USE WORDY PHRASES

17.19   One finds in contracts circumlocutions and overly formal words and phrases that characterize not just legal writing but stuffy writing generally. Some examples are listed below; using instead the suggested alternatives (in the *Better* column) would make a contract easier to read.

Wordy	*Better*
at that point in time	then
at the place where	where
at the time at which	when
at the time that	when, once
at the time when	when
by means of	by
by reason of	because of
by virtue of the fact that	because
commensurate with	equal to, appropriate for
despite the fact that	although
due to the fact that	because
during such time as	while, during
during the course of	while
following the conclusion of	after
for the purpose of [verb]ing	To [verb]
for the reason that	because
in combination with	with
in furtherance of	furthering, to advance

Wordy	*Better*
in lieu of	instead of
in order for	so
in order that	so
in order to	to
in the course of	while, during
in the event of	if
in the event that	if
is binding upon	binds
is unable to	cannot
per annum	a year, per year, annually
period of time	period, time
previous to	before
prior to	before
pursuant to	under, in accordance with, authorized by
set forth in	stated in, in
subsequent to	after
under the provisions of	under
until such time as	until
with the exception of	except for

17.20   Below are other wordy phrases, ones that merit explication.

To the Extent That

17.21   The phrase *to the extent that* is appropriate when the degree to which a provision applies depends on some variable: *This agreement is governed by the laws of the state of New York, except to the extent that the federal securities laws apply.* But the phrase is often used even when satisfying a condition results in the provision being applied to its fullest, rather than incrementally; in such contexts, *if* would be more appropriate. One example: "*To the extent that* [read *If*] any document is required to be filed or any certification is required to be made with respect to the Issuer or the Notes under the Sarbanes-Oxley Act, the Seller shall prepare and execute that document or certification." Another example: "*To the extent that* [read *If*] the Company has not paid the Investor's fees and expenses, the Investor may deduct from the Advance the amount of any unpaid fees and expenses."

The Fact That

17.22   You can almost always improve on constructions containing the wordy phrase *the fact that*. One example: "Executive acknowledges that Acme's

Confidential Information would be valuable to the Company's competitors *by virtue of the fact that* [read *because*] it is not generally known to the public or in the industry." Another example: *The fact that there may be no Loans outstanding* [read *Whether any Loans are outstanding*] at any given time will not affect the continuing validity of this agreement."

17.23   And the phrases *notwithstanding the fact that* and *regardless of the fact that* can always be replaced by *although, even though,* or *even if.* An example: "Doe will be entitled to receive the stock dividend on the shares of Common Stock acquired upon that Option exercise, *notwithstanding the fact that* [read *even though*] those shares were not outstanding on the record date for the stock dividend."

There Is and *There Are*

17.24   Whenever you start a clause or sentence with *there* or *it* followed by a form of the verb "to be"—*there is, there are, it is*—you are lumbering the front end of the clause or sentence with a fake subject and a weak verb. Instead, find the real subject and the real verb and use them to start the sentence or clause; sometimes this requires significant restructuring. Below are three sentences beginning with *there is*, along with a proposed alternative for each.

There Is	***No* There Is**
If *there is* a conflict or inconsistency between this agreement and any other Loan Document, the terms of this agreement will control.	If this agreement conflicts with or is not consistent with any other Loan Document, the terms of this agreement will control.
There is no fact that is known to any Seller or that reasonably should be known to any of them that has not been disclosed to the Agent in writing with respect to the transactions contemplated by this agreement and that could reasonably be expected to result in a Material Adverse Change.	Each Seller has disclosed to the Agent in writing all facts that that Seller knows or reasonably should know that relate to the transactions contemplated by this agreement and could reasonably be expected to result in a Material Adverse Change.
There is no ongoing audit or examination or, to the knowledge of the Borrower, other investigation by any Governmental Authority of the tax liability of the Borrower and its Restricted Subsidiaries.	No Governmental Authority is currently auditing, examining, or, to the knowledge of the Borrower, otherwise investigating the tax liability of the Borrower and its Restricted Subsidiaries.

With Respect To

17.25   A less wordy alternative to *with respect to* is *regarding.* But *with respect to* can sometimes be replaced by a single preposition:

> The holders of certificates previously evidencing shares of ABC Stock outstanding immediately before the Effective Time will cease to have any rights *with respect to* [read *in*] those shares of ABC Stock … .

> ... and the continued employment of each such executive officer does not subject the Company or any of its Subsidiaries to any liability *with respect to* [read *for*] any of the foregoing matters.
>
> No dividends or other distributions declared or made after the Effective Time *with respect to* [read *on*] XYZ Stock ... .

17.26 Or a shorter prepositional phrase:

> "**Affiliate**" means, *with respect to* [read *as to*] any specified Person, any other Person ... .

17.27 Or a bigger fix might be in order:

> ... the CIO may revoke or change *Borrowing Instructions with respect to a Fund* [read *a Fund's Borrowing Instructions*] by notifying the Credit Facility Team.
>
> "**Prospectus**" means *with respect to each Borrower the prospectus required to be delivered by the Borrower to offerees of its securities under the Securities Act of 1933* [read *a prospectus that under the Securities Act of 1933 a Borrower is required to deliver to offerees of its securities*].

USE POSSESSIVES

17.28 One simple way of making contract prose less wooden is to use possessives, as in these examples:

No Possessive	Possessive
the board of directors of Acme	Acme's board of directors
the shares held by Smith	Smith's shares
the obligation of the Lender to make Loans under this agreement	the Lender's obligation to make Loans under this agreement

DON'T OVERUSE INITIAL CAPITALS

17.29 Contract drafters tend to overuse initial capitals. Use of initial capitals in references to agreements is one example of that (see 2.20). Discussed below are additional examples. Those who overuse initial capitals presumably think that if something is important, it's best to give it initial capitals. This overuse is essentially trivial, but not without cost, because initial capitals make a document less easy to read. As it is, the typical contract is not wanting for initial capitals used appropriately. So be restrained in using initial capitals. This manual follows the guidelines in *The Chicago Manual of Style*.

17.30 Drafters generally add initial capitals to *board of directors*, but it's a generic term, so lowercase letters are appropriate. And drafters invariably use initial capitals when referring to officer titles (*The certificate must be signed by the*

President of Acme), but it's preferable to do so only if the title is followed by a name (*President Jane Roe*), which is never the case in contracts. The same applies to other titles, such as *director* and *secretary of state*.

17.31   Initial capitals are often used in references to a company's organizational documents (*Acme's Restated Certificate of Incorporation and Bylaws*). But you're referring not to the title of a work but to a category of document, so use lowercase letters.

17.32   Words denoting political divisions are capitalized when they follow a name and are used as an accepted part of the name. When they precede the name, such terms are usually capitalized in names of countries but lowercased in entities below the national level—hence *New York State* but *the state of New York*. Drafters tend to capitalize *state* whatever the context.

17.33   Many drafters also use initial capitals when referring to a company's capital stock (*the Common Stock, par value $0.01 per share, of Widgetco*); use lowercase letters instead.

17.34   The recommended practice in general English usage is to use lowercase letters when referring to parts of a work. This is mostly the practice in legislative drafting. Contract drafters should fall in line and use lowercase letters for article and section cross-references (*Acme's obligations under section 12.4*) and for references to exhibits, schedules, and other attachments (*an employment agreement in the form of exhibit C*) (see 4.111, 5.82).

THE EXTRANEOUS *THE*

17.35   Drafters often place an extraneous *the* in front of some abstract nouns; the result is ponderous prose. In the examples below, which come from a credit agreement, each extraneous *the* is shown in strikethrough italics.

> upon ~~*the*~~ satisfaction of the conditions stated in section 4.2

> with respect to ~~*the*~~ execution and delivery of Borrowing Notices

> for ~~*the*~~ purposes of calculating Consolidated EBITDA for any period of four consecutive fiscal quarters

> any agreement to provide financial assurance with respect to the financial condition of, or ~~*the*~~ payment of the obligations of, that other Person

> net of amounts required to be applied to ~~*the*~~ repayment of Indebtedness secured by a Lien

> damages suffered by the Borrower or that Lender to the extent caused by ~~*the*~~ willful misconduct or gross negligence of the LC Issuer

CONTRACTIONS

17.36   Don't use contractions in contracts. It's generally accepted among commentators on English usage that contractions—including *it's, that's, isn't, won't*—are suitable in all but the most formal kinds of writing. (That's why this manual uses contractions.) Contractions help you achieve a more natural, conversational rhythm. But that doesn't mean that they're suitable for business contracts. The prose of business contracts is like computer code—it should be devoid of tone or rhythm. So using contractions in business contracts is inconsistent with the nature of contract prose.

PUNCTUATION

17.37 The law has a long tradition of disdaining punctuation. See *Garner's Dictionary of Legal Usage*, at 730. That view has thankfully all but disappeared—rational drafting requires that one use punctuation consistent with standard English, but without relying on it unduly (see 12.36, 12.37, 12.55, 12.76). But you might come across the following internal rule of interpretation, most likely in a contract drafted by an English lawyer: *Punctuation and headings used in this agreement are for the purpose of easy reference or reading only and do not affect its interpretation.* Insist that it be deleted.

AMENDMENTS

18.1   It's commonplace for the parties to a contract to want to amend—that is, make changes to—the contract to fix errors, to address circumstances that hadn't been contemplated in the original negotiations, or to change the deal terms.

18.2   Amending a contract is accomplished by a new writing, which can be in the form of a regular contract or a letter agreement. This chapter considers usages relating to effecting an amendment by means of a regular contract.

AMENDING, OR AMENDING AND RESTATING

18.3   Parties who wish to make changes to a contract can either amend it or amend and restate it. To amend a contract, the parties enter into a new contract that contains only the changes being made to the original contract. To amend and restate a contract, the parties enter into a new contract that consists of the original contract revised to incorporate any amendments that the parties had made since it was signed and any further amendments that the parties wish to make. In theory, the parties could simply restate a contract, in other words incorporate in a new contract, without making any further changes, all amendments that had previously been made to that contract, but that's done rarely, if at all.

18.4   When only a few discrete changes are being made, it usually makes sense simply to amend a contract rather than requiring that lawyers and clients add to their files another copy of the entire contract, slightly revised. By contrast, amending and restating a contract is likely to be the more efficient option when the parties wish to make extensive changes or when the proposed changes come on the heels of other amendments, making it awkward to keep track of the changes.

TITLE

18.5   If a contract amends, or amends and restates, another contract, it's conventional to state as much in the title, and the title should also refer to the type of agreement involved: *AMENDED AND RESTATED MERGER AGREEMENT*. It's helpful to number each amendment to a contract, or at least the second amendment onward: *AMENDMENT NO. 4 TO CREDIT AGREEMENT*. As with titles generally (see 2.2), don't include party names, because doing so makes the title unwieldy. (Regarding use of *allonge* instead of *amendment* in titles, see 13.14.)

INTRODUCTORY CLAUSE AND RECITALS

18.6   The introductory clause to an amendment or a restated and amended contract should follow this manual's recommendations for introductory clauses generally (see 2.15–.128). In particular, in the introductory clause you don't need to refer to the contract that's being amended, or restated and amended, as the case may be. Instead, the recitals should refer to that contract and, if feasible, state briefly why the parties wish to amend it or amend and restate it. Also, don't create in an amendment the defined term *this Amendment* (see 2.124).

THE LEAD-IN

18.7   The lead-in to an amendment should be the same as that for any other contract (see 2.160–.213), with the exception that if only one simple change is being made, it could conceivably be wrapped into the lead-in: *The parties therefore amend the Employment Agreement by deleting section 13 in its entirety.* The lead-in would then constitute the entire body of the contract, with the concluding clause following. But if you wish to add general provisions addressing matters such as the law governing the contract—and most drafters would—this approach wouldn't work.

18.8   The lead-in to an amended and restated contract should look like this: *The parties therefore amend and restate the [contract being amended] to read in its entirety as follows: … .*

LANGUAGE OF PERFORMANCE

18.9   The language used to state an amendment is an example of language of performance. (Regarding language of performance, see 3.33.) So it's preferable to have the parties state that the contract or provision, as the case may be, *is hereby amended*, as opposed to *is amended* or *is amended as of the date hereof* (see 3.35). It would be appropriate to use the passive voice, because there wouldn't be any question who's doing the amending (see 3.22).

DISTINGUISHING BETWEEN AMENDING AND SUPPLEMENTING

18.10   An amendment changes the original agreement; a supplement simply adds to it. Acme and Doe are party to an employment agreement that provides for Acme to pay Doe an annual salary. Acme and Doe enter into another agreement in which Acme agrees to pay Doe an annual bonus. One might term the second agreement an amendment of the employment agreement, but it doesn't amend the employment agreement unless it states that the new provisions are being added to the employment agreement. If the provisions in the second agreement are freestanding, the second agreement is best considered as supplementing the employment agreement. If that's the case, call it a supplement rather than use the fusty Latinism *addendum*.

ADDING, DELETING, AND REPLACING LANGUAGE

18.11   In an amendment, the parties can add or delete language or replace existing language with new language. How this process is handled is a function of whether entire provisions are involved.

Change Affecting Part of a Provision

18.12   When a change involves adding, deleting, or replacing less than an entire section or subsection (a word or two, a phrase, a sentence, or an enumerated clause), the distinction between amending, on the one hand, and amending and restating, on the other hand, can be applied, albeit on a smaller scale: the drafter generally has a choice between specifying only the exact change being made or restating the entire provision.

18.13   Assume, for example, that an agreement contains this definition: *"Termination Date" means 11:00 a.m., Houston, Texas, time, on 28 February 2017 or any earlier date on which the Commitment terminates under this agreement.* The parties agree to postpone the termination date by two months. The agreement could be revised in two different ways to reflect this change. The parties could substitute one date for the other: *The definition of "Termination Date" is hereby revised by replacing "28 February 2019" with "30 April 2019."* Or they could restate the entire definition, revised to include the new date: *The definition of "Termination Date" is hereby amended to read in its entirety as follows: … .*

18.14   The former approach is more concise and has the benefit of highlighting the change that was made. But that change is presented out of context, so a reader can't be sure of understanding its significance without referring to the underlying agreement. Restating the amended provision in its entirety avoids that problem, but at the cost of making the amendment longer and less specific, although the reason for the amendment could be stated in the recitals or in the amendment proper. Which approach is preferable in a given context requires balancing the pros and cons of each.

Change Affecting an Entire Provision

ADDING

18.15   An amendment can add a new section, subsection, or enumerated clause: *The Agreement is hereby amended by adding after section 10 the following new section 11: … .* Unless the new section, subsection, or enumerated clause is inserted at the end of the agreement, section, or series of enumerated clauses, respectively, contract enumeration would be affected. The amendment necessary to change the enumeration would generally follow immediately after the amendment requiring the change in enumeration: *The Agreement is hereby amended as follows: (1) by adding after section 10 the* *following new section 11 and (2) by renumbering sections 11 through 19 as sections 12 through 20.*

18.16　It could be that the original contract's internal cross-references, or references to the original contract that are in another contract, would be rendered inaccurate by a change in enumeration. That problem could presumably be addressed by further amendment (of both the original contract and any referencing contract), but it would be best if you could avoid the problem by inserting the new section, subsection, or enumerated clause at the end of the agreement, section, or series of enumerated clauses, respectively.

18.17　Adding an enumerated clause as the penultimate or last in a series of enumerated clauses requires some fine-tuning to address the fact that in the penultimate clause the semicolon is followed by *and* or *or* and the last clause ends in a period. For example, adding an enumerated clause at the end of a series of enumerated clauses would, strictly speaking, require amending language along the lines of the following: *Section 9 is hereby amended as follows: (1) by deleting the word "or" at the end of clause (4); (2) by deleting the period at the end of clause (5) and replacing it with "; or"; and (3) by inserting the following as a new clause (6): … .* But inserting an enumerated clause without doing this fine-tuning wouldn't change the meaning of any provision and so couldn't harm a party's interest.

DELETING

18.18　An amendment can delete a section, subsection, or enumerated clause of the original contract: *The Agreement is hereby amended by deleting section 10 in its entirety.* Unless the section, subsection, or enumerated clause being deleted occurs at the end of the agreement, section, or series of enumerated clauses, respectively, enumeration in the contract would be affected. One could address this by tacking on a further amendment: *The Agreement is hereby amended as follows: (1) by deleting section 10 in its entirety; and (2) by renumbering sections 11 through 19 as sections 10 through 18.* But you might find it simpler to retain the enumeration of the provision being deleted and replace the provision itself with the bracketed notation *Intentionally omitted*, which acts as a place-filler (see 4.114). This would have the added advantage of leaving unaffected internal cross-references in the original contract and any references to the original contract that are in another contract (unless any of those references is to the deleted provision).

18.19　Deleting the next-to-last or last in a series of enumerated clauses requires fine-tuning of the sort required when you add such a clause (see 18.17). For example, deleting the last of a series of enumerated clauses would require amending language of the following sort: *Section 9 is hereby amended as follows: (1) by adding the word "or" at the end of clause (3); (2) deleting the "; or" at the end of clause (4) and replacing it with a period; and (3) deleting in its entirety clause (5).* Here too, omitting such adjustments when deleting an enumerated clause couldn't harm a party's interests.

LAYOUT

18.20   If an amendment is adding an entire section, subsection, or tabulated enumerated clause to the contract that's being amended, indenting that block of text, stating it in italics, and otherwise formatting it as you would if it were being stated in the contract being amended would help distinguish it from text that pertains to the amendment itself. This approach is shown in sample 15.

SAMPLE 15   ▪   **USE OF ITALICS IN AMENDMENTS (USING *MSCD* HANGING-INDENT ENUMERATION SCHEME)**

1.   **Amendment to Section 4.1**

Section 4.1 of the Supply Agreement is hereby amended by replacing "16 July 2017" with "16 September 2017".

2.   **Amendments to Article 5**

Article 5 of the Supply Agreement is hereby amended as follows:

(1)   by inserting after section 5.2 the following new section 5.3:

    5.3   ***Transition Services Agreement***

       Subject to the transition services agreement dated 12 March 20017 between Waferco and Digital, Waferco shall comply with exhibit G (Delivery and Logistics) in its shipping and handling of finished Wafers.

(2)   by renumbering sections 5.4 through 5.10 as sections 5.5 through 5.11.

LETTER AGREEMENTS

FUNCTION

19.1   Instead of being in the form of a regular contract, an agreement might be embodied in a letter agreement, which is a letter that contains the terms of the agreement and is signed by the sender and the recipient. By convention, some categories of agreement, notably letters of intent, are generally in the form of a letter agreement. Don't give a regular contract the title "letter of intent"—it sends mixed signals.

19.2   Usually the letter-agreement format is used for short agreements, but sometimes they can be lengthy. For example, it's not unusual for credit agreements to be in the form of letter agreements.

COMPONENTS

19.3   A letter agreement will typically contain the following: the sender's address; the date; the recipient's address; the salutation; an introductory sentence; the substantive terms; a closing sentence; the sender's signature; and the recipient's signature. A letter agreement might also have a subject line, but it shouldn't bear a title.

Sender's Address

19.4   The sender should be the individual or entity that's party to the agreement and not, in the case of an entity, a representative. The sender's address can be typed or included in preprinted letterhead.

Date

19.5   What date you use in a letter agreement involves the same considerations as what date you use in the introductory clause of a regular contract (see 2.23–.47).

Recipient's Address

19.6   The recipients of a letter agreement would be those one or more persons or entities, other than the sender, that are to be bound by the letter agreement. If a recipient is an entity, usually one would include in an "Attention" line the name of a representative of the recipient.

Salutation

19.7   If the recipient is an individual, use as a salutation *Dear* and the individual's name. A salutation is standard in correspondence with an individual, and it would allow you to reflect the nature of the relationship: in a letter to Jane Doe, the salutation would presumably refer to *Jane* or *Ms. Doe*.

19.8   If the recipient is an entity, you can dispense with a salutation—it would be pointless to use a salutation such as *Dear Acme Corporation*, as the reader would know from the recipient address stated above the salutation that the recipient is Acme Corporation. A traditional choice for a salutation to an entity would be *Dear Sirs*, but it's gender-specific (see 17.10), it's old-fashioned, and it suggests you're writing to a group of individuals. *Dear Sirs and Madams* (or *Mesdames*) and *Ladies and Gentlemen* exhibit the second and third of those problems. *To whom it may concern* suggests that you either don't know to whom you're sending the letter or don't care.

Introductory Sentence

19.9   The introductory sentence is often something like this: *The purpose of this letter agreement is to state the terms of* [*the transaction*].

Substantive Terms

19.10   The substantive terms of a letter agreement should be phrased just as they would be in a regular contract. In a letter agreement one can dispense with section numbers and headings, but generally it's helpful to retain them.

19.11   Use the third person instead of *you*, on the one hand, and *we* and *us*, on the other hand (see 3.8).

Closing Sentence

19.12   The closing sentence would normally be like that in sample 16, although it could also refer to return of an original signed copy.

Sender's Signature

19.13   The sender's signature block is placed where the sender usually signs a letter (see sample 16). A closing formula such as *Yours sincerely* isn't necessary. Letter-agreement signature blocks use the same format as signature blocks in regular contracts (see 5.29). You would use a different arrangement if the letter agreement were signed electronically (see 5.68).

19.14   If the sender is an entity, the sender's signature block should be in the name of the sender rather than a representative of the sender, although a representative would sign.

Recipient's Signature

19.15   A letter agreement should contain a signature block for each recipient. They're usually placed under the sender's signature block, flush left (see sample 16).

19.16   Each recipient's signature block should be preceded by text indicating that the recipient is agreeing to the terms of the letter agreement. *Agreed to* is adequate; adding *and accepted* does nothing. And it's generally helpful to include a date. In the absence of a date a court might conclude that the date at the top of the letter applies, but there's no point in leaving that to chance.

SAMPLE 16   ▪   LETTER AGREEMENT

Dynamix Corporation
710 West Jefferson Street
Shorewood, IL 60431

20 September 2017

Excelsior, Inc.
599 Lexington Avenue
New York, NY 10022
Attention: Ms. Jane Doe, President

The purpose of this letter agreement is to state the terms under which Dynamix Corporation, a Delaware corporation ("**Dynamix**"), is to retain Excelsior, Inc., a New York corporation ("**Excelsior**"), as a consultant.

[Insert substantive provisions]

If this letter agreement accurately reflects the terms agreed to by Dynamix and Excelsior, please have it signed in the space provided below and send a copy by email to jroe@dynamix.com.

DYNAMIX CORPORATION

By: _____
      John Roe
      Chief Financial Officer

Agreed to on 20 September 2017:

EXCELSIOR, INC.

By: _____
      Name:
      Title:

19.17   If it's important that the date be a particular date (for example, the same as the date at the top of the letter agreement), the drafter should include that date rather than leaving it blank for the signer to fill in by hand. Saying *Agreed to on the date of this letter agreement*—assuming that's appropriate—would leave the drafter only one date to adjust—the one at the top—when finalizing the letter agreement. It would be preferable not to use an *as of* date (see 2.35).

A P P E N D I X 1

This appendix consists of two versions of a template of a "golden parachute" termination agreement—a contract between a company and one of its employees in which the company agrees to provide the employee with various benefits if the employee's employment is terminated after a change in control of the company. This template was prepared by lawyers at a national U.S. law firm. It can be said to be representative of mainstream contract drafting, to the extent that any one contract can be said to be representative.

Appendix A is the "before" version annotated with footnotes to show its drafting shortcomings. Many footnotes cite relevant paragraphs of this manual.

Appendix B is the "after" version—the contract redrafted consistent with the recommendations in this manual. As noted in the footnotes to appendix A, sections 8 (Arbitration), 10 (Notices), 11 (Severability), and 13 (Governing Law) in appendix B replace the corresponding sections in appendix A, because readers would likely find the author's versions of those boilerplate provisions more helpful than cleaned-up but still problematic versions of the corresponding appendix A sections.

The difference between appendix A and appendix B demonstrates the cumulative effect of a rigorous approach to the full spectrum of drafting usages. For one thing, appendix B is 86% the number of words of appendix A, even though the notices and severability sections in appendix B are twice as long as their counterparts in appendix A—informed drafting results in shorter contracts.

Furthermore, appendix B is much clearer and easier to read, and it fixes some significant problems of structure and logic present in appendix A. Such problems are easy to miss in the murk that is mainstream contract language.

Most contracts could be redrafted to similar effect. If an organization were to experience improvements on that scale in all its contracts, its contract process would operate faster and more cost-effectively, with less confusion. And the likelihood of drafting problems metastasizing into contract disputes would be significantly reduced.

Neither appendix A nor appendix B is included for use as a template. For appendix B, the language and structure of appendix A were retooled, but not the deal terms. This manual offers no opinion regarding whether the deal terms are appropriate or could be improved. And appendix A first appeared in this manual in the second edition; since then no attempt has been made to revise it to reflect changes in how such transactions are handled.

APPENDIX A: BEFORE, ANNOTATED

TERMINATION AGREEMENT[1]

This Agreement[2] is made[3] as of[4] _____, 20 __,[5] between RMA WIDGETS, INC., a Delaware corporation, with its principal offices at 500 Third Avenue, Suite 400, New York, New York 10022[6] (the "Company")[7] and _____("Employee")[8], residing at _____.[9]

WITNESSETH THAT:[10]

WHEREAS,[11] this Agreement is intended to specify the financial arrangements that the Company will provide to the Employee[12] upon Employee's separation from employment with the Company under any of the circumstances described herein; and[13]

WHEREAS, this Agreement is entered into by the Company in the belief that it is in the best interests of the Company and its shareholders to provide stable conditions of employment for Employee notwithstanding the possibility, threat or occurrence of certain types of change in control, thereby enhancing the Company's ability to attract and retain highly qualified people.[14]

NOW, THEREFORE,[15] to assure the Company that it will have the continued dedication of Employee notwithstanding the possibility, threat or occurrence of a bid to take over control of the Company, and to induce Employee to remain in the employ of the Company,[16] and for other good and valuable consideration,[17] the Company and Employee[18] agree as follows:

---

[1]   There are better font choices than Times New Roman (see 16.2–.14).

[2]   Don't use a capital *A* in references to "this agreement" (see 2.123–.127).

[3]   Use instead *is dated* (see 2.22).

[4]   Using *as of* with a date in the introductory clause is a loose convention used to indicate that one or more parties signed the agreement on a date other than the date stated in the introductory clause. This manual recommends not using *as of* dates (see 2.35). Furthermore, it doesn't make sense to use an *as of* date in a template.

[5]   This manual uses the day-month-year format to state dates (see 10.8).

[6]   It's unnecessary to state in the introductory clause the address of a party that's a legal entity. To distinguish a U.S. legal-entity party from any other entity sharing the same name, it's sufficient to state its jurisdiction of organization (see 2.68).

[7]   Consider using as the defined term for RMA Widgets a name based on that party's name rather than "the Company" (see 2.97).

[8]   Because this is a template that is to be used in transactions with different employees, it's appropriate to use the defined term *Employee* (see 2.97–.98). But using the definite article *the* with the defined term would make the prose a little less stilted (see 2.105).

[9]   In the case of a party that's an individual, in the U.S. stating their address is usually the simplest way to distinguish them from any other person bearing the same name. But if, as in this case, the contract contains a notices provision, nothing would be served by stating an address twice in the same contract—leave the address out of the introductory clause (see 2.71).

[10]   Use of *WITNESSETH* is archaic (see 2.136–.137).

[11]   This use of *WHEREAS* is archaic (see 2.142).

[12]   The defined term is *Employee*, but this contract refers sporadically to *the Employee*. Be consistent (see 2.105).

[13]   End recitals with a period, not a semicolon (see 2.143).

[14]   These recitals would be improved by making them more concise.

[15]   *NOW, THEREFORE* is archaic (see 2.166).

[16]   Buried in the lead-in is a purpose recital (see 2.131). It would be clearer to state it as a separate recital.

[17]   Use the *MSCD* form of lead-in (see 2.159) and eliminate the traditional recital of consideration (see 2.165–.209).

[18]   Don't refer to the parties by name in the lead-in, as doing so would serve no purpose and would just make the lead-in longer (see 2.163).

1.[19] Term of Agreement[20]. The term of this Agreement shall[21] commence on the date hereof as first written above[22] and shall[21] continue in effect through December 31, 20__ [year of execution][23]; provided that[24] commencing on January 1, 20__ [year following year of execution] and each January 1 thereafter,[25] the term of this Agreement shall[21] automatically be extended for one additional year unless not later than twelve months[26] prior to[27] such[28] January 1, the Company shall have given notice[29] to Employee that it does not wish to extend this Agreement (which notice may not, in any event, be given sooner than January 1, 20__ [year following year of execution] such that this Agreement may not terminate prior to[27] December 31, 20__ [year following year of execution])[30]; and provided, further, that[31] notwithstanding[32] any such notice by the Company not to extend, this Agreement shall[21] automatically continue in effect for a period of 24 months beyond the then current term[33] if a Change in Control (as defined in Section[34] 3(i) hereof[35])[36] shall have occurred[37] during such[28] term.[38]

---

[19] Use the *MSCD* first-line-indent enumeration scheme, "sections" version (see 4.2–.3). The *MSCD* hanging-indent enumeration scheme would be equally acceptable, but this contract was drafted by U.S. a law-firm; a law firm would be more likely to choose the first-line-indent scheme.

[20] To emphasize section headings, use bold rather than underlining (see 4.20–.21).

[21] This is language of policy, so *shall* is inappropriate (see 3.307–.308).

[22] It's sufficiently obvious that a contract becomes effective once the parties have signed it that nothing is gained by saying so (see 2.30). And "the date hereof as first written above" is archaic (see 5.27).

[23] It's misleading to say that the initial term ends on 31 December of the year of execution (in other words, the year the contract is signed). The proviso that follows says that the agreement will automatically be extended for an additional year unless at least 12 months before the beginning of the new term the company notifies the employee that it doesn't want to renew. Because it would be impossible for the company to give 12 months' notice to prevent the contract from being extended for an additional year commencing 1 January of the year following the year the contract is signed—the end of the year the contract is signed will always be less than 12 months away—it's inevitable that the agreement will renew for at least one year. It would be clearer to have the initial term run through 31 December of the year after the year the contract is signed.

[24] Using *provided that* is an imprecise way to signal the relationship between two conjoined contract provisions (see 13.663). In this case, the provision that follows *provided that* can stand on its own.

[25] The phrase "commencing on … and each 1 January thereafter" is unnecessary.

[26] In this context, *one year* would be the simpler and therefore better choice.

[27] *Prior to* is wordy; use instead *before* (see 17.19).

[28] Don't use *such* instead of the "pointing words" *this*, *that*, *these*, or *those* (see 13.767).

[29] The clause beginning "unless" is a conditional clause. The present perfect tense (*has given*) would be acceptable in this context, but the present tense (*gives*) is the simpler choice, as it works in all contexts (see 3.321). Using *shall* isn't appropriate, as no duty is being expressed (see 3.322).

[30] This parenthetical is redundant, because notice given sooner than 1 January of the year following the year in which the contract is signed would in any event be ineffective to prevent the contract from being extended for an additional year. See note 23.

[31] Using *provided, further, that* suffers from the same shortcomings as *provided that* (see note 24). In this case, the provision that follows *provided, further, that* can stand on its own.

[32] There's always a clearer alternative to *notwithstanding* (see 13.599).

[33] In this context, "will automatically be extended by two years" would be more concise.

[34] Don't use a capital *S* in *section* (see 17.34).

[35] Don't use *hereof* after cross-references (see 4.105).

[36] This sort of parenthetical is an inefficient way of cross-referencing, particularly when used to excess, as in this contract (see 6.111–.114).

[37] The clause beginning "if" is a conditional clause, so the present perfect tense (*has occurred*) would be acceptable in this context, but the present tense (*occurs*) would be the simpler choice, as it works in all contexts (see 3.321). Using *shall* isn't appropriate, as no duty is being expressed (see 3.322).

[38] It's not clear whether after a two-year extension the agreement would be subject to further one-year extensions.

2. Termination of Employment[39]

(i) Prior to a Change in Control. Prior to[27] a Change in Control (as defined in Section 3(i) hereof)[36], the Company may terminate Employee from employment with the Company at will, with or without Cause (as defined in Section 3(iii) hereof)[36], at any time[40].

(ii) After a Change in Control

(a) From and after[41] the date of a Change in Control (as defined in Section 3(i) hereof)[36] during the term of this Agreement,[42] the Company shall not terminate Employee from employment with the Company except as provided in this Section 2(ii)[43] or as a result of Employee's Disability (as defined in Section 3(iv) hereof)[36] or his[44] death.

(b) From and after[41] the date of a Change in Control (as defined in Section 3(i) hereof)[36] during the term of this Agreement,[42] the Company shall have the right to[45] terminate Employee from employment with the Company at any time[40] during the term of this Agreement[42] for Cause (as defined in Section 3(iii) hereof)[36], by written notice[46] to the Employee, specifying the particulars of the conduct of Employee forming the basis for such[28] termination.

(c) From and after[41] the date of a Change in Control (as defined in Section 3(i) hereof)[36] during the term of this Agreement:[42] (x) the Company shall have the right to[45] terminate Employee's employment without Cause (as defined in Section 3(iii) hereof)[36], at any time[40]; and (y) the Employee shall, upon the occurrence of such a termination by the Company without Cause, or upon the voluntary termination of Employee's employment by Employee for Good Reason (as defined in Section 3(ii) hereof)[36], be entitled to receive[47] the benefits provided in Section 4 hereof.[43] Employee shall evidence[48] a voluntary termination for Good Reason by written notice[46] to the Company given within[49] 60 days after the date as of which the Employee knows or should reasonably have known an event has occurred which[50] constitutes Good Reason for voluntary termination. Such[28] notice need only[51] identify the Employee and set forth in[52] reasonable detail the facts and circumstances claimed by Employee to constitute Good Reason.[53]

---

[39] Taken together, the elements of section 2 in effect state that both before and after occurrence of a Change in Control the company may terminate the employee for any reason. Section 2 would be much clearer if it were rewritten to say exactly that. One would also need to retain the notification requirements that apply if the company terminates for Cause or the employee terminates for Good Reason.

[40] The phrase "at any time" is redundant (see 10.128).

[41] It's redundant to use both "from" and "after" in this context.

[42] In this context, the phrase "during the term of this Agreement" is redundant (see 13.254).

[43] Stating that certain rights or obligations are as stated elsewhere in a contract is a reliable sign of inefficient structure.

[44] Because this is a template that is to be used in transactions with different employees, it would be best to use gender-neutral language (see 17.11).

[45] This is language of discretion rather than language of obligation, so use *may* instead of *shall have the right to* (see 3.188–.189).

[46] If the notices provision says that all notices must be in writing, elsewhere you can simply use *notice* rather than *written notice*.

[47] Use of *is entitled to* and *receive* obscures who has the duty (see 3.151, 3.152). Use instead language of obligation imposing the duty on the company (see 3.72).

[48] Instead of imposing on the employee an obligation give notice of termination for Good Reason, it would make more sense to have it be a condition.

[49] Use instead "no later than" (see 10.68).

[50] Use *that* instead of *which* (see 12.43).

[51] Using "need only" isn't the clearest way to express a condition (see 3.359).

[52] *Set forth in* is wordy (see 17.19).

[53] What constitutes proper notice could be stated more succinctly.

[54]Any notice given by Employee pursuant to[55] this Section 2 shall[21] be effective[56] five business days after the date it is given by Employee.

3.[57] Definitions[58]

(i)[59] A[60] "Change in Control"[61] shall[21] mean[62]:

(a) a change in control[63] of a nature[64] that would be required to be reported in response to[65] Item 6(e) of Schedule 14A of Regulation 14A promulgated under the Securities Exchange Act of 1934, as amended[66] (the "Exchange Act")[67], or successor provision thereto[68], whether or not the Company is then subject to such[28] reporting requirement;

(b) any "person"[69] (as such[28] term is used in Sections 13(d) and 14(d) of the Exchange Act) is or becomes the "beneficial owner"[69] (as defined in Rule 13d-3 promulgated under the Exchange Act), directly or indirectly, of securities of the Company representing 35% or more of the combined voting power of the Company's then outstanding securities;

(c) the Continuing Directors (as defined in Section 3(v) hereof)[36] cease to constitute a majority of the Company's Board of Directors[70]; provided that[71] such change is the direct or indirect result[72] of a proxy fight[73] and contested election or elections[74] for positions on the Board of Directors; or

---

[54]   With only a few exceptions, all text in the body of the contract should be enumerated (see 4.27). This sentence doesn't constitute one of the exceptions. But more to the point, it would be more efficient to integrate this sentence with the rest of this section.

[55]   Don't use the wordy *pursuant to* (see 17.19).

[56]   It would be clearer to say that termination, rather than the notice, will be effective after five business days.

[57]   Because the defined terms are interrelated, relatively lengthy, and are used in three different sections, it would make sense to collect the definitions as autonomous definitions within a separate section (see 6.86). And because the defined terms don't have a universally accepted meaning, it would be best to place them "on site" rather than tucking them at the end of the contract (see 6.88). So retain the section containing definitions—which is more modest in scope than a conventional definition section (see 6.87)—and move it further back in the contract, but not to the end.

[58]   Add introductory language (see 6.31).

[59]   Nothing is gained by enumerating the autonomous definitions in a section composed entirely of autonomous definitions (see 6.32).

[60]   Omit the indefinite article (see 6.30).

[61]   Put in alphabetical order the autonomous definitions in a section composed entirely of autonomous definitions (see 6.32).

[62]   *Refers to* would be a better definitional verb, because in this case the defined term isn't equivalent to all elements of the definition (see 6.45).

[63]   This defined term refers only to changes in control of the company, so add "of the Company".

[64]   The phrase "of a nature" is redundant.

[65]   Awkward wording.

[66]   The "as amended" is unnecessary (see 13.54).

[67]   Don't include an integrated definition within an autonomous definition (see 6.59).

[68]   The "thereto" is unnecessary.

[69]   The quotation marks are unnecessary.

[70]   Don't use initial capitals in *board of directors* (see 17.30).

[71]   Instead of stating a general proposition, then narrowing it by means of a proviso, it would be more logical to make the proposition narrower. To do that, put first what had been the proviso, but have it begin "as a result of".

[72]   "Direct or indirect result" is an example of needless elaboration (see 1.53). Refer just to "result" or be more specific.

[73]   The reference to "a proxy fight" is redundant, because a proxy fight entails a contested election.

[74]   The formula *one or more Xs* is simpler than *X or Xs* (see 11.7).

(d) the majority of the Continuing Directors (as defined in Section 3(v) hereof)[36] determine in their sole and absolute[75] discretion[76] that there has been a change in control of the Company.

(ii) "Good Reason" shall[21] mean[62] the occurrence of any of the following events[77], except for the occurrence of such an event in connection with the[78] termination or reassignment of Employee's employment by the Company for Cause (as defined in Section 3(iii) hereof)[36], for Disability[79] (as defined in Section 3(iv) hereof)[36] or for death:

(a) the assignment[80] to Employee of employment responsibilities which[50] are not of comparable responsibility and status as the employment responsibilities held by Employee[81] immediately prior to[27] a Change in Control;

(b) a reduction[80] by the Company in Employee's base salary as in effect immediately prior to[27] a Change in Control;

(c) an amendment or modification[80] [82] of the Company's incentive compensation program (except as may be required by applicable law)[83] which[50] affects the terms or administration of the program in a manner adverse to the interest of Employee as compared to the terms and administration of such[28] program immediately prior to[27] a Change in Control;

(d) the Company's requiring[80] Employee to be based anywhere other than within 50 miles of[84] Employee's office location[80] immediately prior to[27] a Change in Control, except for requirements of[85] temporary travel on the Company's business to an extent substantially[86] consistent with Employee's business travel obligations immediately prior to[27] a Change in Control;

(e) except to the extent otherwise required[87] by applicable[88] law, the failure[80] by the Company to continue in effect[89] any benefit[90] or compensation plan, stock ownership plan, stock purchase plan, bonus plan, life insurance plan, health-and-accident plan or disability plan in which Employee is participating immediately prior to[27] a Change in Control (or plans providing Employee with substantially[86] similar benefits), the taking[80] of any action by the Company which[50] would adversely affect Employee's participation in, or materially[91] reduce Employee's benefits under, any

---

[75]   This is rhetorical emphasis (see 1.58).

[76]   Either this is redundant or it represents a problematic attempt to skirt the implied duty of good faith (see 3.255–.257).

[77]   Each element of this definition relates to a Change of Control. It would make those elements more concise if the reference to Change of Control were moved to the introductory language.

[78]   The "the" is extraneous (see 17.35).

[79]   Once section 2 is cleaned up, this is the only place where the concept of disability is referred to. Rather than create a defined term that is used only once, incorporate the definition here and eliminate the defined term.

[80]   Use a verb rather than a "buried verb" (see 17.7).

[81]   Awkward wording.

[82]   The "or modification" is redundant.

[83]   Move this phrase to the beginning of this element, eliminating the parentheses.

[84]   It would be more direct and concise to say "more than 50 miles from".

[85]   Awkward wording.

[86]   *Substantially* is vague and so leaves room for dispute (see 7.42, 7.46). But it's retained in appendix B, as replacing it wherever it occurs would require extensive changes.

[87]   Saying "except as required" would be more concise.

[88]   In references to *applicable law*, the *applicable* is redundant (see 13.33).

[89]   The "in effect" is redundant.

[90]   The following plans all constitute employee benefit plans; revise accordingly.

[91]   The "materially" is ambiguous, as is the "material" used later in the sentence, so use unambiguous language instead (see 9.8).

of such plans or deprive Employee of any material[92] fringe benefit enjoyed by Employee immediately prior to[27] such[28] Change in Control, or the[78] failure by the Company to provide Employee with the number of paid vacation days to which Employee is entitled immediately prior to[27] such[28] Change in Control in accordance with the Company's vacation policy as then in effect; or

(f) the failure[80] by the Company to obtain, as specified in Section 5(i) hereof, an assumption[80] of the obligations of the Company to perform this Agreement by any successor to the Company[93].

(iii) "Cause" shall[21] mean[62] termination by the Company of Employee's employment based upon[94] (a) the willful[95] and continued failure by Employee substantially[86] to perform his[44] duties[96] and obligations (other than any such failure resulting from his incapacity due to physical or mental illness or any such actual or anticipated failure resulting from Employee's termination[80] for Good Reason) or (b) the willful engaging by Employee in misconduct which[50] is materially[97] injurious to the Company, monetarily or otherwise. For purposes of this Section 3(iii)[98], no action or failure to act on Employee's part shall[21] be considered "willful" unless done, or omitted to be done, by Employee in bad faith and without reasonable belief that his action or omission was in the best interests of the Company.

(iv) "Disability" shall mean any physical or mental condition which would qualify Employee for a disability benefit under the Company's long-term disability plan.[99]

(v) "Continuing Director" shall[21] mean any person who is a member of the Board of Directors[70] of the Company[100], while such[28] person is a member of the Board of Directors,[101] who is not an Acquiring Person (as hereinafter defined) or an Affiliate or Associate (as hereinafter defined)[102] of an Acquiring Person, or a representative of an Acquiring Person or of any such Affiliate or Associate, and who (a) was a member of the Board of Directors on the date of this Agreement as first written above[103] or (b) subsequently becomes a member of the Board of Directors, if such[28] person's initial nomination for election or initial election to the Board of Directors is recommended or approved by a majority of the[104] Continuing Directors[105]. For purposes of this Section 3(v): "Acquiring Person"[106] shall[21] mean any "person"[69] (as such[28] term is used in Sections 13(d) and 14(d) of the Exchange Act) who or which, together with all Affiliates and Associates[102] of such[28] person, is the "beneficial owner" (as defined in Rule 13d-3 promulgated under the Exchange Act) of 20% or more of the shares of Common Stock[107] of the Company[100] then outstanding, but shall[21] not include the Company, any subsidiary of the Company or any employee benefit plan of the Company or of any subsidiary of the Company or any entity holding shares of Common Stock[107] organized,

---

[92] See note 91.

[93] The "to the Company" is redundant.

[94] Because "Cause" is used only in the phrase "termination for Cause", there's no need to refer to termination when defining "Cause".

[95] Don't use *willful*—it's ambiguous (see 13.896).

[96] The reference to "duty" is redundant (see 3.172–.173).

[97] The "materially" is ambiguous, so use unambiguous language instead (see 9.8).

[98] Say instead that it's for purposes of this definition.

[99] This defined term is unnecessary (see note 79).

[100] Use the possessive (see 17.28).

[101] The immediately preceding phrase is unnecessary.

[102] Don't make these defined terms. Instead, say in parentheses that they have the meaning given them in the statute.

[103] "First written above" is archaic and imprecise (see 5.27).

[104] Insert *then*.

[105] Reverse the order of the *(a)* and *(b)* enumerated clauses, to make clear that the modifiers after the *(b)* enumerated clause don't also modify the *(a)* enumerated clause (see 12.10).

[106] State this as a separate definition.

[107] Don't use initial capitals (see 17.33).

appointed or established for, or pursuant to[55] the terms of, any such plan; and "Affiliate" and "Associate" shall have the respective meanings ascribed to such[28] terms in Rule 12b-2 promulgated under the Exchange Act.[108]

4. Benefits upon Termination under Section 2(ii)(c)[109]

(i)[110] Upon the termination[80] (voluntary or involuntary) of the employment of Employee pursuant to Section 2(ii)(c) hereof,[111] Employee shall be entitled to receive[47] the benefits specified in this Section 4.[112] The amounts due to Employee under subparagraphs (a), (b) and (c) of this Section 4(i)[112] shall be paid[113] to Employee not later than one business day prior to[27] the date that[114] the[78] termination of Employee's employment becomes effective. All benefits to Employee pursuant to this Section 4(i) shall[21] be subject to any applicable payroll or other taxes required by law to be withheld.

(a) The Company shall pay to Employee any and all[115] amounts payable[116] to Employee pursuant to[55] any standard or general[117] severance policy of the Company or its Board of Directors;[118]

(b) In lieu of[119] any further base salary payments to Employee for periods subsequent to[120] the date that the termination of Employee's employment becomes effective, the Company shall pay as severance pay to Employee a lump-sum cash[121] amount equal to twenty-four (24)[122] times the Employee's monthly base salary (as in effect in the month preceding the month in which the termination becomes effective or as in effect in the month preceding the Change in Control, whichever is higher);

(c) The Company shall also pay to Employee all legal fees and expenses incurred by Employee as a result of such[28] termination of employment (including all fees and expenses, if any, incurred by Employee in seeking to obtain or enforce any right or benefit provided to Employee by this Agreement whether by arbitration or otherwise); and

(d) Any and all[115] contracts, agreements or arrangements[123] between the Company and Employee prohibiting or restricting the Employee from owning, operating, participating in, or providing employment or consulting services to, any business or company competitive with[124] the Company at any time or during any period after the date the termination of Employee's employment

---

[108] Delete the definitions of *Affiliate* and *Associate* (see note 102).

[109] It's odd to include a cross-reference in a section heading.

[110] The enumeration in this section is unhelpful—because the *(i)* hierarchy has the same layout as the *(a)* hierarchy, the reader cannot determine based on layout alone which takes precedence.

[111] State what kind of termination entitles the employee to benefits, rather than relying on a cross-reference.

[112] Instead of referring indirectly to the benefits, say what they are.

[113] Use the active rather than the passive voice to express an obligation (see 3.142).

[114] Using "the date that" is redundant.

[115] Eliminate redundancy by using one or other word in this traditional couplet (see 1.38).

[116] *Payable* is a feature of "buried-actor policies" (see 3.309). Rephrase this to make clear that it is a duty that is being referred to.

[117] The word "standard" adds nothing.

[118] It's sufficient to refer to a severance policy of the Company.

[119] This is a wordy phrase; replace it with *instead of* (see 17.19).

[120] This is a wordy phrase; use instead *after* (see 17.19).

[121] The words "lump-sum cash" are redundant (see 13.385).

[122] For numbers over ten, use digits only (see 14.13).

[123] Eliminate the redundancy by using only "agreements" (see 1.38).

[124] *Competitive* means "likely to succeed in competition"; use instead "that competes with" (see 13.149).

becomes effective[125], shall be deemed terminated[126] and of no further force or effect[127] as of the date[128] the[78] termination of Employee's employment becomes effective, to the extent, but only to the extent[129], such[28] contracts, agreements or arrangements so prohibit or restrict the Employee; provided that[130] the foregoing[131] provisions shall[21] not constitute a license or right to use any proprietary[132] information of the Company and shall[21] in no way affect any such contracts, agreements or arrangements insofar as they relate to nondisclosure and nonuse of proprietary information of the Company notwithstanding the fact that[133] such nondisclosure and nonuse may[134] prohibit[135] or restrict the Employee in certain competitive[136] activities.

(ii) Employee shall[21] not be required to mitigate the amount of any payment provided for in this Section 4 by seeking other employment or otherwise.[137] The amount of any payment or benefit provided in this Section 4 shall[21] not be reduced by any compensation earned by Employee as a result of any employment by another employer or from any other source.

(iii)[138] In the event that[139] any payment or benefit received or to be received by Employee in connection with a Change in Control of the Company[140] or termination of Employee's employment (whether payable[141] pursuant to[55] the terms of this Agreement or pursuant to[55] any other plan, contract, agreement or arrangement[142] with the Company, with any person whose actions result in a Change in Control of the Company[140] or with any person constituting a member of an "affiliated group" as defined in Section 280G(d)(5) of the Internal Revenue Code of 1986, as amended[66] (the "Code"), with the Company or with any person whose actions result in a Change in Control of the Company[140] [143] (collectively, the "Total Payments"[144])) would be subject to the excise tax imposed by Section 4999 of the Code or any interest, penalties or additions to tax with respect to such[28] excise tax (such excise tax, together with any such interest, penalties or additions to tax, are collectively referred to as[145] the "Excise Tax"), then Employee shall be entitled to receive[47] from the Company an additional cash payment (a "Gross-Up Payment") in an amount such that after payment by Employee of all taxes (including any interest, penalties or additions to tax imposed with respect to such taxes),

---

[125]   Make this more concise.

[126]   *Deem* serves to establish a legal fiction. Here, the parties don't need to rely on a legal fiction; they can instead just say that the contracts in question will terminate (see 13.216).

[127]   The phrase "and of no further force or effect" is redundant.

[128]   Say instead "when".

[129]   Eliminate the rhetorical emphasis—say "but only to the extent" (see 1.58).

[130]   *Provided that* is an imprecise way to signal the relationship between two conjoined contract provisions (see 13.663). In this case, the employee could simply acknowledge, in a separate provision rather than a proviso, the limitations in question.

[131]   Make it clearer what is being referred to (see 7.25).

[132]   Because the concern here is confidentiality, use the word "confidential" instead of "proprietary" (see 13.660).

[133]   Saying "notwithstanding the fact that" is wordy; use instead "even if".

[134]   This "may" is unnecessary (see 3.459).

[135]   Nondisclosure or nonuse can't prohibit anything—"prevent" would be a better word.

[136]   *Competitive* is the wrong word to use, as it means "likely to succeed in competition" (see 13.149).

[137]   Express this more concisely.

[138]   Carve out the rest of this section as a separate section with the heading "Gross-up Payment."

[139]   This is a wordy phrase; instead use "if" (see 17.19).

[140]   The defined term is *Change of Control* and it's defined with respect to the Company, so "of the Company" is superfluous (see 6.118).

[141]   *Payable* is a potentially confusing word (see note 116) so it's best to avoid using it. Here, it can simply be omitted.

[142]   Eliminate the redundancy by using just "agreement" (see 1.38).

[143]   The immediately preceding phrase is superfluous, in that it also occurs earlier in the parenthetical.

[144]   This provision would be easier to read if *Total Payments* were defined using an autonomous definition rather than an integrated definition, and if a more informative defined term were used.

[145]   Wordy; replace everything in these parentheses up to this point with "collectively".

including any Excise Tax, imposed upon the Gross-Up Payment, Employee would retain an amount of the Gross-Up Payment equal to the Excise Tax imposed upon[146] the Total Payments, as determined in accordance with the provisions of[147] this Section 4(iii).

(a) All determinations required to be made[148] under this Section 4(iii), including whether a Gross-Up Payment is required and the amount of such[28] Gross-Up Payment, shall be made by[149] the independent accounting firm retained by the Company[150] on the date of the Change in Control (the "Accounting Firm"[151]). The Accounting Firm shall[149] provide detailed supporting calculations of its determination to both the Company and the Employee within[49] 15 business days of the Employment Termination Date[152], or at such earlier time as is requested by the Company[153]. For purposes of determining the amount of any tax pursuant to[55] this Section 4(iii), the Employee's tax rate shall be deemed[21] to be the highest statutory marginal state and Federal tax rate (on a combined basis and including the Employee's share of F.I.C.A. and Medicare taxes) then in effect.

(b) Employee shall in good faith[154] cooperate with the Accounting Firm in making[155] the determination of[80] whether a Gross-Up Payment is required, including but not limited to[156] providing the Accounting Firm with information or documentation as reasonably requested by the Accounting Firm[157]. A determination by the Accounting Firm regarding whether a Gross-Up Payment is required and the amount of such[28] Gross-Up Payment shall[21] be conclusive and binding upon[80] the Employee and the Company for all purposes[158].

(c) A Gross-Up Payment required to be made pursuant to this Section 4(iii)[159] shall be paid[113] to Employee within[49] 30 days of a final determination[160] by the Accounting Firm that the Gross-Up Payment is required. Employee and Company shall report all amounts paid to Employee on their respective tax returns consistent with the determination of the Accounting Firm.

(d) The Company and the Employee shall promptly deliver to each other copies of any written communications, and summaries of any oral communications, with any tax authority regarding the applicability[80] of Section 280G or 4999 of the Code to any portion of the Total Payments. In the event of any controversy with the Internal Revenue Service or other tax authority regarding the applicability of Section 280G or 4999 of the Code to any portion of the Total Payments[161], Company shall have the right[45], exercisable in its sole discretion,[76] to control the resolution of such controversy at its own expense. Employee and the Company shall in good faith[154] cooperate in the resolution[80] of such[28] controversy.

---

[146] Use "on"; *upon* is best used to refer only to the simultaneous occurrence of events.

[147] The phrase "the provisions of" is redundant.

[148] The phrase "to be made" is redundant.

[149] Don't use "shall"—the Accounting Firm isn't a party and so isn't assuming any obligations (see 3.149).

[150] Make it an obligation of the company to retain an accounting firm.

[151] This defined term doesn't add enough value to offset the cost of adding another defined term to the contract (see 6.115).

[152] This term isn't defined.

[153] The passive voice is unhelpful here (see 3.11). A good alternative to using the active voice would be to use "unless".

[154] The reference to good faith is redundant, as good faith is inherent in the notion of parties cooperating (see 13.552).

[155] This construction suggests, inappropriately, that the employee will be involved in "making the determination."

[156] Omit "but not limited to" (see 13.353).

[157] Use the active voice (see 3.11).

[158] The phrase "for all purposes" is unnecessary.

[159] It would be better to say "any Gross-Up Payment".

[160] In this context it wouldn't be feasible to use a verb rather than the buried verb *determination* (see 17.7), in that "determine finally" would convey a different meaning than "final determination".

[161] Needless repetition; instead say "in that regard".

(e) If the Internal Revenue Service or any tax authority makes a final determination[160] that a greater Excise Tax should be imposed upon the Total Payments than is determined by the Accounting Firm or reflected in the Employee's tax return pursuant to[55] this Section, the Employee shall be entitled to receive[47] from the Company the full Gross-Up Payment calculated on the basis of the amount of Excise Tax determined to be payable[116] by such[28] tax authority. That amount shall be paid[113] to the Participant within[49] 30 days of the date of such[28] final determination[160] by the relevant tax authority[162].

5. <u>Successors and Binding Agreement</u>[163]

(i) The Company will[164] require any successor (whether direct or indirect, by purchase, merger, consolidation or otherwise[165] to all or substantially[86] all of the business and/or assets[166] of the Company[100]), by agreement in form and substance[167] satisfactory to Employee, to expressly[168] assume and agree to perform this Agreement[169] in the same manner and to the same extent that the Company would be required to perform it if no such succession had taken place. Failure[80] of the Company to obtain such[170] agreement prior to[27] the effectiveness of[80] any such succession shall[21] be a breach of this Agreement and shall[21] entitle Employee[171] to compensation from the Company in the same amount and on the same terms as Employee would be entitled hereunder if employee terminated Employee's employment after a Change in Control for Good Reason, except that for purposes of implementing the foregoing[131], the date on which any such succession becomes effective shall[21] be deemed the date that the termination of Employee's employment becomes effective.[172] As used in this Agreement, "Company" shall mean the Company and any successor to its business and/or assets[166] which executes and delivers[173] the agreement provided for in this Section 5(i) or which otherwise becomes bound by all the terms and provisions[174] of this Agreement by operation of law.[175]

[176](ii) This Agreement is personal to Employee[177], and Employee may not[178] assign or transfer any part[179] of Employee's rights or duties hereunder, or any compensation due to Employee hereunder, to any other person.[180] Notwithstanding the foregoing,[181] this Agreement shall inure to the

---

[162] The subsection would be more concise if the essence of the second sentence were incorporated into the first sentence.

[163] Split this into two sections.

[164] This is language of obligation; use *shall* (see 3.72).

[165] This is where the closing parenthesis should be, not after "Company".

[166] Regarding *and/or*, see 11.86. Rather than saying "the business or assets or both," a simpler fix would be to omit "business" (see 1.38).

[167] *In form and substance* is redundant (see 13.306).

[168] Instead of using "expressly", state that the agreement has to be in writing.

[169] One doesn't assume or perform an agreement but rather obligations under that agreement.

[170] Use instead "any such".

[171] Use of "shall entitle" is a wordy and unclear way of expressing an obligation. Use instead language of obligation imposing the duty on the company (see 3.72).

[172] The preceding sentence is unnecessary, as the definition of "Good Reason" includes breach by the company of its obligations under this subsection. Move to the definition of "Good Reason" the part stating when termination for Good Reason will be deemed to have occurred.

[173] Use "enters into" instead of "executes and delivers" (see 13.278).

[174] Use "terms" instead of "terms and provisions" (see 13.807).

[175] This sentence is unnecessary.

[176] This is an appropriate place to put the "Definitions" section.

[177] To make this provision easier to read, make the preceding language a separate sentence.

[178] Because *may not* is ambiguous, *shall not* is a better choice for language of prohibition (see 3.279).

[179] The word "part" is redundant.

[180] For an explanation of the alternative language used in appendix B, see Kenneth A. Adams, *Rethinking the "No Assignment" Provision*, Adams on Contract Drafting (20 Nov. 2012), http://www.adamsdrafting.com/rethinking-the-no-assignment-provision/.

[181] Use instead "except that", and join the second sentence to the first.

benefit of and be enforceable by[182] Employee's personal or legal representatives, executors, administrators, heirs, distributees, devisees and legatees[183].

6. <u>Arbitration</u>.[184]Any dispute or controversy arising under or in connection with[185] this Agreement shall be settled[157] exclusively by arbitration in the Borough of Manhattan, in accordance with the applicable rules of the American Arbitration Association then in effect. Judgment may be entered[186] on the arbitrator's award in any court having jurisdiction.

7. <u>Modification; Waiver</u>. No provisions of this Agreement may be modified, waived or discharged[187] unless such[28] waiver, modification or discharge is agreed to in a writing signed by Employee and such[188] officer as may[134] be specifically[189] designated by the Board of Directors[70] of the Company. No waiver by either party hereto[190] at any time[40] of any breach by the other party hereto[190] of, or compliance with, any condition or provision of this Agreement to be performed[191] by such other party shall be deemed[192] a waiver of similar or dissimilar[193] provisions or conditions at the same or at any prior or subsequent time.[194]

8. <u>Notice</u>.[195] All notices, requests, demands and all other communications required or permitted by either party to the other party by this Agreement (including, without limitation, any notice of termination of employment and any notice of intention to arbitrate) shall be in writing and shall be deemed to have been duly given when delivered personally or received by certified or registered mail, return receipt requested, postage prepaid, at the address of the other party, as first written above (directed to the attention of the Board of Directors and Corporate Secretary in the case of the Company). Either party hereto may change its address for purposes of this Section 8 by giving 15 days' prior notice to the other party hereto.

9. <u>Severability</u>.[196] If any term or provision[197] of this Agreement or the application hereof[198] to any person or circumstances shall[21] to any extent be invalid or unenforceable, the remainder of this Agreement or the application of such[28] term or provision[197] to persons or circumstances other than

---

[182] Because this is an exception to a restriction on transfer, it's confusing to use wording that evokes the pointless traditional successors-and-assigns provision (see 13.449).

[183] This string of nouns is confusing; express instead the underlying concept (see 1.48).

[184] In appendix B, this section is replaced by one based on language proposed in Kenneth A. Adams, *The AAA Standard Arbitration Clause: Room for Improvement*, New York Law Journal, 9 Mar. 2010.

[185] "Arising under"—or rather "arising out of"—is sufficient (see 13.37).

[186] This instance of the passive voice is unobjectionable (see 3.22).

[187] It would be simpler to refer to amendment rather than modification, and the concept of discharge is both unnecessary and overbroad. And rather than expressing this sentence as a prohibition, it would make more sense to address effectiveness of any amendment or waiver. (Regarding confusion between obligations and conditions, see 3.356.)

[188] In this context, use "any" instead of "such".

[189] Delete "specifically"—it's an example of rhetorical emphasis (see 1.58).

[190] The "hereto" is unnecessary, as it would be unreasonable to think that without it this would constitute a reference to parties to some other agreement (see 2.110).

[191] You don't *breach*, *comply with*, or *perform* a condition, you *satisfy* it.

[192] *Deem* serves to establish a legal fiction (see 13.216). Here, no legal fiction is required.

[193] "Similar or dissimilar" is needless elaboration (see 1.53).

[194] This sentence is unnecessarily wordy and legalistic.

[195] In appendix B, this section is replaced by one developed for the author's automated confidentiality-agreement template. It is beyond the scope of this appendix B to address all the drafting issues raised by this section.

[196] In appendix B, this section is replaced by a severability section developed by the author. See *Kenneth A. Adams, OK, Let's Try That Again: Revising My Severability Provision*, Adams on Contract Drafting (3 Feb. 2017), http://www.adamsdrafting.com/revisiting-my-severability-provision/. It's not clear whether this kind of severability provision is helpful in this context, but that analysis is beyond the scope of these annotations.

[197] The word "term" is redundant (see 1.38).

[198] The phrase "or the application hereof" is redundant.

those as to which it is held invalid or unenforceable[199] shall[21] not be affected thereby, and each term and provision[197] of this Agreement shall[21] be valid and enforceable[200] to the fullest extent permitted by law.

10. <u>Counterparts</u>. This Agreement may be executed[201] in several counterparts, each of which shall[21] be deemed an original, but all of which together shall[21] constitute one and the same[202] instrument.

11. <u>Governing Law</u>.[203] This Agreement has been executed and delivered in the State of New York and shall in all respects be governed by, and construed and enforced in accordance with, the laws of the State of New York, including all matters of construction, validity and performance, and without taking into consideration the conflict of law provisions of such state.

12. <u>Effect of Agreement; Entire Agreement</u>. The Company and the Employee understand and agree that[204] this Agreement is intended[205] to reflect their agreement only with respect to payments and benefits upon termination in certain cases[206] and is not intended[205] to create any obligation on the part of either party to continue employment. This Agreement supersedes any and all[115] other oral or written agreements or policies made relating to the subject matter hereof[207] and constitutes the entire agreement of the parties relating to the subject matter hereof; provided that[208] this Agreement shall[21] not supersede or limit in any way[209] Employee's rights under any benefit plan, program or arrangements[210] in accordance with their terms[211].

IN WITNESS WHEREOF, the parties hereto have caused this Agreement to be executed, all as of the date first written above.[212]

RMA WIDGETS, INC.[213]

By   _____

Janet Doe
Its Vice President, Human Resources

             [214]
_____

Employee, _____

---

[199] Eliminate the redundancy by using just "enforceable" (see 1.38).

[200] "Valid" is redundant.

[201] Language of policy (see 3.305) makes more sense here than language of discretion.

[202] Eliminate redundancy by deleting "the same" (see 1.38).

[203] In appendix B, this section is replaced by one developed by the author. See the following blog post and two others linked to in it: Kenneth A. Adams, *Simplifying Governing-Law Provisions, Part 3 ("Governs" and the Alternatives)*, Adams on Contract Drafting (15 July 2015), http://www.adamsdrafting.com/simplifying-governing-law-provisions-part-3-governs/. It is beyond the scope of this appendix B to address all the drafting issues raised by this section.

[204] This is throat-clearing (see 3.25).

[205] This should be language of policy (see 3.305), not language of intention (see 3.442).

[206] This concept is adequately addressed in the recitals.

[207] Be restrained in using *here-* and *there-* words (see 13.349).

[208] Use instead "except that" (see 13.663–.666).

[209] Delete "in any way"—it's rhetorical emphasis (see 1.58).

[210] The term "benefit plan" is by itself sufficiently broad.

[211] The phrase "in accordance with their terms" is superfluous.

[212] This is a traditional concluding clause (see 5.19–.20). Use instead the *MSCD* form of concluding clause for when the date of the agreement is stated in the introductory clause (see 5.4).

[213] Use the *MSCD* form of signature block for companies (see 5.30 and sample 8).

[214] Use the *MSCD* form of signature block for individuals (see 5.38 and sample 8).

APPENDIX B: AFTER

TERMINATION AGREEMENT

This termination agreement is dated _____ 20__ and is between RMA WIDGETS, INC., a Delaware corporation ("**RMA**"), and_____, an individual (the "**Employee**").

The Employee is an employee of RMA. To give the Employee additional incentive to remain an employee of RMA, RMA wants to specify what payments, if any, RMA will be required to make to the Employee if RMA ceases to employ the Employee in the context of a change of control of RMA.

RMA and the Employee therefore agree as follows:

     1.   **Term.** The initial term of this agreement ends at midnight at the end of 31 December 20__ [year following year of this agreement]. The term of this agreement (consisting of the initial term and any one-year extensions in accordance with this section 1) will automatically be extended by consecutive one-year terms unless no later than one year before any such extension begins RMA notifies the Employee that it does not wish to extend this agreement. If a Change of Control occurs, then (1) any notice that RMA previously delivered in accordance with this section 1 that would preclude any extension commencing after the Change of Control will be deemed ineffective and (2) the term of this agreement (consisting of the initial term and any one-year extensions in accordance with this section 1) will automatically be extended by two years and will then terminate without the possibility of automatic extension.

     2.   **Termination of Employment.** Each of RMA and the Employee may terminate the Employee's employment with RMA at any time and for any reason, except that (1) for RMA to terminate the Employee for Cause after a Change of Control occurs, RMA must notify the Employee of that termination and specify in reasonable detail the conduct of the Employee constituting the basis for termination for Cause, and (2) for the Employee to terminate for Good Reason after a Change of Control occurs, the Employee must, no later than 60 days after the date that the Employee knew or should reasonably have known of the one or more events or circumstances constituting the basis for termination for Good Reason, notify RMA of the Employee's termination for Good Reason and specify those events or circumstances in reasonable detail, and the Employee's termination will be effective five business days after the date that notice from RMA or the Employee, as applicable, is delivered.

     3.   **Benefits on Termination.** (a) If after a Change of Control RMA terminates the Employee without Cause or the Employee terminates for Good Reason, then RMA shall pay the Employee, no later than one business day before termination of the Employee's employment becomes effective, the following amounts, subject to any applicable payroll or other taxes that RMA is required by law to withhold:

(1)   all amounts that RMA is required to pay the Employee under any general RMA severance policy;

(2)   as severance instead of any further base salary for periods after the date that termination of the Employee's employment becomes effective, an amount equal to 24 times the Employee's monthly base salary (as in effect in the month preceding the month in which the termination becomes effective or as in effect in the month preceding the Change of Control, whichever is greater); and

(3)   all legal fees and expenses that the Employee incurs as a result of termination of the Employee's employment, including any fees and expenses incurred by the Employee in seeking to obtain or enforce, including by arbitration, any right or benefit under this agreement.

(b)   If after a Change of Control RMA terminates the Employee without Cause or the Employee terminates for Good Reason, then all agreements between RMA and the Employee prohibiting or restricting the Employee from owning, operating, participating in, or providing employment or consulting services to, after termination of the Employee's employment becomes effective, any business that competes with RMA will automatically terminate when termination of the Employee's employment becomes effective, but only to the extent those contracts so prohibit or restrict the Employee. The Employee acknowledges that nothing in this section 3(b) constitutes a license to use any confidential information of RMA or affects any provisions of any such agreement regarding nondisclosure or nonuse of confidential information of RMA, even if any such nondisclosure and nonuse prevents the Employee from competing with RMA or interferes with the Employee's ability to do so.

(c)   The Employee will not be required to mitigate the amount of any payment under this section 3, including by seeking other employment. The amount of any payment or benefit under this section 3 will not be reduced by any compensation the Employee earns from any other employment or from any other source.

4.   **Gross-Up Payment.** (a) If any Employee Change-of-Control Payment would be subject to the excise tax imposed by section 4999 of the Code or any interest, penalties, or additions to tax with respect to that excise tax (collectively, the "**Excise Tax**"), then RMA shall pay the Employee an additional amount of cash (a "**Gross-Up Payment**") such that after the Employee pays all taxes (including any interest, penalties, or additions to tax imposed with respect to those taxes), including any Excise Tax, imposed on the Gross-Up Payment, the Employee would retain an amount of the Gross-Up Payment equal to the Excise Tax imposed on the Total Payments, as determined in accordance with this section 4.

(b)   On the day a Change of Control occurs, RMA shall retain an independent accounting firm. RMA shall cause the accounting firm to make all determinations required under this section 4 (including whether RMA is required to make a Gross-Up Payment and the amount of that Gross-Up Payment) and to provide detailed supporting calculations of each such determination to both RMA and the Employee no later than 15 business days after the date of termination of the Employee's employment, unless RMA requests that it does so sooner. For purposes of determining the amount of any tax in accordance with this section 4, the Employee's tax rate will be deemed to be the highest statutory marginal state and Federal tax rate (on a combined basis and including the Employee's share of FICA and Medicare taxes) then in effect.

(c)   The Employee shall cooperate with the accounting firm as it determines whether a Gross-Up Payment is required, including by providing the accounting firm with any information or documentation that the accounting firm requests. The Employee and RMA will be bound by any determination by the accounting firm regarding whether a Gross-Up Payment is required and the amount of any Gross-Up Payment.

(d)   RMA shall pay any Gross-Up Payment no later than 30 days after the accounting firm determines that RMA is required to make that Gross-Up Payment. The Employee and RMA shall report any Gross-Up Payment on their respective tax returns consistent with the determination of the accounting firm.

(e)   RMA and the Employee shall promptly deliver to each other copies of any written communications, and summaries of any oral communications, with any tax authority regarding whether section 280G or 4999 of the Code applies to any portion of the Total Payments. In the event of any controversy with the Internal Revenue Service or any other tax authority in that regard, RMA may elect to control, at its own expense, resolution of that controversy, and the Employee and RMA shall cooperate in resolving that controversy.

(f)   If the Internal Revenue Service or any other tax authority makes a final determination that the Excise Tax to be imposed on the Total Payments is greater than was determined by the accounting firm or reflected in the Employee's tax return in accordance with this section 4, RMA shall, no later than 30 days after it receives notice of that determination, pay the Employee any additional amount required to ensure that RMA has paid the Employee a Gross-Up Payment calculated on the basis of the amount of Excise Tax that the tax authority determines must be paid.

5.   **Successors.** By means of a written agreement satisfactory to the Employee, RMA shall require any successor (whether direct or indirect or by purchase, merger, consolidation, or otherwise) to all or substantially all of RMA's assets to assume RMA's obligations under this agreement and agree to perform them in the same manner and to the same extent that RMA would have been required to if that succession had not taken place.

6.   **Definitions.** For purposes of this agreement, the following definitions apply:

"**Acquiring Person**" means any person (as that term is used in sections 13(d) and 14(d) of the Exchange Act) that, together with all affiliates and associates (as those terms are defined in Rule 12b-2 promulgated under the Exchange Act) of that person, is the beneficial owner (as that term is defined in Rule 13d-3 promulgated under the Exchange Act) of 20% or more of the shares of RMA common stock then outstanding, but does not include RMA, any RMA subsidiary, any employee benefit plan of RMA or of RMA subsidiary, or any entity holding shares of RMA common stock that is organized, appointed, or established for, or in accordance with the terms of, any such plan.

"**Cause**" refers to (1) the Employee's intentional and continued failure to substantially perform the Employee's duties as employee (other than any such failure resulting from any physical or mental condition of the Employee or any such actual or anticipated failure resulting from the Employee's having terminated for Good Reason) or (2) the Employee's engaging in intentional misconduct that, from the perspective of a reasonable person in RMA's position, is sufficiently harmful to RMA, monetarily or otherwise, as to merit attention, with any action or failure to act on the Employee's part not being considered intentional for purposes of clauses (1) and (2) of this definition if that action or failure to act was in good faith or if the Employee reasonably believed that the action or failure to act was in the best interests of RMA.

"**Change of Control**" refers to occurrence of any of the following events and circumstances:

(1)   a change of control of RMA that falls within the scope of item 6(e) of Schedule 14A of Regulation 14A promulgated under the Exchange Act, or any successor provision, whether or not RMA is then subject to that reporting requirement;

(2)   any person (as that word is used in sections 13(d) and 14(d) of the Exchange Act) is or becomes the beneficial owner (as defined in Rule 13d-3 promulgated under the Exchange Act), directly or indirectly, of securities of RMA representing 35% or more of the combined voting power of RMA's then outstanding securities;

(3)   as the direct or indirect result of one or more contested elections for positions on RMA's board of directors, the Continuing Directors cease to constitute a majority of RMA's board of directors; and

(4)   a majority of the Continuing Directors determine that a change of control of RMA has occurred.

"**Code**" means the Internal Revenue Code of 1986.

"**Continuing Director**" means any person who (1) is a member of RMA's board of directors, (2) is not at the same time an Acquiring Person or an affiliate or associate (as those terms are defined in Rule 12b-2 promulgated under the Exchange Act) of an Acquiring Person, or a representative of an Acquiring Person or of any such affiliate or associate, and (3) either (A) became a member of RMA's board of directors after the date of this agreement, if that person's initial nomination for election or initial appointment to RMA's board of directors was recommended or approved by a majority of the then Continuing Directors, or (B) was a member of RMA's board of directors on the date of this agreement.

"**Employee Change-of-Control Payment**" means any payment or benefit received or to be received by the Employee in connection with a Change of Control or termination of the Employee's employment (whether under this agreement or any other plan or agreement with RMA, any person whose actions result in a Change of Control, or any person constituting a member of an affiliated group, as that term is defined in section 280G(d)(5) of the Code).

"**Exchange Act**" means the Securities Exchange Act of 1934.

"**Good Reason**" refers to occurrence of any of the following events after a Change of Control (or, in the case of clause (8), in connection with a Change of Control), except in connection with termination or reassignment of the Employee by RMA for Cause or in connection with the Employee's death or any physical or mental condition of the Employee that would permit the Employee to qualify for a disability benefit under RMA's long-term disability plan:

(1)   RMA assigns the Employee employment responsibilities that, when compared to the Employee's responsibilities immediately before the Change of Control, are commensurate with reduced status or seniority or both;

(2)   RMA reduces the Employee's base salary to below what it was immediately before the Change of Control;

(3)   except as required by law, RMA amends RMA's incentive compensation program so as to affect the terms or administration of the program in a manner adverse to the interest of the Employee, as compared to the terms and administration of that program immediately before the Change of Control;

(4)   except for purposes of temporary travel on RMA's business to an extent substantially consistent with such travel by the Employee during the period immediately before the Change of Control, RMA requires the Employee to be based more than 50 miles from where the Employee's office was located immediately before the Change of Control;

(5)   except as required by law, RMA fails to continue any compensation plan, stock ownership plan, stock purchase plan, bonus plan, life insurance plan, health-and-accident plan, disability plan, or other employee benefit plan in which the Employee is participating immediately before the Change of Control, or fails to implement plans providing the Employee with substantially similar benefits;

(6)   except as required by law, and in each case to an extent that, from the perspective of a reasonable person in the Employee's position, is sufficiently important to merit attention, RMA takes any action that would adversely affect the Employee's participation in, or reduce the Employee's benefits under, any such plans or deprive the Employee of any fringe benefit enjoyed by the Employee immediately before the Change of Control;

(7)   except as required by law, RMA fails to provide the Employee with the number of paid vacation days to which the Employee was entitled immediately before the Change of Control in accordance with RMA's vacation policy as then in effect; and

(8)   RMA breaches its obligations under section 5, in which case RMA will be deemed to have terminated the Employee for Good Reason on the date on which the succession in question became effective.

7.   **Assignment.** This agreement is personal to the Employee. The Employee shall not transfer to any other person, other than by will or intestate succession, (1) any discretion granted under this agreement, (2) any right to satisfy a condition under this agreement, (3) any remedy under this agreement, or (4) any obligation imposed under this agreement.

8.   **Arbitration.** As the exclusive means of initiating adversarial proceedings to resolve any dispute arising out of this agreement or termination of the Employee's employment with RMA, a party may demand that the dispute be resolved by arbitration administered by the American Arbitration Association in accordance with its commercial arbitration rules, and each party hereby consents to any such dispute being so resolved. Judgment on any award rendered in any such arbitration may be entered in any court having jurisdiction.

9.   **Modification; Waiver.** No amendment of this agreement will be effective unless it is in writing and signed by the parties. No waiver under this agreement will be effective unless it is in writing and signed by the party granting the waiver (in the case of RMA, by an individual authorized by RMA's board of directors to sign the waiver). A waiver granted on one occasion will not operate as a waiver on other occasions.

10.   **Notices.** (a) For a notice or other communication under this agreement to be valid, it must be in writing and delivered (1) by hand, (2) by a national transportation company (with all fees prepaid), or (3) by registered or certified mail, return receipt requested and postage prepaid

(b)   Subject to section 10(d), a valid notice or other communication under this agreement will be effective when received by the party to which it is addressed. It will be deemed to have been received as follows:

(1)   if it is delivered by hand, delivered by a national transportation company (with all fees prepaid), or delivered by registered or certified mail, return receipt requested and postage prepaid, upon receipt as indicated by the date on the signed receipt; and

(2)   if the party to which it is addressed rejects or otherwise refuses to accept it, or if it cannot be delivered because of a change in address for which no notice was given, then upon that rejection, refusal, or inability to deliver.

(c)   For a notice or other communication to a party under this agreement to be valid, it must be addressed using the information specified below for that party or any other information specified by that party in a notice in accordance with this section 10.

To RMA: RMA Widgets, Inc
                    500 Third Avenue
                    Suite 400
                    New York, NY 10022
                    Attention: Board of Directors and Corporate Secretary

To the Employee: [Name]
                    [Address]

(d)   If a notice or other communication addressed to a party is received after 5:00 p.m. on a business day at the location specified in the address for that party, or on a day that is not a business day, then the notice will be deemed received at 9:00 a.m. on the next business day.

11. **Severability.** The parties acknowledge that if a dispute between the parties arises out of this agreement or termination of the Employee's employment with RMA, they would want the court to interpret this agreement as follows:

(1)   with respect to any provision that it holds to be unenforceable, by modifying that provision to the minimum extent necessary to make it enforceable or, if that modification is not permitted by law, by disregarding that provision;

(2)   if an unenforceable provision is modified or disregarded in accordance with this section 11, by holding that the rest of the agreement will remain in effect as written;

(3)   by holding that any unenforceable provision will remain as written in any circumstances other than those in which the provision is held to be unenforceable; and

(4)   if modifying or disregarding the unenforceable provision would result in failure of an essential purpose of this agreement, by holding the entire agreement unenforceable.

12. **Counterparts.** If the parties sign this agreement in several counterparts, each will be deemed an original but all counterparts together will constitute one instrument.

13. **Governing Law.** New York law governs all adversarial proceedings brought by one party against the other party arising out of this agreement or termination of the Employee's employment with RMA.

14. **Scope of Agreement; Entire Agreement.** This agreement does not grant the Employee any rights with respect to continued employment by RMA. This agreement constitutes the entire understanding between the parties with respect to the subject matter of this agreement and supersedes all other agreements, whether written or oral, between the parties, except that this agreement does not supersede or limit the Employee's rights under any benefit plan.

The parties are signing this agreement on the date stated in the introductory clause.

RMA WIDGETS, INC.

By: _____

Janet Doe
Vice President, Human Resources

_____

[EMPLOYEE]

The works listed below are cited more than once in this manual, using a shortened form of citation.

Black's Law Dictionary (10th ed. 2014).

Butterick, Matthew, *Typography for Lawyers* (2d ed. 2015).

The Chicago Manual of Style (17th ed. 2017).

Committee on Mergers and Acquisitions, Section of Business Law, American Bar Association, I *Model Stock Purchase Agreement* (2d ed. 2010).

Corbin, Arthur L., *Corbin on Contracts* (Joseph M. Perillo ed., rev. ed. 2016).

Felici, James, *The Complete Manual of Typography* (2003).

Garner, Bryan A., *Garner's Dictionary of Legal Usage* (3d ed. 2011).

Garner, Bryan A., *Garner's Modern English Usage* (4th ed. 2016).

Huddleston, Rodney & Pullum, Geoffrey K., *The Cambridge Grammar of the English Language* (2002).

Lord, Richard A., *Williston on Contracts* (4th ed. 2016).

Murray, John E., Jr., *Murray on Contracts* (5th ed. 2011).

Buck v. Scalf, No. M2002-00620-COA-R3-CV, 2003 WL 21170328 (Tenn. Ct. App. 20 May 2003), 10.110

Carteret Bancorp v. Home Group, Inc., No. 9380, 1988 Del Ch. LEXIS 2 (Del. Ch. 13 Jan. 1988), 8.64

Cecil Lawter Real Estate School, Inc. v. Town & Country Shopping Center Co., 694 P.2d 815 (Ariz. Ct. App. 1984), 13.433

Chandelor v. Lopus, 79 Eng. Rep. 3 (Ex. Ch. 1625), 3.408

Charles R. Tips Family Trust v. PB Commercial LLC, 459 S.W.3d 147 (Tex. App. 2015), 14.11

Chartbrook Limited v. Persimmon Homes Limited and others [2009] UKHL 38, 14.39

City of Santa Barbara v. Superior Court, 161 P.3d 1095 (Cal. 2007), 13.560, 13.564–.567

Coady Corp. v. Toyota Motor Distributors, Inc., 361 F.3d 50 (1st Cir. 2004), 8.39, 8.43

Coast Oyster Co. v. Perluss, 32 Cal. Rptr. 740 (Ct. App. 1963), 13.360

Consult Urban Renewal Development Corp. v. T.R. Arnold & Associates, Inc., No. CIV A 06-1684 WJM, 2007 WL 1175742 (D.N.J. 19 Apr. 2007), 13.421

Continental Savings Association v. U.S. Fidelity and Guaranty Co., 762 F.2d 1239 (5th Cir. 1985), 10.115

Coral Production Corp. v. Central Resources, Inc., 273 Neb. 379 (2007), 11.4, 11.6, 11.8, 11.10

Corporate Lodging Consultants, Inc. v. Bombardier Aerospace Corp., No. 03-1467-WEB, 2005 WL 1153606 (D. Kan. 11 May 2005), 8.43

County of Du Page v. Illinois Labor Relations Board, 900 N.E.2d 1095 (2008), 11.40

Crowe v. Trickey, 204 U.S. 228 (1907), 13.202

Cussler v. Crusader Entertainment, LLC, No. B208738, 2010 WL 718007 (Cal. Ct. App. 3 Mar. 2010), 3.237, 3.253–.253

Dean St. Capital Advisors, LLC v. Otoka Energy Corp., No. 15-CV-824 (RJS), 2016 WL 413124 (S.D.N.Y. 1 Feb. 2016), 7.24

Denil v. DeBoer, Inc., 650 F.3d 635 (7th Cir. 2011), 8.55–.56

Dennison v. North Dakota Department of Human Services, 640 N.W.2d 447 (N.D. 2002), 13.715

Department of Treasury of Indiana v. Muessel, 32 N.E.2d 596 (Ind. 1941), 13.358

Diamond Robinson Building Ltd. v. Conn, 2010 BCSC 76, 8.72

DIRECTV, Inc. v. Crespin, 224 F. App'x. 741 (10th Cir. 2007), 13.356

Doe Fund, Inc. v. Royal Indemnity Co., 825 N.Y.S.2d 450 (App. Div. 2006), 10.110

Dooba Developments Ltd v. McLagan Investments Ltd [2016] EWHC 2944 (Ch), 11.105–.111

Dresser Industries, Inc. v. Page Petroleum, Inc., 853 S.W.2d 505 (Tex. 1993), 16.25

Dwoskin v. Rollins, Inc., 634 F.2d 285 (5th Cir. 1981), 10.115

East Texas Copy Systems, Inc. v. Player, No. 06-16-00035-CV, 2016 WL 6638865 (Tex. App. 10 Nov. 2016), 3.14–.21

Edwards v. Skyways [1964] 1 All ER 494, 2.88

Ellington v. EMI Music, Inc., 21 N.E.3d 1000 (N.Y. 2014), 10.150

Ener-G Holdings plc v. Hormell [2012] EWCA Civ. 1059 (31 July 2012), 3.200, 13.644

Exxess Electronixx v. Heger Realty Corp., 75 Cal. Rptr.2d 376 (Ct. App. 1998), 13.658

Federal Land Bank of St. Paul v. Bismarck Lumber Co., 314 U.S. 95 (U.S. 1941), 13.354

FH Partners, LLC v. Complete Home Concepts, Inc., No. WD 74653, 2012 WL 4074530 (Mo. Ct. App. 18 Sept. 2012), 2.47

First Union National Bank v. Steele Software Systems Corp., 838 A.2d 404 (Md. Ct. Spec. App. 2003), 8.62

Total Recall Technologies v. Luckey, No. C 15-02281 WHA, 2016 WL 199796 (N.D. Cal. 16 Jan. 2016), 3.337, 17.18

TPTCC NY v. Radiation Therapy Services, 784 F. Supp. 2d 485 (S.D.N.Y. 2011), 8.96

Trecom Business Systems, Inc. v. Prasad, 980 F. Supp. 770 (D.N.J. 1997), 8.44

Triple-A Baseball Club Associates v. Northeastern Baseball, Inc., 832 F.2d 214 (1st Cir. 1987), 8.39, 8.40, 8.57

TSC Industries, Inc. v. Northway, Inc., 426 U.S. 438 (1976), 9.3, 9.5

T.S.I. Holdings, Inc. v. Jenkins, 924 P.2d 1239 (Kan. 1996), 8.42

UBH (Mechanical Services) Ltd v. Standard Life Assurance Co., T.L.R., 13 Nov. 1986 (Q.B.), 8.67

UBS Securities LLC v. Highland Capital Management, L.P., 906 N.Y.S.2d 784 (Sup. Ct. 2009), *rev'd*, 893 N.Y.S.2d 869 (App. Div. 2010), 3.28

United Rentals, Inc. v. RAM Holdings Inc., 937 A.2d 810 (Del. Ch. 2007), 7.7, 7.36, 12.15–.16, 13.613

United States v. Contract Management, Inc., 912 F.2d 1045 (9th Cir. 1990), 13.423

Urban Sites of Chicago, LLC v. Crown Castle USA, 979 N.E.2d 480 (Ill. App. Ct. 2012), 2.177

VTR, Inc. v. Goodyear Tire & Rubber Co., 303 F. Supp. 773 (S.D.N.Y. 1969), 3.250

Waters Lane v. Sweeney [2007] NSWCA 200, 8.74

Weichert Co. of Maryland, Inc. v. Faust, 419 Md. 306 (2011), 7.23

Western Geophysical Co. of America v. Bolt Associates, Inc., 584 F.2d 1164 (2d Cir. 1978), 8.40

Williams Companies, Inc. v. Energy Transfer Equity, L.P., No. 330, 2016, 2017 WL 1090912 (Del. 23 Mar. 2017), 8.48–.49.

Williams v. CDP, Inc., No. 10-1396, 2012 WL 959343 (4th Cir. 22 Mar. 2012), 4.14

Wilson v. Gentile, 10 Cal. Rptr. 2d 713 (Ct. App. 1992), 10.70

World of Boxing LLC v. King, 56 F. Supp. 3d 507 (S.D.N.Y. 2014), 3.147

Yosemite Insurance Co. v. Nationwide Mutual Insurance Co., No. 16 CIV. 5290 (PAE), 2016 WL 6684246 (S.D.N.Y. 10 Nov. 2016), 7.26

Zilg v. Prentice-Hall Inc., 717 F.2d 671 (2d Cir. 1983), 8.62

INDEX

References are to paragraph numbers except where specified as a page number (p.) or a range of page numbers (pp.).

A

absolutely, 1.59
according to, in accordance with, 13.351–.352
acknowledge. See acknowledgments
acknowledgments, 3.436–.441
  acknowledge used with other verbs, 3.375, 3.441
  relation to recitals, 3.438
  rhetorical emphasis in, 3.440
  used inappropriately to introduce other language, 3.25, 3.439
acronyms. *See* initialisms
action or proceeding, 13.1–.3
actively, 13.4–.5
active voice. *See* voice
actual, actually, 13.6–.8
address of party, whether to include in introductory clause, 2.69, 2.70, 2.72
affiliate
  example of a defined term with a definition that's largely clear, 6.92
  having a parent enter into a contract on behalf of an affiliate, 2.57–.60
  referring to, in the introductory clause, 2.54, 2.83–.84
  incorporating, in the definition of defined terms for party names, 2.95
  time of determination, 10.149–.153
affirmatively, affirmative, 13.9–.13
after, 10.24, 10.26, 10.62
agreement
  in title, 2.11–.12
  not using defined term *this Agreement*, 2.124–.128
  not using initial capital in, 2.20, 2.125
  versus *contract*, 2.11
agrees that, 3.25, 3.28, 3.441

agrees to, 3.40, 3.109–.111
all, 11.102, 11.104, 11.105–.111
all capitals
  don't for party-name defined terms, 2.97
  don't use for entire provision, 16.29
  for party names in introductory clause, 2.52
  for party names in signature blocks, 5.30, 5.38
  in article headings, 4.10
  in title, 2.2
allonge, 1.15, 13.14
also, 13.17
ambiguity, p. xxxix, 7.5–.22. *See also and; or;* references to time; syntactic ambiguity
  and, 11.20–.45, 11.92–.96, 11.145–.153
  and/or, 11.86–.91
  and ... or, 11.92–.96
  antecedent ambiguity, 7.14–.22
  any, 11.103–.104
  comma, 4.40, 4.43, 10.9, 12.18, 12.25–.30, 12.32–.42, 12.43–.56, 12.57–.76, 13.517, 13.760
  "creative" ambiguity, 7.6–.7
  each, 11.101–.102, 11.104
  every, 11.101–.102, 11.104
  in formulas, 14.23
  latent ambiguity, 7.34
  lexical ambiguity, 7.10–.13
  material, 9.7–.9, 9.10, 9.17–.23, 9.24
  may, 3.206–.208
  may not, 3.268, 3.279
  may ... only, 3.201–.205
  notice, 13.585–.592
  notice periods, 10.65–.66
  or, 11.46–.85, 11.92–.96, 11.112–.141, 11.145–.153
  plural nouns, ambiguity relating to, 11.15–.20

T

Kenneth A. Adams is a consultant, writer, and speaker on contract drafting.

Through his company, Adams Contracts Consulting LLC, Mr. Adams helps companies improve their contracts and their contract process. He gives "Drafting Clearer Contracts" seminars internationally, for the public and for companies, law firms, and government agencies. He also acts as an expert in contract disputes.

Mr. Adams has taught as an adjunct professor at Hofstra School of Law, the University of Pennsylvania Law School, and Notre Dame Law School. And he's a pioneer in online contract automation.

As part of its "Legal Rebels" project, in 2009 the ABA Journal, the flagship magazine of the American Bar Association, named Mr. Adams one of its initial group of 50 leading innovators in the legal profession. And in 2014, the Legal Writing Institute awarded its Golden Pen Award to Mr. Adams, "to recognize his exemplary work in contract drafting."

Mr. Adams writes extensively on contract drafting. In addition to this manual, he's author of *The Structure of M&A Contracts* (Thomson Reuters 2011). In 2015, the ABA Journal named Mr. Adams's blog to the hall of fame of the "Blawg 100"—its list of the hundred best law blogs.

A U.S. citizen, Mr. Adams was raised in Africa and Europe; he received his secondary and college education in England. After graduating from the University of Pennsylvania Law School in 1989, he practiced as a transactional lawyer with major U.S. law firms in New York and Geneva, Switzerland. He currently resides in Garden City, New York.

For Mr. Adams's blog and information on his seminars and his writing, go to www.adamsdrafting.com. For information on his consulting, go to www.adamscontracts.com. He can be reached at kadams@adamsdrafting.com.